ELEGANT PEOPLE

A HISTORY OF THE BAND WEATHER REPORT

CURT BIANCHI

Backbeat Books

GUILFORD, CONNECTICUT

Backbeat Books
An imprint of The Rowman & Littlefield Publishing Group, Inc.
4501 Forbes Blvd., Ste. 200
Lanham, MD 20706
www.rowman.com

Distributed by NATIONAL BOOK NETWORK

Library of Congress Cataloging-in-Publication Data available

ISBN 978-1-4930-5999-7 (hardcover)
ISBN 978-1-4930-6000-9 (e-book)

The paper used in this publication meets the minimum requirements of American National Standard for Information Sciences—Permanence of Paper for Printed Library Materials, ANSI/NISO Z39.48-1992

Visit the author's website at www.weatherreportdiscography.org.

Weather Report is the greatest fucking band in the world, man.

—Joe Zawinul

Brian Risner collection.

Contents

Foreword

THE WRITER TERRY BOOKMAN SAYS, "There is beauty in not knowing, in being awash in the mystery of being." Part of the allure of Weather Report, from its inception, was the band's innate sense of mystery. Joe proclaimed that Weather Report was both a big band and a small group. And while Chick Corea's Return to Forever group promised *No Mystery*, Weather Report was the *Mysterious Traveller*, and Joe Zawinul and Wayne Shorter extolled Zen koans as revealing as, "We never solo, we always solo." Which, if you think about it, neatly strips away all of the mystery while preserving the mythology.

As an ardent fan from 1971 onward, I thrilled to hear the rare stories about Weather Report in the recording studio, word being that no outsiders were ever allowed to set foot in the room when Weather Report was working. Who doesn't love a top-secret laboratory? Zawinul, more than anyone, understood the dynamics of mystery and art, curiosity, and cats. Wayne seemed a natural magician to Joe's manufactured Machiavellianism, but the combination worked wonders. Weather Report fans awaited the release of each album with the same amount of enthusiasm and need as a tribe awaiting word from an absent leader. More often than not, each new album revealed a change in the band's lineup. The secret lab had a serious revolving door as part of its architecture.

I suppose I should be pleased when someone tells me that their favorite version of the band was the one with me and Jaco, but I frankly have trouble understanding it. I mean, I get that someone else liked or likes that band, but it was not my favorite version of Weather Report by any means. I loved the band with Eric Gravatt. Wait, I loved the first recording with Alphonse Mouzon. But *Mysterious Traveller* was a total game-changer. Wait, the band that made *Heavy Weather* with Alex Acuña was the version of Weather Report I'd been waiting for my entire life—at least, that's what I told Jaco when I first met him. And *Sportin' Life* was a great album with Omar Hakim somehow making the drum chair sound and feel easy. Much credit to Victor Bailey. And let's not forget Miroslav Vitous (not that he'd let you).

Most bands whose legacy survives the test of time had a stable lineup or cast of characters. Weather Report was, indeed, like a big band. Joe and Wayne both played in Maynard Ferguson's big band. (Come to think of it, so did I.) Joe's hero was Duke Ellington. Duke's rhythm section changed over the years, too. But even the mercurial Miles Davis kept his bands together longer than Joe and Wayne did. And since Weather Report? Joe's bands changed with just about the same frequency as Weather Report, while Wayne's quartet has been a unit now for twenty years.

Elegant People sheds more than just some light on the inner workings of the band, and the minds and souls that created it. Curt Bianchi has shown the kind of perseverance, determination, and moxie necessary to pierce the veils of mystery and misinformation that have plagued other recountings of the band's history and ways. This book is the first telling of Weather Report that did not make me cringe, and it actually taught me something new about the band with each turn of the page.

Curt is a fan, and no doubt being a fan is a necessary attribute to take on such a story. More than that, Curt Bianchi is diligent, ethical, a great interviewer as well as storyteller. *Elegant People* tells a story that has long needed telling. As Jaco once said: "This shit is **correct**, man." As Wayne Shorter told me: "Peter! BIG BANDS!" And, as Joe Zawinul told anyone and everyone: "This is the greatest band in the history."

From start to finish, *Elegant People* tells the story beautifully.

Peter Erskine, drummer & author of No Beethoven

Josef Zawinul (left) and Wayne Shorter perform at Wolf Trap in Vienna, Virginia, June 15, 1982. Photograph: Michael Wilderman.

Introduction

Wayne and I had a sort of telepathic understanding. We never had
to talk about music.

—Joe Zawinul

ON JULY 6, 2003, one day before Joe Zawinul's seventy-first birthday, I received
an email from Brian DiGenti, the editor of a relatively new publication called
Wax Poetics. He had seen my websites about Zawinul and Weather Report, and
wondered if I would be interested in writing an article about Joe's pioneering use
of electric keyboards. I told him no.

Let's all say it together: Curt, what were you thinking? To be fair, I had never
heard of *Wax Poetics*, and my work commitments made taking on a feature article,
with its attendant deadlines and stress, a challenge. Nevertheless, Brian persisted,
sending me copies of the magazine and asking me to think it over. When I got
them, I was impressed. The production values were top notch and the depth and
care that went into the content was equally impressive. It was evident that despite
being a commercial product, *Wax Poetics* was a labor of love. The clincher was
when Brian offered to arrange for me to interview Zawinul at his home in Malibu.
It isn't often that we get to meet our musical heroes, let alone interview them. I
knew then that this was a project I had to do.

It took a while to get things lined up, but in September I called Joe to arrange
the visit. When I got to his house, high on a bluff overlooking the Pacific Ocean,
he greeted me in the courtyard and led me into his office. It had the untidiness
of a place where things get done. Just inside the entrance hung gold records for
"Mercy, Mercy, Mercy" and *Heavy Weather*, as well as several Grammy nominations, most of them perched a tad crooked. There were also a number of framed
Down Beat Readers Poll certificates. I pointed out that he must have many more.
"Yeah, twenty-nine of them," he replied. "I don't know where the other ones are."[1]

While Joe fetched me a bottle of water, I had a look around. At the far end of the room sat Joe's grand piano, and on the wall behind it, a set of shelves. The uppermost ones housed a collection of small statues depicting musicians, arranged to tell the story of black music migrating from Africa to North America, ultimately evolving into jazz. Below them were half a dozen accordions. When Joe returned, I asked him if any of them were ones he played in his youth. I don't remember for sure if any of them were, but my question prompted him to start telling me stories of his childhood in Austria.

For the next hour we sat on opposite sides of a chest as he told me of growing up under the Nazi regime during World War II, the aerial bombing that took place in his neighborhood in Vienna, the first time he heard jazz played on the piano, of having nothing to eat, and his first gigs after the war. I was mesmerized. Joe leaned into me as he spoke, his unblinking eyes boring into mine with great intensity. I still remember the way his voice trailed off after he finished describing a day of camp life, where he was forced to endure a regimen of war training and musical studies. "Man, that was rough," he said, his eyes gazing elsewhere as the images replayed in his mind.[2]

All the while I realized that this had nothing to do with the article I was supposed to write. The few times that I tried to gently move on to other topics, he told me that he hadn't finished the story yet. "This all connects very nicely," he insisted, as though he was improvising a long through-composed piece of music. I grew concerned that at any moment he would declare the interview over and I would be dismissed without a single germane quote for my article. Sure enough, he concluded his story and said, "I think you've got enough, don't you?" I protested that I needed to ask a few more questions, so we continued.

At one point, Joe showed me some framed photographs that were displayed on a table. His favorite was the one in which he is hunched over a piano, head down in concentration, playing "Come Sunday" for its composer, Duke Ellington. Ellington was Joe's musical hero. I knew the story behind the photograph, so I asked the leading question: "And what did Duke say when you finished that tune?" A childlike expression came across Joe's face as he replied: "Duke said I played it better than he did!"[3]

Joe invited me over to his computer because he wanted to show me how he conceived his music. Since the Weather Report days, all of his compositions came from recording his improvisations at his piano or keyboard rig. Now Joe's laboratory was a laptop computer connected to a portable keyboard, the kind with two or three octaves of miniature, toylike keys. He played several pieces for me. Some of them were just single tracks rendered through a piano sample. Others were further along, with percussion and countermelodies. All of them bore the unmistakable stamp of Joe's rhythm and phrasing.

Afterward, we sat down for one more session across the chest, jumping from one topic to another. On making music with samples: "*Why not?* Let people express themselves. These kinds of things are like an instrument. It's like a language." On how he consistently found such great bass players: "That's my soul. Actually I am the best bass player of them all in terms of concept." On inspiration: "Oh, that's no problem, man." On bebop: "Improvising on changes and playing on changes—to me that is nothing." On Japan's love of smooth jazz: "It doesn't bother me a bit, man. If soft jazz is what makes them happy, and they don't go out there and kill somebody because they are so frustrated, then let it be the best music in the world."[4]

It was well after lunchtime when I finally turned off the recorder and we walked out to the edge of the cliff overlooking the ocean. Joe nonchalantly mentioned that he had recently killed a couple of rattlesnakes in the yard because he didn't want his grandchildren to encounter them. Then he took me into his state-of-the-art studio, dubbed the Music Room, which was located in a large outbuilding. Joe's son Ivan was inside setting up the keyboard rig, which had recently been shipped back from Paris. Ivan showed me around the studio like a proud papa, having designed it and installed the equipment himself. Three and a half hours after I arrived, I bid them both goodbye. It was a good day.

After the *Wax Poetics* piece was published, I had several more encounters with Joe. These interviews were a window into the inner workings of his music and that of Weather Report, but I was also a voracious collector of written material about the band. For a long time, I was content to let my website, Weather Report: The Annotated Discography (www.weatherreportdiscography.org), serve as the outlet for this research. Then I was asked to write the liner notes for a CD reissue of Weather Report's fifth studio album, *Tale Spinnin'*, which gave me the opportunity to interview Joe's musical partner in the band, Wayne Shorter. I was warned that interviewing him would be a challenge. When I told a former band member that I would be calling Wayne the next day, he let out a hearty chuckle and replied, "Good luck!"

Like everyone else, I quickly discovered that conversations with Wayne are an adventure, veering in unexpected directions like a pinball careening off bumpers. He shifts from one metaphor to another, punctuated by spot-on and often hilarious impersonations of past bosses Miles Davis and Art Blakey, not to mention actors like Bela Lugosi and Slim Pickens. But I found Wayne to be a delight. Yes, he sometimes answered my questions as if I had asked a different one. And yes, his speech is peppered with non sequiturs and lots of Buddhist philosophy. But talking to Wayne is *fun*.

I also spoke with Alphonso Johnson and Leon "Ndugu" Chancler, both of whom made significant contributions to *Tale Spinnin'*. The concept of my website is to let the musicians do the talking, and for that I relied on their comments in print. Now I began interviewing them myself. Sometimes it was easy to make a connection; other times it took years. But one thing led to another, and I managed to interview nearly all of Weather Report's members, as well as many other individuals associated with the band. This was no easy feat, as some two-dozen musicians graced the bandstand or figured prominently in the band's recordings.

Especially in its early years, Weather Report's lineup changed with every album, as the band evolved from its freewheeling, avant-garde roots into a grooving juggernaut that combined elements of jazz, funk, and rhythm 'n' blues to create a style of music that was wholly their own. They went from performing in smoky clubs to commanding the world's largest concert halls, from manhandling their own equipment to traveling with a crew of sixteen, replete with lights and sound systems. Fueled by the popularity of "Birdland" and the charismatic stage presence of Jaco Pastorius, Weather Report took on the aura of rock stars.

Of course, the constants amidst this churn were Joe and Wayne. For fifteen years their vision guided the music and gave it cohesion, shaped by a conviction that each album should be different from the others. Even after they hit pay dirt with *Heavy Weather* (the band's only gold record, signifying sales of 500,000 units), their attitude didn't waver. One CBS executive remembered Joe complaining that the label didn't know how to market Weather Report's music. "What do we need to do to sell more records," Zawinul demanded to know. Give us a song like "Birdland," the exec suggested. "Just one, man. Give the people what they want on one song. The rest of the album, you guys do you. Pure, unadulterated Weather Report." Joe seemed to ponder the idea for a moment before shaking his head. "Another 'Birdland,'" he muttered. "That's bullshit. Man, get the fuck outta here."[5]

As first-time bandleaders, Joe and Wayne came to the task with impeccable credentials. Born a year and an ocean apart, they met in 1959, not long after Joe arrived in the United States. After briefly playing together in Maynard Ferguson's orchestra, they each embarked on parallel careers with the leading jazz bands of the day. Zawinul accompanied the popular blues singer Dinah Washington for eighteen months before spending nearly a decade with Cannonball Adderley, where he gradually assumed much of the band's musical direction and became its principal composer. Wayne filled a similar role with Art Blakey's Jazz Messengers, and later with Miles Davis. In 1968, Joe began collaborating with Miles as well, and his compositions served as the raw materials that Davis used to explore the boundaries of jazz. Out of those sessions came two groundbreaking albums, *In a Silent Way* and *Bitches Brew*, which launched the jazz-rock subgenre.

Working with Miles reunited Joe and Wayne for the first time since their Maynard Ferguson days, and their shared musical affinity was apparent. In the fall of

1970 they joined forces with a young bass player from Czechoslovakia named Miroslav Vitous. Determined to forge a path of their own, Weather Report's intentions were made clear by the first song on their inaugural LP. "Milky Way" is a piece that could only be constructed in the studio and bears none of the traditional hallmarks of jazz. Likewise, the rest of the album is a manifesto for a new kind of music. The group espoused an egalitarian attitude in which any instrumentalist could take the lead at any time. Left behind were conventional song forms and the solo-after-solo format that was de rigueur for small jazz bands. Instead, Weather Report's pieces seemed to grow organically, often fueled by the rhythmic intensity of rock and funk, while other tunes were delicate, expressive tone poems.

The most distinctive aspect of Weather Report's sound was Zawinul's use of the Rhodes electric piano and synthesizers. He got his first Rhodes in 1967, while synthesizers became accessible to working musicians a few years later. These instruments spurred Joe's imagination and creativity, and he took on the role of orchestrator, enveloping Weather Report's songs with timbres that were at times reminiscent of big band horn sections, but more often sounded unlike anything previously heard. As synthesizers increased in sophistication, Joe absorbed their capabilities as well as any musician of any genre, becoming one of the few musicians to create a personal, identifiable voice with them.

As much as Zawinul dominated the music, Weather Report could not have existed without Wayne. It's true that he receded into the background at times, but Wayne's lyricism and wit imbue nearly all of Weather Report's pieces, while his unique compositional pen complemented Joe's to achieve a sum greater than their parts—a hallmark of all great songwriting duos. Wayne rejected the traditional soloist role of a jazz horn player, much to the consternation of those who viewed him as a leading voice of the tenor saxophone. Once "the hardest of hard bop players," as Bob Blumenthal described him[6], Wayne now favored the use of space and color as opposed to technical virtuosity, his playing given over to the needs of the compositions and that of the ensemble. Wayne could still blow hard—one need only listen to recordings of Weather Report's live shows to be assured of that—but he also created art with the simplest of phrases.

While Weather Report enjoyed popular and critical acclaim (five of its first seven LPs received *Down Beat* magazine's highest rating of five stars, denoting a masterpiece), it was also the subject of criticism (the eighth album received a rare *Down Beat* one-star drubbing). Depending on one's point of view, Weather Report either expanded jazz or abandoned it. In a 2001 *Down Beat* retrospective on the band, Josef Woodard wrote, "From this historical juncture, it's reasonable to say that Weather Report is the finest jazz group of the last thirty years. They managed, better than anyone else did, a delicate balance of elements: improvisation and structure, electric and acoustic textures, melodic and atmospheric qualities."[7]

Not long before that, the esteemed writer Gary Giddins was asked by filmmaker Ken Burns if "Birdland" is jazz. That was the wrong question, Giddins replied. "The question about whether 'Birdland' is jazz should be changed to, 'Is it music?' . . . It doesn't have the spontaneity, it doesn't have the invention, it doesn't have the vigor that jazz ought to have."[8] Ironically, those were exactly the qualities that Weather Report's fans found so appealing in its music.

By the time Wayne and Joe parted ways in 1985, Weather Report had produced fifteen albums, plus one for release in Japan—a body of work that historian Stuart Nicholson called one of the most significant in post-1960s jazz.[9] They also performed live nearly a thousand times together. For many Weather Report fans, the highlight of those performances was Joe and Wayne's duet. Often they would improvise using Zawinul's tune "In a Silent Way" as the vehicle. Other times they would create an entirely new piece on the spot. It might start with a few bleats of Wayne's saxophone, or Joe would initiate their dialogue with some stabs at his keyboards, taking inspiration from a sound he dialed up on one of his synthesizers.

And it isn't just the fans that remember those duets as high points; the other band members do, too. "Their duets were absolutely amazing," bassist Victor Bailey told me. "When you do a tour and you have a break like this duet, you normally go backstage, maybe get some water, something to eat. But we would stand right there and listen to these guys every night. It was completely different every time, completely improvised. They would shift, change keys, change melodies, change timing, change key signatures, and to this day I marvel at how well those two guys could play together, because it sounded like a composition but it never was composed."[10]

Chester Thompson played drums in the band for a year. "My favorite moment in the show was when the two of them would play 'In a Silent Way,' because I never heard it played the same way twice. *Ever.* Some nights it would be classical. Some nights it would be acoustic. Some nights it would be electronic. But they never even *approached* it the same way twice, which was just amazing to me. And they always read each other exactly. I was just grateful to be on the stage with those guys."[11]

Wayne and Joe's deep musical connection was all the more remarkable because they were so different from each other. Growing up in a time of war, Joe developed the street smarts needed to not only survive, but to thrive in that kind of environment. He carried himself with a confidence that many saw as arrogant and egotistical. He could be impatient and demanding, even intimidating. With Weather Report he quickly assumed the role of straw boss, negotiating with managers and record companies and hiring and firing band members. He had no qualms about telling other musicians what to play and how to play it. In photographs he scowls at the camera, his demeanor that of a serious musician, a serious man. And yet, he also had a warm, gregarious side, a youthful spirit, and a keen sense of humor. He loved sports and a good drink of slivovitz, the plum brandy his grandfather brewed at the family farm. Many of Weather Report's musicians formed close relationships with Joe that lasted for life.

Wayne was reserved and introspective. On the road, he tended to stick to himself while Joe and the other band members explored the town or engaged in athletic games of one-upmanship. Wayne's practice of Buddhism, which he took up in 1973, became a major part of his life during the Weather Report years, and some band members—including Joe, at first—were quick to dismiss it. Whereas Joe was direct, Wayne was enigmatic. As one writer charmingly put it, Wayne "operates on a more intuitive level than the rest of us usually do."[12] Wayne loves movies, and his direction to other musicians often came in the form of theatrical references, with the band members left to interpret his meaning.

When it came to their duets, Wayne and Joe had an uncanny ability to anticipate each other musically, to intuit what the other needed in the moment. "Wayne and I had a sort of telepathic understanding," Joe confirmed. "We never had to talk about music. We never spoke about what we were going to do, what key we were going to use, when we played duets. We just had a musical conversation. In that respect, Wayne Shorter is the greatest musician I've ever played with."[13]

Wayne described their playing in similar terms. "The duet process that we had was just something very . . . it's like what you *wished*. We were actually wishing on the same level, the same intensity, what our wishes were musically, just for that moment. But not *every* wish. Just do a duet, no discussion, and when it's done, we didn't talk about it. We didn't say, 'I should have, I could have.' We just let it be."[14]

"When Wayne says that Joe played what he wished for, well, that's camaraderie," drummer Omar Hakim said. "That's understanding. That's a deep connection. I was really impressed as a young musician by this experience of watching these two masters and their friendship. Un-freakin-believable, those duets every night. They were a conversation of camaraderie and love."[15]

A similar camaraderie exists among the Weather Report alumni themselves, even if it's largely unspoken. It's an exclusive club. Virtually every member prominently touts the band in their biography, even the ones whose experience ended badly or merely had bit parts. There's a shared connection among these musicians, of having survived the Zawinul gantlet and deciphered Wayne's cryptic instructions. Mostly, it's the conviction of having done something meaningful that will outlast their natural lives. Each of them has a story to tell, and you'll find them in the following pages. But at its core, Weather Report is the story of Joe and Wayne, and that is where we begin.

PART I

Roots

1 Joe

When I came over on the boat, in January of 1959, I did it with the purpose to kick asses.

—Joe Zawinul

JOSEF ZAWINUL COULD ALWAYS MAKE MUSIC. At the age of four, he surprised everyone when he picked up a harmonica and developed a knack for playing it. A little later, some family friends had an accordion and Joe was able to play that, too. Young Josef even found music in the most ordinary of sounds. One of his earliest memories was riding along with his grandfather, who drove a truck for a living. "I used to really get on with the rhythm of the windshield wiper," Joe quipped.[1]

"That boy has some talent for music," his grandfather said, so he bought Josef a small violin.[2] It didn't take because he was already enamored with accordions, so his grandfather bought him one of those, too. At first he got along playing by ear, but after a while his parents scraped up some money for lessons. Josef was a quick student and within a year he exhausted what his teacher had to offer. He even developed an unorthodox way of playing, using the buttons for melodies and the keyboard for accompaniment—in effect, playing the instrument upside down.[3]

Perhaps Joe's favorite story had to do with modifying his accordion when he was around seven years old. One time he came across a billiard table that was being reconditioned in a coffee house. Spotting some scraps of green felt left on a chair, Joe swiped a piece and put it in his pocket. "I took one of my accordions, a little Hohner I had with forty-eight bass notes and a couple of registers, and glued it into the soundboard, and I got this beautiful sound," Joe remembered. "And that was always my thing. The sound. The sound for me was automatic music."[4]

As an only child (a twin brother died at the age of four), Josef lived with his parents in a two-room apartment in Vienna's working class district of Erdberg. Though they weren't musically trained, Joe recalled that his father was "a great harmonica player," while his mother "could sing like a bird."[5] She did domestic work for a well-known physician in Vienna, who introduced her to opera and sent her to concerts from time to time. He "instilled a love of music in her," Joe said. "I am grateful to them for what I am today."[6]

Weekends, holidays, and summers were spent at his maternal grandparents' farm in the village of Oberkirchbach, then an enclave of some sixty people in the Viennese woods. His mother was one of sixteen children. It was a lot of mouths to feed, especially in the devastated economic climate of the 1930s. Joe often traced his work ethic back to his days in the village, where his summers were hardly vacations. "I was up at six working with the animals. I picked apples from trees, berries in the woods; I hunted for mushrooms in September. We had an outhouse with grass for toilet paper. Neighbors paid me in potatoes for chopping wood and plowing their fields with an ox."[7]

The farm was a gathering place for the extended family. Many nights the small kitchen would be stuffed with people and Josef would be called upon to entertain them on the accordion. Sometimes they would demand that he play "something proper," but other times "it would be nice, the big, big family sitting around together after dinner. My grandfather would be distilling schnapps and smoking a long pipe, and I'd play and everyone would sing, all drunk on the fumes of the schnapps." With so many people joining in, "the rhythm was catastrophic . . . So I learned how to deal with the beat, because I had to hold it all together, and that's where I got my inner strength for rhythm."[8]

The music he played at the farm, and later as a young man playing casual dates, stuck with Joe for the rest of his life. It was a mixture of Hungarian gypsy music, Yugoslavian music, and polkas. "Polkas have a good rhythm if you play that good. Just as difficult as jazz music," he said. "To play a Vienna waltz is just as difficult as to play a bebop tune."[9] Long after he left for the United States, Oberkirchbach remained a special place for Joe. Shortly after Weather Report was formed he said it was where "all my stuff comes from, where I do my best writing. There's a certain peace there . . . nothing but thick woods for a dozen miles. You just walk through it, and all the stuff comes out."[10]

Josef was four months shy of his sixth birthday when the German *Wehrmacht* marched into Austria on March 12, 1938, annexing it into the Third Reich. Three days later, Adolf Hitler culminated a triumphant tour of the country with his arrival in Vienna. Between the *Anschluss* and the postwar occupation by the Allied powers, it would be nearly two decades before Austria regained its independence. A year after the Nazis arrived, Josef was selected by the regime to be a pupil of the Vienna Conservatory of Music, in part because he had perfect pitch, which is the ability to identify the specific note of any pitch without first being given a reference pitch. It's estimated that only one in a thousand people can do this. And it wasn't just isolated notes: Years later, the members of Joe's bands would try to stump him with the most complex chords they could think of, but he never failed to identify each note.

At the conservatory Josef studied classical music and learned to play the piano, violin, and trumpet. But five years later, World War II was at Joe's doorstep as the Allied forces closed in—the Americans and British from the west, the Russians from the east. Vienna came under heavy aerial bombardment, and in September 1944, Josef and his classmates were sent away to ride out the war from a safer location. Nearly sixty years later, he remembered it vividly:

> It was one of those palaces from the Austro-Hungarian monarchy, one of those palaces of a count. And in this phenomenal palace were twenty-nine of the best music students of Austria, incarcerated more or less, to protect us because we had bomb attacks every night, every day. It was the Reich's purpose to keep the talented for the future. I was one of these people.
>
> The regimen was, get up at four o'clock in the morning, wash with the coldest possible water, and then go out and do war training. We had SS officers as our teachers. The Latin professor was the only one who was a woman, a Viennese woman. All the other teachers were war-injured SS officers. The sports teacher had one arm. They were tough. And I hated this. I really hated this stuff. But, okay, we were trained, we were conditioned to do what we were told, and that's what we had to do.
>
> We had school until noon, then lunch. Then we had to lie down for an hour and a half. And then school continued until six o'clock in the evening. After dinner, we practiced. I had to practice in the hunting trophy room of the count. It was huge. There were fifty-seven Bösendorfer grand pianos in there, and all kind of [large game] animal heads on the walls—every damn kind of species from his hunting in Africa. And that was the place.
>
> On Saturdays we went in a bus to where there was a public bathing house and we had three minutes for a shower. It was like prison, but we were not prisoners to speak of. We had our privileges. And we were well respected because we were the best musicians in Vienna at that time.
>
> Every Sunday after dinner we had to listen to the music of the masters: Handel, Beethoven, Mozart, Haydn. One of the music professors was there, and one of the SS guys. There was a picture of Hitler in the classroom. One night after this was finished, this one guy got up and went to the piano. He was a clarinet student, a funny guy, and he sat down and played [Fats Waller's] "Honeysuckle Rose."

I was out of it, man. I was a great accordion player; I played *volksmusik*, and that is fairly rhythmic. But this was the first time I had ever heard anything rhythmic like that. Everybody was fascinated. I was the star in that group, but after this guy played, I was no star anymore. This guy said, "See, you're a fine piano player, but this—you don't have that in you. And by the way, this kind of music is unlearnable—you either have it or you don't have it." I said, "Well, how can you have something that you have never even heard? I like it just as much as you, you know."

I asked him, "What kind of music is that?" He said they call it "jazz." And I said, "How do you write that?" I had never even heard the word. When he spelled it, I immediately saw my name in the word, in the initials. I thought, *that is something*. I liked the music, but I also liked the word.[11]

In late December, the students were sent home for Christmas break. Joe didn't return. "We could hear artillery every night already coming closer and closer as the Russians approached. The war got so bad, I didn't go back. My father was still in the military and my mama worked two jobs. I was out there with my grandmama in the village. And the funny thing is, later on I met guys who went back and they said that when the Russians marched in, they took the covers off the Bösendorfers, bound the horses to the legs of the pianos, and put the hay and the food inside them. It was a horse stable. That's the great culture they brought!"[12]

Joe remained in Oberkirchbach until the fall of 1945. "I was a happy kid in the country," he said. "It was a sad day when I had to move to Vienna 100 percent of the time. The war was over. It was time to get on with my life. To be educated. I was the first member of my family to go to gymnasium [an advanced secondary school]. I was already a very good musician."[13] Joe's parents had managed to buy him a piano, but it was damaged in the bomb attacks and was no longer playable. A nearby friend had a piano in his apartment, so Joe's mother arranged for him to practice there once or twice a week. He worked at it half-heartedly. "I didn't take it that serious," he said. "I practiced maybe a half hour a week, but I was really quick in learning."[14] It was enough that his teacher was convinced that Joe had put in a full week of work.

Jazz records were almost impossible to come by in Vienna, but as luck would have it, Joe found some Louis Armstrong and Duke Ellington discs in the apartment where he practiced. It was the first time he heard jazz since the conservatory camp. "But for some kind of reason, when I heard this music again, as much as I was impressed by this piano playing of 'Honeysuckle Rose,' I really didn't like Louis Armstrong. I didn't like that, for some kind of reason. I can't explain it. Duke Ellington—I just didn't get that."[15]

What he *did* like were the American dance bands. He first heard them on the radio via the Blue Danube Network, which was set up in 1945 to serve American troops stationed in Austria. "There came this radio program, *Strictly Solid*, and they played a variety of jazz music. Tommy Dorsey and Harry James. Count Basie. Duke Ellington. I ran home every day from school to hear it. And by having perfect pitch, I could note down things."[16] Joe developed his own shorthand notation and "within a year, I had about three hundred songs down."[17]

Post-war Austria was occupied by the four Allied powers—the United States, Britain, France, and Russia—and the districts of Vienna were similarly divided up. One of the benefits for a young man like Josef was that he began catching glimpses of American culture, *Strictly Solid* being one example. The movies were another. The first movie he recalled seeing was *Sun Valley Serenade*, with Glenn Miller. "They played 'Moonlight Serenade' and all these beautiful tunes. I was in heaven. And then later on they came out with *Bathing Beauty* with Esther Williams and Red Skelton. When I saw the opening of *Bathing Beauty*—it was in Southern California, with the biggest swimming pool, and the Harry James band played 'Trumpet Blues and Cantabile'—that did it to me. I knew I'm going to go to America; that gave it to me."[18]

Bathing Beauty was but a prelude to the real love of Joe's teen years, *Stormy Weather*. It stood in contrast to the previous movies he had seen because of its all-black cast of musicians and actors, including Bill "Bojangles" Robinson, Fats Waller, Cab Calloway, and the amazing Nicholas Brothers dancing team. It left a deep impression on Joe. "*Stormy Weather* totally changed my life," he said. "I saw that movie twenty-four times. I said to myself, 'This is what I want to do!' I dreamed about this. . . . I would wake up at night, and I saw myself playing with Negro orchestras."[19] It didn't hurt that Joe had a crush on the film's female star, Lena Horne, and he snuck into the theater day after day to take in her charms, convinced that he wanted to marry her.

But that was the fantasy of a teenage mind. Back in the real world, Joe's interest in school was never strong, and at the age of seventeen, the first member of his family to go to gymnasium saw his academic career come to an end. "I was a fuck-up in many ways," he later admitted. "I was on the streets all the time. I was thrown out of school for fighting. I was a restless person. After the war it was rough."[20] By this time, Joe was already doing casual gigs on accordion, but his parents pressed him to take up a vocation, afraid that he'd spend his life in smoky rooms. So Joe tried his hand as an apprentice typesetter. He found it boring and quit after a few months, but kept up the appearance of going to work. When his parents caught him, the jig was up. They pressed him again, demanding to know what he was going to do with himself.

Joe's old piano teacher, Valerie Tschörner, had an answer. He was already an excellent pianist, she told his parents, and if he committed himself to practicing for a year, he had a good chance of winning the prestigious International Music Competition in Geneva, Switzerland. "She said I had a gift to win this contest," Joe remembered, "and it would establish a classical piano career. And Friedrich Gulda, one of the great ones of all time [and a fellow pianist from Vienna who was two years older than Joe], had in 1946 won this particular contest, so my professor always said I could be like Gulda. I didn't want to be like Gulda. I didn't even like classical music. But I felt my parents were really having a hard time, so I said, 'Okay, I'm going to do this, I do this for my parents.' I started that summer.

"I practiced piano every day, eight or nine hours, to prepare myself for the big contest. I didn't do anything else. I didn't even go out. I said, 'I'm going to show I can do this,' and then I'll do what I want to do anyhow, because by that time I liked jazz a lot. But one evening, I said, 'Shit, I'm going to go and see my friend play.' He said he played in a hillbilly band—an American hillbilly band with Austrian musicians. I didn't know what that was. So I went there that evening, away from my studies, and my friend invited me up to play accordion. They had a nice little band, with a Hawaiian type of guitar and my friend was playing accordion—Hank Williams and all this wonderful country and western music. I love country and western still today. So I sat in with them and the leader said, 'Listen, man, we go tomorrow on a tour of American clubs here in Austria. Why don't you come with us?' It was the happiest day of my life. I went the next morning and packed up my little suitcase and went with them."[21]

The movies were one thing, but touring the military bases brought Joe into direct contact with Americans. "What a life," he remembered. "We played hillbilly music in the Officers' Club at night. Just the *smell* in there, to go in there to smell. Of hamburgers and hot dogs, and potato chips and ketchup. *Man.* I never ate like that. My family ate to *survive*; we didn't eat for pleasure. Then we went to breakfast in the Officers' Club. We ate breakfast down there, my friend. The first time I'd ever seen that you eat toast with beautiful butter, and eggs with bacon. I mean, we had no breakfast like that. And then they brought the milk. I thought, *How can people live like this?* It's America, you know? And then the 101st Army band came through, an all-black big band, and that's when I went crazy. I said, man, this is what I'm going to do."[22]

Whether his parents approved or not, Josef had found his vocation; he never earned another paycheck outside of music. He left classical music behind as well, choosing to play popular music at the summer and winter resorts. The experience was invaluable. "I got into an orchestra where there was a lot of reading to do. The reading you do at home, where you can practice, is one thing, but going into an orchestra where you get a score that's nothing but notes is completely different. To be a musician in Austria, you've got to play a lot of different stuff. It's an international place. We used to play in nightclubs, walking around to the different tables playing *horas* and gypsy music. . . . I loved it."[23]

Joe's musical career blossomed. Over the next several years, he played in a series of increasingly high-profile bands. "My goal was to always get on scenes where I was the weakest one going in and the strongest coming out," he explained.[24] Near the end of 1954, he helped establish Austria's first bona fide jazz combo, the Austrian All Stars. They put on a memorable concert at Vienna's prestigious Konzerthaus that reverberated for years among those in attendance. They also cut several studio tracks that are today collected on the compilation disc, *His Majesty Swinging Nephews 1954–57.*

Despite their successes, jazz wasn't popular enough in Austria for Joe and his fellow bandmates to earn a living from it, so they all held other jobs to pay the bills. Joe had a lucrative deal with Polydor doing radio and studio work. "We had a great level of musicians," he said. "There were guys from the Vienna Philharmonic, the Vienna Symphony Orchestra, and the best musicians from the dance bands. So we were able to cut a tune in twenty minutes, with rehearsal. . . . And I had a nice deal with them. I didn't want to be paid by the hour, I wanted to be paid by the title. Sometimes we recorded twenty titles in a day. So I made a lot of money. We played all kinds of things—operas, Gershwin, film music, really difficult classical stuff, but mostly pop. And I played a lot of instruments—vibraphone, accordion, piano, bass, trumpet. It was really an experience to learn a lot in a short amount of time."[25] Overall, Joe's career was thriving. He reckoned he might have been the best paid musician in Vienna at that point.

And then came independence. When the Allied occupation ended, it was as though shackles were removed. "1956 was the turning point," Joe said. "There was *life* in Vienna."[26] That year, he joined up with Fatty George, an accomplished Viennese clarinetist and showman who returned from Germany to open a nightclub and lead a band that mixed traditional and modern jazz. George brought along a Memphis-born singer named Al "Fats" Edwards, and the band caused a sensation. "We were the hottest shit there was," Zawinul remembered.[27]

Vienna had a burgeoning art scene, and Joe found himself drawn into its orbit. There he met Gulda, who by then was an international star in the classical world and had recently made his first jazz record in New York. Gulda gave Joe his first opportunity to compose. The latter had been commissioned by the Vienna Broadcasting Corporation to produce new, original music, and Gulda proposed that they split the compositions evenly between them. Joe wasn't yet the prolific writer he would later become, so Gulda wound up completing the lion's share of the work. Nevertheless, it was a prestigious assignment and good experience for Zawinul.

Around this time, American jazz musicians began making appearances in Ger-

Joe Zawinul plays the piano while Friedrich Gulda looks on. The photo was taken around 1958 at the Club Tabarin where Fatty George held forth. Photo: © Imagno / Hulton Archive / Getty Images.

many and Austria. Joe remembered seeing Oscar Peterson with Norman Granz's Jazz at the Philharmonic, for instance. One break occurred when Joe's trio was hired to tour Germany with the American saxophonists Bud Shank and Bob Cooper. Why did they choose Joe's trio as opposed to a local rhythm section? "We could groove a little better than the German musicians," Joe said.[28]

•

In January 1958, *Down Beat* magazine—the unofficial bible of jazz—announced its first Hall of Fame Scholarship competition. Applicants were asked to submit a recording, either as a composer or instrumentalist, and the winner would receive a full year's tuition to the Berklee School of Music in Boston. Anyone was eligible and there was no upper age limit.[29] The notice caught Joe's eye. He and his musician friends often went to the English reading room in Vienna to thumb through the magazine's pages. "It was our main connection to find out about all the great musicians and maybe gain a little knowledge about the English language," Zawinul said.[30]

Ever since seeing *Bathing Beauty* and *Stormy Weather*, Joe dreamed of going to the United States, but it was a difficult proposition even in the late fifties. In addition to the costs and risks of leaving family, friends, and work behind, immigration quotas restricted the number of Austrian émigrés to a trickle. There was also the problem of making it in America, where Joe would be an unknown competing with the best jazz musicians in the world. His fellow Austrian musicians recognized that while they might be in the upper echelon at home, that didn't mean they measured up to the real thing. Even as late as 1966, Willis Conover, the host of *Voice of America Jazz Hour* heard throughout Europe, described Austria as "a country without a jazz scene."[31] The pond was small, indeed. To most of Joe's friends, the idea of going to the States was inconceivable. But the Berklee scholarship offered a way, even if it was a long shot.

"The deal was free school if you can make it over," Joe said, "and you have to pay your own food and lodging." He had the financial means, but he was conflicted because there were "such good vibes" in Vienna.[32] In the end, that wasn't enough. Jazz in Austria had reached a "cul-de-sac," he said. "I *had* to get to the United States if I was to grow as a musician. I had to have contact with the music as a living force, and I couldn't get this in Vienna."[33]

Joe and saxophonist Karl Drewo, a friend who also played with the All Stars, went ahead and submitted an application. Zawinul included a recording of the Woody Herman tune "Red Top" that he had recently made with Fatty George. Then they waited three months to learn if they won. *Down Beat* promised that the winner would be announced in the April 17, 1958, issue. Who knows how long it took for a copy to get to the English reading room in Vienna. Joe must have been full of anticipation and apprehension when it finally did arrive. He turned every page looking for the results, only to find that they weren't there. It would be another month before it was finally revealed that Nicholas Brignola, a twenty-one-year-old saxophonist from New York, had been named the winner.[34]

But the article went on to say that "the flood of applications for the Hall of Fame scholarship unveiled many fine jazz talents. This led *Down Beat* to name five additional winners of scholarships for study at Berklee." The second winner was Joe's pal, Karl Drewo, who received a $350 scholarship. A high school student who wasn't technically eligible for the competition was also given a special award of $350. That left three $200 winners. The last name listed was Joe's, described simply as "25, a pianist from Vienna, Austria." Drewo didn't go to America. Joe did.

Just after the New Year, Zawinul boarded the SS *Liberté* for the six-day trip across the Atlantic. He brought a suitcase, his bass trumpet, and $800 in cash. "I knew that to be successful in America I would have to do a lot of learning—not in school, but out there with the musicians," he said. "I knew it wouldn't be easy, because I had no relatives, didn't know a single person in America. But when I came over on the boat, in January of 1959, I did it with the purpose to kick asses."[35]

•

The *Liberté* slipped into New York harbor late on a cold and foggy morning. Barely on American soil, Joe nearly got into a fistfight. He shared a taxi with a couple he met on the ship, who paid the full fare when they were dropped off. But when the cab got to Joe's destination, the driver tried to collect again. Fisticuffs were averted when Joe called out to a nearby police officer and the cabbie sped off. "It started immediately," he said.[36]

After checking into his hotel, Joe walked down Broadway toward Fifty-Second Street, dazzled by the neon signs that flickered to life in the late afternoon gloom. The blocks east of Broadway, between Fifth and Sixth Avenues, once teemed with so many jazz clubs that it was known simply as "The Street," and musicians flocked there to learn to play bebop. By the time Joe arrived, New York City remained the undisputed epicenter of jazz, but The Street's heyday was a good decade past, overtaken by burlesque and strip clubs. That didn't matter much to Joe, for he really had only one destination in mind: the famous jazz club, Birdland, located at the corner of Fifty-Second and Broadway.

Joe descended the narrow stairs to the club's basement entrance and entered a world he had only dreamed about. Billing itself as "The Jazz Corner of the World," Birdland was the mecca of modern jazz. Not only did everyone play there, if they weren't on the bandstand they hobnobbed at the bar while a cross section of New York society occupied the tables and "the bleachers" behind them. To Joe, it seemed larger than life.

Still in the thrall of what he saw and heard, Joe took the train to Boston the next morning to begin his studies at Berklee. About two weeks into the semester, he caught a break that launched his American jazz career. Ella Fitzgerald was appearing at Storyville, the Boston jazz club owned by impresario George Wein. The pianist for the house band was ill that night, so Wein called Berklee for a substitute. Ray Santisi, a legendary piano teacher at the school, sent Joe. He impressed the drummer, Jake Hanna, who called his former employer, trumpet player and bandleader Maynard Ferguson, whose pianist was going into the Army. On Hanna's recommendation, Ferguson invited Joe to audition. He went to New York the next day.[37]

That afternoon, Zawinul auditioned with the Ferguson band during its gig at the Apollo Theater. He was announced to the audience as "Joe Vienna" and asked to sit in for a number, sink or swim. "I was scared to death," Joe admitted years later.[38] It was an up-tempo tune, and Joe had a hard time hearing the bassist and didn't play well. "I know I didn't get the gig," he told Ferguson, "but at least let me play one more show and show you. Maybe not play something that fast, where I can feel the band."[39] Maynard gave him another chance and this time Zawinul did well enough to get the job.

The Ferguson outfit was like the blustery teenager of big bands, bursting with youthful energy and fine soloists. Frankie Dunlop and Jimmy Rowser completed the rhythm section, while the horns included Slide Hampton, Bill Chase, Don Sebesky, Jimmy Ford, Don Ellis, Carmen Leggio and Willie Maiden. "The band was on fire," Joe remembered.[40] "It was an exciting and challenging experience for someone like me. And it did wonders for my self-confidence as a musician. . . . I learned a lot; in fact, it was a situation in which someone like myself couldn't help but learn, working regularly with such top musicians."[41]

Ferguson arranged for Joe to obtain his green card, which allowed him to live and work in the United States permanently. With his immigration status assured, Zawinul quickly began to assimilate into the city's jazz community and frequent the clubs, especially Birdland. One night he ran into Booker Little—a trumpet player who died at the age of twenty-three—and a young saxophonist out of New Jersey who was just creating a stir. He was known to some as the Newark Flash. His name was Wayne Shorter.

2 Wayne

You're the kid from Newark, huh? You're the Flash, the Newark Flash.
— Max Roach

WHEN WAYNE MET JOE EARLY IN 1959, he was twenty-five years old. He had recently been discharged from the Army, where he was assigned to the band at Fort Dix, about sixty miles southwest of his hometown of Newark, New Jersey. It was a fortuitous assignment in that he was able to stay abreast of the East Coast jazz scene, even if apart from it. Now that he was a civilian, Wayne made up for lost time, gigging with pianist Horace Silver, exchanging ideas with John Coltrane, and jamming with a new kid in town, trumpet player Freddie Hubbard. Wayne's reputation was rising quickly and it wouldn't be long before a name bandleader snapped him up.

Remarkably, Wayne didn't take up music until his junior year in high school. He originally wanted to be a painter, and his mother encouraged his artistic side—and that of his older brother, Alan—by creating an exceptionally nurturing environment for her sons. Playtime in Louise Shorter's home wasn't a frivolous activity, but a serious pursuit that she zealously guarded. Everything, including household chores, took a back seat. Wayne's creativity flourished. When he was twelve, he won first prize in an all-city art contest for a watercolor painting. Spurred by the honor, Wayne applied to and was accepted at Newark's Arts High School, the first public high school in the United States devoted to the visual and performing arts.

Wayne had an insatiable appetite for comic books and movies, and seeing films at Newark's old Capitol Theater, like *The Wolf Man* or *Captive Wild Woman* (a horror film in which a mad scientist transforms a female gorilla into a human) spurred late night jam sessions of the mind with Alan. "My brother and I used to get up in the middle of the night, at two or three o'clock," Wayne remembered.

"We'd sit up in the bed and rock back and forth and imitate what we had heard in the movies. Like, the sound effects—we'd soundtrack the things we'd seen. . . . Of course, we didn't know these would be the building blocks for a life's profession. We had no intentions of becoming musicians. I was supposed to be a painter."[1]

Wayne's love of escapist entertainment and his artistic abilities came together in a fifty-six-page comic book that he produced while at Arts High titled *Other Worlds*. He described it as "a trip to the moon. In my drawings you can see scientists on the ship with the commander with the speech bubbles. It's about encountering a whole other race on the moon; it's about life and wars."[2]

At around the same time, Wayne took note of jazz, which he first heard on Martin Block's *Make Believe Ballroom* on WNEW. Block was a popular and powerful presence on radio; some called him the nation's first disc jockey. "I remember one week he announced that he was going to play something different, a new music called bebop," Wayne said.[3] Hearing bop on the radio for the first time would have captured the attention of any listener. Wayne was drawn to it immediately.

Bebop's roots grew from after-hours jam sessions in New York City, especially at Minton's Playhouse. Opened in 1938, Minton's became a musicians' hang, where they would go after their regular gigs. The house band was led by drummer Kenny Clarke and pianist Thelonious Monk. Charlie Parker and Dizzy Gillespie regularly joined them. Anyone could come up on the bandstand, but as the story goes, the less talented musicians would "feel a breeze" as Monk and company threw them off by changing keys, employing "weird" chords, and "getting modern all the time." Those who couldn't keep up didn't remain on Minton's bandstand for long. Collectively, they established the foundations of bebop, and it evolved quickly, particularly in the clubs of New York.

When Wayne heard bebop on WNEW in the late forties, it was just gaining currency in popular culture. Most of Block's audience, used to hearing, say, Tommy Dorsey or Bing Crosby, undoubtedly found listening to bebop a challenge; dancing along probably seemed impossible. It was fast and harmonically complex, emphasizing improvisation and virtuosity. In short, it was modern. To Wayne, it was the musical answer to the science fiction he found so enticing in the comics and movies. He described it as "futuristic."[4] "The music had a velocity in there," he said. "Something that meant more than music to me. It was the same kind of velocity that would go on in certain sections of a symphony, but with bebop, this velocity was all in a box—you could take it in your lunch pail!"[5]

Until then, Wayne hadn't thought about being a musician. "But the shapes and pictures of feelings that emerged—some button was pushed, and I felt I must be part of this," he said.[6] He got a Tonette, a small, plastic toylike instrument similar to a recorder and taught himself how to play it. Not long after mastering its possibilities, he graduated to a real instrument when his grandmother gifted him a clarinet for his fifteenth birthday. Wayne had seen one in a music shop window and was taken by its appearance, its silver keys contrasting with its ebony body.

Meanwhile, Wayne found some kindred spirits at Arts High and joined them in forays to the nearby Adams Theatre, where he heard many of the great jazz bands of the day. He played hooky so often that he was eventually called to the vice principal's office where his parents were waiting for him.

"Where do you go when you play hooky?" the vice principal asked.

"The Adams Theatre."

"Oh, do you like movies?"

"Yes, but also the bands there."[7]

As punishment, Wayne was assigned to the classroom of Achilles D'Amico, the school's director of instrumental music and a stern disciplinarian. The first week Wayne was there, D'Amico told his students that music was going in three directions, and played for them selections from *The Rite of Spring* by Igor Stravinsky; the Peruvian vocalist, Yma Sumac; and Charlie Parker. Wayne recognized the latter from the things he heard on the radio. When he received a perfect score on his music theory test, Wayne knew he was in the right place and resolved to pursue music wholeheartedly.

He and Alan became obsessed with bebop, practicing at home for hours every night. He even neglected comic books. His grandmother got him a tenor saxophone, and he and Alan joined a band led by another teenager named Jackie Bland, who, according to Wayne, couldn't read music but "had the look" of a bandleader. Bland already knew many of Dizzy Gillespie's big band arrangements by ear, which the youngsters attempted with varying degrees of success. They called themselves the Group.

"We used to try to play everybody's music," Wayne recalled. "We even tried to play all of the big band arrangements without having the music sheets, just what we heard, harmony and all. It was a *wild* band. We were playing a lot of bebop and just down-to-earth swinging."[8] They rehearsed at a nearby YMCA, where a counselor took notice and helped them get organized, bringing in charts for them to play. When the trumpet players couldn't reach the high notes, Wayne would play their parts on the clarinet.

Bebop was a challenge to orthodoxy, and the Shorters relished its outsider status. "People used to talk about us in those years, say, 'Man, you're crazy, you're weird.' But I didn't even lift my little finger to be crazy or weird or *out*," Wayne said.[9] Alan painted "Doc Strange" on his saxophone case; Wayne followed suit, putting "Mr. Weird" on his. "We'd go to the gig, and my brother would bring his horn in a shopping bag, and play it with gloves on. He'd wear galoshes when the sun was shining; and we'd take the chairs and turn them around and start playing 'Emanon' or 'Godchild' or 'Jeru' by ear, with newspapers on our music stands, making fun of people who read music. We made sure our clothes were wrinkled, because if you played bebop you were raggedy, not smooth."[10]

The popular band among Wayne's high school crowd was the Nat Phipps Orchestra, which he and Alan derisively referred to as the "Pretty Boy Band" for their conformity and popularity. The Phipps Orchestra "had bandstands, uniforms, lights, girlfriends who would carry their instruments, everything," Wayne said.[11] A rivalry developed between the bands, and the YMCA staged a series of battles between them. Phipps always won, but eventually Bland's group started getting a good share of applause, too. At one contest, when the voting suggested that Bland's men might be in the lead, their sympathetic YMCA counselor cut the competition short, declaring them the winner. As Wayne remembered, "Nobody left, but they just looked at each other and said, 'Wow, they're weird, they're crazy,' but people kind of dug us."[12]

Wayne's musical progress was rapid. In his senior year, he packed his schedule with music classes and played in the school bands. The writer Amiri Baraka (then LeRoi Jones) grew up in Newark and remembered hearing Shorter in those days. "Wayne was precocious; I heard many pretty astounding things he was doing at seventeen and eighteen. Even then, when he couldn't do anything else, he could still make you gasp at sheer technical infallibility."[13]

Not long after Wayne took up the tenor, the saxophonist Sonny Stitt came to town for a gig. Stitt possessed bebop bona fides that Wayne could only dream of, having already met Charlie Parker, with whom he shared a similar style, and toured and recorded with Dizzy Gillespie. After Stitt's manager called around for "two of the best players in Newark to stand alongside him on certain numbers during his gig," Wayne joined him on the bandstand. "I was nervous because I could only play in the keys of C, B-flat and G, and I was just working on E-flat," Wayne said. "So Sonny says, 'Okay, we're going to play a blues in E-flat.' And I thought I'd better find the right note to thrill everybody. And the people loved it."[14]

Stitt was impressed enough to ask Wayne to join him in New York, but Wayne couldn't go because he was still in high school. When he graduated, he took a job at the Singer sewing machine factory where his father worked, playing casual gigs on weekends. A year later he had saved up $2,000 and passed the entrance exams for the music education program at New York University. Wayne attended NYU from 1952 to 1956, commuting every day from his parents' home in Newark. Given that Wayne later became known as one of jazz music's greatest composers, it's natural to wonder if he studied composition in college. "They told us that they were actually there to teach us to be teachers," Wayne said. "If we were gonna go composing, and do things on our own, we'd have to do that outside, and we'd have to stick to the lesson plan. But the teachers who knew gave us enough inspiration.”[15]

Wayne got a different education at the clubs, listening to and participating in jam sessions when he could. One time he was nursing a drink at Teddy Powell’s Lounge in Newark. Sonny Stitt was performing, and he invited Wayne up on the bandstand. They took turns soloing on the Charlie Parker bebop standard “Donna Lee.” “The audience was on their heads,” Wayne remembered. “Stitt was playing very smoothly, all the transitions, while I was going for the originality. . . . And I think Stitt must have told people, ‘There’s a bad cat in Newark.’”[16]

Upon graduation Shorter was offered a teaching position, which he barely considered because his heart was set on becoming a jazz musician. But just as he was getting known around New York, he got his draft notice. As his reporting time neared, Wayne paid a visit to the Café Bohemia in Greenwich Village, “just to see some music and musicians for the last time,” he said melodramatically.[17] He ordered a drink at the bar, where the drummer Max Roach spotted him. They hadn’t met, but Roach had heard about Wayne through the grapevine. “You’re the kid from Newark, huh? You’re the Flash, the Newark Flash.”[18]

Roach invited him up to play. It was a big-time jam session, with players steeped in bop: Oscar Pettiford on bass, Walter Bishop on piano, and Cannonball Adderley and Jackie McLean on sax. Jimmy Smith hauled his Hammond B3 over in a hearse, while Art Blakey, Art Taylor, and Kenny Clarke alternated on drums with Roach. Wayne joined them, uncertain of his status among such company. “I did what I could but wondered what kind of contribution I could be making with all of these giants up there. I started to leave the stand, but someone grabbed me by the back of my shirt—I think it was Max—and he told me to play more. It was a great night for me.”[19]

With what felt like his swan song behind him, Wayne reported for basic training, after which he was stationed at Fort Dix. He got to New York whenever he could, “making sessions and getting heard.” Once on leave, he went to Sugar Hill, a club in Newark. Sonny Rollins was playing and asked Wayne to sit in. “We played ‘Cherokee’ at Concorde speed, and ever since then I would see Sonny and I would see that little glint in his eye because he remembered that.”[20] On another furlough he went to hear Lester Young, one of the first giants of the tenor saxophone, who singled out Wayne at the bar between sets and invited him to share drinks in the basement, despite the two having never met.

These experiences left a deep impression on Wayne. In Austria, it was rare for Joe to hear American jazz musicians perform live, but Wayne felt as though he belonged to a lineage stretching back to the great jazz innovators of the thirties and forties. “When you see people like Charlie Parker—I saw him play four or five times—Lester Young, and Billie Holiday who sang at the Sugar Hill in Newark not far from where I lived, it becomes part of your music.”[21]

Wayne also played a few dates with the pianist Horace Silver. After one of the gigs, a woman approached him backstage and said that someone wanted to meet him. The woman was John Coltrane's wife, Naima. Introducing Wayne to her husband, she said, "You all got something in common."[22] They shook hands. "You're playing those strange funny things all over the horn like me," Trane said. "It's not the same way, but like I'm trying—like I'm doing. That's some interesting stuff." He seemed to view Wayne as a kindred spirit.[23]

Seven years older than Shorter, Coltrane was then a member of Miles Davis's band, on his way to becoming the most influential tenor sax player in jazz. As Wayne had yet to establish himself, he looked upon Coltrane as one of the "adults" in the field and admired the seriousness with which he approached his music.[24] Wayne spent several evenings at the couple's apartment in Manhattan, and reciprocated by inviting them to his parents' house for Thanksgiving dinner. Their conversations were far-ranging. "He would talk about his desire to speak the English language backward, and not really in a playful way," Wayne said. "It was like, to speak backwards, to get at something else. To break patterns, I guess. It was that innovative spirit that he had." They also took turns sitting at Trane's piano. Wayne would play "the first thing that came to my fingers" and Trane would respond with his horn. Then they would switch roles.[25]

For years, Wayne's playing would be linked to Coltrane's. It would have been impossible for any tenor saxophonist, especially one playing hard bop, not to be influenced by John Coltrane. But while Wayne owed a debt to Trane, he also absorbed all of the preceding tenor sax giants and ultimately forged a style of his own. Branford Marsalis, who followed in Wayne's Jazz Messengers footsteps a generation later, noted that Wayne had a way of "internalizing the history of the music by learning how to play while [listening to] a lot of different guys. He was a master mimic—he could play like Bird, he could play like Lester, he could roll like Coltrane; that's what enabled him to play the way he did, because he had many more reference points than everyone else."[26] Joe remembered that while "Trane was doing a lot of arpeggiating, running the chords," Shorter "had a wonderful way of blowing chords, but he wasn't just arpeggiating. Wayne could already weave melodies as a part of the chords." Trane himself saw that Wayne was onto his own thing, too. "Yeah, you're scramblin' those eggs," he told Wayne. "You're scrambling them differently than me, but you're doing it, too."[27]

Wayne emerged from his Army years with a fresh voice. He "started writing, practiced a lot and, most of all, came out of it his own man, playing his horn like *nobody else* around," Amiri Baraka wrote in 1959. "He had passed through two very critical stages of his life: the young precocious imitator of Bird, and the 'good' young session musician whose ideas have not quite jelled. He is, now, almost at that third even more critical stage of his career: the Innovator. He still has a little way to go, but not so much as to make anyone who's heard him recently doubt for a second that he'll make it." As Wayne's brother, Alan, told Baraka, "Man, he went to the Army and took care of a lot of business."[28]

•

Joe had been in the United States for about a month when he first met Wayne. They were introduced one evening at a diner called Ham and Eggs, down the street from Birdland, where Joe and Booker Little were sharing a late night meal. Afterward, they headed over to the Green Lantern, a bar nearby. Joe was impressed by Wayne's expansive knowledge of music. He even knew about Friedrich Gulda—a sure conversation icebreaker for Joe. Zawinul's grasp of English wasn't so good yet, but that didn't seem to pose much of a barrier between them.

"When I met Joe, I thought he was speaking English," Wayne admitted. "But he said no, he was *learning* English. It was a while before I realized that we were communicating maybe just by thought, 'cause I could bet a whole lotta money that he was speaking English, 'cause he was already in the rhythm of what was going on, you know? Like certain body language, or something like that."[29] Downing a few drinks didn't hurt, either. It was a pastime the two would enjoy often over the years.

A few months after their first encounter, a slot opened up in Maynard Ferguson's band for a tenor saxophonist. By then, everybody in New York was talking about Wayne, Joe remembered. He and Slide Hampton, Ferguson's musical director, persuaded Wayne to audition, along with Eddie Harris and George Coleman. Shorter got the job, his first regular gig with an established band.

By this time, Joe and Slide were good friends, and for a short while Wayne and his brother Alan lived at Hampton's Brooklyn house along with Joe. It was a big brownstone with thirteen rooms, which the Hamptons rented out to other jazzmen. Curtis Fuller, Eric Dolphy, Wes Montgomery, and Freddie Hubbard also lived there. When they weren't playing gigs, they all jammed together. Another tenant was John Coltrane's cousin, Mary Greenlee, and her husband, Charles, a trombone player. Consequently, Coltrane used to drop by and Joe would hear him practicing with Wayne. "It was a very inspiring period in my life," Zawinul recalled.[30]

Joe and Wayne became running buddies. Wayne recalled the two of them "[going] from one place to another—myself, him and Slide Hampton, and some of the other guys. Freddie Hubbard. We'd just move around, runnin' around, and I didn't realize that what we were doing was in place of talking, the action. There was a lot of action going on. Now that I think back, we were always with people and running into people and things. 'There's Thelonious Monk. There goes Miles. There goes—hey! Sonny Rollins!' And then we'd go in a place to eat, and while we were eating, late at night, everyone came in there—Dizzy Gillespie, all of them—and it seemed, like . . . They say a picture's worth a thousand words? Well, we viewed. And to me, I thought it was language."[31]

Wayne lasted only about a month with the Ferguson band, but Amiri Baraka caught them one night at Birdland. Wayne told him that he had already gotten a few of his tunes in Ferguson's book. Maynard was open to audience requests, Wayne said, and he recommended a couple that Baraka should ask for. Ferguson obliged. Baraka later recalled the performance in an article for *The Jazz Review*, writing, "It was apparent to everyone in Birdland that [Wayne's] playing was the most exciting thing that had happened all night."[32]

A few weeks later, Ferguson played the four-day Toronto Jazz Festival (the first of its kind in Canada, which must have delighted Maynard, who was Canadian). The next afternoon, Art Blakey's Jazz Messengers took the outdoor stage without their saxman, Hank Mobley, who suffered from drug addiction and failed to show. Wayne listened from the grandstands, where Lee Morgan, Art's trumpet player, spotted him. Morgan had been keeping tabs on Wayne since his Army days. After the Messengers' set, Morgan ran across the dirt track separating the makeshift bandstand from the spectator area.

"Hey, Wayne, you want to play with us?" he asked.

Wayne didn't hesitate. "Shit, yeah," he responded.[33]

Of course, Blakey knew Wayne, too. "You know, the big band is a bomber aircraft; Wayne is a fighter pilot," Art told him.[34] His message was clear: With his improvisational gifts, Wayne belonged in a small band. He played one last engagement with Ferguson opposite the Messengers at Birdland. Without a sax player of his own, Blakey asked Wayne if he would play for him that night. As Joe recalled, "Wayne happened to know every tune and played with them like he was there all his life, you know? And that was it for Wayne Shorter. He left Maynard's band."[35]

3 Apprenticeship

I had to pay a whole lot of dues to learn this way to express myself.
—Joe Zawinul

NOT LONG AFTER WAYNE BOLTED FOR THE JAZZ MESSENGERS, Zawinul found himself out of a job. In his telling, he was fired after Maynard Ferguson became suspicious that he and Slide Hampton were trying to take over the band. Ferguson's own explanation was simpler: "Joe Zawinul, I felt, was ready for other things, so I let him go."[1] Regardless of the reason, Joe spent the summer of 1959 lounging at the beach during the day and jamming at Slide Hampton's brownstone at night. He also occasionally checked in at the musician's union, which led to his first record date. A singer asked Joe to accompany him for an audition at Strand Records, a new budget label. When they were done, one of the label men suggested they do an album of Joe's. So he rehearsed a band for two or three days at Hampton's house, then cut the record in two hours—the first under his own name.[2]

Joe's easygoing lifestyle changed in October when he ran into his next boss, Dinah Washington, at Birdland. They were already acquainted. At one point, the Ferguson band was booked for some shows with Washington in Atlanta. Impressed with Joe's playing, she stopped by the hotel bar where Zawinul and a group of musicians were holding forth. She lingered for a while before walking up to Joe, who was seated at the piano. Putting a business card in his shirt pocket, she said, "I sure like the way you play," and urged him to call her when he got back to New York.[3] Dinah was steeped in gospel, blues, and jazz; her interest in Joe indicated just how well he could handle those forms after only a few months in the States.

Joe didn't follow up, but now that they were face-to-face, Dinah stopped her entourage and said, "Aren't you the guy I heard play at a party? Why don't you come tomorrow—I'm opening at the Village Vanguard."[4] Joe did as instructed, and Dinah asked him to sit in. After a few numbers in which he played "some of the funkiest blues you ever wanna hear," according to one observer, she was ready to hire him.[5] "You want to be the piano player?" she discretely whispered.[6] Joe started the next day, bringing along Jimmy Rowser, who had also been fired by Ferguson. They remained with Dinah for the next eighteen months.

At the time, Washington was at the peak of her popularity. Earlier in the year, her single "What a Diff'rence a Day Makes" had risen to number four on the pop charts, establishing her appeal beyond the mostly black audience that was her bread and butter.[7] She excelled in a variety of styles, but the blues was always at her core. She had a high-pitched voice that could cut through a noisy room and sang with exquisite diction, time and phrasing. Not only was she one of the outstanding female vocalists of her era, she was also extravagant. She loved her furs, her shoes, her jewelry—even her wigs. She was a diva before popular female vocalists were known as such.

Washington traveled with a trio, which gave Joe ample opportunity to shine. She described him as having the touch of George Shearing and the soul of Ray Charles, and engaged him in stage banter that revealed his Austrian accent, much to the surprise and delight of the audience. The band worked regularly and was "in super shape," Joe said. As Washington's biographer, Nadine Cohodas, wrote, Zawinul was having the time of his life.

> The musicians were well paid, and he got extra because he wrote the arrangements for the live shows. Like other musicians before him who had played with Dinah, Zawinul looked at the job as a tutorial. 'I learned a lot about phraseology, using the lyrics,' he said. 'There was always a lyricism in her phrasing.' He knew, too, that he and bassist Jimmy Rowser had to be ready for on-the-spot changes if Dinah was feeling tired or hoarse. 'We could drop it down a third with no problem,' he explained. 'We were so in tune with each other.'"[8]

As the only white musician in Dinah's band, Joe experienced the working conditions of black entertainers. They worked along the Chitlin' Circuit, a string of nightclubs and theaters in the Eastern and Southern states where black musicians performed during the time of segregation. Joe stayed in the black hotels or in the homes of black families right along with the rest of the band, and drew solidarity from it. Washington was a big enough star by this time that she also performed at mainstream venues, but even there, black entertainers were welcome only on the stage—"idolized and demeaned at the same moment," Cohodas wrote.[9]

In early 1961, Washington took over the Roberts Show Lounge in her hometown of Chicago, where she installed a revue with a cast of forty, including other musical acts, comedians, and her latest husband (one of seven), who served as host. She dubbed it "Dinahland." By this time, Joe was growing dissatisfied with the emphasis on entertainment at the expense of stimulating music. "I'm getting tired of this shit," he confided to Rowser. "I came to America to play jazz."[10] Joe's favorite drummer in those days, Philly Joe Jones, stopped by one night and admonished him: "It's time for you to play some real music."[11] Perhaps that was the nudge Joe needed, for he gave notice shortly after Dinahland got underway and went back to New York.

Ironically, Zawinul then joined Joe Williams, the Count Basie singer who had formed a band with Harry "Sweets" Edison. Jones was incredulous. "Are you nuts?" he exclaimed. "You walk away from the best singer out there to get back to playing with another singer. What is this?"[12] But it was "a great fuckin' band!" Joe protested, so he toured with them for a month.[13] In his mind, it was another chance to learn, another rung up the ladder. When he returned from the road, the phone was ringing in his apartment. It was Cannonball Adderley, asking if he wanted a job. Joe didn't hesitate, even if Edison didn't take the news well. "He wanted to take me to the union and sue me," Joe recalled. "I said, 'You got to understand. This is my shot.'"[14]

•

Wayne officially joined the Jazz Messengers on August 1, 1959.[15] The band included Lee Morgan on trumpet, Bobby Timmons on piano, and Jymie Merritt on bass. Art Blakey was a generation older than most of them; only Merritt was over thirty. Morgan, at twenty-one, was the youngest, a prodigy who at the age of eighteen had cut his first records as a leader for Savoy and Blue Note. Surrounding himself with young talent was a pattern Blakey would maintain throughout his career.

If one were to name the quintessential hard bop drummer, it would be Art Blakey. He earned his bebop bona fides in Billy Eckstine's band and was soon in demand by the best jazz musicians in New York. In the 1950s, he teamed with pianist Horace Silver, performing under the name Horace Silver and the Jazz Messengers. Silver brought an R&B funkiness to bebop, and after Silver left, the Messengers carried on in that vein. Their music was more accessible than bebop while retaining its excitement and vitality, all undergirded by Blakey, who radiated "sheer drive, swing, strength, power, and excitement" from behind the kit.[16] It's been said that even though Blakey didn't write the Messengers' tunes, they were *all* Blakey tunes, such was his ability to dictate to the rest of the band.

Wayne came to the Messengers with a book of compositions that Blakey quickly tapped. Three months after Wayne's first gig, the band went to Rudy Van Gelder's New Jersey recording studio. Among the tunes committed to tape were

Wayne's "Africaine" and "Lester Left Town," the latter a tribute to the tenor great Lester Young, who had died in March. The song lopes along in an easy-going fashion, with a descending chromatic melody that Wayne said represented the way Lester walked.[17] Wayne's songs always seemed to have a story behind them.

The results of the session were not released until 1981, when Blue Note issued the album *Africaine*. Alfred Lion, Blue Note's co-owner, evidently found the music less than satisfactory, in part because Wayne's new music was . . . different. "I wonder if this is too avant-garde," Lion mused in his German accent. "Can you give me some grease?" By grease, Lion was thinking of the Messengers' previous (and first Blue Note) studio album, *Moanin'*, and the title track that became a hard bop anthem and remained in their repertoire to the end. But Blakey wasn't accepting any interference, even from his label head. "This is my band, and we're gonna do these tunes," he insisted. As Wayne put it, "No matter how different something was, Art would stay with it."[18]

"Lester Left Town" became a hard bop standard, too, and a more up-tempo version appeared on the Messengers' next album, *The Big Beat*, recorded four months later. Though the relaxed pace of the earlier version seemed to better evoke Young's shuffling gait, Wayne's more assured solo on *The Big Beat* demonstrated his growth in just a few months' time. The album got a timely release from Blue Note, perhaps because of the inclusion of Timmons's funky tune "Dat Dere," a sequel to his "Dis Here," which had been a hit for Cannonball Adderley the year before. *The Big Beat* also included two more of Wayne's tunes, "The Chess Players" and "Sakeena's Vision"—more evidence of his imprint on the Messengers' music early on. As for Wayne's playing, Nat Hentoff wrote in the album's liner notes: "While it's true he has clearly listened with concentration to Coltrane and Rollins, Wayne is one of the few of the younger tenors who is already his own man. He plays with striking strength and consistent logic. And, like Coltrane and Rollins, he has that 'cry' at the core of his playing that separates the jazzman who has something to say from the musician who knows his changes but not himself."[19]

The Messengers returned to Van Gelder's studio nine times in 1961, recording enough material for six albums. That was a lot for such a short period of time, so several albums were held in the vaults for later release. All told, Blakey recorded over twenty of Wayne's tunes in just two years. Cedar Walton, who took over the piano chair that year, explained, "You couldn't write enough music for Art. You'd write it now, you'd get it played now, and you'd get it recorded now."[20] Wayne became the band's musical director, and when the group was expanded to a sextet, the third horn afforded him more arranging possibilities.

Being a Messenger instantly raised Wayne's profile and he secured a recording contract with Chicago-based Vee-Jay Records. Wayne's book of tunes was so thick that he filled his debut album, *Introducing Wayne Shorter*, with five more compositions. All told, Wayne got nearly fifty compositions recorded by the time he left the Messengers in 1964. He was so prolific that Curtis Fuller remembered him writing two or three tunes a week, most of which he threw away.[21]

The five years Wayne spent with the Jazz Messengers are considered by many historians to be the band's most creative period—high praise, considering Blakey kept the Messengers going for over three decades. Art once said that when Shorter joined the band, he was so shy that the bandleader had to bring him out of his shell. But by 1964, it seemed as though the Messengers could barely contain him. The road he traveled after "Lester Left Town" might be best illustrated by one of his tunes the band recorded shortly before he left. "Free For All," from the album of the same name, is eleven minutes of joyous music. Wayne is in complete command of his instrument, with no inhibitions, unfurling a solo that, in Kenny Mathieson's words, is "breathtakingly turbulent, twisting and turning the material through ever-increasing degrees of density and abstraction."[22]

•

When Joe Zawinul got the call to join Cannonball Adderley's band, the saxophonist was one of the biggest names in jazz. His 1959 album *The Cannonball Adderley Quintet in San Francisco* sold 80,000 copies in its first year, fueled by the Bobby Timmons tune "This Here" (a.k.a. "Dis Here"). That was an impressive figure in an age when successful jazz albums sold in the six to eight thousand range, making the saxophonist a star in the emerging soul jazz market, a term used to describe jazz inflected with a healthy dose of rhythm 'n' blues. Adderley excelled at it. His bebop chops were unquestioned, but he also loved to get down and dirty, and he would straddle the line between the two genres throughout his career. Cannonball's next album made the connection explicit in its title, *Them Dirty Blues*, which included an even bigger hit in "Work Song," which was composed by Cannon's brother and musical partner, Nat Adderley.

Dinah Washington was a star in her own right, but the piano chair in the Adderley Quintet was unquestionably a step up. In a rare moment of self-doubt, Joe worried if he was up to it. With so many of his peers hanging out at Birdland, "it used to freak me out" to play there, he later admitted. "But after awhile it got to the point where I really didn't give a shit. I said to myself, 'Either you do it or you don't do it.'"[23]

A week after getting hired, the quintet recorded with vocalist Nancy Wilson. The resulting album, *Nancy Wilson / Cannonball Adderley*, helped launch Wilson's national career and remains one of her finest recordings. Having spent eighteen months accompanying Dinah Washington, this was right up Joe's alley, and he sounds like he's been a part of the band for much longer. It's also notable for including the first of Joe's many compositions for Adderley, "One Man's Dream." The style is reminiscent of two funky pianists Cannonball knew well, Bobby Tim-

The Cannonball Adderley Quintet, 1964. Left to right: Joe Zawinul, Nat Adderley, Sam Jones, Cannonball Adderley, and Louis Hayes. Photo: © David Redfern / Redferns / Getty Images.

mons and Horace Silver, both of whom Joe acknowledged as early influences.

In fact, Zawinul was influenced by many pianists, to the extent that he once described himself as "a total copyist."[24] But that wasn't going to cut it in New York. "Every guy on the streets was a piano player," Joe said. "I remember hanging out with Phineas Newborn, Wynton Kelly, Barry Harris, Tommy Flanagan, Walter Davis Jr., Walter Bishop, Sonny Clark, Cedar Walton, Bobby Timmons, Bill Evans. . . . All these guys could really play, and none of them played like the other ones did."[25] Joe tried to soak them all up, but one style he was particularly keen to absorb was bebop, having had little exposure to it in Austria. To do so, he began practicing with Barry Harris, whose style was patterned after the pioneering bebop pianist Bud Powell. Within a few years, Joe had essentially mastered the art of modern jazz piano. According to a 1966 profile in *Down Beat*, he commanded the idiom with "exceptional authority," and to his peers he sounded as American as they did.[26]

But as time passed, Joe reached a point of disenchantment. He began to chafe at the band's repertoire, which he felt required him to "play roles" while performing the band's hits.[27] Cannonball was keenly aware of his audiences, and while he didn't pander to them, he understood that they were there to be entertained. But Joe wanted to push into more modern things. After a while, he "started messing up. Goofing." He turned to alcohol and his playing suffered, which he blamed on "tensions I had developed over what I was playing—or, rather, wasn't playing."[28]

At around this time, an incident with Barry Harris, who preceded Joe in Adderley's band, forced Zawinul to take a closer look at himself. One day he was hanging out near Birdland when an excited Harris ran up to him, exclaiming, "Joe! I gotta tell you something! It's killing me, man!"

"Yeah, what's that?" Joe asked.

"The tune I just heard on the radio in the cab, it was Cannonball, and I swear to God I thought it was me playing. And then they announced it was you, man. Congratulations!"

"I said, 'Thank you, Barry.' And I was flattered for a minute. But when I thought about it, I said, 'Well, now, what the hell does that mean? He's already copying Bud Powell and I'm copying him. What the hell is *this*?'"[29]

To Joe, it was a catalyst for change. For one thing, he stopped listening to other people's music. "I went home, right then and there, and put all my records in boxes, and they are still stashed away," he said.[30] But it also led to a period of deeper introspection from which he emerged a more mature person and musician. At the recommendation of Friedrich Gulda, Zawinul began weekly lessons with classical pianist Raymond Lewenthal, whom Joe called "the greatest technician in the world."[31] He nailed metal bars to the hammers of his piano to strengthen his fingers.

And there was one other thing: "We had a couple of days off and I took some acid. And we were in this guy's house, on a houseboat, and he had a nice piano and I played. And all of a sudden I started playing different than I've ever played all my life. And that was it. That's exactly what I do now. I just went—*bam*—in one switch. And I never went back to anything, and things just came to me."[32]

•

By 1966, Joe was "brimming with ideas, interested in hearing and experiencing new music, eager to play and experiment," according to the *Down Beat* profile.[33] That year, the quintet recorded five of his compositions—more than in all his previous years combined—and Joe took his first step toward establishing an independent career, making his first album for Atlantic Records, which included three more of his pieces. By this time, Joe had married a beautiful African American woman named Maxine, and writing was partly a matter of economics. "I had a family and I asked myself, 'What is the future going to be like if I'm just going to be a sideman, even in a great band like Cannonball Adderley's group?' So, I started writing; but without those years of learning how to play bebop, it would have never happened quite that way."[34]

Joe also began working with a young gospel singer named Esther Marrow. "Not gigs, just going to the house and practicing with her," he explained. "I needed the extra money and at the same time we developed a nice repertoire which we could bring on stage."[35] Joe recorded their sessions, and one time he was listening to one of the tapes. "We were improvising around, and I played this little background, and it was nice. So I played it again, and all of a sudden it was a little tune."[36] Joe began playing it during Cannonball's shows, often as the background while Adderley chatted with the audience. "Somehow people liked it," Joe remembered. "People would come up and ask us to 'play that tune you don't have a name for yet!'"[37]

One night in New England, the basketball player Bill Russell drove down from Boston to see the band with Olympian John Thomas, a former high jump world record holder. "They were big fans of Cannonball's, and they sat down at the front table," Joe said. "I started playing it, the first few bars, and John Thomas stood up and said, 'Mercy, mercy, mercy.' So I said to myself, 'Well, I'm going to put a bridge to that, and boom, from then on we played it."[38]

Joe worked up an unorthodox arrangement. The piece was built around his gospel-inspired piano lines, while the horns merely stated and restated the theme, with no solos other than Joe's. Cary Ginell, in his Adderley biography, *Walk Tall*, describes the song as "a modern-day version of the *kyrie*, a lament impelling black Americans to turn mercy into activism; it is a statement of Zawinul's musical identification with African Americans' struggle for equality."[39] It's doubtful that Joe consciously had such a lofty purpose in mind when he came up with "Mercy, Mercy, Mercy"—after all, to him it was just "a little tune"—but after years of working closely with black musicians and marrying a black woman, he certainly was sympathetic to their plight.

In October 1966, the quintet gathered at the Capitol Records building in Hollywood to make their seventh album for the label. Cannonball's best LPs had been recorded live, when the band thrived on audience feedback. So for this session, producer David Axelrod transformed Capitol's cavernous Studio A into a temporary nightclub. He placed the band on risers, set up stage lighting courtesy of Capitol's art department, and provided seating and an open bar for an audience. It gave the session the energy of a club, but in the controlled environment of a recording studio. Urged on by an enthusiastic audience of Capitol employees and their friends, the result was Adderley's most successful record, *Mercy, Mercy, Mercy! Live at "The Club."*

Like virtually all jazz pianists at the time, Joe stuck to the acoustic piano, even on "Mercy."[40] But for this session he thought of the Wurlitzer electric pianos he'd previously seen at the Capitol studios. It was an instrument he knew well, going back to the fifties. "They had a lot of those instruments at the camps for the soldiers, and I played them on those shows often times, for GIs and all that."[41] Later, he occasionally played one with Dinah Washington. "We toured a lot with Ray Charles, and he did a couple of the songs, you know, 'What'd I Say,' with a Wurlitzer. And sometimes when the pianos were not in good shape—in the South it happened quite often—Dinah asked Ray to let me play on it. I always liked that sound from way back, and I really knew how to play it."[42]

That sound was on Joe's mind as he drove with Adderley to 1750 Vine Street. "I said to Cannon on the way to the studio, 'Cannon, if I find this instrument I'm looking for, I will play that tune on this instrument, and I guarantee we have a smash hit.' And I go to Studio A and I look around, and in one corner, man, I see it. I opened it up and it was in great, great tune. I had 'em take it out on the bandstand and we rehearsed it one time through, and I knew it was all over. It was a live recording. We had about eighty or ninety people out there, with catering and a lot of friends. History, man."[43] Indeed, when Joe played the opening strains of "Mercy" behind Adderley's sermon-like spoken introduction, the reaction of the audience was immediate.

At the end of the year, Capitol released an edited version of "Mercy" as a single. David Axelrod realized they might be onto something special when he heard it played on late night radio seven times in a row. It took off "like a rocket," he remembered, garnering airplay around the country and reaching an impressive number eleven on the *Billboard* Hot 100 chart.[44] Three quarters of a million singles were sold in six months, while the album topped 300,000 units by summer.[45] Within weeks two vocal versions, each with different lyrics, were made, and at one point all three of them occupied spots on the *Billboard* R&B Singles chart. But the highest chart-topper of all came in August, when the Buckinghams reached number five on the Hot 100 with their rendition.[46]

"Mercy" was a watershed in Joe's career because it unequivocally established his ability to tap into the American musical experience in a way that belied his background. It also put him on the path of electric keyboards from which he never returned. It wasn't the first time an electric piano was used in jazz, but it proved to be the most influential, leading the way to the instrument's broader adoption. At the time, his peers dismissed such instruments as toys unworthy of serious music. Joe didn't care about that; he was simply interested in the sound.

With audiences demanding to hear "Mercy, Mercy, Mercy" live, Joe needed to carry an electric piano on the road. He started with a Wurlitzer, but soon found a better instrument, one that became his mainstay for years to come. "I was very lucky that Victor Feldman was a close friend to me and my family and one of the best musicians around," Zawinul said. (Feldman played piano for Adderley before Joe took over.) "After I started playing the Wurlitzer, Victor said, 'Man, there's this guy, Hal Rhodes, and he's working on an instrument that you should check out.'"[47]

One of the legendary figures of the musical instrument industry, Harold Rhodes invented his first electric piano out of old B-17 airplane parts while stationed in Europe during World War II. A music teacher by trade, Rhodes used his small, suitcase-sized instrument to teach music to convalescing soldiers. In the years after the war, he continued to evolve and refine his ideas, ultimately creating one of the classic instruments of the twentieth century. The seventy-three-key Fender Rhodes electric piano was introduced in 1965. That model and its successors would be produced for the next twenty years, becoming nearly ubiquitous in pop, jazz, and R&B.

Joe also reaped the financial windfall that came from writing a hit song. At the time, he was making $300 a week with Cannonball while paying for his own lodging and meals. It didn't stretch far. At one point he was offered the piano chair with Ella Fitzgerald at the considerable salary of $1,400 a month, plus hotels and expenses. The per diem alone was almost double his current salary. It was a tough offer to refuse. But he was also moving forward in headstrong fashion; accompanying a vocalist would have been a step backward. Still, he felt obligated to run it by Maxine. "You do what you have to do," she said. "I can make do with $300 and I have time to wait until you have your thing."[48]

Then "Mercy" hit. In Gunther Baumann's book *Zawinul: Ein Leben aus Jazz*, Joe described the impact it had on his family:

> At one point I had to go on a tour and there was hardly any money in the house. We paid the rent and only had a few dollars left—that was it. I had already received an advance and we didn't even have money to eat. My wife always accompanied me with the kids to the front door when I left, and that was the first time I saw tears running down her cheeks. She never complained. She had this quiet strength, but I couldn't forget that face. So I went to the office of our manager, John Levy, and when I arrived, he told me that I should immediately call home. That gave me a pang; what happened? I went to a pay phone and called my wife, and she said, "Honey, our problems are over. I just got a check for $13,000." That was my first royalty check. . . . A huge weight was lifted from my heart. Basically, from that moment on we were never poor.[49]

•

Joe was one of the first musicians Herbie Hancock met when he came to New York in 1961. So it was from this perspective that Hancock observed that Joe's "whole being has gone through such a metamorphosis since then. He had certain kinds of insecurities at that time, which since 'Mercy, Mercy' have completely disappeared. He's a European piano player, his roots are not in the music which comes out of America—and he's white, too. Maybe this was the source of the insecurities he had, and then he writes one of the greatest soul pieces of today's music; that completely washed all those other things away."[50]

Any traces of the self-proclaimed "copyist" were washed away as well. From 1966 on, Joe's playing took on a deeply personal style. He no longer fell back on the crutch of imitation. The bebop chops that he had worked so hard to master just a few years earlier melded into a lyrical approach that favored melody, space, and mood. He could still dazzle an audience with his formidable technique, but he now crafted compelling and engaging solos that transcended mere technical excellence. He was becoming a storyteller, imbuing his music with emotion and narrative—a concept that would become central to his music.

Almost a year after recording "Mercy," Cannonball returned to Capitol's Studio A. This time the band recorded Joe's tune "74 Miles Away," the title of which derives from its 7/4 time signature. The bass-and-drum tandem of Victor Gaskin and Roy McCurdy sustain an intense feeling of momentum throughout the tune's fourteen-minute duration. In its length, bass ostinato, and sheer rhythmic energy and drive, "74 Miles Away" is a prototype for later Weather Report pieces such as "Boogie Woogie Waltz" and "Nubian Sundance." It was also one of the more significant pieces Joe wrote for Adderley. When the band needed to come out on fire from the get-go, this is the tune they would pick.

"74 Miles Away" also signaled Joe's move to modal, open compositional forms. Miles Davis and John Coltrane were the central figures in the development of modal jazz, the exemplar being "So What" from Miles's 1959 album *Kind of Blue*. The essence of modal playing is to improvise using a scale or mode, typically over slow harmonic movement or pedal point harmonies (in which the bass note is sustained). Improvising in this fashion is the antithesis of the bebop ethos of "playing the changes," and modal forms served as the basis for much of jazz after 1960. Joe likened it to the *volksmusik* he played in Austria. "We were doing modal stuff in Vienna, you know? We were getting into all these different scales from folk music. . . . I was actually surprised when I came to the States that more people weren't doing this."[51]

"74 Miles Away" stays in one tonal center for its entirety. Joe called it "a very natural groove based just on one chord."[52] Cannonball and Nat deliver fine statements, but the highlight is Joe's marvelous extended solo, in which he skillfully builds and releases the tension until it explodes in a powerful climax before bringing the band back to the main groove. In the album's liner notes, Leonard Feather called Zawinul's performance "a magnificent demonstration of the scope and resourcefulness he can bring to modern jazz piano."[53] Part of that resourcefulness was using a prepared piano to overcome its inherent limitations of tone and timbre. "I had small tambourines duct taped inside the piano, small tambourines with little bells, " Joe said, "and I started already synthesizing my shit, with my acoustic instruments."[54] He was so keen on pulling new sounds out of the piano that Roy McCurdy remembered him shaking it, trying to get the notes to bend.[55]

A few months later, Joe recorded his second album for Atlantic, *The Rise & Fall of the Third Stream*—an ambitious collaboration with saxophonist-composer William Fischer, who wrote all of the material save one tune by Friedrich Gulda. The term *third stream* was coined by composer-conductor Gunther Schuller a decade earlier to describe a fusion of the "improvisational spontaneity and rhythmic vitality" of jazz with classical music's "compositional formal procedures."[56] This album was an attempt to do that, with a string quartet augmenting a conventional jazz combo.

Aside from foreshadowing Joe's embrace of a variety of musical influences, there is one piece in particular that serves as a road map for his later work. "The Soul of a Village" (Parts I and II) is a heavily layered modal performance undergirded by a drone reminiscent of Indian music. Once again Joe uses a prepared piano to good effect, in this case placing wax paper on the strings, which adds depth to the drone and provides color to the string ensemble. In "Part II," he plays electric piano, producing a solo that recalls his *volksmusik* roots while also tapping into the American blues tradition. It is elegant in its simplicity, yet bears the hallmarks of story in its construction and execution.[57]

Reflecting on his musical journey, Joe said, "I had to pay a whole lot of dues to learn this way to express myself."[58] But he also realized that he had it all along, he just needed the confidence to let himself go. Flush with success and equipped with a new sense of maturity that would carry him forward for the rest of his life, Joe took his family to Austria at the end of 1966. The visit turned out to be a highly productive one. Perhaps it was the comfort of being home with his parents, or maybe it was the peace of the Oberkirchbach forests. Regardless of the source of inspiration, when Joe returned to New York a few weeks later, he did so with a cache of new tunes that would help shape some momentous changes in music.

4 Miles

I wasn't prepared to be a memory yet.

—Miles Davis

THE FIRST TIME MILES DAVIS SPOKE TO WAYNE SHORTER, the trumpeter had no idea who he was. It was late 1959, and John Coltrane was preparing to leave Davis's band. He urged Wayne to call the bandleader, saying, "You can have the job if you want it." Wayne did as instructed. "I called and said, 'Hello. I'm Wayne Shorter, and I'm from Newark, New Jersey.' And you know Miles, he said in that voice [a rasp caused by damaged vocal cords], 'Who told you I needed a saxophone player?' And I said, 'Trane. John Coltrane.' Well, Miles says, 'If I need a saxophone player, I'll get one.' Then we kind of measured each other to see who would hang up first."[1]

It didn't take long before Wayne was on Miles's radar. Davis started covertly going to Messengers gigs—"incognito," as Wayne described it.[2] "Lee Morgan would tap me on the shoulder and say, 'Miles is in the club; he's over in the corner. He's checking you out.'"[3] It wasn't just Wayne's playing that Miles found interesting, but also his arrangements and compositions. When Coltrane followed through with his plans the following spring, Wayne got a call from Davis inviting him to join his group. "I had just joined the Messengers, so I told Miles, 'You know I've only been with this band not even a year yet. I don't think it's cool to just run and leave 'em. I don't think anybody likes a Benedict Arnold.'" Miles understood. "When you're ready, call me," he told Wayne.[4]

Losing Coltrane was a significant blow to Davis. In a real sense, he was irreplaceable; there simply wasn't another saxophonist of his caliber. In Trane's absence, Davis entered a period of musical stagnation, and when his working band fell apart in 1963, he set about putting together a new one from scratch. His first hires were George Coleman—the saxophonist Wayne bested for the Maynard Ferguson job—and bassist Ron Carter. Then he nabbed seventeen-year-old drumming phenom, Tony Williams. After trying a couple of piano players, Miles invited Herbie Hancock to rehearse with the band in his apartment. "I knew right away that this was going to be a motherfucker of a group," Davis said.[5] The only problem was that Coleman wasn't a good fit and quit the band a year later, so Miles again set his sights on Wayne. Art Blakey knew it was just a matter time.

If there was a pecking order in jazz, Miles Davis was at the top. Though just seven years Wayne's senior, it seemed as if Davis had already lived a lifetime of jazz. He came to New York in 1944 to attend Juilliard, but his real ambition was to seek out Charlie Parker and Dizzy Gillespie. Davis quickly immersed himself in the city's emerging bebop scene, and a year later he took Gillespie's place in Parker's band. But it was the decade that began just after his association with Parker ended that established Miles as one of the giants of jazz. From 1949 to 1959, he was instrumental in four significant innovations in the music, here summarized by Gary Giddins and Scott DeVeaux in their book, *Jazz*:

> In 1949–50, his nonet helped focus the attention of a generation of musicians looking beyond bebop and launched cool jazz. In 1954, his *Walkin'* session acted as an antidote to the cool school's increasing refinement and reliance on classical music, providing an impetus for hard bop. From 1957 to 1960, Davis's three major collaborations with Gil Evans enlarged the scope of jazz composition, big band music, and recordings, projecting a deep, meditative mood new in jazz. In 1959, *Kind of Blue*, the culmination of Davis's experiments with modal improvisation, transformed jazz performance and replaced bebop's harmonic complexity with a scalar approach that favored melody and nuance.[6]

In addition to all of that, Davis's 1950s quintet, with John Coltrane, Red Garland, Paul Chambers, and Philly Joe Jones (later augmented to a sextet with the addition of Cannonball Adderley), was one of the foremost combos in the history of the genre. It became known as Davis's first great quintet, challenged in supremacy only by his second great quintet, the one that was established when Wayne came into the fold.

It took a year for Davis to get his man. When he learned that Wayne had left the Messengers in July 1964, he put on the full-court press and had the rest of his musicians recruit Wayne, too. Davis had just returned from a tour of Japan and had an upcoming performance in California when Wayne finally called. "I sent that motherfucker a first-class ticket so he could come out in style. That's how bad I wanted him," Miles later wrote.[7]

In September, Wayne flew to Los Angeles and made his way to the Hollywood

Bowl, where Davis was set to open a show called "Modern Sounds '64" with Gerry Mulligan, João Gilberto, and Nina Simone.[8] When he got there, Wayne found the rest of the band gathered in the trumpeter's dressing room. "The first thing Miles said to me was, 'You know my music?' I said, 'Yeah!' He said, 'Uh-oh,' like, 'You think you bad, huh?' I had this book under my arm. He looked at the book before we went on stage—I had a lot of stuff I was writing in there."[9]

Wayne's new surroundings inspired him from the start. In his book, *Possibilities*, Herbie Hancock recalled his reaction upon sharing the stage with Wayne for the first time.

> We got up to Wayne's solo, and he was about to do what we called "strolling," which meant that all the rest of us would drop out and he'd be playing completely alone, with no accompaniment. And suddenly Wayne started playing these weird, ghostly tones, blowing into the horn so you could hear the air going through with just the faintest suggestion of a note. When he started doing that, Tony and I just looked at each other like, *Whoa! Where did that come from?* It was strangely beautiful, almost like whispering. I'd never heard anything like it.[10]

After the performance, Wayne went back to his hotel room, unsure of how he'd done, when the phone rang. It was Miles. "We're gonna record Monday. Bring the book," he said, matter-of-factly. *He must have heard something worth recording*, Wayne thought.[11] Indeed, he had. "When we went out to the Hollywood Bowl to play it was bad from the beginning and it just got better," Miles wrote in his autobiography.[12]

With the Jazz Messengers, Wayne played within a fairly rigid format imposed by the leader. Miles encouraged his musicians to experiment. If he caught them practicing prearranged parts or licks ahead of time, he would admonish them: "I pay you to practice *on* the bandstand."[13] "The beauty of playing with Miles was that he gave us so much freedom," Hancock wrote. "He never told us what to do or how to do it—he just gave us a platform to explore. We would start playing a song, and the deeper we got into it, the more each player would branch out into new improvisatory places. No song ever sounded the same twice, and often they wouldn't even be recognizable by the time they ended. Even the most familiar jazz standards became swirling, unpredictable explorations—'controlled freedom' was what we called it."[14]

Controlled freedom was an allusion to the avant-garde or free jazz school that came into prominence—or perhaps more accurately, ignited a firestorm—in late 1959 when a relatively unknown, self-taught saxophonist named Ornette Coleman brought his band to New York City for an extended engagement at the Five

Spot. His music instantly polarized the jazz community. Coleman dispensed with the usual harmonic, rhythmic, and metric constraints of jazz to produce music that seemed to evolve spontaneously by instinct, without hewing to form.

Some prominent critics declared it the first great advance in jazz since bebop; hence it was commonly called "the New Thing." But most jazzmen weren't convinced. "I don't know what [Coleman's] playing, but it's not jazz," Dizzy Gillespie groused in *Time* magazine.[15] Miles was dismissive as well. "Hell, just listen to what he writes and how he plays. If you're talking psychologically, the man is all screwed up inside."[16] Nevertheless, by 1964, the avant-garde was firmly entrenched in the jazz landscape, and Davis's old tenor player, John Coltrane, was about to become its leading exponent.

Miles had been at the forefront of all of the major developments in jazz since bebop, with the exception of the New Thing. Even though he publicly disparaged it, one way for Miles to reinvigorate his music was to adopt elements of the avant-garde into his own aesthetic. His young rhythm section was already pushing him in that direction. They were thoroughly versed in hard bop, but crucially came of age when the avant-garde was the most exciting thing in jazz. As a consequence, the group tried, in Hancock's words, to "take these influences that were happening to all of us at the time and amalgamate them, personalize them in such a way that when people were hearing us, they were hearing the avant-garde on the one hand, and they were hearing the history of jazz that led up to it on the other hand—because Miles was that history. He was that link."[17]

Four months after playing the Hollywood Bowl, the band recorded its first studio effort with Wayne. "I brought the book with me and [Miles] looked at the music," he recalled. "The first thing he saw was 'E.S.P.' He said, 'Let's try this.' So we did it."[18] The LP took its title from that tune, which was an apt description of the group's seeming telepathic ability to improvise off each other. In addition to the title track, Wayne contributed a ballad called "Iris," which features some of his characteristic harmonic devices that leave the tune's tonal center ambiguous. The album was a departure from Miles's earlier recordings and his first move toward adopting avant-garde sensibilities, which *Down Beat*'s review picked up on.[19] In his liner notes for the 1998 CD remaster, producer Bob Belden hyperbolically described it as "light years ahead of anything that had previously been released."[20]

•

Not long after recording *E.S.P.*, the quintet had to suspend performances as Miles underwent hip surgery; he wouldn't resume playing for seven months. In the interim, the rest of the band took gigs where they could and kept busy recording for Blue Note at Rudy Van Gelder's. Wayne was a frequent visitor there during Miles's hiatus, making three more albums to go along with the trio he had made the previous year. "I had nothing to do but record," he recalled. "I had no band or anything, and I was just home and was going through material that I had tested out, written at the piano. I didn't even realize that all that went down in such a short period of time."[21]

Alfred Lion was more than happy to record Miles's sidemen. When he felt a musician was hot, he would "record the hell out of him because it's not going to last forever," Van Gelder said.[22] And the musicians were just as happy to be recorded because it was an important source of income when they were off the road. "Blue Note was like going to the bank for us," Wayne told his biographer, Michelle Mercer.[23] With rehearsals, they could get a record done in a week and pocket $500 in the process.

Wayne was quick to employ his new bandmates on his Blue Note projects. In particular, he established a lifelong musical partnership and friendship with Herbie Hancock, later bound together by their common practice of Nichiren Buddhism. Initially, though, Hancock wasn't sure what to make of the saxophonist. "Even after Wayne had been playing with us for a while with Miles, I often couldn't follow what he was saying," Hancock recalled. "I just figured, 'Well, Wayne's a little out there.' One day I decided: 'I've got to find out whether this guy is a genius or just a little crazy!' We had a few days off, and I decided to hang out with him until it was clear to me. So we hung out all night, had something to drink, and I went along with the conversation and figured out a little more about how to listen and follow and play the games. And my conclusion was, 'Yup, he's a genius!'"[24]

The Blue Note albums are showcases for Wayne's writing, as nearly all of the tunes are from his hand. Wayne possessed a singular compositional voice that continues to inspire jazz musicians and academics alike. His pieces deviate from conventional form and employ harmonies devoid of the predictable close-to-the-melody chord progressions of popular songs. "I don't like that approach because thereby, the listener can just about anticipate what's going to come next," he once said.[25] Instead, Wayne's chord choices often rely on atypical resolutions and tonal ambiguity that jazzmen find rich in improvisational possibilities.

Victor Bailey, Weather Report's last bass player, was also a lifelong student of Shorter's work. "What's great about Wayne's music is that, as sophisticated as it is, he writes *songs*. And what's been lost since that era—maybe starting with my generation in the eighties—the idea of actually writing songs. People are writing to show how deep they can be, or how sophisticated harmonically they can be, whereas with every Wayne Shorter composition, the chord changes—and where they go harmonically—are very unusual, but the melody is a *song*. 'Footprints' is a song. 'Witch Hunt' is a song. A person who knows nothing about music can listen to them and hum them back. So Wayne manages to accomplish that while having incredibly sophisticated harmonic qualities."[26]

Members of the Miles Davis Quintet in 1967. Left to right: Miles Davis, Ron Carter, Wayne Shorter. Photo: © Heritage Images / Hulton Archive / Getty Images.

Wayne made seven albums for Blue Note in less than two years, although some of them weren't released until much later. Their scope touches on each of the major jazz movements of the time: hard bop, post bop, and the avant-garde. They became more and more appreciated over the years and cemented Wayne's standing as one of jazz music's most distinctive composers. At the time, though, such thoughts were hardly on his mind. "When all those records came out, I didn't know that they would be thought of as classics or ABCs of modern jazz," Wayne said years later. "Most of those tunes came just like that—real quick. And if anything was behind them, it was like a wish that was manifested musically: Maybe a wish for eternity or a beautiful girl."[27]

•

Davis returned to the stage in late 1965, leading up to a December appearance at the Plugged Nickel, a small club in Chicago that held about a hundred people. Miles had been playing the same standards for years, and despite the layoff, the band was, in Hancock's words, "a little too comfortable."[28] Tony Williams was always up for a challenge, and on the flight to Chicago he threw out an idea: "Let's play some anti-music." According to Hancock, "He wanted us to promise that during our sets at the Plugged Nickel, whatever anybody in the band expected us to play, we would play the opposite."[29] But when they arrived at the club, they saw recording equipment being set up. Hancock wondered whether they should follow through, but Williams was adamant. Just before hitting, they let Wayne and Ron Carter in on the plan, but Miles was kept in the dark. The first tune they played was "If I Were a Bell," a Broadway show tune that had been a part of Davis's repertoire for years. But after the signature piano introduction, the band abruptly veered from the usual script, leaving Miles to negotiate a new reality.

Columbia recorded seven sets over two nights, eventually releasing all of this material as the box set, *The Complete Live at the Plugged Nickel 1965*. It documents the quintet revolutionizing the way in which a small combo consisting of standard instrumentation could approach the jazz repertoire. The music radically changed from set to set as the band stretched the tunes to their breaking points. And while Miles wasn't in top form following his illness, Wayne more than made up for it, "virtually reinventing the vocabulary of the tenor saxophone," according to Davis biographer Ian Carr.[30]

Wayne remembered the Plugged Nickel as the point at which the quintet's musical concepts began to crystallize. "We knew that everyone was taking a lot of chances. We were chance-taking anyway but we were taking some real chances now. I would hear Herbie and myself at certain junctures, struggling with something. Miles would be grappling with something and when we finished, it was like he came out of the boxing ring, but something refreshing was going on. The 'arrival' started to happen at the Plugged Nickel and we couldn't stop that arrival and everybody was celebrating individually in his own way."[31]

The next fall, the quintet recorded its second album, *Miles Smiles*. Unlike its live appearances, the studio albums focused on new material written by the band members themselves. Wayne was responsible for much of this new music. Over the course of the three albums that followed *E.S.P.*, recorded during a ten-month period, Wayne contributed more than half the compositions. "Wayne would just write something and give it to me and walk off," Miles said. "He wouldn't say shit. He'd just say, 'Here, Mr. Davis, I wrote some new songs.' Mr. Davis! Then I'd look at the shit and it would be a motherfucker."[32]

Miles Smiles represented a distillation of the quintet's direction, starting with *E.S.P.* and forged on the bandstand at the Plugged Nickel. In his book analyzing the album, Jeremy Yudkin writes that *Miles Smiles* constituted a "new vision, a sudden understanding of a way forward, one that did not completely follow the old conventions of bop or the apparently formless freedom of the new jazz. The vision was inspired by his band members, and it was one that would result in a new style, one to which we can apply the term *post bop*."[33] As the group's most prolific composer, Wayne played a key role in these developments. Miles described him as "the idea person, the conceptualizer of a whole lot of musical ideas we did."[34]

Given his policy of not listening to records, Joe Zawinul was somewhat oblivious to these developments. That changed one day in 1968, when he happened to be at the home of Bill Russell, listening to music on the basketball star's state-of-the-art hi-fi system. He donned a pair of headphones as *Nefertiti*—the fourth studio album by the second great quintet—spun on the turntable. Joe's interest was piqued.

He first met Miles when he was with Dinah Washington. Back then, he saw Davis at Birdland almost daily, but kept his distance. Miles was a star, but Joe wasn't one to curry favor. If they were going to establish a relationship, Joe intended it to be on equal terms. Inevitably, they bumped into each other at the club one night, and Washington's manager introduced them. The next evening, Miles went to see Dinah's band and subsequently invited Joe to work with him. In Austria, Zawinul used to boast that he would play with Miles one day. It was such an outlandish idea that his buddies laughed it off, but now that he had his chance, he passed. "That set him back," Joe said. "But I told him when the time was right that we would work together and make history. He liked that. We started a friendship that lasted until the day he died."[35]

Back in Bill Russell's basement, listening to *Nefertiti*, Joe was struck by what he called Wayne's "new thinking."[36] Joe later said there were "certain things I heard, certain concepts, which were very, I wouldn't say similar, but complementary" to his own evolving approach.[37] Shorter's title track is distinctive in that there are no horn solos. Instead, he and Miles repeat the haunting melody over and over in unison, but never the same way twice, while the rhythm section serves as the improvisational focal point. When Joe heard it, he kept "waiting for the music to start." It was only when the song ended that he realized that the music had been happening all along.[38]

"Nefertiti" is followed by another of Wayne's tunes called "Fall." He conceived both of them quickly, in a moment of clarity. "One night I'm sitting at four o'clock in the morning with the candlelight and I just drew my hands up and ['Nefertiti'] came. And 'Fall' was like that. I just moved my hands, and there it was."[39] "Fall" is most often described as a tone poem, a term that was being used for some of Joe's pieces as well. By this time, Zawinul had largely abandoned traditional song forms in his own writing, and like Wayne's role with Miles, Joe had become Cannonball's principal writer, shaping much of the group's music. "Mercy, Mercy, Mercy" was his best-known piece, but others, like "74 Miles Away," "Rumpelstiltskin" or "Hippodelphia," moved the quintet away from standards and "gutbucket" (Joe's word) tunes into modal, open forms.

Joe knew he wouldn't be a sideman forever, and listening to *Nefertiti*, he thought, *Wayne is the guy I should do something with.* But for now, he remained happily employed by Adderley, as was Wayne with Miles. Joe filed the thought away for another day.

•

When Joe met Miles in 1959, the trumpeter was at the peak of his popularity. His collaborations with Gil Evans—*Miles Ahead* (1957), *Porgy and Bess* (1959), and *Sketches of Spain* (1960)—were masterpieces, while his small combo LP, *Kind of Blue*, was destined to become the most beloved jazz record of all time, with over five million copies sold as of this writing. These albums appealed to casual and hardcore jazz fans alike, making Miles a celebrity when jazz as a whole enjoyed a golden age amidst an emerging recognition as a true American art form.

But by the time *Nefertiti* was released, the cultural terrain had shifted dramatically. Between 1946, when Davis made his first records with Charlie Parker, and 1964, when Wayne joined his band, seventy-six million children were born in America, making up 40 percent of the nation's population. They became known as the baby boomers, distinguished not only by their numbers but also by their affluence. Raised in the era of postwar prosperity, these youngsters spurred a huge juvenile market made up of everything from diapers to toys. As teenagers and adults, they exerted an outsized influence on popular culture.

The music that gave voice to the boomers was rock 'n' roll. It became a distinct genre in the mid-fifties, exemplified by Elvis Presley, whose style mixed country with rhythm 'n' blues. As historian James T. Patterson wrote, rock 'n' roll's rise was "one of the most shocking cultural phenomena" of the time, "especially to people over the age of twenty-five. Like jazz in the 1920s, the new music seemed to separate young Americans from their elders and to usher in the beginnings of a strange and powerful 'youth culture.' Rock 'n' roll gave millions of young people—especially 'teenagers' (a noun that came into widespread use only in 1956)—a sense of common bond: only *they* could appreciate it."[40]

Initially, the jazz community dismissed rock 'n' roll as unworthy of serious consideration.[41] Eventually, the thinking went, many of the kids would acquire a taste for jazz as they matured into college students and young professionals. A 1960 *Down Beat* news item appeared to confirm it. Reporting on the findings of a poll of six hundred young people, "rock 'n' roll appeals primarily to the pre-teener and the young teenager," the article said. "At about fourteen or fifteen (however) he suddenly becomes interested in jazz."[42]

But the report failed to anticipate the extent to which the boomers would reject anything that smacked of their parents' culture, and just a few years later it was clear that the younger generation had almost entirely ignored jazz. The British invasion, led by the enormous success of the Beatles, ignited a surge in record sales that continued unabated for the rest of the decade, eventually reaching $2 billion by 1972, at which point jazz represented just 1.3 percent of all records sold in the United States.[43] Ten years after Presley recorded his first number one hit, "Heartbreak Hotel," in 1956, rock so thoroughly dominated the marketplace that it crowded out just about all other forms of music from jukeboxes and radio airplay.

Contemporary black music underwent its own revolution. Detroit-based Motown Records, established in 1959, became a rhythm 'n' blues force, creating a new style called *soul* (which, despite the similarity in terms, could hardly be confused with soul jazz). Several Motown artists crossed over to mainstream appeal, producing twenty number one singles during the ensuing decade. At the same time, James Brown evolved his R&B and gospel roots into a unique brand of funk exemplified by his singles "Papa's Got a Brand New Bag" and "I Got You (I Feel Good)." Brown's music in turn influenced newer artists such as Sly and the Family Stone, who produced their own number one hits a few years later.

The toll on jazz was significant. The writer David Rosenthal remembered the black music of the early sixties as "a cornucopia" of jazz, urban blues, soul, and gospel, but the one-two punch of rock and popular black music soon relegated jazz to the fringes. "The effect was economically and psychologically devastating," one musician told Rosenthal. "It was almost as though jazz had had a stroke in late 1967."[44] Sure, there were occasional instrumental hits like "Mercy, Mercy, Mercy" or Ramsey Lewis's "The 'In' Crowd," but it was, as the writer Nat Hentoff summed up, "a bleak decade for jazz."[45]

Like the jazz world, Miles's label, Columbia Records, was caught flat-footed by these developments. Internally, Columbia's A&R (artists and repertoire) heads viewed rock with disdain, believing it to be a passing fad.[46] For years, Columbia had thrived on classical and middle-of-the-road fare, such as Broadway cast albums, Mitch Miller sing-alongs, and vocalists like Johnny Mathis, Andy Williams, and Barbra Streisand. But whereas cast albums for earlier shows such as *My Fair Lady* and *South Pacific* sold in the millions, Columbia's latest offerings topped out at 300,000 or less. Likewise, Miller's string of eleven consecutive gold records came to an abrupt end as sales collapsed to five figures.[47] This was more than a wake-up call for Columbia: the dominance of the youth market, and Columbia's reluctance to enter it, posed an existential threat to the company.

Clive Davis, a young corporate lawyer who was elevated to the role of vice president and general manager in 1965, set about restocking the label's roster. His first signing was the Scottish singer-songwriter Donovan, but his eyes were truly opened to the potential of rock artists when he attended the Monterey International Pop Festival in June 1967. "It was a glimpse of a new world," he wrote in his memoir.[48] More than thirty bands took the stage over the three-day weekend, including Jimi Hendrix, the Grateful Dead, and Jefferson Airplane. Impressed with the excitement and energy generated by these performers, Davis signed the charismatic singer Janis Joplin of Big Brother and the Holding Company. From there, he aggressively steered Columbia into the rock and contemporary arena. By 1973, when Davis was fired, corporate profits had increased tenfold, making

Columbia the largest and most successful record label in the world.

Faced with this climate, jazz was becoming marginalized, "increasingly associated with a middle-aged, middle-class audience positioned in antagonistic opposition to the youth of the times," wrote Kevin Fellezs in his book, *Birds of Fire*.[49] Rock was "alive, the 'art that expresses the experience of living,'" while jazz "was thought of as a 'quaint anachronism' by the youth of the time."[50] By that formulation, Miles himself was in danger of becoming one of those quaint anachronisms. He could see the signs well enough. While his current quintet represented a creative highpoint, his public acceptance was on the wane. His more recent records struggled to sell 25,000 copies—respectable numbers for a jazz artist at the time, but a sizable decline from his heyday. Attendance at his live appearances dropped off as well. Dave Holland, who replaced Ron Carter in 1968, observed that while the band performed in some packed houses, they also played "a lot of clubs where there were sort of thirty or forty people in the audience."[51]

It was inevitable that some musicians would attempt to bridge the divide between jazz and rock, and the term *jazz-rock* first began to appear in the entertainment press in the mid-sixties.[52] Some attempts were facile, motivated by a desire to capitalize on rock's burgeoning popularity. Count Basie, for example, recorded an album of Beatles originals (*Basie's Beatle Bag*, 1966), treating the material as he would Tin Pan Alley standards. Guitarist Wes Montgomery made a series of commercially successful records consisting of anodyne treatments of current pop and rock tunes ranging from "Chim Chim Cher-ee" (from the 1964 movie *Mary Poppins*) to the Beatles' magnum opus "A Day in the Life." They sold well, but suffered from a formulaic approach that made them unsatisfying as either jazz or rock. A true rapprochement would require more than subjecting rock tunes to full-fledged jazz arrangements or, worse, treating them as "innocuous background music," as one critic referred to Montgomery's efforts.[53]

Miles had long paid attention to popular music, and he began thinking about how to incorporate elements of it into his own music. His decision to do so is one of the most discussed topics in the jazz literature, but at root it seems to have been a quest to remain relevant. As he wrote in his autobiography, "I wasn't prepared to be a memory yet."[54] Following a prolific period in the studio during the spring and early summer of 1967, culminating in *Nefertiti*, the quintet didn't record again for nearly five months. When Miles took them back to Columbia's Thirtieth Street studio in December, he had some changes in store. For the first time in over a year, he brought in one of his own tunes, "Circle in the Round." Until then, Miles had relied almost entirely on the quintet's other members—especially Wayne—for new material. But with this session, he initiated a shift that emphasized his own writing, signaling his intent to assert more control over the music.

Davis also began experimenting with new timbres, directing Hancock to play the celeste while he played chimes and trumpet. He brought in a young electric guitarist named Joe Beck, who kept up a low-register, drone-like figure. An even more radical change is the way in which the finished product was constructed. Instead of Miles's usual practice of rehearsing material in the studio as a lead-up to a complete take, engineer/producer Teo Macero assembled "Circle in the Round" by splicing together parts from thirty-five takes.[55] Thus, the finished piece was realized through post-production as opposed to a single, real-time performance—a process that Miles and Macero would return to with considerable success later.

Miles also became intrigued by the Fender Rhodes electric piano. He first heard its cousin, the Wurlitzer, when "Mercy, Mercy, Mercy" was released in 1967.[56] Later, when Joe used the Rhodes regularly, Davis made sure to attend Adderley's gigs when they were both in New York. "He used to come to the clubs constantly where we played with Cannonball and record only the parts with the Rhodes," Joe remembered. "On the breaks he would call me out to the street to play it for me!"[57] The Rhodes was a very flexible instrument. It could provide sharp, barking rhythmic accompaniment, swirls of ringing sound, or layers of dark, sustained chords. It could add depth to the bottom of a band, or lend a gritty, down-and-dirty feel to a tune. Miles loved it. "For me, it was the future," he said.[58]

Davis introduced the Rhodes to his own music at a studio session in May 1968. Later that summer, *Miles in the Sky* was released. It was dressed in a psychedelic cover—a not-so-subtle effort by Columbia to link the album to the younger set. The title didn't refer to any cut on the LP, but brought to mind the Beatles song "Lucy in the Sky with Diamonds," which had come out the previous year. Upon dropping a needle onto the record, listeners heard "Stuff," a seventeen-minute soul jazz composition with a Motown-like groove.[59]

Miles in the Sky and its successor, *Filles de Kilimanjaro*, are now generally seen as transitional works, "emerging between the twilight of post bop jazz and the dawn of fusion," as Keith Waters wrote in his book, *The Studio Recordings of the Miles Davis Quintet, 1965–68* (fusion being the term that would come to replace jazz-rock).[60] Miles's band didn't survive this transition. Ron Carter was the first to go. He had a thriving career as a New York studio musician and became less inclined to go on the road, forcing Miles to use substitutes until he found a permanent replacement in Dave Holland. Herbie Hancock was next, dismissed by Davis after he failed to return from his honeymoon in Brazil in a timely manner. Then Tony Williams started his own band with guitarist John McLaughlin and organist Larry Young. Wayne stuck it out the longest, surfing the sea changes in Miles's music that would position him as the father figure of jazz-rock.

•

Not long after Joe returned to New York from his family trip to Austria, he walked the mile and a half from his apartment on 104th Street to Davis's brownstone on West Seventy-Seventh near the Hudson River.[61] It was a beautiful day and he brought along some wine and hors d'oeuvres that he had purchased overseas. When he arrived, Miles asked him to play something—as he always did—so Joe sat down at the built-in upright piano and said, "This is a little piece I wrote in Vienna."[62]

Joe composed it on the first night back in the city of his birth. "The children were with my parents in Vienna, where we had had a wonderful afternoon," he recalled. "It was maybe a week before Christmas. My wife was so exhausted from the hardships of the trip, she had already gone to bed and slept peacefully, like a baby. I sat by the window and thought about my life, and it started to snow. And from the hotel window I could see the house where my parents lived when they got married, where I was conceived. What a ridiculous coincidence. I have always felt like a very happy person, but maybe this was one of the happiest moments in my life, because the circle was completed. I left home, immigrated to America and stayed there for almost ten years. And I looked out of the hotel window to the Stadtpark in Vienna, and thought to myself how nice it is that the whole family was together."[63] Filled with a feeling of contentment, supplemented by a few cognacs, the song came quickly and Joe jotted it down on manuscript paper without the aid of a piano.

As Zawinul played, Miles wandered out of view and Joe wasn't sure he was even listening. But Davis, sitting right behind the piano, soon stood up and said, "Man, this is a beautiful song. I've *got* to record it."[64] Thinking of his future, Joe recognized that collaborating with Miles at this stage of his career would be beneficial, so he agreed. Meanwhile, Joe began playing the piece at sound checks with Cannonball's band. When Nat heard it, he said, "Hey, this is beautiful, like in a silent way."[65] Joe co-opted the phrase for the tune's title. The Adderleys wanted to record it, too, and when Joe told them he had already promised it to Miles, an argument ensued. Joe held his ground. Sometime later his telephone rang in the wee hours. It was Miles, asking him to come to the studio the next day. A few minutes after hanging up, Davis called back. "Bring some music," he told Joe. "And bring that nice tune."[66]

Joe's first session with Miles was on November 25, 1968. Davis already had two keyboard players on hand: Chick Corea, who was now his regular pianist, and Herbie Hancock. They were both stationed at electric pianos, so Joe sat down behind an organ. They didn't take up any of Zawinul's music that day, but forty-eight hours later they recorded two of Joe's compositions: "Ascent" and "Directions." The pair of tunes form a study in contrast: the former an atmospheric tone poem, the latter a driving piece that Miles liked so much that he began using it to open his live sets.

It was the start of a fifteen-month collaboration in which Joe served as a primary musical stimulus to Miles, much as Wayne had done with the second great quintet. Miles recorded nine of Joe's compositions (and rehearsed a few others), and though he never joined Davis's live band, Zawinul was a steady presence at the studio sessions that produced the music for *In a Silent Way* and *Bitches Brew*, the albums widely credited with launching the jazz-rock movement. For Joe, giving over so many of his compositions must have given him pause. While he wanted the prestige of working with Miles, he was also sitting on material—much of it written on his prolific Christmas trip to Vienna—that he intended for his own use. "I almost didn't record with Miles in '68," he later acknowledged. "My wife told me not to do it because they were all pieces that were ready for my own *Zawinul* album [which he recorded in 1970], but I really wanted to do something with Miles—not because it would have been a springboard for my career, but just because I really admire the man."[67]

The sessions also reunited Joe and Wayne for the first time since their Maynard Ferguson days. It was also the first time that Wayne recorded on the soprano saxophone, an instrument that would come to define him as much as the tenor. For years the soprano was a neglected instrument in jazz. Its sole, identifiable voice was Sidney Bechet, a contemporary of Louis Armstrong's, and it figured little in the bebop and post bop developments of the 1940s and beyond. It wasn't until John Coltrane took up the soprano on his 1961 album *My Favorite Things* that it began to find a place in small jazz ensembles again.

Wayne got his first soprano shortly before playing it on "Ascent."[68] The soprano is the wild beast of the saxophone family. Its narrow conical shape and small mouthpiece make it notoriously difficult to achieve good tone and proper intonation, but Wayne took to it immediately. It reminded him of the clarinet, and it added another dimension to his music. There was also a practical reason to adopt the soprano. With Miles's music becoming denser, the tenor could get lost in the mix whereas the higher-pitched soprano cut through it. This would remain an issue with Weather Report, where Wayne's horns competed with Joe's electric piano and Miroslav's electronically processed bass.

The November sessions were but a prelude to February 18, 1969, when Miles and company spent three-plus hours creating the music for *In a Silent Way*. As before, there were three keyboard players, including Joe, but this time the band was augmented by guitarist John McLaughlin, who had just arrived in New York from England. The night before the session, he dropped by Miles's brownstone with Tony Williams, who was scheduled to make the date the next morning. Miles invited McLaughlin to come along, too. "Why don't you bring your guitar?" he suggested.[69] It proved to be a stroke of genius.

All the elements that Miles had experimented with over the past year came together on *In a Silent Way*. And yet, even as it was evolutionary, it was also revolutionary. Nothing he had previously recorded sounded like *In a Silent Way*. Nothing *anyone* had recorded sounded like it. His use of the studio as a creative tool truly came to the fore. Once the session was complete, he had forty reels of tape, but no complete takes of anything. How was Teo Macero going to turn that into a set of tunes for an LP? He didn't intend to do it alone, telling Miles, "This is a big job, get your ass down here." Miles had never come to the studio for post-production work, but this time he agreed. Together they went through all the tapes, ultimately cutting them down to seventeen minutes of music, at which point Miles turned to Macero and said, "That's my record." Macero was incredulous. "I said, 'Go to hell!' because it wasn't enough music for an album. So I ended up creating repeats to make it longer."[70] In the end, Bob Belden noted, they used thirty-three minutes of tape to make a forty-minute album from forty-six minutes of usable music—"a landmark in minimalism."[71]

The second side of the record is a medley of Miles's "It's About That Time" sandwiched between two identical takes of "In a Silent Way," the making of which has become a part of jazz lore. As the composer, Joe was given the opportunity to rehearse the band, which played it with his original chord changes intact, undergirded by a bossa nova rhythm, as indicated on his handwritten score.[72]

But Miles wanted something different. As was his custom, he pared the tune to its essence, eliminating the drums altogether, cutting out the introduction, and stripping the harmonies in favor of a single chord and pedal point. The overall effect was to put the entire focus on the beautiful melody that Joe had written. The reconceived version starts with McLaughlin's hesitant, fragile playing, which is one of the most memorable parts of the album. The key was Miles's cryptic instruction: "Play it like you don't know how to play the guitar."[73]

"Today, many people consider Joe's tune a classic and the beginning of fusion," Miles wrote in his autobiography. "If I had left that tune the way Joe had it, I don't think it would have been praised the way it was after the album came out."[74] Based on the rehearsal take, it's hard to argue the point. Davis's version of "In a Silent Way" has the quality of a beautiful, ethereal hymn. Nevertheless, Joe resented the idea that his composition *needed* editing. "The section of the tune he used, and which now has become famous, never had any [chord] changes, apart from a couple of chords going up," he insisted to Paul Tingen. "Until today I believe that Miles was wrong in taking these two chords out, because the tune does not have the climax it could have had. But there was no note in the melody changed, and no chords were stripped."[75]

Released in July 1969, *In a Silent Way* is jazz-rock's first masterpiece. As such, it was controversial. While it wasn't rock (or R&B or funk), to the purists it wasn't jazz, either, so the response from jazz critics was lukewarm. The most positive reception came from the rock press—listeners less likely to hold previously established convictions of what jazz should be. Lester Bangs wrote a glowing review for *Rolling Stone*. At the time, the publication was barely two years old, with a fraction of *Down Beat's* circulation, but well on its way to becoming the authoritative source for rock coverage. "This is the kind of album that gives you faith in the future of music," Bangs wrote. "It is not rock 'n' roll, but it's nothing stereotyped as jazz either. . . . It is part of a transcendental new music which flushes categories away and, while using musical devices from all styles and cultures, is defined mainly by its deep emotion and unaffected originality."[76]

•

For all the attention that *In a Silent Way* generated, an even bigger jolt awaited the jazz world with the release of *Bitches Brew* the following spring. Whereas *In a Silent Way* was marked by a level of restraint that made it a prototype for ambient music—meaning, music that could be listened to passively—*Bitches Brew* was provocative; it demanded a response from listeners. As if to emphasize the point, Miles used the working title *Listen to This* during its development. To some it was thrilling; to others, disorienting. Jim Szantor captured both reactions in his review for *Down Beat*. He gave it five stars but struggled to explain why. "Trying to describe the music is something else again—mainly an exercise in futility," he wrote. In the end, he urged readers, "You'll have to experience this for yourself—and I strongly advise that you do."[77]

The album would forever divide Miles's fans into two camps—those who loved him even after his turn to rock, and those who felt he had sold out. Some long-time fans were so disappointed by *Bitches Brew* that they returned the record to Columbia. Those complaints landed on Macero's desk, who politely responded by offering other albums in exchange.[78] But Miles also gained legions of new fans as sales of *Bitches Brew* neared 400,000 units by the end of 1971, making it one of the best, if not *the* best selling jazz record up to that point in time. (It eventually reached platinum status, indicating sales of over one million.)[79]

Once again, Joe figured prominently in the end result. His tune "Pharaoh's Dance" consumes the entire first side of the double LP. It is a complex, thematic piece consisting of two parts. The first is clearly spelled out in Joe's handwritten score, but he intended for the second part to be loosely interpreted, with notes such as "keep developing," "play whenever," and "play your own way."[80] Davis liked the tune when Joe brought it to his brownstone, and he deconstructed it, reducing it to a few sketches. The band gave it a try on the first day of recording. Apparently, there was no lead sheet at the studio, as Dave Holland can be heard on the session tapes teaching the melody to the other musicians. After struggling through Part I, they set it aside.

The ensemble took it up again on day three, but never recorded an entire take of it. Instead, Macero kept the tapes rolling while they played it in pieces, skipping some sections entirely, with Miles tossing off instructions to Macero for how the takes related to each other. In the end, it took nineteen edits to construct "Pharaoh's Dance"—a "tour de force in editing," Belden said, speculating, "Maybe it was a source of pride for Miles and his production team to lead off an important album with this 'composite composition and performance.'"[81]

Given the nature of the sessions, it's not surprising that the musicians walked out of the studio wondering if what they had played was any good. All they really knew was that Miles was happy. After one session, Joe shared a ride home with Davis, not saying a word. Finally, Miles broke the silence, asking, "What's the matter?"

"I don't like what we're doing here," Joe replied.

"[Miles] was very hurt," Joe said. "He thought it was really something special. And I had an idea of how this music should be done. I didn't say too much more; just for me it was too much noodling around and not enough strong melodies."[82] Six months later, Joe was at the Columbia building when he heard some "enormous, fantastic music" wafting out of an office. He poked his head inside the door and asked, "Wow, what's that?"

"Well, Mr. Zawinul," Teo Macero's secretary responded, "that's you playing with Miles on *Bitches Brew*!"[83] Joe walked away thinking, *Damn, that's great.*[84]

•

Miles wasn't the only (or even the first) jazz musician to take a serious approach to fusing jazz and rock, but his stature, coupled with *Bitches Brew*'s commercial success, made it the "big bang" of jazz-rock. *Down Beat*'s readers voted it their album of the year, as did *Playboy*'s, who named it Record of the Year by a Big Band (for lack of a better category). Those honors were capped with a Grammy Award for Best Jazz Performance by a Large Group, Davis's first Grammy since 1960 for *Sketches Of Spain*. Some reviews positioned the album as a significant step forward in music. The composer Carman Moore, writing in the *New York Times*, described it as "a landmark of recorded music."[85] Even today, *Bitches Brew* stands as a unique document that continues to be cited for its influence by musicians ranging from Carlos Santana to Thom Yorke of the alternative rock band Radiohead.

Almost immediately, however, a backlash arose among those who felt that *Bitches Brew*'s rock-inflected polyrhythms and electric instrumentation excluded it from the jazz tradition, and the claim that Miles sold out—that is, put commercial considerations ahead of artistic ones—gained currency among writers and critics who invariably projected their own biases onto Davis's motivations. Musician and educator Bill Cole wrote one of the first biographies of Davis in 1974. Dismissive of Miles's electric period, Cole considered *Bitches Brew* to be "artistically far beneath [Davis's] potential." The root of the problem, as Cole saw it, occurred when "Clive Davis advised Miles to change his music to accommodate a larger audience," after which Miles informed the CBS executive that he was "prepared to overhaul the music so it would have more broad-based appeal."[86]

The source behind Cole's allegation was a 1971 *Down Beat* article in which Clive Davis said he "encouraged Miles to go in a new direction" and, according to the executive, Miles eventually told him that he was "prepared to embark on this route, which has proven beautiful for him, for us, for people, for music."[87] But Clive chose his words loosely and later acknowledged that he "certainly wasn't going to tell Miles Davis what kind of music to record."[88] What he *did* suggest was that Miles could reach a larger audience by playing rock venues, and that "being in new environments with new listeners on bills that featured artists who admired him but who were not jazz musicians might even affect the music he himself would make. Whether it did or not, I was confident that it would increase his sales."[89]

He had a good reason for thinking so. Starting with *Filles de Kilimanjaro*, Columbia recognized the appeal of Miles's music to "serious rock buyers" and began marketing him in the rock and underground press.[90] *In a Silent Way* produced much better numbers than Davis's previous efforts, and with *Bitches Brew*, Columbia felt they had "a monster in our hands." "This is not a jazz album," urged one sales executive. "Sell it like you sold Blood, Sweat & Tears and Santana."[91] As to the notion that Clive Davis had an effect on his music, Miles was clear: "I had seen the way to the future with my music, and I was going for it like I had always done. Not for Columbia and their record sales, and not for trying to get some young white record buyers. I was going for it for myself, for what I wanted and needed in my own music. *I* wanted to change course, *had* to change course for me to continue to believe in and love what I was playing."[92]

Cole's claims continued to be amplified in subsequent years. In his book *The Freedom Jazz Principle*, John Litweiler makes the following assertion as though it is self-evident: "As Miles Davis's music declined in the late 1960s, the sales of his records declined, too, and this was during the period when the new management of Columbia Records was raising sales quotas. Davis's bosses ordered him to make a hit record or else; *Bitches Brew* was his response."[93] Later came a personal attack by Stanley Crouch masquerading as a review of Miles's recently published autobiography. Miles was "intimidated into mining the fool's gold of rock 'n' roll," according to Crouch. "Desperate to maintain his position at the forefront of modern music, to sustain his financial position, to be admired for the hipness of his purported innovations, Davis turned butt to beautiful in order to genuflect before the commercial."[94] Each of these writers drew lines defining what jazz was and wasn't—a debate that continues to this day.

Regardless of the controversy that followed, *In a Silent Way* and *Bitches Brew* had an enormous impact on the jazz scene. Many of the musicians Miles assembled for those recordings established the leading jazz-rock bands of the 1970s: Herbie Hancock's Mwandishi and Headhunters bands (Hancock, Bennie Maupin), John McLaughlin's Mahavishnu Orchestra (McLaughlin, Billy Cobham), Return to Forever (Chick Corea, Lenny White), Lifetime (Tony Williams and McLaughlin), and of course, Weather Report, which outlived them all.

For Zawinul, the success of these albums raised his profile and set the stage for the next chapter of his career. But it also came with a price tag as writers implicitly or explicitly tied his subsequent success to having worked with Miles. So Joe's relationship with Davis was marked by ambivalence. Miles was one of his heroes—"my first hero," he said after forming Weather Report—and when Zawinul finally did work with him, "it was a dream come true."[95] But as much as he respected Davis, Joe bristled when interviewers asked how Miles influenced him, often flipping the script. For instance, when a reporter wondered if Weather Report grew out of the concept formulated with *Bitches Brew*, Joe responded, "I don't think so. I went to Miles and played him the ideas for my *Zawinul* solo album, and *that's* where his other stuff started happening. I'm not saying that's how it all began, but I had a lot to do with it."[96]

That said, Joe never doubted Miles's greatness. "To me, when I give you an overall view of Miles Davis, I'd say . . . maybe the best musician I've ever played with in my life. Not just a musician, but an artist who made music. There's a difference. There are a lot of great musicians but very few artists, and he was one of them. A real artist."[97]

5 Miroslav

Infinite Search was way ahead of its time, and it still is.
—Miroslav Vitous

MIROSLAV VITOUS FIRST CAME TO THE ATTENTION of American jazz fans when Willis Conover wrote an article for *Down Beat* about the second International Festival of Jazz in Prague, Czechoslovakia. The festival, which took place in October 1965, was organized by Dr. Jan Hammer, "Prague's leading cardiologist—and a bassist, vibraharpist, singer, composer, the head of a family of four jazz performers, president of the Prague Jazz Club, and emcee of the festival."[1] Just seventeen years old, Vitous appeared as part of the Junior Trio with his older brother, Alan, on drums; and Dr. Hammer's teenage son, Jan Jr., on piano. Vitous played "with exceptional technique, intonation, and cello-like purity," Conover wrote. "An admirer of Scott LaFaro and Steve Swallow, Miroslav played bass while seated on a stool. If he ever stands up and learns to swing a line of horns, too, he will make the front rank anywhere."[2]

When Conover heard him, Miroslav had been playing bass for about four years. His introduction to it was a bit of a lark. While visiting his uncle one day, he spied a double bass lying in a corner. "I just went to it and started playing it," he recalled. "I played it for two hours and my uncle said, 'You know what? Just take it home with you.'"[3] Miroslav was already an accomplished musician by then, starting on violin at age six and moving to piano a few years later. As a tall, athletic kid with big hands, the bass fit him physically. He loved it from the first moment. Within a year of taking it up, he was accepted to the Prague Conservatory, a prestigious institution that dates back to Napoleonic times, where he studied the acoustic bass and classical music.

Jazz was forbidden at the conservatory, but Prague had a small jazz following, and Miroslav began performing publicly with his brother in the band of trumpeter Jiří Jelínek, who patterned himself after Louis Armstrong.[4] Living behind the Iron Curtain, American records were hard to come by, as they were for Joe two decades earlier, so Miroslav's main link to the music was Conover's radio program, *Voice of America Jazz Hour*, which was broadcast to Eastern Europe over shortwave radio. It was so well known to jazz fans there that impresario George Wein once claimed, "Eastern Europe's entire concept of jazz comes from Willis Conover."[5]

"The greatest thing we had was Radio Free Europe," Miroslav said, referring to the United States government-funded broadcasts to the Soviet bloc. "There was a show on every night at midnight, most of the week, so we taped all of the stuff because he was playing all of the new releases—Duke Ellington, Miles Davis, Bill Evans—everybody who released a new album, he played it. And this was great for us over there because when I came to America and I spoke to my American colleagues, they didn't know half of the material that I knew. They got a few albums from the local store, but they didn't hear anywhere near what I heard in a communist country."[6]

Seven months after the Prague festival, Vitous got the opportunity to perform before some of the leading names in jazz when Friedrich Gulda used his star power to will into being a first-of-its-kind competition hosted in his home city of Vienna. The International Competition for Modern Jazz attracted nearly one hundred young musicians from nineteen countries, competing in six categories: piano, bass, drums, saxophone, trumpet, and trombone. Among them was a contingent of a dozen or so Czech musicians, including Miroslav and Jan Hammer.

The judges were J. J. Johnson, Art Farmer, Mel Lewis, Ron Carter, Cannonball Adderley, and Joe Zawinul—all well-known luminaries in American jazz, each representing one of the instruments of the competition. In the preliminaries, each musician played three numbers for the jury, which listened behind a screen. Forty contestants made it into the finals, including nine Americans and eight Czechs. Dr. Hammer must have been proud. For their final performances, they came face-to-face with the jury, which was instructed to listen impassively, silently filling out their ballots.

Miroslav won first place in the bass category—the youngest winner in the competition—netting him a $1,000 cash prize and a scholarship to the Berklee School of Music. "How did the jury sit still through Vitous's set?" Conover marveled. "It was as close to perfect as one could expect a bassist to be—sensitive, swinging." The judges shared his enthusiasm. "The bassists were the best," Zawinul said. Cannonball agreed, adding, "I was astounded to find that the bassists were fully as good as we expect professionals to be."[7]

Like Joe, the Berklee scholarship was Miroslav's ticket to the States. Not only that, Adderley was so impressed that he wanted to hire him. Cannonball's interest factored heavily in Miroslav's decision to leave home, and he made plans to depart that summer. "I got the visa and I got permission to leave from the communist country. But they didn't know anything about the engagement with Cannonball Adderley. Somebody betrayed me and told them that I wasn't coming back. The soldiers came for me the day after I left for the United States. They came to get me. That was very close. I would have been in a military jail somewhere instead of going to the United States."[8] When Miroslav arrived in New York in August, he discovered that Adderley was scheduled to go to Japan that month. "It was impossible for me to get a Japanese visa with a Czech passport, and it was even more impossible to return to the United States coming back from Japan. So the whole thing fell through."[9]

Unable to secure the gig, Vitous enrolled at Berklee and tried to focus on his studies, but he quickly realized that the classes were well below his abilities. "I was really surprised about the level of the school," Miroslav said. "They were teaching things that I learned when I was eight or nine years old when I started on violin."[10] He went to the school's director and asked in his broken English to be moved up, but he was told that it wasn't possible. His bass teacher was more sympathetic. "I went to him and I played a classical concerto with arco, and then I played 'Days of Wine and Roses' in double stops. He looked at me and said, 'You know what? You don't have to come here. I don't have anything to teach you. It's a waste of time for you. I'll give you an A+, and don't say nothing to nobody.' So I just stopped coming altogether."[11]

Instead, Miroslav holed up in his Boston apartment and practiced on his own, maintaining a rigorous, self-imposed schedule. "I got up in the morning, ate breakfast, and then went straight to practice, working on technical things like études, fingerings, and the pizzicato. Then I listened to albums for the purpose of pursuing walking and accompanying—studying the lines and playing along with them. Then there was lunch. After that I took a walk to get some movement. When I returned, I started up again, doing improvisation practice—lines, ideas for phrases, working on my solos, and still playing with the albums. By the time five o'clock came, I was finally free to play whatever I wanted to play. I ended up playing ten or eleven hours a day, and it was incredible."[12]

Miroslav was a member of the Czech national swim team, and his training gave him a firm grounding in endurance, discipline, and hard work—all qualities he called upon during this time. "You learn how to pace yourself, to keep going," he said. "You have to drive yourself just as hard to start practicing long hours as you do to drag yourself out of bed before dawn to swim laps."[13] It was an isolating time for him. Back home the Junior Trio was a sensation; here he was mostly ignored, without classical music or swimming to fall back on. When the school year ended, Miroslav decided to make the move to New York. "I had met [bassist] Walter Booker in Boston, and when it was time, I just called him up and said, 'Listen, could I come and stay with you for some days before I get some stuff happening?' And he said, 'Yeah, come by and stay with us.' So I went to New York on the bus with twenty dollars in my pocket and my bass and suitcase."[14]

Booker, who took over the bass duties for Cannonball Adderley during Joe's final years with the band, shared a large apartment with his wife, Maria, on the Upper West Side of Manhattan. It was a lively gathering place for musicians. "That place was history," Maria remembered. "Unbelievable music was done there. Musicians dropped by because there was always a good joint to smoke and food and music and good people—beautiful people. It would start at one, two o'clock in the afternoon and end up at six in the morning—every day. And everybody passed through that house—John Coltrane, Miles Davis—everybody. It was a place where you came to get a job. And there was always a good ambience—food, drugs, music and love. But elegant drugs! [*laughs*]"[15] When Miroslav got there, the studio was just a room with a tape recorder, a piano, and a set of drums. Booker eventually transformed the space into the Boogie Woogie Studio, with two recording rooms outfitted with consoles.

Not long after getting to New York, Bob Brookmeyer and Clark Terry hired Miroslav for an engagement in Chicago. It turned out to be the break that launched his career, coming almost exactly a year after he arrived in the United States. They were performing at a club called the London House. As it happened, Miles Davis and Herbie Mann were in town for a benefit concert dubbed "Newport in Chicago," at the Civic Opera House.[16] After his concert, Miles dropped by the club to see Terry, one of his oldest friends, but his attention soon focused on Miroslav. Davis had an engagement at the Village Gate coming up and he needed a substitute for Ron Carter. The next morning, he called Terry.

"Hey, man, that bass player you got is a motherfucker!"

"Yeah, he can play his ass off," Terry replied.

"Will you ask him if he wants to play with me?"

That night after their set, Clark told Miroslav to sit down; he had something to tell him. At first Miroslav wondered if he'd done something wrong. Then Terry broke the news: "Miles wants you to play with him next week." Upon hearing that, Miroslav was so excited, he "screamed and moaned and jumped up and down so much, I thought he was going to pass out," Terry said.[17]

For Miroslav, playing with Miles was an exhilarating experience. "That was the first time I played with Wayne, the first time I met everybody. It was out of this world. I played with some great bands already by that time, but when I walked on the stage with that band, I can compare it to suddenly being on the sixth floor of a building, whereas with the other bands I was never higher than second, maybe the third floor. This was like double that—just the height of the musicianship, the feeling of it. We were playing maybe 30 percent standards and 70 percent new music, so it was really taking off. That band was capable of having conversations within the standard forms and taking it to a level which I really looked at as creative music. This was the top of modern jazz, to me."[18]

The gig with Miles was short-lived, but the night after Davis had seen Miroslav in Chicago, Herbie Mann also stopped by the club and sought him out during a break. "My bass player is leaving," he told Miroslav. "Would you be interested in joining the group?"

"Literally, within two days, I had a career breakthrough," Vitous remembered.[19]

Mann was a popular and prolific flutist who seemed to indulge his every musical interest, which was so broad that he described it as a "smorgasbord table."[20] At around the time Miroslav joined him, Mann was producing overtly commercial albums laden with three-minute easy-listening versions of current pop hits. Whereas critics speculated about Miles's motivations for going into jazz-rock, Mann was completely upfront about his. He later called himself "the Kenny G of the sixties, except he was a much better player than I was then."[21] He even hired Zawinul on one album, 1967's *A Mann & A Woman* with vocalist Tamiko Jones. Joe arranged and played on three tunes, including a peppy version of the Beatles' "Day Tripper." But Mann's live band was considerably more daring than such material. Sandwiched among his commercial fare were albums like *The Wailing Dervishes*, a live set that melded Middle Eastern instruments to his working combo, even including a blues tune with the unorthodox sound of Rufus Harley on bagpipes.

Mann put together a tight quintet that included Miroslav, the avant-garde guitarist Sonny Sharrock, drummer Bruno Carr, and Roy Ayers on vibes. It was later enlarged to a sextet with the addition of saxophonist Steve Marcus. Mann described his new musicians as "a great brand-new thing again, like finding a new food."[22] His fans, accustomed to his more accessible side, weren't as enthusiastic. Sharrock's unique and polarizing style was a tough sell, and some fans angrily demanded to know why he and Miroslav were in the band at all. "Well, what was Coltrane doing in Miles's band?" Mann said. "Miles was a melodist and Coltrane was this 'out' saxophone player. You need foils. And besides, they were originals. How many originals are there in the world?"[23]

One of the first published reviews of Mann's reconfigured band—and therefore, of Vitous—was by Leonard Feather in the *Los Angeles Times*, who caught them on Miroslav's twentieth birthday, December 6, 1967. Miroslav "[turned] his listeners on with a maturity that belied his youth," Feather remarked. Of the band as a whole, he found it to be a refreshing change from previous Mann congregations—"shorter on quantity [of musicians] and longer on quality."[24]

Meanwhile, living with the Bookers put Miroslav in contact with New York's best jazz musicians, and those jams led to his participation on Chick Corea's album *Now He Sings, Now He Sobs*. "When Chick was getting ready to make a recording, he remembered that we had something going there, and he called me for the date," Vitous explained.[25] The album is now considered a classic of the piano trio genre, and it marked Miroslav as a special talent. By the middle of 1969, he was considered a rising star, combining prodigious technique with melodic, imaginative lines. He most assuredly could swing a line of horns, even though he still preferred sitting on a stool.

•

A week after the *Bitches Brew* recordings, Wayne made his next Blue Note album, which he called *Super Nova*. It had been more than two years since he last recorded under his own name, and his personal life had undergone a significant change. In 1967, he met Ana Maria Patricio, a Portuguese woman who had immigrated to the United States with her family at the age of twelve. Maria Booker, who was Ana Maria's sister, introduced them at one of Wayne's gigs. That night they went back to the Bookers' place and hung out, initiating a romance that culminated in their marriage. At the time of the *Super Nova* sessions, Ana Maria was pregnant with their only child, who was born the next month.

Wayne also gave his first interview to *Down Beat*. The interviewer, Larry Kart, remembered Wayne initially turning him down, claiming that he had nothing to say. But he soon changed his mind and invited the journalist to his hotel room the next day. Once he got there, Kart barely got his portable reel-to-reel tape recorder started before Wayne embarked on a long soliloquy. It turned out that he had *a lot* to say, and *Down Beat* wound up running his remarks as an expansive, 5,000-word essay titled "Creativity and Change." Among other things, Wayne reminisced about watching and participating in jam sessions with his jazz elders. "That kind of getting together is not going on too much now," he lamented. For his next record, "I'd like to create the atmosphere that we're not just at a recording session. I've written something down, but we'll have a jam-session spirit."[26]

That was Wayne's state of mind when he brought together an unorthodox group of musicians for what was, per Herb Wong's liner notes, "a very loose date with no rehearsal."[27] Joining him from *Bitches Brew* were Jack DeJohnette, John McLaughlin, and Chick Corea, who played drums and vibes instead of piano, plus Miroslav and Sonny Sharrock. On the second day, they were joined by percussionist Airto Moreira and the Bookers, producing a timbral quality that was a departure from Shorter's previous records and a definitive move away from the conventional hard bop sound. Wayne even eschewed Rudy Van Gelder's, choosing instead A&R Recording Studio in New York City.

The fact that *Super Nova* was made so soon after *Bitches Brew*, and with many of the same musicians, led some to consider it the first offspring of *Brew*. But compared to Miles's effort, *Super Nova* has what one writer called "a heads-down-and-play quality."[28] Group improvisation is at the core of both, but the pieces on *Super Nova* were recorded live, in whole, without relying on post-production to sort it all out. As the main soloist, Wayne had ample opportunity to dissect his themes, loose as they may have been, in a setting that sometimes approached the avant-garde in its freedom. He gives an impassioned performance, sticking entirely to the soprano, thoroughly exploring the horn's dimensions.

To some critics, the results weren't entirely successful. *Jazz Journal* called *Super Nova* a "largely baffling" record of "weird 'space music'"[29]—a term then being used to describe improvisational music that was hard to categorize, ranging from the Grateful Dead to Pink Floyd, and later, Herbie Hancock and Weather Report.[30] *Down Beat*'s John Litweiler, a champion of free jazz, criticized "the confusion and niggling of the accompanying group," specifically "the glaring inability of any but bassist Vitous to play *with* Shorter"—and this was in a five-star review. But in singling out Miroslav for his "marvelously unfailing" support, Litweiler's assessment was prescient, as Vitous became the saxophonist's first-call bassist.[31]

Including *Super Nova*, Miroslav recorded some twenty albums between 1968 and 1970, but the one that stands out above the others is *Infinite Search*, the first release under his own name. (It was later repackaged with an additional track as *Mountain in the Clouds*.) The opportunity to make it came courtesy of Herbie Mann, who started the Embryo label in 1969. At the time, recording sessions led by bass players were rare, so Miroslav's association with Mann was fortuitous. Beyond leading the date, Miroslav took on the additional challenges of composing nearly all of the material and assuming the role of primary soloist. He succeeded on all counts.

Infinite Search is Miroslav's first truly personal musical statement. He enlisted some of the best musicians in New York, including Herbie Hancock, Jack De-Johnette, and John McLaughlin. Wayne was asked, too, but he declined, claiming that he only recorded with Miles or on his own projects. So Miroslav turned to Joe Henderson, who meshed so beautifully with the group that one reviewer lamented that he appeared on only two tracks (plus the one added to *Mountain in the Clouds*).[32] Those two tracks—"Freedom Jazz Dance" and "I Will Tell Him On You"—are the centerpieces of their respective sides of vinyl. The entire ensemble plays cohesively, and there's a consistent vibe throughout the album, which Miroslav described as "a mix of American jazz and the strong influence of European melodies and culture."[33] It's a tribute to the caliber of musicians that the music comes off so well despite no rehearsals, but the star of the album is Vitous, whose playing is at the forefront of every tune. He gives a marvelous performance, showing off his big, woody tone and technique, while also revealing a sensitivity and inventiveness in his solos.

"I think it was a revolutionary kind of a step," Miroslav said of the album. "Instead of playing the role of a bass player, I was talking to the other musicians directly. That was the difference. It is a much more liberal, democratic arrangement between the musicians than the traditional jazz roles." He was inspired by Scott LaFaro, whose playing in the Bill Evans Trio emancipated the bass from its timekeeping function to a full-fledged partner in the interplay with the other musicians. "They were having multiple conversations, nonstop, already at the Village Vanguard in 1961," Miroslav said. "And Miles didn't get to this point until some years later."[34]

Even today, *Infinite Search* stands out as Miroslav's musical manifesto. "*Infinite Search* was way ahead of its time, and it still is," Miroslav said decades later. "When you play it today, it actually sounds extremely modern. They are not there yet, the rest of the crowd. It wasn't a beginner's album. I set a very high standard for myself, almost unfortunately, in a way, because it's so hard to achieve something like this again."[35]

•

Miroslav continued gigging with Herbie Mann into 1970. The flutist was as popular as ever. At one point that spring he simultaneously held five spots on the *Billboard* top twenty jazz albums chart, paced by *Memphis Underground*, one of the best-selling jazz albums of the time. Mann followed that up with *Muscle Shoals Nitty Gritty*, another nod to his populist roots that, like its predecessor, relied on an R&B rhythm section. There was a growing disparity between his records and his live band, with the latter more interested in testing boundaries than replicating Mann's studio efforts.

By late that summer, Miroslav, Sonny Sharrock, and Steve Marcus were dominating the band to the extent that Mann said he "felt like a sideman in my own group" and grew tired of their freewheeling ways. "I found that freedom by itself turns me off," he said. "Maybe one solo at the end, as part of a tune; that was fine—but then it became like two or three solos. Sonny and Steven and Miroslav would solo, and everybody forgot about the beginning of the tune or the end, and the whole thing was just that way."[36] Mann's fans were likely turned off, too. It's telling that in describing *Muscle Shoals Nitty Gritty*, *Billboard* seemed relieved to note that it "[toned] down the usual instrumental anarchy rampant in his sidemen."[37]

This was the situation as Mann embarked on a tour of Japan at the end of August. He later told *Down Beat* that he was already preparing to make some changes when they departed, but while they were on tour Miroslav and Sharrock got an offer to join Miles.[38] Miroslav accepted immediately, giving Mann his three-week notice.[39] However, the band that Vitous had been invited to join was vastly different from the one he'd enjoyed so much in 1967. The second great quintet had long since passed, and Miles was getting heavily into funk and looking for a purely rhythmic function from the bass. He'd soon find such a player in Michael Henderson, because that wasn't going to work for Miroslav. He lasted just one concert.

"I was not very suitable for what Miles wanted to do at that time," Vitous acknowledged. "He was moving in the direction of having the bass player hold the bass line steadily, repetitively playing the same thing over and over with no communication between the players on a compositional level, which is what I wanted to do. I started to 'talk' with Miles, instead of keeping the bass line. The music was fantastic, but Miles didn't like it because that wasn't what he wanted to do. So he fired me right after the concert. I remember Jack DeJohnette telling Miles, 'Well, why don't you talk to him to let him know what you want?' And Miles said something very interesting. He said, 'Well, if the guy's not gonna do it by himself—what I need to be done—then it doesn't make any sense.'"[40]

So Miroslav returned to New York without a steady gig for the first time since his Boston days. Going back to Herbie Mann wasn't an option. He'd done some tours with Stan Getz, but he didn't want to return to that, either. Instead, he had an idea: *Wayne isn't doing anything. Why don't I give him a call and see if he'd be interested in putting something together.*

6 Shoviza

Gimme your card, man. Wayne and me are startin' a new band.
—Joe Zawinul

1970 WAS THE YEAR THAT JOE, WAYNE, AND MIROSLAV finally shed their side-man roles and established themselves as bandleaders in their own rights. They each ended associations with long-term employers, trading security and familiarity for the ability to control their music. Throughout the year their paths crisscrossed in the recording studios, culminating in a series of phone calls in early fall when they "circled around something," as Wayne put it.[1] In later telling the story, Joe often made it sound as though he and Wayne were destined to join forces—that there was a straight line from Miles to Weather Report, if not all the way back to their first encounter in 1959. Even the band name was said to come to them almost cosmically in a single evening of inspired brainstorming. But events weren't quite so tidy, with the three men exploring other options before Miroslav acted as the "trigger man" in bringing them all together.[2]

•

On September 29, 1969, just after Wayne returned from a two-week engagement in California, Ana Maria gave birth to their daughter, Iska. The couple enjoyed nearly a month with their newborn before Wayne embarked on a lengthy tour of Europe with Miles. Another short break led to an six-day appearance in Toronto, followed by stands at the Village Gate before and after Christmas. The pace of touring, coupled with the new addition to his family, factored into Wayne's sense that it was time for a change. As with Art Blakey, he felt that five years in one band was long enough. With Miles, it was going on six. Besides, Davis had been needling him about his future. "Don't you think it's time for you to get your own band?" he'd say. "I had so many ideas," Wayne remembered, "and the music was coming out like water and everything, and I said, 'Yeah. I think it's really time.'"[3]

Then a personal tragedy shook up Wayne's life. Right after the New Year, he and Ana Maria took Iska to the doctor for her routine three-month examination. She was given a tetanus shot, and later that day they put her down for a nap. When Ana went to check on the infant a short time later, she found her in the midst of a seizure. They rushed Iska to the hospital, but she had suffered irreparable brain damage that left her developmentally disabled and prone to seizures for the rest of her life. It was a devastating prognosis for Wayne and Ana Maria. The crisis strengthened Wayne's resolve and he finally gave notice to Miles, making his last public appearances with him at New York's Fillmore East on March 6 and 7.

Wayne left with a great sense of accomplishment, but moving forward he was determined to break from the past. He said he needed to "get rid of that sound that I had with Miles, to get the sound of the musicians, and the compositions I wrote during that time, out of my system. I wanted to rid myself of any one association—so that people can look at anything new that I do with a bit of objectivity, without connecting me with Miles or Art Blakey, as everyone always has." Among other things, this meant resisting Davis's continued requests that he remain a part of his orbit. "Miles would call me up and ask if I wanted to make a record date, or write something for his band, and I had to refuse, because it was necessary for me to break that connection completely."[4]

Less than a month after his last gigs with Davis, Wayne brought a group of Miles Davis alumni (plus Miroslav and a young Belgian drummer named Micheline Pelzer) to A&R Studios to record another Blue Note album, titled *Moto Grosso Feio*.[5] Like *Super Nova*, the instrumentation is unconventional, including marimba, cello, percussion, and guitars. From the moment the needle drops on the LP, it's clear that Wayne has transported listeners to a world far removed from his hard bop roots, with his lush soprano saxophone carving a path through the rest of the band's exotic sounds. It was, he said, a period of "searching and experimenting."[6]

After the session, Wayne took a holiday, relaxing in the Caribbean Islands. He brought his saxophones with him, but needn't have bothered. "I just looked at the horn every once in a while," he said. When he got back to New York, he "started playing a lot of other things, not jazz, but stuff from Yma Sumac, music from Peru, a lot of Latin stuff."[7] One day, Wayne invited guitarist Ralph Towner over for a visit. "We got together at his apartment and spent a whole afternoon together just playing each other's cassettes and pieces," Towner remembered. It felt to him as though Wayne was "sort of putting out feelers for putting together a band."[8]

Canadian Sonny Greenwich was another guitarist who caught Wayne's attention, and he began rehearsing a group that included Greenwich, drummer Billy Hart, and bassist Cecil McBee. Wayne even had a name in mind for them: The

New York Art Quartet. The absence of a pianist was consistent with his previous two studio efforts as well as his next. Evidently Wayne found the guitar more in line with his evolving aesthetic; it opened up the music harmonically, and the use of guitar-mallet combinations could be viewed as his response to the broadening sound canvas that musicians were employing at the end of the sixties.

The group didn't go further because Greenwich had difficulty securing a green card and wound up returning to Canada. But Hart and McBee joined Wayne for his next recording session in late August. Wayne also brought in Ron Carter (he tried to get Miroslav, but he was en route to Japan with Herbie Mann) and a quartet of musicians with whom he had little or no previous connection: Gene Bertoncini (guitar), David Friedman (electronically processed vibes and marimba), Frank Cuomo (percussion), and Alphonse Mouzon (drums). None of them knew what to expect upon walking into the studio. "I had no idea what was going to happen," remembered Bertoncini, who got the call from producer Duke Pearson. "I'd never met Wayne before. I'd done a couple of things for Duke, so I guess he believed in me and had me come over there. And it seemed a little strange, with two bass players and three drummers, but Wayne was going after something."[9]

The most notable newcomer was Alphonse Mouzon, who would become Weather Report's first drummer. He came to New York in 1966, fresh out of high school where he won South Carolina's scholastic drum competition four years running. Within a few weeks of arriving, he found work with the Ross Carnegie Orchestra, performing at social functions with moonlighting members of the Duke Ellington and Count Basie bands. An old high school buddy of Wayne's, drummer Bobby Thomas, took Mouzon under his wing, eventually recommending him for the pit band of the Broadway show *Promises, Promises*.[10] Now he recommended Alphonse to Wayne.

If there was a theme to Wayne's recent recordings, it was the freedom he granted his musicians, and *Odyssey of Iska* was no different—"loose, free and inspiring," Mouzon remembered.[11] All of the compositions were Wayne's except for "De Pois do Amour, o Vazio" (After Love, Emptiness), which was written by Thomas. Wayne had lead sheets for everybody, "but it wasn't structured like everything was written out," Bertoncini said. "Wayne was saying things like, 'Let's make this sound like the wind.' He was trying to get us to feel certain effects."[12] (The titles of his pieces are "Wind," "Storm," "Calm" and "Joy.") "The tune that Bob [Thomas] wrote was pretty well defined, but on the other ones I was just reacting. I had never played any of them before, so a lot of it was going by the seat of my pants. I listened and tried not to throw anything in there that was going to conflict with what Wayne or anybody else was doing. I had no idea if I did well when I walked out of there."[13] Friedman felt the same: "Wayne gave very little direction, and I remember playing more or less what I felt was appropriate for the music."[14]

Wayne described his objective in the album's liner notes. "I'm trying to get what you might call more of a sheer sound instead of a hard and solid instrumentation. . . . I think the time has come for more content, from the compositional standpoint. But at the same time we need not be restrictive in the sense of adhering to the traditional song form, like, say, Burt Bacharach or the Beatles. We have to rearrange the concept of melodic, harmonic, and rhythmic ideas as they have been dealt with in the past and come up with something fresh. We've been working hard on it."[15]

While some listeners, such as *Rolling Stone*'s Lester Bangs, luxuriated in *Odyssey*'s "visually tangible earthly landscapes,"[16] Wayne's desire for "sheer sound" and "more content" wasn't convincing to all. Larry Kart, a perceptive critic, wrote the review for *Down Beat*. He was disappointed by Wayne's "devotion to sonic color, virtually at the expense of any other kind of energy and invention." Kart attributed this to Wayne's "seeming desire to renounce the notion of the improvising musician as the purveyor of a competitive, flamboyant ego." But it was the last two lines of Kart's review that seemed prescient as Wayne's career with Weather Report unfolded and he appeared to retreat into the background, ostensibly subsumed by Joe's vision. "What I hear on this album is a musician trying to disappear. I wish he wouldn't."[17]

•

Zawinul's last session with Miles Davis took place in February 1970. In the meantime, he still had his gig with Cannonball. With three young children to support, leaving the security and steady income that Adderley provided wasn't an easy decision. Even Miles couldn't tempt him away. But at this point Joe wanted control over his music, which he couldn't get with Cannonball *or* Miles. "Cannonball gave me plenty of opportunity to write," Joe said, "but it's not the same thing as writing for yourself. So, no matter how great the band was, there still was a great difference between the way they did it and how I would have expressed it."[18] Seeing Miles run roughshod over his compositions just reinforced the feeling.

The negative vibes from the dispute over "In a Silent Way" lingered and Joe later cited it as his impetus for leaving Cannonball, even though it took him more than a year to follow through. Joe also felt held back by the band's repertoire. "We had fine music, believe me," he said. "But sometimes the band relied too much on playing the hits. About this we had quite a few arguments during those years, especially with Nat. I used to say, 'Hey, man, we are the hit, not the hits.' The band was such a good band. We had so much to offer, we didn't have to play 'Dis Here' and 'Dat Dere' and 'Mercy, Mercy, Mercy' all the time."[19]

"Joe was always thinking about different things other than playing just straight-ahead 4/4 stuff," Roy McCurdy recalled. "He wrote a lot of music like 'Doctor

Honoris Causa,' '74 Miles Away,' 'The Painted Desert,' which were the lead up to the Weather Report period. Joe was thinking ahead because he had that sound in his head. I used to go over to his house all the time when we lived in New York, and he had all this experimental music that he wound up playing with Weather Report. I couldn't sit down and have a conversation with him until he made me hear what he was playing or what he had written. They were all just spectacular things."[20]

So Joe made plans to record his most personal and substantial album to date. He called it, simply, *Zawinul.* If Wayne's sessions were somewhat offhanded in their preparation, Joe's method was anything but. His purposeful intent is reflected in his formal description of the album that appears on the back of the jacket: "Music for two electric pianos, flute, trumpet, soprano saxophone, two contrabasses, and percussion." The striking black-and-white portrait of Joe on the cover also conveys a work of substance. Before settling on that image, Zawinul first approached Pablo Picasso for art (he was told the artist didn't do such things), and then Ansel Adams, who happily sent a set of prints that didn't quite convey the feeling that Joe was looking for. He also prevailed on Miles to write a liner note. At first, Davis wanted to play on the record, but Joe turned him down, realizing that the trumpeter's name would overpower his own.

By this time, Zawinul had earned a reputation as a first-rate musician and composer, but one still laboring in the shadows of Cannonball and Miles. He was best known for his soul jazz tunes such as "Mercy, Mercy, Mercy," "Walk Tall" and "Country Preacher." And while his work with Miles revealed other facets of his writing, the dominance of Davis's vision and Teo Macero's editing blurred his contributions. Even Joe's previous Atlantic album, *The Rise & Fall of the Third Stream,* was a collaborative effort with William Fischer. But with *Zawinul* he enjoyed complete creative control. As such, it serves as an undiluted expression of his personal style just before Weather Report.

"I was really happy [with *Zawinul*]," Joe said shortly after its release. "Although it was not as perfect as I would have liked, it was so human and really me. It gave me the feeling of 'I did what I wanted to do,' a freedom which really helps. The music was not written for others. I mean it was only subject to my interpretation. Also I don't think that the music would have stood up in 1967 when I wrote most of it. I would not have received as much acceptance as now, when everyone's head is opening up."[21]

The album unfolds like a suite grounded in conceptual continuity. The music is richly layered, but not in a dense-sounding way, with a spacious, relaxed feel—swinging but unhurried. The first track, "Doctor Honoris Causa," sets the tone. After an introduction, it proceeds in a stately manner befitting its title, which refers to an honorary degree that Herbie Hancock received from his alma mater,

Grinnell College. A second piece, "Double Image," is similarly built around elegant themes and modal tonalities that provide the framework for the individual soloists. In this case, Miroslav Vitous puts his expressive arco playing to good use. The doubling of instruments allows the rhythm section to improvise while also maintaining a strong rhythmic pulse.

"In a Silent Way" and "His Last Journey" highlight Joe's lyrical side, sharing a pastoral, romantic quality. The last track, "Arrival In New York," is a piece of *musique concrète* of which Teo Macero would have been proud. It was created by splicing together slowed-down tapes, evoking the sounds of the city as the *Liberté* anchored in the harbor.[22] It isn't known what kind of help Joe received in assembling it, but it certainly showed a creative use of studio technology, and Joe's skill with the razor blade was later acknowledged by Weather Report's recording engineers.

The sessions took place over three days in August, a few weeks before Wayne recorded *Odyssey of Iska*. The first tune the ensemble tackled was "In a Silent Way." If Joe was unhappy with Miles's version, then surely this was the corrective, and the care Zawinul took in its recording reflected its importance to him. When the other musicians arrived at the studio that day they found it lit by candles, with incense smoke wafting through the air. Billy Hart, one of three drummers on hand, described the scene to Zawinul biographer Brian Glasser: "It was an amazingly creative session. It was almost spiritual, that day. Earl Turbinton was chosen to play the 'In a Silent Way' theme, and the way he played it was so beautiful. Everyone was just stunned. That was the first time the full version of 'Silent Way' had been played. Everyone left the studio knowing something special had happened."[23]

They performed the song as a ballad, well removed from the samba rehearsal take included in *The Complete In a Silent Way Sessions*. Joe included a lengthy introduction (which Miles recorded as the long, meditative track "Recollections") before moving to the now-familiar theme.[24] And while Joe restored the harmonic movement that was missing in Miles's version, the renditions are similar in many respects. There is no rhythmic accompaniment, and an acoustic bass establishes a pedal tone for much of the main theme. The other bass improvises a counter to the melody while Zawinul and Hancock create a bed of swirling tones on Fender Rhodes pianos. Most importantly, like Miles, Joe found no need to embellish the melody with improvised solos.

In hindsight, it seems surprising that Joe would use Turbinton on such an important project. The saxophonist was not well known then or now, but the quality of his performances on "Silent Way" and "Doctor Honoris Causa" speaks for itself. It also caught Miles's ear. "Dig the clear funky black soprano sound," he wrote in his liner notes. Turbinton was one of three New Orleanians Joe employed on the album, the others being multi-instrumentalist George Davis, who played flute, and drummer David Lee. They were among a group of musicians who revolved around Earl and his younger brother, Wilson, a pianist and vocalist whose stage name was Willie Tee. Joe got to know them during his years with Adderley. They all had an affinity for each other and, at least in the case of Tee and Zawinul, a friendship formed for life. There's a photograph taken at radio station WDSU, circa 1967, in which Willie plays the piano while Joe watches over his shoulder. It's only conjecture, but it stands to reason that the "master of funk,"[25] as *Down Beat* once described Joe, might have gotten some of that funkiness by rubbing elbows with musicians from the funkiest place on earth.

A last intriguing topic regarding the personnel on *Zawinul* is the inclusion of Wayne, making this the first time that the three founders of Weather Report played on the same record. However, there's conflicting information regarding the extent of Wayne's role and when it took place. The album jacket credits him on "Double Image," but Michel Ruppli's Atlantic Records sessionography indicates that Turbinton played on that track, whereas Wayne was only present for an overdubbing session ten weeks later. Miroslav also did the overdubs, so that *was* the first time that the three Weather Report founders performed together, but by then they had already agreed to form their new band. There's no saxophone solo on "Double Image," so Wayne's role was limited regardless of the inconsistent documentation. In any event, it would be misleading to characterize *Zawinul* as the moment when they collectively recognized their musical rapport.[26]

Zawinul wasn't released until the spring of 1971, at about the same time as Weather Report's debut album, so it got lost in the blizzard of publicity generated by Columbia's press and marketing departments and failed to make the impact it deserved.[27] Nevertheless, it was universally acclaimed. Lester Bangs covered both albums in a joint review for *Rolling Stone*, and it's clear which of the two was his favorite. *Zawinul*, he wrote, is an "absolute cathedral of an album," one that "will remain a classic jazz album of the type that transcends our narrow conceptions of what jazz has become."[28] Doug Ramsey was equally effusive in *Down Beat*, calling it "the work of a complete musician who has transcended categories and is certain to have a profound influence on the direction music will take in the '70s."[29] Those were prophetic words.

•

Just before leaving for Japan with Herbie Mann, Miroslav finished some tracks that he had been working on at Apostolic Studios with engineer David Baker, whom he had met earlier in the year while working on Larry Coryell's album *Spaces*.[30] Billy Cobham joined him on drums, and he enlisted Joe on a couple of tunes and John McLaughlin on another. Miroslav also overdubbed himself on several pieces, playing arco bass or electric piano.

"I just went to the studio and did some experimental tracks," Miroslav later explained, "and then when something came out of it, I happened to have it with me when I was in Japan, and I sold it there. It was not really an album like *Infinite Search* was. That was seriously prepared for one year, and this one was like experimental things which happened."[31] The tracks became the album *Purple*, which was initially released only in Japan. But when Weather Report hit, the interest in Vitous magnified, and *Purple* was released in Europe in 1972 as part of Epic's short-lived Jazz on Epic series.[32]

Meanwhile, Wayne started considering his next steps in earnest. It had been several months since he had been on a bandstand, and it was time to get something going. He checked in with Jack Whittemore, the agent who booked many of the top jazz acts, including Miles Davis and Art Blakey. Whittemore "called around to the club owners in the United States to see how they would react to having the 'Wayne Shorter Quartet,'" Wayne said, but the clubs were noncommittal, preferring to stick with proven name acts.[33]

Among the factors working against him was the number of jazz-oriented venues that closed in the 1960s, partially caused by inner city urban renewal projects that claimed their premises, but also the result of lost patronage due to the ubiquity of television and white flight to the suburbs. Some observers, including many mainstream musicians, also blamed avant-garde artists for driving audiences away.[34] Birdland closed in 1965, the Five Spot two years later. According to Stuart Nicholson, by 1970 just six jazz clubs remained in Manhattan, survivors of nearly thirty that prospered earlier in the decade.[35] It was the same story in other major cities. With so few opportunities to perform publicly, one *Down Beat* writer worried that he'd have to go to a Broadway show just to hear jazz musicians play.[36]

As for what Wayne might expect as a bandleader, the experience of his friend, Herbie Hancock, offered a case in point. When Hancock struck out on his own in 1968, he had more name recognition than Wayne, thanks to his years with Miles and the success of his own albums, some of which produced moderate hits like "Watermelon Man." Now in the summer of 1970, bookings for Hancock's band were sparse, leading some members to seek other sources of income.[37]

Aside from economics, there was another reason Wayne didn't form his own band. "It was hard to find a bunch of musicians who were willing to stop playing like they used to," he acknowledged.[38] His ideas were radical enough that he needed musicians who could break free from convention, and do so naturally without being told what to do. For the most part, those musicians were either still with Miles or had already established their own groups.

While Wayne pondered his next move, Joe plotted his end game with Cannonball. Shortly after recording *Zawinul*, the Adderley quintet hit the road, arriving in California for a two-week engagement at Shelly's Manne-Hole on September 1.

While they were there, Joe got a call from Miles. "[He] told me Miroslav Vitous was joining him," Joe recalled. "I'd already decided to leave Cannonball, so I told Miles I'd join, too."[39]

Davis's recent albums used two and sometimes three keyboard players and he had both Chick Corea and Keith Jarrett on the bandstand throughout the summer. As Holland's departure precipitated the recruitment of Miroslav, Corea's led to Joe's. Miles and Adderley were scheduled to perform on back-to-back nights at the Pacific Northwest Jazz Spectacular in Seattle in early October, so Joe made plans to sit in with Davis.[40] But by the time he got there, Miroslav had come and gone. Besides, by then Joe had something else up his sleeve. He pulled aside one of the promoters: "Gimme your card, man. Wayne and me are startin' a new band."[41]

Exactly how the discussions went down among Joe, Wayne, and Miroslav is lost in the fog of time, but after Miroslav's offer from Miles failed to pan out, the first person he called was Wayne. "I'm free!" the bassist told him.[42] Wayne took it to mean that he was available to record, but Miroslav explained that he had left Mann for good. "Wayne, what would you think about putting a band together?" Vitous asked.

"You know, this is interesting," Wayne replied. "Let me think about that for a while and call you back."[43]

Then Joe rang him up the very next day, suggesting that *they* get together.[44] Teaming up addressed both of Wayne's concerns about leading a band of his own. Their combined star power was enough to draw an audience, and adding Vitous gave them a third musician who had already demonstrated that he fit into their music. Joe had long considered Wayne to be a potential music partner, and Miroslav was a musician "who didn't have to be told at every turn what you're looking for."[45] Shortly after their initial conversation, Wayne called Miroslav back. He had talked to Joe, and asked the bassist what he thought of the three of them having a band. "If it's okay with you that Joe comes with us, then let's do it," Wayne said.[46] That was a curveball Miroslav didn't expect, but he was amenable, and a new band was born.

From the outset, they agreed on a cooperative arrangement in which they would all be co-leaders. Cooperative bands—those lacking a hierarchical organization headed by a traditional leader—were uncommon, but a contemporaneous example was Circle (consisting of Chick Corea, Dave Holland, Barry Altschul and Anthony Braxton), in which the members shared the duties of running the band.[47] A longer-lived model was the Modern Jazz Quartet, whose members set up their own corporation, the Modern Jazz Society, and served as its officers. The corporation paid them a weekly salary and even funded a pension plan.[48]

Along those lines, Joe, Wayne, and Miroslav formed their own production company, Shoviza Productions, Inc. (the name was derived from their surnames), of which they were each one-third owners. They also set up a publishing company, Barometer Music. It was an idealistic arrangement, but eventually these business affairs would prove problematic. Initially, Barometer distributed the writing royalties equally among the three of them, but it wasn't long before Joe suggested that each writer collect for his own tunes, rationalizing that if one of them had a strong piece, the weaker ones would automatically benefit because of increased album sales. A bigger problem occurred when Miroslav was ousted from the band at the end of 1973. But for now, they moved forward enthusiastically.

That fall, they grabbed some studio time to jam and get a feel for what this new band might sound like. "We never talked about a concept," Joe said. "We went down into the studio the first time—Billy Cobham, Wayne, Miroslav, and myself—and made a tape. . . . Immediately we knew that that was gonna be it."[49] From the start, a form of group improvisation took hold that would characterize their early albums. "It was immediate," Wayne remembered. "We had a rehearsal, and just immediately that kind of collective thing, just like, BAM!"[50] Joe called it "instant experimentation."[51]

The drum chair was filled by Alphonse Mouzon. "We tested a few drummers to see how it would work out," Miroslav recalled. "Alphonse seemed to be the most suitable drummer for the band because Billy Cobham was too . . . I wouldn't want to say *stiff*, but kind of not flexible enough—that would be a better way to put it. Billy was more into rock-jazz than really swinging kind of stuff, and Weather Report was heavily swinging at the beginning. Alphonse was much looser than Billy and he could do both."[52]

Other musicians seem to have been considered as well—if not for Weather Report, then for the possibility of Wayne's and Joe's own bands had they gone that route. Gene Bertoncini remembered Wayne getting in touch with him around this time. "He called me a couple of months after recording *Odyssey of Iska* and said, 'I like what you did on the album. I'm putting this group together to record and maybe then go on the road a little bit.' And he started naming the guys: Miroslav and Alphonse Mouzon—I think he said Joe Zawinul. I told him that I didn't think I could get involved in anything on a semi-permanent basis because I was really trying to do my own thing at that point. So basically I turned down the first Weather Report album. Later on, I was on the road with my trio, with Joe Corsello and Michael Moore, and Joe was listening to this record. 'Man, you got to hear this, it's a great thing.' And he was listening to Weather Report. And I said, 'Wow, that's Wayne?' I realized then that I kind of had a chance at that."[53]

Woody Shaw, the trumpet player on *Zawinul*, was named as the fifth member in the first press item about the new band, printed in the October 24 issue of *Melody Maker*.[54] A similar blurb appeared in the December 10 issue of *Down*

Beat (which hit newsstands about a month before the issue date). It described the trumpeter as "New Orleanian David Lee, who has played with Willie Tee and the Souls," mistaking either the musician or his instrument.[55] The best explanation for Shaw and Lee popping up in these announcements is that before hooking up with Wayne and Miroslav, Joe considered forming a band populated by musicians he had employed on *Zawinul.* Along these lines, Earl Turbinton often told the story that *he* was asked to join Weather Report but turned down the offer, choosing instead to tour with B. B. King—a gig that would have been more lucrative and stable at the time.[56]

•

Some unfinished business remained before the yet-to-be-named band could get started in earnest. In order to fulfill his Blue Note contract, Wayne went back to A&R Studio with Miroslav and Mouzon, pianist McCoy Tyner, and percussionist Barbara Burton. The resulting tracks, collectively known as *Creation,* have never been released and are the subject of much speculation, coming just before Weather Report's founding and given the presence of three of the band's charter members, plus Burton, who played on Weather Report's first album. According to those who have heard the tracks, the music is farther out than anything Wayne had previously done—so far out, in fact, that Wayne has resisted its release all these years despite intense interest in *anything* he did for Blue Note.[57]

The other issue was that Joe was still a part of Cannonball Adderley's band. Zawinul broke the news to his boss while they were on the road in the Midwest. After nine and a half years of working closely together, traversing the country by automobile—*living* together—it was an emotional moment. They shared tears and drinks and hugs, but Cannon acknowledged that Joe had assembled a formidable team. "This will be something to reckon with," he told Zawinul, using a favorite expression of approval.[58] Joe had already planned a trip to Europe with his family at the end of the year, so his last appearance with Adderley was a weeklong stint at New York's Apollo Theater in early December.[59] (Miroslav and Mouzon were on the same bill, supporting vocalist Eugene McDaniels, with whom they cut the album *Headless Heroes of the Apocalypse* in October.[60])

Although Cannonball died in 1975, Joe's love for him remained undiminished decades later.

> He was my favorite, man. He was the most incredible instrumentalist. I worked for almost ten years with him, and we played so many concerts in those days, clubs mostly. We worked very, very hard. And making hardly any money, you know? Just to survive with the family. The man was a master. He never made one mistake as long as I played with him. We played the fastest, the slowest—never out of tune, never a *doubt,* man.

He was family. He was my best man, my witness, when we got married, the wife and I. He bought bicycles for my kids. We were together a lot, you know? He was a great friend. He was like a brother to me. He was a superbly intelligent man. Educated. Worldly. Funny. He had it all. He was one of the few who was the full package. A *master*.

Cannonball. I miss him every day. My wife and me, we talk about him somehow every day.[61]

With that, one phase of Joe's life came to an end. He had proved that he belonged on the American jazz scene. Now he was poised to become one of its leading figures. It was time to kick asses.

PART II

Weather Report, 1971–1975

7 Weather Report

We always solo and we never solo.

—Joe Zawinul

SID BERNSTEIN WAS ALWAYS ON THE HUNT FOR THE NEXT BIG ACT. A soft-spoken man with a quick smile, he was a beloved figure to many, from music-industry titans to high-rise doormen. A tireless promoter, he was so well connected that a friend later joked that Bernstein invented networking long before the word became common. He began staging shows while stationed in France just after World War II and never stopped, eventually booking the biggest names in the music business. But he was best known as the man who brought the Beatles to America, first to Carnegie Hall in 1964 and then to Shea Stadium a year later.

By 1970, Bernstein was still putting on big shows, but he also managed a handful of music acts. His best moneymaker was the Rascals, which had nine top twenty singles from 1966 to 1968. But just after they moved from Atlantic Records to Columbia, the group's lead singer and half of its songwriting duo quit the band. The Rascals soldiered on, but when word got out about the defection, bookings dried up, along with Bernstein's cash flow. His other clients at the time—the funk band Mandrill, and two rock groups, Rhinoceros and Ten Wheel Drive—failed to make up the deficit, a fact underscored by their absence in his autobiography. So when Joe came along, waxing enthusiastically about the fantastic new group he was forming, Bernstein was eager to sign him. And Joe was eager to be signed. To him, Bernstein represented the crème de la crème of the music world, having worked with the likes of Duke Ellington, Ray Charles, Judy Garland, Tony Bennett, and the Rolling Stones, to name a few.

One of the first things Bernstein did for his new clients was get them in front of Clive Davis. Having negotiated a million dollar contract for the Rascals, Sid had the mogul's ear. Though Joe had a handshake deal with Atlantic, and Wayne had a long history with Blue Note, neither label could compete with Columbia's prestige and marketing muscle. Under Davis's helm, Columbia projected a forward-thinking image that stood in stark contrast to its earlier reputation as a stodgy upholder of tradition. Columbia still maintained a stable of top-notch jazz artists, but they were going to have to change with the times if they expected to be retained.

"We're really not interested in signing artists still involved with traditional jazz," Davis said in 1971. "I fully recognize the talent of the traditional jazz artist . . . but I am really interested in communicating to new audiences; in people using their skills, using their ideas to communicate to new audiences in terms that new audiences can understand and accept."[1] Davis felt that there was "a marvelously rich new opportunity for the brilliant progressive music artist. The public had grown much more sophisticated and so encouraged by the audiences being reached by Miles Davis with *Bitches Brew*, I felt keenly that another major trend was in the making and planned accordingly."[2] Wayne, Joe and Miroslav fit the bill perfectly.

They all gathered in Clive Davis's office at Black Rock, CBS's corporate headquarters in Manhattan. The room was so crowded that some of the attendees sat on the floor. At first, Bernstein gave the pitch on behalf of the band, but the longer he went on, the more Joe thought, *He might be a great manager, but he doesn't know how to sell our kind of music.* So Joe took over, his confidence and enthusiasm carrying the day.

They brought along a demo tape (from the first rehearsal with Billy Cobham), but it wasn't needed. "Their verbal descriptions of what they wanted to do musically were exciting; I didn't have to hear them play," Davis recalled. "These were brilliant names—Joe Zawinul, Wayne Shorter, Miroslav Vitous—and they represented quality and virtuosity to me. It was enough to know that they were moving in the right direction."[3] They agreed to a long-term deal for five records and $90,000.[4] When the meeting adjourned, Zawinul made a solemn promise. "Mr. Davis, you will not regret it—this band will be special."[5]

According to Wayne, the only thing Davis asked was, "How could we give some name to this music in order to sell it? Where are we going to put it in the record stores? Are we going to put it in the classical thing?"[6] They spent a good part of the meeting "thinking and thinking and thinking," trying to come up with a name for the group—something so unique that it would defy categorization. "It was the only creative process that happened between us and the executives," Wayne later quipped.[7] Finally, someone suggested the Audience. It was an awkward name, to say the least. No one was happy with it, but lacking a better alternative, it stuck long enough to show up in press items as late as March.[8]

Nevertheless, they all knew the Audience wasn't going to cut it, so Joe, Wayne and Miroslav went back to the drawing board, trying to find something better. One afternoon they all sat around Joe's apartment, yet another name-the-band brainstorming (or head scratching) session underway, when Zawinul suggested they choose something people hear every day, like the Daily News. He was on the right track, but it wasn't catchy enough. Then Wayne had an idea.

"They have the news about the weather every evening," he offered. "And the weather is something that nobody can predict. And this music we are doing has something about not being predictable. How about the Weather Report?"

"And then we took the 'the' off it: Weather Report. And everybody said, 'Yeah!' It all clicked. The weather report can be an analogy to almost anything if you stretch it out."[9] It was a distinctive name that would forever serve the group well, especially as the band underwent numerous personnel and stylistic changes. The only downside was an endless supply of weather-related headlines over the years: "Weather Report Plays Up a Storm," "Weather Report: Outlook Sunny," "Weather Report's Cloudy Image," "Weather Report: Singing in the Rain," and on and on. Excited by their breakthrough, the guys celebrated with drinks of slivovitz before heading to the nearby Wienerwald restaurant for some dinner.

Columbia wanted to get a record out as soon as possible, so when Joe got back from Europe in January 1971, the group started rehearsing in earnest, four days a week, leading up to a mid-February studio date. There really was no plan going in and it was an intense feeling-out period. "Every day when we got home we'd be exhausted, there was so much music going on," Joe remembered.[10]

Miroslav recalled those early days as his favorite time in the band. "It was really wonderful because we were all creating together. Joe brought a tune and we all worked on it, did our best. I brought a tune, we all worked on it and everybody did their best to have the tune come off, and the same with Wayne's tunes. It was a very creative process and everybody gave 100 percent to the other. It was about communication and sharing more than anything else."[11]

From the start—and this is what must have appealed to Clive Davis—Weather Report challenged conventional notions of jazz. Wayne and Joe each expressed this intention in their own individual ways—Wayne in the abstract, Joe grounded in tangibles. "We were talking about writing another vocabulary, a language," Wayne said. "Musically expanding the vocabulary *as a group*, not as just a soloist. You know, everyone takes a solo, and then you come back and play the theme, and you go home? No. We said this is music with valleys, streams, lakes. And no commas, no periods, and maybe music with a paragraph."[12]

Joe's translation: "Wayne was coming at it independently of me, but he had that same kind of openness, with no limits. I was tired of [the] standard jazz form—you know, the AABB and the changes—sax, trumpet, bass solo, then drums, then back to the melody. That bored the shit out of me after years of do-

Miroslav Vitous, photographed at the Berkeley Jazz Festival in 1973. Photo: Michael Wilderman.

ing it. I wanted to play music which had drive, which was melodically interesting. Harmony wasn't that important. Music which was melodically and rhythmically present, which had tone, color, and space, so that you could find silence with it, not being hectic."[13]

As a quartet, they were a nimble, streamlined unit compared to the larger ensembles of their recent projects (and those of Miles). It was a fluid approach to improvisation in which any member of the band could take the lead at any time, shifting the mood of the music or changing the harmonies or rhythms on the fly. As Joe famously put it, "We always solo and we never solo."[14] Weather Report long outlasted Miroslav's involvement, so his contributions are sometimes overlooked, but he was highly instrumental in creating the music's distinctive character. "Listen to the bass," Alphonse Mouzon later said. "You hear Miroslav leading where we were going with the bass."[15]

Miroslav himself is clear about his role in the band's identity. "This is not something coming out of my ego, but the way I play the bass—at that time and I still do—is that I am not like a background bass player. I was like another voice, so when I played with Joe and Wayne, I answered them, and they had to answer me. And this is actually what created the new sound of Weather Report, the fact that they had to respond differently. I don't want to take the whole credit for it, of course, but it was the biggest reason why this happened, this music."[16]

Seeking to add more color to the ensemble, two percussionists came to rehearsals just before recording commenced. Miroslav invited Don Alias, a friend who specialized in Afro-Cuban rhythms on congas and the drum kit. Wayne brought in Barbara Burton, a young, classically trained musician who had played vibes on his *Creation* tracks the previous October. He first heard her at the Village Gate when she performed with a loose-knit group of studio and Broadway musicians known as the Seventh Century.[17] The next morning, Burton got a call from her friend, Al Mouzon, wanting to know if he could pass along her phone number to Wayne. "Now listen, Barbara," Mouzon cautioned her, "Wayne doesn't talk a lot. He's not like me. He's very laid back. He'll probably ask you to play a gig with him or something, but don't be upset if he doesn't say a lot to you."[18]

As Burton remembered, Wayne called, "and we were on the phone for three hours talking about music. I think I was at Juilliard at the time, so we talked about classical music, and boy, we just had a ball." A few months after the *Creation* session, Wayne called her back. "Hey Barbara, I'm putting together a group. This is going to be the *baddest* group ever. It's going to be just what you want to do. You like sound effects, you like inventing things. You're going to love this group. I want you to come and play with me."[19]

By this time, Burton was working for the New Jersey Symphony, but she was so enamored by the idea of Wayne's band that she quit her job in order to join him. She didn't realize that Wayne was just one of the leaders of his new group. That omitted detail would prove crucial later on, but for now they all entered the recording studio on February 16, cutting half the tunes for Weather Report's eponymous debut album. Two more pieces were completed over the next two days. Wayne and Joe returned on the twenty-first to record their duet "Milky Way," and one last track was made on March 17 in order to fill out the LP. Burton shared her observations of the process:

> We went in the studio and it was *magical.* The music was just outrageous. We played things that none of us had heard before. It was just glorious. I had the feeling that they had gone over the music a few times, but due to the nature of the musical experience they were trying to invoke, it was never quite the same all of the time. That's what made it exciting. Sometimes someone would hit a note that really had not been in, but it worked, so it would find its way in. And that's what made the whole process so great. It felt like we were on a carpet of music, like we were in space, and these sounds were just shooting past you, and you just added when you could.
>
> It seemed to me that everybody was busy trying to make sure they

knew where their track was, like a piece of a puzzle. Joe spent a lot of time working on the sounds he wanted. Miroslav was great. He's just a committed musician—a fabulous player. I never heard anything like him. He could just come in and play with anybody doing anything. Al was a very fiery player and he was having a ball.

There were lots of colors and things, and it caused you to really think about what you wanted to add. At one point, I think I had a gong that I was dipping in water—just doing all kinds of crazy stuff, things that you don't get to do in an orchestra. It felt wide open, like the entrance to a new frontier; that's what I thought. It was terribly exciting.[20]

The first track on the album, "Milky Way," is unique, yet sets the tone for what's to come. As its title implies, it sounds as if it emanates from the heavens, leaving listeners wondering what they are hearing and musicians trying to figure out how it was done. Above all, it serves notice that Weather Report would defy convention. In the album's liner notes, Don DeMichael writes that "Milky Way" was "made by acoustic piano and soprano saxophone. It has to do with the overtones and the way one uses the piano pedals."[21] That hardly explains its construction, though, and for years Joe refused to divulge its secrets.

For instance, when asked about it for a 1977 *Keyboard* magazine interview, he demurred, noting that there are "certain things that should be left alone, left unsaid."[22] But when he made a return appearance in the magazine seven years later, he was more forthcoming. "I silently held a chord down on the piano and had Wayne play an arpeggio of the same chord, blowing his saxophone right inside the piano at the soundboard. The tape recorder was started on the echo at the end of the sound, not when he was playing. We played different chords and edited them together. It was definitely not magic."[23]

Faint clicks and pops can be heard on the track, perhaps from tape splices or Wayne releasing the keys on his saxophone. At one point a bleep from his soprano darts past. He and Joe were too careful to leave that in by mistake, so perhaps it was meant to be a hint to the listener. Wayne had a better explanation: "You can say, theatrically, it's an asteroid!"[24]

Inspired by "Milky Way," some listeners thought the album cover depicted some sort of celestial body. But its origin is far more earthbound, based on a photograph by Ed Freeman, who shot the portrait for Joe's eponymous album. At the time, Freeman made his living as a record producer (most notably, Don McLean's *American Pie*), but he also did photography on the side and has since become a professional fine art photographer.[25] He didn't even hear the music before submitting his image. "I guess Joe liked what I did for *Zawinul* and he just said, 'Hey, why don't you do the cover.' They didn't tell me anything. I don't think they

Joe Zawinul sits behind his Fender Rhodes electric piano in 1971. On top of the Rhodes is an Ober-heim ring modulator. The lid of the Rhodes, which was arched, has been removed to create a stable base for the ring modulator. On the chair behind Joe is a Watkins Copicat, a tape delay unit similar to an Echoplex. Photo: © United Archives / Hulton Archive / Getty Images.

even saw the cover before I submitted it. I had no idea [about the music]; I heard it later. I just thought, well, some kind of abstract image. I had never done an abstract before in my life—that's not what I do—but I had been playing around with this technique of putting distressed plastic between two pieces of polarized plastic. And so I did that and I took it to Columbia and said, 'Here you go; here's the cover.' There was absolutely no intent on anybody's part to interpret any of the songs on the record."[26]

"Milky Way" is followed by "Umbrellas," a tune that came about during a rehearsal jam. "I had Don Alias come down to play with us, to try out, to see how it would be," Miroslav recalled. "Don started to play a beat and I picked up the bass and I started to play this bass line, and then Joe and Wayne jumped in. Joe played a chord, Wayne played a few notes of melody, and that was it. That's how it happened."[27]

In less than three and a half minutes, "Umbrellas" establishes many of the essential characteristics of Weather Report's music: the importance of space and texture (that is, sound itself as a compositional element), the use of electric instruments to create new timbres, a reliance on group interplay, and allusions to funk and blues. The tune begins with an up-tempo drumbeat that Mouzon said came directly from his rock influences.[28] At about the thirty-second mark, the feel shifts abruptly as he raps out a syncopated groove while Joe lays down some funky lines on his electronically processed Rhodes. There are no harmonies to lead the listener, nor are the melody lines particularly memorable. In their absence, the drumming holds the tune together, establishing its atmosphere and even informing its title, which came from the musicians hearing the sound of raindrops in Mouzon's playing.

One of the hallmarks of Weather Report—and jazz-rock in general—is the application of rock and funk rhythms in a jazz context. Alphonse Mouzon was well suited to this task. "When I was in the South, I was a funk drummer—jazz and funk," he said. Those roots led to his first gig in New York, shortly after he moved there:

> Right across the street from my flat was the Ross Carnegie Orchestra playing in the basement. I was seventeen, going on eighteen, trying to get the ball rolling, so I knocked on the door and introduced myself. I said, "I'm from Charleston, and I've been here for three weeks. I don't have drums, but I have drumsticks." I sat in with them, and Ross, who was the organ player and the leader, liked the way I grooved. I had played with organ players in the South, so I hit that Charleston funk beat and locked that pocket in, and he just fell in love with that groove. He hired me on the spot. "Y'all gonna be the second drummer, twenty dollars a night." The regular drummer was Frankie Dunlop, Thelonious Monk's drummer, but I had never heard of him. He would do the casual date and I would play on his drums. I had a suit, but I had to go get me a tuxedo because they all played in tuxedos. And I had to get drums. I went back to South Carolina a week later and my mom took me to Fox Music and we got a drum set—Ludwig, I still have it. Put it on layaway, sent her money and paid it off, and brought the drums on the train all the way back to New York.[29]

Alphonse had an adventuresome spirit, always willing to try new things. He'd say, "I got an idea" and just jump in and do it.[30] And while he sometimes felt like locking in the pocket with Weather Report, too, it wasn't that kind of band. "We

Alphonse Mouzon in 1971. Photo: © United Archives / Hulton Archive / Getty Images.

had our signature, so I had to take my groove and alter it and make it different. Whatever I played normal, Joe wanted to have the reverse of it. So I had the attitude that whatever I played had to be different, like [something] no one had ever heard. That's why my stuff would sound funky and backwards; I'd come up with different beats."[31]

"Umbrellas" also features Miroslav playing melody lines on distorted electric bass, an instrument he started playing at the behest of Herbie Mann. In Weather Report, he processed both of his basses through electronic effects like the ones rock guitarists used. He especially liked using a wah-wah pedal when bowing to create a singular sound on acoustic bass.

Joe was using a collection of effects boxes as well. One was a tape delay unit called the Echoplex. When coupled with the Rhodes, it created the swirling or cascading sound that Joe and Herbie Hancock used to good effect on *Zawinul*. Another favorite was an Oberheim ring modulator, which can be seen sitting atop his Rhodes in photos and videos from 1971 or 1972.[32] It worked by modulating an external audio source with an internal waveform, and had sliders to vary the waveform frequency and the amount of modulation, plus a toggle switch to activate or defeat its circuitry. Joe began using it late in his Cannonball days. "I did a lot of groundbreaking stuff [with Cannonball] on the electric piano, but nobody paid any attention back then," he remarked.[33]

The ring modulator hardly seems like a candidate for producing music, rendering what most people would consider unpleasant, grating sounds. But gifted musicians like Joe used it to expand their timbral range. On "Umbrellas," he adds a slight amount of modulation to give his Rhodes a metallic character. But on the next track, "Seventh Arrow," he manipulates the settings as he plays, creating wild, sweeping pitch changes that transform the Rhodes from a fixed-pitch instrument to something unrecognizable. In a sense, it allowed him to fly alongside Wayne's saxophone.

As for "Seventh Arrow" the tune, it was brought in by Miroslav. "I recorded it on *Purple*, and then I rewrote it and added that big line to the tune. And then we went into the melody, and it took off from there."[34] Joe called it "a masterpiece"—"a constant interplay of motives."[35] As with "Umbrellas" before it, "Seventh Arrow" is moored by Mouzon's drumming, leaving the rest of the band free to roam, occasionally unifying on a composed riff to give the tune some structure.

Standing in contrast to "Umbrellas" and "Seventh Arrow" is Joe's tune "Orange Lady," which has no rhythmic pulse at all. It's a rubato tone poem based on an elegiac melody in the mold of "In a Silent Way" or "His Last Journey." Like those tunes, it was conceived during Joe's prolific winter holiday a few years earlier. He said he wrote it for his wife; when she was melancholy, he would get her out of the city and take her to the countryside. "That's what the middle part is about," Joe said. "And then you come back to New York and it's like the same thing all over again."[36]

Most memorable about this tune is how Wayne and Miroslav play the melody in unison on saxophone and arco bass—a spur-of-the-moment suggestion by Vitous. Eliciting a horn-like quality from his instrument, it was such a novel sound that *Down Beat*'s editor, Dan Morgenstern, considered it "quite beyond description."[37]

Side two of *Weather Report* leads off with a pair of companion pieces, "Morning Lake" and "Waterfall." Miroslav wrote the former, explaining that it had "an identical skeleton"[38] to a tune on *Purple* called "Water Lilie." Zawinul remarked that it created the feeling of "being somewhere very early in the morning on a nice day."[39] This leads to "Waterfall," an impressionistic piece written by Joe. The tunes are conceptually similar, with Wayne playing drawn-out, wistful melodies on soprano that reinforce the dreamlike quality.

Closing out the album are two of Wayne's compositions. "Tears" shows off Weather Report's funky side. It includes Mouzon's wordless vocalizations, which Wayne said were meant to add a spiritual quality to the album's story arc. As Mouzon recalled, "Wayne didn't have a title. He didn't know what to call it; I said, call it 'Tears.'" As far as his vocals, "That's all my melody. I should have gotten composer credit. That was like a solo, but I sing almost like an opera. It's pretty cool."[40]

The album finale, "Eurydice," is the closest *Weather Report* gets to straight-ahead jazz; as if to say, *We can swing, too, in case you were wondering*. The released track begins somewhat abruptly because it is the last half of a near eleven-minute performance that was later included in full in the box set *Forecast: Tomorrow*. Joe called it "very hip swing," adding that "this is really the only track where we solo a little bit, 'cause on all the other tunes, we don't solo; we just play with one another—like an orchestra."[41] He plays straight Rhodes, letting its percussive, ringing sound inform his solo. With little to no left-hand chord jabs, it retains an airy feeling, letting the music breathe.

•

At the end of the third day of recording, with most of the tunes in the can, Barbara Burton was packing up her instruments when Joe introduced her to Airto Moreira, whom he described as "a great Brazilian percussionist." Unbeknownst to Burton, Joe had called him down to the studio to do some overdubs. Joe and Wayne were well aware of his talents, having heard him often at Walter Booker's place. In fact, one of Airto's first sessions in the United States was for Wayne's album *Super Nova*. So in hindsight, it seems surprising that they didn't use Airto from the start. Perhaps they wanted to find someone able to tour with the band, and knowing that Airto was then with Miles, they looked elsewhere. Or maybe Wayne was presently enamored by the unusual sounds that Burton created.

At any rate, when Airto listened to the tracks he thought they sounded complete as-is. "There was no space for my tastes. There was no space for me to play there," he said. Nevertheless, Zawinul insisted, and he asked the recording engineer to mute Burton's tracks so that Airto could hear how he might contribute. At Joe's urging, Airto spent the next few days overdubbing onto the music. Zawinul gave him a free hand to play as he wished, after which Joe directed him to replace or add certain parts. "I played through a tune, and then they would play it back, and Joe would say, 'Okay, from here to here, you play this shaker,' and this and that," Airto recalled. "It was almost like patching. There were certain things that Joe heard, specifically, so he was kind of directing me to a point, though not all the time."[42]

As a consequence of Airto's participation, most of Burton's playing is left out of the final result. "You hear nothing. Zilch," Mouzon said. "They erased her tracks along with Don's, except for Don's congas on 'Tears.' You can still hear it because

I had my mikes live so I could hear him. They never got rid of it, and it sounded so good." Burton can be heard on "Morning Lake," wiggling a sheet of Formica to create a bubbling effect, but that's about it. Asked if the co-leaders were unhappy with what she did, Mouzon is clear. "*Joe* wasn't happy with it."[43]

We don't have the benefit of hearing the music as it was originally recorded with Burton and Alias, but the quality of the released tracks make it hard to second-guess Zawinul's instincts. Airto adds immeasurably to the final result, the most impressive part being how organic he sounds considering that he wasn't in the studio with the rest of the band. "He did an *excellent* job," Mouzon said, "like he was there. He was like a painter."[44]

His additions to "Orange Lady," in particular, constitute a clinic when it comes to overdubbing hand percussion. The tune was a particularly fertile canvas for Airto because of its spaciousness. He doesn't enter until the song transitions to its middle section, when the distinctive sound of a berimbau is heard. From there, he imbues the music with emotional resonance. "Percussion is a complement to everything," Airto said. "If you play the wrong sound in the wrong place, the whole thing can change to a different mood, but if you pick up the right instrument and make the right sound in that spot, you raise the music so much it's unbelievable, just with little percussion instruments."[45]

It's telling that Airto's involvement played out through Joe. Despite the cooperative nature of the band, Zawinul assumed a great degree of control from the beginning, even when it came to selecting musicians. For example, Frank Cuomo, who played on *Odyssey of Iska*, followed up with Wayne a few months later when he heard that the saxophonist was forming a new band. "He told me that Joe was making the decision who would join the group, so it was left at that," Cuomo said.[46] And while the three leaders shared the writing credits equally, Alphonse Mouzon clearly recalled the dynamics in the studio: "They got along well—mutual respect for one another—but Joe was in control. Somebody had to be the leader, and he was like the leader."[47]

Given the personalities involved, it's hardly surprising that the band would evolve this way. Miroslav had just turned twenty-three years old, and while he possessed a powerful musical voice, he was clearly the junior partner of the enterprise. Wayne had plenty of experience, but he wasn't the type to seize the reins or even tell others what to do (at least not directly). He was "so soft-spoken and shy that he took a backseat," Mouzon said.[48] Even on his own projects, Wayne gave musicians considerable latitude to express themselves, confident in his own ability to hear and react. Part of the beauty of his playing is how well he adapts to just about any situation. As one Weather Report musician said of him, "Wayne was the explorer of the band. When we played a song, as far as Wayne was concerned, it didn't matter to him if we ended up in India or back in the States—or for that matter, on Jupiter. He just loved the exploration and enjoyed the ride."[49]

But it mattered to Joe. With Cannonball, he felt like his music never got played the way he heard it in his head. That was okay; he was a sideman and understood his role. But he also thought, *There will be a time when I will have a group of people play the music exactly like I want it.*[50] Joe knew what he wanted and didn't hesitate to express it, so he easily filled the void. *Somebody had to be the leader.* Joe's assertiveness would lead to great music, but not everyone appreciated his approach. Don Alias wound up cutting his involvement short after the two disagreed on what he should play. "He started to control everything," Alias recalled. "Now that's his prerogative. You know, he's the leader and stuff like that. But man, don't take away from what we've got to give you."[51]

Later on, when the record came out, Burton and Alias were left off the credits. Burton took it in stride, regarding it as a learning experience. Alias was less forgiving. When he got the record and noticed his name was missing, he figured it was because they didn't use his tracks. Then he put it on the turntable and heard himself on "Tears." "So I called up Alphonse Mouzon and I said, 'What's the deal here, man?' And he said, 'Yeah, yeah, yeah, you're playing on it.' I said, 'Did you know that Zawinul did not put my name on there, he put Airto on there or something like that?' And he didn't know that. So we had this falling out for years. I didn't want to have nothing to do with that kind of thinking."[52]

Meanwhile, Joe was so pleased with Airto's work that he pressed him hard to join the group. "We're going to be the best in the world," he boasted. "Miroslav is the best in the world. I'm the best in the world. You're the best in the world." Airto liked the music, but he worried about Joe's big talk and heavy-handed approach. Plus it would mean leaving Miles. "I was going to make it, because the music the group was playing was so beautiful. I said to Joe that I wanted to make it, but that I wanted to think about it for a little bit longer. And Joe said, 'Hey man, why think about it? Let's just go.' But I took two or three more days and decided not to make it. We had already taken the album cover shots and recorded the first Weather Report album. It caused real bad vibrations."[53]

If Joe couldn't have Airto, he insisted on getting the next best thing and tasked Moreira with finding another Brazilian percussionist even though he wasn't a member of the band.

•

Columbia didn't waste much time getting the record to market (in contrast to Blue Note and Atlantic, which sat on *Odyssey of Iska* and *Zawinul* for many months), and they had an aggressive marketing campaign in store. *Billboard* noted that the label had "instituted a mass merchandising campaign for any album product regardless of music category, which the company feels can appeal to major disk and concert audiences. A jazz group, Weather Report, will be the first group treated to this contemporary music-level promotion."[54] It was evident that Columbia had high hopes for the album, viewing it in the same vein as *Bitches Brew*.

The LP was due for release at the end of April. The timeline slipped a month, but at the end of May, Columbia ramped up its publicity machine with a week-long series of luncheon interviews aimed at introducing Weather Report to the music press. The group, sans percussionist, sat alongside Columbia publicity functionaries, sandwiches piled high on a conference table while a shoeshine boy plied his trade beneath it.[55] When one writer raised an eyebrow at being told that Clive Davis signed the band without having heard its music, Columbia publicity director (and jazz aficionado) Bob Altshuler was quick to jump in. "I'll tell you what it was really based on: he felt the right vibrations. . . . He felt the creative vibrations from certain things that were said by Joe and Miroslav and Wayne. . . . It was instant recognition of their creativity and he did not hear a note of music."[56]

Sid Bernstein sprang into action, too, inviting his music business pals to his Manhattan office where he did his best to promote the group. Among them was pop writer Al Aronowitz, who, like Bernstein, flaunted his connection to the Beatles—in his case, introducing them to Bob Dylan and marijuana. Aronowitz wrote a dispatch about "the Weather Report" for *Melody Maker* that was as much about Bernstein's current financial woes as it was the band. "Like a desert, it's been. Just like a desert," the impresario told him. As for Weather Report, "To me, this is the super super-group of America," Bernstein declared. "I believe it is America's first super super-group. It's truly a super super-group."[57] That statement goes some way toward explaining why Joe thought Bernstein didn't know how to sell Weather Report's music.

The meetings were capped by a couple of live performances for the press at Columbia's famed Thirtieth Street studios. It was the only time Airto performed with the band.[58] One writer claimed that they played their entire album "straight through with virtually no deviation from the recorded version," causing him to conclude that though their music "sounds thoroughly improvisational, everything is fixed, arranged, consistently repeatable."[59] Of course, it wasn't fixed, but perhaps one explanation for this perception comes from critic Hollie West, who heard the band a few months later. He noted that the group "deals in compositions that sound almost formal. They sound orchestrated even when there is abundant improvisation, because all the performers have a highly developed sense of melody."[60]

Another reporter who attended the press gig remembered it being "outrageous"; Wayne, in particular, was "unbelievable." The group "played and expanded upon basic themes from virtually every cut on their first LP," he said.[61] Dave Holland crashed the affair along with some other musicians. "Right away we knew it was a great band and had wonderful potential," he recalled.[62]

At around the same time, *Down Beat* published an atypical interview-cum-record review penned by Dan Morgenstern. "An extraordinary new group merits an extraordinary review of its debut album," he wrote.[63] Later in the summer, *Jazz & Pop* ran a profile by Michael Cuscuna, who couldn't help but notice the musicians' "glowing enthusiasm and satisfaction with Weather Report." Cuscuna considered their cooperative character "a small miracle." "We are doing it," Zawinul told him. "We are working together. One of us will bring in a tune and the ideas seem to develop by themselves. But there's a great respect for one another, so it's very easy to cooperate."[64]

Columbia made good on its marketing promise with an advertising blitz in the leading music magazines, featuring full- or half-page advertisements tailored to each publication's readership. The *Down Beat* version emphasized the band members' jazz credentials as "poll winners" and "pioneers," while describing the album as music they had "bubbling and churning inside them for years."[65] In *Rolling Stone*, Columbia appealed to open-minded, adventurous listeners, calling *Weather Report* "a feast for the human mind."[66] The full-page ad in *Record World*, a trade journal for retailers, ran with the title "Why you're probably having a hard time keeping this mysterious-looking album in stock." It played to the idea of a grassroots demand for the album fueled by things like the glowing *Down Beat* review the previous month.[67]

Weather Report was the most talked about new jazz band of the year, and anticipation was high as fans eagerly waited for the LP to reach store shelves. A young drummer by the name of Peter Erskine was just finishing up his high school years at Michigan's Interlochen Center for the Arts when he heard the album for the first time. "From 'Milky Way' into 'Umbrellas,' I was like, 'Wow, what chords were those?' And that drumbeat. Then when it goes into tempo, the beat changes, the tempo changes, and the whole band just turns left on a dime. That's kind of a Miles thing. And I thought, 'That's the shit!' And in fact, it's not only a Miles thing, it's very similar to the Beatles' *Magical Mystery Tour*. I was like, 'Oh man, here we go.' The way that entire album opened, it's like a Broadway musical. It was like, 'This is an overture to the music of the future.'"[68]

There were also some tepid responses to the album. Some reviews cited a lack of emotion compounded by the fact that none of the players stepped up and *blew*. "It's all beautiful, lush, hypnotic, mostly quite soothing, but I can't help feeling that something is missing," wrote Lester Bangs in *Rolling Stone*. On the other side of the Atlantic, *Melody Maker* titled its review "Weather Report: A Bleak Outlook." "Everything sounds so detached," Richard Williams complained. "The players are ultimately concerned with creating 'spacey' textures, with those lightning-fast responses to each other, that nobody really has a chance to play."[69]

Dom Um Romão performing with Weather Report in 1971. Note the table of hand percussion instruments. Photo: © United Archives / Hulton Archive / Getty Images.

•

As Weather Report prepared for its first public appearances, they still didn't have a percussionist. At the press conferences they told reporters that Carmelo Garcia would be their man.[70] But Garcia was best known for playing timbales with Mongo Santamaría, and Joe really hoped to find a player in the mold of Airto—someone who could add color to the music without cluttering it. The problem was, there was only one Airto, and he remained loyal to Miles. Nevertheless, the press gigs went so well that Joe made another run at him. "You gotta go on tour with us!" he insisted. Airto turned him down again, but this time he offered an alternative. Since overdubbing on *Weather Report*, Airto had recorded his second stateside release, *Seeds on the Ground*. For that session, he brought an old Brazilian friend up to New York.

"Listen," Airto told Joe. "I can do one thing. I will get somebody to play with you. This guy is a *great* player. He is in Miami right now and he would be glad to come here and play with the Weather Report."

"What's his name?" Joe asked.

"Dom Um Romão."

Joe had never heard of him. "How old is he?"

"Well, I don't know how old he is," Airto replied, "but he's older than I am."

Apparently, that was enough to convince Joe. "Okay. Call him."[71]

Sixteen years Airto's senior, Romão was considered one of the best drummers in Brazil, steeped in the nation's musical traditions. For years he played on the *samba-enredo* (song samba) records for Carnival, playing drums and overdubbing all the percussion. He made his first visit to the United States in 1962 with Sérgio Mendes's *Sexteto Bossa Rio*, which was among a contingent of Brazilians who performed at Carnegie Hall, a milestone concert that helped establish the international popularity of bossa nova. Based on that visit, Romão decided to move to the United States permanently. He returned in 1965, gigging with Astrud Gilberto and doing session work, most notably the *Francis Albert Sinatra & Antônio Carlos Jobim* bossa nova album. In 1968, he reunited with Mendes, who by then was leading the popular band Brasil '66.

Working mainly as a drummer since immigrating to the States, Dom Um didn't have the percussion instruments that the Weather Report job demanded. "We talked about the whole thing," Airto remembered, "and he said, 'Well, I have to buy some stuff.' I said, 'You can't buy this over here, but you can use some of my stuff,' and I gave him all the things that I had."[72] So Romão packed up his car and made the twenty-hour drive to New York City. Once he got settled, he met Joe and Wayne at a club. "They both talked to me about playing percussion with them and asked me to come to a rehearsal with them the next day," Romão recalled. "We played for about an hour before Zawinul suddenly said, 'Yeah, man, we don't need to rehearse anymore. That's good just like that, man. Leave it just like it is! Anyway, tomorrow we'll be leaving on a tour.'"[73]

Shortly after Romão's audition, Weather Report staged its first public performance, at Penn State University. Promoted by the school's jazz club, the free admission helped attract 170 audience members, most of whom were undoubtedly members of the club.[74] Listening to a tape of the gig, Joe later said, "It was mean. . . . And right after that we went to Europe, incredible."[75]

8 I Sing the Body Electric

Let's hit 'em hard, right from the first note.

—Joe Zawinul

THE CENTERPIECE OF WEATHER REPORT'S FIRST TRIP TO EUROPE was its appearance at the Third International Music Forum, held at the lakeside resort village of Ossiach, Austria.[1] It was arranged through Joe's old friend, Friedrich Gulda, who served as the festival's artistic director. Gulda was nothing if not ambitious, and he assembled a ten-day event that was indeed international in scope, combining classical, jazz, and folk music from around the world. Some of the better known names that appeared there were Jean-Luc Ponty, Tangerine Dream, and Pink Floyd. The latter came at a cost of 300,000 shillings—an impressive sum at the time—and the highlight of their concert was a performance of their suite "Atom Heart Mother," backed by a sixty-member orchestra and choir.

During its eighty-minute set, Weather Report played all of the pieces from its album except "Milky Way," plus Joe's tune "Early Minor," which he had previously recorded with both Nat Adderley and Miles Davis, and another piece that has been identified as "Firefish." Information about the band's early European tours is scant. It's not clear how many performances they had under their belt by the time they got to Ossiach, but there couldn't have been many. So it's striking how together the band sounded and how well Dom Um Romão integrated with his bandmates.

Weather Report returned to the States in July, just in time for the Newport Jazz Festival. With their first LP in store bins, Columbia had high hopes for the band's appearance there, viewing it as a kind of coming-out party. Then in its seventeenth year, the festival was a major happening in the jazz world, attracting worldwide attention. All the music publications, as well as major newspapers and entertainment trade journals, sent representatives. Scheduled over the long Fourth of July weekend, the musical acts were grouped in themes. For the Monday afternoon slot, Columbia lined up three of its progressive jazz bands: Miles Davis, the British group Soft Machine, and Weather Report. They never took the stage.

A sold-out crowd of about 18,000 fans squeezed onto the festival grounds on Friday night, while a growing contingent of young people camped out on the hill beyond the fences, lured there by the prospect that Newport was the closest thing to a rock festival that they would see that year. For promoter George Wein, their presence was a disturbing reminder of the near-riot that occurred two years earlier as Sly and the Family Stone finished their set. That was the first time the festival featured rock acts, and the chaos prompted the city to ban rock 'n' roll from future events. What started out as a hopeful co-mingling of jazz and rock ended with further polarization among their fans—a generational clash that played out in the pages of *Down Beat* and *Rolling Stone* magazines, among others.[2]

By Saturday afternoon, the number of "hill people" had swelled to several thousand and Wein's worst fears were realized later that evening when hundreds of kids began milling around the gates, demanding free entrance. Wein pleaded with them through a bullhorn, encouraging them to remain where they were and simply enjoy the music for free from their encampment. With the rabble-rousers undeterred, Wein issued one last appeal: "You can destroy the festival or you can stay and have a good time."[3]

"Fuck the festival" came the response.[4] Soon the fences were breached and a swarm of gatecrashers surged through the audience as Dionne Warwick finished her set singing, of all things, "What the World Needs Now Is Love." After a quick consult with city officials, Wein grabbed the microphone from Warwick's hand, declaring that the evening's performances were over and instructing concertgoers to leave in an orderly fashion for their own safety. In their wake the mob commandeered the stage, destroying whatever equipment they could get their hands on and refusing to leave. Wein canceled the remainder of the festival the next morning. For Columbia, it was a bitter pill to swallow. The Monday afternoon concert "was very important to us," lamented Bob Altshuler. "This was the first year that we had made strong efforts to get major rock critics to attend Newport. I'm terribly saddened by the whole episode."[5]

So Weather Report cooled its heels for a few days before heading up to Boston for a weeklong stand at the Jazz Workshop. Gigs like this were how bands honed their sound, and the regular patrons couldn't help but notice how Weather Report got tighter as the week wore on. Presciently, one observer noted that the band "has no leader but you can still feel the dominating personality of Joe Zawinul."[6] The most curious thing about this gig is that Barbara Burton was back, "augmenting the drum parts with horns, scrapers, bells and assorted gear," according to the *Boston Globe*.[7]

It isn't clear why she replaced Dom Um Romão for these shows. Perhaps he was unavailable, but a possible clue comes from an interview Joe gave to *Billboard*, which appeared a few weeks later. Talking about Weather Report's next LP, he said it would "probably" include Romão.[8] Probably? That suggests that Joe wasn't yet sold on the Brazilian and was willing to give Burton another try.

Adding color to a constantly improvising jazz band was different from Romão's previous experience, and it must have required an adjustment. "He had his groove and stuff," Miroslav said, "but I think the music was so strange for him that he really didn't know what to do with it. We found out that he was just picking something from the table and shaking it for a while, throwing it back on the table and picking another one because he didn't know what to do. Joe got pissed off many times, saying, 'Hey, why don't you just pick one thing and play some music with it, stick to it?'"[9]

Burton recalled that things went well enough in Boston to receive an invitation from Joe to tour with the band. Then an odd thing happened: At the end of the gig, she didn't get paid. "The club owner said that they didn't make enough money," she recalled, "but the place was packed every night." That, coupled with the unwanted advances of one of the band members, convinced her that her future lay elsewhere. Burton did find a silver lining to the events in Boston, however. "The last night, when we were supposed to come home that week, I met my husband," she recalled. "I never would have met him if I had not taken that gig."[10]

Late in the summer of 1971, Weather Report returned to Europe, once again with Romão onboard. Among other things, the band was invited to take part in Germany's NDR (Northern German Radio) *Jazzworkshop*, a long-running series that started in 1958, in which leading jazz musicians from around the world were brought together for a one-week residency in order to develop a concert program for radio and television broadcast. In this case, Weather Report was joined by trombonist Eje Thelin from Sweden, and saxophonists Alan Skidmore and John Surman from the United Kingdom. Billed as "Weather Report Plus Three," the resulting performance was carried over NDR on September 3.

Romão and Mouzon traveled to Europe ahead of the rest of the group, but upon arriving they discovered that they didn't have hotel rooms. "We had to find a place to stay, me and Dom Um," Mouzon recalled. "I said, 'I know where I'm going to find me a place. I'll go to the jazz club.' I had my suitcase and my drumsticks—they were shipping the drums over—and I sat in and I met these girls. I don't know where Dom Um went, but I wasn't going to stay out in the cold freezing to death. I got a place to stay and the girls got something."[11]

That episode reinforced some resentments that had been building within Mouzon, stemming from what he perceived to be unequal treatment of the band members. While Weather Report was established as a collective band, in practice it was only applicable to the founders. "It was like Weather Report with Alphonse Mouzon as a sideman. I was there when they signed the contract, but my name wasn't in the contract."[12] Another issue was the lack of opportunity to get his compositions played by the band. "I wrote songs that I still haven't recorded—music that I wrote for Weather Report and never had an opportunity to present to them, because I was a writer, too."[13]

The three additional musicians for the NDR *Jazzworkshop* also rankled Mouzon. "They had no business being there with us," he insisted years later. "They interfered with the band's sound. And Joe didn't like the way I was treating those guys, I guess. I was very protective because we rehearsed so much and we had our own sound, and nobody could just come in and join us. This was a special thing we had going, and they came in there and there was no place for Wayne. It had nothing to do with what we were doing. Wayne was the horn player, and he's taking a back seat. I said, 'What is this?' And I guess they overheard and the guy felt bad."[14]

Word of his drummer's unhappiness about the situation got back to Joe in an unpleasant way. "This man Mouzon goes in the bar and gets a little drunk and really puts down Skidmore and Surman," Joe complained. "That's okay if he feels like that, but these guys thought it came from Wayne and me, and it really hurt 'em. And later on, we came to talking and I said, 'What's the matter, Alan?' And he said, 'Well you know, Joe, I don't know. Maybe we shouldn't have been here,' and so on. I said, 'What did this?' He said, 'You know the drummer, man? Said yesterday that we can't play shit, and we're in the wrong place.' And that was it. I don't need somebody like that."[15] As the band flew back to New York, Mouzon's days with Weather Report were over.

•

Alphonse Mouzon's departure opened a revolving door through which drummers passed with regularity until Peter Erskine stabilized the position in 1978. The first to follow in Mouzon's footsteps was twenty-four-year-old Eric Kamau Gravatt. He grew up in Philadelphia's Germantown neighborhood, an area with a rich jazz tradition. "I started playing trumpet in elementary school," Gravatt said, "but my dog wouldn't let me practice because every time I played, he would howl. So I transferred to drums and played in the orchestra in junior high school."[16] By the time he got to high school, Eric was good enough to attract the attention of older musicians who hired him for their gigs.

Gravatt gravitated to jazz and was especially drawn to John Coltrane's music. He practiced to Trane's records so much that at one point he played hooky from school twenty-five days in a row. When his parents caught him, the punishment was harsh: No touching the drums for a year. "The drums were set up in the dining room, and I had to walk past them every day," he said.[17] When he was allowed

to play again, Gravatt met another like-minded young musician in the neighborhood, saxophonist Michael Brecker, and they jammed together often, just drums
and sax. Even then, Eric was "a fantastic drummer," Brecker remembered.[18]

After high school, Gravatt attended Cheyney State College before transfer-
ring to Howard University in Washington, D.C., where he pursued a philosophy
degree. There he indulged many pursuits, including acting, writing, voiceover
work, and teaching at the New Thing Art and Architecture Center, which offered
cultural programs for inner city youth.[19] A 1975 profile described Gravatt as "a
twentieth century Renaissance man with many interests and abilities, high intelligence, a keen wit; a deep man with a lot to say and a knack for saying it well; a
man of humility but not false modesty; a man who puts himself and his music in
perspective."[20]

Gravatt soon found his way into D.C.'s avant-garde jazz community, and met
Zawinul at a gig in 1967. Impressed, Joe recommended him to Miles Davis when
Tony Williams left the trumpeter the following year. But the two never quite
hooked up. One night Miles invited Gravatt to sit in, but Gravatt's wife had to be
rushed to the hospital, scuttling that opportunity. Another time, he was supposed
to audition at a local club, but when he got there Miles said he didn't feel like
hearing anybody play that night.[21] Yet another time Miles offered Gravatt a tour,
only for it to be called off.[22]

These missed opportunities are emblematic of Gravatt's career, in which his
talent was undermined both by circumstances beyond his control and his own
prickly nature. "I have always suffered a bit from the fact that I am my own man,"
he once said. "And when I was younger I was full of piss and vinegar—you know,
a little too strong-willed. I have always been the guy who'd be happy to play with
you, but after the gig, I'm not hanging out and drinking and smoking with you.
This has unsettled more than a few people throughout the years, and that's fine.
I'm a quiet guy, and sometimes being quiet and confident can be misperceived."[23]
As a consequence, Gravatt is now remembered as "possibly the least known highly
influential drummer in history," as one writer described him.[24] But that's getting
ahead of the story.

Gravatt's big break came late in the summer of 1970, when McCoy Tyner
asked him to join his group. Tyner was Coltrane's pianist, so this was a dream
assignment. "It was a turning point for me," Eric acknowledged. "In fact, that
first tour I did with McCoy was the first time I went to Minneapolis [where Gravatt later settled]. It was with [saxophonist] Byard Lancaster and [bassist] Herbie
Lewis. McCoy had a big station wagon and I had the backseat facing backwards.
And when we drove up to Minneapolis from New York, my job was to round up
Herbie and Byard every time we stopped, because they stopped at every bar they
could."[25]

In those days, Tyner frequently worked at Slugs' Saloon, a notorious dive of a jazz club in the East Village. Years later, Gravatt recalled this time fondly. "It was popping—that's where all the action was. When McCoy played there, oftentimes there would be twenty or thirty people waiting to sit in. I remember playing with Marzette Watts, Giuseppi Logan . . . They were just lined up to sit in."[26] Gravatt was still living in D.C. at the time, so he hauled his drums up to New York by bus, playing from ten at night until four in the morning. Eventually, the grind became too much and Gravatt gave Tyner his notice. Not long afterward, Wayne rang him up and invited him to a rehearsal.

Weather Report didn't have many gigs that first year, but on October 23–24 they opened for Dr. John the Night Tripper at the Beacon Theatre, an opulent Rococo-style movie palace on Manhattan's Upper West Side. The appearance was arranged not by Sid Bernstein, but by Bow Wow Productions, a new promoter that leased the Beacon on weekends in the hopes of establishing it as a concert venue. One of Bow Wow's principals was Wayne's sister-in-law, Maria Booker. She made a point of booking jazz bands to support the rock and pop headliners. "What I wanted to do was to fuse jazz and rock," she said, "because the jazz musicians are the best, but who makes all the money? The rock musicians. So I tried to put them together so that people learned about jazz."[27] Weather Report benefited from its familial connections and got some of these gigs.[28]

The band's slim bookings led to a falling out with Bernstein. "Sid had great influence in the music business," Joe recalled, "but he never got business for us. All the offers came directly to Wayne or to me, and we even sent him money from Europe when he did nothing. When we first won the critics poll in *Down Beat* magazine, the highest award for a jazz band, he said, 'That's quite nice, but . . .'" Joe told him this couldn't continue and they agreed to part ways with a handshake, but soon Bernstein claimed that he was contractually entitled to receive his percentage as long as the band existed. "If you insist, we'll look for a new name and still be successful," Joe told him. Bernstein realized that Joe was right and they concluded their business relationship over some beers. "He wasn't a bad guy," Joe said, "but he had no idea about our music."[29]

Eric Gravatt was just coming on board as the Beacon dates approached, so Joe asked Alphonse Mouzon to do the gig. He wouldn't have it. "They were getting another drummer, rehearsing behind my back, and I found out," Mouzon said. "They weren't ready yet, so they called me and wanted me to play the concert. I said, 'No, I quit.' Rehearse somebody behind my back? Nuh uh. Forget it."[30]

Losing Mouzon might have provoked a crisis in the band if it weren't for the fact that Gravatt was so superb himself. "Eric's one of those rare individuals with feeling and intelligence," Joe remarked at the time. "And it's even rarer to find those qualities in a drummer. When you start looking, you can count on one

Eric Gravatt on the bandstand with Weather Report in 1972. Photo: Lee Tanner.

hand the drummers who can stay on top of it like he does."[31] Joe and Wayne both remembered him as their favorite drummer the band ever had. "Eric was the one," Wayne said. "He had bounce in his rhythm that would bounce off the floor and carry the music up to the ceiling. He had this ethnic sound—the continent of Africa—but with grace. He has a dignity and the flavor of Africa, and of metropolitan cities, all with the element of surprise."[32]

Drummer drama aside, the band was thrilled to finally play before a hometown audience, despite the many empty seats in the theater. Joe's old bandmate, Roy McCurdy was on hand with some musician friends. "We loved it," he recalled. "We thought it was great."[33] Critics were a bit mixed. One reviewer noted that Weather Report "gave an exceptional instrumental jazz performance,"[34] but its music went right past the *Village Voice's* Richard Nusser, who wrote that the band "left me cold with a lackluster set of undistinguished melodies that seemed to be nothing more than garden variety progressive jazz, with a bossa nova percussionist providing a few bird calls."[35]

As Weather Report held forth at the Beacon, one of Dr. John's musicians listened from the wings. "Those guys were killing it on that gig," guitarist Kenny Klimak recalled. "I thought they were amazing. But what I'll never forget [is that] when they walked off stage at the end of their set Zawinul started bitching at the guys as soon as they were out of the audience's view, and he continued bitching all the way up several flights of stairs to their dressing room. At least that's what it sounded like to me. That one instance made me a better musician because I thought what they just played was incredible, but clearly I wasn't hearing what Zawinul was hearing—he was hearing something more. That made me want to up my game."[36]

Right after the Beacon gigs, Weather Report hit the road, spending a week in Boston at Lennie's on the Turnpike, followed by another week at the Cellar Door in Washington, D.C. Over Thanksgiving weekend, Bow Wow gave them another slot at the Beacon, this time as one of the opening acts for the Ike & Tina Turner Revue. Bow Wow's previous events had difficulty filling the 2,800-seat theater, but this one sold so well that a third date was added. However, a ticketing snafu on the first night resulted in an overflow audience and some people ended up without seats. By the time Weather Report took the stage, the audience had already sat (or stood) through two rock groups. With their nerves frayed from the seating problems, they greeted Weather Report with what *Variety* described as a "rude response."[37]

"They were booing," Maria Booker confirmed. "The crowd got very mad. I went to the stage and *I* got mad. You have to learn about music, you know! I was very upset about that."[38] Such was the hazard of performing before someone else's fans. After the show, Gravatt ran into Miles Davis backstage, wearing a big fur coat and oversized glasses. "Eric! Eric!" he called in his raspy voice. "You sound like a motherfucker. The rest of the band sounds like shit."[39] Such was the hazard of performing before Miles Davis.

Weather Report had one more club date at the Colonial Tavern in Toronto during the first week of December before taking the rest of the year off. The next time they performed live, it would be in Japan.

•

While Weather Report was ensconced at the Jazz Workshop in Boston earlier in the year, Joe received a visitor to his hotel room. It was Roger Powell, a twenty-two-year-old clinician from nearby ARP Instruments. He came lugging two black, Tolex-covered cases via their plastic handles. The bigger one, about the size of a suitcase, housed an ARP 2600 music synthesizer fresh off the factory floor. The other case contained its four-octave keyboard. Powell put the larger case on a table, unhooked its silver latches, and removed the lid, revealing the 2600's control panel with its dozens of sliders labeled in terminology that derived from audio engineering. Here was an instrument that, save for the piano-style keyboard, must have seemed totally alien to Zawinul. Unlike an electric piano, you couldn't merely turn it on and get a pleasing sound. You *had* to learn how it worked or you had nothing. As Powell put the machine through its paces and Joe took in its incredible range of sounds, it must have been immensely intriguing and intimidating at the same time. It was an instrument he had waited for since his days in Austria.[40]

"I will tell you something," Joe said years later. "I was interested in synthesizers, or what became synthesizers—in the possibility of having many sounds to deal with—when I was a kid. I was playing accordion, and on the better accordions they have what we call registers. That means buttons, which when you press them down the sound changes completely. That was for me why I liked to play accordion much more than piano." Even better was the Hammond organ, which he discovered in Austria during an engagement for American servicemen. "In the bottom of the hotel was an American chapel where they held their church service, and there was a Hammond down there," Joe recalled. "They allowed me to go down there, and I played for hours. Every day. I fell in love with it."[41]

Zawinul considered the synthesizer to be the spiritual, if not technical successor, of those instruments. "My whole concept was, an accordion is a wonderful instrument, but awfully clumsy. And the Hammond organ is also clumsy, because how do you take this with you? I said there has got to be a way one day that I have an instrument where you have something shaped like a piano, that has many of these registers like a Hammond organ, but not as clumsy and big. And I had this in my mind all my life."[42]

At the time Powell showed the 2600 to Joe, few musicians had seen a synthesizer, much less played one. The best-known and most successful use of the instrument, both commercially and artistically, was Wendy Carlos's *Switched-On Bach*. It was released in late 1968 and captured the public's fancy, selling over a million copies and garnering three Grammy Awards.[43] There had been other synth-based recordings on the market, but they tended toward the gimmicky or experimental, neither of which appealed to mainstream listeners. *Switched-On Bach* exhibited such a high level of taste and craftsmanship that it transcended the technology used to produce it.

Carlos's synthesizer was designed and built by Robert Moog, whose pioneering work in voltage-controlled oscillators and filters led to the release of his first modular synthesizer in 1965. The term *modular* refers to the fact that each synthesizer consisted of independent electronic circuits that were connected together via patch chords. The fundamental modules were oscillators, which generated a waveform of a given frequency or pitch; filters, which colored the timbre produced by the oscillators; amplifiers, which governed the volume of the sound; and envelope generators, which determined how quickly the volume rose and fell.

Each module was controlled by variable voltages generated by other modules or manually using knobs or sliders. In addition, a piano-style keyboard generated a voltage and a trigger; connecting it to an oscillator and envelope generator caused individual notes to sound as the keys were pressed and released. Such synthesizers are now known as analog synthesizers because they relied on voltages to define state as opposed to binary data used by digital circuits.

Moog's synthesizers were custom built, intended for use in large recording studios. Despite their apparent complexity, they seem comically primitive by today's standards. Carlos had to painstakingly record each piece one note at a time because the Moog keyboard was monophonic—that is, it produced only one output no matter how many keys were pressed. Furthermore, Carlos had to pause every few minutes in order to retune the oscillators because they drifted out of tune so quickly. It was a tedious process; it took Carlos the entire spring and summer of 1968 to complete *Switched-On Bach*.

A few rock musicians also acquired Moog modular systems, like George Harrison of the Beatles, who used it on their album *Abbey Road*.[44] Pete Townshend of the Who and Keith Emerson of Emerson, Lake & Palmer even ventured on stage with theirs. But for the most part, these machines were behemoths—Emerson's weighed hundreds of pounds and stood ten feet tall—whose use required the assistance of an expert. Naturally, the idea occurred to Moog to produce a pared-down model that could be used in live settings. Thus was born the Minimoog, perhaps *the* classic analog synthesizer of all time. It had a three-and-a-half-octave monophonic keyboard with internal modules that were hardwired together in a package small enough to sit atop a Rhodes electric piano. Though it lacked its big brother's flexibility, it was far more approachable. Jazz pianist Dick Hyman, who had already recorded with the Moog modular, debuted the Minimoog in public performance in the summer of 1970.[45]

Among the many individuals inspired by *Switched-On Bach* was Alan R. Pearlman, an electrical engineer who had designed amplifiers for the Gemini and Apollo space programs. After tinkering with some ideas in his garage workshop, Pearlman invested $100,000 of his own money and founded ARP Instruments. In 1970, ARP unveiled its first synthesizer, the 2500, which was a competitor to Moog's modular systems. Determined to build a product for use by small to medium-sized higher-education music departments, ARP's second synthesizer was the 2600, which was introduced that fall, though it took several more months before they were produced in quantity. Like the Minimoog, its modules were pre-connected in a standard way, allowing users to get started fairly easily. But the unique thing about the 2600 was that those connections could be overridden with patch cords, giving it the flexibility of a modular system. It, too, became a classic, manufactured for ten years and widely used by educators and performing artists.

With Moog's name recognition and head start in the marketplace, ARP adopted a strategy of getting its products into the hands of influential musicians. Joe Zawinul was one such beneficiary.[46] The 2600's price tag rivaled that of an automobile, an amount beyond Joe's reach. So the one that Roger Powell brought with him was given to Zawinul "on evaluation." Powell, a synth pioneer in his own right who later played keyboards for Todd Rundgren's Utopia, spent the week teaching Joe how to use it.

"You didn't really need patch cords to get a basic sound out of the 2600," Powell said, "but you did need to know how to move the sliders. The way we worked together is, I would show him a patch and explain why you had to push each slider up to a certain point, and then I would just push all the sliders back to zero, and say, 'Okay, Joe, now it's your turn.' And he would stare at the machine for a little while; I wasn't giving him any help. So then he started glancing back and forth, and finally he would pick a slider that he thought was part of the patch, and he would look at me and go, 'Push this one up?' I think it was really twisting his brain, but he was such a smart and talented guy that it didn't stop him. And he really had a vision for it."[47]

In those days, synthesizers didn't have memories, so every patch had to be configured from scratch, slider by slider. In order to record these settings, ARP provided patch sheets, which were paper facsimiles of the instrument's front panel on which one could mark the locations of the various sliders and patch connections. Eventually, ARP produced a book containing one hundred patches, but for now, Joe was on his own. Powell recalled an incident that illustrates the challenges of the 2600 compared to an electric piano or organ. Buried among the many sliders on the 2600's control panel was one that, if raised, made the sound stay on whether a key was pressed or not. A week or two after Joe took it back to his apartment in New York, he called Powell. "I went to the phone, and all I could hear was a blazing, droning oscillator. So I said, 'Hey, Joe, how ya doin'?'"

"Oh man, I'm doin' great! Let me tell you, the sound is *fantastic*," Zawinul said. "But let me ask you, man, how do I make it stop?"[48]

•

In November 1971, Weather Report returned to Columbia's Fifty-Second Street Studios to record tracks for its second album, *I Sing the Body Electric*. Wayne came up with the title, which no doubt appealed to him because of its allusion to the band's contemporary sound. He got it from a short story in Ray Bradbury's 1969 book of the same name, which co-opted the title from a Walt Whitman poem. The story, which was also made into an episode of *The Twilight Zone*, revolves around a father who purchases a robotic grandmother to care for his children after his wife dies suddenly. Presumably that story inspired the album's cover art, which is based on a collage by artist Jack Trompetter. A Columbia art director happened across it, and the next thing Trompetter knew, it was on the front of Weather Report's new album, which tickled him because he was a fan of their music.[49] It's the kind of cover that made record shop browsers do a double take.

One of the first pieces the band tackled was Joe's composition "Unknown

Soldier." Like many of his tunes from this period, it is autobiographical in nature. The title refers to the monuments memorializing the deaths of unidentified soldiers that developed in the aftermath of World War I, but Joe had a broader idea in mind. "It was also about the fact that in the war we were also unknown soldiers without being soldiers," he said. "We lived in the war and for two years we were bombed almost every day. The many people who died in concentration camps were also unknown soldiers."[50]

Joe experienced a particularly close call on September 10, 1944—a date that was etched into his memory. When the air-raid sirens began wailing, he was hanging out on the street with his best friend. "We were standing on the corner, and all of a sudden the bombs were falling, and he ran home and I ran home. I grabbed my momma and took her down to the shelter, and the moment we hit the shelter, a thousand-pound bomb flew in front of the house." The bombing lasted ninety minutes. When it finally subsided, Joe ventured outside to survey the damage. "The crater was five or six meters deep," he recalled. "The water hydrant was on our terrace [on the fourth floor], and a whole cornerstone was on the roof. When I walked outside the dust was [up to my knees]. And in the park, next to the school, was an arm sticking out of the debris. I tried to get underneath to get that person out, but it was only an arm, ripped off."[51] That bombing led to Joe's evacuation to the hunting lodge in the Sudetenland.

When the war ended in the spring of 1945, Josef was tasked with burying the bodies of dead soldiers that were left behind in the woods. He recalled the experience vividly decades later. "It was one of the hottest Mays in history. There were hundreds and hundreds of corpses on the sides of the roads. Blown up, with gasses—millions of flies. It was horrible. We had to dig the grave. We didn't have any gloves and things like that. All barefoot, with just some shorts, you know. And with fire hooks. And we had to break off the [dog] tag. And those bodies were so decayed in the sun, spiders coming out of 'em from the eye sockets. I buried one guy, he was obviously rolled over by a tank. And his head was as wide as a table, all spread out like a Picasso painting, eyes here, and shit like that. So it was. That was my upbringing."[52]

All of these memories inform "Unknown Soldier." As the tune unfolds, it takes on an increasingly ominous tone. Then one hears the explosion itself, the chaos of armed conflict happening all around him, the ghostly apparition of the deformed bodies that he buried, and the healing that began in the war's aftermath. It was Joe's most ambitious work to date—a complex composition structured in distinct movements, with a middle section that combines an avant-garde free jam with percussion and elements of *musique concrète*. It significantly raised the level of sophistication in Weather Report's music, revealing an ambition well beyond musical sketches designed for improvisatory exploration.

Joe conceived "Unknown Soldier" for larger instrumentation than Weather Report offered, so he brought in a small horn section and a choir to sing the wordless vocals, which he described in his score as "voices praying in an unknown language." Joe had just gotten his ARP 2600 and wasn't comfortable using it yet, so he invited Roger Powell to the session to program some sound effects, such as the air raid sirens that are heard in the second movement. "I guess he still felt like a neophyte, and he requested that I come down for a day to help him make sure he could get the sound," Powell recalled. "I helped him out with some patches, and they were into this whole thing of, like, almost improvised tone poems, so the music had a kind of dramatic, almost orchestral, classical structure to it, and yet there was a lot of improvisation.

"[On 'Unknown Soldier'] he was playing some other instrument, and when he wanted something out of the 2600, he would point at me. One time I did this really weird thing with the sample-and-hold circuit, a totally randomized thing, and it came in a big hole in the music where they stopped playing and there was silence [at about 5:05 into the piece]. I thought, *Oh, God, that's not what he wanted*. But after we did the take, he jumped up and said, 'That was amazing!' He loved it. So it stayed in the recording, and I got a credit as 'consultant.' I think they did that so they wouldn't have to pay me as a musician on the session. Not that they didn't have the money, but it would have involved musician union paperwork and stuff like that."[53]

The second tune Weather Report recorded that fall was Wayne's piece "The Moors." The most distinctive part of the track is Ralph Towner's introduction, which he played on twelve-string guitar. When Towner came to New York in 1968, he was primarily known as a piano player, but by the early seventies he had created a singular guitar style based on his classical training, especially on the twelve-string. Towner recalled how "The Moors" came about:

Wayne called me to come try this piece of his in Weather Report. And strangely enough, my twelve-string guitar had gotten stolen about a week before, so I rented one from the Music Inn down in the Village for $10. I didn't even bother to change the strings; I just took it to the recording session.

I got to the studio, and I had a whole score sitting in front of me. In fact, an interesting thing: When I showed up, I tuned the twelve-string down a whole step so it was like a B-flat instrument. So if I played an E major chord on the guitar, it actually would be a D major chord. The score was very complicated—just notes that Wayne had written out. I said, "Oh God, I'll have to transpose this," and he said, "Well, I can write it out for you." So he copied it down and transposed the entire tune.

So we started to try to figure out how to play it, and Joe said, "You can't play just free, we have to have some rhythm," and stuff like that. Joe was sort of taking charge. Everybody was trying things. I don't know how many hours we were in the studio, just trying different things. It was all notes, very dense, so that was one of the reasons we were trying to make it work as a Weather Report tune. It wasn't coming together very easily, and Joe kept suggesting things.

At first Wayne wanted to do it sort of rubato, just tossing things around. And I think I was just improvising on what was suggested on the page, really. I wasn't reading it literally after a while, because we were trying so many different things. But the flavor of the tune was there and I just did a long series of improvisations on the idea of it, sort of unwittingly, because suddenly I looked up and people had left the room—it was just me all alone. So I stopped after a bit and went to the recording booth where the console was, and everybody was there and they were just blown away by this. So they decided to cobble it together; Joe did some editing. Then we went back in and did the second part.[54]

Unbeknownst to Towner, Joe took a page out of the Miles Davis playbook and recorded Towner while he was rehearsing. "When he came into the studio, he was nervous," Zawinul recalled. "So I said to the engineer when he tuned up, 'Don't put the red light on, I better get him early.' He played for about twenty minutes, practiced, and said, 'I'm ready,' and I said, 'That's very nice, but Ralph, you are ready now to pack up your guitar because it's done!' And that was the introduction to 'The Moors.'"[55]

"I wasn't aware that I was being recording," Towner confirmed. "It didn't dawn on me that Joe said to leave the tape recorder on, which probably led to it being so relaxed. Because I was just off in a world there, and for some reason that ten-dollar rental guitar sounded just great. I was as excited to hear back my own playing as everybody else was. I was in a zone. But it was all triggered by the tune, the atmosphere, and being around these great musicians. It really was an example of the creativity of that group. They were willing to try things. There weren't any preconceived notions about what they wanted to do, so it was fantastic."[56]

•

Weather Report's first order of business in 1972 was to go to Japan. Anticipation for their visit was high, as they swept the end-of-year awards in *Swing Journal* magazine, Japan's equivalent of *Down Beat* but with the heft and production values of America's best glossies. Weather Report's first LP garnered the magazine's Grand Prix award, given for winning both its readers' and critics' polls. It was also named Japan's best selling jazz album of the year, despite having been released mid-year. The magazine also lauded Weather Report as its band of the year.[57] As far as jazz in Japan was concerned, there was no hotter ticket to be had than for one of Weather Report's concerts.

The tour came nearly a decade to the day after Art Blakey and the Jazz Messengers (with Wayne in tow) famously took the country by storm, opening the floodgates to numerous American jazz and pop acts in what was known as the "*rainichi* (literally 'come to Japan') rush."[58] As with Blakey before them, Weather Report was treated like royalty. In a nod to the band's name, each of the musicians was given a *kasa*, an umbrella made of bamboo and oilpaper. (This custom continued in future visits, though the later umbrellas weren't made with traditional materials.)

Joe, Wayne, and Miroslav had previously been to the island nation, so they had an idea of what to expect, but Eric Gravatt had not, and the band's reception stood in stark contrast to what he experienced in the States. When they landed in Tokyo, for instance, hundreds of fans were waiting to greet them. "It was tremendous," Gravatt said shortly after the tour. "I'd never seen anything like it. People had told me it would happen, but I didn't believe it. The Japanese had five limousines waiting for us at the airport, one for each man. There was a reception committee, flowers. They gave us a dinner."[59]

Even Joe was impressed. "We didn't know what kind of a response we would get," he recalled, "but I couldn't believe what happened. We thought, 'What are we gonna do with these Japanese people, man?' They're so beautiful, such wonderful listeners, but laid back. That was their culture. So we said, 'Let's hit 'em hard, right from the first note,' and we hit 'em hard!"[60] Indeed, they did. If the criticism of Weather Report's first album was that it was too cerebral, almost clinical, the Japanese concerts crackled with energy. The band was riveting on stage, playing long, suite-like medleys that showed off its incredible range with a take-no-prisoners attitude. Joe would tell subsequent band members that their gig in Sapporo was the best one the band ever played.

The last of Weather Report's eight performances was recorded and released in Japan a few months later as the double LP *Live in Tokyo*.[61] The opening medley is a good representation of the entire concert. Consuming an entire side of vinyl, the performance begins with the controlled aggression of an imaginative, polyrhythmic drum solo by Gravatt. Two minutes later, the rest of the musicians take the stage to applause, joining Gravatt in a free jam that segues into Joe's tune "Vertical Invader"—a swinging jaunt in which he overdrives his Rhodes, giving it a harsh edge. That sound is all over *Live in Tokyo*. At the time, he was using a "suitcase model," which included its own amplifier and speakers. In what was the start of a never-ending quest to get as loud as possible, Joe turned the piano's volume knob all the way up and kicked in his Vox wah-wah foot pedal, overloading the

Rhodes's circuitry to the point that it became distorted. In essence, Joe turned a flaw into a feature.

At about the 7:50 mark, Joe swivels over to the acoustic piano, where he coaxes a variety of unorthodox sounds from the instrument. At various times he placed objects across the strings to create folk-like timbres. Other times he plucked or struck the strings with mallets, or dragged metal bars across them. He used rubber wedges to hold down keys, or blocked the hammers from the strings with felt or pieces of paper. Many of these techniques are heard on the album.

Eventually, the piano interlude turns into a frenzied jam until the band suddenly breaks into "Seventh Arrow," followed by Miroslav strolling on arco, propelled along by Gravatt. Finally, the medley concludes with Joe's composition "Doctor Honoris Causa." Pared down to svelte quintet form, the elegance of the studio track on *Zawinul* is replaced by an aggressive, highly improvisational take. In sum, this medley has just about everything Weather Report could offer (although some wished for more from Wayne, who skates around the music, never busting out a solo in the conventional sense).

Elsewhere, "Orange Lady" is rendered as an eighteen-minute elegy, with Dom Um Romão soloing on berimbau midway through the tune. Romão is generally credited as the first person to play that instrument in the United States (when he was a part of Brasil '66) and his solos soon became a highlight of Weather Report shows, adding a touch of theater that Joe appreciated. Many reviews of the band's live performances mention it, even if the reporters didn't always know what Romão was playing.[62]

At other times, we hear Romão use his cheeks as drums, slapping them with his hands while changing the shape of his mouth to produce a variety of popping sounds and vocalizations. An excellent example of this can be heard during the introduction of "Surucucú," the title of which Wayne took from the Spanish word for a venomous snake found in South America. "It winds around, zig zags, and it's fast," he said of the snake, which must have been how he heard the lines of this particular tune.[63] "Surucucú" is largely a feature for Wayne, but it is also notable for the way in which Miroslav carries the bottom while simultaneously injecting his own commentary.

With his avant-garde background, Gravatt was in his element, reveling in the inventiveness around him. "We were in uncharted territory and I was loving every minute of it," he said.[64] Despite his quiet, introspective demeanor offstage, he was a dynamo behind his small Gretsch drum kit—"a spirited percussionist who could swing Guy Lombardo if he were given the task," remarked one reporter.[65] Perhaps the most common word used to describe Gravatt's playing was "explosive." Not that he was loud all the time, but his energy and drive filled the entire stage. He placed his ride cymbal high on its stand, perpendicular to the floor,

未来のジャズを予言する
ウェザー・リポート
《天気予報》東京公演

1月4日(火)pm6:30 渋谷公会堂

主催●ニッポン放送／ユニバーサル
後援●CBSソニーレコード／平凡パンチ／スイングジャーナル
協賛●パンアメリカン航空

¥2,000

2 階 た 列 55 番

WEATHER REPORT

UNIVERSAL ORIENT PROMOTIONS PRESENTS

Ticket stub for one of Weather Report's 1972 Japanese concerts. Curt Bianchi collection.

making it seem like he was reaching for the sky when he struck it.

"Overall, it was an exhilarating experience," Gravatt said of Japan. "We had gone past the sawdust on the floor, the backdoor being opened, and the doorman kicking people out. It was a different atmosphere altogether. And it was amazing to me, because the people in Japan had researched me. They knew what high school I went to and all kinds of stuff. I had no idea that they would go that far. In fact, I still have the chanchanko [a traditional vest] that some fans at the Shibuya Kōkaidō gave me. The guy said, 'We don't have much to give you, but we want you to accept this chanchanko.' It's a gift that I still have."[66]

Gravatt elaborated on his early experiences with the band:

> I relished every minute I could spend on the same bandstand with Wayne Shorter. When we got into town, Wayne would turn on the TV and turn down the sound, pull out his soprano, and start writing music. And it would be perfectly playable—just magnificent music. He was shy; he kept me at arm's length—not distasteful; he was into his own things.
>
> Dom Um was my anchor in the band because he was older. We always got along very well. He had played with Sergio Mendes and Brasil '66, so he was slumming by the time he came to play with Weather Report. [And Miroslav], it was nice playing with somebody who could manipulate his instrument so well. From the first time that we played together it was notable; I knew that he was something special. In fact, I was kind of amazed that Miroslav's comments [at the first rehearsal] were, "Well, now we can play fast," because I had thought Alphonse was playing fast enough. Evidently I was doing a little better at playing fast.[67]

Later in the year, Gravatt spoke with the *Washington Post*'s Hollie West about how the band created its cohesiveness. "We're all trying to hear a composition in totality and make it seem as if we were one person playing a piano or saxophone," he explained. "So many groups fall back on clichés. They don't invent. We're trying to make it impossible to play the same way twice. . . . The different pieces have their own character. All of us compose and we try to take into account how each person wants his music played. We may talk about how Wayne or Joe would play the piece if they were the only soloist, and we try to capture their character and imagination."[68]

Left unsaid was that the drummer's relationship with Joe was already fraught with drama. They both possessed strong personalities that led to a test of wills almost from the start. For example, when the band arrived in Japan, Gravatt elected to forego the hotel, as well as the limousine ride from the airport, in favor of accepting an offer to stay at the home of Terumasa Hino, a trumpeter with whom he had recorded in the States several months earlier. Gravatt's natural inclination to go his own way off the bandstand didn't sit well with Zawinul, who perceived it as aloofness. According to Gravatt, Joe began playing mind games with him. "It got to be that whenever me and Zawinul were together it was always a head trip. All the time a head trip unless I could see it coming and go off and be on my own."[69] As far as Gravatt was concerned, they didn't have to be friends; so long as he met his professional obligations, that should be enough.

•

Going back to the previous fall, Joe had talked about including some live material on Weather Report's second album. At the time he said it would be excerpts from their European performances, some of which had been professionally recorded for radio or television broadcast.[70] But the Tokyo date provided a wealth of new material to choose from and, more importantly, reflected the current makeup of the band. So the decision was made to fill the second side of *I Sing* with edited excerpts from Tokyo, while side one would be new studio material. With two studio tracks already in the can, they needed a few more to fill out the LP, so they headed back to the studio shortly after returning to the United States.

The first piece they tackled was "Crystal," an improvisation among the three leaders that is reminiscent of the duets that Joe and Wayne later recorded. "I think we had never played it before," Miroslav recalled. "I had a melody and some chords and some structure—basically, the format of the tune, which we played over and over and did whatever we could with it. It was very much improvised. In fact, I think Wayne played some of the most beautiful things on this. It was a wonderful piece of music, I thought. And it was a very unusual direction, too, because the bass was playing the melody and then we all just played together. Again, it's coming from this point that the bass was playing something, and Joe and Wayne responded to it."[71]

They also recorded another of Joe's compositions, "Second Sunday in August," which captures the joyful spirit of the harvest festivals in Oberkirchbach. "Second Sunday" is rarely included in discussions of Joe's formative songs, but of all the pieces on *I Sing the Body Electric*, this one most points toward Weather Report's future. After a brief introduction, it stays in one tonal center, undergirded by an even beat and a simple repeating piano riff that harkens back to Joe's *volksmusik* roots—fitting given its inspiration—while powerful percussive elements maintain a delightful dance-like quality. It's also the first Weather Report track in which layered keyboards figure prominently. In addition to acoustic piano, Joe overdubs organ and adds some synthesizer accents, his facility with the 2600 starting to take root. Wayne soars over the thicket of sound, playing the beautiful clarion-like themes with long, bluesy lines on soprano.

One other studio track was not included on the LP, but has since seen the light of day. "Directions" is yet another tune that Zawinul wrote in Vienna when he took his family there a few years earlier, and it became a staple of Weather Report's performances. The studio take wouldn't have fit on side one of *I Sing* without dropping something else, so the decision was made to go with the live version from Tokyo, and it's a smoker.[72] Played at a breakneck tempo, "Directions" is a great example of Weather Report's brand of swing at the time. On top of Miroslav and Gravatt's ferocious drive, Wayne unfurls one inventive line after another, utterly devoid of clichés and licks, while Joe eschews accompaniment in favor of delivering his own lines in response—a characteristic of Weather Report's "we always solo and we never solo" ensemble sound. As one fan remarked, this was savage Weather Report.

•

Columbia assigned an executive producer to *I Sing the Body Electric*, a music industry veteran by the name of Bob Devere. He began his career in record distribution, eventually establishing his own distributorship in upstate New York. In 1968, Devere joined Columbia's Artists & Repertoire staff as a manager of independent projects.[73] In this role, he purchased the masters of regional hits that he thought could go national, which Columbia then put out on a subsidiary label, Date Records. The band was impressed enough with Devere to hire him as their new manager. Although he had no previous experience as such, he loved the music business and took to the task enthusiastically.

Largely thanks to Devere's efforts, Weather Report booked well over a hundred dates in 1972. At least in the States, most of these gigs were in small clubs, a circumstance the band hoped to avoid. During the press conferences the previous year, they talked about how clubs were "not the best for listening to music" and also a grind, mentally and physically.[74] Regardless of their desires, Weather Report didn't have a big enough following to book larger venues. So it was that Weather Report's first New York appearance of its own (as opposed to opening someone else's show) took place at the Gaslight Au Go Go in Greenwich Village at the end of March. The Gaslight was primarily known for folk and rock, but since taking over the old Café Au Go Go location the previous April, it had hosted Miles Davis several times, as well as the first appearances of an upstart band, John McLaughlin's Mahavishnu Orchestra, which was held over twice on its way to becoming known to its fans as "the greatest band that ever was." (Joe Zawinul would certainly argue that point.)[75]

After the sold-out concert halls in Japan, the first night at the Gaslight was a letdown as the engagement wasn't well publicized and the house was nearly empty. (The Gaslight regularly advertised in the *Village Voice*, but the first ad mentioning Weather Report didn't appear until the first day of their four-night run.[76]) Nevertheless, the audience grew each night thanks to word of mouth, and the stand proved so successful that Weather Report was brought back three weeks later. This time the press also showed up, and the band got positive reviews from the *New York Times*, *Variety*, and *Record World*. In the latter, Martin Snider wrote that "it's rare when you can sit and listen to a group of superb musicians bringing you into a totally new world of music. There was a time when I thought the music of Miles Davis was the limit, but Weather Report has introduced me to one of the highest forms of music ever made."[77]

Immediately after the Gaslight gigs, the band flew to Mexico to begin a three-week tour of Central and South America. Once again, Weather Report was the beneficiary of Joe's relationship with Friedrich Gulda, who headlined the tour. They played to mostly sellout houses, enjoying the leisurely pace that the star attraction preferred. He and Gulda played a duet each night, but outside of the concerts, Gulda kept to himself, even flying first class while Weather Report flew economy.[78]

Weather Report and a classical pianist must have made for an odd pairing. "The reception of this group was not too good, because the audience here is not much on the avant-garde side of things," a reporter in Argentina wrote.[79] Nevertheless, Wayne, especially, was taken by South America, even if the local music lovers were less enthused by him. While they were in Rio de Janeiro, the band made a point to hear the Brazilian singer Milton Nascimento, who at the time was not well known outside of his own country. As the story goes, Weather Report cut short its own set so they could hop in a waiting cab to get to Nascimento's show as quickly as possible. Wayne was so enthralled by Nascimento's music that it made him "feel reincarnated."[80] Two years later, the two collaborated on Wayne's only album as a leader during his Weather Report years, *Native Dancer*.

After returning from South America, the band performed a series of club dates, usually weeklong residencies. In July, they played Carnegie Hall as part of the Newport Jazz Festival, which moved to New York after the previous year's debacle made it unwelcome in Rhode Island. Weather Report then went to London, holding forth at Ronnie Scott's for a fortnight before embarking on a tour of Europe.

Meanwhile, *I Sing the Body Electric* was released to generally excellent reviews. "Approach this music as the sixth musician," Michael Cuscuna urged. "The empathy among these five men is awesome and thrilling."[81] In *Rolling Stone*, Bob Palmer called it "a beautiful, near-perfect LP" by "one of the most exciting groups in contemporary music."[82] Jack Chambers of *Coda* gushed about "the mind-blowing originality of their group conception," adding, "You are not likely to hear a better set of recorded music for a long time. Possibly not until their third LP is released."[83]

•

In September, Weather Report was booked into a small club in Cleveland that had opened the previous October. The Smiling Dog Saloon was a funky place on a seedy stretch of road near Interstate 71, housed in an old bowling alley in which the lanes had been ripped out and replaced by a stage and tables and chairs. It was noisy, sweaty, and smoky—just the kind of scene the band hoped to get away from.

The Dog was owned by Roger Bohn, a rough-looking character who wore biker leathers and a bowler hat, with his hair pulled back in a long ponytail. But his physical appearance betrayed his good intentions, especially when it came to helping local musicians. Late in the summer of 1972, he began booking nationally known jazz acts, hoping to establish the club as a way station between New York and Chicago. And for a few years, despite operating on the margin of profitability, he succeeded. By the time the club closed in 1975, virtually every big-name jazz artist had passed through its doors. Weather Report was the first.

Bohn wanted to make a good impression with this show, so he called on two young men that he knew could handle the live sound: Alan Howarth and Brian Risner. Howarth led a Pink Floyd–inspired experimental group called Braino. Risner was their soundman, an appellation that fails to convey the scope of his contributions. They had a sophisticated setup, running quadraphonic sound and echo effects. In addition, Risner created tape cues and clever audio hacks that the band would incorporate into their live sets. His technical abilities were so integral to Braino's music that they considered him a full-fledged member of the band. Years later, local musicians remembered him as "our George Martin" and even gave him co-composer credit on some of their tunes.[84]

Braino sometimes served as the house band at the Smiling Dog, and Risner did live sound for other gigs there as well. With their gear already in place, Risner and Howarth gave Weather Report the full Braino treatment with the quad sound and all. It was well beyond the normal sound reinforcement that Weather Report typically enjoyed, and they were impressed. At the time, they had no roadies, and

Bohn thought they could use some help. "You know, we've got these two guys, Alan and Brian," he told Bob Devere. "These guys really know what they're doing. You need somebody like this out on the road with you."[85] With the band's approval, Devere approached the two young men to see if they would be interested. Howarth had a full-time job as a music store repair technician, but Risner was available; plus, he was "totally knocked out by the group."[86] So at the age of nineteen, Risner decided to join the circus, as it were. He stayed nearly to the end, eventually earning the informal title of chief meteorologist. Only Joe and Wayne exceeded his longevity with the group.

At first, Risner performed the usual roadie duties, setting up the band's gear before gigs and packing it up afterward. Pretty soon he was also handling travel logistics, getting the equipment on and off airplanes and arranging ground transportation. "Basically, I did everything," Risner recalled. "They would book the hotels, but as far as getting the band around and getting them set up, and doing their sound, and keeping all the electronics going, I was it. We traveled in one car or one van. Or sometimes I'd get two cars, or a panel van to fit the gear in, and they'd get a rental car. That's how we traveled. It was the classic band in a car."[87]

On the road, Risner roomed with Dom Um Romão, "probably so he could save some money and charge it back to the band," Brian said, chuckling at the memory. "I learned a lot from that guy; he was a very special cat. And I had to set his stuff up, too. I mean, it was one thing to take care of the electronics, but he had me setting up his gear, too. I set up everybody. He had these two funky-ass fiber drum-type suitcases held together by bungee cords, with all these exotic instruments inside that I wasn't up on. I learned them all, and how to set up the percussion table, though every day would be different, so I never quite had it perfect. But he was really good to me. He was a life mentor in a way, into yoga and eating right—chicken and fish, and that's it. No hard alcohol. He might have a little bit of wine, but hardly ever. Yeah, he was a heavy cat."[88]

It wasn't long before Risner proved his worth far beyond the typical roadie tasks. For instance, Joe still wanted to get as loud as possible, so Risner built a custom speaker setup for his Rhodes to replace the ones that resided in the factory cabinet, which also served as the keyboard's stand. The new setup was loud all right—so loud that it had the unintended consequence of producing feedback on the piano's tines, causing them to howl. But better ideas soon followed, and it wasn't long before Joe had one of the best Rhodes sounds in the business. Joe now had a technical accomplice willing and capable of pushing the envelope. In many ways, they were partners; Zawinul supplied the musical vision, and Risner provided the technical expertise to help him bring it to fruition.

•

After a short tour opening for Santana, followed by some rock-venue gigs in

California, Weather Report's last shows of 1972 took place before packed houses at the Bitter End, a small club in Greenwich Village that mainly booked folk singers and comedy acts. By then, Risner had been to Joe's apartment and seen the gear he had there, including the ARP 2600. At this point, Zawinul considered it too delicate to withstand the rigors of the road. Instead, his stage setup consisted of the Rhodes (with the Oberheim ring modulator, Vox wah-wah pedal, and Echoplex), a small Farfisa organ, and an acoustic piano when it was available. In lieu of using the 2600 live, Joe made pre-recorded tapes with it, which he cued on stage. But Risner thought the Bitter End gigs would be a good opportunity to try it out on stage. They were in town, so they wouldn't need a road case for it. "Let's bring it down to the club," he suggested.

Joe worried that the 2600 was too fragile even for that, but Risner soon won him over. The afternoon of the first gig, Risner came by in a taxi, and Zawinul brought the synthesizer down from his apartment, wrapped in a blanket. "Take care of this, man," Joe said as he handed it over.[89]

Dan Nooger of the *Village Voice* was on hand and took note of the auspicious occasion. "'Crystal,' which featured Josef Zawinul on synthesizer, was built around repeated cycles of ascending arpeggios, recalling Terry Riley's experiments in the area of 'trance music.' The high, keening sounds, offset by Romão's percussive effects, established a pervasively mysterioso atmosphere for a graceful, leaping tenor solo by Wayne Shorter that developed into a free-blowing conversation among the players."[90] Nooger was likely describing the 2600's sample-and-hold feature, which could create repeating sequences of ascending or descending notes, or rapidly triggered random tones, depending on how it was configured.

Sample-and-hold sounds were often used in the early days of synthesizers because they were easy to create and didn't require playing the keyboard. At first it sounded like a futuristic space age effect, but it quickly became clichéd. "Herbie Hancock was really big on it," Roger Powell remembered. "He'd put the machine on automatic sample-and-hold and he didn't have to play the keyboard at that point. I remember him getting up and walking around the keyboard and mystically gesticulating at it, like he was drawing the sound out of it. And I was like, oh man, you've come a long way, dude, from playing all that really cool stuff with Miles to now being this 'magician' of the synthesizer!"[91]

One of the earliest extant recordings of Joe using the 2600 live includes an improvisation largely built around the sample-and-hold feature. Joe incorporates it into a performance lasting several minutes, spurring the band into a free jam. Listening to it, one pictures Zawinul playing the keyboard with one hand while hunched over the 2600's control panel, inserting and removing patch chords and nudging sliders to create a dynamic performance that varies between his own lines and those produced by the sample-and-hold circuitry. "Sometimes I had a jack chord over my neck in order to patch something, and it must have looked pretty comical because I had to do so much," Joe later remarked.[92]

Regardless of how silly Zawinul thought he appeared, things took a decisive turn at the Bitter End. "Riz, we *have* to use this," he told Brian after the gig, pointing to the 2600.[93] Risner made a mental note to order a custom flight case after the holidays. His life was about to get more complicated.

9 Sweetnighter

I just know nobody played that beat before I did.

— Joe Zawinul

AFTER THE BITTER END GIGS, the band took its first extended break since finishing *I Sing the Body Electric* the previous spring. Wayne spent the time planning his move to Los Angeles. He and Ana Maria were enticed there by Herbie Hancock and his wife, Gigi, who left New York at the end of 1972. They extolled Southern California's mild climate as well as its lifestyle. "In New York, no matter how much money you have, you're just surviving," Herbie told Wayne. "Come out to California and start living."[1] It didn't require much arm-twisting. Beyond the obvious benefits, the New York City jazz scene that Wayne grew up with had largely drifted away. He considered himself lucky to have seen "the change of hands" from the original beboppers to the avant-garde modernists, but now the old clubs were gone, along with the appeal of hanging out in them. So the Shorters made the move, temporarily living with the Hancocks until they found a house of their own to rent.

Joe used the break to appraise the band. He was pleased to see *Down Beat*'s end-of-year issue, which brought the news that its readers voted Weather Report their favorite jazz group—a title they wouldn't relinquish for thirteen years.[2] But Joe also found some things he didn't like. He was well aware of what was written about the band, including the not-infrequent criticism that it played for itself more than its audience. For instance, the *New York Times*'s Don Heckman, who saw the band at the Gaslight Au Go Go, wrote that while the music was "magnificently executed," he "couldn't help but feel that it was more enjoyable to the musicians than to the listeners."[3] This didn't sit well with Joe. "For me, happiness has something to do with getting across to people," he said.[4]

Joe was also frustrated by the creative tightrope the band walked, dependent on the illusive nature of collective inspiration. When it was right, it was thrilling. But trying to maintain that edge night after night could be exhausting. A pair of *Down Beat* concert reviews neatly encapsulated the hit-and-miss nature of their music. Bob Protzman caught one of those magical nights, calling it "one of the greatest concerts I've ever heard."[5] A few months earlier, Jim Szantor found them groping in the dark. "A postmortem discussion with Zawinul indicated that the magic, brought about by inspired interplay and so plentiful and joyous the previous [opening] night, was most elusive this night. And with a group like Weather Report, if the rabbit doesn't appear, all you have left is an interesting-sounding hat."[6]

Then there was the question of finances. Near the end of 1972, Joe was asked how things had gone so far. "It was rough," he admitted, "We starved half to death."[7] To compound matters, their deal with Columbia was far from secure. Columbia's measuring stick for success was not five-star reviews, but record sales, specifically those of Miles Davis. By the end of 1972, *Bitches Brew* had surpassed 400,000 units sold, on its way to gold. It was the reason Columbia was willing to sign unheard both Weather Report and John McLaughlin—not to mention modern jazz luminaries Ornette Coleman, Charles Mingus, Bill Evans, and Keith Jarrett, all of whom joined the label at around the same time as Weather Report.

About a year after its release, CBS publicly pegged sales of Weather Report's first LP at 40,000 units, while also stating that the Mahavishnu Orchestra's debut album, *The Inner Mounting Flame*, had surpassed 50,000 copies in less than two months.[8] Miles's albums could blow past that amount in one week, Columbia claimed (although Davis would never make another gold record after *Bitches Brew*).[9] To put those numbers in perspective, Joel Dorn, Joe's old Atlantic producer, put the average sale of a jazz LP in 1972 at 35,000 (though straight-ahead jazz efforts were lucky to crack five figures).[10]

In other words, sales for *Weather Report* were better than the average jazz album, but not by much, and lagged behind both Miles and Mahavishnu. This would have been welcome news at an independent label, but a major label like Columbia—*the* major label at this point—hoped for better, and it's doubtful that it was breaking even on the band. One contemporaneous analysis indicated that record companies made about seventy cents per unit sold.[11] Given that, Columbia would have generated about $28,000 in revenue on 40,000 units—probably not enough to offset its contractual advances and production costs.

When Clive Davis talked about artists "using their skills, using their ideas to communicate to new audiences," he expected it to translate into increased sales, specifically to young people. Asked if he would drop an underperforming jazz artist, he said no, "unless [they] were not willing to grow on their own." He used the case of rock musician Edgar Winter to illustrate his point. Winter's first album sold just 20,000 copies, but his latest had sold 60,000 in its first four weeks. "He learned," Davis said.[12] Columbia's ultimate response for artists who didn't learn was to give them their release, and in the coming year it unceremoniously dropped Coleman, Mingus, Evans, and Jarrett—reportedly all on a single day.[13] The same fate awaited Weather Report if things continued on the present path.

Joe took all of this into account and resolved to change the band's direction. He later explained that while *I Sing the Body Electric* was "a good record, we had to make a living. I have a big family and Wayne has a big family. Somehow we had to survive. I had come out of Cannonball's band, and naturally, I wanted to play a little funkier than we were playing at the time."[14] In January, the band spent a week rehearsing new material at Tom Di Pietro's studio in New York City—"ten hours a day for five days straight," according to Eric Gravatt.[15] Everyone brought in some music, including Gravatt, who was encouraged to do so by Joe and Wayne.

But in the two weeks between the rehearsals and the recording date, Joe decided that he wasn't happy with what was going down. He specifically zeroed in on the playing of Vitous and Gravatt. As Zawinul put it, "Miroslav, being a great bass player in one way, was not the bass player for other things we wanted to do."[16] He also complained about Gravatt's drum sound. "I needed a low bass drum. Eric had one of those long small little things that went 'boop.'"[17] When Gravatt suggested that he "could make my little bass drum sound just as big as anything, [that] it was just a matter of tuning it," Joe remained unconvinced.[18]

So to make the music come off, an entirely separate rhythm section was brought to the studio, largely replacing Miroslav and Gravatt. The rest of the band didn't know they would be shadowed, and it doesn't take much imagination to realize how it went over with them. "It was an awkward situation," Joe later acknowledged. "Here we had a band and we had to hire outside musicians to play instruments, which were already supposed to be played by the members of the band—it started getting weird."[19] That the music wasn't well fleshed-out beforehand only added to the sense of unease. An air of tension pervaded the studio as the band went through reel after reel of tape, trying to create the feel that Joe heard in his head. More than once, he and Wayne holed up in the engineer's booth listening to playbacks, frustrated that the music wasn't coming together.

Despite it all, they produced another album that was critically well received. Perhaps more important, record sales mushroomed, saving Weather Report's contract with Columbia and setting the stage for the band's success that followed. But the transition also came with casualties. The studio musicians were a temporary fix. On the road, Miroslav and Gravatt struggled to cope with their roles in the band's new music. The chemistry the group enjoyed the previous year was permanently damaged, and Gravatt wouldn't last the summer. As a partner in the band's contracts and businesses, Miroslav's situation was more complicated, but he, too, would be forced out by the end of the year.

•

After the holidays, Weather Report resumed performing with a late January return to the Smiling Dog, followed by three nights at the Twelfth Gate in Atlanta, which at the time was one of the city's few truly integrated venues for jazz and blues. Situated in an old house, the stage occupied a corner of the dining room. With the audience crammed inside and spilling out onto the front porch, it was all Brian Risner could do to snake his way through the bodies to get the band's equipment on and off the stage.[20] After the Atlanta gig, the band wended its way up the East Coast, arriving a few days later in Connecticut, where they sequestered themselves to record *Sweetnighter*. Wayne copped the title from a children's anti-bed-wetting medication.[21]

Sweetnighter is where Bob Devere proved his mettle as Weather Report's manager. Aside from keeping the band's calendar booked, he now faced two additional challenges. The first was to produce Weather Report's new record on a shoestring budget. Their standing with Columbia had fallen so precipitously that Devere had to smooth-talk his way into getting *any* kind of budget from the label. To save money, he prevailed on a friend, songwriter/producer Paul Leka. He and his partner Billy Rose owned Connecticut Recording Studio.

Located in the city of Bridgeport, some sixty miles northeast of New York City, the studio was a small, unassuming place on the second floor of an old building on Main Street. Leka and Rose let Weather Report record there at no upfront cost to the band, with the understanding that they would be compensated later.[22] The studio had the added benefit of being close enough to New York to be convenient, but far enough to escape the scrutiny of CBS executives. The band didn't want anyone forming opinions before they were finished.

Devere's second challenge was finding musicians who could provide the funkiness that Joe wanted. His first call went to Herschel Dwellingham, a drummer who originally hailed from Bogalusa, Louisiana, a small town north of New Orleans. After attending the Berklee School of Music in Boston, Dwellingham quickly became a fixture in the city's soul scene, leading the house band at the Sugar Shack, a club that hosted touring R&B and funk acts. But Dwellingham's true passion was producing his own records. Devere handled some of those records during his distributorship days and thought the drummer on those tracks could work.

Devere and Dwellingham also had some personal history at Columbia. At one point Herschel paid a visit to Black Rock, shopping a single he had produced. He met with Devere, who wanted to buy the rights to the song so that he could re-record it with R&B singer O. C. Smith. But Dwellingham was intent on releasing his own version and wound up selling it to RCA instead. When Devere called

Herschel shortly before the *Sweetnighter* sessions, he didn't remember previously meeting with him. Furthermore, he asked for "Herschel Dwellingham Jr.," not realizing that the drummer and producer were the same. Confused, Dwellingham asked what this was about.

"I'm Bob Devere. I manage Weather Report."

"Bob Devere? First thing, Herschel Dwellingham Jr. doesn't play drums; he's only four years old. You want to talk to me. But Bob, you don't remember who I am? I'm the guy whose tracks you wanted to buy for O. C. Smith."

"No you're not! You're the same guy? I thought you just produced."

"Yeah, I'm an arranger/producer. On most of the stuff I produce I play drums or keyboards. And sometimes I do both."[23]

That confusion cleared up, Devere got to the point of his call. "Can you come to Connecticut? I would like for you to play with Weather Report and do an album. I'll pay you scale or whatever you want, your hotel and everything—you won't have to spend a dime. When you get there, I'll see you at the desk. There will be a per diem there, just ask for your mail."[24]

"He told me to come on a Thursday," Herschel recalled, "so I did, and I set up my drums over at the studio. They didn't show up until late the next day. That's when I first met them. Now the ironic thing is, when Bob said 'Weather Report,' I didn't think of Wayne Shorter or Joe Zawinul. I didn't think of any of them guys until I got there and saw who it was. And I was in shock. I said, 'These guys want me to play with them?' They were just happy to see me there."[25]

That Friday, Dwellingham recognized a familiar face at the hotel. It was Andrew White, a multi-instrumentalist from Washington, D.C. "I had played with Andrew before," Dwellingham said. "My orchestra played behind Stevie Wonder when he came to Boston [at the Sugar Shack] and Andrew was the bass player with Stevie."[26] White was a familiar face to Weather Report, too, having played English horn on "Unknown Soldier" a year earlier.

A tall, slender, bespectacled man with a hearty laugh, White once said he started playing the electric bass "by accident." "Stanley Turrentine came to town one week back in 1967 and his bass man was late, so I filled in. I didn't know much about the instrument." A year later, he landed the gig with Stevie Wonder, moving over to the Fifth Dimension in 1970. "I still haven't studied [the bass] outside what I've taught myself, and I don't practice," he said. "I play bass by the law of physics—the shorter the string, the higher the pitch."[27]

Those cavalier comments might lead one to assume that White didn't approach music in a serious way, but the opposite is true. He was a music scholar, graduating cum laude from Howard University in 1964 with a major in music theory and a minor in the oboe. He continued his academic career at the Paris Conservatory of Music, Dartmouth College, and the State University of New York, and

Herschel Dwellingham circa 1973. Photo courtesy Herschel Dwellingham.

became the principal oboist for the American Ballet Theatre Orchestra in 1968. White made his first mark on the jazz scene while at Howard, playing saxophone in the JFK Quintet, which is when he met Joe and Wayne. The Fifth Dimension gig allowed him to fund his personal projects, such as painstakingly transcribing hundreds of John Coltrane saxophone solos. He established Andrew's Music in 1971—a one-man shop that he used to produce and sell his own records and publications until his death in 2020. He billed himself as "the most voluminously self-published artist in the history of the music business (so I've been told)."

Just after the New Year, White got a call from Wayne, asking if he could do another session with Weather Report—and to bring his bass this time. White knew the band as "an expansive jazz thing," so he was perplexed about the bass part. When Bob Devere picked him up from the airport, White told him, "I don't know what y'all want 'cause you got Miroslav Vitous. That mother plays his ass off on the bass, you know. I ain't doing that. You got a virtuoso bass player in there doing all that stuff."

"Well, we just want to try you out and do something," Devere replied. "We'll just try it out." If it didn't work out, Devere assured him, there would be no hassles or problems.[28]

Later, White found out that his participation was Joe's idea. "After I got up there, we had a meal one night and I was sitting next to Joe," White said. "I asked him, 'Why'd you call me for this?' And he told me that he saw me on television with the Fifth Dimension and said, 'Shit, that sounds like what we need.' So he told Wayne to call me to come up there and be on the date, and I just happened to be off during the time that he called."[29]

Devere recruited a third musician for the session, a versatile drummer named Steve Booker. His earliest gigs were playing Russian folk music on accordion, but his professional career spanned several genres, including the folk duo Jim & Jean and the Paul Winter Consort. In New York, he hung out at the Café Au Go Go, jamming with the likes of Jimi Hendrix. At Woodstock, Booker met the Indian guru Swami Satchidananda, who gave him his spiritual name, Muruga, which he adopted as his stage name.

Unbeknownst to Devere, Muruga also knew Joe. They met in 1970 at a jazz festival in Detroit. "He first saw me play there at Cobo Hall," Muruga remembered. "I was with the jazz bagpipe player Rufus Harley and he was with Cannonball. I did a solo on Moroccan clay drums, which is what I used on *Sweetnighter*. I got a standing ovation and Joe took notice and got my number." They kept in touch and Muruga went to Joe's apartment a few months before the *Sweetnighter* sessions. "He played me this album that was very spaced out—abstract, timeless, classical jazz–orientated, dreamy, meditative jazz music. They told him, 'If you keep going in that direction, you don't get no more contract. We like you because you wrote "Mercy, Mercy" with Cannonball.'"[30] Dwellingham and White heard much the same story.

Muruga was at the Record Plant recording with Al Kooper when Devere happened to hear him. As Muruga remembered it, "He said, 'Hey man, do you play funk?' Yeah. 'You play jazz?' Yeah. 'Cool, give me your number. I've got Weather Report and we're going to do some stuff, but we need funk *and* jazz.' When he said 'Weather Report,' I didn't put two and two together that it was Joe Zawinul."[31]

Muruga recounts how Devere called him on the eve of the session:

I was in Detroit, literally on an acid trip—this is the '60s going into the '70s, remember—and I went to this hippie house and my friends said they were going to New York, so I hopped in the car and went with them. When we arrived, I said, "Let's go to Perry's house." Perry Robinson was a *Down Beat* poll winner I used to play with in Darius Brubeck's group. He had a cot and I could sleep there. And just as I walked into Perry's, he said, "Hey bro! Weather Report's manager just called you!" I said, "Cool!" I called him back and he said, "Yup, we're going to record. Can I pick you up in a couple of hours?" I said, "Absolutely." But oh crap, man, I didn't even have my drums. I didn't have *any* drums. I'm off an acid trip. I just drove all night. I read a yoga book and got enlightened by the yoga on the way to New York, and it talked about inner light, and now I walk in and this guy says we're recording.

So months earlier I gave Perry an Israeli clay doumbek—a beautiful one—and it was sitting in his living room. I said, "Perry, you gotta let me use that clay doumbek." Then I went to the Music Inn on Fourth Street and bought a Moroccan clay drum for twenty or thirty bucks, and I bought some little bells and a microphone gooseneck. And I went to a toyshop and got a Fisher-Price roller toy [known as a Melody Push Chime]. So here I was, a young kid, having the time of my life, playing with the best musicians on the planet, and I didn't even have my instruments![32]

On Saturday morning, everyone assembled in the small recording room—Wayne and Joe, a pair of bass players, a pair of drummers, a pair of percussionists, and some pretty raw feelings. For Eric Gravatt, the presence of the additional musicians came as a shock. "When I got up to Connecticut to do the recording for *Sweetnighter*, there were three extra people there!" he recalled. "I would have expected at least a message on my key equipment [a telephone connected to his answering service], but nobody had told me about that. And to make matters worse, Herschel and I were separated by a bunch of baffles. They wanted two drummers, but they only wanted one drum sound."[33] Then, after a perfunctory run-through of his tune, it was thrown out along with most of the other music that had been rehearsed. Gravatt was not happy. "After all that rehearsing . . . yeah, I was pissed."[34]

At one point, noticing Gravatt's lack of enthusiasm, Joe stood up from behind his piano and asked, "Eric, what's the matter with you? Don't you know we love you?"

"I don't know what you're talking about," Gravatt tersely responded.[35]

Dom Um wasn't happy, either, making it clear that he wasn't sharing his table of percussion instruments with anybody. So Muruga looked around the studio and found a set of cymbals and timpani that he claimed for himself. As for Miroslav, "Well, I was surprised. I mean, Joe said before the session that this guy [Andrew White] was coming. I knew that Joe wanted to go a more funky way, and somehow it just wasn't coming out of me. I think that my spirit denied going this way, because I *could* do it, really. But somehow it wasn't coming out, and there was also a very negative influence from Joe for me; he didn't even want me to do it. I think I was too much of a musical threat for him. Joe knew that if he got rid of me, he would have control of the whole band, because Wayne was not the type of person to be a leader."[36]

The first track on *Sweetnighter* is "Boogie Woogie Waltz," the centerpiece for where Joe wanted to take the music.[37] It's a thirteen-minute groove grounded in Dwellingham's drumming. He raps out every beat on his snare drum, while his bass drum never deviates from emphasizing the *and-one*, giving the tune its forward momentum—*ba-BOOM-two-three, ba-BOOM-two-three*. On top of Dwell-

スーパー・グループ、ウェザー・リポートの快作！

BOOGIE WOOGIE WALTZ

来日記念盤

ブギ・ウギ・ワルツ

ウェザー・リポート
WEATHER REPORT

C/W アディオス ADIOS ￥500

"Boogie Woogie Waltz" 45rpm single. Pictured on the jacket are, left to right, Eric Gravatt, Wayne Shorter, Joe Zawinul, Miroslav Vitous, and Dom Um Romão. Brian Risner collection.

ingham's beat is a layered polyrhythm thanks to Muruga's hand drumming, Herschel's cymbal work, and Romão's shakers.

Joe only had a sketch for the tune, which he said consisted of five sentences. Those sentences give the tune its structure. For instance, during the introduction an ascending figure is repeated several times—independently and jointly—by Joe, Wayne and Miroslav. At just over the one-minute mark, Joe plays a new motif on his electric piano, which is picked up by Andrew White on bass, whose playing is especially integral to *Sweetnighter* in that he provides a Motown-like bottom replete with improvisations.[38] This motif informs the music for several minutes; even when it isn't clearly delineated (or played at all), it's still in the listener's mind as the band improvises around it. After a short interlude that includes a key modulation, the tune returns to the original key and Joe's four-bar main theme reveals itself, ultimately becoming the tune's closing anthem before the introduction's ascending figure is reprised one last time, bringing the song full circle.

As for preparation with the new rhythm section, Dwellingham claimed there wasn't any. "They just started. He gave me the count off and I played what I was going to play. The only thing he told me he wanted was a side stick in 'Boogie Woogie Waltz.' That's all he told me about. There were no rehearsals, no nothing. Just, this is the song, we're going to do it, and we did it. It was so natural and spontaneous—that's what made it so great."[39]

At other times, Muruga remembered, "Joe would say, 'Here's this riff, whaddya got to put with it?' And then we'd find a riff, and we'd record it. Sometimes he would gather us and say, 'Okay, Herschel, hum your drum part. And Muruga, hum yours.' And then he'd get the bass player to hum his part, and while we're singing our parts, we walked out of the engineering room to our instruments and started playing what we were singing.

"'Boogie Woogie Waltz' was very interesting. Joe had these funk lines and these charts that had numbered signals with Wayne Shorter, and each number meant a different lick, so they had those kinds of signals. They didn't even tell me it was in 3/4. See, this was put together so fast and we were smoking joints, you know. So I'm listening through earphones and I hear *boom-boom, boom-boom*. Everything else was pretty vague, so I just followed the bass drum. It was so funky I thought it was a weird way of playing four, so I started playing 4/4 on my Moroccan clay drums against Herschel's *boom-boom*, which put it three against four, which is what Africans do. It happened because I didn't hear where it was!"[40]

The group jammed until the tape ran out, then the engineer mounted another reel, and they jammed some more. "To say we made multiple takes is an under-statement," White recalled.[41] Nor is what we hear on the LP a single take. Brian Risner, who spent much of the sessions in the control booth, remembered there being a lot of editing to create the composition after the fact.

In addition to the rhythms, the funkiness of "Boogie Woogie Waltz" also owes to Joe's playing on electric piano. By this time he had mastered, if not invented, a remarkable range of sounds on the instrument, and while he had been funky be-fore, he topped himself on *Sweetnighter*. In part, this was enabled by the electron-ics that he brought to the studio. His new toy was a Maestro PS-1 phase shifter, another Tom Oberheim design intended to simulate a Leslie rotary speaker. It was a simple device that effectively thickened or warmed the piano's sound. Coupled with his masterful use of the wah-wah pedal, Joe's Rhodes took on an entirely new character.

"I don't think there's any better guitar wah-wah around than what I had going on 'Boogie Woogie Waltz,'" Joe said years later. "It was really fine."[42] So fine that some musicians were convinced that Joe possessed a secret ingredient to get his sound. "I got a call once from a guy in Iowa," Risner recalled, "who had tracked me down all the way from the East, wanting to know what kind of wah-wah Za-winul was playing through. You know, how does he get that sound? When I told him it was just a plain Vox wah-wah, he wouldn't believe me."[43] In other words, the secret ingredient was Joe.

Sweetnighter was also the first time Wayne electronically processed his saxo-phone. "We brought in a Maestro woodwind box," Risner said. "We actually had to drill a hole in Wayne's sax so we could put a Vox pickup on it, and it would drive this box. It was basically like an envelope follower, like a tracking box—the

Wayne performing on soprano in 1973. Note the pickup near the mouthpiece, which was connected to the Maestro Sound System for Woodwinds box. A hole was drilled into Wayne's saxophone in order to mount the pickup. Photo: Michael Wilderman.

harder you blew, the more you brought out that particular effect. And that's how he came up with all those subtones on 'Boogie Woogie Waltz.'"[44]

In addition to this gear, Risner hauled the ARP 2600 up to Connecticut. By this time, Joe had developed a feel for programming it. While the 2600 came with a detailed 120-page owner's manual (which included the admonition, "putting it all together is your job"), Joe preferred the trial-and-error method to methodical study, fueled by his innate curiosity for sound. When a reporter asked him if he approached it mainly as an electronic instrument, Zawinul responded, "I'm not really thinking like that. I don't read books about it because I would get completely confused and it would take me so long. I just find what I want to hear by doing it and coordinating it."[45]

Joe uses the 2600 on "Boogie Woogie Waltz," but it figures more prominently on the album's next tune, Wayne's composition "Manolete." Although the 2600 was monophonic, its three oscillators could be tuned to different frequencies to produce two- or three-note chords of fixed intervals. For instance, as "Manolete" closes out, Joe plays rapidly ascending and descending chromatic lines on the 2600 with two oscillators tuned a whole step apart, creating a rolling dissonant sound. At about 2:19 (and later at the 4:45 mark) he creates an unusual stuttering effect using a low-frequency oscillator.[46]

On the next track, "Adios," Joe produces a timbre that is right at home alongside the horns of Wayne and Andrew White. Zawinul realized early on that a key to creating natural sounds from synthesizers was to generate movement in timbre or articulation, either subtly, as in the filtering on his "Adios" lines, or more overtly in the case of "Manolete." Early synthesizer keyboards lacked velocity and pressure sensitivity, so developing "touch" was a challenge because the keys generated simple on/off signals. But Joe varied the dynamics with volume foot pedals and relied on other features of the synthesizer to alter the shape of the timbre over time.

"Adios" is a beautiful, meditative piece that was improvised in the studio. It stands in contrast to *Sweetnighter*'s groove-laden tunes in that it has no drums and really no rhythmic pulse at all. It could just as easily have been at home on *Zawinul*. The timbre Joe achieves from his Rhodes is almost unrecognizable, with long, sustained tones. For years Weather Report audiences filed out of auditoriums serenaded by its calming sounds. "'Adios' was a favorite song of mine," said Brian Risner, who handled Weather Report's house sound for many years. "It was just great, because after the whole event, this big huge sound, and the final number, the lights would come up and 'Adios' would come on. It was kind of a signature that I used for years. It was a perfect feeling."[47]

"Adios" is also notable for one of the more unusual instrument credits in Weather Report's discography: the roller toy. "Joe said 'Adios' was really laid back," Muruga recalled, "so I snuck the roller toy out for that one and I said I wanted to use it. Joe heard it and said, 'Oh wow! See those four notes there? That's in the scale of my song!' So now I had to play the doggone roller toy staying in between those four notes! And the bells I held in my mouth, and with the other hand I was flexing a flexatone. And I had a whistle in my mouth, and I was shaking my head with the bells. So it was this multitasking, textural thing I was going for."[48]

Anchoring side two of *Sweetnighter* is Joe's tune "125th Street Congress," named for the street in Harlem where the Apollo Theater is located. Like "Boogie Woogie Waltz," it's a long (twelve-minute) groove, with Joe's motifs darting in and out as he and Wayne improvise over the constant, funky rhythm. "I wanted the band to get stronger rhythmically," Joe said of this tune. "Even stronger than Cannonball and Miles and all those. But there was just one thing, I just didn't like the backbeat, that two and four backbeat, it destroys [any] sensibility of rhythm because it is not rhythm, it is time, and time and rhythm in music are two different things. A groove is a groove, but time doesn't give you a groove, time gives you a certain exactness. '125th Street Congress' is a groove and that is what I wanted—I come from Cannonball, I come from Dinah Washington, everything I ever grew up with and liked about jazz is in there."[49]

Until this point, Weather Report's rhythms had been firmly rooted in the jazz aesthetic in terms of improvisation, dynamism, and complexity. Now Joe felt that traditional jazz rhythm patterns were "old stuff."[50] Nevertheless, he still wanted it to swing, even if not in the jazz sense. To do that, he had a specific feel in mind. "The beat which I used on '125th Street Congress' and also on 'Boogie Woogie Waltz,' but in three-four, is a beat I never heard nobody play before, and nobody else heard," he later said. "And it has such a groove if it is played correctly—with another little hump in the beat, which takes away what you have to always play with backbeats. It depends on where you place the bass drum and where you place your snare drum. It's not something you can really write down. The bass is a little earlier than it is written, and the snare is a little later. It's a feeling thing. And a lot of people don't have that; if you don't have the rotation in your being, that shuffle rotation, you cannot play it."[51]

To later Weather Report drummers, it came to be known as the "Zawa beat," the joke being that whenever Joe was unhappy with a drumbeat, he'd get on the drum set himself to demonstrate what he wanted, only to play the same beat every time. "It was this kind of boogie-woogie groove," Peter Erskine said, "and it took me a while to figure out what he was trying to get. I'd go, 'Well, Joe, that's a different tempo.'" Omar Hakim experienced the same thing and realized that it was "the attitude he was trying to lay on us, more than the groove."[52]

According to Joe, Dwellingham didn't initially feel the rhythm, either. So Joe sung it to him until he had it.[53] If only things were that simple. As Muruga tells the story, "We did this one tune ['125th Street Congress'] and Joe said, 'Give me a rhythm for this.' So Herschel had this really cool, funky rhythm. And being from Detroit, I associated, and so we laid that down. And Joe said, 'No, do something else.' And he took us on a half-hour to an hour tangent looking for another rhythm. And you know, after about forty minutes of grueling rhythms, Herschel came up and whispered in my ear, 'Hey bro, you remember that beat that we did in the beginning, the first one that he didn't like? Let's lay that motherfucker on him again. We're going to lay that same beat on him.'

"So we gave him the first rhythm again and Joe said, 'That's it! That's the rhythm I want, man! That's perfect!' And Herschel just stood up and yelled, 'You motherfucker!' And he started running and rushed him right through the center of all of the instruments, right through the whole studio and up against the wall. And he said, 'Look motherfucker! You ain't telling me what to play anymore! We gave you that an hour ago and you made us go through all that shit and waste our time. You could've had that track done!' And I was just cracking up because Herschel is twice as big as Joe and I saw that Joe was a domineering person. Joe said, 'Okay, man, we're cool! I know! You're right, man! Everything's cool!' Joe listened to Herschel a little bit better after that. [*laughs*]"[54]

Andrew White observed the interactions between Joe and Herschel, and while Joe was funky in his own way, White is quick to point out that it had nothing to do with the genre of music known as funk. "Joe had a feeling, he had ideas," White recalled, "but he did not have any indoctrination into funk at all; he was pulled into that by Herschel. And they had many, many minutes together with all of us in there—and this was during studio time—working this out, and working that out. Wayne was trying to figure out what Joe was talking about, and I was sitting there laughing because in the funk community, we don't say nothin' about funk; we just do it."[55]

Despite such birthing pains, Joe must have gotten what he wanted, because he forever took credit for the beats on *Sweetnighter*. And when hip-hop artists started sampling "125th Street Congress" many years later, Joe's penchant for self-promotion led him to grandiosely claim that he invented the first hip-hop beat. "It *was* [the first hip-hop beat]," he told me in 2004. "When rap became really something big, a lot of rap groups used that soundtrack of '125th Street Congress' from *Sweetnighter*. And I think I have about fifty recordings of that, fifty CDs by rap groups, and I just know that nobody had done that before. Everybody else knew that, too. And if it is not so, I don't care either. I just know nobody played that beat before I did."[56]

The next tune on *Sweetnighter* is "Will," Miroslav's only composition on the album. It's a spacious, melancholy piece that takes listeners to an entirely different place from "125th Street Congress." Together with Wayne, Miroslav plays the long-limbed melody lines on bass guitar processed through a Fender Fuzz Wah pedal. "I gave Joe [the line he repeats throughout the tune on electric piano] and he seemed to enjoy that very much because he kind of grooved with it and kept going with the phase shifter," Miroslav said. "And then I had the melody and there were a few things played with that. And that's the way we played the tune."[57] Although the LP jacket doesn't list Muruga on "Will," he says he "played the original doumbek drum part before anybody overdubbed on top of it, and they need to credit me for that."[58]

The final track is "Non-Stop Home," an uptempo piece that Wayne said was written for his grandmother. "She used to belong to the Baptist church, the Black

Andrew White and Miroslav Vitous at Connecticut Recording Studio. Photo courtesy Andrew White.

Baptist church, and that was like her church's song. If you take the rhythm off and let the melody play, that's her song, man."[59] It begins abruptly with an up-cut midway through a studio jam, and then at 1:44 there's a jarring splice where the feel suddenly changes. Usually edits are done in a way to mask their presence, but that was not Joe and Wayne's intent here. "An edit isn't always about not being able to tell it's there," Risner said. "Sometimes you do things for effect. It was so cool."[60]

The tune is largely characterized by the funky drumbeat that Dwellingham lays down with Eric Gravatt. "That's me playing a combination of funk and a hip jazz groove," Dwellingham said. "I established the tempo and the groove, and Eric played like a saxophone player would play against it. The only reason I could do this so well is because I had the Elvin [Jones] thing, too. I played a lot of jazz gigs at the Jazz Workshop in Boston with people like Wes Montgomery, Roland Kirk, Sonny Rollins. If Alan Dawson [a legendary instructor at Berklee] couldn't make it, he would ask me to do it. I'm not known for that because all people hear is me playing funk. But that funk is really what Alan Dawson taught combined with my Southern R&B feeling."[61]

Meanwhile, Joe had crazy fun conjuring up all manner of strange sounds from his Rhodes. It's like he took all of his modifiers and said, *Let's see how wild this rig can get.* "One of the great things about these old devices is that they were real hands-on units," Brian Risner said. "Joe would get into using the whammy bar on the Echoplex, as in this song. This was the control that would slide the playback head in the tape loop path. You would get wow and flutter from the [Echoplex] tape speeding up and slowing down. Sometimes he'd just reach over there and grab the throttle and *wham*, the sound would stretch and snap. Joe would perform with the tape loop for effect! It was all improvisation and a lot of discovery. At the time, it was often jaw-dropping, seat-of-the-pants driving. Between the ring modulator and the wah-wah pedal, that was a whole lot of shaking going on there. And he had such a brilliant compositional ear, he knew where he was going, the sound that he was going for."[62]

As with everything else on *Sweetnighter*, Wayne only had a sketch for this tune, leaving much to the rest of the musicians. With no bass line to read, White improvised his part. "That was my audition take," he said. "That was my first piece. I asked, 'What do you want me to do?' And Joe said, 'Just do your thing.' And that's what I did. I didn't even know the tape was rolling. I just thought we were trying to feel something out and get some ideas. When the record came out, you could have knocked me over with a feather. But whatever it was that I had was what they wanted, and that's what they put on the record."[63]

•

The additional musicians were so integral to *Sweetnighter* that it wasn't lost on Joe that he would have trouble playing the music live without them. So overtures were made in Connecticut, none of which panned out, in part because the studio guys found their existing gigs more lucrative than hitting the road with Weather Report. One evening they were eating dinner together when Zawinul made a pitch to Dwellingham. "Herschel," he suddenly blurted out, "would you like to join the band?"

Since Eric Gravatt was sitting at the table alongside him, Dwellingham was taken aback. "What?" he answered, unsure if he heard correctly. Joe may have had in mind taking two drummers on the road, with Herschel playing the bottom, as Joe put it, and Gravatt playing the top. It was an idea that Zawinul had toyed with before. Gravatt remembers Billy Cobham coming in for a rehearsal after Weather Report's tour of Japan. "That didn't work out because we just couldn't play together," Eric recalled.[64] Of course, by the time of *Sweetnighter*, Gravatt was no longer the new guy, but an integral part of the band, so Joe's invitation to Herschel must have stung.

"I'm asking you to join the band," Zawinul repeated. "We love the way you play. You sound great. From this day on, you go on tour with us."

Dwellingham was flattered, but it would mean leaving his studio gigs and family behind. Plus, he had some concerns about Joe's interactions with the other musicians, especially Miroslav. "Well, I'll tell you, man," Herschel responded. "I've got a good career as a session player, and that's really what I do as an arranger/producer. And I have to stay stable somewhere to do that. I appreciate you offering me to come with you all, but I've just got too much going."[65]

Andrew White was also approached. "I couldn't do it because the economics of jazz ain't got *nothing* to do with rock 'n' roll," he explained. "I made the record with my friends from the Art Blakey and Cannonball days, but it ain't got nothing to do with me leaving the Fifth Dimension to make some gigs with a wanna-be rock and fusion band or whatever they call it. I had no interest in doing that. And they were desperate because Bob Devere was hittin' on me the whole summer. I said, 'Man, I can't do nothing. Plus, you have no money. You need to pay me more than you're paying the whole band.' Joe understood that."[66]

Nevertheless, White was quick to leverage the gig to his benefit. Late that summer, *Down Beat* ran its review of *Sweetnighter*—two reviews, in fact—that relegated White's role to the English horn, despite the track-by-track personnel listing on the album jacket.[67] Recognizing the value in setting the record straight, White immediately dashed off a letter to *Down Beat* in response, which the magazine printed under the heading "Who Brought the Funk?" "With all due respect to Miroslav Vitous, who I think is a fine bassist, I played all of the funk on the bass on that album. But to be more specific, I played electric bass with Miroslav on 'Boogie Woogie Waltz' and 'Manolete,' and I played bass alone on '125th Street Congress' and 'Non-Stop Home.'"[68]

Andrew White the businessman knew to strike while the iron was hot. At the first opportunity, he took the Fifth Dimension band into a recording studio and had the resulting record, *Who Got de Funk?*, on the market—that is, available by mail order from Andrew's Music—seemingly before the ink was dry on his *Down Beat* letter. It quickly sold out the first pressing. He also transcribed his bass part on "125th Street Congress," which he sold for decades. "It's been just as popular as my Coltrane transcriptions," White said. "Every time they come out with another [Weather Report] anthology, I get a big bump in sales. People call me and say, 'Are you the bass player that played on "125th Street Congress"?' I tell them, 'I am. And if you buy the transcription, you can sound just like me!'" [*laughs*][69]

Dwellingham felt the benefits of his Weather Report association as well. "From that connection with Weather Report, Paul Leka started calling me to do sessions. I was doing a lot of stuff for him: REO Speedwagon, Peter Nero. The biggest thing was 'Cat's in the Cradle' with Harry Chapin. So it opened doors for me." Dwellingham began working so much in New York that he soon moved there. "Later, Bob Devere told me, 'Herschel, you did the right thing, moving to New

York. They only get about $5,000 to $10,000 per concert. You're making more than them in one week.' In some ways I wish I had [toured with Weather Report], because I would have had the fame and I could probably have had my own group. But I was just trying to make money to feed my wife and three little kids. I got $1,300 for the session. It was just another session. I didn't think anything would come from it. I was just trying to keep money in the house."[70]

•

Immediately after wrapping up in Connecticut, Weather Report hit the road for a couple of shows in the Midwest before continuing to the West Coast for ten days. Bob Devere kept the band pretty well booked through the spring and into the summer, mostly in clubs with some college dates thrown in. Any lingering friction from the *Sweetnighter* sessions didn't manifest itself to the audiences, judging by published descriptions of their appearances. One of Weather Report's first post-*Sweetnighter* gigs was at the Guthrie Theater in Minneapolis. This was the concert that Bob Protzman waxed so enthusiastically about in *Down Beat*. Among other things, he was particularly impressed by the way Eric Gravatt and Dom Um Romão meshed together, as well as Joe's solo rendition of Duke Ellington's "Sophisticated Lady." Protzman thought the latter was inspired by a television special about Ellington that aired the same night, but Joe often played Ellington pieces on the piano.

The next week, Jon Hendricks attended one of Weather Report's gigs at Keystone Korner in San Francisco. "It is wonderful. Superb. Brilliant. Beautiful," he wrote. "The compositions are perfectly crafted symphonettes, encompassing every musical form extant and some unheard before."[71] Days later, the band took the stage at the Whisky a Go Go, a rock 'n' roll club on the Sunset Strip in Hollywood. Dennis Hunt of the *Los Angeles Times* called their performance there "enthralling and exhausting."[72]

Joe was now traveling with the ARP 2600. At first he used it sparingly, relegating it to a corner of his stage setup—"a mere gadget for the unimaginative," according to one concert review.[73] One problem was that it quickly proved to be less than roadworthy. "The very first concert, we had technical issues," Brian Risner recalled. "The oscillators wouldn't keep in tune through the octaves, and the keyboard wouldn't track properly. Internally, there were little adjustment controls—trim pots—to calibrate the modules. It was totally sensitive to vibration, and all of this stuff would go out of whack on the road."[74]

All of the 2600's modules relied on precise voltages for their settings. For example, each key on the keyboard generated 1/12th of a volt more than the previous one; that is, one volt per octave. Maintaining the accuracy of these voltages across the keyboard was crucial to ensuring that it played in tune. "They were lab instruments," Risner said. "And even then, they weren't stable. I had to do a field service on the 2600 before every gig. Every day I had to pop open the lid and do a scaling on the keyboard and tracking on the oscillators. I made an investment in digital test equipment and frequency counters, as well as a Strobotuner to field service the 2600. And since it allowed you to get a visual tuning of the oscillators, Joe could retune them silently between songs."[75]

Joe's first 2600 was an early unit that predated improvements made to manufacture them in quantity. "The oscillator modules were hand-wired boards," Risner said. "Eventually we got into more-stable modules. I was at the ARP factory all the time, getting new parts and getting new modules. I would be up there every other week; they got tired of seeing me. They would send me new modules and I would replace stuff. I rebuilt those things a lot. I found out what their weaknesses were. For instance, the connectors between the keyboard and the synthesizer were really crappy. It was a bad design in their production, and they weren't going to change it, but I had to deal with it on a daily basis. So I changed out the type of connectors because any kind of deviation in the contact in terms of resistance or capacitance would affect the tuning on the keyboard."[76]

Despite these trials, the 2600 soon became an indispensable part of Zawinul's rig, which made those times when Risner couldn't fix it all the more glaring. "On one show it broke down, and I couldn't get it in tune," Risner recalled. "Joe said, 'Riz, it's part of my sound now. I can't be without it.' It wasn't optional anymore. For the integrity and the orchestration of the songs, he needed the 2600 just to be able to play them. I thought that the only way we could continue to use it in live performance was to get a backup. So the next day we went out and somehow spent the money and bought a second synthesizer and got some road cases built for it.

"So now we had the spare, and if the synth went down during the set, I had to pull the other one out to replace it. Here I am mixing the show and he's having trouble with the synthesizer, and I have to go up and replace it during the gig. That wasn't going to work, so I put them both up on stage next to each other so that Joe could plug the keyboard of one into the other." But relegating one as a spare "didn't last but one show. As soon as Joe figured out he could get them both working, he said, 'Forget about it being a spare.'"[77]

Risner stacked the two 2600 keyboards on top of the Rhodes—"the first and only dual manual 2600s," he joked. Being built before the uniformity of integrated circuits, each 2600 had its own unique character. In order to keep them straight, Risner christened them *Eins* and *Zwei* (German for 'one' and 'two'). Zawinul commented on this in an ARP advertisement, calling Eins his "soft synthesizer, with a clear, clean sound I have never heard on any other," while Zwei gave him a harder edge.

Risner devised a clever approach for making both front panels easily accessible

Weather Report at the UC Berkeley Jazz Festival, Apr. 26, 1973. Zawinul still has one ARP 2600, whose keyboard sits atop his Fender Rhodes electric piano. The pedestal in front of Wayne holds the Maestro Sound System for Woodwinds box. The base of the pedestal was the case for the ARP 2600's keyboard, stood on end. Brian Risner ran an efficient operation. Photo: Michael Wilderman.

to Joe on stage, arranged one atop the other at an oblique angle, just to the left of the keyboards. "I flipped one around in its chassis. I think I changed some woodwork inside, but I didn't have to reengineer the case. So that's how we set it up. We stacked them [instead of placing them side-by-side], and that way I could crosspatch between the two, and it was all right there. It was really cool, actually."[78] To mount them on stage, Risner built a frame out of aluminum piping that, because of its appearance, became known as "the electric chair." He also fashioned a tray that sat below the synthesizers for outboard effects.

With all this gear, the technical demands on Risner escalated. "Very quickly the curve went up. All of a sudden I had the Rhodes, which at some point we hot-rodded, a pair of 2600s, dual manuals, the Maestro phase shifter, the same stuff on the Rhodes."[79] All of the effects were in separate boxes, connected together via audio cables, and with their own power supplies. "It ended up being quite a kludge up there, in part because Joe found something essential in every effect that he tried. Once we brought out one of those gizmos, it remained there. It became rather elaborate."[80] At this point, Risner was a one-man sound engineer, logistics manager, and electronics technician, sharing the rental car and truck-driving duties with Miroslav. It was pretty heady stuff for a twenty-year-old. Later in the year, recognizing that the band's needs were becoming substantial, Bob Devere added a road manager to take some of the burden off Risner.

•

Sweetnighter was released in May and quickly lodged itself near the top of the *Billboard* jazz chart, where it remained for over a year. By the time it drifted out of the top ten, Columbia claimed to have sold 300,000 copies of the album. [81]

Weather Report had finally produced commercially in a way that Columbia had hoped it would from the beginning.

1973 was a banner year for jazz, which was in the midst of a marked turn-around from the "bleak decade" of the sixties. Just a few years earlier, its image among industry executives was so bad that "confronted by the word *jazz*, [they] immediately react as though they had heard the word *leprosy*," wrote the promi-nent journalist Leonard Feather.[82] Now a recurring storyline within the entertain-ment press was the music's favorable economic climate. One headline read, "As Rock Stalls at Crossroads, Jazz Breaks Through All Across Board,"[83] while the lead of another article announced, "Jazz in the early '70s is reaching a new audience of enthusiastic young listeners."[84]

Right about the time Weather Report was ensconced at Connecticut Record-ing Studio, the Mahavishnu Orchestra's second album, *Birds of Fire*, landed in re-cord stores. It quickly exceeded the sales of its predecessor and ultimately became one of three jazz albums released in 1973 to be certified gold by the Recording Industry Association of America, the others being Herbie Hancock's *Head Hunt-ers*; and *Love, Devotion and Surrender* by Carlos Santana and John McLaughlin. All three were Columbia products. Meanwhile, Donald Byrd's album *Black Byrd* became far and away the best-selling record in Blue Note's history to that point, with sales in excess of 300,000 units.[85]

Whether these records should even be considered jazz was a matter of debate, as they drew heavily upon popular music influences ranging from soul to rock. Leonard Feather remembered having spirited arguments while participating on the committee of the National Academy of Recording Arts and Sciences (NARAS) whose task was to determine which recordings qualified for the Grammy jazz cat-egories.[86] The hardliners carried the day, as none of the albums mentioned above received such a nomination.[87]

When *Sweetnighter*'s successor, *Mysterious Traveller*, was also snubbed, Bob De-vere went public with his gripes, complaining that NARAS "failed to give recogni-tion to some of the most creative forces which are bringing a new form of jazz to a new generation of listeners."[88] NARAS brushed off those concerns. "A judgment was made that Weather Report did not belong in the jazz category," a spokesman told *Variety*.[89] (After *I Sing the Body Electric* was nominated in 1973, Weather Report didn't receive another nod until it won the newly created Best Jazz Fusion Performance category in 1980.)

Grammy nominations were just one manifestation of the struggles over genre and terminology when it came to the music that was nominally produced under the jazz banner. "Space music," "energy jazz," "Afro-American music," "jazz-based music," "jazz-rock," "crossover albums"—all of these terms were bandied about by writers groping for a way to describe a range of hybrid music that wasn't necessarily jazz, but wasn't rock, either. When quizzed about the music that had blossomed forth from Miles Davis's former sidemen, Joe simply said, "No one can say what it is."[90] At the time, he seemed unconcerned about the business of labeling Weather Report's music. "Whatever somebody wants to call it is okay with me," he told one reporter.[91]

But the media needed a way to describe it, and by this time it more or less settled on the term *jazz-rock*. In November 1972, *Down Beat* ran its first jazz-rock issue with the phrase emblazoned on the front cover.[92] In its second jazz-rock issue a year later, the publisher, Charles Suber, offered his explanation for the term, which was probably as good as any other. "'Jazz-rock' is a fusion of music and technology. Jazz itself has three basic criteria: improvisation, swing, and individuality of expression. Today's rock has formed its own character from a rhythm 'n' blues base to which has been added the technology of amplification, electronic tone production and modification, and the creative use of the new instruments: i.e. synthesizers of various kinds. Put them all together and you get a music that is coded 'jazz-rock.'"[93]

Columbia Records was well aware of how labels affected public perception. Bruce Lundvall, Columbia's marketing vice president, stated that everything had to be aimed at the "young rock buying public as opposed to the pure jazz buying public."[94] Concerned that the word *jazz* carried a stigma with its target audience, CBS explicitly avoided using it in its Weather Report marketing efforts. Instead, it adopted the phrase *progressive music*, which went back to the days when Clive Davis signed the band. This applied to Columbia's jazz artists, in general. For instance, one merchandising theme was "The Progressives: Yesterday and Tomorrow," which promoted Weather Report, Miles Davis, Duke Ellington, Thelonious Monk, Billie Holiday, Ornette Coleman, Bill Evans, Maynard Ferguson, John McLaughlin, and Charles Mingus.[95]

"Today's music audience is more sophisticated and better educated than ever before," read another full-page advertisement. "People no longer accept what is thrust upon them, they care about music and become involved with it. They are demanding higher and higher standards of musicianship and artistic excellence. Which in part explains the phenomenal commercial success of the Mahavishnu Orchestra, Miles Davis, Weather Report and other groups whose aesthetic value was never in question, but who were considered 'too far out': or 'ahead of their time.'"[96] In other words, Columbia positioned its progressive jazz offerings as cutting-edge music that appealed to open-minded listeners who valued quality. The upshot was that young people accounted for 90 percent of Weather Report's following, per Columbia's own estimate.[97]

Meanwhile, the critical reception to *Sweetnighter* was positive, if somewhat mixed, as the pair of *Down Beat* reviews illustrated. Published in the same issue,

Joe Klee rated it five stars, praising Weather Report as "truly a band for which there is no pigeonhole." Will Smith gave it three stars, writing, "There's no doubt that the group has its own bag. But there's not that much in this bag."[98]

With *Sweetnighter*'s release, Weather Report's live book was updated as well. "Boogie Woogie Waltz" now served as the concert closer, sometimes prompting the audience to get out of their seats and dance. Enthusiastic crowds and outstanding reviews greeted Weather Report at nearly every stop. Nancy Ball caught them in Kansas City, writing, "The temptation to rant on in jubilant superlatives is almost uncontrollable." Wayne brought along the Maestro woodwind box, which, Ball said, caused him to sound like a "clutch of oboes; and when that comes together with the fast, smooth work of Zawinul on electric piano and synthesizer, the effect is pretty devastating."[99]

The response was validating for Joe, but as spring turned to summer, audiences expected to hear the music played in the style of the LP. Of course, the band on stage wasn't the one that produced the record. Bob Devere kept pestering Andrew White to join them on the road, but that was a nonstarter. Meanwhile, the tension between Joe and Eric Gravatt mounted. To Joe, Gravatt resisted playing the grooves he wanted. "Not that he couldn't have done it, but with him it was a mental thing. He just didn't have his heart in it."[100] Gravatt put the blame on Zawinul. "Joe was the leader, and I had no problem with that. But in order to be a leader, you have to *be* a leader. If you can't write out what you want me to play, and you can't tell me verbally what you want me to play, then I have to play what I know how to play."[101]

It led to problems on and off the bandstand. "Joe was so strong and Eric was so sensitive that as time went along [Joe] made [Eric] more and more insecure," Miroslav said. "Joe was doing things on stage. Like Eric would play something and Joe's shoulders would drop down and he would look like, 'Oh, Jesus Christ, what is this?' very visibly on the bandstand several times through the concert, which is absolutely insane and disrespectful. But he did that, and because musicians respected Joe, they took it very personally, and it started to mess with their own security. After a while the guy didn't know how to play or what to play, so it just started vanishing. He even started to do it to me, which also made me feel terrible."[102]

Earlier in the year, Miroslav had met Greg Errico, the former drummer for Sly and the Family Stone. Their connection was through Doug Rauch, who was then the bass player for Santana. "I had a music room downstairs, and Doug used to come over and jam all the time," Errico recalled. "He would bring different people over, and he started bringing Miroslav Vitous around. We had a few jam sessions, and Miroslav would bring his upright with his bow and everything. Miroslav loved funk. He wasn't a funk player, but he loved it."[103]

Miroslav and Errico got on so well that they talked of doing an album together.[104] Then one day Vitous called the drummer with a different offer. "You know, Joe's looking for a new guy. We're doing a Japan tour, would you like to come out?" Having spent the past year decompressing from the Family Stone whirlwind, Errico was getting the itch to perform again. "Truthfully, I had heard about Weather Report, but I wasn't really familiar with the music at that time," Errico admitted. "But I said, 'Yeah, I'd be interested.'"[105] Shortly thereafter, Gravatt got a phone call from Bob Devere. "Eric, the guys decided they want to use another drummer. We'll send your drums." Click.[106]

Gravatt was shocked by the swiftness with which his time came to an end. The band's next gig was just a few days away, after all, and he was looking forward to a return trip to Japan the next month. And judging from an unpublished interview he gave in 1980, his resentment toward Joe and the music business in general remained palpable for years. Nevertheless, with the passage of time Gravatt eventually viewed the experience from a more balanced perspective. "Most of the problems we had were off of the bandstand," he said in 1996. "I think that when people work with you they try to get inside your head, and sometimes they find out they don't like what's in there. Then they go through a process of trying to change you, which is the worst thing they can do. That was one of the things that baffled me when I got the call saying I was no longer in Weather Report. I wasn't playing any differently. If anything I was playing more confidently."[107]

Gravatt's immediate reaction to his ouster was to quit the music business altogether, but he soon moved to San Francisco to play with pianist Todd Cochran, who then performed by the name Bayeté.[108] While he was out there, Eric also did sessions with Eddie Henderson (*Inside Out*) and Joe Henderson (*Canyon Lady*). The next year, Gravatt made his way to Minneapolis to join the band Natural Life. He even had plans to record his own album and was writing lyrics to go along with his music. "I want people to hear my views on life. I have some things I want to say," he said.[109] But the opportunity to produce it never materialized. So he got back with McCoy Tyner, doing a couple of records (*Focal Point* and *Inner Voices*) and another tour with the pianist. None of it was enough to sustain him economically.

A newborn daughter intensified the need for a steady income, and a friend helped Gravatt get a job as a prison guard at the Lino Lakes facility of the Minnesota Department of Corrections. "It's a good thing I did," he later explained. "Because my wife got sick and she died nine years later. I wouldn't have been able to pay for that if I had tried to be a musician."[110] With that, Eric Gravatt disappeared from the national music scene, popping up every now and then for a local gig in the Twin Cities where few in the audience knew of his résumé.

"There was one year when we just lit up the planet, man," he said. "That year we did Japan, we were second only to Miles in popularity. I wasn't quite prepared for the adulation that the Japanese had for us—limousines, roses, and stuff waiting for the band. . . . I wouldn't trade that whole experience with Weather Report for anything. In retrospect, I guess I have mellowed with age. I can look back at the head-butting I did with Zawinul with fondness now because I can recognize it for what it was—two rams amongst the sheep."[111]

Twenty-five years after they first played together, the magazine *Modern Drummer* asked Joe if there were any drummers he would yet like to play with. The first words out of his mouth were, "There's still Eric Gravatt."[112]

10 Mysterious Traveller

Mysterious Traveller was another kind of story. All of a sudden we were a power band.

—Joe Zawinul

GREG ERRICO'S FIRST CONCERT WITH WEATHER REPORT was at the 1973 Newport Jazz Festival on a double bill with Chick Corea's Return to Forever. In place of Eric Gravatt and his small jazz kit, Errico filled a good chunk of the stage with a full-bore rock set that included large-diameter clear acrylic shells and a twenty-four-inch bass drum whose *boom* Joe must have loved, all surrounded by a forest of cymbals. Joe told one reporter that Errico and the band only had time for "a little get together half an hour beforehand."[1] No matter. Errico jumped in and the music took on new life.

According to an account in *Melody Maker*, Weather Report opened the show and played an hour-long set built around two numbers: "Boogie Woogie Waltz" and "In a Silent Way."[2] The author ascribed the latter tune to Miles Davis, but he probably meant "It's About That Time," which was a common item on Weather Report's set lists in those days. There's also an unofficial recording that purports to be from this gig, which includes "125th Street Congress," "Doctor Honoris Causa," "Directions," and "Seventh Arrow." Weather Report regularly performed all of these tunes in 1973.

Errico's addition to the group came as a surprise. Although jazz-rock was the buzz at the time, in practice there wasn't much commingling between rock and jazz musicians. Essentially, they worked in separate networks, each with their own venues, fans, and media. (To illustrate the point, Errico remembered meeting the band in New York just before his first gig and being introduced to "a whole different circle of people in relation to where I had come from."[3]) Of course, there was overlap among these constituents, but it wasn't hard for listeners to distinguish, say, Chicago or Santana from Miles Davis or the Mahavishnu Orchestra. Despite the deep grooves of *Sweetnighter*, Weather Report was still a jazz band, but the new drummer had neither a jazz pedigree nor any formal training on the drums. What he did have was five years of experience maintaining the pocket for one of the funkiest bands then in existence.

At its peak, nothing compared to Sly and the Family Stone. It was a genre-busting congregation that transcended categorization. They dressed in eccentric outfits and performed dance steps like their rhythm 'n' blues counterparts, with gospel-like shouts and screams, all elevated to an outrageous degree. They were also very serious about their music. Sylvester Stewart, a.k.a. Sly Stone, brought a songwriter's craft to funk, creating an infectious, upbeat brand of music that was embraced by mainstream America and served as a template for black music in the seventies. By the time Sly and the Family Stone took the stage at Woodstock in 1969, performing an electrifying set in the dead of night, they were on their way to becoming one of the biggest names in the business. Between that year and the next, they sold eight million records and changed music in their wake.

When Sly tabbed Errico for his new band in 1966, he was seventeen years old and fresh out of high school. A self-taught drummer, Errico picked up his first pair of sticks just three years earlier.

> I started playing when I was fourteen. I'd come home from school, put on some 45s in the rumpus room downstairs where my drums were set up, and I'd start playing to them. My first inspirations were from the jazz world. It was Buddy Rich and Joe Morello. I had everything from Xavier Cugat to Aretha Franklin, Ray Charles, Wilson Pickett. I'd practice with Dave Brubeck's "Take Five" and then some Ray Charles stuff. Fortunately, my dad had good taste so there was always good music around. My brother was six years older than me, so he had all the cool 45s. And growing up in San Francisco, which is a world intersection of characters and music and everything, I was exposed to all of this, and I gravitated to it. I just got into it from playing and listening to different music.[4]

Three weeks after the Newport Jazz Festival, Weather Report went to Japan, where they performed in the best concert halls before sold-out, attentive audiences. Like Eric Gravatt, Errico came away impressed by the experience. "I remember it was large theaters," Errico said. "The place would be packed and they'd be sitting there, knees together, hands folded on their lap—not a peep. At first I wasn't sure if it was respect or boredom. But no, it was respect, for sure. They would wait until the end of the song and there would be a pause—you could hear a pin drop—and then all of a sudden they would break out into a cheer."[5]

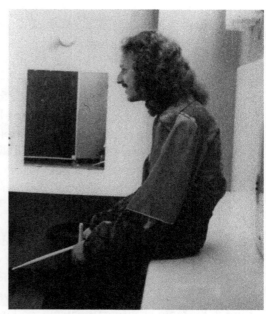

Greg Errico backstage in Japan. Photo: Brian Risner.

After performing seven concerts in Japan, the band flew to Hawaii for a few days of R&R before a concert in Honolulu. Wayne stayed behind. Early in the tour, he received a visitor backstage. It was Nobu Urushiyama, a Japanese drummer and practitioner of Nichiren Buddhism. He was there at the urging of Ana Maria, who asked him to seek out Wayne and encourage him to become a Buddhist. Herbie Hancock had introduced Ana Maria to the practice several months earlier. She immediately found comfort in the daily ritualistic chanting of the mantra "Nam-myoho-renge-kyo." According to Soka Gakkai International, the lay organization of Nichiren Buddhists, "By chanting Nam-myoho-renge-kyo, we awaken to the reality that within our life is unlimited reserves of courage, wisdom and compassion—that we are in fact Buddhas. Based on this conviction, we can transform any suffering, lead those around us to happiness, and create peace in our communities and the world. Nam-myoho-renge-kyo is a declaration of the inherent dignity and power within the lives of all people."[6]

Beginning Buddhists are encouraged to chant for anything that will bring them happiness. Hancock credited the practice for the creative shift that led to *Head Hunters* later that year.[7] It was a musical departure for him that became the best-selling jazz record of all time to that point. He even credited the record's title to an epiphany he had while chanting.[8] Ana Maria's chanting centered on seeking improvement in Iska's condition. But as her even-syllabled cadence became a routine sound in the Shorter home, Wayne remained skeptical. He tried chanting with her on occasion, but kept it at arm's length, leery of taking it seriously. His full immersion took place in Japan. Nobu convinced him to remain there after Weather Report's tour concluded, and he gave Wayne a gentle but deep introduction to Nichiren Buddhism. The culmination was a ceremony at a small temple, where he received his *Gohonzon*—a calligraphic scroll that contains the main tenants of Nichiren Buddhism and serves as the focus of one's practice.[9]

Buddhism became the center of Wayne's life—more important than music. He chanted at home and on the road. He explained that chanting "is akin to the rhythm of everything in life, and if you're off the track it puts you back on, gets all the cobwebs off the brain and polishes you so that things shine, get brighter and brighter." The rest of the band didn't join in, he said, "but they're listening to me. Like Joe will say, 'Very interesting.' He said, 'I'm gonna ask you some questions from time to time,' or 'I'm gonna challenge you on this, Wayne,' but sometimes when I'm chanting I know he's listening outside the door. Then when I finish he'll say, 'Hey, there's a lot of rhythm in that thing you're doing,' and there is."[10]

"When Wayne wasn't playing a note on the reed, he was chanting," Greg Errico recalled. "You could walk down the hallway in the hotel and hear it; he'd be sitting in his room chanting. I remember asking him once, 'Wayne, what are you chanting for, man?' He'd say, like, a million dollars, or something to that effect. I said okay. And he finally got it, I guess. He was an interesting cat, more or less quiet, but when we got on stage and played, everybody had a voice and everybody conversed musically; it was just an unspoken understanding. I never quite met anyone like him."[11]

Being a working musician didn't make it easy for Wayne. "In the beginning I was struggling on the road to do this thing all alone, by myself, and it seemed a very lonely thing," he said in 1975. "I remembered Herbie saying, 'You do this thing to attain happiness, enlightenment,' but it was rough doing it. Then as time went on the same kinda change happened in me that I'd seen happen in Herbie Hancock."[12] When Wayne made the album *Native Dancer* with Milton Nascimento the next year, he called it "actual proof of something changing in my life and being reflected musically."[13] He introduced journalists who visited his home to his *Butsudan*, the altar where he chanted, and his speech was spiked with references to "human revolution" and the advantages of Eastern "unity" versus Western "separatism." Wayne joined the local chapter of Nichiren Shoshu Buddhism, which was run by Herbie Hancock.[14]

Meanwhile, with Errico in the fold, Wayne noticed more young people filling the audiences, attracted to Errico's rock 'n' roll persona. He certainly looked the part, with his sandy-colored hair draped over his shoulders atop a mod stage wardrobe that included colorful long-sleeve shirts and flared pants. The band was still highly improvisational, but it was on top of a driving beat that Errico laid down *and maintained*, especially at the fast tempos that Joe liked. Weather Report rocked hard in the summer and fall of 1973.

Errico was the ideal drummer for tunes like "Boogie Woogie Waltz" and "125th Street Congress"—or "It's About That Time," for that matter. "Greg played the hip-hop rhythm on 'Boogie Woogie Waltz' better than any Weather Report drummer before or since," Zawinul later acknowledged. "He was a great musician." [15] As the concert closer, it could go on for twenty minutes or more, invariably bringing the audience to its feet. "Musically, it was like he threw me the keys to the car, and I just had a lot of fun," Errico said. "It was challenging, but it all worked. The chemistry was good. Dom Um had a small set of traps up there, and once in a while he would jump on them, too." [16]

Miroslav also got into it, even if he still refused to accept what he called "the slave rhythm section" role. "Miroslav was very unconventional," Errico remembered. "At first I thought, *Well, this is going to be a little weird*, but I found it delightfully challenging, and it really turned out to be kind of a cool thing. I mean, he'd whip out the bow sometimes, and we'd be in these hellacious uptempo grooves, and he would just float over the top of it. It was kind of the opposite, the antithesis of what I would do with Larry Graham [the bass player in Sly and the Family Stone]. It just worked in its own way because Miroslav had a passion for it, but he couldn't do it in a conventional sense; it wasn't him. It created this other element that was very interesting, and he understood what I was doing and just applied his perspective on it." [17]

With Errico providing a foundation of unyielding grooves, the rest of the band soared. Even longtime jazz critic Leonard Feather bought into the "stronger rock tinge," as he put it. Seeing them at UCLA's Royce Hall in September, he wrote, "The climactic 'Boogie Woogie Waltz' was a dizzying sonic maze," with "a hypnotic buildup that became deafening—but just as the threshold of pain seemed imminent, pow! The music stopped. In response to a tremendous standing ovation, Weather Report played a brief encore and an extraordinary evening was over—except for the sounds it left spinning in your brain." [18]

Joe's expertise with his ARP synthesizers grew rapidly as the year progressed. Their lack of memory meant that reconfiguring them required moving a series of sliders and potentially rearranging patch cords. With the music flying by, there wasn't a lot of time for that sort of thing on stage, so having two 2600s afforded him the flexibility to pre-configure each of them before the show. He also took advantage of down times, such as when Miroslav gave a solo reading of "Days of Wine and Roses" on acoustic bass, to reconfigure or retune the synthesizers—a sleight-of-hand trick while the audience's attention was elsewhere.

The 2600's large control panel, with the sliders laid out in schematic fashion, proved to be quite useful because Joe could tell at a glance how the machine was set up. To ease his performance burden, Risner marked the slider locations for important patches. "At first I cut up pieces of colored tape," he recalled, "but it didn't work under stage lights, so I went with shapes. You could probably find those same pieces of tape on them to this day."[19]

In addition to reprogramming the synthesizers, Joe also had a cassette deck on stage that he would use to play pre-recorded tapes. Some of them were made with the 2600s, but other times he would play "Milky Way" as the background for a percussion improvisation, or even one involving the rest of the band. In time, the task of playing tape cues was handed off to Risner, who eventually gave the job to a member of the stage crew.

After Japan, the band went to Europe, hitting the summer festivals there. They returned to the States in late August and began a tour of colleges and universities—a clear indication of who their audience was.[20] Clubs became a less frequent part of their itinerary as they performed in medium size halls and auditoriums in the Midwest and East Coast. Often these dates were shared with other bands. At various times they opened for Fleetwood Mac, the Buddy Miles Express, Paul Butterfield, B. B. King, Deodato, and the Mahavishnu Orchestra. Other times a local band would open for Weather Report.

Zawinul liked Errico enough to ask him to stay on permanently. "Joe said, 'Okay, we want you to join the corporation and be in the whole thing,'" Errico recalled. "But I didn't believe in the manager and I also had a bunch of production commitments at the time. Now, had one of the elements not been present? I would say it most likely would have happened, because I loved the guys. I enjoyed playing with them, traveling with them, the whole thing. I remained very close with all of them; we kept in touch. I was doing my thing and they were doing their thing."[21]

Errico made plans to leave the band at the end of October. At around the same time, Joe heard a tape of a drummer out of Philadelphia. He had no idea who it was, but he liked his style. Joe put in a call to Bob Devere to get this young man to a gig.

•

Ishmael "Butch" Wilburn grew up in the Pentecostal church. His father was a deacon and his mother was a minister who also sang and played the piano and organ at Sunday services. Young Butch began playing snare and tambourine by her side, eventually moving to the church's drum set. At around the age of fifteen, he put some drums on layaway at the local Sam Goody store with the intention of buying them with money he earned from a weekend job. His father had a different idea. "He knew that I really wanted them," Wilburn recalled decades later, "and I came home one day and that set of drums was in the living room. He had already cleared it with all the neighbors. Buying me that set of drums set me off."[22]

Butch learned by ear, playing along to James Brown, Motown, and Jackson 5 records, and began hanging out with a group of older musicians which included a bass player named C. J. Clark, who went on to do a lot of Philadelphia sound session work. In 1973, Wilburn was in an R&B band with Clark, doing originals with a female vocalist. That fall, the band's manager met up with Weather Report. "This guy was somehow related to Wayne Shorter," Wilburn recalled. "And he let them hear a tape—a demo of some originals we were working on—and they liked the drumming. He said, 'Hey man, those guys want to talk to you. Joe really likes your foot'—how I played my kick drum, where I dropped and the feel of how I played. I said, 'Wow, my foot!'" [*laughs*][23]

Wilburn agreed to meet the band in Washington, D.C. "I took the Amtrak down and I think I was going to sit in or do something at sound check so they could get a feel for me. But something happened and they didn't get into town, so I came back to Philly and started doing my daily thing. And then one day I got a call from their manager. He said, 'Listen, they want you to play a gig with them.'"[24]

Wilburn was flabbergasted. "You've got to be kidding me," he replied. "I have never even played with them. I have never met them." Nor did he consider himself a jazz drummer. "I was coming from a gospel background. I was more into funk—Earth, Wind & Fire, Rare Earth, Chicago, that kind of thing. I think it was six months before I started playing with them that I heard *Sweetnighter*. And I thought, wow, this is different stuff. And then somebody turned me onto *I Sing the Body Electric*, and that's when I really started stretching my ears."[25]

Wilburn gave another listen to *Sweetnighter* and *I Sing the Body Electric* before flying to Dayton, Ohio, in early November to meet the band. "My first time on an airplane," he recalled. "I went to the hotel, then went for sound check. I was actually playing on Greg Errico's drums—*huge* drums—and I'm not very good at playing other people's drums. I'm tall, long, and I hate playing somebody else's kit. But anyway, I went and did the sound check for about forty minutes, and I was nervous as hell. I was twenty years old. I don't read music; I'm all ear.

"Then we did the concert. I had never played a room that size. Scared as hell. That was really something. It was a standing ovation. I really hadn't understood how big they were in the jazz market. And afterwards Joe told me how fucking great it was. Joe Zawinul was a character. Oh my God, man! He took a tape off the soundboard and gave me a cassette of it and said, 'This is you. Listen to this. *This is you.*' I didn't even recognize me playing the drums with them. I said, 'No, this is not me.' He said, 'Yeah, that's you!'"[26]

And so launched a whirlwind that found Wilburn playing drums for one of the hottest jazz bands of the day. Within a month, he was in a recording studio in Los Angeles cutting Weather Report's fourth album. "It was a crazy, crazy ride," he marveled years later. "We were doing these college gigs, bouncing all over the country—some were flying, some were by van, some were by car. It was a really great experience, just getting thrown right into the mix at twenty years old. I had never really been out there, doing that kind of work. I was signing autographs—people wanted me to sign albums that I never even played on. And the next thing I knew, we're opening up for Herbie [Hancock], we're opening up for Chick [Corea]. It was just surreal, it really was."[27]

Meanwhile, Wilburn wasn't the only one to make his Weather Report debut in Dayton. The opening act was a college group called the Pyramids. They had a conga player named Bradie Speller who was also part of Cecil Taylor's ensemble at nearby Antioch College, where the pianist was in residency. Whereas Ishmael Wilburn knew little about Weather Report beforehand, Speller was a huge fan, with a strong premonition that he would one day play with them. He bought a copy of *Sweetnighter* earlier that year, and after listening to "Boogie Woogie Waltz," he said to himself, "Okay, that's the song that I'm going to play with Weather Report."[28] When a friend got the Pyramids on the Dayton gig, the stage was set.

After the Pyramids' set, Joe walked up to Speller and, "Look, we just got a brand new drummer, we're breaking him in. I like the way you play, man. When I give you the signal, you bring your shit out on the stage and play."[29]

Speller picks up the story:

> So during the middle of one of the songs, as he's going into "Boogie Woogie Waltz," Joe turned to me and gestured with his head, *come on.* I brought two congas out on the stage, and one of the sound engineers brought me a chair because I didn't bring one out. I started playing and I was right in time with that song and the rest of the music that they did because I had listened to the album every freaking day, practicing to it every freaking day. I knew every note, every lick, every change, the whole nine yards. I could play it by ear.
>
> And here's the thing. I had been telling people on campus that I was going to play with Weather Report. So it was almost like a self-fulfilling prophecy. I didn't know how it was going to happen, but I knew it was going to happen. And then finally, when it did happen, jaws were dropping in that concert hall—mostly students from Antioch who knew me. Even the band that I had been playing with, they were like, Oh. My. God. Is this guy a prophet or what? We thought he was crazy! I was on cloud twenty-eight—way past cloud nine. It was dream accomplished.[30]

Joe invited Speller to Weather Report's next show in Gambier, Ohio.

My friend and I packed up our stuff and drove out there. We got to the gig a little bit late because it was a lot further away from Dayton than we had anticipated. They were already playing, so I just brought my stuff on stage and jumped right in. There was a very mystical, deep cosmic connection with those guys, playing with them that night. As we were leaving the concert hall, we were driving—Joe was in the backseat with Miroslav, and I was in the front seat with Dom Um Romão—I'm listening to them talk in the back, and Miroslav asked Joe, "How do you remember this guy's name?" referring to me. And Joe said, "You never forget a bad motherfucker." Those were his exact words.

So I did several gigs with them. We did Kent State, where Return to Forever opened up for us. That was a disaster. It was excruciatingly painful, even to this day, because Return to Forever knocked the ball out of the park, and then we came on and Butch was playing so strong that he pushed a hole into the kick drum itself. Fortunately, Dom Um had a drum set on stage and he jumped off the percussion and onto the drums. It was not the same, so we had trouble.

The last gig I did with Weather Report, we opened up for Earth, Wind & Fire. It was another college or stadium somewhere in Ohio. And that night we ripped it up. We were on fire. I remember I was sitting next to Joe and he was animated, man. "Come on, God dammit! Play! Play! Play!" I'm playing my ass off, motherfucker, what else you want? I've only been doing this for two years! After the gig, Joe walked up to me and said, "Okay, my man. You did your thing. Thank you very much. We love you. We appreciate you. It's time to go back to school." [31]

•

During the summer, Joe moved his family out to the West Coast, attracted to the same California lifestyle as Wayne. Maxine took the lead in finding a home for the family, and she fell in love with a sprawling white 1924 Spanish Colonial Revival house in Pasadena, a suburb just below the San Gabriel Mountains northeast of Los Angeles. The house was designed by the prominent Southern California architect Wallace Neff, situated at the end of a quiet cul-de-sac on an arroyo overlooking the Rose Bowl. Joe immediately claimed the living room for his own. It had a view of the swimming pool through a large arched window, beyond which were fruit trees and space for a vegetable garden. Soon a pet goat rummaged around the yard. It was perfect for the Zawinuls. When he wasn't on the road, Joe divided his time between the pool and garden—sometimes even sleeping on the outdoor terrace—and the music room just inside.[32]

With Joe and Wayne in Los Angeles, the band's center of gravity moved west

Dom Um Romão gets in some time behind his drum kit during a sound check in Japan in 1973. Photo: Brian Risner.

along with them. This was one of the factors that ultimately led to a parting with Bob Devere. The move also provoked a change of recording venues. Joe and Wayne wanted someplace close to home, so Devere hooked them up with engineer Ron Malo, whose base of operation was Devonshire Sound Studios in North Hollywood, just a twenty-minute drive from their houses.

Malo was a highly respected engineer who made his name at Chess Records, where he engineered most of the label's classic sixties rhythm 'n' blues sides by legendary artists such as Howlin' Wolf, Bo Diddley, Muddy Waters, and Chuck Berry. Malo's sound so impressed the Rolling Stones that when they came to America in 1964, they specifically sought him out, looking to get the same treatment as the American R&B greats. After Chess was sold in 1969, Malo moved to California, working mainly out of Devonshire Sound. It was a small, family-run facility, lacking in pretense, with recording credits going back only a few years. When Brian Risner walked through Devonshire's doors for the first time, he noticed a record cover mounted on one of the walls. It was Billy Joel's breakout album, *Piano Man*, which he had recently recorded there. Joel was so impressed by Malo's work on the album that he gave him the credit "Engineer Par Excellence."

Weather Report settled into Devonshire Sound during the second week of December. Joe and Wayne found it to be a comfortable place to work, and the band was pretty much left to itself, which suited them just fine. The success of *Sweetnighter* made more financial resources available, and they spent ten days at

Devonshire before taking a break for Christmas. The result was the album *Mysterious Traveller*, arguably Weather Report's first masterpiece.

Of course, that assessment depends on whether one likes the direction the band began pursuing with *Sweetnighter*. Like Miles Davis's turn to jazz-rock, some fans of Weather Report's early music didn't come along for the rest of the ride. Nevertheless, from the moment "Nubian Sundance" explodes out of the speakers, there's no denying that *Mysterious Traveller* carves out new territory to stunning effect. Every track is a gem. Wayne called the album "kaleidoscopic," an apt description given that the music evokes joyous celebration ("Nubian Sundance"), mystery ("Scarlet Woman"), funk ("Cucumber Slumber"), sublime grace ("Blackthorn Rose"), and old-world charm ("Jungle Book").

Mysterious Traveller was largely shaped by Joe's vision. He wrote or co-wrote five of the album's seven tunes, while stamping his imprint on the other two. Aided by the expertise of Ron Malo, Zawinul exploited the studio as a creative tool like never before. He took full advantage of the possibilities offered by multitracking, layering additional parts of his own as well as those of other musicians, seventeen of whom were involved in the production. At various points, Joe played acoustic piano, electric piano, tack piano, organ, synthesizer, guitar, kalimba, tamboura, clay drum, melodica, miscellaneous percussion instruments, and sang. He harnessed the full potential of his synthesizers, creating signature sounds on "American Tango" and "Scarlet Woman." He was still using his ARP 2600s, meaning he was limited to playing one note at a time on each of them, but through overdubbing, clever programming, and studio processing, he created a soundscape that was far richer than his previous work.

Joe was certainly pleased. "It was a hell of a record," he said a decade later. "Sure, we had three albums out, and the third album did sell much better than the first two, but the recording company was not all that interested. They knew they had a prestige band and had faith in us, because we won record of the year awards in different countries, and so on. However, at that time, they didn't know what to do with us. *Mysterious Traveller* was another kind of story. All of a sudden we were a power band."[33]

When Weather Report began rehearsing the album's material, it was with the current band—Joe, Wayne, and Miroslav, along with Dom Um Romão and Ishmael Wilburn. But like *Sweetnighter*, Joe had a surprise in store when they got to Devonshire: he brought in another drummer. His old bandmate, Roy McCurdy, knew just who to call. McCurdy had gotten friendly with an impressive young drummer in Cleveland named Skip Hadden, who played in the house band at the Smiling Dog with guitarist Bill DeArango and saxophonist Ernie Krivda. One night while Cannonball Adderley was in town, they were hanging out between sets when McCurdy said, "We got to get you out of this city. You should be out playing." Hadden was open to the idea. "You want to do Frank Zappa or you want to do Weather Report?" Roy asked.

Although McCurdy had connections to both groups (Zappa's keyboardist, George Duke, had taken Joe's place in Adderley's band), Hadden didn't take him seriously. Still, he gave him an answer. "Well, I think there's too much structure in Zappa's stuff for me," he said. "So I think I'd like to do Weather Report." McCurdy nodded and Hadden assumed nothing would come of it. But a couple of months later, as he was getting ready for a gig, Hadden's mother-in-law told him he'd missed a call from "the weatherman." Initially, he wasn't sure what to make of that. "And then it dawned on me that it wasn't the weatherman, but Weather Report. She said, 'Oh, don't worry. They said they'd call back. I told them you're in the shower.'" Hadden continues the story:

> About twenty minutes later Bob Devere called me back and wanted to know if I could send him and Joe a tape so they could hear my playing. I said, "Yeah, I tape every night. But it's not going to be like the Weather Report stuff. Weather Report is way different than what I'm doing, but I'd be glad to send you a tape. Where do I send it?" He said, "No, wait a minute. I'll call you right back." I thought that was the end of it, but a couple of minutes later he called back and said, "The ticket is at the counter. United Airlines, tomorrow morning, nine o'clock."
>
> It was already four or five in the afternoon. I was playing that night, so I did the gig, tore down my stuff, stayed up all night, and just went to the airport and took everything with me to L.A. When I got there, Brian Risner picked me up. He said, "What are you doing here?" He didn't know that I was the drummer that was coming. We drove straight to the studio. I was totally fried. I stayed there for eight hours, and we just did that one tune, and what you hear on the record is from that.[34]

That one tune is "Nubian Sundance," the first cut on *Mysterious Traveller*. It was based on a cassette tape that Joe made in his home music room, and marked the beginning of a new composing paradigm for Zawinul. "I wrote 'Nubian Sundance' in ten minutes, and it's a smoker," he said. "Every bass line, every statement was originally improvised. I rarely sit down and compose. I just turn on the tape recorder and play my instrument, and when a moment of inspiration comes I keep playing, and transcribe from the tape later on. You don't concentrate on one little element or another; just open up and let it all come through you."[35]

Scott Kinsey, a keyboardist who has extended Zawinul's synthesizer legacy as much as anyone, became close to Joe in his later years and helped produce his 2002 album *Faces & Places*. "I've heard the old tapes," Kinsey said. "He would just record to cassettes. Like, if he had a Rhodes and a synthesizer, he would have that coming through a small PA, and he would just use the little microphone built into the cassette recorder and capture it that way, and then transcribe it by ear. So he would improvise by playing and playing, and then he'd listen back and say, 'Right here it got good.'

"And it's uncanny how this would happen, because I've heard certain things that were on *My People* [from 1996]—I heard the whole improvisation, the natural state. And he would be playing along and noodling a little bit, just getting a few ideas. He would stop, then he'd play a little more. And then all of a sudden, maybe twelve minutes in, he would just play the entire tune, and it would come out complete. Then there would be a little pause, maybe an extra two bars that weren't part of it, and then again, it would be another eight bars of complete, beautifully constructed music. And that's the genius of Joe Zawinul; most people can't do that."[36]

It may have taken only ten minutes to conceive "Nubian Sundance," but the band spent days working on it. By the time Hadden arrived, Ishmael Wilburn had already come up with the underlying groove. "I remember one day, we were in L.A. in the studio," Wilburn recalled, "and Joe said, 'Ish, I feel this. You feel this?' And he sang 'COO-LOO-DOON, ca-CHA. COO-LOO-DOON, ca-CHA. COO-LOO-DOON, ca-CHA.' Guys sing music. They'll put a chart in front of you, but they'll sing a phrase, and how you interpret their phrase is how they build songs. So I sat down, and the next thing you know, it was 'BL-BLOOM, chicka-bot. BL-BLOOM, chicka-bot,' almost like a shuffle. You can't imagine rehearsing that song over and over and over. That song is ten minutes long, and he'd start it from the top again. My hands would be cramping up, but I'd keep that groove, keep the feel, keep the pace. But there was something missing to it. He wanted something else, like a swing to it, and that's when he called in Skip Hadden."[37]

Hadden didn't expect to find another drummer when he got there, so whatever expectations he might have had for the session were dashed right away. Plus, the music wasn't what he anticipated. "I was coming more from the Alphonse Mouzon or Eric Gravatt side of it," Hadden said. "I had seen those guys play in the group, so I knew the music from that standpoint. But when I got there, it was totally different. Butch was already there in the studio, so it was a big surprise to me, and he already had his part. He had a really big drum set; I had a small Slingerland jazz kit—eighteen-inch bass drum, really bright cymbals—totally different sound, but it worked with his really deep, fat sound. And I knew right away what I could do. I had to play in between what he was doing. If you listen closely you will notice all of those smaller or lower in the mix bass drum notes. That's what I came up with, and the jazzy kind of hi-hat thing and phrasing to make it flow smoothly and seamlessly forward. But it was always in the context of working within what Butch played. I tried to complete what I was given to work with. I thought, 'Okay, this is the way the thing is dealt to me, so how can I make this work?'"[38]

One of the fascinating things about Weather Report is that the first nine albums each featured a different drummer (or drummers), but they all sound right in the context of the music. Rhythm was extremely important to Joe and he spent a lot of time on it, to the point of being a perfectionist. For years afterward, he bragged about how he taught the drummers various grooves. And yet, the drummers say he didn't tell them specifically what to play, and it was no different here. Instead of giving Wilburn a drum pattern, Joe and Wayne asked him what *he* heard. When Hadden got to the studio, it was the same. "No instructions were ever given about what to play on the tunes," he said. "I remember Joe gave me a lesson about how to set up and how to play the drums [as if Hadden needed such tutoring], but never *what* to play. It was always about the energy."[39]

One way that Joe inspired Hadden's playing was by giving him reference points. "He would play me music," Hadden recalled. "Source recordings from Africa, tribal things with scores of drummers, things like that. But he didn't want those particular beats. He was not playing them for me to cop those grooves and then play them. He just wanted all that energy. And I could do lots of energy. I was told that that was the reason I was there."[40] Later in the week, Joe took the guys to the Whisky to hear George Clinton's Funkadelic and Larry Graham's Graham Central Station, two of the leading funk bands of the day.[41] "It was wild." Hadden recalled. "So he didn't tell you what to play, but he would show you by what he pointed out to you."[42]

Day after day, Joe kept returning to "Nubian Sundance." "They played for hours on this stuff trying to lock in," Risner recalled. "It was crazy—the old 'fall over at the drum kit' kind of stuff. We did tons of takes—tons being more than one, less than a hundred. And just to give it to Ron Malo, he helped *Mysterious Traveller* quite a bit. A lot of that album was done on the editing block just to make the song forms work. But what happened was, they used so much tape on the *Sweetnighter* sessions—because they were building those songs as they were going along—that there was this edict to keep the tape costs down. It sounds crazy now, but if you used twenty-four reels of tape, that's two- to three-thousand dollars in tape costs. So we had a lot of tape from the *Sweetnighter* session sent out—all those failed grooves—and we recorded over some of it. That would be something to hear now."[43]

Malo cut a stereo mix of each day's takes so that Joe could listen to them at home—the equivalent of motion picture dailies. "Ron would say, 'Okay, we just did twelve takes on this—go and listen to them, and the next time we come in, let me know which ones are circle takes so I can go over the other ones,'" Risner said.

If Joe didn't want to keep what was recorded, they would reuse the master tape on another day. "Well, Joe didn't listen to him, and he came back and told Ron, 'Yeah, just go over that stuff. We don't need any of it.'

"So we burned it, right? Gone. So now we're on take twenty-five, take twenty-six. Joe's like, 'I'm just not getting this shit.' He finally goes home and listens to the first tape and comes back and says, 'Hey man, do you still have that take from Tuesday?' And Ron says, 'Uh, no, you said to go over it.' And Joe says, 'Oh, man, that was the shit! Man, did I make a mistake.' So Ron took that two-track, where it was just the groove that these guys had, and spun it back over onto the multitrack. Now we had maybe eight tracks or twelve tracks of a tracking session—stereo drums and keyboard accompaniment—mixed down to two tracks. And so we just started overdubbing on top of it, playing more synths on top of it, playing the bass on top of it, throwing more onto it so it was actually like thirty tracks. If you listen to this thing, it's really dense."[44]

Indeed, "Nubian Sundance" is the densest track Weather Report had produced to that point. Like many of the band's early recordings, Dom Um Romão is an unsung hero, contributing some ferocious triangle and tambourine work, while Joe adds a variety of electronic textures on top of his acoustic piano base. He incorporated crowd noises that led some listeners to believe it was a live recording.[45] In addition to his own singing, Joe brought in five vocalists who call out in celebratory fashion. All of it—the crowd noises, the vocals—was meant to convey a specific story Joe had in mind. "The music isn't about Nubia, really," he told Conrad Silvert. "It's a wedding dance. You can hear the man's voice calling Godinia, and later on she calls him, Accru. And then you hear the people cheering and applauding—that's like a toast, a certain ritual. The moral of the story is that if you meet the right person in your life, you always know from the very beginning."[46]

Hadden also figures prominently in Wayne's title track, which leads off the second side of the LP. It's written primarily in 7/4, with an idiosyncratic groove that relies on the deft combination of Hadden and Wilburn. The foundation of "Mysterious Traveller" is the opening piano riff, which Wayne played in the studio on an upright tack piano (one with nails or tacks affixed to the hammers to brighten its sound) while Joe played the other keyboard parts. (Wayne also played this riff live on stage before switching over to his saxophone midway through the tune.)

Wilburn remembered Wayne working on the composition while the band was on the road. "One day we were packing up in the morning, getting in the car, and Wayne walked up to me and pulled this chart out and he said, 'I've got this in my head.' And as I mentioned, I don't read, so I'm looking at it and I'm going, 'Um . . .' So he started singing it, the opening line. He said it was in seven. I don't think I'd ever played in seven. Maybe five—you know, 'Take Five.' So he sang it, just like Joe did with 'Nubian Sundance,' and I heard a drum track in my head, and that's the groove on it."[47]

As with "Nubian Sundance," Hadden was thrust into the role of adapting to what Wilburn had already come up with. "I asked Joe if there was anything written down, because it was a quirky kind of tune. It had different sections, different time signatures in it. And he said, 'No, I don't have any charts. I don't need you to read any kind of charts. I just want you to do that energy thing. The best readers in the world are in L.A. If I wanted them, I would just write it out and have them play it. But that's not what I want.' So I'm playing the thing, and then later I'm in the booth and I'm listening to the playback with Wayne and I said, 'Oh wow, this is in seven!' They looked at me like, 'What?' I wasn't approaching the music from anything like that. They said they didn't want that."[48]

As far as the tune's construction, Joe took the lead in arranging it even though it was Wayne's composition. ("That didn't have much to do with it," Hadden said, regarding the composer. "Wayne didn't have much to do with what was going on. He didn't really say anything."[49]) The eerie, ethereal sounds that envelop the start and end of the track stem from the same technique as that of "Milky Way," with a healthy dose of studio effects thrown in. "I can't tell you all the tricks on that," Risner said, "but basically, it's the same trick [as 'Milky Way'], but some of it's reversed and slowed down. Wayne would play into the piano, and you'd have these open chords that he would excite the piano with. And some of it was the Rhodes where you'd have the echo on it. So he made a loop out of it that we ran on the machine."[50]

Meanwhile, the band worked out a few other tunes at Devonshire. "American Tango" is Miroslav's only composing credit on *Mysterious Traveller*, which he shared with Joe. It was mostly improvised in the studio, combining a background of Miroslav's with an old melody that Zawinul thought of. As for Wilburn's part, "It was just an easy, laid-back groove; he said a tango. Joe would sit down at the piano and play something—guys mess around in the studio like that, trying to get a feel for something, and you just start playing and coming up with grooves. Whatever he was playing, you hear what you feel complements that." Later, when Joe played him the finished version, Ishmael barely recognized it. "Every time I heard all the overdubs I thought, *God, how do you guys do that?* It was just a straight drum track, and when I came back and listened to it, it was like, wow."[51]

They also tracked another of Miroslav's tunes that didn't appear on the album but was released years later as a bonus track on a Japanese CD reissue. It was never given a proper title, going by the nondescript "Miroslav's Tune." Although it's an excellent example of Hadden and Wilburn working together, the tune has an unfinished quality (probably because it *was* unfinished) and never seems to go anywhere. It sounds out of character with the rest of the album, in part because Vitous wrote string parts for it, which he recorded with a live string ensemble.[52]

Hadden spent ten days in Los Angeles, but the immediate rush of playing with musicians he greatly admired quickly gave way to unease. He was uncomfortable being thrust into a competition with Wilburn, with Joe pushing him to be more aggressive on the drum kit. "They were trying to talk me into blowing this guy away, and that wasn't part of my personality," Hadden said. "I had done other projects with other drummers, and it was not to just go there and dominate the thing, it was to figure a way to make the music better. So it was strange. And it was a little bit frosty because nobody really was talking to me. I don't remember even speaking to Butch the whole ten days I was there." The endless takes also left Hadden uncertain about his playing. "Joe kept telling me, 'Come on, we hear you can play,' because Roy had told him I played like three Tony Williamses. If you listen to the music I did with Bill DeArango, you'll have an idea, because I had lots of chops. But I couldn't do any of it with Ishmael."[53]

Hadden's gut told him his time with Weather Report would be short, a hunch that was confirmed when photographer Norman Seeff showed up to shoot the portraits for the back of the album jacket. "I was there, but they never took my picture. I held the clouds that were on the cardboard that was the backdrop. So I knew it wasn't happening. It was a lesson in humility."[54] A similar lesson occurred when the LP came out. The first thing Hadden noticed was that his name wasn't on the back cover along with the rest of the band.[55] "It turned out that because I wasn't on it, it really didn't have any impact [on Hadden's career] for a long time about what could happen," he said. "I only talked to Joe in the ensuing years a couple of different times, and when I did talk to him, he'd say, 'Oh yeah! You're the 'mysterious traveller!' That was his line for me. So that [not being on the back cover] was part of the gag about me being the 'mysterious traveller.'"[56]

As soon as the sessions were over, Hadden went back to Cleveland and the Smiling Dog. His first gig was the last week of December, working with organist Jimmy Smith. A few months later, Cannonball Adderley came to town. "We were hanging out in the funky dressing room that they had, talking about the experience, because he knew that I had done the thing with Joe. I said I just couldn't get a handle on what the vibe was. And he said, 'Well, maybe this will help: Joe Zawinul worked with me for ten years and he always had something to say after every set. And it was always negative.' So that put a different spin on it for me. There was never good enough; it was that kind of vibe. It really didn't matter what you did, it only had to do with Joe's perception of what it was. And that kind of concreted for me that I always wanted to play with people that I got along with—that I wanted to play with friends. It didn't have to be at that level for me to be able to play."[57]

Nevertheless, Hadden has good memories of his time in L.A. "We went to Joe's house, we had dinner there. He was very nice. Met Max and the kids and all that. When I went home it was going to be Christmas. I hadn't been working, and I didn't have any idea when I'd get paid for this—and it took months to get paid. So Joe gave me cash so I'd have Christmas when I got home. It was a great opportunity. It was like seeing the top of things from a different angle, from all these other perspectives."[58]

•

Midway through the first week of recording, Hadden noticed that Miroslav wasn't in the studio. When he went outside for a breath of fresh air, he saw the bassist sitting in his car. "And it was hot, even though it was December," Hadden recalled. "He was there all day in the parking lot, in his car. I didn't know until later on that he was gone. Nobody was talking to me about any of it."[59]

Like Eric Gravatt, the parting came suddenly. "One afternoon I received a call from Joe Zawinul telling me that he and Wayne had decided that they don't want to work with me anymore," Vitous remembered.[60] No further explanation was offered, but clearly the issue had been building since *Sweetnighter*. When Greg Errico joined the band, the musical direction was even more apparent. Miroslav hung in there, attempting to meld his own musicality with the band's new approach. "I was trying to march with that and see what was happening, see how I could play with this, but it really wasn't going for me," he said. "It was like the spirit didn't want me to touch this."[61]

Fundamentally, he didn't want to give up his role as an equal voice alongside Wayne and Joe. According to Zawinul, Miroslav went so far as to suggest that they hire another bassist to hold down the bottom, freeing him of that chore, but Joe wasn't interested. "Why don't we get one bassist who can do all of that?" Zawinul retorted.[62] Ultimately, it became a test of wills. "There was really no confrontation or blowup between him and me," Miroslav said. "He wanted to control the music, and I was controlling the music with my bass playing; that was the problem."[63]

There's no question that Miroslav played a significant role in shaping the band's music, but now Joe wanted the bass to provide what he called a base or root. "Miroslav didn't have what we needed," Zawinul later said. "We needed a fundamental bass player with imagination, a bass player who holds the band together. A band has to have bottom and he didn't have that—he should have been a guitar player. He could play, believe me, he's a helluva musician, but he didn't have what I call a bass concept."[64]

Miroslav sat in his car that day, numbed by what had just happened. "I was devastated," he later admitted. "I was in shock for about two years. There was a lot of drugs around, so I was taking coke. I was drinking pretty heavily. I couldn't really deal with it at the time. It was just too much. It took me two, almost three years to get out of California and start all over again in New York."[65]

Miroslav's financial difficulties were exacerbated by the fact that he wasn't receiving his royalties from Shoviza and Barometer Music. "I was having a really tough time with my family," Vitous said. "They were shutting off the lights because I couldn't pay the bills sometimes."[66] Eventually, he cornered Joe at a festival and pleaded his case. "Look, man, we've been friends for a long time, and we've been cooperating together, so there's no reason why I have to go to court to get my money."[67] Joe realized that Miroslav was right and made arrangements for him to receive monthly payments for the money he was owed, which according to Vitous totaled over $40,000.

Given Miroslav's perceived commercialization of Weather Report's music, the first album he made on his own seemed an odd choice. *Magical Shepherd* is replete with funky grooves and pop-like vocals by rock singer Cheryl Grainger.[68] Vitous ignores his acoustic bass in favor of the electric, and plays an unusual combination electric bass and guitar with two necks. On top of that, he overdubs a variety of synthesizers and was one of the first instrumentalists to play a guitar synthesizer. Perhaps Miroslav took to heart Joe's admonition that he should be a guitar player, because he solos on that instrument or one of its relatives on every track.

The album was poorly received. Critics had a hard time reconciling it with Miroslav's previous work. "Something is wrong," wrote *Down Beat*'s Russell Shaw in his two-and-a-half star review. "Vitous is a bass player of uncommon dexterity and skill, yet he avoids all but the elementary here." Shaw described Miroslav as "a man in search of an idiom. As a funkmeister, he fails miserably."[69] Another album, *Miroslav*, fared no better.

Ironically, when Vitous performed live, he encountered the same problem that Joe identified with Weather Report. On records, he was able to overdub himself and fulfill as many roles as he wanted, but live performance was another matter. "There is a basic role for the bass in the whole music spectrum," Miroslav acknowledged not long after *Magical Shepherd* was released. "When you have a band you need bottom as well as harmony and melody. There are a few people that have turned the bass into a melodic instrument. I, personally, run into a problem when I do change to a lead instrument with a bow, say. There is a bottom missing. As a result, I am getting another bass player to play the bottom for me, the basic bass."[70]

Miroslav returned to his artistic roots in 1978 when ECM label head Manfred Eicher invited him to record an album with Terje Rypdal and Jack DeJohnette. Titled *Terje Rypdal / Miroslav Vitous / Jack DeJohnette*, the album is a highlight of Miroslav's discography and includes an exquisite rendition of "Will." Subsequently, Eicher agreed to record Miroslav's own group, "and we started a beautiful relationship," Vitous said. "When I started working with ECM, it sort of confirmed in the public's eye that I am again playing acoustic bass, and that I'm playing my music rather than trying to do some commercial stuff."[71] He never returned to the funk forays of his seventies albums.

•

Making it possible to push Miroslav out of the band was another bass player that Wayne and Joe heard that fall. His name was Alphonso Johnson—a tall, lean young man whom they referred to as "Slim." He was part of trumpeter Chuck Mangione's band when they opened for Weather Report in October 1973, the only bill they ever shared. As it happened, the show took place in Johnson's hometown of Philadelphia, making it a kind of homecoming for him. There couldn't have been a better platform for Alphonso to display his talents.

"I was in one of those special moments when you're not only playing in your hometown, but all your high school buddies are there, and your mom is there," Johnson recalled. "And either everything is going to go totally wrong, or you release yourself and something special happens. So it was one of my best nights with the band, and after I finished taking this bass solo, I glanced off to my left and there was Wayne Shorter standing there. So then I got really nervous. I'm a big fan of Wayne's music; have been for ages. After we finished our set, I went backstage and asked the promoter to introduce us. He took me to Wayne's dressing room, and after a couple of minutes of conversation that didn't make sense, Wayne asked me if I'd ever been to California. I said no, I'd like to go, and he just kind of shook his head. And then I met Joe, and he was the opposite of Wayne, more direct. He said, 'What are you doing next month? We want you to come out and audition.'"[72]

It took a couple of months to arrange, but in January Johnson traveled to Los Angeles, still under the impression he would be auditioning. "I thought it was going to be in a rehearsal hall setting, but when I showed up, the road manager said, 'Just catch a cab to the studio.' So I went to Devonshire and we just started cutting tracks. They would pull up tracks—some of them still had Miroslav playing bass—and I would just add my thing. And some worked out, some didn't. So I guess when they went in to mix, they would decide which tracks were the best ones to use for the recording."[73]

Nearly twenty-three years old, Johnson started on his musical path at the age of nine. As the tallest youngster in class, he was handed an acoustic bass, an event that changed his life. Variety was the watchword of Johnson's early musical years. "I always listened to a lot of music, but in the very beginning I listened to the music that my brothers and sisters would play around the house, and that was mostly the doo-wop groups like Little Anthony and the Imperials. I listened to a lot of Motown back then, and that's where my roots really lie. When I got to school, I started playing classical music in order to learn to play the upright bass, and then I started getting into whatever was on the radio. At that time there was a station in Philadelphia that broadcast from Temple University, and they played everything—Coltrane, Hendrix, Otis Redding. It was a great time for me because all the stuff they played I loved."[74]

Johnson's professional career began in earnest the day he graduated from high school. "I was with a group called the Majestics. I got my diploma, gave my mom a hug and a kiss, and jumped in the car and we drove ninety miles to Atlantic City. That was my first professional gig. Never looked back. That was a great moment for me, to know that I could do what I really wanted to do right out of high school. I can't describe the feeling."[75] After stints backing vocalists and working with the Philadelphia funk-jazz group, Catalyst, Johnson hit the road with Woody Herman's Thundering Herd. In 1973, he joined Mangione, with whom he recorded the popular album *Land of Make Believe*, laying down the memorable bass riff on the title track.

Johnson was a perfect fit for where Joe and Wayne were going. He was funky, but in a melodic way. He could hold down a groove without seeming to ever repeat himself. He had a strong harmonic sense, honed when Mangione, who doubled on piano, soloed on his horn, leaving Alphonso to fill out the harmonic content. In short, Johnson was the linchpin that set Weather Report on its mature course, leading to everything that followed. "Alphonso Johnson had a lot," Zawinul said. "He was young, he was bright, he was disciplined, and he could lay down a groove that hurt, and that's what I wanted."[76] Years later, after some of the best players of the electric bass had passed through his bands, just the mere mention of Johnson's name could cause Joe to pause mid-thought and exclaim "Ohh! He had the *funk*, man! He was the funkiest of 'em all—even more than Jaco."[77]

"We liked the way he set a groove," Wayne said. "We used to call it a 'loping' kind of groove. And we liked *him*, as a person. He was *well mannered*. He was tall and he carried his height well. He didn't have a problem with self-esteem—you know, if you're too tall you kind of curve over when you stand up, trying to get lower, hiding. He didn't hide behind the bass, the instrument, or hide behind being a musician."[78]

In addition to his playing, Johnson brought in some musical ideas that immediately paid dividends in the form of the atmospheric tune "Scarlet Woman." Alphonso explained how it came about: "I was working on this song, and I had a pretty definitive melody, but it didn't have a direction; it was kind of like a ballad. So I played it for Joe and Wayne, and of course Joe had his own idea about what the chords and harmony should be. Which was great for me, because who am I to tell Joe Zawinul what to play? And it just so happened that what he came up with was perfect."[79]

Joe latched onto Johnson's four-note descending melody and went from there, eliminating the other sections of the tune and paring it down in Miles Davis fashion. "Al Johnson brought the melody in, the first melody," Zawinul said. "That's the only thing he brought in. I put in the harmony, the bridge, and I arranged it, and Wayne Shorter played the beautiful solo on it."[80] Wayne's solo only lasts for ten measures or twenty-five seconds, but it was considered so crucial to the end result that he received co-composer credit with Joe and Alphonso.

Wayne's economical playing led to a sense that he was being overshadowed by Zawinul's orchestration skills, but his contributions went a long way toward distinguishing Weather Report from its jazz-rock peers. In describing how they worked together, Joe once referred to himself as "the base-giver" and Wayne as "a great, great painter." "I constructed the building, and he painted it. I don't mean that in a derogatory way; that's how it was. Miles often said to me, 'You don't really need Wayne.' I said, 'You're wrong, man.' And I knew he was wrong because, when you hear it like that, as just *blip-blop* on a saxophone . . . but those *blip-blops* were very fuckin' important, you know what I mean?"[81]

Wayne provides much more than *blips* and *blops* on "Blackthorn Rose," an intimate, exquisite duet that he performed with Joe. The tune was written by Wayne, but his manuscript was merely the starting point for what transpired in the studio. "That song—what you hear on record is not what's on paper," Johnson said. "The paper was like a foundation for what Joe and Wayne did and how they interacted with each other. I didn't even realize they were recording. I was in the studio packing up my gear, and I could feel the presence of the genius that was going on. So I stopped, and I just sat down right next to the piano while they were recording. They had kind of blocked everything out once they started on this journey together. It's amazing. I looked at the music, and I just went wow; it was nothing like what happened."[82]

While Wayne's playing left many of his fans wanting more, Weather Report's emphasis was never on virtuosity for virtuosity's sake. From the beginning, all of the band members played to serve the needs of the music, which Joe once described as "a soundtrack for the mind."[83] As Wayne explained at the time of *Mysterious Traveller*'s recording, "You don't need to have other people recognize your virtuosity, because instinctively you know your own worth. Life consists of individuals and groups, and we're more interested in doing things as a group. And we're aware of our responsibilities within the group."[84]

Blue Note released Wayne's 1970 recording, *Moto Grosso Feio*, at about the same time that *Mysterious Traveller* came out, prompting comparisons between the two. *Down Beat* ran a dual review of the albums in which Marv Hohman ranked Wayne's solo effort above Weather Report's, in part because *Moto Grosso Feio* was "Shorter's show." Taken together, the two albums "showcase the steady growth of Wayne Shorter into the most authoritative soprano sax force since [John] Coltrane," Hohman wrote.[85] After Coltrane revived the soprano's use in jazz, many saxophonists took it up, including Joe's old employer, Cannonball Adderley. But in the wake of Trane's death in 1967, Wayne emerged with the most individual sound. His tone was pure and sensuous, his playing replete with an expressive lyricism that was reminiscent of Miles. Besides, as one Weather Report engineer dryly noted, "Wayne is one of the few people on the planet that can actually play a soprano sax in tune."[86]

If Wayne wasn't soloing in the traditional sense, neither did Joe solo on synthesizer. In fact, a true synth solo doesn't appear on a Weather Report record until 1975's *Tale Spinnin'*. In that regard, Joe set himself apart. By the time of *Mysterious Traveller*, several prominent jazz pianists were using synthesizers, the best-known (aside from Joe) being Herbie Hancock, Chick Corea, and Jan Hammer. But their individual approaches differed in significant ways, in part dictated by their choice of instruments.

Corea and Hammer played the Minimoog. An important performance element of the Minimoog was the pair of wheels next to the keyboard. The leftmost wheel allowed the player to bend the pitches of notes. Corea and Hammer were masters at using it to play in a style similar to lead guitarists. Instead of a wheel, the ARP 2600 had a knob for bending notes, which in practice was much harder to use. Although Joe once took a Minimoog on the road, he never warmed to it.[87] "I didn't like the sound of it," he later confirmed. "A few people played it, and I didn't like the way they played the instrument. Jan Hammer was a great player, and there were a few. But I always thought the sound had nothing. They all sounded alike. They all played great and all that, but in general it was one sound. The sound had nothing from the person."[88]

"We carried it for a while," Brian Risner remembered. "I brought it out to replace the Farfisa because I was still carrying it with the Rhodes and ARPs. At one point I said, 'Well, let's check out the Minimoog. It's got some neat shit going on with it, bass lines and stuff.' But the Minimoog was a different thing. It didn't have the graphic programmability like the ARPs. Basically, you kind of set it up for one sound and that was it. And as it turned out, Joe just didn't dig the filtering as much. And really, it was a solo instrument when it comes down to it. Chick soloed on it. George [Duke] did. Jan did. And that became their thing. Your expression was in how well you played the pitch bend, and Joe was not about that at all. He was about orchestration and timbre, and how you stack the voices. If he soloed, it was how it fit within the orchestration, not how fast and cool it was."[89]

Like Joe, Herbie Hancock played ARP instruments, including the 2600 and its newer, smaller brothers: the Odyssey and Soloist. Hancock also made frequent use of the Hohner Clavinet, an electrically amplified clavichord that was prominent in funk and soul music, Stevie Wonder's "Superstition" being the definitive example. On *Head Hunters*, Hancock heavily used electric keyboards, but his synthesizer parts often seem ornamental to the music, whereas Joe's were thoroughly

ARP Instruments advertisement that appeared in various music magazines in the mid-1970s. The set-up was created specifically for the ad. On stage, the 2600 keyboards were stacked on Joe's Rhodes electric piano. Courtesy the Alan R. Pearlman Foundation.

organic, to the point that the sounds are inseparable from the compositions. This was perhaps the most compelling aspect of Joe's synthesizer style, and it went a long way toward preventing his playing from sounding dated in future years.

Joe brought one other tune to Devonshire. Like "Nubian Sundance," "Jungle Book" is based on an improvisation that he made at home on his piano. It was the first piece that he recorded at the Pasadena house.[90] As he played, his youngest son, Ivan, pestered him to read from Rudyard Kipling's *The Jungle Book*. Despite Ivan squirming beneath the piano to get his father's attention, Joe maintained his focus for several minutes. When he finally turned off the recorder, he had improvised another complete composition.

"Jungle Book" was a special piece for Joe, largely because his original improvisation, with Ivan crying in the background, is preserved on the released track (whereas the cassette recording of "Nubian Sundance" was transcribed so that it could be reproduced in the studio). In other words, it is a pure representation of what transpired during a moment of transcendent inspiration. Joe wasn't a religious person, but his ability to improvise in this way led him to "trust in some creative power up there somewhere higher than ourselves."[91]

Joe's tape was made on a small cassette recorder that Brian Risner described as "a little mono thing that you would buy at the drug store now for $20. It wasn't even stereo. I remember him bringing in that tape. His kids were there and he thought, 'Man, this is the greatest thing!' And it wasn't a very good recording, in an ambient room. But it was beautiful; you've got all the emotion. We put it over on quarter-inch tape and did whatever we could."[92] Once the improvisation was transferred to multitrack, Joe went to work at Devonshire, overdubbing himself playing guitar, sitar, and a variety of percussion instruments. He wrote woodwind parts that were played by Don Ashworth, a studio musician who was part of *The Tonight Show* band. It is a tour de force performance that is one of Zawinul's finest works.

•

By the end of January, the band was on the road again, playing the college circuit. The lineup included Ishmael Wilburn and Alphonso Johnson, though the latter remained uncertain of his status. "I still didn't know if I had the gig, even though I was recording on the record," Johnson recalled. "And right after that session there were some dates. I think the day before, Bob Devere called and asked if I was available. But again, I was never told that I had the gig."[93]

Johnson's first performance with the band was an eye-opener. "I got slaughtered," he recalled, chuckling at the memory. "Joe just blew me out of the water. I mean, it was unbelievable how loud he was. I heard them in Philadelphia when we opened for them, but to be on stage was a whole different thing. I had one double-15 cabinet—the Kustom cabinets with the Naugahyde tuck-and-roll sparkle covers—and I was so loud that the bass was distorting and you *still* couldn't hear me. It was like the louder I turned up, the smaller my sound got. I was really unprepared. After the first couple of gigs, I went out and got some gear and Brian Risner said, 'No, no, we don't want more gear on stage. Let me handle it.' Because you could just see that it was going to start escalating. Pretty soon we would be so loud on stage that we would be competing with the house sound. That's when the band really started growing and blossoming sound-wise, and Brian really contributed a lot towards that."[94]

With their work at Devonshire behind them, the original plan was for *Mysterious Traveller* to consist of six tunes: "Nubian Sundance," "American Tango," and "Jungle Book" on side one, with "Mysterious Traveller," "Blackthorn Rose," and "Scarlet Woman" filling side two. We know this because that sequence was printed on early inner sleeves of the LP. However, it turned out that there would be one more addition to the album. In late February, the band had a gig in Westport, Connecticut and booked a day at Connecticut Recording Studio. "I think Joe and Wayne were thinking, *Hey, the band is starting to feel pretty good; let's go in and do something*," Johnson recalled. Perhaps cognizant of how the band sounded with Bradie Speller, Joe also invited an old friend, Ray Barretto, to play congas.

On the spot, the group collectively produced one of the funkiest tunes Weather Report ever recorded. "We were in the studio, testing all the lines and everything, and I started messing around with this bass line," Johnson recalled. "And before I knew it, Joe was playing along with me. I just saw him look inside the studio and put his finger down—you know, to start recording—and that's what came out of it: 'Cucumber Slumber.' Joe and Wayne pretty much improvised the melodies. I think Joe came up with [the main] melody, and then Wayne came up with [the melody part starting around 2:08]. And the solos are classic. For a guy who's not known to be a funky player, Wayne's solo is one of the funkiest solos on soprano I've heard in *years*. It's just masterful."[95]

Ever since his first sessions at Devonshire Sound, Wayne and Joe's freewheeling methods had struck Johnson as unusual, but this was on another level. "We just went right to the studio, which was kind of new for me. I'm used to rehearsing and preparing everything, but it really opened up my eyes to a whole new way of capturing music and recording. Because you capture the spontaneity and then you build on *that*. What a lot of groups or bands would consider mistakes, Joe and Wayne saw as opportunities, and they would exploit them. And it would be something simple, a little nuance—they didn't make a big deal out of it. And I went wow, that's pretty hip, you know?"[96]

With "Cucumber Slumber" in the can, Columbia move quickly to get *Mysterious Traveller* into record stores that spring. It was Weather Report's most powerful statement to date, and Columbia had hopes that it would go gold like Herbie Hancock's *Head Hunters*. That didn't happen, but Joe later claimed that the album eclipsed 400,000 units sold, so they were getting closer.[97] *Rolling Stone*'s Bob Palmer called *Mysterious Traveller* "far and away Weather Report's most complete and perfect statement,"[98] and at the end of the year *Down Beat*'s readers voted it their album of the year.

•

In March, a young man named Shawn Hart took over Weather Report's road manager duties. In that role, Hart wore many hats, but his main job was getting Weather Report on stage, on time, every night. With Bob Devere booking gigs all over the United States, it wasn't easy. "It seemed to me that we were doing twenty-eight dates in a month, and the logistics required a lot of flying," Hart recalled. "Many times I had to pass twenty or forty bucks to a baggage handler to get our gear on a plane as extra baggage, because we'd never make it to the gig if we had to truck it there." At one point, Hart was sure they'd miss a gig when the band was delayed for ninety minutes after airport security officials mistook Dom Um Romão's berimbau for a weapon. It didn't help that Romão's pronunciation made it sound like he was saying "beer-im-bomb."[99]

Another time Weather Report had a show on the same night as the Muhammad Ali–George Foreman fight known as the "Rumble in the Jungle." Joe was a huge boxing fan, and much to Hart's consternation, he determined that the fight was more important than the gig, so the entire band watched it in an auditorium via closed circuit TV before hitting the stage forty minutes late.

Aside from logistical snafus, the memory that Hart retains most strongly is how daring the band was musically. "I've worked for a lot of startup companies in the publishing business, and I never saw a creative ensemble take risks like Weather Report—and they did so nightly," Hart said. "When they prepared to come on stage, they were like a five-member, highly competitive fighting team. Backstage, Joe would inflate his chest with deep inhalations of the surrounding atmosphere and roll his head on his shoulders like a boxer. He brought that competitive and combative nature to every show.

"And the demands that he made on the rest of the band were so instrumental to their success. The motif of the band was 'excellence at all costs,' even to your ego. Until they lifted off, musically, there was so much intrinsic tension with Joe forever forcing the issue. The envelope was never large enough for Joe, and he pushed it every night. I often thought he badgered Wayne—'Wayne, don't noodle, man!'—to make him respond, but in the process they created this unique and elevated sound. And it didn't always work. I saw the backs of a lot of patrons heading for the exits on those rare occasions when the musicality wasn't equal to the effort and they just couldn't find one another."[100]

During the gigs, Hart walked the room, estimating the crowd size (the band's payment was often predicated on how full the house was) and evaluating the sound from different vantage points for Brian Risner. Eventually, he ended up next to the stage, where he watched the band as well as the crowd reactions. Hart particularly remembers how physical Ishmael Wilburn played. "I couldn't believe the perspiration that would pour off this guy during a show," Hart said. "He just completely committed to delivering the drive for this band. When they did 'Nubian Sundance' or 'Boogie Woogie Waltz,' I would watch from stage left or stage right and I could almost see the weight dropping from his frame. He was a big man and I'll bet he lost eight pounds a night playing the music." So it was a surprise to Hart when Joe told him to send Wilburn home. "I remember thinking, what was it about this guy that was inadequate? I didn't understand it."[101]

Zawinul was always hard on drummers, and Wilburn caught some of that flack. "Joe was a taskmaster," Wilburn acknowledged. "Some nights we would have a great concert, standing ovation and so on, and I'm saying, 'All right, I'm going to play just like that the next night.'" But keeping it the same wasn't Weather Report's way, and Joe would challenge Wilburn on a nightly basis. "He'd get up on his feet, live, on stage, and come up in front of me and tell me, 'Give it! Give it! Come on!' He was not afraid to do that. It could get annoying, especially when you're trying your best."[102]

Wayne tried to get him into chanting, but Wilburn took his cues from fellow Philadelphian Alphonso Johnson, who was just a few years older, but far more experienced. "I enjoyed playing with him," Wilburn said. "He was so accomplished. I was unused to traveling, living out of a suitcase, so I mimicked his professionalism. A bass player and a drummer need to have a feel, and he would encourage me, show me different things when we were going through rehearsals and stuff. Or when it was one of those moments when I'm like, 'Oh my God, Joe's losing it,' his calmness would help me."[103]

With Wilburn back in Philadelphia, the band tried out drummers, one after another. "We were changing drummers every two or three days," Johnson recalled. "Wayne and Joe just weren't happy. I mean, they were flying guys in, and they would know after the first two bars if he was happening. Sometimes Wayne could tell just by watching the guy set his drums up. 'No, Joe, I think we need to get on the phone.' So Joe would have all these numbers. He would be upstairs meeting the new drummer, and Wayne would be downstairs telling the guy from last night that he's going to have to go home."[104]

It wasn't that the drummers weren't good. "It's like they were all specialists," Johnson said. "They focused on one thing and did it really well, like a heart surgeon. But after playing with someone like Tony Williams or Jack DeJohnette, or even Eric Gravatt—they're masters. I could see that Wayne and Joe's ears were yearning to hear something on a broader scope, so we just kept searching and searching. Eventually, I think they got burnt out on changing because the material—the book—wasn't growing. We would pick songs that at least we could have fun playing, and all the drummer had to do was keep up. Finally, Joe said, 'You know, we're going to have to nurture one of these guys,' and Wayne agreed. And that's what they tried to do."[105]

11 Tale Spinnin'

If we have a cult following, it's getting bigger.

— Joe Zawinul

AFTER ISHMAEL WILBURN'S DEPARTURE, the band didn't work much, which was probably a good thing considering they didn't have a permanent drummer. But with a two-week tour lined up for July 1974, followed by an extensive performing schedule through November, finding a permanent drummer took on more urgency. Furthermore, *Mysterious Traveller* was moving up the charts and it was time to retool the live book and incorporate some new material. So Joe and Wayne came up with a novel way to find their next drummer. In June, they gathered at Bob Devere's Long Island home, where they holed up for a week, auditioning as many drummers as it took until they found one who could hang with the rest of the group.

The Deveres lived in an older center hall colonial in the hamlet of Port Washington. Upon the band's arrival, they cleared the furniture out of the living room except for the family's upright piano and set up their own equipment in its place. The Devere children were temporarily farmed out to friends, and the band members moved into their upstairs bedrooms. It was a retreat and audition rolled into one. Drummers came in during the day, while Joe and Brian Risner tiptoed downstairs at night to fool around with the synthesizers. Bob's wife, Jerri, made sure everyone was comfortable and arranged for catered meals in the dining room. That's not to say they didn't get out of the house from time to time. One drummer who tried out played in the pit band of the Broadway musical, *The Magic Show,* starring magician Doug Henning. He got everyone tickets, so they all went into the city to see it one evening.

Finding a drummer with all the qualities that Joe sought was going to be a challenge. Ideally, it would be someone with the improvisational abilities of Eric

Gravatt, the pocket of Greg Errico, and the youthful vitality of Ishmael Wilburn. Joe also wanted someone malleable. The best-known drummers, like Tony Williams or Jack DeJohnette, wouldn't do, he said, because they would be too strong in their own ideas.[1]

Peter Erskine wouldn't join the band until 1978, but his description of what Weather Report demanded of a drummer was applicable here as well. "They wanted me to always be composing, to be rhythmically creative, to never play unimaginatively, but not to play miscellaneously," he said. "It had to be clear, it had to be solid and strong—in other words, it had to be supportive. It's like the thing Zawinul said years ago about Weather Report—'we always solo and we never solo.' And that's the way the drums had to be: always creative but never just bashing all over the place or taking up too much musical space."[2]

One young man who made his way to the Deveres' living room was Darryl Brown. Despite having just turned legal drinking age, Brown was already experienced, having done tours with Natalie Cole and Grover Washington Jr. At the time, he was back in his hometown of Philadelphia working in a local band named Good God, which opened for Weather Report a couple of times at the end of 1973. He must have made an impression, because some months later he got a call from Alphonso Johnson inviting him to audition.

"There were drummers everywhere," Brown remembered. "I don't even know how many they auditioned, but there was a rumor that they had at least a couple hundred or more. [Joe said there were nine or ten.] Anyway, I sat down at the drums—and I remember this vividly—I looked and I saw what I considered to be legends—especially Joe Zawinul and Wayne Shorter—and Dom Um Romão, who I had admired coming up because he used to play with Brasil '66.

"So, I said to myself, 'Don't play it like it's an audition. You've got a chance to play with these great musicians, so just play to make music.' I treated it like a recording that, when played back, would be very musical and you would enjoy, which was not a typical approach for me. Usually I would try to impress people with my technique and things I could do. So I did that and the music felt good, and things seemed to go well. When I finished playing, I remember Joe coming over to me and saying, 'Man, you've got some big ears.'"[3]

Coming from one of his idols, Brown was gratified by that comment, but he went back to Philadelphia having no idea how he fared against the others who auditioned. Two days later, he got a call from Bob Devere. "Get your drums, get your clothes, and come to New York. We're going to rehearse. You've been hired."[4]

One of Brown's earliest gigs with the band was at the Bottom Line, a relatively new venue in Greenwich Village that held about four hundred people. At least that many packed the club on each of Weather Report's two nights. The *New York Times* sent critic John Rockwell to the club, and he found that Brown "seemed fully settled in." Rockwell observed how much Weather Report was then relying on groove, with Brown and Dom Um Romão providing an "infectiously steady beat" for Joe and Wayne to improvise on. The result, Rockwell wrote, was one of "dense excitement." It "may not be to everybody's taste, but it makes a genuine impact in its compulsively intense way."[5]

The next week, Weather Report played the Lisner Auditorium in Washington, D.C., a 1,500-seat venue on the campus of George Washington University. Despite its size, the band had no trouble filling the auditorium for two shows with what the *Washington Post* called "the sort of people who would blend right in with the crowd at a War or Led Zeppelin concert."[6] In those days, the band generally led off with "Nubian Sundance," while one could count on "Boogie Woogie Waltz" as the climactic closer. In between, audiences were almost sure to hear a piece or two from *Mysterious Traveller*, an acoustic piano rendition of Duke Ellington's "Sophisticated Lady," and highly improvisational takes on "In a Silent Way" and "Doctor Honoris Causa." Other tunes that might be played on any given night included "It's About That Time," "Directions," and "125th Street Congress."

A bootleg recording from the Lisner shows how the band didn't always hew to form. They began not with "Nubian Sundance," but with a synthesizer introduction backed by a tape of "Milky Way." It soon segued to the main theme of "Manolete" from *Sweetnighter*, then a full version of "American Tango," before closing with a brief reprise of "Manolete" and "Milky Way." "Cucumber Slumber" followed, then a percussion and synthesizer duet led to a medley of "Doctor Honoris Causa" and "Directions." Another percussion interlude gave way to Joe's acoustic piano solo, which also served as the introduction to "In a Silent Way" and "It's About That Time." The closer, as usual, was "Boogie Woogie Waltz."

Dom Um Romão's percussion solos continued to be a highlight of Weather Report shows. He didn't adhere to any routine in his song introductions and interludes, which could last several minutes and often wound up involving the entire band. He had gongs, flutes, whistles, and assorted other percussion gear, all of which he used effectively. "It may be difficult to imagine a creative solo on Chinese gong and Indian cowbells, but seeing is believing," wrote one observer.[7]

Darryl Brown was as impressed by Romão as anyone. "Dom Um was simply amazing. He was pretty much the spices and flavoring of the band. He sounded like a Brazilian forest, if you can imagine being in a forest and hearing all of the natural sounds of the animals and the water. The atmosphere he created for the band was just unbelievable. He taught me a lot about the subtleties of percussion instruments. And of course, he was most famous for playing the berimbau, and he was a master of it. He had a gift for showmanship. He would just light up the room, particularly when he would go down the steps, off the stage, and into the audience, going row to row, playing that berimbau. It was just incredible. I mean, I'm on the stage and I'm looking at him out there, and it's like I'm at a concert myself. That's how it was with him."[8]

Joe and Wayne surely kept the band's newcomers on their toes. With no pattern for how the tunes would develop live, the challenge was to listen and react. "They could make a ninety-degree turn at any minute, so you really had to have a big ear to play in that band," Johnson said. "And a lot of it was instinctive. It's not like you hear, *Oh, okay, they just moved up a major third*. It's like they moved up a major third, but the feeling changed, or the tone changed—it's not a continuation of where we were. A lot of it was body language and reading moods, and you learn to do that after you're with somebody on the road for a while. That had more to do with it than anything."[9]

Brown's ability to roll with these changes was a big reason he got the drum chair. "I think that was something the band heard in me when I auditioned with them, because that's exactly what they did. They weren't doing the songs like you were reading a chart. We would play a song, and in the middle of it they would come in with the melody from 'American Tango' or something like that—just unbelievable how they would move around. And they would change keys and put melodies on different rhythms that were happening to myself, Al, and Dom Um.

"'Directions' was pretty awesome," Brown continued. "That was loud and crazy—one of those tunes where you never knew where you were going to end up. It was the ultimate improvisational experience. In fact, I think that's how Wayne enjoyed it the most. Because I remember one time when Joe was starting to get more exact about who should do what when, and Wayne said it felt really good when we were just winging it. And that's all he said. He would kinda say something like that, or he would speak through metaphors. On the road it was more formatted, except for songs like 'Directions,' or some songs where they would just kind of really let it go with improvisation, and wherever it ended up being, it ended up being."[10]

Like Ishmael Wilburn, Darryl Brown received plenty of Joe's drumming advice. "Yeah, I did, very much so. And sometimes I have to admit it was challenging, because we would work out things in rehearsal, and then we'd get to perform it, and he would want something different. And it wasn't always real clear exactly what he wanted. So that was a challenging part for sure."[11]

Also like Wilburn, Brown gravitated to Alphonso Johnson. "Alphonso was close to me in age, so we were kind of like buddies; similar life experiences, particularly being from Philadelphia. Al was very unique— a tremendously influential bassist. He would get this crystal-clear tone on the bass at the most amazing volumes. I'm talking about Led Zeppelin–loud. And at the same time, even though he was that articulate and that clean, he could create a tremendous feel of funk. It

Weather Report in 1974. Left to right: Dom Um Romão, Alphonso Johnson, Wayne Shorter, Joe Zawinul, and Darryl Brown. Photo: © Echoes / Redferns / Getty Images.

sounds like they wouldn't even go together, the tone I'm describing and the funk and blues and jazz that he played, but he did it so well. And he could go from there to whisper time—just utter silence. And then he would play some really subtle, lyrical stuff.

"One of the things that I really enjoyed about Alphonso—and he did it the best, I think—is that he created tremendous room for interplay. He was the master of this. It was almost as though he had manuscript paper, and he was writing out bass parts as he went along. And if you looked at the tape you would find big gaps between the notes, and as a result of this, the music always breathed. It was never cluttered with a lot of notes, with the musicians fighting for space. It sparked a lot of creativity from me because of the room that existed. Listening to him influenced me a lot on the drums—playing with space and not just being all over the drums all the time. I'll never forget that."[12]

Joe also experimented with two drummers on the bandstand. None of them stuck, which Brown took as a good sign. "Yeah, that was very uplifting for me, and motivating. I think it made me a lot stronger as a drummer, because there were times when they did things like that, but they didn't tell me. Almost out of the blue one day, another drummer showed up who I hadn't met, which turned out to be Ishmael Wilburn, and he did a couple of concerts with us. And then Joe decided to go back to one drummer, which was me. And it was kind of like that. These guys were twice my age, and I didn't really understand everything that was going on with their thoughts and processes. But it was an invaluable experience, and I just welcomed it and embraced it and just tried to give it my best."[13]

Perhaps the most memorable episode of the one-and-done drummers occurred in October at the University of Miami's Gusman Auditorium. "I think the craziest night was when one guy was flown in from Switzerland, because Joe said he was an African drummer," Brian Risner recalled. "He came straight from the airport and he turned out to be white and when he set up he asked for an electric cord and proceeded to put Christmas tree lights on his clear Fibes drum kit!"[14]

"For some reason he was under the opinion that he had the job," Brown said. "He even came over with his family. So, same thing, that didn't work out, and they sent him back. So these things were happening and at one point I didn't like it so much, because it told me they potentially had eyes for somebody else. But at the same time, as these guys were being rejected, I kept saying, 'Well, I must be doing something right,' because they've got to be comparing them to me. And obviously, if a guy came along that they thought was doing a better job, they would have probably hired him."[15]

Nevertheless, the constant churn inevitably wore on the band members. It was counterproductive to fostering the type of cohesion that would normally develop over the course of touring. Alphonso Johnson said he eventually left the band because he was burned out on "the whole switching drummers episode."[16] Dom Um Romão also wasn't happy about it. In addition, Joe had grown more domineering and often showed his unhappiness with Dom Um on the bandstand. Romão threatened to quit the band more than once, only to stick around each time. But the last straw came late in the fall of 1974 when Zawinul was again on Romão's case. "Joe was kind of frowning and unhappy," Brown remembered, "and he was pointing at the tambourine for Dom Um to play. Well, Dom Um finished the performance and he was really pissed off. Afterward, he packed up all his instruments and told the roadies where to send them, and he just took off."[17] He never came back, thus abruptly ending his Weather Report career.

•

As was their custom, Weather Report took a break at the end of the year, during which they recorded their fifth album, *Tale Spinnin'*. Darryl Brown didn't know whether he figured in their future plans, so he checked in with Bob Devere. "I called him, just wondering what was going on with the band, 'cause different drummers were coming in, and I didn't know how that was going to play out. He said that they were talking about going back into the studio, and they were looking at some studio drummers, and that's how it ended. I never got official notice."[18] So when Joe and Wayne began preparing the music for *Tale Spinnin'*, they didn't have a band together. As usual, the task of finding a drummer fell to Alphonso Johnson, who once again tapped his Philadelphia connections and found Chuck Bazemore, who was best known as the drummer with the R&B vocal group, the Delfonics.

The percussion chair was filled by a young Brazilian named Alyrio Lima. Devere had heard him in June when he attended the wedding of Sly Stone and actress Kathy Silva at Madison Square Garden. Lima was part of the Webster Lewis Band, which provided the reception entertainment at the Waldorf Astoria Hotel, a star-studded affair that included a who's who of the record industry. Perhaps cognizant of Dom Um Romão's increasing unhappiness, Devere introduced himself to Lima, and the two exchanged phone numbers. At the end of the year, Devere got back in touch. "There's a vacancy in the band," he told Lima. "Would you like to join?"[19]

Devere didn't have to ask twice. Lima later said he was inspired to come to the States after seeing Weather Report during its 1972 tour of South America. He described himself as "a rock-influenced drummer" with hopes of playing with Jimi Hendrix, but his influences were broad and included Miles Davis, Philip Glass, John Cage, the Beatles, and Indian music. He was talented enough to get a full scholarship to the New England Conservatory of Music in Boston, where he studied classical percussion while gigging on the side with the Lewis band.

Bazemore and Lima came out to California, and the band began rehearsing at Studio Equipment Rentals in Hollywood. But just about the time they were ready to record, Bazemore got a call from Bob Devere, who notified him that his pregnant wife was in the hospital. Bazemore flew home hoping to welcome a new daughter to the world, only to learn that she had been stillborn. After that, "everything just changed," he said. "I couldn't think. I still stayed in contact with the guys, just talking to them and everything, and I said 'I would love to come back, but right now, I can't do it.'"[20]

With Bazemore out of the picture, a parade of drummers auditioned, none of whom made the grade. No sooner would one start playing than Joe would stop the band and say, "Nah, that ain't working. Thanks for comin' in, man. Next."[21] By this time, Alphonse Mouzon was also in L.A., having just recorded his album *Mind Transplant*, and Joe and Wayne asked him to come back, but he was intent on pursuing a solo career.

So it was serendipity that they found Leon "Ndugu" Chancler, who was next door recording Jean-Luc Ponty's *Upon the Wings of Music* at Paramount Recording Studios. As luck would have it, one night Ndugu walked out of Paramount and ran into Alphonso Johnson on the sidewalk. The two had recently met while playing on George Duke's album *The Aura Will Prevail*.[22] As they chatted, Joe and Wayne joined them. "Ndugu, what are you doing the next two days?" Zawinul asked. Chancler said he was finishing up with Ponty, but would be free the following week. "Come and do a session with Weather Report," Joe suggested.[23]

Though just twenty-two, Ndugu was already a veteran of Herbie Hancock's and Miles Davis's bands, and was then a member of the rock group, Santana. When Santana was off the road, Ndugu returned home to L.A. and did recording sessions. It was a way to indulge his wide-ranging musical interests. He was fluent in the fusion styles of the day and had a keen sense for balancing jazz with contemporary rhythms. As for Weather Report, "I knew their music from the beginning," Ndugu said. "I followed Zawinul with Cannon, and Wayne from way back in the Jazz Messenger days. So I was very familiar with the music and I had seen all of the earlier Weather Report bands."[24]

Once Ndugu got to the recording studio, he immediately impressed, despite having not rehearsed any of the music. "He was the first drummer that just came in and got it," Johnson said. "He understood what was going on right from the start. You could tell by the way he tuned his drums, how he set his drums up. And I think the other thing is, he wasn't intimidated by Joe and Wayne. He was, but he didn't show it. And that was 80 percent of the gig. Most of the drummers who came in wanted to please Wayne and Joe so much that they wound up *not* pleasing them. They couldn't please themselves. Ndugu came in, he set up, and all right, let's hit it."[25]

The engineer for the session was Bruce Botnick, best known for his work with rock bands, especially the Doors. Botnick had just signed on as a staff producer for Columbia Records when the label's A&R head, Don Ellis, threw out an idea. "How would you like to do Weather Report?" Ellis asked. To some high profile engineers and producers, Weather Report wasn't exactly a plum assignment. Upon learning of his latest project, a friend of Botnick's scoffed, "Oh, lucky you. *Somebody's* got to do it." But Botnick was excited to do the session. "I love adventurous stuff—the more adventurous, the better, because it takes me out of my box," he said. "And that's one of the things I loved about Joe and Wayne: They were never in the box. I had a great time because I was so enamored with the musicians."[26]

Once he showed up at Wally Heider's Studio, Ndugu might have expected someone to run over the charts or give him some direction before they got started, but that wasn't the Weather Report way. "No one's talking to me, and I have to make some real quick creative decisions," Ndugu said of his first session. "The engineer got a drum sound, and everybody's kind of walking around, and no one's saying anything, and all of a sudden they struck up the band. They had rehearsed this music, so they're ready to go. The drummer they'd had before me was from a group called [the Delfonics], so I'm thinking, *Maybe they want a serious pocket.* But when they took off, nothing gave me any indication of pocket. They were playing that tune 'Freezing Fire,' so I just started bashing. And I got in a backbeat every now and then, but I'm doing a Jack [DeJohnette] fusiony kind of thing. They're diggin' it, and they never stopped. They ran out of a roll of tape, and they put another roll of tape in and were still playing."[27]

It was like that for the rest of the sessions. "By the third day we're doing a Wayne Shorter tune, 'Lusitanos.' And Wayne writes everything out. But he didn't write a drum chart, so you're reading from the melodies and harmonies and all of that. So me, being of a studio mentality, I say, 'Wayne, what do you want me to play on this?' And he says, 'Well, like Gabby Hayes said, "Let's go get these Indians."' That was *it*! [*laughs*] So at that point I'm like, 'Okay, I'm not going to get any help. I'll just wing it.' . . . I was like the Lone Ranger in there. My direction was based on them just taking off and playing. So Zawinul never really said anything to me, but then we'd finish a take, and he'd say, 'This is Weather Report, the greatest band in the world.' And then he'd say, 'This album is going to be the baddest bleep bleep in the world.'"[28]

As it turned out, Ndugu integrated so well with the band that words weren't needed. As a consequence, the creativity flowed freely and the music evolved naturally. It made for a happy studio, and Botnick definitely felt the vibe from his side of the glass. "You know, it's a funny thing about dialogue," he said. "That's one of the things that happened with Ndugu, that they didn't have to speak about that stuff. I've been on numerous albums or movie scores where you didn't have to talk, you just knew. You communicated by listening and embellishing. I've always felt in my talks with musicians, be it jazz, rock, or classical, they're all that way. They really like that unspoken communication where they just respond, that they understand where to go and they just do. And my recollection is that Weather Report was like that."[29]

The one lifeline that Ndugu latched onto was Alphonso Johnson. "I leaned on Alphonso a lot. He was a bass player that I could play with easily. He was also a bass player that I had worked with extensively on sessions. So all I had to do in the first couple of days was follow him. That's all I had to do. I mean, Alphonso—let's be real about this: The concept that everyone talks about with Jaco was set up with Alphonso—the role of the bass in Weather Report. Of course, Miroslav pioneered the bass in the band, but Alphonso took it to the next level, especially the electric bass as a distinctive voice. And I was familiar with Alphonso's concept and playing with that voice already, so it was just a natural thing for me to lean on him."[30]

Alphonso turns in an outstanding performance on *Tale Spinnin'*, exhibiting the clean, warm tone that Joe and Wayne found so attractive when they hired him. That Johnson did so largely on the fretless electric bass has gone underappreciated, obscured by the sheer virtuosity and charisma of his successor in the band, Jaco Pastorius. So overwhelming is Pastorius's imprint on the fretless that it leads even knowledgeable observers to incorrectly credit him with inventing it.[31]

Johnson is too modest to take credit as a fretless pioneer himself. In fact, he is so unassuming that when asked to describe his role in Weather Report, he once

Alphonso Johnson. Photo: © Heritage Images / Hulton Archive / Getty Images.

responded, "I'd have to say that my function was to stay out of the way, both in frequency and register, from an orchestration perspective."[32] But Alphonso *was* a pioneer because there just weren't many others playing fretless when he took it up. Bill Wyman of the Rolling Stones might have been the first. He famously converted a cheap Japanese bass by pulling out its frets in 1961 and used it on all of the Stones' albums and many of their singles up to 1975.[33]

In 1966, Ampeg began manufacturing the first commercially available "unfretted bass" and Rick Danko of the Band began using one a few years later. Fender didn't introduce a fretless model until 1970, when it made a smooth-necked version of its industry-leading Precision Bass. The next year, nineteen-year-old Al Johnson went shopping for a new bass and came home with one. "I figured since I already played upright I would have some affinity for it, but the main reason I bought it was because no one else I knew of was playing one—sort of the novelty of it," he explained.[34]

One reason fretless electrics are not as popular as fretted models is that they are considerably more difficult to play. The main challenge is intonation; that is, playing in tune—something even the best players can struggle with. On a fretted bass you can press a string anywhere between two frets to produce a given note, but a fretless requires pressing the strings at precise locations on the neck in order to play in tune. It takes a lot of practice, and Alphonso was no different from others in that regard, though his upright bass experience gave him a leg up. At the time he got his first fretless, he was doing club gigs, which involved a lot of reading. "I had to woodshed around the clock to get my intonation together without looking at the neck," he said.[35]

The reward for mastering the neck is a beautifully expressive instrument with a warm, woody tone and more creative choices, such as coloring the notes (playing in between them), uninterrupted slides, and employing true vibrato. Within a few years of getting his fretless, Johnson's tone and technique were so strong that Woody Herman told him to leave his acoustic bass at home.

In 1974, Johnson had a custom fretless bass built for him by guitar-maker Charles LoBue. "All Charlie did was, he gave me a piece of wood and he said, 'Just pretend that it's going to be your neck, and just play on it.' So that's what I did. So he got an idea of my hand's shape, and the length of my fingers, and how I would be playing, and that was the first part of the bass he built, the neck. After he finished the neck, he started working on the body, and put it all together, and the bass is his creation."[36] You can see Alphonso play his LoBue bass throughout the video *Live in Berlin 1975*. The only time he switches away from it is for the final tune, "Boogie Woogie Waltz," where he deemed his fretted Fender more appropriate because of its percussive sound.

When Jaco Pastorius revolutionized the electric bass a few years later, it led to a wave of imitators. Alphonso stayed the course, maintaining his own style and sound. "Tone is a tricky thing because the player really gets the tone out of the instrument more than the instrument dictates," Johnson said. "When you listen to Jaco play fretless, or listen to me, or probably any other fretless player, you can really hear the distinction and the personality, even though the instruments can have the sustain and the tonal quality of the fretless bass. Our sounds were just different, just like listening to Coltrane play tenor and Wayne play tenor."[37]

Alphonso would probably find it ironic to read about his playing in the context of *Tale Spinnin'* because it is his least favorite of the Weather Report albums that he played on. "I've got to tell ya, that was not my best performance," he said decades later. "It's a great recording as far as the compositions and everything, but I never felt I could get myself to play 100 percent of what I was capable of playing. I don't know if I went in with the wrong attitude or what it was, but I could tell that I wasn't up to 100 percent."[38] Not that it's apparent listening to the record. "Well, you know, I tell people that, and they don't get it. I can't explain it. I just wasn't at my best. I thought I could have played a lot better. Maybe Ndugu psyched me out because he came in and he was so ready. But I think where I was in my life was not a healthy place, and therefore it was reflected in my music."[39]

Johnson kept his concerns to himself, only confiding in Ndugu. In any event, Wayne and Joe were pleased with both of them. "Ndugu and Alphonso worked well together," Wayne said. "They had a good sound. They interlocked. And the other thing is that Ndugu was laughing. He had a personality that was injected into the album."[40]

•

The title, *Tale Spinnin'*, is obviously a nod to storytelling. "We were sitting around in the studio, talking about how people told tales in the old days," Wayne said. "Folk tales, spinning tales. We actually started talking about these stories, and we went from one story to another, and everybody started contributing. And we arrived at that name, *Tale Spinnin'*."[41]

Like its predecessors, *Tale Spinnin'* has a character of its own. Its light, sunny disposition is established by the festive nature of the first track, Joe's "Man in the Green Shirt," an improvisation that was inspired by a scene he saw at a carnival in the Virgin Islands. Joe said it was "about his seeing a man in a green shirt," Wayne recalled. "Sometimes he would disappear and then he would always show up. And Joe said there was something funny, something rhythmic about how he would disappear and appear, and he said it was a man in a green shirt. So a simple thing like that became a title."[42]

It's an ideal opener in that it shows off the entire band to superb effect. Wayne gets all of the solo space, his soprano flitting about in a series of extended statements interspersed among the tune's composed lines, which Joe doubles on melodica. Ndugu inhabits the tune so thoroughly that it's hard to imagine it played with another drummer, while Alyrio Lima adds a range of colors. And despite his reservations regarding his performance, Alphonso Johnson undergirds the entire tune with funky, riffing bass lines.

The second track, "Lusitanos," takes its name from Ana Maria Shorter's native country. "That was the original name of Portugal, before the Romans got there," Wayne said. "They were called the Lusitanos among themselves. It means 'light,' the people of light."[43] His inspiration for the tune was the traditional Portuguese folk music fado. Although "Lusitanos" sounds nothing like fado, which is typically sung by a female vocalist backed by stringed instruments, especially the Portuguese guitar, it does have a dramatic narrative arc that honors its inspiration. "I wanted to make it kind of sweeping, epical," Wayne said. "No kind of cute melody or hook."[44]

The track begins with a simple drumbeat coupled with Johnson's slinky wah-wahed fretless bass. A low-pitched synthesizer drone soon enters, leading to a fully orchestrated piece. Wayne is featured throughout on tenor saxophone, unadorned by electronic effects, at times soaring over the band, at other times painting with elegant economy. A further treat is Joe's acoustic piano solo, which by this point was becoming a rarity on Weather Report records.

Tale Spinnin' marks the first time that Zawinul is credited with "orchestrations," reflecting the increasingly rich soundscape he was creating. A striking quality of his arranging skills is how well he blended acoustic and electronic instruments into an organic whole. Of course, he had done this to limited effect on *Sweetnighter* and more so on *Mysterious Traveller*, but he took it to an entirely new level on *Tale Spinnin'*. "Lusitanos" is a good example of the attention to detail that he brought to the task. The electro-acoustic textures were unimaginable just a few years earlier, the sound much bigger than that of five musicians.

As orchestrator, Joe wielded significant influence on all of the band's music, not just his own compositions. He shed light on his methods in an interview in *Jazz Forum* published the year after *Tale Spinnin'* was released. After the band recorded a piece like "Lusitanos," Joe would return to the studio without Wayne, and "let the tape run and orchestrate, improvise, on top of it. That's my way of 'orchestration,'" he said. "You know, from all we record we get tape cassettes. I take them home, listen to them again and again, think about it and begin to hear many things that would go along with it, melodies and sound that would get different vibrations of it."[45]

As for his own music, Joe brought in orchestral sketches. "He wrote his music out on a full score page," Alphonso recalled, "as if you were writing for a full orchestra. And the score paper would just have parts, not like a full score. It would be like a bass idea, and then a flute idea, or a trumpet idea, or a voice, or oboe. Whatever he was hearing, he would just kind of jot it down. And he would have the bass part written down in the bass clef, and he would have some melodies written. So he was already hearing his songs orchestrated."[46] When Joe overdubbed on his synthesizers, he would make reference to the "horn" or "string" parts he was about to lay down, and the engineers would label the tracks as such.

Joe still relied on the ARP 2600s, but at one point during the production of *Tale Spinnin'*, Brian Risner had the idea of getting him in front of Malcolm Cecil and Bob Margouleff's TONTO synthesizer in order to expand his tonal palette. TONTO is an acronym for The Original New Timbral Orchestra. At the time, it was the largest analog synthesizer in existence, combining modules from Moog, ARP, and other manufacturers, as well as components that Cecil and Margouleff designed and built themselves, all enclosed in a towering nine-foot-long wooden cabinet with hundreds of knobs, most of which were unlabeled. Its four keyboards moved around on dollies in order to get from one end of the system to the other. Imposing wouldn't begin to describe it.

At first, Cecil (who was a professional bass player back home in Britain) and Margouleff used TONTO to produce their own album, *Zero Time*, which came out in 1971 on Herbie Mann's Embryo label. On the heels of its release, Stevie Wonder came knocking on their door. Ever since hearing *Switched-On Bach*, Wonder had been keen to explore synthesizers himself. In collaboration with Cecil and Margouleff, Wonder made four hugely successful albums: *Music of My Mind* (March 1972), *Talking Book* (October 1972), *Innervisions* (1973), and *Fulfillingness' First Finale* (1974). As Zawinul did with his synthesizers, Wonder, Cecil and Margouleff brilliantly harnessed TONTO to produce music that manages to not sound dated.

Their creative process was highly interactive. In the book *Analog Days: The Invention and Impact of the Moog Synthesizer*, Cecil described how everything "flowed" between the three men:

> One of us would work on the knobs, one of us, Stevie, would play the actual notes, and one of us would work on the keyboard. I would usually work either on the knobs or the keyboard things, switching in the portamento [causing notes to slide from one to another] and switching out, watching his line, knowing what he was going to play, so the portamentos were in the right place, switching it in and out, turning the hold, no-hold on and off in the right places so the right effects were happening. So as a player, you couldn't have done it—one person could not have played that. . . . It was the three of us together doing it that made the thing happen.[47]

That description explains why little came of Joe's sessions with TONTO. He couldn't drive TONTO himself, which eliminated the process of self-discovery. Nor was Zawinul going to let someone else copilot while he played, like Wonder did. "Joe really didn't have a hands-on with the TONTO," Risner remembered. "Malcolm was there and he would dial up a sound, and Joe would play it and say, 'Oh yeah, that's kind of cool' or whatever. But it wasn't a sound *Joe* came up with. He wasn't turning the knobs, and he wasn't interested in having a programmer get his sounds, and that was it. So even though it was a bitchin' instrument, and we gave credit to it, I don't think much of that was used. I couldn't even listen to the tracks now and say, 'Oh, there's TONTO.'"[48]

The last track on side one is Joe's tune "Between the Thighs." It starts out as a funky groove, with a catchy riff played by Joe and Alphonso. As with Joe's other tunes, the band only had a sketch to work with. This was the first piece that Ndugu played on, where they "rolled tape until the tape ran out and then we put another reel in and did it again."[49] Given that, there's a remarkable amount of cohesiveness by everyone involved, but especially Ndugu's hookup with Alphonso. And once it seems like the tune will stick to its funky underpinnings for the duration, the mood changes dramatically for several minutes before returning for a funk reprise. As for the title: "Yeah, it's what you think it means," Wayne said with a laugh. "Joe came up with that title himself. We said, 'You think it will go?' He said, 'Yeah, I don't think it will be censored.'"[50]

Side two begins with one of Joe's most enduring pieces: "Badia," which he continued to play to the end of his life. Although there are contributions from the rest of the band minus Wayne, "Badia" is largely the work of Joe himself. Like *Mysterious Traveller*'s "Jungle Book," he overdubbed himself playing a variety of instruments, once again demonstrating that his range extended well beyond keyboards. Indeed, the genius and beauty of "Badia" lies in Joe's mastery of texture and the delicate touches that envelop what is at heart a very simple form. With its vaguely Middle Eastern vibe, many consider "Badia" to be Joe's first foray into world music, a term that didn't come into widespread use until the 1980s. Although he eventually claimed to have invented the genre, Zawinul was quick to point out that Weather Report's brand of world music came directly from within, inspired by his observations and interactions with people of different cultures.

Joe conceived the melodies for "Badia" while he was still living in Austria. He was inspired by a girlfriend who had a volatile personality, whom he described to Gunther Baumann:

Badia was a belly dancer from Cairo, a beautiful black woman who I met in Vienna. We fell in love, and I usually went to get her from the club where she danced when I was done playing. She lived with an Egyptian friend, also a belly dancer. One night I was dancing with this girlfriend. Badia saw us, and all at once I heard a crack. She tossed champagne glasses and bottles at me because she was so jealous. Then she wanted to hurt me with a knife. I had to fight back, of course, and that wasn't good for me, because I got a lifelong ban from the club. Badia was a really dangerous woman. The love was over, but I still wrote a piece for her.[51]

When it came to recording the piece, all Zawinul had was those melodies. In lieu of written charts, he gathered the musicians around him and played the lines while explaining the background to them. As Ndugu remembered, it was the only time Joe talked about music. "He just described this feeling and these characters. He had this Moorish idea that he was singing, and then he sang [the descending] phrase. That's what he kept singing, and that gave us the idea for how the tune was." After listening to Joe's concept, Ndugu felt like drums would just get in the way of the vibe, so he provided the lightest of touches. "It was a melody that really didn't need rhythm; one of those singable melodies that didn't need a lot from the drums," he said. "It needed more shading than a rhythmic pulse, because the rhythmic pulse was so dominant in the melody."[52]

"Badia" begins with the vaguely familiar yet unidentifiable sounds of plucked strings and metallic plinks. Joe produced them on his Mzuthra, a unique percussive instrument that he discovered five months earlier when the band played three nights at the Town and Country Lodge in Ben Lomond, California. (The gig is remembered by some for two things: First, it seemed like it was in the middle of nowhere, deep in the Santa Cruz Mountains. And there was also the couple copulating right in front of Joe's Rhodes, setting a new bar for audience participation.)

The Mzuthra's inventor, a local musician named Bradley Dupont Blanchard, had heard that Weather Report was coming to town, so he stopped by the club on the afternoon of their first show. There he found Joe alone, fiddling with his synthesizers. Blanchard approached the stage and boldly declared, "I've got a sound-effects instrument that is better than that, and it's acoustic." Joe turned around and fixed him with a stare. Blanchard quickly told him about his mission to "create sacred objects for the greatest musicians on the planet." One instrument, he said, was carved from wood that he brought back from an ancient temple in Mexico. As an inveterate collector of all kinds of musical instruments, especially ethnic percussion, Joe was intrigued. "I want to see this," he told Blanchard. "Bring it to me about an hour before the gig."[53]

Blanchard hurried home and grabbed every playable instrument he had. By the time he returned to the club, the rest of the band had assembled and Joe wasted no time getting to the point. "Let's see what you got in there," motioning to one of Blanchard's cases. He opened it up and took out a box made of dark, varnished wood, about 8 by 12 inches in size. It looked like it could have come from Africa, but Blanchard had designed and constructed it himself.

He explained how to play it. "Joe, these lamellae [keys] are made of German clock spring, easily tunable by sliding them back and forth. You can play both ends of the metal keys. Underneath you have a bank of strings tuned sympathetically, which can be manipulated by moving these beads. I have pickups mounted inside on both the key and string banks, so it plays acoustic-electric. You can add effects to it if you want to."

Joe gave it a try and immediately fell under its spell. "No effects," he said approvingly. "I like it acoustic. You can mix and match tones like you would on the synth. What do you call this?"

"It's called a Mzuthra," Blanchard replied. The name was derived from the two African instruments it resembled, the mbira and zither.

Joe's face warmed as he repeated the name. "Yeah, man. M-zootra!" Blanchard passed out more instruments to the rest of the band, and soon they were all jamming backstage. "Don't stop!" Joe said. "Let's go through the crowd like we are in a parade!"

"So out the door we went, and the crowd went nuts," Blanchard remembered.

"It was standing-room only, but everyone made room to let us pass and we ended up on the stage, where I joined in for the first couple of tunes."[54]

Just before recording *Tale Spinnin'*, Joe telephoned Blanchard. "Brad, bring all of your instruments here to the studio. We're recording." As Blanchard's wife was late in the pregnancy of their first child, he couldn't leave town. Instead, he sold Joe the Mzuthra and shipped it to L.A. in time for the sessions, where Zawinul used it to good effect. For years afterward, it occupied the same spot atop Joe's Rhodes, specifically to play "Badia" live.[55]

The other memorable part of "Badia's" introduction is the strange, high-pitched, vocal-like line. It is woven into the tune so well that it sounds like something Joe might have produced on his synthesizer, but it is actually a field recording of an Islamic call to prayer, sped up on playback so as to disguise its origins. It is perhaps *the* signature Weather Report sound effect, recognized by virtually every fan of the band, and Joe included it whenever he performed "Badia" live, even with his post–Weather Report bands.

The next tune on *Tale Spinnin'*, "Freezing Fire," was brought in by Wayne. He described it as a vehicle for blowing. "It was meant for different members of the band to go out and solo, to fly over it and fly around it—kind of standing on the running board. When we played it in public, it was more like a carpet from which to take off on and go here and there. It didn't have a guardrail."[56]

Notably, "Freezing Fire" contains the first synthesizer solo that Joe ever recorded. It starts out with a kind of pure, bright, square-wave tone. Later, he switches to another timbre that is reminiscent of a fiddle until it transforms into something almost akin to a ray gun in an old science fiction movie. Throughout, Joe adds various flourishes that bring the sound alive. He even uses the ARP 2600's awkward pitch-bend knob ever so briefly, at one point suddenly twisting the knob all the way to the right to produce a rapid octave-pitch rise.

The closing piece on *Tale Spinnin'* is "Five Short Stories," which Joe wrote and performed as a duet with Wayne. Shorter described it as "a lot of themes that [Joe] played on the piano, on the keyboard, the thematic material, and I was kind of soloing around it. Not soloing, but flying, embellishing, and all that. And he had probably been working on that. You know, things that came to him, came to him from childhood, would come out in that kind of thing."[57] Ironically, many years later, when asked about the tunes on *Tale Spinnin'*, Joe attributed this composition to Wayne, a comment that reveals the cooperative nature of their duets.[58]

•

"When I first heard the album, I didn't like the drum sound," Ndugu recalled. "That was my first reaction, the reason being, I didn't feel like I had at that point the Weather Report drum sound. I played great, but I had the session sound versus the Weather Report sound. That was because I was used to hearing non-session drummers play with Weather Report, and I was used to that sound, and not a more polished studio sound. I really liked it, but at the time I thought it was different from Weather Report."[59]

It could be said that *every* Weather Report album was different from Weather Report; *Tale Spinnin'* just lived up to tradition. The days of avant-garde-like freedom were long gone. Even the funk grooves of *Sweetnighter* had given way to complex fusion rhythms.[60] The tunes were more structured than ever, lengthy yet compact, the music itself the story rather than straight-out blowing. Joe, especially, insisted on never straying too far from the point. In that sense, Weather Report separated itself from its jazz-rock peers, most of which relied on flaunting technical chops to wow audiences.

By this time, true jazz-rock bands, like Chick Corea's Return to Forever, were becoming an endangered species. The classic lineup of John McLaughlin's Mahavishnu Orchestra flamed out after a couple of years, done in by sheer exhaustion and internal strife. Miles Davis continued to pursue his own unique brand of jazz-funk until health issues forced him into retirement midway through 1975. Meanwhile, the record labels found success in the modern equivalent of soul jazz that marketers described as "crossover music" because of its ability to appeal to mainstream (white) audiences. When *Tale Spinnin'* first entered the *Billboard* jazz chart, on June 14, 1975, it was dominated by such fare, with Grover Washington Jr.'s *Mister Magic* at the top (as it was all summer), followed by *Two* by Bob James, a pianist who came to personify instrumental pop in the seventies.

Though Weather Report's music was aesthetically on another plane from those offerings, the band had become a reliable commercial success in its own right. Things had come a long way since the days of struggling to pay for studio time. Now their records could be counted on to sell hundreds of thousands of copies. That summer, a reporter encountered Zawinul at the CBS building on Sunset Boulevard. Thumbing through a copy of *Billboard*, Joe paused to check out the top LPs chart. His index finger led him to *Tale Spinnin'*, listed at number thirty-one with a bullet. Zawinul looked up casually. "If we have a cult following," he quipped, "it's getting bigger."[61]

The album received the band's third five-star review from *Down Beat*, and once again the magazine's readers voted it the best album of the year, this time by a two-to-one margin over its closest competitor. Without a doubt, Wayne and Joe were on a creative roll, the beauty of which was that no one else came close to sounding like them. "It is as if these men one day met and collectively decided to define a new trend in music," *Audio* magazine's Fred De Van marveled.[62]

Audio billed itself as "the authoritative magazine about high fidelity," and its record reviews were accompanied by two grades, one for the quality of the recording and the other for the performance. *Tale Spinnin'* received an A+ for both.

"The sound quality in this disc is so markedly superior, it can *only* be described as state of the art," De Van wrote.[63] Like *Mysterious Traveller*, *Tale Spinnin'* was mastered in SQ quadraphonic sound, a short-lived vinyl format that produced an early version of surround sound. *Audio* called the quad version of *Tale Spinnin'* a "technical tour de force" and an instant demonstration album for evaluating high fidelity equipment.[64]

Bruce Botnick was proud of the result, and to this day he still cites *Tale Spinnin'* as an example of high resolution audio with a lot of dynamics. When asked what makes the LP special, Botnick reaches for an analogy from the visual arts world. "To me, Joe, Wayne, and I were able to realize negative space." Asked to explain, he continued: "It's all the interesting stuff—the light, the darkness, the shades, the reverb, the room tone, all that kind of stuff. That's negative space. That album in particular has a great deal of it. There's a lot of depth. You can walk around inside the mix. You can walk around the instruments. I like to think it's very three-dimensional from that standpoint; it's all there. I know if Joe was here right now and I could talk to him about it, he would go, 'Yeah man! Yeah! Yeah!'"[65]

Given that, it's surprising that Botnick and Weather Report didn't work together again. "Why we never made another record together or spent any time together, I have no idea," Botnick said. "Probably because I was busy producing other acts and just wasn't available. I would have loved to do another record with them." Not that he looks back with regret. "It was probably good that we only did one record together. Sometimes those things are good. There's a reason for that stuff to happen."[66]

Joe was so pleased with Ndugu's playing on *Tale Spinnin'* that he offered him the gig using the same pitch he gave to Airto four years earlier. "He made it very simple," Ndugu remembered. "He called me up and said, 'What do you want to do with your life? Do you want to stay with Santana or do you want to join the greatest band in the world?'" Had it been a different time in his life, Ndugu would have loved to do it, but he was heavily involved with Santana at that point. "I said, 'I'm sorry Joe, I've got to stay with Santana.' And it wasn't just Weather Report. I'd gotten the same kind of offer from Earth, Wind & Fire at the time, but I couldn't go. I was a part of the new Santana band, with profit sharing and everything. So it was a business decision more than a musical one. I had a great deal with Santana, and I had a commitment. I wasn't going to just walk out on that."[67]

So once again the band was back to square one when it came to a drummer. Would this problem never be solved?

•

Alphonso Johnson had been trying to get Chester Thompson to jam with the band for months. They knew each other from when they each played in different bands managed by the same agency. Thompson played drums in a group

Weather Report in 1975. Left to right: Chester Thompson, Wayne Shorter, Joe Zawinul, Alyrio Lima, and Alphonso Johnson. Photo: © Gems / Redferns / Getty Images.

fashioned after the Supremes, while Johnson's group was modeled on Sly and the Family Stone. Sometimes their bands would get booked at the same venue, and they would jam together between shows. Chester and Alphonso hit it off and became friends. When Johnson got the Weather Report gig, one of the first people he called was Chester, telling him how excited he was to be headed to L.A. the next day.

By the time of the *Tale Spinnin'* sessions, Thompson was a member of Frank Zappa's group. It was one of the most technically demanding gigs in rock and drew upon all of Thompson's training, which was primarily rooted in jazz. His first professional engagement was with the organist Jack McDuff. After a year on the road, Thompson settled back in his hometown, attending the Community College of Baltimore for two years. The music department was run by professors from the nearby Peabody Institute, a prestigious performing arts conservatory. Thompson got a thorough grounding in all aspects of music, even taking up the flute because of the school's requirement that he play a second instrument.

Right after that, he went to California to audition for Zappa. "He gave me a chart to look at that night to see if I could play it the next day," Thompson recalled. "I had never seen a mess like that in my life! It definitely was the hardest piece of music I had ever looked at, including any orchestral music I had ever played."[68] Thompson was a good reader, but this was more than he could handle in a single night. Nevertheless, Zappa was impressed by Chester's playing and hired him.

When Weather Report finished recording *Tale Spinnin'* in early 1975, Zappa was on hiatus. "Frank had just canceled a tour," Thompson said. "He had gotten a film-editing machine and wanted to take some time to really learn how to use it, because he did get quite heavily into that later. And unfortunately for me, I wasn't established enough in L.A. at that point to get a lot of work. We had been touring so much that I hadn't really met very many people. So as it turned out, I was looking for something to do until Frank started touring again."[69] That's when Johnson called. Thompson continues the story:

> Alphonso kept asking me if I wanted to come down and jam with the guys. I said, "Well, I'm fine to do that, but I need to let you know that I don't really care to audition." Alphonso insisted it was not an audition, just jamming with the guys. And of course, I get there and there's another drummer set up, and he's been playing through stuff. So, so much for the "no audition" thing.
>
> Weather Report was my favorite band, so of course I knew who they were. I was a little bit nervous, but not really. I had played in a lot of pretty intense situations. As far as first reactions, it was a pretty magic moment because what we were doing was totally free. It wasn't like they were calling tunes; they would just play, which was something that I had a lot of experience with. So that felt really good.
>
> The other drummer was pretty amazing. I fully expected that he would be the one to get it. But at one point they decided to do an ethereal kind of ballad, and whereas this guy had all the fire in the world and was really impressive, when they played this ballad, he had no idea what to do, and that kind of freaked them out.
>
> At first they asked if I would consider playing with two drummers. I had done that the first year with Zappa, so I wasn't really interested in doing that again. I said to them, "This guy [the other drummer] is amazing, why don't you go ahead and go with him. I've already got a gig as soon as Frank gets back on tour." I was just grateful for the opportunity to play with those guys. And I was pretty serious about that. But I think the fact that the other guy didn't quite know what to do in that other setting really freaked them out, so that's how I ended up getting the gig.[70]

Alphonso's recollection was more succinct. "When Chester showed interest, I just told Joe, 'This guy is going to blow you away.' And that's what he did."[71]

The next week, Thompson began rehearsing with the band, which was preparing for a quick trip to the South before a long tour of Europe beginning in mid-March. (Demand for Weather Report's two concerts in Paris was such that tickets sold out in just three hours.[72]) "They weren't using charts for the tour," Chester recalled. "I had a list of stuff to listen to, and they made sure I had recordings of everything before rehearsals. I already knew everything up to *Tale Spinnin'*, anyway, because I was a real fan. All the descriptions for the tour, there were no musical terms. Every single tune that we talked about, I was given a visual perspective on how to play it. Like, one tune Wayne would say, 'Picture a caravan going across the desert.' They were both big movie buffs, and they would usually relate to some movie or some scene, and that would be how they wanted the tune played."[73]

Thompson had a huge rock kit with eight tom toms and double bass drums—unusual for a jazz band to be sure, but he liked the flexibility. "You don't play all the notes on the piano all the time, but when you want them there, you want them there," he explained by analogy.[74] He also had an undeniable rapport with Alphonso. "It had been pretty firmly established years before. I mean, when we jammed it was just never this typical, 'Let's play a funk groove for nine hours.' He always had this amazing sense of space, and I don't think we played any backbeats that whole year that I toured with those guys—very rarely, if ever. There was so much freedom there. And the grooves were pretty deep, but they were never the typical sort of grooves."[75]

Alyrio Lima took over Dom Um Romão's role, even playing the berimbau. The guys called him "junkman" because he would pick up anything and treat it as a percussion instrument.[76] Although he had "a blast playing with those music geniuses," he initially struggled to understand his role in the music, and Joe was on his case nightly. "It was scary for a young man like I was," recalled Lima. "Joe was all the time pushing, exploring my abilities to fly into their vast music concepts. He would say, 'Alyrio! Play in front. This is not the James Brown band. It can be funk, but in front and not with a backbeat. Relax, man, and kick ass tonight.' Wayne took me under his wing and spent lots of time honing my skills, sharpening my musical understanding. He would say, 'Don't talk about music. Play it. Forget about all those silly academic ideas.'"[77]

Lima vividly remembered one instance when the band was in Copenhagen, and Wayne showed him what it meant to play in front of the beat. "It was a continual harassment to have Joe almost every night say something about that subject. Then at the dressing room before the concert Wayne asked for a bottle of cognac, and when the waiter brought it Wayne took the bottle just before it touched the table and, smiling, said, 'This is in front of the beat.' At that moment I understood something that I still cherish in the depth of everything I do in life. 'Be ahead without rushing.' It's almost a Zen koan. Wayne is like that, like an old soul who is caring and loving, compassionate with the ones that are behind and truly grateful to the ones that have gone ahead."[78]

Thompson had heard stories about Zawinul's treatment of drummers, but he

Alyrio Lima and Alphonso Johnson. Photo: Brian Risner.

mostly escaped Joe's ire. One advantage he had over his predecessors is that he lived in Los Angeles. "Joe would have me come over to his house sometimes, and we would just jam, we would just play. So we developed this kind of understanding. Sometimes he was working on something, or sometimes he just wanted to jam. I think I got to know him pretty well, and those times we did that were pretty significant for me. One thing he told me, for example, is that he thought a drummer should play like a boxer. You've got to have the element of surprise. You can't be repetitious, because you'd get knocked out. He would say things in a descriptive way, and I really took those things to heart."[79]

With Chester and Alphonso in the fold, the music took off. Leonard Feather, who had observed the band for years, caught them in Santa Monica, California shortly after their return from Europe. He called Weather Report more compelling than any other group on the contemporary scene. "The quintet painted sound pictures that shot off wildly in unpredictable directions, starting with a high voltage supersamba in which the theme's fragmentary phrases left room for percussion comments that stressed one centrally important fact: This edition of Weather Report swings."[80]

Joe called it "a great period" and described the new lineup as "a powerful, modern rhythm 'n' blues band." Wayne shared his enthusiasm. "Instead of going out on stage and getting through something and saying, 'Hey, okay,' because we knew we could do it the next day, for the first time I had that *feeling*."[81] It was a point of pride for both of them that Miles Davis, who was in poor health at the time, made the effort to see the band at the Bottom Line that October. "When the set was over, Miles jumped on the chair and started a standing ovation," Zawinul recalled. "Miles was loving this band, because it was a hard-grooving band."[82]

"Musically," Thompson said, "this phenomenon used to happen live, where we would just all do things that were never talked about at the exact same time— really complex, rhythmic things, or some kind of hit that would happen in a really complicated place, but which was never, ever planned. And we did that stuff together all the time. The communication was pretty intense." One might think that after such moments the band would get backstage and congratulate each other over what had just transpired, but nope. "I got the impression that they expected no less," Thompson said.[83]

Chester was older and more experienced than the band's recent string of drummers, and he was secure enough to speak up when he felt the situation called for it. "There would be times when Joe's solos were just too long," he observed. "I mean, brilliant stuff that he's playing, but I like the idea that you build to a climax, and then it's time for something else to happen. And I felt like sometimes we would build to a climax in Joe's solos, but then he would just keep going and going. And if there was a point where it wasn't magic, he would inevitably kind of blame Alphonso. And one night, because Alphonso was a friend of mine, I guess I felt like Joe was bullying him. I probably spoke out of turn, but I said to him, 'Sorry Joe, but the thing that happened there, man, is we built up to the climax, the groove was perfect, and you wouldn't stop soloing, and so the groove fell apart.' And he gave me the strangest look. But I was pretty angry that he was treating Alphonso that way, so I didn't care if they fired me or what. I don't think we had many more of those conversations." [*laughs*][84]

•

As was par for the course in those days, the post–*Tale Spinnin'* lineup didn't last long, as Alyrio Lima left the band at the end of the summer, tired of the road life. In order to fill the vacancy, Joe checked around with friends in New York who told him about a percussionist in Las Vegas by the name of Alejandro Acuña. Joe didn't know who he was, but the New York guys were high on him, so Zawinul cold-called him with a job offer. The conversation went something like this:

"Hello?"
"Mr. Acuña?" Joe asked.
"Yes. Who's this?"
"Joe Zawinul."
"Joe *who*?"
"Joe Zawinul."
"C'mon, man. Are you really Joe? Who is this?"

"Yes, I'm Joe."

"How do you know me?"

"David Liebman. Miroslav. Don Alias. They told me who you were and gave me your number. Do you want to play with the band?"

"What band?"

"Weather Report."

"Are you serious?"[85]

Although Acuña thought he might be pranked, he definitely knew who Joe Zawinul and Weather Report were. When the band's first record came out, he was living in Puerto Rico and remembered how impactful it was to him. "I had an incredible desire to play with this band because it was the music that really touched me. It knocked me out. I said, 'This music has beautiful melodies, great harmony, and great rhythm. This is exactly the music that I want to play.' So it became my passion, it became my dream, my vision."[86]

By the time Joe called, Acuña had been a professional musician for two decades, despite being just thirty years old. He came from a large family in Peru, the tenth of eleven children. His father led the family band, teaching each of Alex's older brothers how to play the various instruments. At first, his mother didn't want the musician's lifestyle for her youngest son, insisting that he become a tradesman. So Alex remained on the sidelines, watching his father rehearse the band at home. One day one of his brothers couldn't make a gig, so ten-year-old Alejandro volunteered to take his place. Everyone laughed at the idea until they realized he could really play. "I was there listening, just sitting under the table. That's how I learned," he recalled.[87] His mother gave in, her only stipulation being that Alex be paid just as much as everyone else despite being the youngest.

At sixteen, Acuña left home to join his older brothers in the broadcast and recording studios in Lima. He got work immediately and eventually caught the eye of Cuban bandleader Pérez Prado, who offered him a nine-month tour of the United States playing drums. Shortly after that ended, Acuña moved to San Juan, Puerto Rico, where he remained for eight years, studying classical technique at the music conservatory while playing every gig he could, soaking up the full range of Latin rhythms.

In 1974, Acuña returned to the United States, intent on getting into the jazz scene. By this time, he had his own family to feed, so he took a job as the house drummer at the International Hilton Hotel. One night in the summer of 1975, Don Alias happened to hear him there. The opening act was Olivia Newton-John, who had just come over from Australia. Alex played drums during her set, then switched to congas for the Temptations, who traveled with their own rhythm section. Alias thought, *Wow, I know of only two guys who are good drummers and good conga players*. One was Walfredo de Los Reyes, Sr., an internationally renowned drummer from Cuba who was also in Vegas. The other was Acuña, whom Alias had only heard about. They met backstage and hit it off. Acuña subsequently did a short tour with Alias, Dave Liebman, Richie Beirach, and Miroslav Vitous, returning to Las Vegas when the gigs dried up. A week later, Joe called.

After their telephone chat, Zawinul decided to pay Alex a visit. Acuña picks up the story:

> I told him, "I'm not working, so you won't be able to see me play. Is that okay?" He said, "No, no, that's okay." He came with his road manager [at the time, Jim Rose, best known for fulfilling the same function for Miles Davis]. I said, "Joe, let's go some place and have a drink." So we were walking to the parking lot and he said, "Alex, let me see you walk." I said, "Come on, man. What do you mean, let me see you walk?" He said, "No, I want to see the way you walk." So I started walking and he's checking me out, the way that I'm walking. I came back and he said, "Alex, you can play, man. I know just by the way you walk, you can play."
>
> So we hung out that night. We went to see Bill Cosby and B. B. King and talked with them a little bit. Joe told me, "I would *love* to play with B. B. King one day." We had a great time. We became very good friends right away.[88]

A few days later, Acuña flew to L.A. for his first rehearsal with the band.

> They brought me to the studio and everything was set up already—all my gear, everything that I asked for. Joe was playing with Alphonso Johnson and Chester Thompson, and Wayne was writing music at the table while the other guys played. And they were burning! I never heard anybody play in that way. There was a lot of music from three guys. I thought, *Wow, it sounds sometimes like an orchestra, sometimes like a trio—a very modern fusion band trio.*
>
> All of a sudden, I thought I better join them. So I went up on the stage and started playing with them, just trying to fit what I was hearing. They liked it, and we kept playing. When we finished, the first one to get up from his chair was Wayne. He said, "Alejandro! Nice to meet you! If I were a percussionist, I would play exactly the way you play!" That was the first thing he told me.
>
> I said, "Were you guys auditioning me?" Joe said, "No, no. We didn't audition you. You were already highly recommended by Miroslav and all those guys." Then they said, "Well, do you have a passport so we can start

working on the visa and getting you tickets? In two weeks we're going to Europe."[89]

With Acuña on board, Joe and Wayne had a truly crack rhythm section. Alex brought an entirely new approach to percussion, one the band hadn't experienced before. By playing an array of Latin drums including congas and timbales—pounding the congas with one hand while striking the cowbells or timbales with a drumstick in his other hand—he effectively helped Joe realize his goal of having two drummers on the bandstand. "Alex is an amazing drummer," Thompson said. "He came in with all this fire and aggressive playing and it really worked. And he complemented; I don't think we ever competed. We both really listened to each other and played off of each other. That's what I feel like happened. We were both big Tony Williams fans, too, so that probably helped."[90]

The band hit the East Coast for a short tour billed as the "World Series of Jazz"—a handful of marathon concerts involving five bands. The shows dragged on so long that one reporter likened them to "an eighteen-inning tie game with everyone hoping and wondering when it will end."[91] That was just a warm-up for a return to Europe, where Weather Report performed more than twenty times in one month. For the band members, the highlight of the trip was when Joe took them to visit his parents in Vienna. They all remembered it decades later for the bits of insight into Joe's background.

"Joe was both European *and* American in his heart," Alphonso said. "When I met his mom and dad in Austria, I totally got it. His dad would be drinking slivovitz and doing chin-ups on the doorjamb. I mean, his dad looked like this frail old guy, and he said something to Joe in German, and Joe said, 'Watch this.' And to see this old guy do chin-ups, I thought, *Wow*. I was impressed."[92]

The band's last concert of 1975 took place in London on November 27. It was Weather Report's first visit to the United Kingdom since their two-week engagement at Ronnie Scott's three years earlier. Anticipation was high, with London's best musicians among those packing the New Victoria Theatre to capacity. They didn't leave disappointed, as the band roared through a two-and-a-half-hour set that "doubtless sent the cream of London musicians scurrying back to their rehearsal rooms, shaking their heads in amazement," Steve Lake wrote in *Melody Maker*.[93]

Everybody was in good spirits, despite being on the road for so long and having to endure a seemingly endless gantlet of press interviews the day of the show. "Man, I've never been happier," Wayne gushed to reporters while extolling the virtues of Buddhism. Joe waxed enthusiastic about a film sequence by computer-animation pioneer John Whitney that he hoped to incorporate into Weather Report's future shows.

Wayne engages with reporters in London. Photo: © Heritage Images / Hulton Archive / Getty Images.

Meanwhile, the London gig turned out to be the final one for Alphonso Johnson and Chester Thompson. "It was a shame that Chester joined when he did," Johnson said. "By that time I was so burned out on the whole switching-drummers episode that I had pretty much started thinking that it was time to move on. But when Chester joined, and with Alex playing percussion, those were to me the best moments of being on the road playing music with Weather Report. That was a phenomenal band. Chester and I had an immediacy that transcended having to say anything on stage. There would be a lot of smiling and gestures. It was fun—a lot of fun."[94]

As for Thompson, he had no plans to leave, but a one-of-a-kind bass player was about to enter the picture, leading to Chester's ouster and a new era in the band's fortunes.

PART III

Weather Report, 1976–1981

12 Black Market

My name is John Francis Pastorius III, *and I am the greatest bass player in the world.*

—Jaco Pastorius

TALE SPINNIN' COMPLETED WEATHER REPORT'S CONTRACT with Columbia on a high note, and Columbia was keen to re-sign them. Despite the ever-changing cast of sidemen, the presence of Joe and Wayne assured a high level of musicianship. But the label also wanted to hook them up with more substantial management than Bob Devere could provide, so they approached the team of Bob Cavallo and Joe Ruffalo about taking on the band.

At the time, Cavallo-Ruffalo managed one of Columbia's most profitable acts, Earth, Wind & Fire. In the spring of 1975, EW&F simultaneously had the number one album and number one single in America in *That's the Way of the World* and "Shining Star." Bob Cavallo enjoyed a close relationship with the group, having engineered their signing with Clive Davis in 1972 and guided them on their road to stardom. Building on EW&F's burgeoning popularity, the group's founder and leader, Maurice White, established a production company called Kalimba Productions, signing new talent such as singer Deniece Williams and a female vocal group called the Emotions, both of which were in turn managed by Cavallo-Ruffalo.

Although Cavallo-Ruffalo's clients operated in the pop realm, Bob Cavallo was well-positioned to represent a jazz band with crossover aspirations. For starters, he was a jazz buff going back to his teenage years in 1950s New York, when he was a frequent visitor to the clubs. Sixty years later he vividly recounted seeing Thelonious Monk at the Five Spot, Lennie Tristano at the Half Note, Nina Simone at the Village Gate, and the Gerry Mulligan Octet at the Village Vanguard ("the band was bigger than the room"). When Cavallo moved to Washington, D.C., to attend Georgetown University, he found the club scene lacking, so he and a classmate started the Intercollegiate Jazz Festival and established a club called the Shadows, which booked folk, jazz, and comedy.

Through the club, Cavallo met John Sebastian and Zal Yanovsky, two Greenwich Village musicians who went on to form the folk-rock group the Lovin' Spoonful. Cavallo took on their management, signing them to Kama Sutra Records, a subsidiary of MGM. When their first album, *Do You Believe in Magic*, hit big in 1965, Cavallo moved back to New York City and subsequently managed Sebastian's solo career after the Spoonful broke up in 1968. Cavallo later relocated to the San Fernando Valley north of Los Angeles where EW&F was based, as well as Little Feat, another rock band that Cavallo-Ruffalo handled. Being in close proximity to Joe and Wayne was a big point in the agency's favor.

"We were asked by Columbia Records to manage the band because they were so good, and they weren't accomplishing what they would like," Cavallo said. He had reservations. His love of jazz made him like the idea, but his business sense did not. *These guys are great, but we'll never make a real buck*, Cavallo remembered thinking. Nevertheless, he set up a meeting with Joe, Wayne, and Ruffalo at Zawinul's house in Pasadena.[1]

"Maurice White said you have the best band in the world, and we would like to manage you," Joe recalled Cavallo telling him. "And it was funny, we were supposed to meet those guys at three o'clock in the afternoon, and Wayne and me were drinkers, heavy drinkers. By the time they arrived we were totally drunk. So this was our audition. We had to really audition for this, you know. But somehow they were so down to earth there was no problem."[2]

Drunk or not, Cavallo came away convinced they should get involved. "We have to do this," he told Ruffalo. "But we have to think of them more as a state band. They should be protected, they're so great." He told Bruce Lundvall, who was now general manager of CBS's record division, "We'll take them on. But it's going to cost you some money, because *we're* not going to make any money."[3] Cavallo urged Lundvall to think of Weather Report as a prestigious asset rather than as a profit center. Instead of a traditional record deal with advances against royalties, he proposed that Columbia pay a monthly stipend to meet the band's operating expenses. "Any money we take in, we will put towards this shortfall. But this is what they need to keep the band together."[4] Lundvall, a jazz lover himself, agreed to the arrangement.

With Cavallo-Ruffalo behind them, Joe and Wayne signed another contract with Columbia, during which the band enjoyed its greatest success. "We didn't really make a buck," Cavallo remembered. "I mean, most of the time I didn't take a commission. I just made sure they made enough money along the way. If there wasn't enough money, I went to Walter [Yetnikoff, president and CEO of CBS

Records Group] or whoever and got some from Columbia."[5]

The arrangement yielded immediate dividends as Cavallo-Ruffalo booked Weather Report on a tour with Earth, Wind & Fire. A few years earlier, the two bands had done some college gigs together, but now EW&F was such a huge box office draw that they sold out venues like Madison Square Garden and the Hollywood Bowl. Serving as an opening act can be an uneasy fit, with audiences paying little attention as they file in, but the band was too busy putting on a good show to notice. Besides, most of the members of Earth, Wind & Fire were next to the stage listening in.

Joe and Wayne must have felt pretty good about things. In Europe, the band killed, motivated by large and enthusiastic crowds. Upon returning to the States at the end of November 1975, they learned that *Down Beat*'s readers named Weather Report their favorite jazz group for the fourth year running. With the band functioning on a high level and eager to record, they spent a week rehearsing before making their sixth album for Columbia.

"I'll never forget the first rehearsal," Thompson recalled. "I was a little intimidated by Wayne. I didn't quite know how to relate to him, because he's a different kind of guy, with the clipped way that he speaks and stuff. And it's like he doesn't seem to say much, but it's always pretty deep when he does say things, which to me is the same way that he plays. But that first rehearsal, Wayne got this gleam in his eye and he said, 'Let's run over the music!' We were pretty much reading the music on the floor; there weren't music stands all over the place, so all their handwritten charts were laying on floor—Wayne and Joe's both. And Wayne led it off and literally ran over the music. I wasn't ready for that. I thought that was the most amazing thing I'd ever seen, especially coming from Wayne Shorter."[6]

The LP was dressed in yet another eye-catching cover—this one painted by Dave McMacken—and printed on heavy matte paper with a glossy inner sleeve. It was first class in all respects. A versatile artist and illustrator, McMacken created dozens of album covers over the years, and is probably best known for his work with Frank Zappa. As was typical in those days, McMacken knew nothing about Weather Report's music and never even met the band. Instead, a Columbia art director named Nancy Donald gave him a call one day. "I've got a thing for you," she casually told him. When McMacken dropped by her office, she handed him a clipping to work from. It was an idea that Joe's wife, Maxine, had put together.

"It looked like it had been cut out of a magazine or something," McMacken recalled. "There weren't any people, just the front of a truck and a little bit of the back, so I just made up all the rest. She knew I could vary my style, and I came up with a kind of 1940s illustration, and the idea of the truck as a bus. The front of the truck is almost the same as the one that was in the clipping. The number on top was my street address. I created all of the characters and the Caribbean look with the palm trees, and what I did helped inspire the album name. 'You created a whole market place,' they said. 'Why don't we call it Black Market?'"[7]

Black Market is arguably the quintessential Weather Report album—all the more remarkable because, like so much of the band's early music, it was recorded with shifting personnel. The mix of composed themes, improvisations, textures, and colors blend into a thoroughly unique and vibrant form that Joe and Wayne called "folk music of the future."[8] With its hummable melodies and vigorous grooves, *Black Market* is an outstanding expression of Weather Report's ability to make accessible music without sacrificing artistic merit; "neither difficult to listen to nor dull," as one writer appraised it.[9]

Like *Tale Spinnin'*, Joe took credit as orchestrator, and more significantly, sole producer (Wayne was relegated to co-producer)—an indication of the strength of his vision and his role as the group's leader. Once again, his arrangements were richer and denser than anything the band had previously produced. This was due in part to two newly invented instruments that Joe and Wayne introduced on this record.

That fall, Tom Oberheim—he of the ring modulator and phase shifter—began producing the Oberheim Four Voice synthesizer. Joe and Brian Risner dropped by his Santa Monica facility and picked up one of the first ones made. As the name connotes, it was capable of playing four notes at a time and was among the first commercially available synthesizers that could do so. Not only was it polyphonic, it was also polytimbral, meaning that each of the four voices could be programmed to a different timbre. This is because the Four Voice was actually four independent synthesizers (which Oberheim called SEMs, an acronym for Synthesizer Expander Modules) connected to a single keyboard. As such, it occupies a unique niche in synthesizer history: a hybrid of the original monophonic analog synthesizers and the microprocessor-based polyphonic instruments that were just around the corner.[10]

That each module was independent of the others had its plusses and minuses. The flexibility enabled creative options that weren't possible otherwise, but it also meant that each module had to be configured separately, even if the desire was for them all to produce the same timbre. It was akin to programming four 2600s. The Eight Voice, released shortly after the Four Voice (with a retail price topping $10,000), was even more onerous in this regard. This problem was not lost on Tom Oberheim, who realized that without memory it was nearly impossible to change settings on stage. This gave rise to the Oberheim Polyphonic Synthesizer Programmer, which could store sixteen patches (although not all of the settings were storable). When Joe got his Four Voice, the Programmer didn't exist yet. Nevertheless, it was a big step forward and it lit up *Black Market*.

Meanwhile, Wayne acquired a Lyricon and experimented with it throughout

the second half of 1975. As the first commercially available wind-controlled synthesizer, it was a breakthrough in its own right and generated considerable interest
among saxophonists. It was played via a soprano-like body and a bass-clarinet
mouthpiece fitted with sensors that detected wind and lip pressure, giving it an
expressive, dynamic quality that couldn't be achieved by the on-off nature of a
piano-style keyboard. Wayne got one of the first ones made.

The Lyricon, too, proved cumbersome in live performance because like the
other early synthesizers, it had no memory or preconfigured patches. "It was a
difficult instrument to get a sound on," Risner said. "So once you got one, it
was there and you couldn't change it easily. It wasn't graphic, just a bunch of
knobs, and the settings were very delicate." As a consequence, it saw limited use
in concert. "Wayne pretty much used it on one song. It didn't become part of the
repertoire. That was just the nature of the machine."[11]

But on *Black Market*, Wayne used the Lyricon so effectively that it seamlessly
blends into the overall soundscape. It is heard most prominently on his tune
"Three Clowns," in which Wayne explained that he "turned some knobs between
the restatements of the theme, and without really knowing what each knob was
for, bam! Some marvelous sounds were created."[12] Of course, some jazz purists
detested it, and Wayne could have played his beautiful, haunting melody on saxophone, but the Lyricon gives "Three Clowns" an entirely new and unfamiliar
character that fits the overall theme of *Black Market*.

Less obvious is how the Lyricon pops up on most of the album's other tracks,
including "Barbary Coast," "Herandnu," and even the title track. As Brian Risner
notes, "It's all over that record."[13] In this regard, *Black Market* is an anomaly in
Weather Report's discography—the only one on which Wayne used an electronic
wind instrument. Wayne stuck with the Lyricon for part of the subsequent tour,
but after that he set it aside. (It resurfaced years later on Wayne's 1986 album
Phantom Navigator.) Although a few musicians carried on with the Lyricon—
most notably Tom Scott—it failed to achieve more than niche status, and by 1980
the company that manufactured it went out of business. The instrument's inventor, Bill Bernardi, never gave up on his dream, however, maintaining a repair shop
in his basement and harboring hopes of making a modern version of his classic
instrument until he succumbed to cancer in 2014.

Joe and Wayne exhibited an exquisite level of taste when it came to using their
electronic instruments. Even other musicians marveled at the richness of sound
they produced. That many of the synth tones were created by Wayne was lost on
most listeners (the album credits offer no help in this regard). To Joe and Wayne,
that was about as relevant as the old head-and-solo format. "I've been playing our
new album for some other musicians," Joe said shortly after *Black Market*'s release,
"and even some of *them* can't always tell who's playing what, or what instruments

Joe Zawinul and Wayne Shorter, November 1975. Wayne is playing his Lyricon. Atop Joe's Rhodes are the two ARP 2600 keyboards. The ARP control panels are to Joe's left. Above them is a Stro-botuner and a Mu-Tron Bi-Phase phase shifter. Partially seen in the bottom-left of the photo is a Moog Minimoog, which Joe carried for a short time in 1975. Photo: © Picture Alliance / Getty Images.

are being used at a given time. I like that. I like that a lot. Why *should* people know? We're not a bunch of individual musicians. We're a *group*."[14]

For the recording sessions, the band went back to Devonshire Sound with Ron Malo behind the console. Before breaking for the holidays, they cut five of *Black Market*'s seven tracks. The first side of the LP is turned over to Zawinul, who delivers a suite-like trio of compositions rich in narrative values, full of interweaving melodies and orchestral voicings that cemented his status as one of the leading composers/arrangers working in contemporary jazz. It is perhaps the finest slab of vinyl that Zawinul ever produced—the personification of what Bob Belden called "postcards home from wherever [Joe] was in his musical world."[15]

The title tune, in particular, held great significance to Zawinul. Years later, when asked to name a single song that best represented Weather Report, he didn't have to think about it.[16] "Black Market" embodies much of what Joe wanted to achieve in music. The folk-like melodies harken back to his days in Austria. It is rhythmically vigorous, with the excitement and energy that Joe found appealing in rock music. As usual, Joe eschews making the song a showcase for himself, instead providing a platform for Wayne to rock on soprano. If Joe has a solo on this tune, it's near the end, when Wayne and the synthesizers lay out, and he plays some elegantly simple lines on his Rhodes, hinting at the repeating motifs while bringing the intensity down to a simmer.

"Black Market" has vaguely African rhythms and instrumentation, with seemingly unidentifiable ethnic horns or reeds adding to the vibe. Of course, these sounds emanated from Joe's ARP 2600 and Wayne's Lyricon. "I call them natural yet unknown, beautiful sounds," Joe said.[17] It was partly a case of technology influencing the creative process. For instance, the sound Joe uses on the melody starting at about 0:30 is one he could only get on the 2600 "because of a certain twang that only the ARP has."[18] Its tone reminded him of the felt-modified accordion of his youth and brought him right back to those days.

Not only did Joe create an organic sound on the 2600, he played it in the most unorthodox of ways. One of the techniques for which he is best known is the inverted keyboard, which he accomplished by running the ARP's keyboard through its voltage inverter so that as he played up the keyboard, the pitches descended. Zawinul improvised the melody line for "Black Market" this way. Afterward, he listened to the tape and played the same melody on a normal keyboard, but he felt like it didn't have the same feeling, so he relearned it on the inverted keyboard. Joe continued this practice when he played the tune live, while playing the accompaniment as normal. "It takes a little while to get used to thinking in the mirrored system," he told Len Lyons. "The chord is going upwards and the melody is going downwards—in contrary motion. It's beautiful to challenge yourself visually. It makes you play new things."[19]

The second of Joe's trilogy is "Cannon Ball," a tribute to his former employer, who died on August 8, 1975. Joe first learned of Cannonball's condition in July, when he got a distressing phone call from Roy McCurdy after Adderley had suffered a stroke. McCurdy managed to get him to the hospital, despite a car accident on the way, but Cannonball slipped into a coma the next day and never recovered. He died nearly four weeks later at the relatively young age of forty-six, just four years older than Zawinul himself.[20]

Joe knew that Adderley's diabetic condition and obesity put him at risk, but the news still stunned him. A few days later, he improvised a poignant piece that had nothing to do with the style of Cannonball's music and everything to do with Joe's love for him. Zawinul was always a perfectionist, but he was particularly intent on getting this tune right. "I was with Joe when he first heard the news," Brian Risner recalled. "And this song was very personal to him. It was important, so *very* important in how it was going to be presented. Everything had to be right."[21]

In the studio, the tune didn't come together easily. "We rehearsed it," Chester Thompson said, "but that one was a little bit difficult for me to find what Joe was looking for. I had kind of a wrong concept because I had listened to a lot of Cannonball and I feel like a lot of what Cannonball did was some of the first true fusion things that really came about, like that 'Money in the Pocket' song of Joe's—really funky. So I tended to play it with a backbeat, and Joe was like, 'No, it's not a backbeat.' I never quite settled into the right feel, because I was trying to relate to it like it was a Cannonball song." Consequently, the band set it aside, returning to it later.[22]

The last of Joe's tunes is "Gibraltar," which he described as an "improvisation from beginning to end. It was one of those things I put together and then I wrote it out for the band and we played it—as simple as that."[23] The chart itself wasn't so simple, though. As good a reader as Chester Thompson was, even he was thrown by its difficulty. Fortunately, Alphonso Johnson and Alex Acuña were also excellent readers and the band quickly got a grip on it. Like many of the tunes on *Black Market*, "Gibraltar" has a highly atmospheric quality, starting with the sounds of a harbor, including a ship's horn. That is followed by a lovely introduction by Wayne on soprano, before the full band blasts into action.

Side two of *Black Market* leads off with two of Wayne's pieces that are as brilliant as Joe's: "Elegant People" and the aforementioned "Three Clowns." The seeds of "Elegant People" date back to Shorter's days at New York University. The title, he said, refers to "that state of living where one can say, with no regrets, 'I reached the point of pride and elegance of being a human being.' It's so elegant to be a human being—'elegant' meaning 'good fortune.' We are very fortunate to be born as human beings. So if we realize that fortune, why not strive to be the most elegant in everything we do?"[24]

Throughout "Elegant People," but especially during Wayne's tenor sax solo, Alex Acuña improvises a sort of percussion concerto. He was particularly inspired by this tune, to the point that he believes that Wayne wrote it for him. "If you listen to the percussion part, I'm just reacting to the music," Acuña said. "Wayne came to me and said, 'Hey Alex, that's exactly [right], I cannot write those things that you play.' I said, 'No, it's not about writing. You wrote the tune and I'm reacting to what the tune is screaming for from the percussion.' And I loved that. Maybe I play only four bars of congas, and then I play six bars of timbales, and then three bars of congas, like that. I didn't play like a rhythm machine from beginning to end because the music required that."[25]

The last piece on *Black Market* is a fitting swan song for Alphonso Johnson. "Herandnu" was the first tune he brought to Joe and Wayne since *Mysterious Traveller*'s "Scarlet Woman." He was keeping most of his compositions to himself because he had signed a deal with Columbia's subsidiary label, Epic Records, and was about to record his first album under his own name.[26] But Alphonso thought "Herandnu" sounded like a Weather Report tune and he brought it to rehearsal. Joe loved it—"a great fucking tune by Alphonso Johnson," he said years later.[27] It's written in an odd time signature and serves as a vehicle for Joe and Wayne to cut loose on ARP and Lyricon—Joe's only extended soloing on the album.

Alphonso explained the origins of the tune: "We were in Copenhagen and we had a day off, and I was out shopping for clothes. I went into this one store called Herandnu, and I asked the owner what the name meant. He said, 'Here and now.' I went down to the basement of the store, and I noticed back in the corner they had this little play area for kids, with coloring books and toys and stuff. And I just thought, *Wow, that's so cool, so forward-thinking.* As I left the shop I started hearing this melody, and that was the beginning of 'Herandnu.' So I brought it in to Joe and Wayne, and again, they put their own take on it, which was great, and that's what you hear on the record."[28]

As Thompson recalled, "'Herandnu' was significant, especially for Alphonso, because it was the first time he got to bring in a tune and it was really *his* tune. The whole idea of 'Cucumber Slumber' started as a jam, and he brought in another tune. But basically, Joe and Wayne would kind of tweak it and turn it around so that it was truly a Weather Report tune with that special flavor. And so this was the first time he brought in a tune and they accepted it as he brought it, without having to change anything. And I love odd time signatures. I played a lot of those with Zappa, so it was pretty normal for me at that point in life. I always felt like it was really different from the rest of the album. I guess for me it has a special flavor.

"And see, the other hassle—I don't know if it ever got talked about, but Alphonso was eagerly waiting for membership, because they had been saying that he was going to become a full member of the band. And when management changed, the new managers were like, absolutely not, you guys keep it the way it is. I mean, Alphonso had been there for two years, and I totally get it. All the years I spent with Genesis, I was never a member of the band; I was a hired gun the whole time. So for me the significance and importance of that song is what it represented for Alphonso."[29]

The other musicians might not have liked it, but Bob Cavallo understood that more owners would create difficulty when it came to decisions and setting direction, to the point that it could easily undermine the entire enterprise. So he gave Joe and Wayne the same advice he gave Maurice White when Earth, Wind & Fire signed with Columbia in 1972. White had intended for all eight band members to sign contracts until Cavallo pulled him aside and convinced him to retain total ownership and control of production, publishing, and the band name. White followed that advice, and so did Joe and Wayne.[30]

•

With several tunes in the can, the band took its customary end-of-year break. By this time, Alphonso Johnson had given notice that he was leaving, so when Weather Report regrouped in January, Joe and Wayne began auditioning bass players. They were also under the impression that Chester Thompson was departing with Johnson, so they began looking for a drummer as well.

Alex Acuña recommended Narada Michael Walden, who had just left the second edition of the Mahavishnu Orchestra. (Narada, pronounced "Nar'da," was bestowed upon him by John McLaughlin's spiritual guru, Sri Chinmoy.) Like a lot of drummers who came of age in the sixties, Walden grew up playing a wide range of musical styles. As a consequence, he didn't think of himself as a jazz drummer or a rock drummer, or any other kind of drummer. It was the ideal attitude for Weather Report because their drummer needed to be all of those things.

When Walden arrived at Devonshire Sound, the first tune he was asked to play was "Black Market." Of course, the band had already recorded it with Chester Thompson, but Joe wanted to see what this new drummer could bring to the table. Zawinul played the song on his Rhodes while Walden recorded it on his portable cassette deck. "I'm a quick study," Narada explained. "I don't read music on those kind of sessions. Never. Mahavishnu Orchestra, Weather Report—you just learn it, memorize it by heart. And then once I learned it, we cut it a couple of times, and that was it. Boom. That's all it is. You count how many times a section repeated, and then you're gone. And from there on, it's really improvised."[31]

As the band started jamming, Narada immediately impressed and the recording light went on. "I'll never forget just looking across the room and seeing everybody so happy," Narada said. "And it was all live. I mean, that's Wayne playing live, that's Joe, everyone playing live. Alex Acuña's percussion is so genius. Everyone was just so happy. And I also remember the intensity of Joe. When you look at him, you know you're playing with somebody. You know he's hearing everything, feeling everything, anticipating like a boxer. That whole thing with him was just magical.

"And Wayne, to me, is a genius. He can go way out there, but with me he played things I completely understood right away. He played like he played in a funk band. I was surprised. If you listen to the sax playing at the end of 'Black Market,' it's like he's in a funk-soul band, like a James Brown band. You think Wayne Shorter, you think *space guy*. But really, he was just as down to earth as he wanted to be whenever he wanted to be. I wouldn't have known that had I not done 'Black Market' with him. And Joe, too, for that matter. Joe shifted into doing that early stuff he would do with Cannonball, that comping that made the whole place go crazy—not trying to be all tricky or slick, just laying it down. I couldn't believe how hard-core funky they would get."[32]

At Joe's urging, Narada brought a fire to "Black Market" that hadn't existed in the previous takes. Joe liked it so much that he used it on the LP, but with a twist: He spliced together an earlier take with Thompson and one with Narada. The first part of the released track, which is played by Thompson, has a relaxed feel. Then a cymbal crash masks a hard cut at about 2:29, and the rest of the tune is with

Joe Zawinul plays the acoustic piano at the 1976 Montreux Jazz Festival. Behind Joe is his Rhodes electric piano and the two ARP 2600 keyboards. To the left of the 2600 keyboards is the Mzuthra, and to its left is a custom six-channel mixer that Brian Risner designed and had built. It was connected to the house PA system as well as the stage monitors. It also had outputs for two Echoplexes, allowing Joe to feed multiple devices to each. Photo: Brian Risner.

Narada and all the fire. "I wasn't so much aware of Chester's recording," Narada said. "I mean, no one explained anything to me; I just went in and played it. Then I heard it later, how they edited it together, and I come splicing in on the bridge part [sings it] for all that high-flying stuff.

"So I played through the song and Joe was very happy. He said, 'Would you consider joining the band and bringing a bass player?' I said, 'Well, that's a very sweet compliment, thank you. But I'm not sure about joining the band.' And I was very candid. I had just left Mahavishnu Orchestra and the fusion thing. I wanted to do more of a rock thing, with girls' panties on stage. I'd never experienced the rock thing. I was very impressed by the offer because I loved them, but I wasn't sure about it yet."[33]

"I don't know about being the drummer," Narada told Joe. "But I know a bass player by the name of Jaco Pastorius, who I jammed with in Florida, and he's really something."[34]

•

Today Jaco Pastorius is universally recognized as a legendary figure of the electric bass. His innovation and mastery of the instrument was profound, influencing virtually everyone who has played it since, across all genres. In fact, upon hearing Jaco's 1976 debut album now, it is difficult to appreciate how groundbreaking it was because it has been so thoroughly absorbed into the bass lexicon. But as Joe and Wayne mulled over bringing Pastorius to L.A., he was barely known outside of south Florida, where his singular tone, boundless virtuosity, and brash personality made him something of a cult figure among local musicians.

Born on December 1, 1951, John Francis Pastorius III was the oldest of three boys raised by Jack and Stephanie Pastorius. The family lived near Philadelphia, but when Jaco was eight they moved to the Fort Lauderdale area. Jack was a professional musician who played standup drums and sang in a style similar to Frank Sinatra's, punctuated by a steady stream of hip stage banter. Though he did lounge gigs around town, Jack was more often on the road. His absences, combined with his drinking, led to a strain on his marriage with Stephanie, and they separated when the boys were still in grade school, with Jack returning to Pennsylvania while Stephanie and the boys remained in Florida.

Jaco was an intensely competitive, precocious youngster who excelled at everything he tried. His closest sibling, Gregory, remembered being depressed at how easily things came to his older brother. But it was music, Gregory said, that was most natural to Jaco. "He said he heard music in everything," Gregory recalled to journalist, Pat Jordan. "A baby crying. A car passing by. The wind in the palm trees. All of a sudden, he'd say to me, 'Shhh!' and he'd listen. I didn't hear a thing."[35]

At the age of thirteen, inspired by his dad, Jaco bought a small drum set with money he earned from his paper route. Shortly thereafter he made his first public appearance as a musician. This being 1965, the trio donned Beatles-style wigs and performed a couple of the group's hits. Jaco was good enough that people walked away commenting, "Wow, not only is Jaco the best athlete in school, he's the best drummer, too!"[36]

A little later, Pastorius joined a group of teenaged musicians who called themselves Las Olas Brass. Soon a more experienced drummer came along, and it looked as if Jaco was out of the band. But as luck would have it, the bass player left at about the same time, so his bandmates asked Pastorius if he could play the bass. As Jaco later told the story: "I went out and bought a brand-new Fender bass, took every penny out of the bank that I had from my paper route, and that was it. I have this super-analytical mind—my whole family have it. I can figure out how to play any instrument in an hour. I can figure out how to play the trombone, in one key at least, in an hour. It's just the way I am. I had to ask someone to tune the bass for me, then I just sat there and played."[37]

It was clear that Jaco had a gift, but he also put in a tremendous amount of work. He became obsessed, practicing for hours on the living room couch or playing along with 45s in his bedroom. He could barely hear the bass on his cheap record player, so he copied the melodies instead. Not only that, Jaco was keen on understanding how music worked, so he learned all of the parts of the latest James Brown or Beatles tunes. Within a few months, Jaco said, "I knew every rhythm 'n' blues tune there was in the world, and I could play 'em on the bass, drums, guitar, piano, and saxophone. I was a fanatic."[38]

By the time Jaco finished high school, he had formed a couple of funky bands of his own and recorded his first version of "The Chicken," an R&B tune by James Brown guitarist Pee Wee Ellis that became a staple of Jaco's live performances. The recording is notable for the fact that he played all of the parts—bass, drums, guitar and saxophone—overdubbing himself on his friend Bob Bobbing's reel-to-reel tape deck.

In 1970, Jaco's girlfriend, Tracy Lee Sexton, became pregnant. They married that summer and their daughter Mary was born in December. At the time, Jaco was working at a car wash to make ends meet. It "wasn't much fun," he later said. About a month before Tracy gave birth, Jaco took the $700 he had saved up for the anticipated hospital bills and spent it on a quality amplifier instead—an Acoustic 360, which became an integral part of his sound. "I needed it," he explained. "We needed it. Playing was my life, and if I didn't have a good amp, I realized no one was going to hear me. And by the time [Mary] was born, I had already earned about $500 back, working with that amp. It was a decision forced on me by the realities of the situation."[39]

With a family to feed, finding steady gigs became paramount. One was aboard a cruise ship that plied the Caribbean. Another was with the local funk band Tommy Strand and the Upper Hand. But the most formative of Jaco's early gigs was the five months he spent with the C.C. Riders in the late summer and fall of 1972.[40] The Riders were a stone-cold R&B horn band led by their flamboyant front man, Wayne Cochran. On stage, Cochran was a sight to behold, dressed in over-the-top wardrobes capped with an immense, gravity-defying blonde pompadour that David Letterman once described as "the biggest hair on a human you're ever going to see." Backed by a crack ten-piece band, Cochran belted out tunes in his gravelly voice, with gospel exhortations sprinkled in along the way.

Cochran was called "the white James Brown," whose mannerisms he freely copped. He was extremely popular in Miami due to his frequent appearances on the old Jackie Gleason Show, which was taped there. "He was just an amazing performer, and the C.C. Riders had a great horn section, really funky," recalled one Floridian who took in his shows. "And as the night progressed he'd just get even more intense as a result of God knows what. It got to where he would be out in the audience, standing on people's tables and knocking bottles over, walking on top of the bar. The crowd would go nuts. You had all these tourists in there from Europe, and they'd never seen anything like it. They were just going bonkers."[41]

Musically, the Riders were a tight group led by its young musical director and guitarist, Charlie Brent. When the bass spot opened up, Brent and drummer Allyn Robinson heard about Jaco and went to see him one night. *This is different,* they thought. Jaco had obviously listened to R&B players like Jerry Jemmott, but he also had a unique staccato groove that Brent and Robinson liked. They invited Pastorius to a rehearsal and put him through Cochran's entire show. He "burned it to pieces," Brent later remarked. So when Pastorius auditioned with the full band the next day and Brent brought out the chart for a new tune that he wanted to try, it came as a great surprise that Jaco couldn't read it. Stunned, Brent asked him how he played all those tunes the day before. "I caught the show a couple of weeks ago," Jaco replied nonchalantly. He had done it entirely by memory.[42]

For Jaco, the C.C. Riders was like a rolling twenty-four-hour music laboratory. The band was constantly on the road, playing five sets a night, six nights a week, often in roadhouses packed with boisterous crowds. They logged miles in an old Greyhound bus, grabbing food and perhaps a quick shower at truck stops along the way. Jaco even convinced Cochran to waive his rule prohibiting women and children on the band bus, so Tracy and baby Mary joined the roadshow in order to save money on living expenses. Brent, who was just a few years older than Jaco, became his running buddy. They encouraged outrageous behavior in each other in a good-natured form of one-upmanship. It was what Brent called a "you got no fuckin' balls unless you do this" kind of relationship.[43]

Brent also became Jaco's mentor, tutoring him about chords and music theory. Jaco had an insatiable appetite for music, and it was a period of intense growth. After one all-night session in which Brent told Jaco "everything" he knew about arranging, Jaco went off and wrote his own chart, a tune called "Domingo." Brent also observed Jaco's transition to the fretless bass, which he recounted to Jaco's biographer, Bill Milkowski:

> We were somewhere in the Midwest, and Jaco said, "Man, I wanna try one of these fretless basses." So he goes down to the hardware store and buys some alligator pliers and wood compound. He takes those pliers and goes at the bass, tearing all the frets out—I mean, wood was flying. I was going crazy, yelling, "Don't do this! That's the only axe you got on the road—you ain't gonna be able to play the gig tonight!" But I swear, that night he played better than he ever played. He was doing slides and all the other things he couldn't do on the fretted. I guess he had been thinking about how he'd play a fretless, but he had never really screwed around with it before. It was fucking amazing.[44]

Jaco's musicianship exploded in Cochran's band. The Riders always played a few instrumentals before Cochran took the stage, and Brent wrote a tune called

"Rice Pudding" that included a spot for Jaco to stretch out. Pretty soon he was getting standing ovations for his solos. Coming from New Orleans, Charlie Brent and Allyn Robinson knew how to put the grease into the music; Jaco fit right in, providing a never-ending motor that propelled the band. But eventually, Jaco's "monstrous ego," as Brent described it, led to his dismissal from the band. He chafed at wearing the band uniform (a tuxedo) and acted out in various ways, clashing with everyone including the bus driver, undermining Cochran's authority as the unit's leader. Brent managed to keep the peace, but when he left in November, there was no one to run interference, and Jaco was fired a few weeks later.

Back in Florida, Jaco became determined to forge a singular path on his instrument. In 1973 and 1974, he made several connections that expanded his musical range beyond his R&B roots and put him on the path to the big time. One was with a young French pianist named Alex Darqui, who lived in the apartment adjacent to Jaco's. Darqui's tastes ran to modern jazz, and he and Jaco jammed for hours, the privacy of the apartment facilitating unfettered experimentation. Later, they joined the band of Ira Sullivan, an elder whose roots reached back to the birth of hard bop.

Jaco also established an important relationship with Peter Graves, who ran the house band at Bachelors III, a nightclub that hosted national touring acts ranging from the Temptations and the Supremes to Phyllis Diller and Charo. Although Jaco's cockiness put many people off, Graves liked guys who "played with attitude" and started giving Pastorius gigs. Aware that Jaco was scuffling financially, Graves also paid him small sums to write horn arrangements. Jaco remained friends with Graves for life and was a frequent guest of Graves's orchestra even during his Weather Report years.[45]

Meanwhile, Jaco was building a repertoire of his own, much of which would appear on his debut album. Through a friend he was able to spend time at a Miami recording studio where he cut demo tracks with the intention of using them to secure a record deal. In addition to the local musicians Jaco worked with, Don Alias played on these sessions. They met when the two were briefly members of Lou Rawls's band.

By the spring of 1975, Jaco was well versed in all kinds of music, though at heart he considered himself a rhythm 'n' blues player. Most importantly, Jaco had developed a thoroughly personal style. The only thing missing was the break that would launch a national career. It came via Bobby Colomby, the co-founder and leader of Blood, Sweat & Tears. In a BBC radio documentary, Colomby described how it came about.

> I was playing with Blood, Sweat & Tears in Fort Lauderdale, and during
> an afternoon I was playing softball with the club team. And in the out-

field with me was a blonde girl named Tracy. She had her hands on her knees and she was going, "Hey, batter, batter, come on, batter, batter"—which you don't expect to hear out of a young lady. So I asked her who she was and what her story was, and she said that she was in fact a wait-ress at that club where I was working. And she said, "Yeah, I'm married to a guy that's the best bass player in the world." And I went, "Well, that's very sweet. In fact, I hope if I ever am married, that my wife says that I'm the best drummer in the world, although I know I'm not." And she said, "Well, no, actually my husband *is* the best bass player in the world."

So that evening, a thin, pale, about five-eleven guy shows up in shorts—I'm not even sure he had on shoes—and he walked up to me—and he had these glasses that were made of plastic, they were kind of strange glasses—and he went, "How ya doin', I'm Jaco." I said, "Hey Jaco, how ya' doin." I said, "I heard that you're the best bass player in the world." And he said, "I am." And as he's shaking my hand, I notice his fingers are wrapping around my hand about twice; he had the largest hands I had ever seen. He plugged in the bass and I asked him to play a little bit.[46]

After a brief warm-up, Jaco launched into a solo rendition of "Donna Lee," the bebop standard first recorded by Charlie Parker in 1947 (and on which Wayne Shorter cut his teeth ten years later). All the while, Peter Graves took in the scene. "I'll never forget the look on Colomby's face as Jaco sat there playing solo. The astonishment on Bobby's face was worth a million bucks."[47]

Indeed, Colomby was awed. "Donna Lee" was about the last thing he expected to hear solo on electric bass, and the fact that Jaco could play it with the phrasing and nuance of a saxophonist floored him. "I said, 'Look, I don't know what I can do, but I'm gonna try and get you a record deal; you're amazing.' And he said, 'Yeah, great, okay.' His feeling was that I was just another jerk that had passed through his life, that had said he was wonderful, and then, you know, that was it; it was over right then and there."[48]

Unbeknownst to Jaco, Colomby had a production deal with Epic Records and soon made good on his word. Jaco signed a contract in September and was in New York the next month making his self-titled debut album. *Jaco Pastorius* was a triumph. The breadth and scope of the music was enough to secure its standing as the work of a fresh new musical voice, but of course, it was Jaco's playing on the electric bass that turned the music world on its head. The first thing listeners heard upon dropping the needle was "Donna Lee," which Jaco performed as a duet with Don Alias, who plays congas. Not only does Pastorius demonstrate remarkable fluidity in playing Parker's sax solo, but the arrangement is strikingly original. It became an instant classic. Elsewhere, "Come On, Come Over" and "Opus Pocus" show off Jaco's unique staccato groove. "Continuum" creates an entirely new sound on the electric bass. "Okonkolé y Trompa" defies genre, its polyrhythms creating a hypnotic mood while Peter Gordon soars on French horn.

"Portrait of Tracy" is a tour de force in the use of harmonics. These high-pitched tones are produced by lightly touching the strings at various points on the fingerboard without pushing them down and plucking with the other hand. Harmonics ring only at certain points on the strings, so the trick is to know where they occur; it's like an alternate instrument within the instrument. Before Jaco, many electric bass players had a limited awareness of harmonics as a way of tuning up, but no one had explored them in any depth on electric bass until Pastorius did. Not only did he figure out how to make music with them, he perfected his technique so that he could make them sing, effectively extending the range of the bass to the treble clef.

Jaco's debut album instantly became the subject of intense study among bass players at institutions like the Berklee College of Music. (The school's name was changed in 1970.) Other young musicians wore out the LP in their bedrooms, determined to figure out how to play Jaco's signature pieces like "Portrait of Tracy" and "Continuum." Overnight, bass players had to rethink the possibilities of the instrument. In the 2000 Sony/Legacy reissue liner notes, Pat Metheny wrote, "The fact that this was his first record is simply astonishing; there's no other way to put it. That this is without question the most auspicious debut album of the past quarter-century is inarguable. As with all great recordings, the force of its value becomes more evident as time passes."

Colomby knew it before anyone else. "Right after we listened to the first play-back of the entire album, I said to Jaco, 'Ssshh—quiet, listen.' He looked at me strangely and said, 'What?' I said, 'I hear the sound of bass cases closing all over the world.' He loved that!"[49]

The rest of the year was a whirlwind for Jaco. At Colomby's invitation, Pastorius spent a few months on the road with Blood, Sweat & Tears. Colomby gave him a tape beforehand so he could learn the music, but Jaco didn't bother listening to it until the afternoon of his first gig. Expecting disaster, Colomby was shocked by Jaco's facility with the music.

Then in mid-December, Jaco flew to Ludwigsburg, Germany to record Pat Metheny's debut album *Bright Size Life*. They met when Metheny came to Florida in 1972, fresh out of high school, to attend the University of Miami. When Metheny saw Jaco with Ira Sullivan. "I almost went and got back on the bus and went back to Missouri," he later said. "It was just shocking to hear somebody playing at that level, who was two or three years older than me." They became close friends and later did trio gigs in Boston. When Metheny got a deal to record his first album, he brought Pastorius along. Joe Zawinul called right after Jaco got back to Florida.[50]

•

Like Narada Michael Walden, Alex Acuña knew who Jaco was, too. He had heard about him from Don Alias, so Alex knew where to get Jaco's phone number. Actually, Narada and Acuña both remember calling Jaco about Weather Report. They also both remember thinking that Joe didn't seem to know who Pastorius was, even though their first face-to-face encounter took place more than a year earlier when Weather Report made its debut in the sunshine state on October 11, 1974. Brian Risner sets the scene:

> We were on a swing playing the East Coast and we had gone down to Gusman Auditorium in Miami. At that time we were carrying a production with sound and lights. So we set up, did a sound check, and then their stage guy said, "Well, can you move the gear now?"
>
> I said, "What are you talking about? We've got all this percussion and electronic keyboard stuff, and drums on a riser. I can't move this stuff."
>
> "Well, we've got a seventeen-piece band that we've got to set up in front of you."
>
> I said, "Are you kidding me?" That was the first I had heard about this. If they had told us beforehand we probably would have tried to get them canceled or something. So we ended up moving our stuff back and made it work, and it turned out to be the University of Miami jazz band.[51]

At the time, Jaco was teaching bass in the university's jazz department. It was a gig borne of necessity. He took it not because he wanted to teach—he hated it, according to his students, and lasted just one semester—but because he needed the money. (Jaco's students invariably remember their one-on-one lessons consisting of Pastorius getting them to hold a groove so that he could solo for the next hour.) That night, Jaco sat in with the university jazz band, which performed two of his numbers, "Domingo" and "Amelia."[52]

No one with Weather Report heard him. "After the sound check, we all split and went to the hotel," Risner said. "I came back early—I had to be there before they finished—but I also wanted to see what was up, so I caught maybe the last half of their set and it was pretty good. I don't remember anything particular about it. So we set up and did our show."[53]

Afterward, Risner was packing up the band's equipment when a young man wearing glasses appeared at the back door of the auditorium. "Hey man, I've got to talk to Joe," he said.

"Well, I'm sure you do," Risner replied. "Hang out here and he'll be out in a little bit. I just can't let you back in."[54]

Of course, the young man waiting outside was Jaco.[55] He stood around a while longer until Joe emerged into the warm night air. Unbeknownst to Pastorius, Joe was in a foul mood. This was the gig when the memorable drummer from Switzerland showed up. Zawinul picks up the story:

> I heard from Slide Hampton, there's a guy from Africa, an African guy who's really great. So I contacted him and flew him all the way over. But while he was already in the airplane, I found out from my manager that the guy has been living in Switzerland for fourteen years, and I almost had a heart attack. I love Switzerland—it's a beautiful country—but any African man who has to live for fourteen years in Switzerland and plays drums there, on the little European thing, he ain't gonna be good enough for this band.
>
> So he comes to the rehearsal and we were rehearsing "Nubian Sundance," and it's *really* uptempo, you know? And he heard it and he was so nervous, he got white in his face. And then finally he sat down at the drums to try to do it and the sticks fell out of his hands. I was really mad—at myself more than anybody—that we had spent a lot of money [to fly him] all the way over from Zürich, and it didn't work out.
>
> So I was kind of mad and I stood there with these two ladies and helped the truck back out onto the street. All of a sudden, this funny-looking guy with glasses approached me.
>
> "Mr. Zawinul?"
>
> "Yes."
>
> "I liked the concert, it was very nice. And by the way, my name is John Francis Pastorius III, and I'm the greatest bass player in the world."
>
> And I told him immediately, "Get the fuck away from me."
>
> But he didn't. He just stood there and looked very innocent. And the one lady, the newspaper writer, gave me a little elbow and said to me, "Check him out. He's a little nuts, but he is a genius."[56]

The irony of Jaco's introduction is that he didn't really know much about Weather Report at the time. By his own admission, he hadn't heard their records, claiming that he "didn't even know what their band was up to until I joined it."[57] At the same time, his boldness was completely in character. When he went to New York to record his debut album, he looked up many of the top names in contemporary jazz. "He decided he had to become more well known," Pat Metheny remembered, "so he called up everybody he could think of—Tony Williams, Ron Carter, Herbie Hancock, and he says, 'Hey man, my name's Jaco, man, I'm the best bass player you're ever gonna hear in your life, man, we should play.' Just calls up all these people, and they're saying, 'Who?'"[58]

As Jaco stood there, shifting from one sneaker to the other, Joe had to admire his moxie, even if he wanted to get rid of him. *Either this guy is crazy or he's got something*, Joe thought.[59] "I'll tell you what," he said, softening up. "Come tomorrow to the hotel and bring a tape or something and we'll talk."[60] Jaco and his brother, Gregory, came by the next morning. After Zawinul offered him a drink, which Jaco politely declined, they listened to the cassette that Pastorius brought with him. Joe was impressed, but he was happy with Alphonso Johnson and had no desire to make a change. Nevertheless, he gave Jaco his address and suggested they stay in contact.

Over the next year, Jaco wrote letters to Joe. He talked about how his family were big Cannonball Adderley fans, and that he hoped they could play together one day. Late in 1975, Jaco accompanied a letter with a rough mix of his Epic album. The first thing Joe heard was "Donna Lee," which bowled him over like it did everyone else. "I was really impressed with the way he played, but I wasn't sure if he could really play funk," Joe said.[61] He must not have listened to the entire tape, for it would have dispelled that concern. Later Joe talked to Tony Williams, who had jammed with Jaco in New York. He assured Zawinul that Pastorius could play anything.

Back at Devonshire Sound, Joe thought of Jaco and Cannonball Adderley. "I said, maybe it's a good idea. He's a Floridian and Cannonball was a Floridian; maybe I'll have this guy come in and play on this tune, and see if he can play. I knew he could play after 'Donna Lee,' but to see the feeling."[62] Joe got Pastorius on the telephone. "You come to the studio and let's see. I've written this song for Cannonball; you take a shot."[63]

•

Right after the New Year, Jaco flew to Los Angeles and headed over to Devonshire the next day for his first session with the band. Meanwhile, Chester Thompson had also returned to L.A. after spending the holidays back home in Baltimore. Eager to get back to work, Thompson left word with Wayne. "I'm back in town. Are we going to the studio?" A little while later, Chester found a cryptic message on his answering machine. "Yeah, this is Wayne. And yeah, we're going into the studio. But don't bother to show up."[64]

"That's what he said," Chester recalled, flummoxed by the memory decades later. "Like, *really*? That was a very strange message to get. So I called Joe immediately and asked him what was going on."

"Well, didn't you quit with Alphonso?" Joe asked.

"I had no idea that he left," Chester replied. "That hadn't been shared at all."

Then Zawinul indicated that Narada Michael Walden was coming in with

Jaco. Thompson wasn't sure where he stood in the band anymore. "So am I fired or what?"

"If you didn't quit, you're not fired," Joe replied. "You're still in the band."

"Well, if you don't mind, can I come in and just play percussion along with Alex?"

"Fine, do that."[65]

The next morning, Thompson gathered his percussion instruments and drove to Devonshire. "So I get there—I'm the first one in the studio because I took my few percussion toys in—and Narada shows up with this look of panic on his face. He says, 'What are you doing here?' I said, 'Well, I'm in the band! What are *you* doing here?' 'Well, they told me *I'm* in the band!' They didn't know that Narada and I already knew each other, so it was obviously very awkward."[66]

Awkwardness aside, this was Jaco's day. Joe and Wayne had never heard him play live, so they were keen on seeing what he could do. For his part, Jaco was intent on making an impression even before playing a single note. Alex Acuña remembered him walking into Devonshire with a cocky air. "He came with his record, his black and white record that he made [it had to be a pre-release pressing because the album wasn't released until April], and threw it across the studio to Joe like a Frisbee. Like, bop! Joe caught it, and Jaco said, 'This is the best stuff you're gonna hear in your whole life.' And then Joe said, 'Man! This guy talks just like me!'"[67]

Jaco took his bass out of its case, plugged in, and tuned up. Ron Malo hadn't heard Pastorius play, either, so as a matter of course he put a limiter on Jaco's signal, not sure what to expect.[68] He didn't need to, because Jaco was fully in control of his sound. "Come here and take a look at this," Malo said, motioning to Brian Risner. "All I have is maybe 3dB of peak limiting and almost no EQ, and it's not even going into limiting. There's only one other bass player I've ever worked with who got this great a sound from his hands, and that was James Jamerson [the legendary Motown bassist]."[69]

As everyone warmed up, Joe taught "Cannon Ball" to Narada and Jaco. "The song was really intricate," Walden recalled. "So I recorded it on my cassette machine while Joe played the song through, so I would at least know what it was. Then I rushed out into the hallway for fifteen minutes and memorized everything. And while we rehearsed it, Jaco was learning it. And as he did at that time, Jaco wanted to Jaco-ize everything and put all kinds of things in there, just because he could; it was so effortless with him, he was such a brilliant cat. But Joe didn't want all that, and he stopped right in the middle of that rehearsal in the studio and said, 'Don't play that shit on my song.' And it was like a knife in the air. Jaco realized he wasn't fucking around, so it made Jaco the best Jaco in the world. It made him settle down, and whatever he *did* play, it was *right*, as opposed to playing just because he could."[70]

Joe made no bones about what he wanted. "I stopped the band and said, 'Now hold it. On one of those tunes you had sent me, you played with this beautiful tone. Why don't you play a nice little melodic line?' And this line, what he played after I told him—I didn't tell him what line to play, but to play around with what I was playing—that was what you really hear on the record. And that was it."[71]

The tone heard on "Cannon Ball" instantly became one of Jaco's signatures. At the time, the knock on the electric bass was that it didn't have the fullness and richness of an acoustic bass. Miroslav Vitous once said that the electric bass, compared to the acoustic, "is flat—completely flat. It doesn't have the overtones and it doesn't have the freedom. It's like half of the instrument, because on acoustic bass I can go all the way up near the bridge and play almost soprano saxophone range."[72] Jaco singlehandedly changed that perception overnight.

Everyone wanted to know what equipment he used. What kind of bass does he play? What kind of effects does he have? They might have been disappointed, then, to learn that he used a beat-up, old sunburst Fender Jazz bass on which the frets had been removed. He filled the empty slots with wood filler (which left lines on the neck, helping with intonation) and then applied several coats of epoxy to the fretboard to protect it from wear caused by the roundwound strings that he favored. For amplification, Pastorius relied on two Acoustic 360s. He settled on this setup early on and stuck with it, perfecting his sound along the way. But the key, Pastorius said, was in the hands. "In order to get that sound, you have to know exactly where to touch the strings, exactly how much pressure to apply. You have to learn to *feel* it. And then it just sings."[73]

With Jaco and Narada, "Cannon Ball" came together. "What Narada played was brilliant, to be honest," Thompson said. "I think he really nailed it. He didn't have that stigma in his head of what he thought Cannonball tunes were, because I was trying to relate to it like it was a Cannonball song."[74]

"Cannon Ball" also benefits from the crystalline tone that Joe achieved on his Rhodes piano, as did all of *Black Market*, for that matter. It was a far cry from the distortion-drenched sounds of *I Sing the Body Electric*. Once again, Joe was well served by Brian Risner's technical know-how. "We were always trying to make things better," Risner said. "And I wanted to clean up [the sound of] the Rhodes. Joe wanted to be loud and not distort it; you could only do so much with a stock Rhodes. The whole thing is just a mono instrument per se, just like a guitar. So we electronically split the keyboard into three sections—low, mid, and high—with separate electronics for each. It gave Joe a lot more control over the tonality that he got out of the Rhodes. It enabled him to create a clearer sound with a bell-like attack in addition to the Rhodes's rich, deep sound. At certain times Joe could turn the quality of the sound down to be softer, and at other times, when he soloed, he could turn it up and really scream. It was like changing the pickup structure on a guitar. And actually, somebody took a similar design and marketed it."[75]

•

Joe and Wayne knew they wanted to hire Jaco almost from the moment he began playing. Zawinul had just one reservation. "He walked so funny that I thought, *Okay, he might be a great bass player, but he looks like a comic.*" Joe was clearly big on walking as an indicator of musicianship. "So I said, 'Can you also walk straight up?' Because he walked very bent forward, like he almost collapses. And he had those funny clothes on—one yellow shoe, one red shoe. And then I thought, *Okay, if he cannot do that, maybe it works for us, you know?*"[76]

After the session, the three of them went outside to have a chat. "I can still see Jaco down the hallway, sitting out in the back of the parking lot at Devonshire, talking with Wayne and Joe after he'd come in and played," Brian Risner said. "They had little poles where the cars would pull up, so they had something to sit on out there, just talking. That's when they asked him to be in the band.

"But what I remember most is when Jaco came into the front [of the building] by the office and called his wife, telling her that he was going to stay here. I think at that time everything was really hand-to-mouth for them. And he was really sweating it, trying to explain to her how he was going to stay in Los Angeles and work on a record while she's back in Florida taking care of the kids. And he stayed for the mix and became pretty integrated into the thing. I don't remember how long he was here, but it was long enough for him to have to explain to his wife."[77]

Jaco told Joe and Wayne that he would join the band, but he wanted to speak with the band's management first. They might have thought Pastorius just wanted to work out the financial terms, but Jaco had something else in mind. Alex Acuña overheard the conversation:

> Jaco was very confident—sometimes overconfident when he talked to the management on the phone—which is okay; it worked for him in those days. He always wanted me to be with him, because we were rooming together, and Jaco and I had a lot of things in common. We had family, we had music, and he knew and played with a lot of people from the islands.
>
> So we were in our room, on the patio, talking to the managers on the phone, and immediately he said, "You know, if you want me to be a part of this band, you have to let me put one tune in the album."
>
> The management said, "Are you crazy? This is Weather Report—Joe and Wayne. There are no other composers who can write better music than those guys. What kind of music are you going to write? Have you talked to them about it?"
>
> He said, "Well, no, *you* talk to them about it! If you don't want me to

join the band, then it's okay. And if you want me on the road, you have to pay me this much money. And also, you have to pay this amount of money to Alex."

So he was being my manager right there. Jaco was no dummy. He read a lot. He was a very educated guy.[78]

And so this is how "Barbary Coast" came to be included on *Black Market*. It was a tune that Jaco began working on shortly before leaving Florida and finished on the flight to California. Fittingly, he called it "Coast to Coast" before the name was changed to better fit the theme of *Black Market*. The "Coast to Coast" working title may also explain the use of the train sound effect, though this also had personal meaning to Pastorius, who as a kid would often sit by the railroad tracks at the end of his street watching the trains roar past.[79]

Whereas "Cannon Ball" took advantage of Jaco's tone, "Barbary Coast" shows off his groove. The funky, mid-tempo number is basically a three-minute form on one chord, bouncing along with Jaco's bass front and center. In addition to his rock-solid time, Jaco's grooves were extremely expressive, in part because of his use of muted notes. These "ghost notes" were made by partially fretting when he plucked, producing a percussive sound that lacked pitch definition. Some likened it to playing congas on the bass. As Joe and Wayne soon found out, Pastorius could maintain these grooves at the fastest tempos all night long, tossing off melodic asides along the way.

Jaco loved steel drums, and Joe evokes that sound with his ring-modulated Rhodes. "At first, I didn't like that tune so much," Zawinul told Bill Milkowski. "It sounded too much like a Horace Silver line to me. But then we worked a little bit with it and got a nice groove happening. And, of course, that became a kind of signature piece for Jaco, and we played it in concert often with Weather Report."[80]

The train sound effect is just one example of the level of detail that Joe and company brought to *Black Market*. The title track opens with the vague din of people speaking, evoking the feeling of an open-air market. These sounds were taken in part from a recording Alex Acuña made of his family, coupled with a tape speed manipulation similar to the one used on "Badia" from *Tale Spinnin'*. The outro includes the pops and crackles of fireworks meant to establish a festive atmosphere. Some fans attributed this effect to Joe's synthesizers, but Brian Risner explained that it came from a sound-effects library, as did the harbor sounds in the introduction to "Gibraltar." "Elegant People" begins with a five-second reversed recording that sounds somewhat like a violin. "It's Wayne's horn," Risner said. "We recorded it straight and then spun part of it off to a two-track, flipped it over [reversed the tape], and flew it back in, cutting the tape at the right point. There might be part of an acoustic piano or a synth, but it's primarily the horn."[81]

With two drummers and two bass players, it's tempting to call *Black Market* a transitional album. But that designation often serves as a euphemism for a substandard effort, which is hardly the case given how well *Black Market* is crafted. Like its predecessors, *Black Market* owes its success to the brilliance of Joe Zawinul and Wayne Shorter, and their ability to enlist an ever-changing cast of sidemen in service to their vision. As Ray Townley put it in his five-star review for *Down Beat*, "It's difficult to believe that one group can remain so bountifully resourceful year after year."[82]

13 Heavy Weather

> We don't play no jazz and we don't play no rock. We play our original music; our category is Weather Report.
>
> —Joe Zawinul

WHILE WORKING ON *BLACK MARKET*, Weather Report remained off the road for over four months, the band's longest such stretch since its inception. In March 1976, they regrouped to rehearse for an eight-week tour of the United States, to be followed by a return to Europe. Jaco was signed to replace Alphonso Johnson, while Chester Thompson and Alex Acuña remained onboard. But as they began running through material with Pastorius, it quickly became apparent that he and Thompson weren't going to work out.

"We started rehearsing for the tour and it was a disaster," Chester recalled. "I'd play the things I played on the album, which Joe and Wayne had been extremely complimentary about. But in rehearsals it was like, no, that's the wrong feel, because Jaco just couldn't really swing that way, I don't think. I can't say he couldn't, but he didn't. There was a radical difference between [him and Johnson]."[1] In short, the space that Alphonso left in the music was filled with notes. There was also a hangover effect from Chester's firing and rehiring, and the vibes never felt right as a result.

As before, Alex and Jaco roomed together. The band rehearsed all day, and it took them a while to unwind before going to bed. One night Jaco put his bass up against the wall (in order to hear it more easily without amplification) and picked out a tune that Wayne had written for Miles Davis.

"Hey, Alex, you heard this tune?" Pastorius asked.

"I know all those tunes," Acuña said. He grabbed his brushes and started tapping out a rhythm on the table.

Jaco raised an eyebrow and shifted his gaze to Alex. "You know *all* these tunes?"

he asked again.

"Of course," Alex said. "I listened to Coltrane and Miles all my life." Then he explained that he played drums as well as percussion. He had his reel-to-reel tape deck with him, so he cued up a recording he made in New York with some Puerto Rican bands that he was in.

"What?" Jaco exclaimed. "You play drums like *this*?"

"Yeah, man. I'm a drummer."

"I thought you were percussion only."

"No, no, no. I'm actually a drummer trying to play percussion."

Jaco suddenly had an idea. "Let's go early tomorrow, before rehearsal, and just you and I jam."[2]

Since joining Weather Report, Alex had been careful not to encroach on Thompson's territory, respectful of the drummer's position in the band. "I never sat on Chester Thompson's drum set because I never liked to show off, or for people to say, 'Oh you play drums.' I was hired as a percussionist. That was my chair. That was my corner. I stayed in my corner because I didn't want to have any discrepancies with Chester or anybody." But at Jaco's urging, Alex made an exception. "Jaco and I went in early and started playing tunes, just following each other. And he was having fun, dancing and playing. And then Joe came in early that day, too, because he was excited that we were rehearsing, excited about the music."[3]

As Joe walked into SIR, he saw Jaco jamming, but Alex was hidden from view, engulfed by Thompson's large kit. When he got closer, Joe saw who it was. "Alex! I didn't know you play drums!"

"Well, yeah," Acuña replied.

Zawinul's eyes lit up. "He said, 'Okay, bring your set. You play drums and percussion with Chester. Just bring your drum set.' I said 'Oh, okay.' But then Jaco said, 'No, I want Alex to play the drums *instead* of Chester.' He probably didn't say it that way, but that's exactly the way it came across. So Joe asked, 'Why do you want Alex?' Jaco said, 'Alex's feel is exactly how I like to play—like Tony Williams with a Latin feel.'"[4]

The next day, Chester came to rehearsal and found Acuña's drums next to his own. "So we both started to play together," Chester said. "And that hadn't been said to me at all. Alex and I were really close friends, and he kind of gave me a look and just went, 'Man, I'm sorry. They just told me to bring my drums because it wasn't really clicking very well.' And I was like, 'Well, if we're going to do this, can we rehearse and work on parts?'"[5]

But by then, Thompson could sense where things were headed. "I contacted the management at the first sign of this thing, because this was coming up pretty quick. They actually had us on salary—a pretty low salary, but I was on a salary. And I basically said, 'I've got a feeling I'm no longer going to be in the band. Is it

Alex Acuña at his drum kit. Photo: © Tom Copi / Michael Ochs Archives / Getty Images.

possible I could get a two-month severance?' Management was shocked because they had even called me [during the recording of *Black Market*] saying how much Joe and Wayne liked what was being played and how great they thought every-thing was. They said, 'Certainly we'll give you that, but we have no idea what you're talking about.' But a couple of days later, they confirmed that I would be getting a check. They were glad that I had called them ahead of time because it was a big surprise to them. It was not a pleasant time, but the previous year had been probably the highlight of my musical life, so I wasn't angry. I just knew that it was time for a change, for them as well as for me."[6]

Alex Acuña's move to drums opened up the percussion slot. Jaco pushed for Don Alias, who had come to Devonshire at the invitation of Wayne (via Alex), playing congas on "Barbary Coast." Alias harbored lingering dissatisfaction re-garding his uncredited playing on Weather Report's first album, but he patched things up with Zawinul and was game to tour with the band. "I'll join, man. I'll join, no problem," he told Joe.

His enthusiasm was short-lived. "Just about an hour later the phone rings and it's Miles," Alias said. "I had to call [Zawinul] back. I mean there's no choice. There's absolutely no choice. Not taking away from Zawinul, not taking away from anybody, but Miles Davis calls you, what are you going to do?"[7] The old pecking order, with Miles on top, remained intact. (Of course, the irony is that Davis's health problems prevented him from touring in 1976, and he didn't re-sume performing live until 1981.)

With little time before the upcoming tour, Joe and Wayne began auditioning percussionists. Some of the best players in L.A. tried out, but the one who struck a chord was an exuberant young man from Puerto Rico named Manolo Badrena. Although he was a little green (he'd never been in a recording studio, for example), Badrena was an excellent musician. He played drums, percussion, piano, and guitar. He also sang and made wind instruments out of pieces of piping. Along with academic training, his experience included rock and jazz, cruise ships out of Miami, and Broadway pit bands in New York.

Manolo didn't know Weather Report's music, but Joe and Wayne were more interested in his musical instincts and how he fit with the rest of the group than anything else. "It was a good thing in a way that I just came in cold," Badrena later recalled. "The other members liked it at first because I just came in and approached it without a preconceived idea. I liked the audition. I went there and jammed with Alex, Joe, Wayne, and Jaco. Joe just took off in an F key, pointed, and said, 'Go!' I got behind the drum set, then I went to the percussion, and then I sat at the piano. From that, Joe said, 'Okay, he's musical.' Then he asked me if I could read, and he put a chart in front of me. I played it and he said, 'Okay, let's work.' So I worked with them until I cracked." [*laughs*][8]

Weather Report launched its U.S. tour at the University of Michigan in Ann Arbor on April 1, 1976. Saxophonist Dave Liebman and his band, Lookout Farm, opened the show with a fast-paced set of funky free jazz. Then, after a brief intermission, the house lights dimmed and the recorded introduction to "Mysterious Traveller" filled the room. Against this backdrop, Joe sat down at his keyboards and improvised a Rhodes/synthesizer solo that eventually revealed the melody of "Directions," and the rest of the band joined in. The Jaco Pastorius era was underway.

He put his imprint on the set list right from the start. After playing "Directions," the band launched into "Elegant People"—which served as the show opener for most of the year—and then segued into "Continuum" from Jaco's solo LP. That was followed by a medley of "Come On, Come Over," sans vocals, and "Barbary Coast." "Continuum" was later dropped in favor of a bass solo that was built around "Portrait of Tracy," but some form of "Come On, Come Over" and "Barbary Coast" was played at every Weather Report show that year. (They even tried a version of Jaco's "Opus Pocus" before giving it up.)

Weather Report marched through the month of April, performing nearly every night, usually with John McLaughlin's Shakti as the opening act. At this point, most of those in the audiences had never heard of Pastorius. Alphonso Johnson had a sizable share of his own fans, and his absence caught them off guard. One young bass player, John Sanna, remembered being "excited for weeks" at the prospect of seeing Alphonso. "So when the band came out and some skinny little

Zawinul at his keyboard rig during a sound check in 1976. The keyboard in front of Joe is the top-most of the two ARP 2600 keyboards. Joe is playing his Rhodes below them. To his left are the two 2600s. Above them is a Mu-Tron Bi-Phase phase shifter. To the right of the 2600s is an ARP Little Brother, which provided another oscillator and LFO (low frequency oscillator) that could be used in conjunction with the 2600s. Below the Little Brother is a Furman pre-amp and a custom mixer built by Brian Risner. At the far end of the ARP 2600 keyboards is the Mzuthra, though it's hard to see in this photo. Photo: Brian Risner.

white kid was on bass, I was outraged. I told the guy I was with that I was going to demand my money back. But after a couple of minutes I was like, 'Whoa, what's going on here?'"[9]

Tom Wilmeth wasn't a bass player, but he also remembered being "stunned" by Jaco. In his book, *Sound Bites: A Lifetime of Listening*, Wilmeth writes that he and his friends had heard rumors that Weather Report had a hot new bass player, but no one knew who he was or if it was true. When the rumor was substantiated on the bandstand, Jaco instantly captured Wilmeth's attention. "For me, the *sound* was the focus. My clear, indelible memory is one of an odd-looking young man bathed in a white spotlight. He was center stage holding a beat-up Fender bass high on his chest, playing like it was an instrument on loan from Mount Olympus. I kept hearing these amazingly fluid solo runs. But that couldn't be the electric bass. Still, Zawinul wasn't even playing at this point. It *had* to be the new guy! Playing those crystal-clear harmonics. On a *bass*? And the speed and cleanliness of each line, even in that fidelity-challenged hall."[10]

Similar reactions took place all spring. In some cases, audience members were openly hostile. At the Roxy, a nightclub in Hollywood, a member of the audience sitting ten rows back chose the beginning of Jaco's bass solo to shout at the top of his lungs, "Hey, where's Alphonso?" Moments later, as Pastorius played the fleet figures of "Okonkolé y Trompa," the same man heckled him. "Tune it, you stupid turkey!" At other times, fans talked among themselves, saying things like, "They're really different."

Pastorius shared a musical connection with Joe that was not unlike that of Joe and Wayne's. Jaco said that when he and Zawinul were improvising, it was "like we're one guy."[11] Gregory Pastorius remembered watching them, thinking "it was almost like two kids playing tag. Jaco would run up, play something—it'd be like he'd run up and touch Joe and take off running, and Joe would chase him. Their level of communication was, Jaco would just look over at Joe, and all of a sudden they'd just be right back to where they needed to be."[12]

Jaco provided a fresh jolt of energy offstage as well. He had a *joie de vivre* and a confidence bordering on arrogance that matched Joe's own personality. Jaco was always *on*, and just plain fun to be around. At nearly twenty years Jaco's senior, Zawinul was like an older brother and father figure to Pastorius. They competed at sports and games like brothers would do, but Jaco also competed for Joe's approval.

Weather Report worked its way down the Eastern Seaboard until it got to Miami on April 30. With both *Black Market* and *Jaco Pastorius* just hitting store shelves, it was a triumphant homecoming for the twenty-four-year-old bassist. Unencumbered by an opening act, Weather Report put on a sizzling two-hour performance. A writer from the *Miami Herald* was left groping for appropriate adjectives, though "incandescent," "hypnotic" and "musical pyrotechnics" sprung forth from his typewriter. Jaco got ample opportunity to shine, and the band drew several standing, stomping ovations accompanied by shouts of "we love you" and "thank you!" It was, in the words of the *Herald*, "one of those singular experiences one knows will linger afterward in the mind."[13]

Jaco's friend, Bob Bobbing, was in the audience. The two had known each other since high school, when Bobbing had the foresight to record Jaco's live performances. (These recordings form the basis of the box set *Portrait of Jaco—The Early Years, 1968–1978*, a labor of love that Bobbing produced and released in 2002.) "It was just great to see everyone supporting him," Bobbing recalled of the concert. "Even before it started, there was a lot of shouting out and enthusiasm. It wasn't just about Weather Report; it was like, 'Yo, Jaco!' And Jaco wasn't hotdogging it. He was doing his thing, but not too many theatrics and stuff. And it made me feel good, in a hard-to-describe way, that he'd finally made it. Something right had happened. He deserved to be in this position, in this band, to get to this level. It was a great hometown-hero-does-well kind of concert."[14]

A crush of well-wishers greeted Jaco backstage, though he didn't have much time for them as Weather Report was off to Orlando the next morning. But several days later, the band had a weeklong break, which Jaco spent in Fort Lauderdale. The local record store held a special event in his honor, where Jaco autographed records beneath a huge reproduction of his album cover, and sunk his hands and feet into a wet slab of cement outside. The *Fort Lauderdale News* ran an article about it, with a photograph of him wearing those big, clear-framed glasses everyone remembered. Jaco must have gotten a rueful laugh at the accompanying headline, however: "A Three-Block Trip from Rags to Riches," which referred both to the proximity of Peaches to Bachelors III, as well as Jaco's supposed new fortunes.[15]

From outward appearances, Pastorius was on top of the world. But internally, he was struggling with being an absentee father and husband. By this time, he and Tracy had added a son to their family. Leaving them wore on Jaco, not to mention the fact that the riches had yet to come. "I'd love to be able just to stay at home with my friends and family all the time," he told a local reporter. "But when you're into music on this level you have to go out on the road. God, I really hate it so much, but I don't have any choice. Right now I'm scuffling. Barely making a living so I've got to go on the road. There's just no other way right now. . . . After all these years you start getting just a little sick of being broke all the time."[16]

•

Joe and Wayne must have been cheered by the retail performance of *Black Market*. Within two months of its release it sold a reported 185,000 copies, well on its way past the 300,000 mark. "Did you ever dream, when you started the group," Zawinul was asked, "that you would reach this level of acceptance?"

"Sure I did," he replied matter-of-factly. "I'm only surprised that it took so long."[17]

Buoyed by *Black Market*'s performance, Weather Report commenced its tour of Europe—eleven countries and twenty cities in the span of a month. Many of these shows were packaged as a night of jazz-rock with Shakti and the Billy Cobham–George Duke band. Demand was huge; they nearly sold out the 10,000-seat Pavillon de Paris, for instance.[18] Alphonso Johnson was with Cobham-Duke, and Duke remembered how the audiences would chant Alphonso's name as Weather Report played its first tune. "However, it didn't take long for the audience to warm up to Jaco," Duke said.[19]

At the Montreux Jazz Festival, the bands each gave separate concerts, all of which were professionally filmed. Weather Report's show was eventually released on DVD. Although the extreme close-up style of the cinematography is off-putting, the video reveals many interesting details about the band. For instance, there are glimpses of Joe playing the melody line of "Black Market" on the inverted ARP 2600 keyboard; he even solos on it briefly toward the end of the tune. The 2600

The Pastorius-Acuña-Badrena band on stage at the Montreux Jazz Festival in 1976. Photo: © Andrew Putler / Redferns / Getty Images.

control panels are just to Joe's left, and he can be seen leaning over there often, manipulating the sliders during songs in order to change timbres. There are good views of the Mzuthra, which Joe plays on the introduction of "Badia." He also turns back to trigger the Islamic prayer effect from a tape player positioned behind him. Meanwhile, the Oberheim Four Voice at Joe's right mostly goes untouched, hobbled by the difficulty of changing its settings.

The video also shows how animated Jaco was on stage, though he was relatively restrained compared to future years. Even so, there are short bursts of Jaco dancing and grooving; it's easy to see why he commanded the attention of the audience. There are many close-ups of him playing his fretless bass, with the filled-in fret lines clearly visible. The video provides a trove of details for bass players, especially on "Portrait of Tracy." Some bass players initially claimed that the recorded version could only be done with studio overdubs, but seeing him play it live dispelled those doubts. The band still played old chestnuts like "Doctor Honoris Causa," but in significantly revised and ultra-funky form, with Alex Acuña and Manolo Badrena's Latin percussion and Jaco's propulsive, driving bass. Over the spring and summer, Joe developed an electric-piano introduction to "Causa" that he later adopted as the introduction to "Birdland."

The European tour concluded at the end of July with Weather Report, Shakti, and Cobham-Duke at the Hammersmith Odeon, London's premier concert venue. Two performances were originally planned for the 3,500-seat theater, but demand was so high that a third night was added. Technically, the bands received equal billing, but Wayne and Joe were thrust into the role of elder statesmen, which meant that they were frequently asked to comment on the state of jazz-rock. Zawinul bristled at the term. "It might fit for some bands, but not for us," he insisted. "If you're trying to put Billy Cobham, Herbie Hancock, and Weather Report under one label, it's bullshit; we don't play no jazz and we don't play no rock. We play our original music; our category is Weather Report."[20]

Unfortunately, the London shows were doomed from the start by their length; one observer referred to them as "five-hour marathons."[21] The format was such that each band had roughly an hour to perform, with interminable stage changes in between. Cobham-Duke opened, and on the first night they ran long, perhaps because they were recording for what became the album *"Live" on Tour in Europe*. It "apparently instigated a touchy 'political' situation," as one reporter diplomatically put it.[22] By the time Weather Report came on, many in the audience had grown weary or left entirely, and the band wound up playing a "sadly short set." Even so, the *Guardian* reported, "They still showed why they are the finest exponents of jazz-rock fusions (with the possible exception of the venerable Crusaders) playing today."[23]

Cobham-Duke's overtime stint didn't seem to cause permanent ill will, for on the last night, as Weather Report closed the show with a rousing version of "Gibraltar," members of the other bands joined them onstage. According to notes that have circulated with an audience recording of the gig, it started with Billy Cobham taking snapshots of Weather Report from the side of the stage. Alex Acuña motioned him out to take over the drumming, while Alex moved to percussion. Then Alphonso Johnson brought his bass on stage, and finally John McLaughlin came on, playing John Scofield's electric guitar. (Scofield was part of the Cobham-Duke band.) They kept up the song's closing vamp for some ten minutes in a raucous jam that brought the house down. It was a rousing sendoff for the return flight home.

•

All told, Weather Report spent about four months on the road in 1976. It was a far cry from their early years, when club dates dominated their calendar. Back then the band often played a week in one city before moving on to another. Now they could entertain more people in a single night than they previously did in a week. All things considered, life was pretty good. With so much time off, a reporter asked Joe what he did with it. He explained that it was "free for creativity, family, and traveling and living for fun." "We don't always make a lot of money," Joe added, "but we've always had enough to keep above water by doing as little work as we have been doing."[24]

Jaco, on the other hand, seemed to be in perpetual motion, in part because money *was* a problem. But he also just craved playing. He claimed to have been home for only three months in 1976, and when he was in Fort Lauderdale, he kept busy doing late night jams with local musicians and filling in here and there with the Peter Graves Orchestra (at one point supporting comedian Bob Hope). That winter Jaco also made several appearances with Herbie Hancock. "If the studio cats want to sit in L.A. making $200,000 a year on those nice little records that all sound the same, that's okay," he said by way of explanation. "But the cats who are making modern music are out beating their ass on the road, having to struggle to keep their families together. That's why their music is so strong, and why studio music will always sound like copy music."[25]

The most significant of Jaco's non–Weather Report activities was his collaboration with Joni Mitchell on her album *Hejira*. One of the great singer-songwriters to come out of the 1960s, Mitchell's early work was essentially performed solo, relying almost entirely on her guitar or piano for accompaniment. But as she grew as an artist, her arrangements took on the greater dimensions of a full band, and she had difficulty finding compatible musicians.

"There were no drummers or bass players that could play my music," she later said in an interview for *Acoustic Guitar* magazine. "They were imposing style on something without seeing what the something was that they were playing to. I thought, 'They're putting big, dark polka dots along the bottom of the music, and fence posts.' I'd end up trying to tell them how to play, and they'd say, 'Isn't it cute, she was telling me how to play my axe, and I've played with James Brown . . .' So it was difficult as a female to guide males into playing [what I wanted] and to make observations in regard to the music that they had not made. Finally a drummer said, 'Joni, you're going to have to play with jazz musicians.' So I started scouting the clubs, and I found the L.A. Express [a Los Angeles–based jazz-rock group led by saxophonist Tom Scott], but that was for my sixth album [*Court and Spark*]. It took me that long."[26]

Mitchell had an unorthodox guitar style characterized by her many nonstandard guitar tunings, which she used to create what some called "Joni's weird chords." And while her harmonies were a long way from folk, they didn't sound like jazz, either. "It's closer to Debussy and to classical composition, and it has its own harmonic movement, which doesn't belong to any camp," she said.[27] It would take someone with big ears to not only support what she was doing, but add to it. She found that person in Jaco.

In one sense, Pastorius wasn't any different from the other men Mitchell had employed, in that his ego wasn't going to let her tell him what to do, either. But unlike them, he immediately and intuitively grasped the nature of Mitchell's songs and created a sound canvas that beautifully complemented her own playing while respecting the emotional content of her lyrics. As musician and journalist Jeffrey Pepper Rodgers observed, "Pastorius both expands on her chords and harmonics and weaves melodies around her vocal line (including several Stravinsky quotes). His rhythmic/melodic approach was so thick and upfront that it demanded new approaches on Mitchell's side. 'Although I wanted a wide bass sound, his was even wider, and he insisted that he be mixed up so that I was like his background singer,' she said. 'So to get enough meat to hold his sound, I doubled the guitar loosely—I just played it twice.'"[28]

Jaco's playing on *Hejira* is one of the high points of his career. He performs on only four of the album's nine tracks, but his contributions dominate the entire album. In Pastorius, Mitchell found a kindred spirit. "There was a time when Jaco and I first worked together when there was nobody I'd rather hang with than him," she remarked after Jaco's death.[29] Ultimately, Pastorius would collaborate with Mitchell on three of her studio albums: *Hejira, Don Juan's Reckless Daughter*, and *Mingus*—a trilogy that ranks among his and Joni's finest work.

Hejira's fall release capped an incredible year for Pastorius. He made substantial contributions to six records—his own, *Black Market*, *Hejira*, Pat Metheny's *Bright Size Life*, Ian Hunter's *All American Alien Boy*, and Al Di Meola's *Land of the Midnight Sun*. On top of those issues, Paul Bley released some tapes that he had made with Jaco in 1974. The *coup de grâce* was the two Grammy nominations Jaco received for his self-titled album. (Weather Report continued to be shunned by the Recording Academy because it still couldn't agree on a category for the band's music.) All of a sudden, the skinny kid with the stringy hair and funny glasses was everywhere. "I'm the baddest," Jaco told Joni (and pretty much everyone else). "I'm not braggin', I'm just telling the truth!"[30] And he was.

•

Joe didn't have much time to explore the Oberheim Four Voice before recording *Black Market*, but when Weather Report was off the road, he called up Tom Oberheim, whose facility was across town in Santa Monica. "Tom, come out and show me how to use this synthesizer of yours," Zawinul cheerfully requested.

"I went out to his house," Oberheim recalled, "and we sat down with it, and I started talking about envelope generators and filter cutoff frequencies, and it was clear after several hours that the technical approach I was taking was not getting anywhere—at least that was my impression. So I left figuring, well, Joe will probably never use the thing. And I figured I'd probably hear later that he sent it back for a refund."[31]

Oberheim's observations reveal how much Joe relied on experimentation and eureka moments as opposed to technical know-how. Fundamentally, the Four Voice shared a similar architecture with the ARP 2600, only simpler. From his experience with the ARP, Joe had an intuitive grasp of how the various oscillator waveforms sounded and how they could be shaped with filtering and envelopes. But the control panels of the two instruments were completely different; it was like learning to finger a new horn. Moreover, Joe needed to explore the Oberheim's *character*; that is, its unique tone.

Not long after Joe's lesson with Oberheim, Bob Cavallo dropped by Joe's house with his junior partner, Steve Fargnoli, who handled the day-to-day management of Weather Report. After dinner, they all smoked a joint and adjourned to the music room, where Zawinul sat behind his keyboards and began to play. Cavallo vividly described it forty years later.

"Steve and I are sitting there on the steps of the sunken living room, and in the midst of this far-out exploration that Joe's doing, at one point he goes [sings the main theme of 'Birdland']. He plays that little riff, and he keeps going. A minute later, Steve goes, 'Joe, that little riff you played, you know that one that went [sings the melody]? That could be a hit.' So Joe noodles around and finds it, and Steve says, 'That could be a hit. You gotta make that into a song.' And that wasn't Joe's bag, right? Joe said, 'You mean this?' And he played it again. And I go, 'Oh yeah, you're right, Steve.' And I started beating on Joe. I said, 'You gotta put it in a three-to-four-minute form, and I think I can get it on the radio.'"[32]

Cavallo was an astute judge of hit potential, and of course his and Fargnoli's assessment proved correct. Whether Joe needed their encouragement or not, he did indeed expand upon that riff, combining it with other compositional elements to create Weather Report's best-known piece, "Birdland." Zawinul said that the tune's starting point was what he called the "fanfare" (heard at 0:43 to 0:55 in the version on *Heavy Weather*). The line reminded him of working with Dinah Washington—not musically, but "the kind of atmosphere we'd have when she was stompin' her heel."[33] To that he added the main theme—the one Cavallo and Fargnoli heard—and the bones of the tune were in place.

In addition to Dinah Washington, Joe drew inspiration from his times spent at Birdland the jazz club. "I wanted to show some of the feeling happening in those days," he said, "when I used to come down the stairs at two o'clock and Count Basie or Duke used to be working there."[34] Heard in this light, "Birdland" is a paean to a bygone era, yet modern and fresh. It's one of the most complex forms Joe wrote, with several distinct sections and variations.

Despite this seeming complexity, it's also one of the most accessible and joyous pieces in the band's discography. Its introduction, in which Zawinul's synthesized bass line underlies Jaco's melodic riff, creates a great sense of anticipation, and when Joe and Wayne shout out the fanfare, it grabs hold of the listener and doesn't let go. The main theme of "Birdland" isn't even introduced until two minutes into the tune. By then, it's gone through several phases, propelled by the drumming of

Joe's keyboards are set up at Devonshire Sound for the *Heavy Weather* recording session. At right is Zawinul's Oberheim polyphonic synthesizer, which by this time has been enlarged to eight voices. Jaco Pastorius and Manolo Badrena chat behind the keyboards. Photo: Brian Risner.

Alex Acuña and Manolo Badrena's tambourine. Together they generate a rhythm that's rock-like in its steadiness, but juxtaposed against the syncopated lines bubbling around it, the overall effect is one of tremendous swing.

The most impressive aspect of "Birdland" is Joe's brilliant use of the Oberheim polyphonic synthesizer. Crucially, he realized that he could program each of the Oberheim's voices independently to emulate the instruments of an orchestra—say, piccolo, flute, clarinet, and oboe—or the horn section of a big band. Joe now had a small ensemble at his disposal, and it was a big leap forward in Weather Report's sound. Two months after Tom Oberheim visited, Joe called him back. "Come out, Tom. I want to play you this latest song I did using your machine." When Oberheim got there, he heard a rough mix of "Birdland." Zawinul's characterization of a big band reed section was so impressive that it surprised even the instrument's inventor. "It blew me away," Oberheim said.[35] Decades later, he still cited "Birdland" as one of a handful of examples that best showed off his synthesizers.

With "Birdland," Weather Report had a bona fide crossover hit on their hands—their first song to garner general radio airplay (that is, beyond FM progressive and college campus stations). This was the tune Weather Report fans played for their friends and relatives, who might suddenly realize they liked jazz after all. The 1970s saw the beginnings of the aftermarket for custom car stereo systems, and blasting a cassette of "Birdland" out of a quality set of speakers was a sure way to impress. In fact, the entire album sounds great; "sparkling" is a word some have used.

Like *Mysterious Traveller* and *Black Market* before it, *Heavy Weather* was recorded by Ron Malo at Devonshire Sound. Its sonic qualities owe in part to Devonshire's echo chamber, which Malo used to create the reverb-drenched ambience that permeates the album. The chamber was a 5,500-cubic-foot room with tile-lined walls. It was fitted with a speaker and a pair of Electro-Voice microphones that picked up the sound echoing around the room and fed it back to the mixing console. Malo described it as "one of the best echo chambers in town."[36]

Its use was encouraged by the way the band recorded. Unlike the classic Blue Note or Miles Davis albums, which were recorded in studios that boasted excellent acoustics, Devonshire's Studio A was a small, narrow room. The acoustic instruments were tightly miked, with the musicians separated by baffles or in adjacent rooms in order to prevent their sound from bleeding into each other's mikes. Joe's Rhodes and synthesizers were recorded direct. Jaco's bass was taken mostly from direct pickups as well, with his miked amplifier added to the mix. One reason for this, Malo said, was that "Jaco creates his sound by hearing what's coming out of his amplifier. . . . If he doesn't have the amplifier out there to work against, he has problems."[37]

With the ubiquity of multitrack tape machines in the 1970s, this was a common way of recording. Since little or no ambience was rendered in the master tracks themselves, it was added in post-production. Some engineers preferred plate reverbs, which emulate a physical space by bouncing sound off of a metal plate, causing it to vibrate. Other engineers were partial to echo chambers and had their personal favorites. Both techniques had their own sonic qualities, and sometimes both were used on the same project depending on the sound the engineer and artist wanted to achieve. Bruce Botnick mixed *Tale Spinnin'* at one of Capitol Studio's eight subterranean echo chambers located beneath the Capitol Tower in Hollywood, each of which had a unique personality. Likewise, Devonshire's chamber had its own personality, too. "Live chambers are something that just breathe and have a unique character unto themselves," Brian Risner said. "You certainly hear it on *Heavy Weather* because so much of that chamber was used, especially with the sax and the acoustic piano."[38]

Applying the echo chamber to the mix, as well as adjusting volumes and panning, and applying other effects to the individual tracks through the course of a tune was a hands-on process done in realtime—a performance in its own right. And if the result wasn't satisfactory, it would be done all over again. (Nowadays, mixes can be programmed so that they are both repeatable and modifiable.) It turned out that in addition to his phenomenal bass chops, Jaco was really good at the mixing console. As a result, he wound up with a co-producer credit on *Heavy*

Weather, which Joe credited to his "workmanship and his input."[39] "Jaco was in the studio with me all the time in those days," Joe recalled. "Wayne was more or less the great 'painter' in the band, not so much involved in the recording. Jaco knew a lot about technology, and he always had a lot of good ideas. He was a very creative guy and fun to work with; lots of energy. . . . We'd be in there, and we'd all have our hands on it—Jaco and me and Ron Malo—doing all the fades by hand. Obviously, there was no memory [automation] or anything like that."[40]

By this time, Pastorius had become a forceful personality in the band, nearly on par with Wayne and Joe, and his playing figures prominently in every piece on *Heavy Weather*. On "Birdland" he plays the introduction using false or artificial harmonics. To do this, Jaco pressed a string to the fretboard with his fretting hand, thereby shortening it. At the same time, his picking hand touched the string lightly with his thumb while plucking behind it with another finger. It required precise finger and thumb placement, and he had to pluck hard to get the harmonic to ring instead of thump. It wasn't an easy thing to consistently pull off in a fluid and musical way, but of course Jaco had practiced this technique so much that he could do exactly that.

The album's second track, "A Remark You Made," is considered to be one of Zawinul's most beautiful ballads. It is an example of how sound itself could inspire him to improvise an entire composition. In this case, the inspiration came on the first day he had his Oberheim synthesizer, when he "found that sound that I use on the song. The next day, Jaco came over and we just *did it*. I knew it was special right away."[41] It is essentially a through-composed piece of music, meaning that it was conceived from beginning to end instead of relying on sections that repeat. This form was common in Joe's work, especially as he relied almost entirely on composition by improvisation. There are many highlights, including Jaco's gorgeous singing bass tone, Joe's artful blending of acoustic and electric pianos, and his ARP 2600 solo at the end.

"A Remark You Made" is followed by "Teen Town," which is now considered an essential track in the electric-bass canon. It took its name from a youth club where Jaco grew up, and it's almost entirely driven by his bass line. As Brian Risner remembered, it had a long gestation period. "We lived with that tune for a month, and nobody was really pleased with it; then one afternoon we went in, brought the tempo up and changed it all around. Sometimes you just wait for something to affect someone's life so that he'll see the tune differently—and then it happens."[42]

Not only did Jaco play bass on "Teen Town," he also played drums. Presumably no one knew the feel he wanted better than he did, but Alex Acuña suggests another reason that Jaco played drums on this track. Having already spent so much time in Los Angeles working on the record, Alex decided it was time to go

Jaco gets in some time behind the drums during a Weather Report sound check in 1978. Photo: Shigeru Uchiyama / Whisper Not Photo Factory.

back home to Las Vegas. "I didn't like to leave my family," he said. "I had a wife and two children, and I said I can't be leaving my home. The music was still a very important part of my life, but I kind of told them I'm not going to finish the album."[43]

Nevertheless, Acuña recognized the beat that Pastorius plays. It came from the tapes Alex played in their hotel room during the rehearsals for the *Black Market* tour. "We did a tune that was kind of a Santana style, but a Tito Puente style at the same time," Alex said. "And in that tune, in the middle of the song, there is a bass solo and me playing the 'Teen Town' beat. And Jaco said, 'Wow! That bass and drums!' And that was the inspiration for him to write that tune." Acuña also notes that Jaco recorded his drum part in separate tracks. "He played the hi-hat and the snare first, and then he played the bass drum and another snare, and the cymbals, doing the fill. He was the first drummer that I recall that was able to overdub drums."[44]

Side one of the LP closes with Wayne's ballad "Harlequin." It was the first tune recorded for *Heavy Weather*, and Zawinul gave Alex some advice before they played it. "Joe came to me and said in a very tenderly way, 'Alex, I don't want a backbeat, you know.' So, hey, I'm going to play this ballad like a Latin *bolero*, like the way a bongo played the *bachata* or *bolero*. So that's the way I played it. The bass drumbeats are in different places, and there is a flow going. There is no click track, the time is perfect, nobody is rushing or dragging. And then Jaco said, 'Alex, play a solo at the end.' So at the end, there is a drum solo, like Tony Williams playing the drums. Peter Erskine called me after he joined the band and said, 'Alex, I didn't know you played like that.' I said, 'Me neither!' But I knew what Jaco wanted, what he liked. It was his idea, so I kind of pleased him, for him to say, 'Yeah! It sounds great!'"[45]

The second side of *Heavy Weather* opens with the unexpected sounds of a live audience, followed by the even more startling full-throated singing of Manolo Badrena on "Rumba Mama." Manolo and Acuña regularly performed a percussion feature during the 1976 tours, and this one can be seen in full on the Montreux DVD. "It was a typical duet, Manolo and I," Alex recalled. "We didn't rehearse anything. Manolo would say, 'Let's do this, let's do that.' Every night was different. Jaco had a solo, and then Joe and Wayne had a duet. And then Manolo and I, we made the concert a little bit theatrical, not just playing tunes. Joe and Wayne loved it!"[46]

"Rumba Mama" is a great scene-setter for the tune that follows, Wayne's "Palladium"—a Latin-jazz smoker with an irresistible groove. While it didn't become the hit that "Birdland" did, "Palladium" is every bit as exciting. And like its better-known counterpart, "Palladium" pays homage to an iconic New York City nightspot. The Palladium Ballroom, located just down the street from Birdland, was the epicenter of Latin dance music in the United States, and the home of the mambo craze that swept the nation in the 1950s. Magazine articles referred to it as "the wildest ballroom in New York."[47] Wayne loved to hang out there and soak up the music, and like every other young man in town, he also knew his way around the dance floor. "You couldn't get a date if you couldn't dance the mambo," he told Michelle Mercer, who added that Wayne's friends "noticed that he danced like he played, with complex flourishes and frenetic outbursts, but altogether slick and controlled."[48]

Inspired by these memories, and perhaps by Joe's love letter to Birdland, Wayne wrote a tune that Weather Report could not have played before Alex and Manolo arrived. There's no question in Alex's mind that he and Badrena were its inspiration. "Most definitely. Wayne used to relate those things [about the Latin bands in New York] to me. He knew who Tito Puente was, who Machito was, and Tito Rodríguez, and all the players. He knew that Charlie Parker played with Machito's orchestra. Doc Severinsen, the trumpet player and leader on the Johnny Carson show, used to play with Tito Rodríguez. So a lot of American jazz players, black and white, were playing with Latin bands because it was Latin *jazz*—big band phrased in Latin ways. It was very hip, and it still *is* very hip!

"Wayne is one of the rare musicians who understood that. There is a live performance of Wayne that we did at the Paramount in Portland, Oregon, and Wayne and I took a sax and drum solo in the middle, just the two of us. And I'm playing

Manolo Badrena and Alex Acuña perform "Rumba Mama" in concert. Photo: Brian Risner.

Latin with the cowbell, and Wayne is soloing like a Latino player. His sense of rhythm is *perfect*. That's why he wrote 'Footprints' and all those tunes—'Palladium,' 'Elegant People,' because he understood that sound really well."[49]

"The Juggler" brings the heat down a notch. It's a tone poem that came about when Joe was improvising at his Rhodes one day. Alex Acuña remembered it being largely shaped during rehearsals. "Joe played it on the piano and Wayne said, 'Wow, that's beautiful.' Joe didn't even put the chord changes in the music. Jaco said, 'There's no chord changes, what do I play?' 'Play whatever you think.' Joe did it intentionally because he knew that Jaco had the eyes and the ears to understand what was needed."[50]

After the introspective nature of "The Juggler," *Heavy Weather* closes with a barnburner in "Havona," a tune Jaco regarded as his best contribution to Weather Report. It predated *Heavy Weather* by a few years and is among the demo tracks he made in Miami in 1974, which can be heard on *Modern American Music…Period! The Criteria Sessions*. Pastorius called it "a simple tune," but Risner remembered it posing some difficulty for the band. "Jaco brought the piece in new, so they were all reading it; I remember it was the most challenging song on the album. They ran it down a few times, and in those days a reel of tape was fifteen minutes, so you'd play the tune twice in a row for each take."[51] Jaco and Alex Acuña lay down a blistering groove (Manolo Badrena sits out), with Acuña cooking in his "Latin Tony Williams" style that Jaco found so attractive. Years later, Acuña called

"Havona" his favorite track on the album. "If you listen to that tune, everybody's soloing, in and out. That's Weather Report right there. It's almost like a free thing with a form. It's fantastic."[52]

Although "Havona" isn't a bass vehicle per se like "Teen Town," Jaco dominates the tune with what *Bass Player* magazine once described as "the consensus baddest bass guitar solo ever put to tape."[53] Bass players rave about his harmonic ideas, speed, and melodic inventiveness. "I can't recall how the bass solo was done," Risner said, "but there were at least three tracks of bass available, so Jaco could have edited it together from different passes."[54] Regardless of whether it was edited or not, this performance convincingly demonstrated that Jaco could hold his own as a third soloist alongside Zawinul and Shorter.

•

Joe and Wayne knew they had something special in *Heavy Weather*, but they didn't necessarily think "Birdland" would become a hit. Cavallo-Ruffalo did. "Birdland" especially seemed like it could appeal to a more general audience, so when the managers learned what Joe intended to name it, they weren't happy. "Who cares about Bird or Birdland?" they scoffed. But Zawinul was adamant. "I don't care what you say, that's what I want to call it," he retorted.[55] This wasn't a small issue for him. "To me Birdland was the most important place in my entire life," he said. "I met everybody including my beautiful wife in this club. I met Miles, I met Duke Ellington. I met anyone I ever cared for in this business. I used to hang out there every night."[56] There was no way he was going to change the title, and in the end it served him well.

Joe supervised the editing of a radio-friendly 45rpm version, painfully cutting ninety seconds from the original. It quickly became a bona fide standard, covered by Buddy Rich, Maynard Ferguson, and Quincy Jones, among others. It has been played entirely on toy instruments, by military pipe-and-drum bands, as a guitar duet, a cappella, and by seemingly every high school and college marching band in the country.[57] Outside of Weather Report's, the best-known version is the one recorded by the Manhattan Transfer for their 1979 album, *Extensions*, with lyrics by Jon Hendricks and an ingenious vocal arrangement by Janis Siegel.

Meanwhile, Columbia produced yet another striking album cover under the direction of Nancy Donald. This time she approached a collage artist named Lou Beach to do the artwork. "I knew the art director, and it was just another assignment that was given to me," Beach recalled. "I wasn't particularly knowledgeable of the music, although I was a jazz fan. I certainly knew Joe's work with Cannonball, but I wasn't all that familiar with Weather Report. They gave me the title and I just conjured up that image. I remember the background image [of the cityscape] came from the cover of some kind of South African business journal. It was large format, and I happened to have the cover in piles of scrap. As a collage

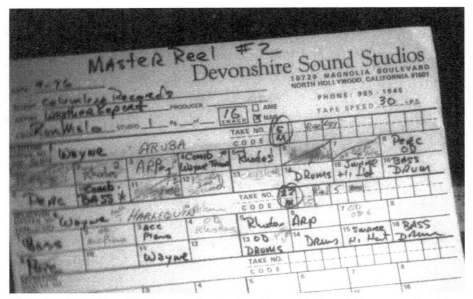

Track sheet from a *Heavy Weather* recording session at Devonshire Sound. Here we see the sixteen tracks for Wayne's tunes, "Aruba" (the working title for "Palladium") and "Harlequin." The "OD" notation on certain tracks indicates that it is an overdub. Photo: Brian Risner.

artist, I work with images scattered all over. The hat came from an old ad in *Life* magazine, and the beautiful leaf came from an *Arizona Highways* cover. So those were pretty much the elements.

"But the interesting part, if you look at the cover to the right of the leaf, there's a little circle the size of a paper punch. I had a bunch of them scattered over the image, and to me it made the eye wiggle a little more and made it seem more like there was rain or storm activity. Well, when Joe saw it, he didn't like all that stuff. He wanted them out. And because this was one of my first record covers, at least of a well-known band, I balked. But then I thought about it for a while, and I changed my mind because I realized that it was not Lou Beach with music by Weather Report. Plus, I needed the dough. *[laughs]* So I took them out, but I left one in, hoping Joe wouldn't notice it, just to get my lick in."[58] Beach was peeved enough at having to make the change that once the artwork was copied and in production, he tore up the original.

Columbia made *Heavy Weather* the centerpiece of a spring 1977 marketing campaign they called "Musical Roots." It was a blitz of so-called "jazz-rock" releases—eleven in all. Released in mid-March, several of these records found commercial success, including *Heavy Weather*.[59] Near the end of April, it reached number thirty-nine on the *Billboard* album chart and eventually topped out at number thirty, the highest a Weather Report album ever achieved. It proved to be Weather Report's first and only gold record (eventually going platinum). In honor of this achievement, Columbia presented each of the band members with a wall plaque upon which a gold record was mounted. Jaco noticed that its grooves didn't match those of *Heavy Weather*, so he removed the LP from its mount and listened to it on a turntable. It turned out to be a nondescript R&B band. That kind of took the luster off the award in Jaco's mind.[60]

By the end of the year, it seemed like Weather Report owned the jazz world. They walked away with virtually all the annual awards, taking best album and best group by huge margins in the *Down Beat* Readers Poll, *Playboy*, *Swing Journal*, and *Jazz Forum*. The Recording Academy still refused to consider Weather Report a jazz band, but it did nominate "Birdland" for best instrumental composition (which was won by John Williams for "Main Title from Star Wars"), and Jaco got a nod for best jazz instrumental performance as a soloist. Meanwhile, Joe and Wayne could cruise down Sunset Boulevard in Hollywood and see the *Heavy Weather* album cover plastered on a huge billboard.

Beyond its popularity, *Heavy Weather* represents the apogee of Weather Report's polished studio sound. "Weather Report has never employed the studio-as-instrument as thoroughly or as well as *Heavy Weather*," wrote Neil Tesser in his *Down Beat* review. "The LP literally explodes with the clarity, separation, and sheer variety of timbres, and Zawinul's arsenal of synthesized tonalities is astounding."[61] Tesser gave the album five stars, the third consecutive Weather Report album to receive that designation.

It seemed as though the band was incapable of a misstep, and everyone—Columbia, Cavallo-Ruffalo, fans, even other musicians—could hardly wait to hear what would come next.

14 Mr. Gone

Anybody who gives this record one star has got to be insane.

—Joe Zawinul

WITH *HEAVY WEATHER*'S 1977 SPRING RELEASE, the band geared up for a ten-week tour of the United States to support it. One of the problems Joe faced was performing "Birdland" live. He called it one of the hardest tunes he ever played as far as hand independence is concerned. "When we did it in the studio, I over-dubbed all the parts, even the solo; but then I realized what I had done. You don't want a record that can beat your performance or not be able to play the tune on stage. So I had to really practice 'Birdland' to get everything to sound like the record, and it wasn't easy."[1]

Fortunately, we can see how Zawinul did it thanks to video that survives from Weather Report's June 10 appearance on the late night television show, *The Midnight Special*.[2] The version of "Birdland" they play is quite faithful to the original, but while Jaco and Manolo Badrena are all smiles, dancing and having a good time, Joe remains focused on his keyboards, his face etched in concentration. And because of the physical arrangement of his keyboards, Joe's back is turned to the other musicians for long stretches while he plays the acoustic piano and Ober-heim. For "Birdland's" climactic solo, he plays an auxiliary synthesizer (an ARP Axxe), which was added to his rig specifically for this purpose, positioned so that he could play it with his right hand while comping on the Oberheim with his left.

By this time, Joe's Oberheim had been expanded to eight voices by adding another bank of SEMs on top of the original four. It was such a large, unwieldy beast that Joe could barely see over the top of it, which might explain why it faced away from the band and the audience. It was also now equipped with the Pro-grammer, which proved crucial to the live show. The tiny knobs on the Oberheim SEMs made it difficult to see their settings, and changing them on eight SEMs was

Weather Report performs at the taping of the *Midnight Special*. Photo: Brian Risner.

an overwhelming task on stage. While the Programmer couldn't save all of the synthesizer's settings, it was enough to do most patch changes with the flick of a switch. Joe can be seen doing that just before the chromatic section of "Birdland," for instance.

Joe's stage setup had grown complicated enough that dealing with it was a full-time task in its own right. So Brian Risner rang up an old friend, Alan Howarth, asking if he'd like to come on the road with Weather Report. Howarth was still working as a technician at a music store in Cleveland. He'd been through the ARP service training, so he knew his way around the inside of a 2600.[3] Plus, he'd hung out with Risner and the band many times, so he knew what he was getting himself into. He came on as Weather Report began rehearsals that spring.

Howarth described his job as Joe's butler. "I really viewed it that way. It was up to me to get all those keyboards up, get them in tune, get them sound-checked, and turn around to Joe and say, 'Okay, it's all set up correctly. You can play now.' And that was my mission. I took that very seriously, and I got really good at it. We were super-consistent."[4] Another crew member, Michael Knuckles, was brought on to handle Jaco and the drums and percussion instruments. Risner was responsible for the house sound while Howarth and Knuckles set up the stage together.

The U.S. tour kicked off in Houston on April 1. Al Di Meola, the young guitarist who made his name as a part of Chick Corea's jazz-rock powerhouse, Return to Forever, opened the shows. As usual, the band was loud—"near Concorde proportions" at "mind-bending volume," according to various reports.[5] They regularly booked large theaters, grossing $25,000 to $40,000 per show (part of which went to Al Di Meola, of course), and the musicians themselves benefited from the improved conditions. "I started with Weather Report playing clubs and colleges, making $350 a week," Alex Acuña noted. "After we made *Heavy Weather*, I started making $1,500 a week."[6]

The audiences were made up of "long-haired rockers" and "aging jazz aficionados," the scent of marijuana wafting through the air.[7] Often demand was such that the band played two shows in one night. If the nightcap wasn't sold out, a healthy number of holdovers from the first show plunked down six bucks or so to watch it all over again. Everyone had a spotlight moment, either performing solo or as a duet. Wayne took the occasion to improvise on everything from "Nefertiti" to, of all things, the old Scottish standby "Loch Lomond." Joe stuck with an Ellington favorite, "Sophisticated Lady."[8]

More than ever, the concerts were programmed with a fixed set list—a consequence of staging a show with more production values. But that didn't preclude spur-of-the-moment surprises. In Royal Oak, Michigan (a suburb of Detroit), audience members were treated to the unique sight and sound of Zawinul commencing the concert by rising from the orchestra pit while playing the theater's pipe organ. In Kansas City, Jaco honored the birthplace of Charlie Parker by playing "Donna Lee" at a breakneck pace, accompanied only by percussion à la his eponymous album. After Wayne joined in, Joe tried to move to "Badia," cueing its signature sound effect, but the rest of the band wouldn't have it and went right on jamming on "Donna Lee."

All the songs from *Heavy Weather* except for "The Juggler" and "Havona" made it into the shows at one time or another. It's understandable why they didn't play "The Juggler" live, given Joe's extensive overdubs on it, but it's unclear why they didn't at least try "Havona." Peter Erskine recalled that when he joined the band a year later, "Havona" was one of the few tunes they never even rehearsed. There were also some holdovers from earlier years, including perennial favorite "Directions." Another staple was "Scarlet Woman," which Joe enlivened with some theatrical flair, introducing it with a countdown and "rocket launch" as smoke and lighting effects emanated from beneath his keyboards.

Most of the time, though, the band's visual interest centered on Jaco and the ever-enthusiastic Manolo Badrena. Sitting behind their instruments, Joe and Alex Acuña couldn't do much in that department. And though Wayne added a touch of style and grace that helped separate Weather Report from its jazz-rock peers, he tended to be impassive in his stage mannerisms. (Joe once likened him to a statue when he played.) But Jaco radiated joy from his position stage right, bouncing and shuffling to the music and delivering sly grins as if to say, "What do you think of me now?" The road crew would sprinkle baby powder on the stage floor so that Pastorius could effortlessly glide around, all the while holding down the groove

Zawinul in the music room at his Pasadena house in 1977, playing his Oberheim Eight Voice. A portable reel-to-reel tape deck can be seen at bottom-left. Photo: Brian Risner.

with his funky lines. In short, Jaco was a crowd pleaser, and the more the audience responded to him, the more he amped up his act. He clearly learned a thing or two from Wayne Cochran.

Weather Report closed its U.S. tour at the Roxy, after which the band took a two-month break. Wayne spent the hiatus with Herbie Hancock as part of his VSOP (Very Special One-time Performance) quintet. It was an offshoot of the previous year's Newport Jazz Festival, where Hancock gave a retrospective concert that included three bands from various stages of his career. One of them was the reunited Miles Davis Quintet, with Freddie Hubbard filling in for the trumpeter, who turned down Hancock's request to be included. Given that Davis and most of his 1960s sidemen had gone on to embrace electric instrumentation, VSOP seemed like a breath of fresh air to the jazz traditionalists, while younger fans got a chance to hear that style of music played live for the first time. The quintet proved to be the hit of the festival, and Hancock had so much fun that he mounted an international tour with it the following summer.

Press reports indicated that Jaco would also spend the summer on the road, in his case with Joni Mitchell, but that failed to materialize, as Mitchell didn't tour at all in 1977 or 1978. Instead, Pastorius recorded her album *Don Juan's Reckless Daughter*, bringing along Alex Acuña and Manolo Badrena for a couple of tunes that required Latin percussion. Wayne also joined Mitchell in the studio for the first time, initiating what would become a long association with her.

When Jaco finally got to Fort Lauderdale at the end of June, there was a buzz around town. Acquaintances, fans, and the just plain curious descended upon Jaco's favorite hangs, hoping to catch a glimpse of the famous bassist sitting in with friends, something he did with regularity. Knowing this, less-than-scrupulous nightclub owners took advantage of Jaco's fame by putting his name on their marquees, claiming that he would grace their bandstands. "There was one case before I got here where a local nightclub put the word out to their customers that I'd be appearing with the house band the following week," Pastorius complained to a local reporter. "Meanwhile, I was in Los Angeles the whole time."

At another point, he planned to attend a concert in Miami and found himself not only a part of the orchestra, but with top billing. "That did not help my friendships with the other musicians," Jaco said. He considered bringing legal action barring the use of his name, "but what I want to do right now is rent one of those airplanes that fly over the beach with a sign saying, JACO PASTORIUS IS NOT PLAYING ANYWHERE IN FLORIDA!"[9]

Jaco also returned home with a taste for alcohol and cocaine. It was a shocking development to those close to him, because up to that point, Pastorius disdained drugs of any kind. As a teenager, he was about the only one in his circle of friends who didn't smoke pot, and he was critical of those who did; likewise with Wayne Cochran. Ira Sullivan remembered Jaco being "straight as an arrow," never drinking so much as a beer.[10]

But in the big-time music business of the seventies, cocaine was in such ample supply that it was nearly impossible to avoid. It was there for the taking at industry events and recording sessions, laid out in lines on coffee tables. On the road, there were always people willing to trade access for drugs. It took a considerable amount of willpower—even courage—to abstain while most everyone else was partaking. Alex Acuña was raised with a strong set of values that have guided him throughout his life, but even he had difficulty navigating the scene, as he related to me:

> As a young person when I came over here, I had no parents, no older brothers to really tell me what to do. I went to sleep at any time. I did whatever I wanted. I got into drugs. I got into the life that the entertainment business sometimes offered, that is available to us as musicians. Especially being from another country, I wanted to be in the circle, so I smoked and I drank, and I dated all kinds of girls.
>
> But when I started playing with Weather Report, that's when I saw very clearly the things that I was not supposed to do. Every time we got together—the whole band and all the guests—Columbia Records threw big parties, and I saw what was going on at the parties. It wasn't because

we really loved it or liked it, but if you didn't do those things, it seemed like you didn't belong there. And I said, "I don't think these are the things that I really want." I wasn't raised this way. I had kids already. I said, "I don't want my children to go through this, so I better start changing my life a little bit." So after I left Weather Report my life really changed for good, for the best. Otherwise, I don't think I would be alive. I would be like Jaco, maybe buried next to him.[11]

Like most everyone else, Zawinul occasionally indulged in cocaine as well, although he was cagey about admitting it. For example, take this excerpt from a 1997 interview with journalist Anil Prasad:

I smoked a little pot here and there and had a little thing [makes a sniffing sound] once a month or something, but it was not a thing to do. I was a busy guy, man. I had a lot of work to do. I was into music. We were in the studio forty-six hours sometimes to mix a record. I'm not stupid. I had a family with three children to feed. I was a real connoisseur about that. I haven't done drugs in twenty-five years, but here and there when the stuff was right and we were very tired, yeah, I had a little blow. But it had nothing to do with being strung-out or needing the stuff every day.[12]

Wayne didn't use drugs of any kind. (It seems almost miraculous in hindsight that he escaped heroin and cocaine, which ravaged so many of his New York peers.) The one time he tried marijuana was at the coaxing of his sister-in-law, Maria Booker, who described herself as Joe's "partner in smoke" during their New York days. "I convinced [Wayne] to smoke and he was so funny with his big eyes," she recalled. "He's telling me, 'How long is this going to last?' He was like, 'Never again.' Wayne was not into that. Wayne never did drugs. Wayne was a drinker."[13]

Drinking was one of the bonds of road life that Joe and Wayne shared. It was nothing for them to knock down two or three shots of cognac before a show, play a two-hour set, and have more drinks afterward. "When you're playing, you'd sweat it out," Wayne said. "We were never blasted on the bandstand. The kind of stuff we were doing, we couldn't afford to go into a blank, y'know?"[14] Herbie Hancock recalled his amazement that Wayne could play in Miles Davis's band "while being ripped. . . . We'd call him cognac man, which he twisted into Corny Act Man."[15] The younger Weather Report band members were equally impressed that Joe and Wayne could play so well under such conditions.

Joe retained a lifelong affection for slivovitz. It started when he was a youngster, playing accordion in the kitchen at Oberkirchbach. His grandfather distilled his own brew of the plum brandy, and as it dripped through the white silk cloth filter, young Josef would catch it on the sly with one hand while playing accordion with the other. Alan Howarth remembers a time when the band played in Vienna and a relative brought Joe a bottle of home-brewed slivovitz. "You could get drunk just getting it anywhere near your nose," Howarth said. "It was like rocket fuel."[16] When both his parents died, Joe reportedly had cases of schnapps aging at the family farm shipped to California.

At first, Jaco didn't join Joe and Wayne in bending the elbow. But one evening in the dressing room, Joe pestered him to have a drink. When Pastorius declined, Joe told him to loosen up a little. One can easily imagine Zawinul posing this as a challenge to Jaco's manhood. Pastorius was nothing if not competitive—he would down a bottle of hot sauce on a bet, Bob Bobbing once remarked[17]—so he had a drink. And then he had another. "He got a little strange after two drinks," Zawinul remembered. "He started throwing things. I knew right away I had made a mistake."[18]

It was a pattern that those close to Jaco would observe in later years, almost like a switch had been flipped. Even in normal circumstances, Pastorius was prone to outrageous and exaggerated behavior—anything to get a reaction, always in fun, even if those around him didn't see it that way. But alcohol brought out a nastier side to his personality, and the good-natured pranks and jibes edged toward cruelty and meanness.

Cocaine was similarly destructive. By the time of the *Heavy Weather* sessions, the party was on. (As one CBS product manager put it, when asked if the band was on time with the album: "I'm sure they were not, because they used to party, my friend."[19]) It wasn't long before the crew had a nickname for Jaco: "P. K.," which stood for Party King. "Joe was great on the hang after the show," recalled Howarth. "But the party went on all night in Jaco's room. You had to really be equipped to hang with Jaco. There was a time when it was really a lot of fun and really enjoyable, but then it became pretty hard to handle—an all-day thing. And once he left the band and kept that lifestyle, it took him to a direction that wasn't healthy for him."[20]

In the meantime, no one knew that Pastorius was suffering from bipolar disorder, a form of mental illness that causes extreme mood swings characterized by extended stints of euphoria and grandiosity followed by long bouts of depression; hence the earlier term for the condition, manic depression. According to Kenneth Alper, the doctor who eventually diagnosed Jaco's illness, manic depression usually manifests itself in males between the ages of twenty-five and thirty-five, when the normal stresses of adulthood emerge. Jaco was twenty-five when Weather Report's 1977 tour commenced.[21]

Beyond the demands of being a husband and father, Jaco bore the weight of fame everywhere Weather Report went. The expectations of being the greatest bass player in the world in the greatest band in the world (as Jaco and Joe were fond of saying) must have been enormous. Deep down, he worried that he wasn't as good as the hype. Pat Jordan relates that at one point Jaco confided to his brother, Gregory, that his greatest fear was that he couldn't repeat his earlier successes, that he wasn't a genius after all. "All I am is clever," he told Greg.[22]

Mike Stern, who knew Pastorius going back to their Blood, Sweat & Tears days, picked up on Jaco's self-doubts early on. Stern recalled how excited Jaco was when his first record came out. "He'd say, 'Man, this is the greatest stuff in the history of music.' That's the way he would talk sometimes." But as Stern got to know Pastorius better, he could see that Jaco was actually insecure. "There were times when he wasn't sure about his own playing and whether or not he was playing well—he was always asking. Meanwhile, he was killin'."[23]

There is a high correlation between manic depression and substance abuse. Some studies indicate that more than half of people with the disorder experience drug or alcohol addiction in their lifetime, so Jaco's vulnerability to them could have been anticipated had he been diagnosed earlier.[24] At the time, though, it just seemed like he really liked to party. Initially, it didn't affect his playing, and his respect for Wayne and Joe kept his behavior toward them in check. But eventually those walls would crack, too.

•

When Weather Report commenced a mammoth eight-week tour of Europe that August, the band had gotten big enough that it no longer needed an opening act, allowing Wayne and Joe to realize a long-held dream of presenting Weather Report concerts as singular events in and of themselves. Billed as "An Evening with Weather Report," the shows now included Ravel's *Boléro* played over the house PA system. Its long buildup created a great sense of anticipation until the piece finally modulated to a new key, releasing the tension in a boisterous finale as the house lights dimmed and the musicians took their places on stage in the dark before blasting into "Elegant People."

The tour concluded with nine shows in the United Kingdom, including three at the three-thousand-seat Rainbow Theatre in London. The Rainbow gigs were recorded with the intention of using them as the basis of a live Weather Report album, but most of the journalists in attendance the first night weren't much impressed. Things got off to an inspired start, but the tone changed with Jaco's indulgent solo, which clocked in at over fifteen minutes and concluded with the audience as good as shouting him off the stage. To them, it came across as a pointless technical exercise, leading one frustrated fan to yell, "Play some music!"[25]

The incident put a damper on the rest of the show. "Maybe they're not used to anything less than adulation," wrote Paul Rambali in *New Musical Express*, "because in the cameos (apart from Badrena's, all no more than perfunctory) and songs that came after there was a strange and saddening lack of intent. The direction and the energy were gone." When the band left the stage after a dull reading of "Badia," someone in the audience shouted, "Is that all we get?"[26]

These might have been the first sour notes voiced in the press about Pastorius, who was the subject of many articles and interviews in 1977. A few days later, Joe acknowledged Jaco's "over-long" bass solo, telling a reporter, "I'm sorry that happened the first night, because I myself was disappointed. Because we were recording he thought he should get enough on tape. I explained to him later that it didn't matter—we're playing for the people, and if it's good it's on the record; if it is not then it won't be. Looking back, I think everything was all right, but it never really took off again, because the feedback was not right after that. Second night, though, from the very first moment on, it was smoking."[27]

In any event, the band played a handful of other gigs before heading home for a couple of weeks of R&R. Then it was back on the road for another swing through the United States and parts of Canada through the end of November. Weather Report wouldn't return to the stage until the following June.

•

In January 1978, Sequential Circuits, a small company located in the heart of Silicon Valley, unveiled its first synthesizer at the NAMM (National Association of Music Merchants) show in Anaheim. The Prophet-5 was a milestone in the evolution of synthesizers—the first commercially viable synthesizer based on microprocessor technology. It had a sound architecture similar to the Oberheim, but the front panel knobs controlled the settings for all the voices simultaneously. In that respect, it was vastly easier to use. More crucially, it could save all the settings in computer memory, allowing the instrument to have a large bank of programs or patches, each of which could be recalled instantly. In short, it gave musicians what they wanted: A polyphonic, fully programmable synthesizer that sounded fantastic. If you were serious about playing keyboards, you had to have one.

When Alan Howarth heard about "this Prophet-5 thing" from his music-store friends in Cleveland, he put in a call to Sequential's Sunnyvale office. "Man, I heard you were at the NAMM show and you had something amazing," Howarth said, asking if he could come up and have a look. "So I went up and visited [Sequential's founder] Dave Smith in his little shop. The Prophet-5 from the NAMM show was sitting on the table. I took one look at it and said, 'We gotta have it.'" Smith pointed out that he was also producing a ten-voice, which was the same as the Prophet-5 but with two voice boards instead of one, so Howarth ordered one of those instead.[28]

When Howarth took delivery of the Prophet-10, he discovered that its bank of programs was empty. "I remember being in the living room of my little rented house in the Eagle Rock area of L.A., and the thing arrived with no sound in it.

Zawinul shows off his recently acquired Sequential Circuits Prophet-5 synthesizer to Japanese electronic music pioneer Isao Tomita during Weather Report's 1978 tour of Japan. Peter Erskine and Alan Howarth listen in. Photo: Shigeru Uchiyama / Whisper Not Photo Factory.

It was blank. So I sat there and dialed up some brass and strings, and whatever synth sounds that appealed to me, and took it to Joe the next morning. He really liked it. He was more than intrigued. It sounded great, but the fact that it was programmable was the big leap forward."[29] Unfortunately, Smith hadn't tested Prophet-10s in real-world use, and the few units he shipped started coming back for servicing. With two circuit boards packed into the case, it quickly overheated, causing tuning problems. Smith realized that he wouldn't be able to deliver Prophet-10s, so Howarth wound up exchanging Joe's for a Prophet-5.

Zawinul took great inspiration from the Prophet-5. He called it "an incredible machine; it has what I've always needed to make the music come off. I have forty-four [sic] different programs, including a string sound that you will not know isn't a symphony orchestra. It hasn't changed the way I write music, it just means there's no limitation."[30] Just the novelty of a new sound was enough to spur Joe's creativity, and coupled with his Oberheim Eight Voice, the Prophet-5 wound up heavily coloring the orchestrations on Weather Report's next album, *Mr. Gone.*

At the time, Joe was working on a solo record—something he'd been talking about for years. When he was off the road and not ensconced in a recording studio or rehearsal hall, Zawinul had his keyboard rig installed in his music room in Pasadena, set up the same as it was on stage. This was the laboratory from which sprang forth virtually all of his compositions from late 1973 on. Shortly after *Black Market* was released, the writer Colman Andrews came by for a visit, and his subsequent article vividly described the scene he encountered. It was, he wrote, "a house which seems, from the inside, to be positively *built* out of musical instruments. An ARP, an acoustic piano and an electric piano, a cello, two guitars, some thumb pianos, a drum kit, amplifiers, percussion instruments of every provenance, and Polyhymnia knows what else, clutter every corner of the living room, looking so much at home that they might as well be pillars and baseboards."[31]

Zawinul was bursting with ideas. He claimed to have enough recorded improvisations to last "for the next five years."[32] He installed an Otari eight-track tape deck, set up such that the output of his keyboard rig's mixer could be recorded to any track, making it easy for him to do multitrack recording on his own. Being "Joe's guy," Alan Howarth spent a lot of time in Pasadena. "I was family, like Brian Risner was family," Howarth said. "And I spent time with Joe, just me and him, fooling around with stuff. I was the chief joint roller; there were a lot of joints that went around. But it was a part of his persona. He enjoyed that stuff. It didn't slow him down at all. If anything, it gave him focus. He got very creative when he was doing that stuff.

"After lunch he would go to the studio and start doing shit. He already ate something, so now it was just a little bit of drinks and smokes and just play in the studio and create. Whatever he had on stage he had right there at the house to play with. And he had a nice Yamaha grand piano parked where the grand piano would have been on stage. It was a full concert monster with red velvet roping on the harp, and it sounded great. And the other thing was just keeping everything turned on and ready to fire up, so he could be inspired. He could just walk up to it and go. Every now and then he would get into a technical thing and start fooling around with sounds, but the main thing was to be inspired and just be able to reach for an instrument and play, 'cause there's no scheduling the muse. It shows up whenever it shows up."[33]

Joe claimed that the next Weather Report offering would be a double album of live material, and probably felt like he finally had time to finish a solo album. But at some point, plans changed.[34] Given the strength of *Heavy Weather*, it seems likely that Columbia pushed for a studio successor instead. (A few tracks from the London tapes later showed up on the 2002 compilation, *Live & Unreleased*.) So in February, it was back to feeding the beast, with the material that Joe had been working on for his solo album forming the basis for *Mr. Gone*. He had three tunes from the previous summer: "The Pursuit of the Woman with the Feathered Hat," "Mr. Gone" (which was initially titled "The Visitors"), and "And Then." He wrote a fourth tune early in 1978, "Young and Fine" (which had the working title "Hi-Life"[35]).

Meanwhile, Joe didn't have a band anymore. The previous November, Manolo Badrena left in the middle of a concert after a blowup with Zawinul.[36] Weather

Report finished the year as a quartet, but by then Alex Acuña had reached the point where he was ready for a change as well. He had moved his family to Los Angeles and was looking to do more studio work there. Plus, he was doing gigs with Diana Ross. If he were to remain in the band, Weather Report would have to work around her schedule, and that wasn't going to happen.

On top of that, when they began rehearsing the material for *Mr. Gone*, Alex just wasn't hearing himself in Joe's new music. "I went to Joe and Wayne and I said, 'Right now I don't have any more beats to play in this song, and I don't want to play the same beats that I played in *Heavy Weather*.' They said, 'Wow, Alex you're so honest.' But music is not supposed to suffer because of our egos. It's not supposed to be a victim. So I said, 'I think I'm done. Maybe I'll come back later, but I'm done.'"[37]

Wayne was missing in action, too. His practice of Buddhism had intensified to the point that music increasingly took a back seat to spiritual growth. It wasn't something he talked about publicly, nor were fans generally aware that he and Ana Maria were raising a child with severe brain damage. As Iska reached school age, the fullness of her disability came into focus. Together with Wayne's extended absences from home, it was a heavy burden for the couple to carry.

Then there was Wayne's five-year rule of band membership. By *Tale Spinnin'*, his internal clock was telling him it might be time to move on. He and Joe didn't plan to be "chained" together forever, he told a reporter in 1975. "We're listening for a total fulfillment of sound, and when we know that is accomplished, we'll disband and go on to create something nobody thought of before, individually."[38]

The previous fall, Wayne said that he had begun work on his own album and hoped to have it out by Christmas.[39] That was optimistic, for sure, but maybe he thought back to his Blue Note days when records were made in a matter of days, not weeks or months. In any event, Wayne didn't produce another album of his own until 1985. Instead, his spiritual quest caused him to rethink fundamental aspects of his life, and he became alienated from even the most commonplace parts of daily living. "I came to a point where I didn't want to see anybody and didn't want to go out anywhere," he told Michelle Mercer.[40]

So Wayne began a period of retrenchment. He later said that for a long time with Weather Report, "I abstained. I elected not to do things. At the same time I was cultivating many other aspects of my life."[41] Most troubling to Wayne was that he lost the inspiration to write music. In a revealing interview that appeared in *Musician* magazine in 1981, Wayne opened up about what he was going through. "I was struggling, trying to write—starting about four and a half years ago—trying to break through, wondering who else is like this, in the world, struggling and struggling. It was very painful trying to write, for the first time. I've heard about painters who would stop in the middle of the canvas and say, 'That's

Wayne finds time for meditation while on the road with Weather Report in Japan.
Photo: Shigeru Uchiyama / Whisper Not Photo Factory.

all—I have nothing more to paint.' That's how I felt. I was worried I'd gone dry, permanently."[42]

Nevertheless, the public perception persisted that Joe and Jaco pushed Wayne aside through the sheer force of their personalities, musical and otherwise. Jaco, for one, rejected that notion. "All the stuff that got written and said about Joe and I pushing Wayne out of the spotlight was totally wrong. We were trying to push him *in*. He'd come to the studio with twenty charts that looked like symphonies, and Joe and I would come in with notes on napkins. Wayne came in for the record after *Heavy Weather*, and his stuff was not together. Everybody has his private life. Wayne had all this music, but it just wasn't connected. It didn't make that much sense, and I said, 'Wayne, you're Mr. Gone,' and Joe said, 'Yeahhh—that's the name of the record.'"[43]

With Wayne preoccupied by "family issues," as those close to the band put it, into the void stepped Jaco. He'd already proved his worth on *Heavy Weather*, and he got another co-producer credit for *Mr. Gone.* (For the first time, Wayne was given no production credit at all.) One of the first things Jaco did was get in touch with Peter Erskine, whom he had heard the year before with Maynard Ferguson. At the time, Ferguson fronted a modern thirteen-piece big band that was riding the success of *Conquistador*, the only gold record of his career. Like *Heavy Weather*, it featured a breakout single "Gonna Fly Now," from the film *Rocky*. It was an even more unlikely success story than "Birdland." Nobody could remember the last time a big band had an instrumental single on the pop charts.[44]

In March 1977, Ferguson's itinerary took him to a place called Joe Rico's Room, a hotel lounge near Miami International Airport that booked national jazz acts. That night between sets, Erskine saw fellow bandmate Ron Tooley talking to an odd-looking guy wearing a Philadelphia Phillies baseball cap. As Peter remembered it, he had long, greasy hair that needed washing, a goofy-looking pair of glasses, and wore a shirt buttoned up to the top. Erskine approached them and playfully blew into Tooley's horn, which was tucked under his arm. Tooley turned around to see who it was. "Peter, hey, say hi to Jaco Pastorius." Erskine knew he might show up, but the fellow standing before him looked nothing like the Jaco Pastorius he expected to see; that is, the one pictured on his album cover. Surprised, Peter's first words to him were, "No shit."

"We chatted for a bit," Erskine recalled, "and it was time to go play the next set, so I excused myself. I was walking to the bandstand, Jaco calls out to me. He goes, 'Hey man.' I turn around. He says, 'Have fun!' Now, no one had ever said that to me. It was always, 'have a good set' or 'play well,' which implied somewhere that there was going to be some scorekeeping going on. And so I had fun. I didn't feel at all self-conscious."

Erskine and a few other bandmates hung out with Jaco after the gig. Pastorius brought along a cassette of *Heavy Weather*, which had just been released, and they listened to it over and over late into the night, fueled by nothing more than cans of soda from a nearby vending machine and the sheer excitement of what they were hearing. "We wouldn't let Jaco leave," Erskine said. "Finally, he said, 'Look, I gotta go home. You guys can keep the cassette.' And I told Jaco, 'This is the version of the band I've been waiting for.' It felt very comfortable and natural to meet Jaco."[45]

Though Erskine didn't realize it at the time, he made an impression on Jaco, too. Pastorius heard a drummer who was adept at driving a big band on bebop staples like Sonny Rollins's "Airegin," but could also muscle his way through the rock-inspired rhythms of Ferguson's contemporary pieces. A Weather Report drummer needed to be well rounded, and Erskine was certainly that. There was also a comfort factor in his playing. Aside from a mutual love of big bands, both men were about the same age and grew up listening to the same music. Jaco immediately recognized someone he could play with. His parting comment to Erskine was, "I'm going to call you one of these days."[46]

Almost a year later, Pastorius made good on his word. Erskine was still with Ferguson when Jaco left him a message at his hotel: Weather Report wanted him to come to Los Angeles and record for a day. Essentially, it would be an audition, a chance to see how he fit in with the band. As was the case with Jaco himself, if it worked out, Peter would be asked to stay on and finish the album.

Ever since spending the evening with Pastorius, Erskine had been listening to *Heavy Weather* nonstop (and driving some of the older Ferguson horn players nuts in the process). A fan of the band from the beginning, Erskine thought Weather Report's albums sounded like the future of music. *Mysterious Traveller* was "stunningly good,"[47] but *Heavy Weather* was so completely fresh that it "mesmerized" him.[48] So the Weather Report drum chair was a dream assignment. He passed.

"It was first day of the *Mr. Gone* recording," Erskine recalled. "I would have been flying out to L.A., renting a drum set, going into the studio for one day. We're in the Midwest. It's January. I can't risk it. Maynard had gigs. I couldn't hang Maynard up; that was my responsibility. And with just one day, I wasn't giving myself any kind of chance. I didn't have studio recording experience where I felt like I could go in. So I told them thanks, but no thanks."[49] In Joe Zawinul's school of macho musicianship, that was probably a point in Erskine's favor. It took some balls to turn down the opportunity to play with Weather Report. It must have reminded Joe of the time he declined Miles's offer way back in 1959. It certainly didn't hurt Peter's chances, because Weather Report would call on him again.

With Erskine unavailable, Joe settled on a tag-team approach for the drums. A case in point is the title track—a delightfully quirky tune anchored by Joe's sixteen-note Oberheim bass line that he programmed into a sequencer. But the drum part never came together. It was one of those elusive grooves that Joe heard in his head but couldn't articulate. Nor, it seems, could anyone play it to his satisfaction. Alphonse Mouzon, Sonship Theus, Steve Gadd, and Alex Acuña all gave it a try, to no avail. (This might have been the point at which Acuña realized he was not destined for this music.) Jaco played it, and even Joe did. Tony Williams came in, but he wasn't good enough, either. Finally, Williams insisted on getting another shot, and after flying out to Los Angeles on his own dime, he did it in one take. (Though even Williams's version didn't quite hit the mark, according to Zawinul. "Tony was the best but still not all the way there."[50])

It was like that for much of the album. Joe wound up using Williams for a pair of tunes. Steve Gadd, a prolific studio drummer with more than fifty recording credits in 1978 alone, played on a few more. Jaco played drums on two tracks, while Peter Erskine eventually came in to add overdubs and record yet

Joe Zawinul has fun behind Peter Erskine's drum kit during a Weather Report sound check. Photo: Peter Erskine.

another. Whereas in the past, Weather Report tunes originated with the entire band recording together, most of the tunes on *Mr. Gone* were built piece-by-piece through overdubbing. Joe made liberal use of sequencers, boasting that his click tracks were "in perfect mathematical time."[51] But of course, musicians don't play in perfect mathematical time. For all these reasons, there's a quality about the music that's different from its predecessors. Perhaps the best way to describe *Mr. Gone* is that it sounds more manufactured and less organic than past efforts.

The album leads off with "The Pursuit of the Woman with the Feathered Hat." That was originally going to be the title of the record, as well. In fact, when Nancy Donald asked Lou Beach to do the artwork, he conjured up a cover on that basis, working into his collage a real ostrich feather and a pair of piercing eyes that command the viewer's attention. Then, when told the title would be *Mr. Gone*, Beach did another cover depicting the title character as a trench-coat-clad Chrysler Building strolling through the neon-lit streets of Manhattan. It was ultra-hip, but evidently Joe liked the first one better, so it remained the front cover while "Mr. Gone" was relegated to the back. Like "Mr. Gone," "Pursuit" is driven by sequenced synth lines, though here they wind up submerged beneath a rich tapestry of textures and dense rhythmic elements that reward repeat listening with headphones.

The sustained suspended chords from Joe's Oberheim Eight Voice announce the next tune, Jaco's "River People." Pastorius wrote it years earlier while on a fishing trip in the Everglades, and he put it together with Joe from an arrangement he had written out. This piece was highly evocative to Jaco; he described it as "a day with the river people," with his bass part meant to evoke their feet plopping through the mud. The introduction represents the sunrise, and by the end everyone is relaxing and partying after a day out on the water. Jaco said he overdubbed himself playing drums in order to capture the feel that he wanted (though it probably also had to do with the fact that Weather Report didn't have a drummer at the time). To a lot of listeners, "River People" veers pretty close to disco, though in concert the band would get a rip-roaring groove going by the tune's end.[52]

Joe's "Young and Fine," comes next. He conceived it just before making *Mr. Gone*, capturing it on his tape deck at home, "humming, accompanying himself on the piano, voicing the chords hesitantly as he went along," according to a profile written by Len Lyons. Later, one of Joe's sons played the melody on trumpet while Zawinul imagined the orchestration and counterpoint. "There are five to eight contrapuntal melodies," Joe told Lyons proudly, explaining that "every leading voice should be a melody that can stand alone as a tune."[53] This was a tenet of his arranging method, and Herbie Hancock later recalled how Zawinul gave him similar advice when Hancock was arranging the horn parts for his 1968 album *Speak Like a Child*. Even if the melodies clash with the harmony, they will sound like "spices to the ear," Joe explained.[54]

"The Elders," Wayne's only original composition for the album, closes out the first side. Its enigmatic, ghostly feel is a departure from the brassy, synth-laden tracks that precede it—so much so that it feels like it could have been lifted from one of Weather Report's early albums. With no drummer, Jaco creates a fascinating percussive effect on his bass, which he described as "almost like a conga. I get it by hitting the strings with my right palm, getting a rhythmic thing going, and then just quickly sliding my palm down the neck, from the bridge down to the nut. It adds some meat in appropriate places."[55]

The flip side of *Mr. Gone* leads off with the title track, discussed above, which is followed by "Punk Jazz." It was Jaco's favorite tune because he expressly wrote it for the record. "It's a satisfaction thing," he explained, "Like 'I came up with the goods,' so you feel like you did your work and it was done specifically for the album. It's just a really well-orchestrated tune—a lot of work went into it."[56] It begins with "some stone jazz," as Jaco put it, in the form of a furious duet between Pastorius and Tony Williams, before abruptly shifting to an orchestrated section that is announced by Wayne's tenor sax.

As the world would soon come to know from Jaco's *Word of Mouth* album, he had a gift for writing for large ensembles. This piece, he said, "sounds like it's written for strings and brass, and Joe's playing all the parts. I brought in the score. He played every note by himself. A thirteen-piece score. I'd say, 'I want a string section here, I want brass here, I want maybe a few flutes here,' and he goes for it."[57] Eventually "Punk Jazz" settles into a wonderfully lopsided mid-tempo groove that one writer described as "reminiscent of an elephant walking with a bad foot,"[58] before giving rise to a classic, concise, blues-drenched Shorter soprano solo, which he announces with an elongated cry that lasts a good eight seconds.

Mr. Gone closes with "And Then," an episodic ballad that includes a brief interlude sung by Deniece Williams and Earth, Wind & Fire's Maurice White. The lyrics were written by a 26-year-old musician from South Carolina named Sam Guest. He had previously written words for a *Heavy Weather* tune, and when Joe heard him sing them, he invited Guest out to California to record. While he was there, Joe asked him to write some more lyrics based on an idea Zawinul had. Guest went to his hotel that night and returned with the words the next morning. Originally, Guest sang those, too, but White happened by the studio and liked the song, leading to Guest's version being replaced by Williams and White.[59]

•

Although *Mr. Gone* remained unfinished, the band had a tour of Japan coming up, and they still hadn't resolved the drum chair. Jaco kept talking up Peter Erskine, so they made another run at him. This time, Joe picked up the telephone himself. He caught Erskine in the middle of a nap. "I felt like a real moron when I spoke with him because I had just woken up," Erskine recalled. "It was just out of the blue and I'm sure he wasn't helpful. But I didn't make too bad of an impression, I guess."[60]

Zawinul was noncommittal, but a few days later Erskine's phone rang again. "Hi, Peter, this is Paul Bruno from Weather Report's management office, and Joe just has one more question he wanted us to ask you."

"Yeah, what is it?"

"Joe wants to know, can you play the beat to 'Nubian Sundance'?"

Erskine knew the tune well. He and Maynard Ferguson's bass player frequently jammed on it during sound checks. "Yeah," Peter replied, mustering as much swagger as he could. "You tell Joe I can play the shit out of it."

"OK, thank you very much. We'll be in touch."[61]

Zawinul loved people who exuded confidence, so it was the perfect answer. Erskine made arrangements to fly to Los Angeles when Ferguson's tour concluded at the end of May. In the meantime, he had an endorsement deal with the Slingerland Drum Company, and when he told them about the Weather Report gig, they went all out to set him up. "They were incredible," Erskine recalled. "They built a new drum set for me, purchased Anvil flight cases, and shipped it all out to L.A. at their expense. It was quite a big deal."[62]

Peter Erskine, photographed during his first tour of Japan with Weather Report in 1978. Photo: Shigeru Uchiyama / Whisper Not Photo Factory.

Here's Erskine's firsthand account of his introduction to the band:

I flew out to L.A., and I was hoping to run into Jaco at the hotel, but he was up the street at the Roxy where Billy Cobham was playing a re-cord-release party. Jaco later told me that CBS had fruit baskets for the guests and they were taking the grapes from the baskets and throwing them at Cobham while he was playing a drum solo.

The next morning I got up early, ate breakfast, and walked to SIR. It was a helluva long walk from the hotel. I met the crew. It's a new drum set, so I've got to tune it, figure out how it's going to set up, and I'm told they're going to be late. I wait around, and I'm told they're going to be even later.

When they showed up, finally, Wayne was quite friendly; Joe was guarded. He had a dried marijuana roach on his lower lip, kind of look-ing at me with his macho bullshit. And Jaco had a big smile. He popped in and popped right back out. He went across the street to get some Heineken beer. So Joe saunters over to the keyboards and he's working with Alan Howarth. I think they had just got the Prophet back from

Sequential Circuits, and he was just kind of checking it out.

Now, if this had started on schedule, I probably would have politely waited. I was an ensemble player; I wasn't a grab-the-music-by-the-throat guy unless I had the chart in front of me. But I was just so bored. And maybe I sensed that, all right, I've got to show these guys what I can do. And I was comfortable because I had been there all day. So I just hit the drums and started playing. And I remember Joe kind of looked surprised, so that turned out to be the perfect thing. And then Wayne came up and the three of us were jamming.

When Jaco came back to the rehearsal room with the beer, he had a big smile on his face. He came up on stage, turned to his left, and they threw him his bass. He caught it, put the strap on, and we did an impromptu medley of the tunes they were planning on playing. Jaco had invited Tom Scott down, and he was standing there for part of it with his mouth open. It seemed like it was pretty good. I was playing for my life. Whatever I lacked in subtlety, I had a lot of energy. And they liked the power. I was fresh off the Ferguson band; I was in shape.

So we finished with "Gibraltar," and Joe just kind of gave the nod for it to end. Even though *Black Market* was one record I didn't own, I had done my homework. So it was like, wow, it all just clicked right away. They all high-fived each other, and I took that as a pretty good sign. And then I went out with Jaco that night. Michel Colombier was there, and they had an electric piano, but they couldn't find a bass amp. Somehow they eventually got Jaco plugged into the Rhodes cabinet, and they had this little jam. And I don't remember if it was that night or the next, but I hung out with Jaco and Steve Gadd, talking into the night. I had no idea how these people stayed up so late. I kept falling asleep. Naive.

Anyway, the next day at rehearsal we took photos for CBS. As far as I'm concerned, I'm joining the band. There's no doubt in my mind. So as we're posing, I say, "Joe?"

"Um hum."

"I was wondering, can I tell my friends I'm in the band?"

Joe thought for a second and said, "You can tell your friends you're going to Japan."[63]

Even if Joe wasn't sold on Erskine yet, the jam session went so well that Zawinul cut rehearsals short and took the band back to Devonshire Sound, where they continued working on *Mr. Gone*. "I put a hi-hat on a Steve Gadd track because Joe wanted it to have a different quality, kind of a lilt or flow," Erskine recalled. "So they put me in a small isolation booth with a hat, and I did the overdub while they were watching a World Cup soccer game. I don't even know if they were listening. Afterwards, I asked Joe, 'How was it?' He glanced up and said, 'You tell me.' I said, 'I think it was good. It was great.' 'Okay. Watch the game.'"[64]

The next day, someone suggested they try an old tune of Wayne's called "Pinocchio," which was originally recorded by the Miles Davis Quintet. Having come from big bands, Erskine was thrilled at the chance to play this small-band classic—and with its composer, to boot. They gave it a go, ripping through a far more aggressive version than Miles had done. Thinking it was a sound check, Erskine "hit everything in sight." So he was crestfallen when they listened to the playback and someone said, "Hey, we're done. Let's just use this." "I begged them [to do another take]," Erskine recalled. "And Jaco was like, 'No, man, you gotta join the band the same way I did: first take.'"[65]

Erskine went on to do other overdubs, even adding his own voice to the "Pursuit" chant. At one point, Joe invited him to sit in the engineer's booth so he could listen to one of the tracks that Tony Williams had done. "Meanwhile, Jaco had taken a framed *Heavy Weather* gold album off the wall and had chopped up some lines of cocaine for him and Joe and the engineer. Now, you never want your engineer getting high on a date; that's completely ridiculous, but this guy was. Anyway, it was there for their consumption and enjoyment, perched on an old MCI console with a leather-padded elbow. So I'm in the producer's chair—cool. I lean back and cross my legs and my foot hits this thing and it goes flying. And the first sound I hear, other than the 'oh no' inside my head, is the tape going 'boooo' [slowing to a stop] and this engineer yelling across the room at me, 'You motherfucker!'"[66]

•

In mid-June, the band set off for Japan, where they hadn't performed since 1973. In Weather Report years, that was several lifetimes ago. They were always popular in Japan, but it took on entirely new dimensions with Jaco, who was, and still is, idolized there. Two days before their first concert in Tokyo, they met with the Japanese press. After the usual questions about Miles Davis, jazz-rock, Jaco's gear, and why they changed drummers so often—all directed to Joe, Wayne, and Jaco—a reporter stood up and addressed Erskine. "What makes you think, having played with Stan Kenton and Maynard Ferguson, that you're qualified to play with Weather Report?"[67] Welcome to Japan, Peter Erskine.

"I was thinking, *Jeez, give me a break. I haven't even played the first gig yet.* And so I got into this meandering thing about, 'Well, good music is good music, and requires the same type thing . . .' Joe Zawinul interrupted me and said to the guy, 'What are you talking about? Weather Report *is* like a big band. The sound is big and we play like a bunch of guys and it's a small group, too.'"[68]

Nevertheless, it was a fair question, if not artfully asked. "I was an improbable choice," Erskine acknowledged. "Here's a guy that's been on tour with Stan Kenton's big band and Maynard Ferguson's big band. We were doing a lot of the bop book, but we were also recording disco versions of the main title of *Star Wars*—you know, playing a lot of bullshit. So yeah, why did I get called to play that?"[69]

Peter later discovered that although he lacked small-band credentials, Joe and Wayne were intrigued that he had played with Kenton, whose band went back to the 1940s. "I don't think they were at all familiar with the work I had done with Stan, or Stan's band in the seventies," Erskine said. "They were remembering Stan from the fifties and sixties. And they were like, wow, here's a guy who can obviously handle a large ensemble. Can he swing? These were unknowns. But they needed a drummer for Japan. They needed to get somebody."[70]

They discovered pretty quickly that Erskine could swing. Decades after Weather Report played its last note, Sony Legacy released *The Legendary Live Tapes: 1978–1981*. It includes several tracks from Erskine's first tour, and the energy emanating from the bandstand is undeniable. For instance, "Birdland" retains the vibe of the *Heavy Weather* version (that would change later), but on the closing vamp Joe abandons comping on the Oberheim to play a full-throttle synth solo while Erskine leads the group to a frenzied conclusion. Elsewhere, "Gibraltar" is rendered as a twenty-one-minute epic, performed during Erskine's second concert with the band, with a marvelous keyboard solo serving as its introduction.

Joe compared Erskine's dexterity to that of an octopus, and he was pleased with his stylistic breadth. He also liked the fact that Peter was open to suggestions.

Weather Report meets the press at the start of its 1978 tour of Japan. Photo: Peter Erskine.

For his part, Erskine was having the time of his life. "The Japan tour was kind of a spectacularly great honeymoon," he said. "It was fun. It was a lot of excitement."[71] Erskine and Jaco were half the age of Wayne and Joe, so it made for an interesting dynamic—two elders from the hard bop era coupled with a pair of young hot-shots raised on the musical diversity of the sixties. "We got along really well, all of us," Erskine said. "But particularly Joe, Jaco and I were kind of three musketeers. We liked to go out, hit the streets, go to museums, see the sights if we were in a famous city."[72]

Before the trip, Erskine was assigned some reading material. "Joe told me to go out and read some Nietzsche. I guess he was trying to prepare me for the 'what doesn't kill me will make me stronger' kind of thing." Peter realized soon enough that he'd need to lean on some of that philosophy. As many musicians discovered, Joe was from the old school. He'd challenge you, and the trick was to stand your ground and project your own strength and confidence in return. "If there was a weakness or a crack," Erskine noted, "he was going to scratch at it, or poke at it, or, you know, take a knife or a hammer to it."[73]

The set list for Japan was pretty much the same as it was the previous year, meaning there were no tunes from *Mr. Gone* because the record wasn't finished yet. Although Weather Report played its last gigs of 1977 as a quartet, there's some evidence to suggest that Joe sought another percussionist for this tour. In May, the English language newspaper *Japan Times* reported that the band would include Don Alias on percussion.[74] Nevertheless, Joe settled on touring without percussion, and he offered many explanations for this decision, including some pretty flip ones, like, "They never mattered all that much anyway."[75]

Mostly, though, he wanted to take the music in a different direction. Ever since *Tale Spinnin'*, the live band had featured a heavy dose of Afro-Cuban rhythms. It's clear that Joe wasn't hearing that on *Mr. Gone*, and the subsequent band followed through on that. "Since we got a quartet, everything is much more consistent," Joe explained. "Last year we had a great band but at times, with a lot of percussion playing, it got a little carried away. The harmonic factor and the melodic factor at times were pushed to the side for some extravagances rhythmically. Since we got rid of the percussion, I can finally hear what is going on with the rhythm."[76]

Meanwhile, the Prophet-5 assumed a position of supremacy in Joe's keyboard arsenal, sitting atop his Rhodes. This required some surgery because the synthesiz-er's power transformer interfered with the Rhodes and created a hum. Alan How-arth came up with a clever solution that also solved the daily chore of tuning the synths. "My big problem on the road was that everything had to be retuned *every day*, and I was going, what is this?" Howarth said. "And then the light bulb went on: The power was variable; the units were fine. So we wound up taking the power supplies out of the Prophet-5, both 2600s, and the Oberheim, and externalizing them so that I could tune the *power supply* every day. At the same time it got the transformers off the top of the Rhodes so that we didn't have the hum anymore, and it made the 2600s super stable because we put them on an outside box."[77]

Everything was fine until they got to Australia for Weather Report's only tour there. The first concert was in Perth, after which the gear was loaded onto trucks for the 1,700-mile trek to Adelaide. "It was like a two-day trucking journey on the transcontinental road of Australia," Howarth remembered, "and it was brutal on the gear."[78] The Prophet-5's internals shook apart, and when Howarth set up for that night's gig, it wouldn't fire up. A desperate phone call to Dave Smith from the Adelaide Festival Theatre stage got them through the concert, but the importance of the Prophet-5 meant that Joe couldn't do without it. Like the 2600s, the answer was a spare. Howarth had also hooked up Jaco and Wayne with their own Prophet-5s, so he had a flight case made to house two of them, and Wayne's unit was taken on tour as a backup.

•

When the band got back to California (with a gig in Hawaii en route), Joe and Jaco finished mixing *Mr. Gone*. They labored over every track for weeks, and when it was finally released in October it quickly took off, selling a reported 200,000 copies in the first week.[79] Most observers assumed it would be similar to *Heavy Weather*. Even Cavallo-Ruffalo hoped for that, much to Joe's annoyance. "When they first heard it they were scared because there was no 'Birdland' on it. I was shocked. I said, 'What the hell is this?' To imitate yourself is a real joke."[80]

So expectations were high—perhaps impossibly so—and some Weather Report fans were disappointed once they began listening to the record. It sounded . . . different. To synthesizer enthusiasts, *Mr. Gone* is chock-full of delicious, cutting edge electronic texture. But to others, Joe's orchestrations are heavy-handed, the synthesizer timbres at times jarring. The drumming is often static, especially compared to the rhythmic vitality that Alex Acuña and Manolo Badrena provided for *Heavy Weather*. Then there is the pop singing on the closing track, an unforgivable transgression to hardcore fans. Unlike "Havona," which closed *Heavy Weather* on an exhilarating note, "And Then" left many listeners wanting to put the record back in its jacket. Most disconcerting of all was Wayne's absence. The inner sleeve credits him on all the tracks, but it seemed like an error because he's hard to spot on several of them.

The reviews were all over the place. In the *Washington Post*, Harry Sumrall described *Mr. Gone* as "a remarkable record because, rather than being a renunciation of commercial values, it is an attempt to combine profundity with accessibility." On the other side of the ledger, Max Bell of the *New Musical Express* called the LP "infuriating, not willfully obscure but trivial." And on it went. Indeed, *Mr. Gone* is the most polarizing record Weather Report produced.[81]

Joe Zawinul outside the Sydney Opera House during Weather Report's only tour of Australia in July 1978. Photo: Peter Erskine.

One can't help but think that the band missed the firm hand of Ron Malo, whose guidance in the engineer's booth helped make *Mysterious Traveller*, *Black Market*, and *Heavy Weather* successes. Why they didn't work with him for *Mr. Gone* is unknown. One possibility is that Joe and Malo simply got tired of working with each other. "Ron Malo was an exceptional engineer, but he was a total control freak," recalled one of his colleagues.[82] So was Joe. Peter Erskine speculates that because Malo was "an opinionated guy, I think he'd just had it with Joe, and Joe had had it with him."[83] Brian Risner, who enjoyed a good relationship with both Zawinul and Malo, was also left in the dark. (He wasn't involved in *Mr. Gone*, as he was in the San Francisco Bay Area at the time.) "Maybe he wasn't available," Risner said. "Or maybe they wouldn't give him producer credit on *Heavy Weather*. Ron might have been asking for producer credit—and rightly so. It was the biggest record they had."[84]

Nevertheless, as Weather Report embarked on a month-long, twenty-six-date tour of Europe, Joe was confident in what he had produced. He was especially proud of *Mr. Gone*'s accessible complexity. "Anybody can move to this album," he said, "but if you don't want to move, you get *moved* by it. I think it has both these things. You don't have to understand nothing, but if you want to get analytical, you can really get down."[85] Joe insisted to reporters that *Mr. Gone* was a masterpiece. He would soon find out that not everyone agreed with that assessment.

15　8:30

Weather Report is the leader in a field of one.

—Joe Zawinul

LATE IN THE SUMMER OF 1978, Jaco held a *Mr. Gone* pre-release party at his house in Pompano Beach, Florida. Among the guests was Bob Bobbing, the friend who had lent Jaco his reel-to-reel tape machine to record "The Chicken" when they were teenagers. The two hadn't seen much of each other since Pastorius joined Weather Report, and Bobbing was struck by the changes he observed.

"I showed up at the party by myself, and there were people all through the house for the first time," Bobbing remembered. "Jaco used to be a loner. He didn't used to have a lot of people. I walked in and he called out, 'Hey Bobbo!' and I got a nice hug and everything. So we're hanging, and he's Mr. Personality all of a sudden. He's like, 'Yo, baby! What's happening, baby! Who loves ya?' I had never heard him say 'who loves ya' one time in five years.

"Then he took me in the bedroom where he did a long line of coke—it wasn't a little peck—and he looked at me, put his finger in my face, and said, 'You didn't see that!' That was the first time I ever saw him get high. Until then, not only did he not do that, he was kind of anti-drugs."[1] Bobbing left the party downhearted, thinking that the Jaco he knew was gone.

Meanwhile, Jaco's marriage was faltering. His months-long absences had forced Tracy to assume the responsibilities of running the household on her own, and she had become much more independent than the high school sweetheart Jaco had married—a development that was highlighted in a *Miami Herald* article about local show business wives coping with their husbands' fame.[2] At the *Mr. Gone* party, Bobbing couldn't help but notice how unhappy she was with the scene swirling around her, or that Jaco was flirting with an exotic-looking woman named Ingrid Horn-Müller. Tracy noticed, too, and a few days later, Jaco asked Bobbing to help

Ingrid and Jaco Pastorius. Photo: Peter Erskine.

move his belongings out of the house and into Ingrid's apartment. They quickly became inseparable, and Jaco invited her to join him for Weather Report's European tour.

For Europe, the live show was retooled to include material from *Mr. Gone*. "Black Market" replaced "Elegant People" as the set opener, while the "Badia/Boogie Woogie Waltz" medley closed the show. The band left the stage to a recording of a train roaring past—and at the volume of a Weather Report concert, it was a *seat-shaking* roar—until all that was left was the crossing guard bells. Joe took advantage of a beautiful string patch on the Prophet-5 for his duet with Wayne on "In a Silent Way," which usually segued into a reading of "Waterfall" from Weather Report's first album. With so many tunes from the band's back catalog in the set list, the shows resembled a "greatest hits" compilation.

By this time, Peter Erskine had been granted the band membership that had been previously withheld, and his "spectacularly great honeymoon" shifted to what he called "the sophomore phase."[3] Like many band members, he vividly remembers the concert postmortems. "Weather Report was Joe's puppy," Erskine said. "You know, if I played in a certain manner at a concert, it could keep him up all night fretting about it. And then at breakfast, it'd be the first thing he'd say to me before he'd even ordered a cup of coffee for himself. I've never been in a group, before or since, where the music was obsessed over that much. It was everything to him, and if it didn't reach the epitome, or pass the smell test as it were, it really bothered him."[4]

Oftentimes during these critiques, Joe and Jaco would exalt in some deftly executed harmonic interplay, but mostly the conversation centered on the drumming, which Joe dissected in detail. Wayne tended to remain quiet, his suggestions coming obliquely and at unexpected times. A series of photographs taken by Shigeru Uchiyama captures this dynamic. In them, Joe and Peter take turns air drumming, absorbed in the intricacies of some drumbeat, while Wayne stands in the background, leaning against a wall, watching intently. It wasn't until they were all on the bullet train the next morning that Wayne chimed in as Erskine told an unrelated story to his bandmates. "I didn't want to disturb the passengers around me, so at some point I punctuated the story by softly clapping my hands together," Erskine said. "Wayne interrupted me as I'm about to finish this story, and he touched me and said, 'No, man. *CLAP*. Like that.' That was his moment to tell me that I needed to play with more snap."[5]

As Joe had done with other drummers, he made it clear to Erskine that he didn't want any clichés. "It was tricky," Peter recalled, "because you couldn't do the normal. Joe once told me, 'If I ever hear you go sixteenth notes on the tom toms, I'll *kill* you.' Oftentimes you'd catch yourself turning a beat inside out and playing it cockamamie-ass-backwards upside down, just to avoid the normal. It led to some pretty interesting drumbeats along the way."[6]

In an improvising band like Weather Report, one hurdle Erskine faced was becoming an active participant in instigating changes in the music along with Joe, Wayne, and Jaco. "That came gradually," Erskine explained. "I had to learn to contribute to the dialogue without just aping or playing back what they had just done. And sometimes I felt challenged. They would present it as a challenge: 'Come up with something.'"[7]

Eventually, a rite of passage occurred. "On these tours they were getting more and more [stage] lights," Erskine recalled. "I was closer to the lights than anybody, and it was really hot. And at the end of playing 'Badia/Boogie Woogie Waltz,' we kicked it into double-time. It's loud and it's fast. And I made the mistake of going up to Joe and saying, 'Hey listen, do me a favor: If I give you the high sign when we get to the end of the cycle, you've got to take it out. I'll put the afterburners on, but after that, I'm shot, man. It's so hot, you know.' So instantly his gears start turning. That night or the next night we do it. I go into afterburners and I signal Joe, and he just looks at me and kind of smiles, leans down into the keyboards and gets louder, and just nods his head—we're not ending it. So we had to go through another cycle of this thing. And I didn't know at the time how to change direction musically. Once the crescendo began it was hard. I had a lot to learn about pacing and taking musical charge.

"This is the end of the show—the encore, essentially—the last thing we're playing. Now we're past the point of what I thought I could do, and the whole

Peter Erskine and Joe Zawinul discuss the finer points of drumming and rhythm. Photo: Shigeru Uchiyama / Whisper Not Photo Factory.

time I'm trying to get through this I'm cursing him with every stroke. 'You moth-erfucker. You fucking asshole. I can't believe you. Fuck you.' Just to myself. And then he signals, okay, now we're ending. And I'm just like, no. You didn't end it where I asked you to; I'm not going to end it where you're asking me to. Fuck you. So I just started pounding the snare drum—I was really angry. But instantly I could hear it had a little bit of an Eric Gravatt thing to it—it was pretty hip—and the very end of the concert is kind of an odd place to do this. And then I sensed a presence as I'm doing this, so I looked up and Joe has jumped up on this riser and somehow perched himself right in front of me. So I think, 'Wow, what's his reaction going to be?' And he's going, 'Yeah, yeah, yeah!' He thought it was great. He loved it. It was like Peter got the Holy Spirit. He felt I'd graduated finally. I'd finally stopped asking permission to do things."[8]

Two weeks after the band got back from Europe, they commenced a six-week tour of the United States, arriving in New York City on November 3 for two nights of sold-out shows at the Beacon Theatre. New York was always a homecoming for Joe and Wayne—a chance to see old friends and perform before the music world's elite, including the Columbia bigwigs. Everybody was pumped with anticipation until a technical failure at sound check threw things out of whack.

"This was a *major* show for the band," Alan Howarth remembered. "I mean, we had Miles Davis in the wings. Joni Mitchell—all the major people. So we fire up the show, we do sound check, and all of a sudden the Prophet-5 dumps its programs. Joe looks at me like, 'What the fuck, man?' So we hold the doors—we literally hold the doors—and Joe and I are sitting on the stage of the Beacon The-atre programming the synth. This was before any backup—you just had to dial it all in again. So we dialed up enough sounds to do the show and get him stabilized. We're happy, we open the doors, the show starts, and on the first number Joe hits the keyboard and boom—it dumps all the programs again. And of course I'm re-sponsible for this, so I'm getting daggers, like, 'What in the fuck is going on? You trying to mess me up in front of all these people?'

"So, the interesting thing about that event is that because the Prophet was down, Joe played the shit out of the acoustic piano. Every time he was going to play the Prophet he went to the piano and played something amazing on it. All this angst and tension came out in the acoustic piano because he had Miles watch-ing, right? He had all the people from the world of jazz there, so he just became the most un-fucking-believable acoustic piano player that night."

After the show, Howarth opened up the Prophet-5 and had a look inside. "It turned out that one of the nuts had come off the circuit-board stand and was lay-ing on the backside of the circuit board, shorting it out. So I shook the thing and the screw fell out. And that's what fucked us up that night."[9]

Meanwhile, Joe and Jaco visited Miles at his Upper West Side brownstone the day between shows. Davis was in the midst of a five-year break from music, a period marked by heavy substance abuse that left his personal life in shambles. As Peter Erskine remembered it, after witnessing the debased state in which Davis was living, Joe and Jaco swore off drugs themselves, even if only for a few days. "They were like, 'Man, if that's what that shit will do to you . . .'"[10]

Technical snafus aside, the band put on exceptional performances night after night. Brian Risner had the house sound dialed in, and Joe's keyboards had nev-er sounded better. The elimination of percussion revealed a clarity that focused the music exceptionally well. Chip Stern attended one of the Beacon shows and wrote about it for *Musician Player & Listener*: "On stage, if not on wax, Zaw-inul, Shorter, Pastorius and new drummer Erskine are simply the best live band around, serving up an almost unbelievable variety of sound from atonal exoticism to fatback funk."[11]

Ten days later, the band pulled into Chicago for three performances at Park West, whose nine hundred seats made it one of the smallest venues Weather Report played at the time. Chicago is the home of Maher Publications, which publishes *Down Beat*, and the magazine sent over a young writer named Larry Birnbaum to do an interview for a cover story. Over the years, *Down Beat* had treated the band well. Its readers were about to vote Weather Report their favorite jazz group for the seventh year in a row. Likewise, Joe, Wayne, and Jaco were each voted to the top slot on their respective instruments. Furthermore, all four of the band mem-

Brian Risner mounts a reel of tape onto a reel-to-reel tape recorder before a Weather Report concert. Photo: Shigeru Uchiyama / Whisper Not Photo Factory.

bers had been the subject of recent feature articles in the magazine. In Zawinul's case, it was a massive two-part cover story by Conrad Silvert that spanned the whole of his life, from his days in Austria right up to making *Mr. Gone*.

As Birnbaum and the band gathered for lunch at a nearby Mexican restaurant, Joe no doubt expected to hear some good news about *Down Beat*'s *Mr. Gone* review. Weather Report's last three albums had achieved the magazine's highest rating, and Joe was convinced in his bones that *Mr. Gone* would merit the same. So after everyone got seated, he cheerfully asked about it.

"Oh yeah," Birnbaum replied. "It's getting a one-star review."[12]

Wait. What? *One star?*

"Weather Report has done to jazz in the '70s what Paul Whiteman did to it in the '20s." So began possibly the most controversial review in *Down Beat*'s history. In it, David Less argued that Zawinul and company had over-orchestrated their music to the point that it "made experimentation sound processed," adding that *Mr. Gone* displayed "the sterility of a too completely preconceived project." In other words, Weather Report had succumbed to commercial excess.[13]

The band felt blindsided. Upon delivering this news, Birnbaum turned on his tape recorder and attempted to conduct his interview, but Joe had a few things to get off his chest first. "We really care, you know? Hey man, *Down Beat* is my favorite magazine. You know why? Because I grew up with it. It was my connection to America and it brought me into jazz music.

"But there is no way in the world that a record like this could get a one-star review. . . .You know what one star means? It means this is a poor record. This band has never put out a record that we didn't believe in, and there's no way in the world that anybody was ever involved in a one-star album. This is a heavy thing, man. I mean, even if somebody doesn't like the record, just for the compositions alone it's got to be five stars. We played it very well; we worked hard on this record. Anybody who gives this record one star has got to be insane."[14]

Those words appeared in *Down Beat*'s February 8, 1979, issue, which pictured the band on the cover beneath the blazing headline, "Weather Report Storms Over 'Mr. Gone.'" Birnbaum managed to get his interview, but needless to say, the guys were in a highly contentious mood. It *did* make for entertaining reading, though, and the publisher later said it was the best-selling issue in the magazine's history. In the aftermath, *Down Beat* wound up printing letters from its readers for months to come.

That review still stuck in Zawinul's craw decades later. "I was angry about it, not because somebody gave it one star," he told Josef Woodard in 2001. "That is totally a reviewer's right and privilege. What I didn't like is that it was such a good production. A lot of effort went into that, and we're no dumb motherfuckers, you know? We tried to do something a little different. Maybe it didn't come off yet as well as it did later. That is also a point. But to give somebody one star is just outrageous. Therefore, I was mad at the time, and I am getting mad now."[15] (Upon reading about Joe's continued ire, Less went back and listened to the album again. "It didn't get any better," he dryly noted.[16])

Perhaps most rankling of the review's claims to Joe was that the band took no chances in making *Mr. Gone*. Whatever its faults, Joe and company didn't take the safe route, which would have been to make a *Heavy Weather* clone. "That was one thing about this album which I think is good, which I really love us for," Joe said. "That we did not try to jump on the bandwagon of a 'Birdland.' Because that was suggested to us. 'Hey man, write another "Birdland" and you'll sell a million fuckin' records.' Fuck you, man—we're gonna do what we're gonna do."[17]

The *Mr. Gone* review wasn't *Down Beat*'s only slam at Joe. In the issue that followed the band's combative interview, Lee Underwood wrote about a Weather Report concert that took place just days after Birnbaum met with the band. Before addressing the performance itself, Underwood took his own swipe at *Mr. Gone*, describing it as "the predominantly pompous preenings and cerebrally sterilized goose-step struttings" of Joe Zawinul. And if the point wasn't clear enough, several times he wrote the band's name as "Weather Report (spelled Z-a-w-i-n-u-l)."[18]

Weather Report sucked up a lot of oxygen in the jazz world and some observers were ready to pounce at the first sign of misstep. Joe was perceived as the overbearing tyrant who wrested control of the band from Wayne, while becoming so consumed with electronic gadgetry and a desire to "cash in" that he lost his way. The band's collective ego also made it a tempting target. As Peter Erskine noted, "Neither Joe nor Jaco were shy to proclaim themselves, their work, or their colleagues as being 'the greatest' in the world or 'in the history' to anyone."[19] ("Wayne didn't waste any air—certainly not any hot air—ever bothering to make those kind of pronouncements," Erskine adds.[20])

One reporter wrote that understatement "is not an element of Joe Zawinul's public personality. Much to the contrary, he wears his superego with pride, fast spouting self-congratulation and hyperbole." This would manifest itself in over-the-top pronouncements to the press, such as, "I have some compositions gonna wipe this world out. I'm very frank with you, I ain't scared of Beethoven or no-body—I don't believe in all this *humble* bullshit."[21] Here are several statements Zawinul made in the summer of 1978 in the course of just one newspaper interview:

> "I think we're the only jazz band alive."
> "We're the only people capable of playing true jazz."
> "We are playing tighter than any group you've ever heard in your life, guaranteed."
> "We are creating works of art every time we play."
> "When Miles Davis's era ended our era started."
> "When it comes to modern music we are the kings."[22]

Joe's take-no-shit, we-are-the-greatest posturing was all part of the macho persona he perpetuated. It was familiar to those who knew him well, but it was bound to rub some people the wrong way, especially those who were skeptical of his motives. Ever since *Sweetnighter*, Weather Report's albums raised the same issues of art versus commerce that plagued Miles Davis with *In a Silent Way* and *Bitches Brew*. Some of Joe and Wayne's contemporaries no longer considered them jazz musicians, to say nothing of conservative critics. Sam Jones, the first bass player Zawinul worked with in Cannonball's band, felt that Joe and Wayne had "moved out into the pop field."[23]

Years later, Barry Harris, who tutored Joe in the ways of bebop, said it made him mad that pianists like Joe were initially "really helping jazz" but then "went over to somewhere else. Now, *that* I don't understand. They were making it with the music—they were making it!" When challenged that maybe his view of making it wasn't enough for Joe, Harris had a ready explanation for what wasn't enough: "*Money!*"[24] Indeed, it appeared to some that the band was raking it in, though Joe disputed that notion.

"This year might be the first time we actually make a little profit from touring," he said in 1978. "Last year we sold out 90 percent of the European concerts, but we barely broke even with it." He went on to enumerate all the expenses that the band racked up while on the road—the musicians, the crew, the equipment rentals, the transportation, the managers and the lawyers. But he also acknowledged that he and Wayne were starting to make some money from royalties. He wasn't rich yet, but he wasn't broke, either. "I'm luckier than most people," he acknowledged. "I'm having a moderate success doing what I want to do, and I'm very happy."[25]

Joe's version of moderate success seemed unobtainable to most mainstream jazz musicians. In 1977, Harris lamented that he had "never made any money in my life."[26] All of this led to a certain amount of resentment among Joe and Wayne's contemporaries. "Some of them were bugged at the success of band, or where the music was going—this kind of stuff," Erskine acknowledges. "And Joe, maybe he might tease them, but I have to say this: Zawinul always showed tremendous patience and respect for these points of view, and if it was a player that he respected, he spent a lot of time honoring who they were and trying to explain what the band was trying to do."[27]

Nevertheless, some cringeworthy encounters occurred, such as the time tour manager Brian Condliffe (who previously crewed for Led Zeppelin) rudely chased drummer and big band leader Mel Lewis out of the backstage area during Weather Report's appearance at the JVC Jazz Festival in New York. Lewis's band was scheduled to perform on the same stage later that evening, but Condliffe was oblivious to who he was. After Zawinul was informed of the episode in excruciating detail during the post-concert ride back to the hotel, he spent the next night at the Village Vanguard paying respect to Lewis's band while attempting to make amends.[28]

Meanwhile, Joe had some resentments of his own. He'd gotten a tad fed up with Weather Report being lumped into the category of music that was now being called fusion. For years the term had occasionally been used in relation to jazz infused with cross-genre influences, but it didn't come to represent a distinct subgenre until the mid-seventies, when it more or less replaced "jazz-rock." (It was endorsed by the National Academy of Recording Arts and Sciences, which established the Grammy Award for Best Jazz Fusion Performance in 1980.)

Like jazz-rock, fusion carved out a wide swath of artists, including Grover Washington Jr., Oregon, Return to Forever, and Weather Report; not exactly a homogeneous style of music. Musicians rightly complained that the word didn't mean anything (although they also used the word in a way that suggests that they recognized fusion when they heard it). Worse, it quickly came to have a negative connotation, most broadly associated with slickly packaged pleasant but unadventurous instrumental music that ultimately spawned the enormously popular subgenre, smooth jazz.

Even the mere suggestion that Weather Report was in any way connected with

Wayne blowing hard on the tenor saxophone. Photo: Shigeru Uchiyama / Whisper Not Photo Factory.

fusion elicited a sharp reply from Zawinul. "Fusion is all crap," he barked at one reporter who had the temerity to use the word. "What's fusion? Can you tell me what it is? I think most fusion music stinks and to be put in the fusion category is an insult. It's the writers who are putting us in this category because it's easy and there's no other place to put us. In Europe they have the right idea. They say Weather Report is the leader in a field of one. There's nobody like us. We don't play rock 'n' roll or jazz-rock or whatever that crap is. We play our own original music and that's that."[29]

•

In late November, the band arrived in California, where their first performance took place at the brand new 3,000-seat Terrace Theater in Long Beach. Weather Report had been on the road for three months, and Joe was keen to record live, so arrangements were made to bring a remote recording truck to Long Beach, Santa Monica, Berkeley, and Phoenix. Most of the concerts had a scheduled start time of 8:00 p.m., but the band was invariably late to the stage; hence the title of the resulting album, *8:30*.

"We recorded four concerts and the very first concert where the guy who recorded it didn't have a clue was the best," Joe later said. "Ninety percent of the music on the *8:30* album was from the very first concert in Long Beach, which was magic."[30] As one of the most respected engineers in the field when it came to recording live concerts, Ray Thompson most definitely had a clue. However, knowing that the band would be recorded three more times, he suggested reusing the Long Beach tapes to save money, figuring they'd get better recordings at the subsequent gigs. Luckily, Joe said, "No way."[31]

8:30 was a vindication for the band, reversing the tide of criticism that *Mr. Gone* had received. It was the first full album with Peter Erskine and it shows just how different the reconfigured band sounded compared to its predecessors. Perhaps the two tracks that best illustrate this are "Black Market" and "Birdland." The former is supercharged with a bouncy, syncopated groove that only Jaco could provide, while Erskine outfits the latter with a new motor that transforms its character.

8:30 also reaffirmed Wayne's standing as a major voice on the tenor saxophone. He blasts through several tunes, including an extended strolling turn on "Black Market" backed only by Erskine's drumming and some percussion provided by the other musicians. Wayne also delivers a tender reading of "A Remark You Made." But most notable is his solo performance of "Thanks for the Memory," which the audience recognized as the theme song from the Bob Hope television specials. As with many tracks on *8:30*, it's a truncated version of the real thing. On stage, Wayne took chorus after chorus, deconstructing the melody before wandering off stage, still playing away to the delight of the audience.

Likewise, "Teen Town" is shortened on the record, but rip-roaring nonetheless. (Left out, for instance, is how Joe often tapped out percussion on the Mzuthra.) Joe called it "a *great* show tune because we played the bass line together, my left hand and his bass line together. And he wanted always to be a little better than me. And it was fun."[32] By this time, Jaco's bass solos had become shows within the shows. In addition to the usual pyrotechnics, he now had a digital delay unit. Using it, he would play a short riff and loop it, then add another part and so on, building his own funky accompaniment right in front of the audience. The crowd loved it, clapping along until Pastorius left the stage with the bass still ringing on the floor.

After parting with the recording truck, Weather Report moved on to Texas before wrapping up its U.S. tour in early December. When Jaco got back to Florida, he and Tracy filed for divorce. It was finalized in January 1979, after which they spent the afternoon reminiscing and celebrating new beginnings at their favorite restaurant. But such appearances masked deep feelings of loss in Jaco. "He lost his house, he lost his wife, and in a way he lost his kids," Bob Bobbing observed. "And the next gig he did on stage, I think it all culminated right there. Something happened. That was the beginning of a whole new set of chemicals in his head."[33]

•

The gig that Bobbing refers to was the Havana Jam. The seeds for the event were planted in 1977, when an American-based cruise ship dropped anchor in the waters of Havana for the first time in sixteen years. It came on the heels of President Jimmy Carter lifting travel restrictions to the communist nation, which were imposed in the aftermath of the Cuban Missile Crisis. Among the three hundred passengers aboard was a contingent of jazz musicians led by Dizzy Gillespie, Stan Getz, and Earl "Fatha" Hines. Though they had a concert scheduled for the next evening, none of them knew what to expect when they arrived. "I feel like Christopher Columbus," Gillespie quipped. "Damned if I know what we're going to discover."[34] As it turned out, hundreds of Cubans were there to greet them at the dock, where an impromptu jam session took place.

The next day, Gillespie and company were invited to a hastily arranged luncheon that turned out to be a showcase for the best progressive jazz outfit Cuba had to offer: Irakere, an eleven-piece group led by a superb twenty-five-year-old pianist named Chucho Valdés, and featuring trumpeter Arturo Sandoval and alto saxophonist Paquito D'Rivera. All three would eventually become international stars. At their concert later that evening, the Americans invited Irakere to join them in a jam session that Leonard Feather described as "one of the most powerful illustrations I've ever seen of the old cliché about the international language."[35]

Upon their return to the States, Gillespie and Getz told Bruce Lundvall about what they had seen and heard. By this time, Lundvall was president of the domestic division of CBS Records, overseeing all of its pop and jazz artists. He undertook an informal scouting trip to Cuba the next year and quickly signed Irakere despite the trade restrictions between the United States and Cuba that remained in place. Irakere's unannounced appearance at the 1978 Newport Jazz Festival electrified the audience. Soon Lundvall set his sights on staging a three-day music festival to be held at the Karl Marx Theatre the first weekend of March 1979.

It was a bold idea. There had been no Cuban-American collaborations of any significance since the 1959 revolution that put Fidel Castro in power. When Lundvall proposed it to CBS president William S. Paley, he was receptive, but he also worried about terrorism—specifically, that the plane carrying the artists might be bombed. At the end of 1978, anti-Castro terrorists struck the Cuban Mission in Manhattan and Avery Fisher Hall, where the Cuban band Orquesta Aragón had just performed. Two years earlier, terrorists brought down a Cuban airliner that was flying from Barbados to Jamaica, killing all seventy-eight people aboard, and damaged another aircraft on the ground when a bomb exploded in its luggage compartment. Despite these concerns, Lundvall received Paley's blessing and plans moved forward.

Since CBS was underwriting the event, Lundvall stocked it with artists from his labels. The biggest name was Billy Joel, whose recent albums had each sold over eight million copies. Others included Stephen Stills, Kris Kristofferson, and the Fania All-Stars. As a passionate jazz fan, Lundvall made sure it was well represented with Weather Report and three all-star aggregations, including the Trio of Doom, consisting of Jaco, John McLaughlin and Tony Williams. The rest of the performances drew from Cuba, including Irakere and Orquesta Aragón.

In addition to dealing with the Cuban bureaucracy, the Havana Jam was an enormous logistical undertaking. Forty tons of equipment and supplies—including a 24-track recording console from the Record Plant—were flown in on three cargo planes. The musicians flew together on a TWA charter along with CBS executives and a pack of journalists—134 passengers in all. (One report indicated that the flight was insured for $120 million.[36]) Most of the delegation had never been to Cuba and the flight had the atmosphere of a grand adventure. Upon arriving in Havana, they were whisked away by bus to the beachfront Hotel MarAzul some twenty kilometers out of town. Although of new construction, the musicians found its accommodations spartan by their usual standards. "They must have thought we'd destroy all their rooms," scoffed Kristofferson.[37] On the other hand, the mojitos flowed freely and the pristine beach outside the hotel proved to be a popular hang.

Jim Jerome filed a colorful report for *People* magazine. It includes a photograph of Jaco wandering the streets of Old Havana, "an object of bystander curiosity" according to the caption. In another photo, Joe sits on the sand outside the hotel putting on swim fins. "The people are great and the weather is great, but the food stinks," he muttered. Jerome also noted that, aside from "soaking up the blistering sun and swimming in clear, green, salty surf," Zawinul spent his time reading the German philosopher Arthur Schopenhauer on the beach while Jaco brought a copy of Friedrich Nietzsche's *Thus Spoke Zarathustra*.[38]

As for the concerts themselves, Weather Report opened the festival on Friday night, its leadoff slot probably dictated by its complicated stage setup. The band hadn't performed live for a couple of months, so they weren't in peak form. Peter Erskine remembered it not being among their better shows, and he's especially harsh about his own performance. "I think I played like an asshole down there," he said. "The band hadn't worked in like three months. We got down there and I hit it hard and my arms cramped up. I wasn't in shape to play. It was a brutal set, I remember, just playing that loud. And I think I was also excited and a little tense because all my musical heroes were there."[39] Erskine's disappointment with his showing was reinforced when he ran into John McLaughlin backstage. "I've heard all these amazing things about you, but you didn't sound that good," the guitarist dryly remarked.[40]

That aside, the Cubans seemed particularly impressed by the showier aspects of Weather Report's concert. The smoke effect on "Scarlet Woman" got wild applause even though (or perhaps because) the fog machine operator got a little carried away, enveloping the entire band and causing the temporary disappearance of the first few rows of the audience.[41] When the fog dissipated, they looked "like they were coming from Mars or something," Paquito D'Rivera recalled. "That makes an impression."[42]

On Saturday, one of the expected highlights was the first and only live performance of the Trio of Doom. (Jaco had a penchant for calling things "this of doom" or "that of doom." He even referred to his fretless Fender Jazz bass as the "Bass of Doom.") The buzz was that the rehearsals were amazing, and indeed, some in the audience were thrilled by the group's twenty-five-minute set. *Rolling Stone*'s Chet Flippo called it "electrifying."[43] But when the trio got off the stage, McLaughlin and Tony Williams were furious.

"Jaco went on a star trip, and musically it was a bit of a disaster," McLaughlin later said. "The three of us are onstage, and all of the sudden Jaco, in the middle of a C-minor blues, starts playing in A-major, real loud, and going up front [*mimes rock-star showboating*]. [Tony and I] did what we could, as best as possible, and when we get offstage, Jaco says, 'You know, you're a bad motherfucker.' And I said, 'I have never felt so ashamed to be onstage . . . If I never see you again, it's too soon.'"[44]

This was the first time that Peter Erskine witnessed Jaco out of control. Bob Bobbing theorizes that it was a consequence of Jaco's divorce, which was finalized weeks earlier. But Erskine observed a couple of other issues that might have contributed to Jaco's erratic behavior. This was one of the rare times that he traveled without Ingrid, whom he sorely missed. Jaco also got into a confrontation with members of the Fania All-Stars.

"Joe had to rescue Jaco from that one because he almost got his ass kicked by those guys," Erskine remembered. "They weren't digging what he was saying and it was spiraling out of hand. So Joe had to broker peace and Jaco lost face. Whenever Jaco lost face like that, then boom. Weather Report had already played, so what could Jaco destroy? He destroyed the Trio Of Doom. He just didn't play the tunes. Jaco just started feedback, playing 'Portrait of Tracy' in the middle of some tune, and Joe and I were thinking, *Oh my God, what's going on?* We were embarrassed. Jaco was self-destructing up there, and Tony was just furious, completely pissed off. They just couldn't get anything going on stage. And then afterwards, Jaco almost destroyed himself by jumping off the dock into the rocky harbor."[45]

Meanwhile, the American musicians as a whole ultimately wound up disillusioned by the event. They were especially disappointed by the lack of interaction with the Cuban people. "We were hoping that we'd be playing for the *gente*, the people, but the audience was very carefully invited," Erskine recalled. "We were put in a hotel way out in the boonies, with minimal interaction with the Cubans. Some musicians kind of snuck in—a lot of Cuban musicians were there, and some fans. But it wasn't for the people like we had imagined it would be."[46]

By Monday morning everyone was anxious to get home, and a heartfelt rendition of "America" broke out on the bus to the airport.[47] Once there, they were delayed for several hours before clearing customs while Russian tour groups waltzed through unimpeded. To compound matters, the luggage-conveyor system broke, so everyone banded together to make a human suitcase brigade. "Looks like the fall of Saigon to me," cracked Kristofferson.[48] When the doors to the gate finally opened, the troupe headed for the airplane singing "I Love New York."[49] "I have never heard as much complaining as I did on that flight back to New York," reported Flippo.[50] Said one exhausted CBS staffer, "I learned a new Spanish phrase this trip: '*Más nunca.*' It means 'never again.'"[51]

Nevertheless, Lundvall had ample reason to be proud of what took place. "Given the logistical complexities of a multi-act jazz-rock show, not to mention dealing with Cuba's Leninist-Latin bureaucracy, the shows were a triumph of cooperation, goodwill, and superb sound quality," Jim Jerome wrote.[52] Certainly the Cuban musicians who were there remember Havana Jam as a significant event in their lives. But in hindsight, the "Bay of Gigs," as one Weather Report crew member dubbed it, isn't much more than a historical footnote. When Ronald Reagan was elected president in 1980, he immediately rolled back U.S.-Cuban relations to the pre-Carter status quo.

•

After Cuba, Weather Report had a couple of other concerts—the U.C. Berkeley Jazz Festival in May and the inaugural Playboy Jazz Festival three weeks later—but the main focus was finishing *8:30*. Meanwhile, Columbia asked the band for a mix of "Black Market" to lead off the first side of the *Havana Jam* album. Instead of the one they played in Cuba, they sent the one from Long Beach. "They were just too busy working on the mixing for *8:30*," Peter Erskine said. "So somebody—maybe it was Jaco—said, 'Fuck it. Let's just send them the Long Beach one.' 'Yeah, okay.' And what was funny, there was one reviewer who contrasted the two versions in a review. I was like, are you kidding?"[53]

Oddly, *8:30* was issued as a double LP with three sides of live material while the fourth side contained all new studio recordings. That none of the live tracks came from *Mr. Gone* led some to speculate that even Joe wasn't so fond of that album, but the plan all along was to include a couple of those tunes until a studio blunder forced their hand. It occurred while they were mixing "Mr. Gone." Joe wanted to combine the Berkeley and Phoenix performances, and he spent days trying to get a good edit point before splicing together the two-inch, 24-track master tapes (yes, they were cutting the masters). Things were in good shape; they just needed to clean up a few details. In the meantime, they were also having trouble with mixing engineers. Peter Erskine picks up the story:

> We were going through engineers like crazy, and management brought in this guy that had worked with Earth, Wind & Fire. I remember he was pretty blasé; you know, "I'm the hotshot engineer." The first work to do that morning was to erase a synth track that was on the right side of the tape edit because Joe hadn't played that keyboard on the other night's performance. Okay, fine. Now, first thing in the morning they had done maintenance on the machine—it was an MCI Recording 24-track machine—and everything was left in ready [as in, ready to record] and the engineer didn't check. So when he hit record, the whole thing lit up like a Christmas tree, and the engineer lunged from his chair. I wasn't that experienced, but I knew what had just happened.
>
> Silence.
>
> Joe was pacing on the other side of the desk where the speakers were, so I said, "Hey Joe."
>
> "What?"
>
> "I think something just happened that wasn't supposed to."
>
> "Oh yeah? What?"
>
> And I pointed at the engineer and I said, "You tell him."
>
> It was one of those times where Joe didn't display any anger, but I

knew he was angry. The happy accident was we made the studio side because we didn't have enough material, and they didn't want to put out a single LP. With "Mr. Gone" out of the picture, Joe said, "Well, let's fill up one side of the album and play some stuff in the studio."[54]

So that's what they did. They set up at Devonshire Sound and one of the toys Joe brought along was a Korg VC-10 vocoder. Vocoder technology had existed for decades in audio laboratories, but the VC-10 was made for musicians, with a two-and-a-half-octave keyboard and a gooseneck microphone that stuck out of the top of the control panel. Speaking or singing into the microphone produced a sound that took on vocal characteristics while following the pitch of the keyboard. When Korg let Joe try one out, he knew he had to have one.

8:30's title track is Joe's first use of a vocoder in a recording. It eventually became one of his most identifiable sounds. "My concept always was that the human voice is the premiere instrument in the world," he explained years later. "Now, I am no Frank Sinatra, because my natural voice is not a pretty voice. It's a different kind of voice. But I can phrase like nobody. I can sing certain old Ellington songs—you'd be surprised—with just my natural voice. I sing low and more like I speak. And my whole concept of making music, when I play and phrase—I have probably learned it through experience, perhaps—is to phrase like I'm singing. And the vocoder allows me to be a singer in the most direct form. That's the most primal thing—the human voice."[55]

While Joe was playing with the vocoder, Jaco hopped on Peter Erskine's drum set, and the impromptu jam led to the tune "8:30." "At one point I think it was Jaco and Wayne," Erskine recalled. "Wayne was hitting a Heineken bottle into the mike and playing a little cowbell, and they got a little thing going; they were sort of trying to show me how to be creative. At any rate, I remember feeling a little envious or jealous because there was Jaco and Joe, and wow, they had a great thing going. They only had a cassette rolling at that point, so I ran and got the engineer, and that's when you hear the audio change [from lo-fi to hi-fi on the record]. And then to start it, Jaco went to some guy's house that had a ham radio, and he recorded maybe forty minutes of random dial turning. He claimed that the little polka thing was the very first thing he got. He was like, 'Man, check this out!' And they cut it all together."[56]

The second studio track, "Brown Street," was a spontaneous improvisation made at Joe's house. "We were fooling around," Zawinul recalled. "My son Erich was with us and he grabbed some shakers. We started a tune, and that's what you hear on the original. I just let the tape recorder roll."[57] Since Jaco wasn't available, Joe played the bass line along with the rest of the keyboard parts. He brought the cassette to Devonshire, and the rest of the band built on it. "I did all the per-

Joe reaches for one of his ARP 2600 synthesizers at his music room in Pasadena. Tape markings are visible on the 2600 control panels, which helped Zawinul quickly find the settings for common patches. To the left of Joe's head is a Sequential Circuits Model 700 Programmer, which could store the settings for 64 ARP 2600 programs. Photo: © Tom Copi / Michael Ochs Archive / Getty Images.

cussion overdubs," Erskine said. "Jaco added a layer of drums at one point, and Wayne redid just about everything he played on the original cassette recording. That's why the tenor has an odd, coarse sound to it—he was trying to match it because they wanted to get a good sound. So we redid it but kept the original cassette performance in there."[58]

Erskine's drumbeat was inspired by some Dom Um Romão albums he had (specifically, the tunes "Salvation Army" and "The Angels"). "We were kind of messing around and I started playing this beat, a combination of those two Dom Um beats, and then Joe started improvising the tune. It wouldn't have happened unless I came up with the beat, so I felt that I was a part of the creative process, that it was a shared composition that brought that up." But when Erskine asked Joe about getting a composer credit, Zawinul wouldn't have it.

"Sing me one melody or part of one melody you wrote," he demanded. "Can you do that?"

"No," Erskine replied.

"Then you didn't write the tune."

"I thought it was unfair, just in principle," Erskine said. "I mean, I was the drum machine that I programmed. I think it's an integral part of the tune, but at the time he didn't see fit to give any credit that way. When we did the albums, I just got paid scale for time in the studio because I was just a sideman. There were no royalties to speak of."[59]

The third studio track on *8:30* is Joe's composition "The Orphan"—a hymn-like duet with Wayne, augmented by a children's choir who were orphans themselves. Like "Unknown Soldier" from *I Sing the Body Electric*, it has to do with Zawinul's experiences during World War II, specifically the children who lost parents fighting the war or closer to home. In regard to the latter, Zawinul remembered how officials came to his school to ask the students what their parents talked about. "If a kid said they don't like Nazis, the parents were gone the next day."[60]

8:30 closes with "Sightseeing," a tune the band rehearsed at Joe's house before taking it to Devonshire. As was often the case, it was part of a much longer score that Wayne brought in. "Wayne's pieces were complexly notated, with mixed accidentals," Erskine recalled. "It was beautiful but ornate penmanship, real clustered—not easy for Joe to read. So we would play everything as a ballad just to try to get through it. And then at a certain point we'd say, 'Okay, what can we do with this?' And they'd say, 'Hey Wayne, this thing on page five is pretty cool. Why don't we just play that?' And he was like, 'Yeah, fine.' And I started wondering, is this what happened in Miles's band? Why some of Wayne's tunes just kind of repeat? Because Wayne was writing much longer, more involved music."[61]

For "Sightseeing," they homed in on two pages of Wayne's manuscript. He didn't have any specific rhythmic ideas in mind, or even a tempo, so once the band got the music under their fingers they collectively came up with the up-tempo version heard on the album. Erskine has always considered it to be his favorite track with the band. Like "Pinocchio," it allowed him to exercise his straight-ahead jazz chops. After they got the tune on tape, Joe felt that it needed another element, so they improvised the odd funky interlude and ending, with Erskine mustering his "best Gravatt/*Mysterious Traveller* beat" while Jaco played a didgeridoo and Erskine's crotales (antique cymbals), which he muted to give them a weird bell sound.

•

1979 was an unusually inactive year for Weather Report. Aside from the Havana Jam and the shows in Berkeley and Hollywood, they did only the summer festivals in Europe for three weeks. In the fall, Jaco toured with Joni Mitchell on her Shadows and Light tour. Mitchell's original plan was to use Weather Report as her backing band like she had done with the L.A. Express. Weather Report would do an opening set, then back Mitchell for hers. Jaco, Wayne and Erskine had all played on her most recent album, *Mingus*, so that was three-fourths of the band right there. Erskine, for one, was excited to do the tour. But just when things seemed set, he got a phone call from Joe.

"The Joni Mitchell tour thing is not happening. I told Jaco that he can do it because of his long association with her, but I don't want Wayne or you to do it."

"What happened?" Erskine asked.

"I just told her we ain't no fucking L.A. Express." Click.[62] Joe's edict left no doubt about who was in charge of the band.

Jaco did indeed do the tour with Joni. In fact, she designated him her musical director. But right about that time, he married Ingrid and wound up missing one rehearsal after another, so a frustrated Mitchell gave the job to Pat Metheny. Michael Brecker took the role that Joni had wanted for Wayne, Don Alias played drums, and Metheny's partner in his own group, Lyle Mays, manned the keyboards. It was a band full of stellar jazz chops, but reined in to support Mitchell. A live double album, *Shadows and Light*, was recorded at the Santa Barbara Bowl in September, and a video of the concert was also produced. These are indispensable documents of Jaco's career.

Around the time Mitchell's tour came to an end, *8:30* was released. It was well received, and even won a Grammy in the inaugural fusion category. (The band was on tour when the winners were announced and didn't even know they had been nominated.) Normally, a new record would occasion a lengthy tour, but Joe and the band elected to remain off the road for the remainder of the year. When they did resume performing in January 1980, it would be with an entirely new repertoire.

16 Night Passage

It started to dawn on me that I was in the most famous jazz band in the world.

—Robert Thomas Jr.

AS THE CALENDAR FLIPPED FROM ONE DECADE TO THE NEXT, a reporter wrote that Weather Report was "probably the only jazz fusion band to make it all the way through the '70s with their reputation intact."[1] Indeed, as fusion became a dirty word, Weather Report stood out not only as a beacon of originality and quality, but also as the lone survivor of the jazz-rock outfits spawned from *In a Silent Way* and *Bitches Brew*. The ten records that Joe and Wayne had produced to this point (including *Live in Tokyo*, which made its way to the United States as an import in the late seventies) represented a sterling and prolific body of work. By now, Zawinul was universally recognized as jazz music's most accomplished practitioner of the synthesizer. His skill at incorporating a wide variety of musical influences and textures was arguably unsurpassed. And while Wayne's direct involvement in the band beyond the concert hall had ebbed, he remained vital to Weather Report's sound. He was their poet—a singular voice on the saxophone that provided a tangible link to the past.

In the jazz world at large, such links seemed strained, at least to some observers. Jazz essentially underwent an identity crisis in the 1970s, running the gamut from the overtly commercial to the highly experimental. The *Billboard* jazz chart for 1979 told one side of the story. At the top were the Crusaders, George Benson, Bob James, Chuck Mangione, and Grover Washington Jr. All were considered "contemporary" or "crossover" artists because they appealed to non-jazz fans. Their popularity fueled surging jazz sales, which *Billboard* claimed now accounted for 17 percent of all U.S. record sales—a vast improvement over the dismal situation a decade earlier.[2]

Joe Zawinul holds the *Swing Journal* Jazz Disc Gold Award, signifying the magazine's recognition of *8:30* as the best album of 1979. Left to right: Zawinul, Jaco Pastorius, Peter Erskine, Robert Thomas Jr., Wayne Shorter. Photo: Peter Erskine.

At the other end of the spectrum was the decidedly non-commercial, but robust free jazz community that gravitated to New York City midway through the seventies. Among the most formidable of the avant-garde groups was the Art Ensemble of Chicago, which very nearly toppled Weather Report in the 1980 *Down Beat* Readers Poll. Then there was ECM, the Munich-based record company founded in 1969 by Manfred Eicher. In the span of a decade, ECM became a highly respected label, known for its uncompromising standards and an eclectic catalog of improvisational music that brought emerging European artists to the attention of American audiences.

That such a diverse range of music was produced under the jazz umbrella revived the "is it jazz?" debate in a way that, according to Leonard Feather, made the bebop versus "moldy figs" debates of the 1940s "seem like ladies' tea party chatter."[3] Perhaps the one point of agreement among critics was the welcome hard bop resurgence that occurred toward the end of the decade, epitomized by saxophonist Dexter Gordon. Ironically, Gordon found renewed success at Columbia, which was the leader of the fusion subgenre. As an unabashed jazz fan, Bruce Lundvall used his position to rejuvenate Gordon's career and champion a small but significant number of musicians who favored a return to the bop-derived music of the fifties and sixties.

Meanwhile, Weather Report failed to fit neatly into any box, at various times occupying each of them. Now Joe was keen to shed skins yet again. "After the *8:30* tour, we were locked in a little bit," he later explained. "Not musically and not like prisoners of success, but the acclaim we achieved led to certain habits.

It's really hard to describe, because the moment we came out onstage, it was as if the Rolling Stones had come out—it was something else! And I think that Jaco, who was very responsible for a lot of the success we had, was susceptible to certain gimmickry, more than anyone else in the band. But we played so well; and I feel that as long as you play well, you can do anything and get away with it."[4]

Peter Erskine remembered Zawinul voicing his concerns to him. "A lot of times Joe would come up to me and say, 'This is not really Weather Report music,' the way we were doing things, so he knew something was missing. The demands of the touring show had kind of taken over, I think, some of the musical decision-making. The show was big. It was loud. It was fairly unrelenting. I would have been *so happy* if I had just had a little four-piece kit like Eric Gravatt had, and I could have played at that dynamic level. But it's hard to do that when 90 percent of the evening is that loud on stage."[5]

Although Joe's response wasn't as dramatic as the changes wrought with *Sweetnighter*, he nonetheless moved the band in another direction, jettisoning nearly all the old music from Weather Report's live shows and replacing it with entirely new material, mostly his own. Joe went about organizing this music toward the end of 1979. The word *organizing* seems appropriate because Zawinul had so many taped improvisations that it was a matter of choosing what to use and shaping it into a form for the band as a whole. In this process he enlisted Erskine, who by then had moved to the San Fernando Valley. His close proximity to Pasadena meant that he spent many afternoons at Joe's house working through tunes.

"I would usually be the first guy that would get to see and hear any of this," Erskine recalled. "Even though I wasn't on any kind of retainer, it was kind of expected because I was living there. I had moved out to California to be with the band. It was just part of my education. I spent a lot of time driving out to Joe's house in Pasadena, but it was always a fun get-together. Sometimes Wayne would come over, but a lot of the rehearsals were just like these incredible jams/drum lessons—just Joe and myself. We might have some lunch, maybe a little slivovitz, and we'd work on the tunes and kind of prepare them for when Jaco would fly out and we'd have a full band rehearsal. And I learned as much as I may have contributed. I mean, Joe worked on the music all the time. I don't know if he ever took a day off in that sense."[6]

The new music debuted on January 17, 1980, when Weather Report commenced an eight-week U.S. tour. They arrived in Virginia Beach three days early, where, in Erskine's words, "Joe, Wayne, Jaco, and I learned a whole new book of music."[7] Even the pre-show buildup was changed, with a cross-cultural selection of songs culminating in Ray Charles singing "America the Beautiful." When the curtains opened onto a darkened stage, Joe was mounted at his keyboards, lit from below through a dry-ice smoke effect, playing the opening strains of "8:30." A

Jaco Pastorius performing on stage in 1980. Photo: Shigeru Uchiyama / Whisper Not Photo Factory.

drummer accompanied him, but as the stage lights brightened, the audience realized that it wasn't Peter Erskine. Their confusion quickly turned to delight when they recognized Jaco throwing down a funky beat. After a bracing ninety seconds or so, Pastorius got up from the drum stool and disappeared backstage while Joe finished "8:30" solo, lit by a lone spotlight. When the stage lights came back up, the full band was in place and jumped into a scorching version of "Sightseeing."

What followed was a raft of new and mostly untitled tunes performed publicly for the first time: "Madagascar," "Three Views of a Secret," "Port of Entry," "Dream Clock," and "Fast City." Most of them were loosely structured, highly experimental works in progress, with more of a jazz edge than before. The writer Jon Pareles caught the band at the Beacon Theatre early in the tour and filed a report for *Musician Player & Listener* magazine. After observing that *8:30* "showed a band caving in to audience demands for predictability," Weather Report was "[sprinting] ahead of their audience once again." He described the new tunes as "more complex" than the band's previous material, with the lines blurred between composition and improvisation. "There was structure aplenty—and the willingness to trash it for the sake of jazz or just plain high spirits."[8]

About an hour into the shows, the rest of the band took a break for Jaco's bass solo. He had curbed some of the excesses that crept into his earlier routine. He was liable, for instance, to play an extremely expressive excerpt from Jimi Hendrix's "Third Stone from the Sun" utilizing his beautiful singing tone. Among the new elements of his performances were portions of Bach's "Chromatic Fantasy" and the Beatles song "Blackbird," both of which would appear on Jaco's 1981 album, *Word of Mouth*. Pastorius also cued a recorded excerpt of Alan Hovhaness's Symphony No. 2, *Mysterious Mountain*, playing along as naturally as if the piece had been written for him. Of course, by this time no Jaco solo was complete without turning up the funk before climaxing in a showy display of fuzzy, loud distortion. These were tour de force performances, and audience members can be heard in bootleg recordings uttering their astonishment.

"Brown Street" followed Jaco's solo, sequenced to give him a break after the rest of the band returned to the stage. As it was originally played on *8:30*, Zawinul handled the bass chores with his left hand. Next came another of Joe's new tunes, titled "Forlorn"—a short, harmonically ambiguous ballad that Joe called an "abstract blues."[9] "'Forlorn' is brilliant because of the multi-tonality of the piece," Erskine said. "It's not quite a dirge, but not quite a blues. There's like three keys happening simultaneously. I remember Joe having a conversation with Julius Farmer, an American bassist living in Italy. He said, 'Man, was that two or three keys?' And Joe said, 'Three keys, man!' And it was like, wow, it's amazing. Not a whole lot of music is written like that. I liked that one."[10]

Early versions of "Forlorn" debuted in the summer of 1979 as a solo synthesizer interlude. Now it largely relied on Jaco's luxurious tones until Joe's keening synthesizer wails seamlessly segued into the biggest surprise of these concerts: A swinging version of Duke Ellington's "Rockin' in Rhythm" with Zawinul's Oberheim synthesizer playing the role of a saxophone section. Zawinul's idea was to pay homage to the old New York jazz scene that greeted him upon his arrival in the United States in 1959, and the performance was accompanied by a visual display of jazz greats projected on screens behind the band.

"Joe wanted to do a tribute to Ellington and all the great jazz masters on Fifty-Second Street," Erskine said. "So they commissioned a woman who was subcontracted by the Showco production company—they did the touring production work, lights, and sound—and she put together a three-screen, computer-controlled slideshow. We were rehearsing in Virginia Beach, and she was running it down for the band, showing photographs of Dizzy Gillespie, Charlie Parker, Louis Armstrong. We stopped everything to watch it and Joe was saying, 'Ah, this is beautiful!' It was like his dream realized, he was feeling so great.

"And then this one photo went by and he went, 'Wait a minute! Stop! Stop! Stop! Go back!' In the midst of all these figures, there was a picture of Chico Hamilton. Chico was incredibly important to the development of the music, but Chico was more West Coast, and Joe had envisioned this as a New York thing. He took great exception that this woman had made the editorial decision to include Chico Hamilton. So Chico had to go, which was too bad. And then Jaco made the joke, 'I wonder who's coming next. Pat Metheny?'"[11]

Chico Hamilton or not, "Rockin' in Rhythm" was a crowd-pleaser every time out and the band enjoyed it, too. In Jon Pareles's words, "it was perfect, not only for its title, but the way the band tore into it. They treated its bluesy line as they'd treat anything Shorter or Zawinul might have come up with, hard and swinging, while behind it Zawinul punched sustained modal Fender Rhodes chords off the beats in trademark style. In totally re-grooving Ellington, Weather Report asserted their continuity with jazz tradition, simultaneously proving they had something of their own to add to it."[12]

After ninety minutes, the main portion of the show climaxed with the obligatory "Birdland," the only nod to pre-*8:30* material. For the half-hour encore, Erskine came out first to perform his drum solo, followed by Joe and Wayne's duet. The grand finale was an extended and reimagined version of "The Orphan." The first part stuck to the contours of the *8:30* recording, though without the choir, before breaking into a furious jam that was reminiscent of "Boogie Woogie Waltz." The band then reprised "The Orphan" before departing the stage to a standing ovation as the train recording blasted through the auditorium. All in all, these were exciting performances that left audiences wowed.

Meanwhile, as happened with many of Erskine's predecessors, Joe began cracking on him more and more. It happened at rehearsals and at sound checks, and even during the gigs. Pretty much anything was fair game for critique. Peter even got flak for the way he walked. ("You take these funny little steps when you walk, man. You should learn to take bigger steps; it will make you a better drummer!"[13])

Such faultfinding was surely instrumental in the departure of some of Erskine's predecessors, but Peter kept it in perspective. "I think part of the reason I stayed in the band so long and enjoyed the longest tenure of any drummer in the group was that, number one, we all liked each other very much. And I also put up with a lot of the bullshit longer than other guys. I would always remind myself: These guys know more about this stuff than I do. And even when I went on the road with big bands—there's a lot not to like about being on the road for fifty weeks a year—but I saw drummers come and go in the other big bands, and I just figured if this is what I'm going to do for a living, and if I'm going to try to establish myself as a player, I've just gotta stick it out a little longer. And there were a couple of times with Weather Report that I just wanted to buy a plane ticket and fly home, but we always worked through those situations."[14]

As frustrating as it might have been at times, Erskine took away pearls of wisdom that stuck with him for the rest of his career. For instance, one time at sound check Joe asked him to play the beat for one of the tunes. "It was something where the hi-hat was closed, so I wasn't having to move the leg or the foot to open and close the hat," Peter recalled. But Zawinul noticed him bouncing his leg in time with the beat. "Joe waits for me to stop and goes, 'What's going on with your leg?'

Zawinul performing in Japan in 1980. Here he's playing his Fender Rhodes electric piano. Atop the Rhodes is the ARP 2600 keyboard and Sequential Circuits Prophet 5. At far left is an ARP Quadra, and the Oberheim 8-Voice is to Joe's right. Photo: Shigeru Uchiyama / Whisper Not Photo Factory.

I said, 'What do you mean?' 'Why you moving it?' 'Just keeping the time, you know. Leave me alone.' He said, 'No. Put that energy into what you're playing.' And it was great advice because it's all about finding your center. It's all about focusing all that energy into what you're playing, into the music. And I still call on that; I'll catch something moving."[15]

Nevertheless, Joe's constant needling sometimes got into Erskine's head. "I was starting to play to try to please him, and that's a big mistake in that band. Because psychically, then you're not in the position he wants the drummer to be in." It began to adversely affect the vibe on stage. At one point, Jaco became so exasperated by the whole thing that he pulled Peter aside to impart some lasting advice. "Sound checks are becoming fucking drum lessons," he complained. "I'm getting tired of it. The whole crew's getting sick and tired of it. Look man, stop thinking so much. Just concentrate."[16]

Another pearl of wisdom. Erskine realized that in his attempts to please Joe, he was losing the qualities that Zawinul appreciated about him in the first place. Jaco's point: Listen to the music, play what you hear, and you'll be fine.

•

About a week into the tour a new musician showed up for a concert. His name was Robert Thomas Jr., and he brought with him a set of congas and other percussion instruments, including cymbals, cowbells, and drums. He played them all with his hands, utilizing a self-taught style that had nothing to do with the Cuban percussionists who dominated the South Florida music scene where he lived. Like Peter Erskine, Jaco recruited him. They met the previous September when Thomas was the house percussionist at a benefit for fellow Floridian Oscar Salas, a friend of Jaco's who had been badly injured in an accident.[17] Puzzled by Thomas's unorthodox methods, Pastorius approached him after the show. "Hey man, what the fuck are you doing? What is that?"

"Well, I'm a bebop hand drummer, a bebop conga player," Thomas explained.[18]

It was a term he invented himself, and if you do an Internet search for "bebop hand drummer" today, the only results will be about Thomas. But what did it mean? Unlike traditional Afro-Cuban percussionists, Thomas didn't fill the music by patting out a constant rhythm. Instead, he valued space and only played what he thought the music needed at a given time. It was his response to the unyielding pulse of the disco era, as well as his interpretation of what it meant to be a jazz musician.

The local Cubans were just as perplexed by Thomas as Jaco was. "Conga players would come see me play on my gigs," Thomas remembered, "and of course, all the Cuban guys would say, 'Hey, man, what are you doing? I've been watching you all night and I don't understand anything you're playing. You're not a *conguero.*' And I'd say, 'Well, first of all, I don't even know what a *conguero* is, and I've never professed to be one.' And they would just get pissed and walk away. I didn't care, because I never wanted to play that kind of music anyway. I like to dance to it, but I don't want to play it." Whatever Thomas was doing, Jaco liked it, and promised to tell Joe about him. Thomas didn't let on that he had no idea who Zawinul was.[19]

Fast-forward four months, and Joe felt that the new music was missing something. As Thomas heard the story, at one point Zawinul and Jaco were talking on the band bus about bringing on a percussionist, and Pastorius suggested Don Alias, one of his favorites. "No, man," Zawinul responded. "I'm tired of all these Afro-Cuban guys. I need something different."

Ingrid was sitting with them. "Hey, what about that hand drummer guy in Miami?" she asked. "I have his card right here in my pocketbook."[20]

Thomas picks up the story:

> I got a phone call from Jaco around midnight, saying, "Hey man, do you want to join Weather Report? You want to come audition?" I said yes. So two weeks later they flew me out to New Haven, Connecticut, and I got off the plane and I saw this nervous guy waiting for me, rushing me and my equipment into the truck. We drove to the venue and I'm thinking, *Wow, what kind of audition is this?* It was straight to the gig, man.
>
> And what was very funny for me is that I'm the first guy to play cym-

bals with my hands. So I'm taking out my cymbals and Peter Erskine is looking over. I had no idea who he was. Nobody spoke to me but Wayne Shorter; he gave me a smile. Peter was pissed because he saw the cymbal stand come out and he thought Joe hired another trap drummer. He was not happy. For me it was just another gig. I wasn't intimidated. I loved jazz. I thought, *Okay, these guys aren't friendly, but I don't care. I'm here; I'll play my ass off anyway.*

So, we started to play, and oh, my God . . . They were working on the *Night Passage* music, even though I was flown out there in the middle of the *8:30* tour. And man, I was so happy because it was just real fast jazz, and I like that a lot. I started playing and Joe Zawinul turned around and he was smiling. And Jaco was laughing at him. I couldn't understand why Jaco kept looking over at this man, laughing at him. Years later, I found out through Ingrid that Jaco had told him that he found the only bebop conga player in the world, and Joe went, "Get out of here. I don't believe you." And Jaco goes, "You wanna bet?" So Joe lost a bet, lost a lot of money, I suppose. And Peter calmed down when he saw the conga drums and my setup, which was very unusual, with the three cymbals and a kick drum. Sometimes I had a snare, but I use my hands for everything, even on the bells.

So Joe came to me after Jaco played this monster solo and said, "Okay, kid, go out there and play some of that hand shit!" He sent me out there by myself. I always play for God, so I didn't worry about anything. I just closed my eyes and let the spirit fly and got a standing ovation right after Jaco just *killed* 'em doing his Jimi Hendrix thing. Afterwards, Joe came over and put his hand on my shoulder, patted me on the back, and said, "Kid, I think you're going to have to go shopping tomorrow. We got to get you some clothes. I heard you only brought a small bag. You're not going home, you're going on a world tour."

And so that was how that went down. I have really big ears. I don't read music, but I listen very well and stay out of the drummer's way. I love bebop, love jazz. And Jaco could see this, and so I didn't have any rehearsal with them, but I played that music like I wrote it, I guarantee you that. It was one of the biggest nights of my life because I had never played in front of so many people before. As time went on, it started to dawn on me that I was in the most famous jazz band in the world. I had no idea who Weather Report was, none at all.[21]

Meanwhile, nobody told Peter Erskine that Thomas was coming. Not that Zawinul was obligated to do so, but it would have been a courtesy, especially since

Robert Thomas Jr. Photograph: Shigeru Uchiyama / Whisper Not Photo Factory.

the band had been a quartet for eighteen months. "The timing was interesting because I had just asked Joe for a raise," Erskine said. "And they were like, 'We can't afford it. We don't have the money.' Shortly after all that, then they decide to hire a percussionist. And Bobby's great. Nobody can swing like he does on the congas, and it was a very cool thing. But my immediate reaction was, *Well, that must mean I'm not cutting it.* I thought everything was feeling pretty cool, and they had talked for such a long time about how they enjoyed the openness of not having percussion in the band.

"But then I went to Joe and I said, 'Hey, Joe, great, but where did the money come from all of a sudden?' And he immediately turned around and said, 'That is the most selfish fucking thing anyone has ever said.' He didn't address my question; he just made me feel like a selfish prick. 'You're not thinking of the band. This is good for the band.' And in fact, who knows, maybe this did add financial strain, because there are a lot of bills when you take a band out on the road. I think the band was making pretty good money. They were adding concerts. I don't know what Jaco's deal was, but I never got paid anything extra if they added another concert. I was still just on a weekly salary. We worked hard, that's for sure. But Bobby was a tremendous addition to the band and we had a lot of fun playing together. It was a very sleek, cool thing. And I think whatever adapting I needed to do happened pretty quickly."[22]

Thomas is indeed a unique player who added a different dimension to Weather Report from anyone who had come before him. But as the new guy, he had his own challenges trying to figure out how to contribute to a tight band that had been together for a while. "My first night, the volume was incredibly loud, and I didn't really hear a backbeat, so that's sort of what was missing. So I made up for that with my left hand on my highest pitch that I have—it's on my bongo drum. I hit that thing and it was like a gunshot, man. And Joe really liked that because it brought some definition to the pulse. I grew up also playing R&B, and I had learned from all the greatest guys from New York City who would come through this club that I worked in Miami—everybody taught me something. So I knew how to play funk really well, and this is what was missing in the music."[23]

The other thing that put Thomas in good stead was his love of the pugilistic arts. "Joe found out that I was a boxer, so we would spar right before curtain; that's how we would warm up. And so when we went out on stage and Joe and I would end up playing duets together, we would keep sparring because I knew how he fought, how he boxed. That's how you know a man's rhythm, his timing. Joe boxed the same way he played piano: very definite, precise, with a lot of power, and very sneaky—some of his punches you really don't see them coming. So I always knew how to counter him."[24]

The U.S. tour took Weather Report from the East Coast to California and back through the Southwest. They traveled in a plush tour bus with sleeping births and two living quarters, playing gigs just about every night. "Joe carried a music room on the bus," Thomas remembered. "He had a chest that was full of cassette tapes, full of snippets of improvisations. I mean, just hundreds and hundreds of cassette tapes. He could just go in there anytime and pull out some improv and put a whole song together from that. It was his private room, his laboratory. It was very cool. I think that's why his music is so interesting.

"And I spent a lot of time in that room because they would keep me away from the adult activities, because I was a young green guy in the band. So they would put me in the back and Joe would make me play piano scales all day. And then Jaco would bring his bass and make me play bass scales all day, just to keep me from the front of the bus. I won't go into that, but they were looking out for me. Making me play that bass so many hours on that bus taught me to expand my vision and become a songwriter. I never wanted to play bass, but he made me do it. Joe made me play piano, made me go out and learn all these other instruments."[25]

Three months after their United States tour ended, the band made its fourth trip to Japan. "We hit Japan, and then I saw all the groupies scratching on the limo windows like we were rock stars," Thomas said. "That's when I realized, 'Hey, this is a big deal.'"[26] Ingrid Pastorius joined them, but Jaco's drug and alcohol use triggered several disturbing confrontations between them, a pattern that continued during the subsequent European tour when an early-morning argument with Ingrid ended with Jaco punching his hand through a hotel door. Only some fast-talking by the band's road manager prevented the entire entourage from getting kicked out of the hotel. Eventually, Jaco's behavior affected his music. "It was still perfect, but it wasn't fresh," Joe told Pat Jordan. "It was like a circus act. Jaco relied on tricks he had done before."[27]

Despite these misgivings, the band was in peak form. Shortly after returning from Japan, they recorded their next album, *Night Passage*, at the Complex in West Los Angeles. It was the newly constructed headquarters for Earth, Wind & Fire and ARC Records, the label that Maurice White established in 1978 after landing a $10 million contract with CBS. Cavallo-Ruffalo was intimately involved in those negotiations and ARC was stocked with many of its artists, including Weather Report. Eagle-eyed fans would have noticed the big blue ARC letters on the center label of Weather Report's LPs starting with *Mr. Gone*. In addition to offices and rehearsal rooms, the Complex housed a recording studio operated by George Massenburg, EW&F's primary engineer.

As Cavallo-Ruffalo was a partner in the Complex, it naturally pushed to have Weather Report's session done there. Joe and Wayne also liked that its sound-stage could accommodate an audience of up to 250 people. In Joe's words, they "wanted to get that feeling of playing it live," the way Cannonball Adderley used to record.[28] However, the Complex wasn't completed yet, and the soundstage was just a cinder-block shell with no acoustic treatment—an empty cavern with chairs. That the band played so loud only made things more difficult for recording purposes.

"We were really looking forward to it because this was a chance to invite as many of our friends as we wanted without worrying about a promoter," Peter Erskine said. "And so Jaco and I had called a lot of people; we were going to have our friends there. And then the management said, 'No, there's all these important people coming.' So we had to call all our buddies and tell them sorry, you can't come. I remember Jaco and I were both really upset before that first concert—and even more so when we got there and the hall was not even half full. And then one of the management people came and said, 'Well, don't worry. We're calling some of the cartage companies. We're just inviting people so we can get some bodies in here.' And like, you motherfuckers, we could have had the best audience in the world, all true fans of the band. So we were pretty annoyed that first night.

"And there were a lot of technical problems with that album. George Massenburg, who was kind of the resident genius at the time, had a number of exotic microphones. I remember one of the drum overheads was distorting. There were

The scene at the Complex before one of Weather Report's sessions. Photo: Brian Risner.

some tape speed issues, and he sort of managed to fix that. You hear a lot of sound anomalies on that album, and that was just the result of one goofy thing or another. But once everything was edited and put together, it's a good album, despite all its little flaws that we were very well aware of."[29]

Most of the pieces on *Night Passage* come from those two nights at the Complex. However, the title track is not one of them, probably because it appears to not have been a part of their concerts leading up to the Complex and therefore wasn't road tested. Joe said it was inspired by a train trip he took from Venice to Vienna, complete with clackety-clack rhythm; hence, the title. As one of his through-composed pieces, it was tricky to play. "It's one of those tunes, if you lose the spot you cannot get back in," he said. Joe improvised the bass and melody simultaneously, not unlike the way he came up with "8:30." He then transcribed the bass part and mailed it to Jaco so that he could learn it. "It's a hard part," Pastorius acknowledged. "It took me about a week to finger that chart."[30]

Its recording proved difficult as well. "We had trouble tracking that tune," Erskine said. "It just wasn't a good session, as I recall. And to be frank, there was a lot of cocaine at that session. You know, wow, great, nighttime session, we'll start late—and it seemed like it kept going downhill from the first note. But we managed to cobble together a tape. I was very embarrassed about the speeding up—some were successive takes, some were takes that just started going faster. Joe just felt like that's the train getting faster. But no, it was the amount of drugs kicking in, I think. I'm not proud to say that, but that's what was going on at that particular session. And I just remember that I was disappointed. We were coming back into the studio, which we hadn't done in a while, and my studio chops weren't where they would eventually learn to be. When you're so used to playing live, it's hard to go into a studio and wait, and then play with the same energy."[31]

After leading off with the title track, the LP continues with "Dream Clock," a contemplative ballad of Joe's that makes good use of Jaco's fretless tone and Wayne's ability to wring emotion from a melody line. Zawinul insisted on keeping the melody of this tune the same each time they played it, but even then, Wayne made it different in the way that he expressed it. For his part, Joe would change the chord progressions in order to keep things fresh.[32]

(As an aside, Scott Kinsey relates this anecdote: "If you ask Joe, 'How does that tune go again?' he'll say, 'Oh, it goes like this,' and he'll play it the way you know it. But then he'll go, 'Or, like this.' And he'll play it five other ways, each totally different, but each just as good as the original composed one. He'll just come up with new progressions that are totally fresh, that sound fucking cool—as good as the original. If you sat down with pen and paper and wanted to reharmonize a song in a new way, it would be tough. But he did it right off the top of his head."[33])

Next is "Port of Entry," Wayne's sole composition on the album. Like a lot of the *Night Passage* material, it was molded into shape on the road with little in the way of a fixed arrangement. "'Port of Entry' was very different in its early incarnations," Erskine said. "In the earlier versions, it reminded me a lot more of older Weather Report. It had more of an open kind of mysterious vibe in terms of the beat."[34] The LP version begins with a funky, swampy feel with Wayne shouting on tenor, before switching to a double-time jam initiated by Bobby Thomas's congas and Jaco's solo. At just over five minutes, it must have been edited from a longer performance because the live versions were long, blowing affairs that typically exceeded ten minutes.

"Forlorn" and "Rockin' in Rhythm" bridge the two sides of the LP, after which comes Joe's aptly named "Fast City"—another improvisation that he transcribed from cassette. It was a fun tune to play, and both Thomas and Erskine remember it as one of their favorites. "Fast City" is most notable for the ferocious soloing that Joe does on his synthesizers, seamlessly switching from one timbre to another. He often cut loose in live performances, but rarely on record, so in that regard, this track is a treat.

In subsequent tours the band opened shows with "Fast City." "That was a challenge," Erskine said. "The recording of Ray Charles singing 'America the Beautiful' would end, and then I would do a short little drum segue, and then we'd do it. And I remember before those concerts, I would do a hundred jumping jacks; I would run in place. I really had to get pumped up because that was a really fast start. And it was fun. It was a fun beat, and although it was super fast, it was my attempt at coming up with a *Mysterious Traveller*-esque beat."[35]

"Three Views of a Secret" follows. It's widely regarded as Jaco's finest composition—a carefully constructed piece of harmonic and melodic ingenuity that he later recorded in fully orchestrated form for *Word of Mouth*. Ingrid recalled how Jaco wrote it. "He had recently moved into my tiny apartment, and it was the newly acquired Prophet-5 that helped him evolve the tune. He initially named the piece after me, but I declined the honor—please don't ask me why, cuz I don't really know, just felt that way at the time. He then decided to name it what it is now, and told me he had 'stolen' the title from [Charlie] Brent." When Jaco brought "Three Views" to Weather Report, "Joe initially wasn't too keen on the tune," Ingrid said. "But Jaco stuck with it. I remember him being in a state of dilemma before submitting the tune to Joe and Wayne."[36]

The album closer is a live version of "Madagascar" that Brian Risner recorded in Osaka, Japan a few weeks before the Complex sessions. It's a highly improvisational tune based around a few simple motifs. The hard-to-identify meter in the introduction stems from some confusion on Erskine's part. "I always heard that note [the fourth note of Joe's synth line starting at 0:29] as the pickup to one, and it wasn't. So I never knew where beat one was until they started [sings the melody line that comes in around 1:52]. Which was good because I played that whole intro kind of floaty, and Joe liked that—it kind of worked. Otherwise, it might have been a little more rigid. But it's funny; even to this day, I still go to the incorrect hearing of the tune, and if I hear it or play it, I'm not sure where beat one is."[37]

•

With a long tour of Europe scheduled to begin on the first of October, Joe and company burned the midnight oil to finish the mixing and editing of *Night Passage* so it could go into production before they left. It was a time-consuming process, especially with the group's perfectionist tendencies, and it dragged out to the very last minute. Every mix would be printed onto tape in order to listen to the result. These could number in the dozens just for one tune, and oftentimes a finished track would consist of parts from one mix and parts of another.

As usual, Joe and Jaco handled the editing and mixing. Wayne was there with them, jotting down possible song titles in a notebook and reacting to the mixing results. Sometimes he would communicate his approval (or not) merely with a well-timed facial expression, and Joe knew to pay attention to them. But like most everything else, mixing became a competition between Joe and Jaco. Peter Erskine: "I remember at one point, they were mixing and they made a deal: We're not going to turn up our own instrument. Jaco and Joe made this solemn promise. This was before automation, so all the mixes were done by hand. But all of Joe's keyboards were grouped into one fader, so you could do a multiple keyboard gain adjustment. So Jaco's sitting by those master faders, and the tune's playing along, and Joe's into it, and he's moving his faders up. Jaco nudges me, and I glance down at his hand and he's counter-riding everything Joe's doing. Joe was going up, and Jaco was bringing the keyboard master down. And of course, they didn't use that take."[38]

By the time the band jetted off to Europe, Joe was exhausted from all the late nights spent getting *Night Passage* in the can. But his self-image didn't permit showing weakness; admitting fatigue was out of the question. As Peter Erskine writes in his book, *No Beethoven: An Autobiography & Chronicle of Weather Report*:

> [Joe] began this tour occasionally giddy, but more mean and short-tem-pered, to the point where all of us were walking on eggshells around the man. There was no pleasing him or curbing his nastiness. It speaks volumes about Jaco's character as well as his relationship to Joe that Jaco had enough balls and sense of what's right to assemble the band and crew following an early concert during this tour, somewhere in Norway as I recall. And there took place a remarkable scene: The entire Weather Re-port band and crew were standing in a large circle, with Joe and Jaco in the center, Jaco addressing Joe, pointing out his behavior and demanding that Joe stop it once and for all: "You're RUDE, Joe. You've been acting like a rude motherfucker for a while now, and it's got to stop." We all stood wide-eyed and in silence. Finally, Joe said, "You're right." More si-lence. And then he continued, "And I would like to apologize to everyone here, right now." It was time to put that in the past, and we continued to tour and play some of the best concerts I remember the band giving.[39]

The tour wound down in the United Kingdom, and the group was in stellar form when it played London's Hammersmith Odeon on back-to-back nights. Like New York's Beacon Theatre or Festival Hall in Osaka, Japan, the Hammy-O was one of those special venues that always inspired the band. It had great acous-tics, and the band had much respect and affection for the audiences, who recip-rocated those feelings. It just felt good to play there. Joe called it a "holy place."[40] "We always had a great show there," Brian Risner confirmed. "There was some-thing about the hall and the people—it was always great. It was the end of the tour and everybody was rocking. They were just *on*."[41]

Certainly the reviews confirmed the greatness of these shows. "Their second night at Hammersmith was simply awesome—no sycophantic bleat from some-one who usually prefers the freer end of jazz," wrote John Gill in *Sounds*, a pop/rock weekly. "They played a grueling set of nigh on three hours, themes from *Mr. Gone* and early works looming and receding in an improvised set, and not once

Weather Report performs in Tokyo during its 1980 tour of Japan. Photo: Shigeru Uchiyama / Whisper Not Photo Factory.

did they take an easy route or lazy option."[42] Andy Gill in *New Musical Express* was likewise effusive, calling Weather Report's performance "a blistering display of sheer technical ability, allied at times to a quite astonishing emotional subtlety."[43]

Meanwhile, *Night Passage* hit the streets and received uniformly excellent reviews. *Melody Maker* described it as "a record that's dense in ingenuity, a work of subtlety that slowly reveals itself to the listener like an onion being peeled layer by layer, showing different nuances and meanings at each successive stage."[44] In *High Fidelity*, Don Heckman called *Night Passage* "one of the finest albums Weather Report has ever made."[45]

Night Passage also convincingly demonstrates that Pastorius remained in peak form. There are the walking bass lines of "Rockin' in Rhythm" and "Fast City," the gorgeous tone on "Dream Clock," the luxuriant long notes of "Forlorn," and perhaps the *pièce de résistance*: his astonishing, lightning-quick solo on "Port of Entry" and the frenetic bass line that follows. In addition to his playing, "Three Views of a Secret" showed his gifts as a composer. That it was his only tune on the record was a function of him saving material for his own use.

Indeed, *Night Passage* finds the entire band rejuvenated. Peter Erskine was more rooted in the jazz aesthetic than any of his predecessors since Eric Gravatt, and Thomas adds just the right touches without becoming too "miscellaneous"—the derisive term Joe used to describe percussionists who he felt weren't being musically smart. Wayne seems particularly inspired, his blowing on tenor suffused with fervor and passion.

As the band concluded performing for 1980, Joe looked forward to Weather Report's future. "Good musicians are a luxury, but it is something you have to find," he told a reporter in London. "There are very few of us to run around, I guarantee you. If someone couldn't handle it, he could never be in this band. It's happened before. You have to find guys who can play. You see, the secret of having a great band and being able to write great is to be able to write for the people you play with, because everyone has a different sound. That's why Duke Ellington was so great. Jaco's bass is his own sound, his own personality. Now we've got a band, and it's going to be for a while, I guarantee it."[46]

Zawinul had no way of knowing it at the time, but by the end of the next year, he and Wayne would be starting over.

17 Weather Report (1982)

It was one of the greatest bands of all time!

— Joe Zawinul

IN THE SPRING OF 1980, Jaco Pastorius signed a contract with Warner Bros. Records. Given his scant discography, it was a remarkable deal that gave him total artistic freedom as a producer and a whopping $125,000 advance against royalties. Warner Bros.' willingness to back Pastorius in such a big way was tangible confirmation of his star power at that point—something that was not lost on Cavallo-Ruffalo. Brian Risner remembered Jaco revealing that the agency had offered to take him on as a solo act. "We'll drop Weather Report in a second if you let us manage you," Pastorius claimed they told him.[1]

Jaco began working on his Warner Bros. debut toward the end of the year. It was an ambitious, sprawling project with sophisticated arrangements that involved dozens of musicians. He called it *Word of Mouth*, a reference to a New York City nightclub gig that couldn't be advertised because of his and Peter Erskine's commitment to Weather Report. Nevertheless, word got out that Jaco would be performing, and the club was filled to capacity.

Pastorius worked closely with Peter Yianilos, a twenty-five-year-old musician and recording engineer who owned a mobile 24-track recording facility that was housed in a converted twenty-seven-foot RV. Yianilos would pull his truck up to Jaco and Ingrid's house in Deerfield Beach, Florida, allowing the bassist to experiment and record in his own living room. When the living room wouldn't do, they headed over to Yianilos's warehouse. More sessions were done in New York, where Jaco brought in some of the elite players of jazz, including Jack DeJohnette, Herbie Hancock, Don Alias, and Michael Brecker. From Weather Report, he enlisted all but Zawinul.

Jaco behaved as if he had a blank check from Warner Bros. No expense was too great, nor was any detail too small to address in pursuit of his vision. At one point, he booked thirty-one members of the Los Angeles Philharmonic at a cost of $9,000 to record the string parts for two tunes, but wound up erasing the tapes because he felt they hadn't played with enough soul and conviction. Jaco loved Toots Thielemans and used him on several tracks. When he decided that Thielemans *had* to play the melody on "Blackbird," Pastorius dropped everything and flew to Belgium, where Toots lived, in order to record him. The short-notice trip wound up costing another $5,000. All the while, Jaco obsessed over the performances and mixes, racking up valuable studio time.

As the overall costs pushed past $200,000, Warner Bros. grew concerned.[2] To make matters worse, Jaco insisted that the record begin with a tune called "Crisis." It was an unusual piece in which he had several musicians independently improvise over his bass line without hearing each other. Sometimes he would give them a peek at what someone else had played, but mostly they just reacted to Jaco. The finished track was brilliant in its own way, but it also lived up to its title with a manic, chaotic feel. In signing Jaco, Warner Bros. expected something along the lines of *Heavy Weather*, not free jazz. They pleaded with him to lead off the LP with a more accessible track, but the more insistent they became, the more Jaco dug in his heels. Any remaining enthusiasm that Warner Bros. had for the album seemed to evaporate at that point.

Then, as *Word of Mouth* neared completion, CBS filed a $1 million lawsuit against Jaco and Warner Bros., asserting that it had an exclusive contract with Pastorius dating back to his 1976 Epic release. Jaco had to engage his own lawyer, who managed to reach a settlement with CBS for the relatively small sum of $25,000. By this time, Warner Bros. was fed up, and when *Word of Mouth* was finally released in July 1981, it was accompanied by little promotion. Despite receiving good reviews, the album failed to gain traction, selling perhaps 30,000 copies according to one Warner Bros. executive.[3]

Nevertheless, *Word of Mouth* is the most complex and personal work that Jaco ever produced. In fact, he never made another studio album of his own. The record contains some of his most endearing and enduring compositions, many of which are treated to lush horn and string arrangements. Jaco's use of Toots Thielemans as a leading voice is brilliant, but it is just one of many unusual colors that he brought to bear on his music, including steel pans, French horn, and tuba. Like Joe, Jaco was a prolific collector of musical instruments, and he used many of them on this project. And, of course, at the center of it all is his bass. The album is beautiful in its range of expression and difficult to classify. Jaco liked to say that he made "modern American music." *Word of Mouth* is what he meant.

Peter Erskine spent a lot of time with Pastorius during its making, recording at Jaco's house in Florida and allowing Pastorius to bunk at his own home for several

Zawinul at a sound check in 1981. His left hand is playing the Prophet-5, which sits atop a Rhodes EK-10 electric piano. In front of Joe, to his left, is the Korg VC-10 vocoder, and behind that a Korg Trident, which was Korg's flagship synthesizer at the time. Joe eventually developed a close relationship with Korg, especially after the demise of the American synthesizer manufacturers. To Joe's right is the Oberheim 8-Voice. Photo: Shigeru Uchiyama / Whisper Not Photo Factory.

weeks while the bassist worked in L.A. "His proudest moment—the happiest I recall seeing him during the entire process of making that album—was when he was doing some work at A&M Studio and Burt Bacharach was visiting," Erskine recalled. "Jaco played 'Three Views of a Secret' for him, and Jaco looked over at me, just beaming. *Check it out: Burt's digging it!* Jaco wanted his tunes to have the timeless melodic quality of the songs that Burt Bacharach wrote, or that Frank Sinatra sang."[4]

As Jaco labored over *Word of Mouth* in the early months of 1981, Joe was busy on multiple fronts himself. In a spring interview for *Billboard*, he revealed that he was working on three projects simultaneously. The first was his long-delayed solo album for CBS. He also planned to make an LP for the CBS Masterworks classical line that would, according to the article, "reflect his roots in European classicism" and offer a more symphonic approach in his use of electronics. And of course there was Weather Report. With another tour of Japan scheduled for the end of May, Joe was prepping new music for the band. "I don't know what I'm working on," he joked. "I've got about thirty tunes I'm working on at the moment, representing material for all those projects."[5]

Zawinul's music room now had a 24-track mixing console, which would soon be paired with a 24-track recorder, in addition to his existing 8-track deck. "Now

316 / ELEGANT PEOPLE

that I have my own studio, the whole business of going to the studio isn't necessary," he boasted. As Joe became more self-sufficient in his production capabilities, his home improvisations became, in *Billboard*'s words, "fully voiced blueprints for what later emerged as Weather Report recordings."[6] With multiple keyboards and sequencers, as well as the recent advent of drum machines, he included counter-melodies, bass lines, and drum parts, all of which he asked the other musicians to learn. If critics complained that his tunes sounded too structured, leaving few opportunities for improvising, Joe countered that the compositions themselves were improvisations; hence, everything was an improvisation.

More and more, Joe regarded his improvisations as sacrosanct. Whereas Wayne would labor over two measures of music for hours, Joe transcribed his playing unchanged. If a melody line seemed awkward, it should be venerated rather than corrected because it was a pure manifestation of whatever spiritual energy he was channeling. As a consequence, his compositions more and more bore the stamp of his idiosyncratic phrasing, which manifested itself on the new batch of tunes that he had for the band.

As the departure for Japan approached, Peter Erskine drove out to Pasadena day after day, learning Joe's music and helping to give it shape. Wayne often participated as well. But completing *Word of Mouth* kept Jaco from joining them until just before the tour commenced, by which time he was well behind the curve. With his mind still on *Word of Mouth* and now confronted with Joe's written bass parts and complex through-composed tunes, Pastorius rebelled. "Jaco was like, I don't want to do this," Erskine recalled. "Jaco wasn't a great reader, and he hated having to read this stuff. And I don't know if Joe originally wanted his keyboards to match the bass, but he didn't feel he could rely on Jaco to play a lot of these things, so Joe doubled a lot of the bass parts, and Jaco really chafed at that."[7]

At the same time, Jaco was negotiating with management for more money. "He'd go up to Joe's bedroom to use that phone, which was really maddening to Joe," Erskine said. "Jaco was not only missing rehearsal, but also going into *his* bedroom and threatening to not go on the tour, because he was holding out for more money. On top of which, he couldn't play the new music, and we were having to go over it by rote. So Joe was angry about the money thing, but he was also angry about the lack of preparation on Jaco's part."[8]

Against this backdrop, the band flew to Japan. During the making of *Word of Mouth*, Jaco would call Joe from Florida and play him tapes over the phone, seeking the elder's approval. Peter Yianilos remembered that Joe was invariably "cruelly dismissive" in his responses, to the point that Yianilos didn't think they should call anymore. But Jaco never gave up, and now that the album was complete, he was anxious to play it for Joe. The twelve-hour flight to Tokyo seemed the perfect time. He waited until after lunch before handing his Sony Walkman over to Zawinul, loaded with a cassette of *Word of Mouth*. Peter Erskine sat nearby as Joe listened to "Liberty City" through headphones.

"Jaco kept looking over at me, winking, like, thumbs up, Joe's gotta be digging the shit out of this. And then Joe took off the headphones, turned, and just said, 'This sounds like some typical high school big band bullshit.' Joe said it just to be cruel because he was getting back at Jaco for not learning the music at rehearsal. And I think he felt that maybe Jaco had extorted the band at the last minute."[9]

Until the end of his days, Joe insisted that he merely gave Jaco his honest opinion—something he was duty-bound to do as Jaco's friend and "older brother." "I didn't like them that much," Zawinul later said of the *Word of Mouth* tracks. "His compositions were good; his arranging was stock—for me. It was not very creative. I thought there was a lot more he could have done with that, and I told him in the airplane. He was very upset."[10]

Stung by the coldness of Joe's words, Jaco retreated to the back of the cabin with the road crew. Sitting on an armrest, partially blocking the aisle, he proceeded to get drunk. The next thing Erskine knew, a teenaged Japanese girl who was seated in front of the band came back from using the restroom, obviously upset about something. "Immediately, I saw this big commotion, and the mother summoned the male steward—it might have been the flight purser—and she said that Jaco had inappropriately touched her daughter as she passed by. All I remember is, it was a scene, and Jaco was accused in front of Joe and all of us of having done this. And Jaco was muttering, 'This is bullshit. I never touched her. I have a fucking daughter of my own,' and he kicked the back of the mother's chair. Well, that was it. The mother and daughter were moved to first class and the police were going to meet the plane when we landed. Somehow Joe defused the situation, but Jaco lost incredible face."[11]

Once the band got to Tokyo, everyone tried to put the incident behind them. "We rehearsed, and everything seemed fine," Erskine said. "But at the first concert, Jaco didn't play any of the new music. He did the same thing he had done in Cuba. He started playing 'Portrait of Tracy.' The bass was real loud and feeding back. He was playing whatever he wanted. He got pretty wasted. I don't know on what—if it was just drinking or it was just his mental state. And it was weird, because we had a set list, and Joe was determined to play this music."[12]

Somehow the band made it through the show, but as everyone took their post-concert bows, Erskine looked over at Joe, thinking, *Holy fuck, what's going to happen now?* Backstage, Brian Condliffe's main concern was keeping Jaco and Joe separated, afraid they would come to blows. "I'm just trying to make sure that these two guys don't encounter each other for the rest of the night," he told Erskine. Perhaps sensing that an altercation was imminent, Jaco quickly disappeared with Ingrid, leaving Joe distraught over what had happened.[13]

Final bows in Japan, June 1981. Photo: Shigeru Uchiyama / Whisper Not Photo Factory.

Later that night, Joe called Erskine and asked him to come to his hotel room. "That's the angriest I ever saw Zawinul," Peter remembered. "Sometimes I had seen him when he was so angry that you almost couldn't tell he was angry, but this went beyond that. He almost broke the phone at one point [slamming the handset onto the receiver]. And he was being sort of calm while we were talking. 'We have to do this tour,' he explained to me. 'We can't afford to cancel the tour. But we can't do it with Jaco, not if he's in this state.' Joe made the compelling case that *we had to do something*. The boy's not well. He needs to get some help, so we need a bass player."

"You made this record with [Japanese guitarist] Kazumi Watanabe. You think he knows somebody?" Joe asked.

"Well, I don't know," Erskine replied. "That was all New York guys. But the guy that played bass on that was Tony Levin."

"Can the motherfucker play?"

"Yeah, Tony's great."

"Let's call him."

So Erskine left a message with Levin, who probably thought it was one of the stranger ones he had received. Meanwhile, the band had a day off and Joe planned to see if anyone in Japan could fill in.

Early the next morning, Peter's telephone rang. It was Joe. "Call your friend Tony and tell him everything's okay. He doesn't need to come out now."

Surprised by the quick turn of events, Erskine asked what happened.

"Jaco knocked on my door at seven o'clock this morning. He was dressed in a three-piece suit. He offered a formal apology and I accepted it. So that's done."[14]

Joe later described the next concert in Osaka as one of the band's best ever.[15] The Japanese press agreed not to write about the first show and review the second one instead. "The rest of the tour was great," Erskine said. "And then at one point, Joe and Jaco were giving *me* shit. I was thinking, *What the fuck? That motherfucker almost sabotaged the whole tour. Just 'cause you don't like the way I'm playing?* I felt almost betrayed—like, I get a pass." [*laughs*][16]

A few days after the band got back from Japan, they headlined the Sunday program at the Playboy Jazz Festival. "It was a late-afternoon set, and we tore the place apart. The band just came out and killed," Erskine said.[17] Leonard Feather was among the sold-out crowd. Aside from complaining that the band tied up one side of the Hollywood Bowl's revolving stage for several hours, he wrote that Weather Report was "the unquestioned crowd killers of the festival. The quintet never lost its grip on an audience clearly ready to explode. It happened when the group concluded with 'Birdland.' Seldom if ever has this reviewer seen or heard such a manic reaction to any performance. Only with great reluctance, and some booing, did the crowd allow the men to leave the stage."[18]

Shortly thereafter, the band embarked on a two-week tour of the East Coast, leading to a recording date in New York City. The trip coincided with Joe's forty-ninth birthday, so on July 7 the band and crew got together for a formal dinner at the Waldorf-Astoria Hotel. "As we were assembling in the lobby, Jaco ran into a couple of people," Erskine remembered. "I don't know who they were or what the story was—it might have been a drug connection for him—but they were hangers-on, and Jaco invited them to join us for dinner. And of course, like good hangers-on, they were the first people to sit down, and there wasn't enough room for everyone. I think Joe didn't have a seat. And so the manager said, 'Wait a minute, there's supposed to be *x* number of people here. Who are you?' 'Well, we're friends of Jaco's.' He said, 'I'm sorry, you'll have to leave.' And Jaco lost face, so he left."[19]

As the dinner went on, Joe grew concerned that Jaco hadn't returned and excused himself to go look for him. "He didn't have to walk too far to find him," Erskine said. "Jaco was just up the block, literally laying in the gutter in his white suit, all filthy, curled up in a fetal position. So he wasn't well, obviously. Cuba, this New York dinner, and the concert in Tokyo all seemed to happen after Jaco had lost face, whatever those dynamics are.

"And then the next day, I met with Don Grolnick at the hotel. We were riding up the elevator, and it stops, and Jaco gets in. And he just says, 'Have you been to Joe's room yet?' I said no, and he took his fist and punched himself in the chest real hard—thump. To emphasize something they'd always punch themselves in the chest; it was kind of funny. And he said [emphatically], 'Check it out!' and

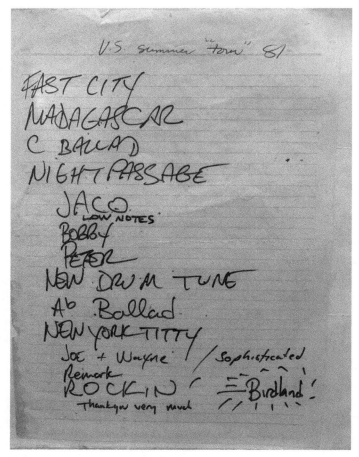

Peter Erskine's handwritten set list for Weather Report's 1981 summer U.S. tour. Brian Risner collection.

stared for a second, then he got off. And Don looked at me and kind of called out to Jaco as the door was closing. 'Nice talking to you!'

"So I went to Joe's room and he pointed to this accordion on the table and said, 'Jaco bought me a birthday gift.' Jaco had purposely left the price tag on the accordion and it was very expensive. Joe was embarrassed by how expensive it was. Jaco had just come in and said, 'Happy birthday, motherfucker,' and kind of threw it on the bed. And Joe said, 'You know, that was really generous of him, but I would have been much happier if he had just signed a birthday card and shook my hand or something.' Joe realized that the monster was out of control. He was blue."[20]

•

There were still a few shows to do and an album to record. The last concert of the Pastorius-Erskine edition of Weather Report took place on July 11 at the

Boston Opera House. Any tensions simmering within the band weren't evident in their performance. Taking the stage while the PA system blasted Wagner, Weather Report "shows signs of renewed vigor and invention," wrote the *Boston Globe*'s Ray Murphy. He singled out Robert Thomas Jr. as the key difference between this performance and the previous year's, supplying "another ensemble voice, separate but equal."[21]

The next week the band settled in at Power Station Studios in New York. Housed in a former Consolidated Edison power relay station (hence the name), it was a relatively new state-of-the-art facility located just a few blocks from the old Birdland jazz club. Jaco had recorded portions of *Word of Mouth* at Power Station, and Erskine had done some sessions there, too. After years of handling live sound and assisting in the studio, Brian Risner was given the task of committing the music to tape as the lead recording engineer, though his role was more akin to that of producer. He arranged all the logistics (in fact, he chose Power Station after Pastorius and Erskine raved about it) and he hired the support personnel. For these sessions, he tabbed Neil Dorfsman, who was a staff engineer at the studio.

The main task at Power Station was to record Joe's new tunes, which the band had been performing that summer. There were four of them, including the three-part "N.Y.C." suite. The piece that serves as the LP opener is "Volcano for Hire," an up-tempo number that never failed to rouse audiences. It's a good example of the improvisations that Joe was bringing to the band at this time. He doubles not only the bass lines on synthesizers, but also the melody lines with Wayne. He also composed a drum and percussion introduction and transcribed it for Erskine and Thomas to learn, but the main beat was something that Peter came up with at one of those Pasadena jam/mentor sessions after Zawinul requested a beat without cymbals.[22]

Joe also composed two ballads for the album: "Current Affairs" and "Speechless." As Erskine remembers, the former was one of those tunes that Joe tended to play the same way every time, like he was reproducing a big band arrangement using brass sounds from his synthesizers. "Speechless" features Jaco's bass tone while Joe sings the melody on vocoder. Erskine called it "absolutely gorgeous. It's one of the more under-recognized pieces. And because there's something reminiscent of 'A Remark You Made,' 'Speechless' seemed an obvious name choice. And 'Current Affairs,' that was just one of the names that was bopping around in the mix room."[23]

The "N.Y.C." suite is Joe's impression of the city that he loved and the jazz scene that he knew there. The abstract, almost random sounds in the introduction were crafted with Risner. "He played around on the keyboard, and I was bending knobs and trying things and reversing stuff," Risner said. "The sirens and horns [in the introduction] came off the Prophet, which I processed through digital

The marquee at the Boston Opera House (formerly the Savoy Theater) marks the date of Weather Report's 1981 performance there as July 11. Photo: Brian Risner.

delays and reverbs and time shifters. It was really a one-on-one collaboration between him and me late in the evening that we just pulled out. Then in the bridge into the second part, there's this suspension of notes—it's almost like a fog or something that was going on. And we actually tried some Foley work. He said, 'You know, I want to carry a microphone of me walking around,' like someone walking into the apartment next door or something. It didn't work out, but that's where it was going. It was like, how do we tie these pieces together?"[24]

The sessions at Power Station went so smoothly that Risner had a couple of takes of each tune in the can with time left on the clock. "We finished early, so I said, 'Well shit, we've still got like two hours with no songs to record,' so they jammed. I'm rolling tape, and Joe started a sequencer. And in a way that's a click track that has melodic movement to it. I think that was on the Oberheim. And I think I recorded for twenty minutes. I know we went through one reel of tape and maybe another one. And we edited it after the fact, and that became 'Dara Factor One' and 'Dara Factor Two.'"[25]

Bobby Thomas also takes some credit for getting these jams going. "They were taking a break, and I always hung out with Joe. I really didn't eat lunch or go hang out and that kind of stuff—I just stayed with him. And I noticed that he was dumping these programs and I said, 'Hey, man, don't get rid of that. Listen to that. Listen to that.' And so he started listening, and I went and grabbed a tambourine, and showed him where the hump was, where the one was for me as a church guy. And he loved it. He loved it so much that we started playing, the two of us. From that spawned 'Dara Factor One' and 'Dara Factor Two,' because when the guys came back from their break, Joe and I had already been recording; tape was rolling. I was playing tambourine and he was getting locked into my groove, and music started pouring out of him. The guys walked into the room, Joe pointed to the booth, and they started playing. No talking, no rehearsing, no nothing. They just locked into my groove and his vibe."[26]

Adds Peter Erskine: "'Dara Factor' was sort of, let's go back to the way the band used to play and improvise. They found the largest reel of two-inch tape that they had, and the instruction was to just put it on the machine and record. Right before that moment, we were playing around with some beats, and at one point I said, 'Hey, Joe, instead of trying to come up with something so upside-down, a backwards groove, how 'bout if we do something that's a little more in the pocket. I think it would be more fun.' He said, 'Let me hear what you have in mind.' So I played this very simple beat, which I thought was kind of hip. He waved me to stop, and he goes, 'Where's the fun in that? I don't hear anything fun in that. Play me something else.' And that's how we came up with that intro to 'Dara Factor.' It's a little bit of a composition right there. And that was the first time that Joe agreed to treat a group improvisation as a group effort [sharing the composer credit with all of the band members on 'Dara Factor Two'], because he wouldn't do it before."[27]

After the Power Station sessions, the group sans Jaco recorded Wayne's sole contribution to the album, "When It Was Now," at Joe's house. (Its working title was "Pipeline," and some reviews described it as such.) The tune's quirky rhythm owes in part to it being the first time the band recorded with a drum machine, in this case a Linn LM-1 Drum Computer. Like the Prophet-5, the Linn was made possible by microprocessor technology. It combined the attributes of sequencers with its own sound-making capability to produce programmable, repeating drum patterns. As the first drum machine to use digital samples of acoustic drums, it was a major breakthrough—"*real* drums digitally recorded and stored in memory," the Linn ad copy went—and its introduction in 1980 sent a shiver down the spine of more than a few session drummers who foresaw the possibility of being replaced by little boxes with buttons. That future didn't exactly come to pass, but drum machines were used extensively in popular music in the 1980s and 1990s.

Although many coveted the Linn, its sky-high price tag of $5,500 kept it out of reach of all but the most affluent musicians (only about five hundred were made before a cheaper model came out).[28] So Weather Report borrowed one for "When It Was Now," which Erskine programmed based on a beat that Wayne had. "I was programming while they were practicing their parts, so when I was finished, they were ready to do a take," Erskine recalled. "The tape started rolling, I pushed a button, the guys played along with the machine, and I played claves

Joe playing the "chicken neck" in Japan. Photo: Shigeru Uchiyama / Whisper Not Photo Factory.

or something, just jamming along with it. And that first take was what we used on the album. . . . It was a different groove, and for that particular tune it worked well. The band was used to working with sequencers, and in essence that's what a drum computer is."[29]

Another new wrinkle in the band's arsenal shows up at about 3:35 into "When It Was Now," when the sounds of plucked strings are heard. It is Joe playing a homely four-stringed instrument with buttons along the neck instead of frets. He found it in a little shop in Cologne the previous fall and began playing it on tour. He would sit at the front of the stage "[summoning] up visions of Old Japan, primordial Africa and wild, folkloric Eastern Europe," according to one account. He also brought it out during his duets with Wayne.[30] One of the crew members dubbed it the "chicken neck" because it had a chicken head carved into the headstock. Its presence on "When It Was Now" is the result of a lucky accident. Joe was playing it in the studio while listening to a playback of the tune and didn't realize that he was being recorded.[31]

•

The new album was given the most pedestrian of titles: *Weather Report*. It seemed a strange and uncreative choice, especially since there was already an album by that name. But Joe and Wayne didn't do things haphazardly, and there was logic behind this, too—specifically that this record concluded their contract with Columbia. Of course, Weather Report was still a very bankable commodity, and CBS would have been happy to ink the band to another deal, but as much as Joe and Wayne had talked about pursuing individual projects in recent years, now seemed the time to do it. Besides, Joe had grown tired of feeling as if he was pulling the band along on his own.

By his own admission, Wayne remained withdrawn from music. And while Joe was respectful of Wayne and sympathetic of his family situation, his annoyance at keeping the band afloat sometimes bubbled over into resentment, and he privately complained about it. At one point, Brian Risner even overheard him talk of replacing Wayne with Michael Brecker, an up-and-coming tenor sax player with a fusion background. So the end of their contract allowed for a clean break, and the title represented the closing of a circle, from *Weather Report* to *Weather Report*—"a wonderful beginning and a wonderful ending to a fantastic career," Joe called it.[32] Their intention was to deliver the album to Columbia and tour in the fall to support it. After that, everyone would be free to go their own way, perhaps to regroup in 1983.

But finishing the album proved to be more difficult than Joe and Wayne anticipated. In September, ads began appearing in local newspapers touting the band's upcoming appearances, and tickets went on sale.[33] With the pressure mounting to get the record done, Joe and Wayne exhausted themselves. "We couldn't finish the album," Zawinul said. "It was very difficult for us. One time, Wayne and I were in the studio for forty-six hours trying to finish it so that we could tour when the album finally came out. Our manager at that time, Joe Ruffalo, said 'I'm going to cancel the tour and we'll make this album right.' And that's what we did—we made a nice album and we canceled the tour."[34]

When it was eventually released, *Weather Report* was met with a lukewarm response. Wayne and Joe had always thrived on the injection of new musicians and ideas; it was part of what made each record different and interesting. But this album was the first to use exactly the same personnel as its predecessor. It was also the first to show signs of stagnation, which is apparent in the reviews. Not that the reviews were bad. In fact, they generally praised *Weather Report* as a singularly good work in the fusion genre. It's just that, unlike the earlier albums, this one broke no new ground. John Stook captured this sense in *Musician* magazine. "The album has a similar feel to *Night Passage*, but few of its surprises and little of its fire," he wrote.[35]

The title also invited comparison to its earlier namesake, which only emphasized the distance that Joe and Wayne had traveled in their decade together. Whereas the first album had no synthesizers at all, now they dominated the music. Conversely, other than the "Dara Factors," the new album showed little of the "miracle of collective improvisation," to quote the earlier album's liner notes. More than ever, Weather Report was Joe's vehicle, collective improvisation having given way to the miracle of Joe's through-composed tunes rendered by the rest of

Last photo of the Pastorius-Erskine band, at Power Station Studios. Photo: Peter Erskine.

the musicians.

Meanwhile, Jaco wanted to lead his own band. Joe and Wayne always supported musicians doing their own thing, but in this case there was also a sense among
all involved that their association had run its course. The bonhomie of Jaco's early
days in Weather Report had given way to discord. Joe and Jaco shared a bond that
was unique in both men's careers, their relationship animated by their egos and
rife with competitive tension. But Joe had already accomplished what Pastorius
sought for himself: standing as a highly respected musician, a degree of financial
independence, and a stable family life. So Jaco saw Zawinul as someone to emulate, and also someone to eclipse.

Jaco accepted that Weather Report was Joe's band, but he chafed at its con-
fines. "Joe has so much music—he's always trying to do his own record," Pastorius
later said. "Every year he would put it off to do another Weather Report album.
He's a consummate writer, so I can understand him wanting to do more of his
own stuff, but I really didn't have much of a chance. I would bring music in and
play one or two notes, and he'd say, 'No, I don't like it,' without even listening to
the whole thing through."[36]

So Jaco made plans to tour with a large ensemble playing his big band charts.
The live debut of this music took place in December, when Jaco held a thirtieth
birthday bash in Fort Lauderdale (immortalized on the album *The Birthday Concert*). The band was stocked with Jaco's friends and colleagues, including members

of the Peter Graves orchestra; Peter Erskine and Bobby Thomas from Weather Report; and Bob Mintzer, Michael Brecker, and Don Alias from New York.

Without question, Jaco cast a large shadow over Weather Report. His musicianship, stage presence, and charisma helped propel the band to its greatest popularity, making him the only band member to approach the significance of Joe and Wayne in the post–Miroslav Vitous years. Many fans, and a good share of critics, thought the Pastorius-Erskine lineup was Weather Report at its best. Joe thought it was special, too. "It was one of the greatest bands of all time!" he told a reporter in 1983.[37] But after six years together, everyone was ready to move on.

PART IV

Weather Report, 1982–1986

18 Procession

We would've really been in trouble if they couldn't play.

— Joe Zawinul

BY THE TIME *WEATHER REPORT* WAS RELEASED IN FEBRUARY 1982, it wasn't clear that the band was still an ongoing concern. They hadn't performed live since the previous July, and they no longer had a recording contract. Meanwhile, Joe and Wayne intended to pursue their own projects while Jaco took a big band on the road early in the year. Rumors circulated that Weather Report had broken up, a circumstance the U.K. magazine, *The Wire*, claimed was corroborated by "a confused CBS press office."[1]

But in the aftermath of their canceled 1981 tours, Joe and Wayne were hit with lawsuits from stood-up concert promoters. The bandleaders knew they were in a bad spot. "There was nothing for us to defend," Joe later said. "We should have played, we had agreed to play, but we did not play." For help they turned to Columbia, which still held an option for an additional Weather Report album. "We told them that we needed so much budget to do the record and pay our debts," and the discussions led to a contract extension for three more albums plus an option for another. Their settlement with the concert promoters was in excess of $100,000. Even at that, they got away cheaply, Joe said.[2]

In essence, it was a new beginning for Weather Report, eventually precipitating a change of management. By this time, Cavallo-Ruffalo was focusing considerable resources on Prince, whom it had signed in 1979, and Earth, Wind & Fire, which remained one of the highest-grossing acts in music. Joe and Wayne felt as though the management group no longer had time for them, so they parted ways with the firm, replacing it with the team of Maria Corvalan, an employee at Cavallo-Ruffalo; and Brian Condliffe, who had served as Weather Report's road manager since 1979.

With a new tour scheduled to commence in June, of greater import was what to do for a band. Jaco was long gone by this point, but management checked in with Peter Erskine. He was in Japan with Steps (later Steps Ahead, with Mike Mainieri and Michael Brecker) when he received a phone call informing him that Joe and Wayne were going to do a summer tour after all.

"The question for me was, did I want to stay in the band," Erskine recalled. "It was hard to imagine being in the group without Jaco there. I wasn't sure where that was going to go. And by this point I had moved to New York, and I was casting my lot in with Steps. I had just agreed to do a summer tour with Steps based on the fact that Weather Report wouldn't be touring until sometime later, and I was going to see what happened, I guess. So I said, 'I'm going to honor the tour commitment I just made to these guys.' And they said, 'Well, okay, if that's your decision, we'll let Joe know.'

"And it felt great. I felt free. I went for a walk and I ran into Michael Brecker in the hallway. I told him and he just looked at me and said, 'What are you, nuts?' And he walked away shaking his head."[3] Brecker's reaction may have given Erskine pause, but he had no regrets. "I just thought it was time. I was in the group almost four years, and I wanted to come to New York and be a jazz musician and start exploring musical things a little bit more on my own."[4]

Bobby Thomas didn't even get the courtesy of a phone call. During Weather Report's idle time, he worked steadily with Herbie Mann and pianist Monty Alexander, among others. One day, word got back to him that Weather Report had a new percussionist. "I was very angry and upset," Thomas said. "It wasn't right. I told Zawinul how I felt, and he was very apologetic and everything and explained to me what had happened. Business-wise, he had no choice. They had to make a move because they were under contract, and they had to get some other guys."[5]

In need of replacements, Joe turned to his New York grapevine for recommendations. One name that came up repeatedly was Omar Hakim, a sought-after drummer on the New York fusion scene, where he was known for his superb technical chops and funky grooves. Though just twenty-two, Hakim had been playing professionally for over a decade. His earliest gigs were with his father, Hasan, a trombonist who played with Count Basie and Duke Ellington. "He had me swinging, playing the modern stuff of the day," Omar said.[6] "But my dad *never* laid any of those jazzman trips on my head, like 'Don't you go listenin' to none of that rock 'n' roll.' My dad was always real open—if it was quality, he dug it. He loved to hear Marvin Gaye as much as I did. So I think I got my attitude from him."[7]

Later, Omar went to New York's High School of Music & Art, where music was such a big part of his life that he likened it to breathing. He did his first professional tour at the age of fifteen and the next year hit the road with La-

Omar Hakim. Photo: © www.markbrady.com.

belle. By the time Joe heard about him, Hakim had worked with David Sanborn, Mike Mainieri, and Gil Evans, to name a few, and was pursuing a solo record in which he played all of the instruments and sang. One night he came home from a mixing session for that project when his mother told him that he had received a phone call. Hakim picks up the story:

> I had just gotten a budget from Warner Bros. It was what they call a development budget. Whenever they were interested in an artist, they'd throw some cash at you to go into the studio and do a serious, record-quality demo. And that would kind of seal the deal—that you came out of there with something usable or whatever. So I had worked really hard to get to that place, and in the usual fashion of life, everything sort of happens at once.
>
> I wasn't even home when Joe called. My mom took the message. When I got home from the studio, she said, "You got a call from a guy in L.A. He had a funny name. It started with a Z and he said something about a weather report." I knew exactly who she was talking about. And I was like, "He actually called here?" So I said, "You gotta find that message for me." And she goes, "Well, it's around here somewhere, give me a moment." Now I'm starting to freak out because she can't find the paper. Eventually, the piece of paper shows up, and sure enough: Joe Zawinul,

with his number in Pasadena.

I called him back and we had a long talk. I asked him how he came to get my number, and he said that he had spoken to three guys in New York and they had all recommended me. One of them was Michal Urbaniak. One of them was Gil Evans, with whom I had toured the year before. And the third name was the biggest surprise: It was Miles. And that made sense to me because I remember playing at Mikell's in New York City, and Miles would be there quite a bit, sitting at the bar, chillin', having a drink, listening to the music. So everybody that Joe mentioned made sense, and they all recommended me.[8]

As for hiring Hakim, Zawinul didn't need a lot of convincing. After some chit-chat having nothing to do with music, Joe suddenly said, "Well, okay, you're in."[9] He then asked about Marcus Miller, a young star on the electric bass who had joined Miles Davis's comeback band the year before. "A lot of people knew that Marcus and I were sort of a team at that time," Omar explained. "We had gone to high school together, and we were doing a lot of work together. We were also the rhythm section for David Sanborn. We did a record around that time called *As We Speak*."[10]

Even if Joe hadn't mentioned Miller, Hakim thought of him, too. "Marcus Miller was my first choice," Omar confirmed. "One, because of our hookup. Two, because of his knowledge of jazz and harmony. Three, because of his knowledge of Weather Report. He and I became Weather Report fans together in many ways. I remember going to his place in Rochdale Village [in Queens] with *Black Market* under my arms in 1976 and we sat in his room and listened to it. And I have memories of going back to that same house right after *Heavy Weather* came out. Marcus was the only bass player in the neighborhood that learned 'Teen Town' the first week it came out, and could play 'Teen Town' and sound like Jaco in high school. My jaw dropped. He was playing along with the record, and I'm like, that's fucking insane. Of course, fast forward a few years and he ended up recording 'Teen Town,' but instead of playing it the way he played it in his bedroom, he played it with his thumb, which is even more insane. So yeah, to me he was the obvious choice because of what I knew and our hookup."[11]

Despite his best efforts, Omar couldn't persuade Miller to leave Miles, so Joe put the decision in Hakim's hands. "He had obviously heard enough of my work and got enough good recommendations that he trusted me for some reason. So I set out looking for a bass player for Weather Report." Hakim was deliberate in his approach. "There were a lot of bad cats in New York," he said, but he realized that whoever followed Jaco in Weather Report would be the subject of intense scrutiny. Such a bass player would need to have a high degree of self-confidence and a thick skin, not to mention exceptional chops and an appreciation of Weather Report's music. Omar found that person in Victor Bailey.[12]

"Right after that conversation with Joe I had some touring dates booked with Hugh Masekela that I had to finish," Omar said. "Now, the last few gigs that I had with Hugh Masekela and Miriam Makeba, the bass player was Victor Bailey. And I knew Victor, but we had never played together. So this was the first time we were playing, and right away I noticed that he and I had a hookup.

"And what really made it evident was the sound checks for the Hugh Masekela gigs. The sound checks would always turn into a jam, and I noticed that as the jams started to get more and more intense, as guys felt satisfied with their sound, they would put their axe down and leave the stage. The guitars would leave first, and then one of the keyboard players would leave, then the horn players would leave, then the other keyboard player would leave, and the only two people left on stage were me and Vic. And this happened more than once. And I thought, hmmm, I think this is our man. So I asked Victor if he would be interested in submitting something to Joe Zawinul. I don't remember his exact words, but I want to say that his answer was something like, 'Hell, yeah!'"[13]

A year younger than Hakim, Bailey also came from a musical family. His father, Morris Bailey Jr., was a songwriter-arranger who was instrumental in developing the Philadelphia sound. His uncle Donald was a jazz and R&B drummer best known for his years with organist Jimmy Smith. In an odd parallel to Jaco's early years, Victor also started out on drums before switching to electric bass under similar circumstances. And like Jaco, he took to the bass immediately. Upon graduating high school, Victor attended the Berklee College of Music. It was a period of intense growth. The school was loaded with talent, and Bailey played non-stop, immersing himself in bebop, before moving to New York in 1980, where he learned that there weren't a lot of jobs for a bebop electric bassist. Nevertheless, Victor quickly established himself with session and club work.

Omar gave Victor Joe's address and encouraged him to send Zawinul a tape. "I had a demo on cassette at the time, and I sent it to Joe the next day," Bailey said. "And interestingly enough, Joe called me two days after talking to Omar and said, 'You're the guy I'm going to hire. I know it.' Then once he got the tape, he and Wayne listened to it, and management called me and said, 'Welcome to Weather Report.'"[14]

Joe also asked Omar to pick a percussionist. He turned to José Rossy. Classically trained at the Conservatory for Music in San Juan, Puerto Rico, Rossy moved to New York in 1975 and began touring with Labelle. In fact, he hired Omar for that band. They had so much fun together that it was an easy decision for Hakim to recommend him for Weather Report.

"I was playing at the Bottom Line in New York City," Rossy said of his recruitment. "It was before Steps became Steps Ahead. It was Warren Bernhardt, Michal Urbaniak, Eddie Gomez. And Omar was playing in the band. We used to do maybe three or four shows in a week. And someone got the call from Joe, saying that they were looking for a drummer and a percussionist and a bass player, and they told us to call. So Omar called, and then I called. From there it was just like, I'm talking to Joe on the phone and I thought it was going to be an audition kind of thing. He said, 'No, you're in the band.' They said, 'How soon can you get here?' It was like, one day you're listening to the band, and then you're talking to somebody who's telling you you're *in* the band. So it was an amazing thing. It was just like reassuring that we were probably doing something right as musicians in New York City."[15]

By May, Weather Report's tour was rapidly approaching, and Wayne and Joe had yet to meet any of their new musicians. "Two and a half weeks before the tour started, Omar, Victor, and José walked in and started rehearsing," Joe said. "We would've really been in trouble if they couldn't play. It was just one of those things, and I call this our real fortunate period, because we could have really been on ice."[16]

What were the rehearsals like? Omar Hakim:

> My last gig with Hugh Masekela was in San Diego. From there, I got on a plane to L.A. with my bags and drums, and the first rehearsals were at Joe's house in Pasadena. I was excited. I felt prepared because I knew a lot of the music. But when we arrived, we discovered that Joe and Wayne didn't want to play any old music; we're going to play new music. So I'm like, okay, that's cool. There was a pile of charts sitting on a music stand, and day one we started playing through a couple of these things. But what was odd about these rehearsals, for me, was that it wasn't being run like a rehearsal that I was used to. We would play through maybe a third of a chart and stop. Then Joe would look at it, and then we would play a couple of pages from the back of the chart. And then he'd say, "Okay, let's take a break."
>
> So then there would be a coffee/tea break out in the backyard. I would take the charts with me on the break so I could look at them. We'd be out there talking and chilling, and an hour later we'd go back in, and I'm thinking, *Okay, we'll continue with this chart so we can get it together.* Well no, he forgot all about that one and we were on to the next chart. And then the same thing happened again. We'd play a quarter of that chart, and then we would stop, and Joe would work on his sounds for a half hour, tinkering with his keyboards. Then we'd count it off again, and maybe this time we'd get through half of it, and he'd say, "Okay, that's

great. You guys hungry?"

So then Maxine would make a big lunch for us. We'd sit outside again, and between the talking and the eating, this break was two hours. So that's fine. This is day one. We've got four or five more days. It's all good. The problem was, it happened like that all week. We'd play through 30 percent of a chart and take a break. Play through half of another chart, then have lunch and talk. We'd go back and we wouldn't even look at those two charts; we'd do another one. We'd play through that one for a half hour, and then we'd tinker with keyboards and sounds. There were some rehearsals that were very productive, and others that felt like nothing was happening. But through it all, there was a lot of talk, a lot of hanging, a lot of tea drinking and eating.[17]

Victor Bailey:

I remember being completely in awe, like, wow, I'm *actually* playing with those guys. My two favorite bands were Weather Report and Return to Forever, so I was a *huge* Weather Report fan. I mean, I would listen to *Mysterious Traveller* or listen to *Heavy Weather* and hold the album cover in my hands the entire time—just stare at the covers, stare at pictures of Joe and Wayne, and think *I'm going to play with those guys one day*.

And it was just the *sound*. There was such a distinct sound that Joe and Wayne had, and sitting in Joe's house and actually playing with these guys. You know, I was a confident kid so I was like, oh, I can play with these guys. And I *could* play with them. But to be in the room and to hear the sound come back was surreal. Literally surreal. It was unbelievable.

And we were able to play. I was still developing, but Omar and I played so well together. I don't remember what we played in the first rehearsal, but whatever little grooves or ideas they could come up with, whatever Omar played, I could find something that fit. Or whatever I played, Omar could find something that fit.

I had an arrangement of the John Coltrane song "Moment's Notice," where I play the chords and the melody and the walking bass line at the same time, and I remember Joe looking at Wayne, saying, "I think we got another Jaco." I was very young, so I still had a ways to go to catch up with Jaco, if you can even catch up with that guy. But it was like a vote of confidence that I needed. It was a very happy moment for me, but at the same time just unbelievable to hear those two guys playing and know that I'm playing with them.[18]

José Rossy:

I had to get the gear together that I thought I might need for the band. I listened to some of the older stuff because I was sure that even with all the new stuff we were rehearsing and recording, we would have to do some of the older stuff. So I listened to what Manolo did, what Bobby Thomas did, and everything that Erskine and Alex did, just to get familiar with how it felt when we were doing that kind of thing.

And then we got to L.A. We went up to Pasadena and they got us an apartment each, got us a rental car each. We started rehearsals and it was just like going to school. You're talking about intense. It was *beautiful*. They just knew what you could do already without you doing anything. They would just throw things at you and let you create on top of that.

You had to forget the rules and just play. That was one of Joe's sayings. The rules are there, but you just play. I loved doing that in other situations and other groups, but you always had to follow certain forms—not forms, but certain pockets, to keep it in the pocket. But with Joe and Wayne, it was like, oh my God, you would hear them do a duet thing just warming up, and they just came up with that. That's how they think. So I had to get myself into that frame of mind and not be tied to anything. Just play. It was an amazing experience. I will never forget that. That was my favorite time in those years that I spent making music.[19]

Meanwhile, Joe's keyboard rig underwent a major overhaul just like the band did. Out went the Rhodes electric piano, the cornerstone of his sound going back to his Cannonball days. He also shelved the venerable ARP 2600s. In their places were a second Prophet-5 and an ARP Quadra, a hybrid polyphonic instrument that combined traditional analog synthesis with technology from electronic organs. Joe also wanted to do something about the Oberheim Eight Voice, which occupied a large amount of space in his stage setup. The obvious solution was to separate the keyboard from the rest of the electronics, like the ARP 2600s, so Brian Risner called up Will Alexander, Oberheim's service manager, asking if he knew someone who could do the job. "Yeah, I do," Alexander replied. "And I've seen the plans for it."

After he got off the phone, Alexander walked down the hall and tapped the shoulder of a young technician named Jim Swanson. "Guess who called me? Brian Risner of Weather Report. They want somebody to modify the Eight Voice, so I gave them your name. Here's your chance, man. Don't fuck up."[20]

As a big fan of the band, Swanson was thrilled to get this news. He'd seen Weather Report several times and spent his spare time working out the details for

Victor Bailey: Photo: © www.markbrady.com.

a separate five-octave keyboard that included controls for performing program changes as well as other performance parameters, allowing the rest of the Eight Voice to remain out of reach and out of view. After meeting Joe and Risner, Swanson took the synthesizer home and undertook the modifications. Impressed with his work, Risner asked if he'd like to go on the road as Joe's keyboard technician. Swanson didn't have to think about it.

Swanson had heard rumors that Jaco and Erskine had gone off to do the *Word of Mouth* tour, so he asked Risner who the bass player and drummer were. "You'll see," Risner replied, leaving the question unanswered. "So these guys showed up for rehearsals at Joe's house and I honestly had no idea who they were. But we all got together and introduced ourselves to each other and shot hoops in Joe's backyard. I thought, *Well, I guess this is the new band.* And they went to Joe's during the day and worked out the material while I came in at night to do the tech work on the keyboards, and it all just kind of came together. And then we packed up and said, 'Let's take it on the road.'"[21]

The reconstituted Weather Report debuted on June 1 at the Starlight Bowl in San Diego, a 4,300-seat amphitheater that sits almost directly under the landing path for the nearby international airport. For years it was home to the San Diego Civic Light Opera, which often paused its performances—sometimes in humorously awkward fashion—when jets passed overhead. While Weather Report was loud enough to drown out the noise most of the time, at one point Joe drew up a synthesizer patch that mimicked the jets during his duet with Wayne.

The band's management had previously stopped by Joe's house to let them know that Leonard Feather would be reviewing the show. That's when Omar Hakim sensed the magnitude of what they were about to do. "I went, 'Oh, shit.' It didn't hit me until the reports of the manager started getting back to the rehearsals, and then I realized what was really happening. For me, it was like, maybe we're not rehearsing enough, or maybe there's not enough time. But it was Joe and Wayne's show. I'm going to do the best that I can with what I'm dealt, but I was honestly getting a little nervous because I didn't feel like we were really rehearsing the music."[22]

As the band took their places on stage against a backdrop of prerecorded fanfare, they looked out at a couple thousand spectators. Sure enough, seated in the first row was Leonard Feather, pen and notepad in hand, along with a handful of other journalists and photographers, including A. James Liska, *Down Beat*'s West Coast editor. While the reporters knew that Joe and Wayne were unveiling a new band, most of the fans in attendance did not. Nor did they recognize the rhythm section. As one writer quipped, the new guys came from "the realm of the unknown sidemen."[23]

Fans were also unfamiliar with much of the material Weather Report played. They led off with one of Joe's new tunes, "Procession," which he announced with a series of low, rumbling moans from his synthesizers that segued into a sustained drone (with a note held down by a matchbook stuck between the keys) that was offset by Omar Hakim's light, almost hypnotic drum pattern. It was an unusually subdued way to open a concert, but it forced the audience to quiet down and focus on the stage. The tune was still being fleshed out and it smoldered along for nearly sixteen minutes, with a lot of swimming and searching, to borrow a phrase from Weather Report's early days. Eventually, it erupted into a full-throated second act that segued into a thunderous, percussion-laden introduction to "Fast City," the kind of up-tempo electro-bop tune that could make or break the new guys in the eyes of fans.

Omar called it the fastest song he ever played—the trick, of course, being to stay loose. "You've got to relax," he explained. "Before you tense up, you've immediately got to say it's not fast."[24] "Fast City" also gave Bailey a chance to show off his chops. While he might not have been Jaco—and to be clear, nobody was Jaco but Jaco—it was at this point that the hard-core fans in attendance knew that the bass was in good hands. Recognizing that the new band members had passed a crucial test, Wayne broke from tradition and announced their names as soon as "Fast City" concluded.

Other surprises followed. Wayne's piece "When It Was Now" was performed live for the first time. And in a strange twist, Weather Report stopped playing its own tunes midway through the set and spent fifteen minutes backing a young

José Rossy. Photo: © www.markbrady.com.

vocalist named Alison Mills on two of her numbers. Meanwhile, the guys seemed to enjoy themselves on stage, hollering at each other while Joe cued them with hand signals from behind his keyboards.

In the course of the evening, Omar's fears that the band wasn't sufficiently rehearsed gave way to a different realization—one that has stuck with him ever since. "It was one of the most amazing gigs I ever did in my life," he said years later. "And what I learned is that rehearsal isn't always playing. When we were talking over drinks and food every day, we were also rehearsing, because we were getting to know each other. And all of the conversations that we had that week, we finished on stage at that gig in San Diego. As a jazz musician, it's almost like you don't want to over-rehearse. You want to leave a little space for the thing to happen, and that's what they were doing. These guys were forty-eight, forty-nine years old, and they knew a lot more than me. I had a lot of experience for someone my age because I had been a professional drummer for more than half my life at that point, but still, I didn't have *their* experience. And because of their experience they were confident that they were getting from us what they needed."[25]

By the time the concert was over, Weather Report had held the stage for over two and a half hours, capping their performance with a medley of greatest hits—the only nod to pre–*Night Passage* material. Afterward, there was a feeling of quiet jubilation backstage. A. James Liska wrote that Wayne "beamed, accepting graciously the compliments being offered," while Zawinul, "posed and intense, smiled broadly, countering each compliment with a reminder that this was the band's first-ever performance." "Just wait," Joe advised. "I think this is the best band; these musicians are the best."[26]

Meanwhile, Jim Swanson spent the night just out of the audience's view, stage left, carefully observing everything Joe did. The only mishap occurred when one of the keyboard stands collapsed, leading to momentary panic on Zawinul's part. "Halfway through the show, as Joe was going to town and banging on the Quadra, the stand came loose and the keyboard dipped down," Swanson remembered. "Joe caught it and looked at me like, *Oh God, what do I do?* So I ran out there and straightened it up while the concert was going. And I realized, no, this is not the keyboard stand *I* want to live with. So I changed to Ultimate Support stands and stuff like that. But all in all, it worked out fine. The audience seemed to like it. The band was smiling afterwards. 'Yeah, we did it. We pulled that gig off.' And it was on to Phoenix."[27]

Leonard Feather's review appeared in the *Los Angeles Times* two days later. While he found nothing groundbreaking in the band's performance, it was reassuring to see that Weather Report was still Weather Report. "This was a reasonably typical evening with a combo that still holds a commanding lead in the jazz-rock fusion field," he wrote.[28]

•

As the tour went on, the music got more focused. "Procession," for instance, was tightened up to nine minutes, about the same length it would be recorded. Joe and Wayne seemed rejuvenated by their young bandmates. These were perceptive, intelligent young men who, while having fun, exuded an almost businesslike demeanor. It must have been a welcome change after the drama that pervaded the Jaco years.

Clearly the newcomer with the most pressure on him was Victor, as there was no escaping Jaco's shadow. Aside from his own formidable chops, one thing Bailey had going for him was youthful confidence. Like Marcus Miller, Victor dissected Jaco's records as a teenager and used them as a measuring stick, figuring that if Jaco could do it, he could, too. "I told everybody since I was fifteen years old that I was going to play with Weather Report after Jaco," Bailey recalled. "It's funny. I remember one guy saying there's going to be a black president before you play with Weather Report. I beat him by about twenty-five years. But it felt great. I thought it was my gig before I had the gig. I saw the band four times—the last two times with Jaco—and I thought they would hire me. I thought it was par for the course."[29]

Nevertheless, Bailey initially struggled with Joe's propensity to stay in one tone center for long periods of time, "Procession" being an example. "The first couple of gigs, I wasn't sure of the music," Victor later admitted. "I knew Weather Report's music, but a lot of the music that Joe had written at that time was vamps.

Weather Report performs at Wolf Trap in Vienna, Virginia, Jun. 15, 1982. Photo: Michael Wilderman.

And at that particular point in my life, all I was practicing was bebop—blowing over chord changes and playing standards. So I wasn't totally comfortable, actually, improvising over those vamps.

"That whole first tour, I almost felt like I was holding my breath. I was trying to figure out what I had to say in this music. And Joe was adamant with me about not playing bebop. Joe was like, 'Wayne and I played that, and we created something beyond that, so don't play bebop here.' I felt like I was learning how to play in the band, trying to figure out what to play and how to play it in the context that I was in. One thing I definitely did not want to do was sound like Alphonso or Jaco, considering those are two of my biggest influences. I thought, *How am I going to play this music and play in this band, and not play like them?*"[30]

While Bailey dealt with the burden of replacing Jaco and finding his way in the music, Omar Hakim wrestled with being a drummer for Joe Zawinul. "I would be lying if I told you he was the greatest guy in the world to play for," Omar acknowledged. "No, there were times when he was a *very* difficult character to deal with. And there were times when you would almost have to get him off of you, because he would ride your ass. And I think he liked me because even though I was young, I had enough confidence to say to him, 'You've got to give me space to develop my place in the band.'

"I remember having a conversation with him about this, because at one point he was almost over-communicating some things, but not necessarily in a clear way. Since he wasn't a drummer, it was like what he was describing wouldn't always jibe with a drummer's language. And I noticed that I was starting to get uptight about it, and I was not one to be uptight because, again, by the time I got there I was twelve years as a professional drummer. So finally I pulled him to the side, and I don't remember the exact words, but the gist of the conversation was,

'Listen, you and I are going to get along great here if you play the keyboards and let me play the drums.' It was said out of a bit of frustration, and after it came out of my mouth, my very next thought was maybe I should just go back to the hotel and pack my bags because I'm probably fired. But I didn't get a call from the manager, so I was still in the band the next day. [*laughs*] And when I got to sound check, Joe pulled me to the side. I don't remember the words, I can just tell you that the feeling was like, 'I can dig it. I appreciate the conversation. Everything is cool. We're going to be fine.'

"As a result, he let it go a little bit, and that was when I could do my thing; I could actually make a contribution to Weather Report. I had enough information that I was bringing to the table that I could make a unique contribution. I mean, I remember the *Down Beat* guy said something really interesting to me. He said, 'Well, how does it feel to be filling the shoes of Peter Erskine?' I said, 'Well, first of all, it would be impossible to fill the shoes of Peter Erskine. I'm not Peter Erskine. Peter Erskine is a brilliant musician, with tremendous experience, who does what he does. I can't do what he does. However, I brought my *own* shoes with me to this gig.'"[31]

After a handful of concerts on the West Coast, the band took a short break before regrouping in Rochester, New York, for a swing through the East Coast. A charter bus was arranged—one of those large motor coaches with "hokey depictions of a Western saga on its sides," per A. James Liska, and "Ego Trips" spelled out atop the windshield where the word "Charter" would normally go. Meanwhile, the band gathered momentum earned via the crucible of the stage. Audiences still didn't know who the rhythm section was, but by the time each show was done, they were won over. At the end of the concert in Pittsburgh, for instance, one fan shouted out, "Jaco who?"[32] And so it went.

Almost three weeks after their San Diego debut, Weather Report was back in Southern California for the Playboy Jazz Festival. With the overwhelming response the band got at the previous year's shindig, George Wein asked Joe if he could do something special, possibly in the form of a guest musician. Zawinul immediately thought of the Manhattan Transfer, which had scored two Grammy Awards for their vocalese version of "Birdland." It was probably the only cover of Joe's tunes that he ever truly liked (though true to form, he complained that there wasn't enough bass).

Joe pitched the idea to Tim Hauser, the Manhattan Transfer's founder, with his customary bravado. "The next time we do the Playboy Jazz Festival I want you to do 'Birdland' with us, and it's going to be recorded on film, and let's make it the only time we do it. We'll never do it again, and it'll have meaning and be a historic thing."[33]

So they gathered for a quick rehearsal at Joe's house and then did it live in front of 17,500 people. "We were all living in L.A. at the time," remembered Janis Siegel, who arranged the tune for the Transfer and sang Joe's synthesizer solo at the end. "As a matter of fact, my place was right above the Hollywood Bowl, so we dressed there and warmed up at my place, and then drove down the hill and bam, just hit the stage. And the audience didn't know what was happening, because they ended their show with 'Birdland,' and then all of a sudden for the encore there was a modulation into our key, and we came out and did it. It was exciting—very exciting."[34]

As for Weather Report topping itself, it was mission accomplished. The crowd reaction to the Weather Report–Manhattan Transfer combination "bordered on hysteria," wrote Leonard Feather in the *Los Angeles Times*, noting that it came at the end of "a generally flawless set by the band that has remained, during the last decade, a whole genre unto itself."[35]

•

Leonard Feather's comments reflected how quickly the band jelled. He observed that there had been "a notable improvement" since he first saw the new configuration in San Diego. Joe and Wayne must have felt the same because they wasted little time getting into a recording studio. A few weeks after their Playboy appearance, they took advantage of a short break in their road schedule and headed to Universal Recording Studios, a legendary studio in Chicago. Then at the end of the tour two weeks later, they went to the Power Station in New York. The band had been playing four new pieces that summer, so those were the ones that were tracked for their new LP, which took its name from Joe's tune "Procession."

As usual, "Procession" was based on an improvisation that Zawinul transcribed for the band. Setting the tone for this piece is a fantastic bit of drumming by Omar Hakim, who subtly builds the energy to the climactic part of the song before dialing it back and taking it out. Joe later described his playing as "a beautiful little composition" in its own right.[36]

"'Procession' was a mood piece that needed to have a really, really slow build," Omar said. "And what they were going for was definitely mystery in the beginning of it. I remember Joe sitting down at the kit at one point, playing this kind of ride cymbal pattern that he was hearing, so I took that pattern and created a kind of—I don't know how I'd describe it—it's a march, but then there's this kind of bebop ride thing, but it's also very quiet. And you had to be disciplined enough to keep this thing moving forward, very softly, and let it build dynamically, ever so subtly, until the thing freakin' exploded in the end. It had an interesting arc to it that was all about drama, mystery, discipline, and then power at a certain point. A very interesting composition."[37]

On the LP, "Procession" is followed by Wayne's tune "Plaza Real." When he brought the chart to rehearsal, it didn't indicate a rhythm, which led to one of

Jim Swanson and Joe Zawinul. Photo: Jim Swanson—Zawinul's Keyboard Engineer.

his cryptic musical directives. "We tried to get him to describe what he wanted groove-wise, how the song should feel," Hakim recalled. "He said, 'Don't think of it as a song, think of it as an adventure,' and then he went into a description of an 'Alice in Wonderland' scene."[38] Omar's response was to not create a groove at all, but to interpret the piece freely, giving it much of its distinctive character. Beyond that, the instrumentation of "Plaza Real" is unique in a number of ways. For one thing, Joe plays the accordion—something he never did in concert and rarely did on record. In fact, it was the same accordion that Jaco gave him the previous year for his birthday—"a gigantic Italian accordion [that was] a great instrument," Zawinul said.[39]

Listeners are also treated to a rare recorded instance of Wayne whistling. In addition, although the main melody was originally conceived for saxophone, Joe asked José Rossy to play it on concertina, an instrument he had never played before. Joe had purchased it from a shop on a little side street off the Plaza Real in Barcelona (probably the inspiration for the tune's title), and he had José try it one day. "The first time he grabbed it he could kind of play it," Zawinul said. "So I said, 'Here, you got it!'"[40]

As Rossy remembered, "Joe looked at me and said, 'Take that concertina to your room tonight, and come back tomorrow like you were born with the instrument.' I thought, holy cow! So I went back to my room, got some coffee, and I just practiced scales and kept practicing. I've got a pretty good ear, and once you find the notes on the instrument, you kind of find where the melody is. And then it's just a matter of putting some feel into it. I came back the next day and played the tune."[41] Rossy played the melody on concertina starting with the first concerts, and he retained a delicate, fragile feeling into the recording studio.

"Plaza Real" was one of those tunes that came from a much longer manuscript, and Victor was taken aback at how Joe would carve up Wayne's compositions. "Wayne's charts were always twenty pages long, and Joe had an unbelievable knack for *instantly*, as you played it down, he would throw seventeen pages away. He would take whatever page it was and say, 'Wayne, this is your song right here.' Like 'Plaza Real' has basically three sections and Joe had a real knack for finding those three things. During my time in the band it used to irk me when Joe would do this. Like, I couldn't believe that you would take Wayne Shorter's music and tell him what's good and what's not, and pick out parts of a sixteen- or seventeen-page thing, and throw those other pages away. However, hearing what Wayne did after that, I thought that Joe helped him a lot, because a lot of the stuff afterwards was a bit rambling, and not getting enough to the point for me. Joe could really find where the point was. So 'Plaza Real' was an example of that—a great composition with three beautiful sections."[42]

Side one of *Procession* closes with "Two Lines," an up-tempo, danceable number that Joe enjoyed playing until the end of his life. It also served as the encore number for much of the 1982 tour. The title came from the two lines on his chart—one for the melody and one for the bass. "The first thing I remember about it was Joe getting the three cowbells for José," Bailey said. "On his demo, Joe had a little part that he played on a keyboard, and I don't know where he went—in his basement or his bedroom or wherever—and he came back with these three cow bells. And that's where that part came from."[43]

Bailey also explained how he interpreted the tune. "I was playing a lot of bebop at that time, so during the melody, even though Omar plays it as sort of a funk groove, I was hearing it like straight-ahead, so I'm swinging. And if you listen closely, a lot of the time I'm playing the chord changes to 'rhythm changes,' but because it's over a funk groove, almost nobody has mentioned that before.[44] So my approach to it was just swinging.

"And then when we got to the solo section where Wayne plays, I remember trying to find all of these crazy, unusual-sounding bass lines, going for almost a hippity-hoppity, Jaco-y kind of thing, and it just didn't work. And Omar said, 'Man, do it like P-Funk, put it on the one.' And that's funk style, like Funkadelic—play the root on one and play a crash on one. So my intention was to play an F on one, every two bars, and that was our funk side coming in. Sometimes you have to go back to the simplest common denominator to make things work, and that made it work. But the whole time I was basically swinging on top of it. If you picture a ride cymbal in jazz, that's the feeling we're creating underneath the whole time."[45]

Side two of *Procession* begins with "Where the Moon Goes," one of the more peculiar tracks in Weather Report's discography. Aside from a melody that is punctuated by Joe's characteristically quirky phrasing, most striking is the inclusion of lyrics sung by an otherworldly chorus. The words were penned by Nan O'Byrne. She was recommended by Cavallo-Ruffalo, having written for Earth, Wind & Fire, among others. Joe invited her to his home in Pasadena, where he played the tune—more like phrases, it wasn't a complete tune in that sense—on piano and explained his idea to create a kind of love letter from the road to Maxine. To that end, O'Byrne's lyrics dutifully name check places around the globe—and not just any places, but ones that meant something to Joe personally—along with autobiographical verses referencing New York and L.A.

Like "Two Lines," Joe worked up a Linn drum part. Of course, when he programmed the drum machine, he was free to come up with all kinds of wacky things that weren't physically possible for a human drummer to play, or even the combination of a drummer and percussionist. "I remember trying to figure out how to play these five-handed Linn drum programs on a drum set," Hakim said. "So my job was to re-create the *feeling* of what was happening, with some of the important sonic elements that would come out of a particular drum program. When we did 'Where the Moon Goes,' there was this one sound on the Linn drum that I decided sounded like a garbage-can lid. I remember going out in Joe's yard looking for something that would make this metallic sound that he was using on the drum machine, and I was like, wow, man, a garbage-can lid sounds perfect. So we drilled a hole in it and put it on a stand, and I figured out how to play that pattern in a way that was close enough to his programming that would make it interesting, but I was still able to add my own vibe to it."[46]

For the vocals, Joe turned to the Manhattan Transfer. Given how Joe and Brian Risner processed their vocals, listeners would be hard-pressed to know who it was without reading the liner notes. "Joe wanted to do another collaboration, and he came up with the idea of this song," Janis Siegel recalled. "And I have to tell you, it was one of the hardest things I have ever sung. And I don't think I'm alone in that. We had trouble with it rhythmically. It was just crazy. We could not get our bearings for much of it, so it took a while. It's such an unusual vocal piece—I wouldn't even call it a song—but it only resolves at the very end. The rest of it is just crazy, nutty, almost spoken-word stuff in unison. He had a very evolved sense of rhythm, and things were just never where we expected them to be.

"And the most interesting thing about it, I have to say, is the way Joe mixed it, which I hated at first. But now I kind of dig it, because he wanted to take us

Weather Report and the Manhattan Transfer at Joe's house after rehearsing for the 1982 Playboy Jazz Festival. Left to right: Victor Bailey, Cheryl Bentyne, Joe Zawinul, Anthony Zawinul, Omar Hakim, Alan Paul (below), Janis Siegel, Ivan Zawinul (above), Tim Hauser, Wayne Shorter, and José Rossy. Photo: Brian Risner.

out of that beautiful, creamy sound that we usually have, and all of a sudden we were compressed and sort of in the background. We were like an effect more than singers, in a way."[47]

That was Joe's intent. He looked at the vocal part as "just another instrument, another timbre."[48] Meanwhile, the idea of coupling Weather Report with the Manhattan Transfer must have had management salivating for another "Birdland," so imagine their reaction to the way it turned out. "We butted heads about that one quite a bit," recalled Brian Risner, who recorded the album and assisted Joe in its production. "I wanted to do this stuff straight, but he kept saying, 'We've got to get it funky, man. We gotta get it sounding like the street.' And he kept pushing it. You couldn't get it mucked up enough for him. Management wanted this hit and Joe just kept wanting to distort the voices."[49]

"Where the Moon Goes" was the last of the four new tunes the band played that summer. To fill out the album, Joe and Wayne included a portion of a duet from a concert in Japan the previous year. They called it "The Well," an allusion to improvisation as "a never-ending source, just like a well."[50] At the time, their duets typically began with a solo performance by Wayne on soprano, after which Joe would join him on stage, playing the chicken neck. Then Zawinul would move back to his keyboards where he and Wayne would fashion a quasi-classical duet like the one heard on *Procession*. These were moments of brilliance, mostly evaporating in the air as soon as they were played. But this recording gives listeners an example of what might have been had Joe and Wayne ever followed through on their oft-stated desire to produce a Masterworks duet album.

Procession closes with "Molasses Run," a funky tune written by Omar Hakim, who explained how it came about. "I played a few tunes of mine for Joe and he dug them, but he really liked that one a lot. And he said, 'Yeah, we'll do one of your tunes.' I felt like he wanted me to feel a part of the band, and he knew that I had stopped doing what I was doing in terms of being an artist, so it was, yes, let's do one of your tunes. The way Joe arranged that song, it was a lot darker harmonically than what I was hearing. He definitely gave it a completely different shape. I even played guitar like he heard me when I showed him the melody and everything. And then he said, 'Oh, why don't you play this on the guitar [on the record].' And they recorded it and used it. So he had a whole other idea with that song mood-wise and atmospherically."[51]

There's one other interesting tidbit about "Molasses Run." When the band played it live the following year, Joe took advantage of a unique feature of the Oberheim Eight Voice called voice rotation, which routed each note played on the keyboard to a different SEM module, one after another in sequence. Because each of the SEMs could be tuned independently of the others, it could be set up so that pressing the same key on the keyboard eight times in a row produced eight different notes. It was even more mind-bending than the ARP 2600 inverted-keyboard technique.

Jim Swanson watched Zawinul improvise solos this way show after show. "Joe started doing the real-time math in his head, and so it enabled him to play a large span of notes knowing that each voice was going to be tuned differently. And so he came up with his own melody lines. It was quite a mind trip. It gave him a whole new performance aspect, playing these wild lines without making it random. You'd watch him do it, and your eyes saw one thing, but your ears heard another. One night Chick Corea came to see our show and he was standing next to me stage right. And when Joe started playing 'Molasses Run' using rotating voices, I said, 'Now Chick—watch this,' and I explained it to him. And he couldn't believe what he was seeing. He said, 'What? That shouldn't be happening.' And I said, 'Yeah, but it is. Isn't it cool?'"[52]

•

Weather Report was on the road for less than two months in 1982, performing roughly twenty-five shows. Joe spent the balance of the year finishing *Procession* and traveling back and forth to Vienna to look after his ailing mother. When she died, Joe brought his father back to Pasadena, where he remained until his own death a year and a half later. Meanwhile, Wayne moved his mother from Newark to California after she experienced a close call with a mugger.

Procession was eventually released in February 1983. It sold well—better than

For the *Procession* album art, a photo shoot was arranged to depict Weather Report's three new musicians springing forth from an Anvil flight case. Brian Risner was on hand to snap this Polaroid. Photo: Brian Risner.

its predecessor, in fact.[53] Within three weeks it was number two on the jazz charts while also cracking the top one hundred albums overall. Wayne described the album as "a universal festive feeling,"[54] and the beautiful jacket artwork by John Lykes harkens back to *Black Market*, depicting a carload of musicians (the keyboardist looks suspiciously like Joe) wending its way through the countryside, enticing the locals to follow. On the flip side, the caravan has reached the city and it's party time in the streets.

The LP's inner sleeve includes a sequence of photos in which Joe and Wayne raise the lid of an Anvil equipment case only to discover—surprise!—a trio of new musicians inside. The entire package suggested a new era for Weather Report, and reviewers heard it as such. In *New Musical Express*, Richard Cook was effusive in his endorsement. "Just when it seemed that the tuneless roar of last year's *Weather Report* had permanently iced over the incandescence of one of the world's great groups, *Procession* torches most of the old brilliance back to life."[55]

But most critics offered somewhat muted praise, such as this from John Diliberto in *Down Beat*: "*Procession* is suffused with a unity and joy that makes this the best Weather Report album since *Mysterious Traveller*. Yet, it lacks the passion of discovery and daring that made Weather Report a landmark group of the 1970s."[56] In *Musician* magazine, Chip Stern managed to condense the same sentiment into eight words: "This sounds just like a Weather Report album."[57]

So *Procession* was seen as evidence that, despite personnel changes, Weather Report remained at the top of its craft, even if it was no longer innovating at every turn. Against this backdrop, the band would spend the rest of 1983 serving notice that its days were far from numbered.

19 Domino Theory

No other group in contemporary music is even comparable.

—Leonard Feather

ON THE HEELS OF *PROCESSION*'S RELEASE, Weather Report embarked on its first world tour since 1980. With Omar Hakim, Victor Bailey and José Rossy back for their sophomore years, they hit the road at the end of February 1983, working their way across the United States, starting with the southern states, then up the Eastern Seaboard and back to California. They drew raves nearly everywhere they went.

Norfolk, Virginia: Weather Report "remains as fine an example as ever of the artistic potential of the fusion field."[1] New York City: Their set "reaffirmed Weather Report's continuing sense of discovery."[2] Ann Arbor, Michigan: Weather Report's concert "showed the current edition of this decade-old band to be the liveliest and most exciting ever."[3] Salt Lake City: "The results were incredible. Weather Report deserves their position as pioneers forging through new musical territories."[4] San Francisco: "That performance was the best Weather Report concert I've ever seen, in fact one of the most explosive concerts by any band that I've seen."[5]

Seven weeks after it began, the band wrapped up its U.S. tour with a home date at the Universal Amphitheatre in Hollywood. Leonard Feather once again took in the show, his third in the span of a year. As with those who had seen the band earlier that spring, his review was generous with praise. Weather Report's two hour and fifteen minute performance "reestablished beyond doubt the quintet's preeminence in its field—or more correctly, its monopoly of a field of one, since no other group in contemporary music is even comparable."[6]

The band was in exceptional form, capable of giving audiences everything they wanted in a Weather Report concert. Omar was a joyous presence on stage, with a touch of showmanship behind the kit. This played out most overtly in a campy,

Three generations of Weather Report bass players at the 1983 Live Under the Sky Jazz Festival. Left to right: Miroslav Vitous, Victor Bailey, and Alphonso Johnson. Photo: Brian Risner.

drawn-out cutting contest with Joe during "Where the Moon Goes" (with Omar, Victor, and Joe on vocoder handling the vocals). Victor proved to be remarkably adept and creative on those endless vamps that Joe liked. José Rossy complemented them both with his versatility and energy, doubling on everything from marimba to concertina. As a group, they smoked tunes like "Fast City."

Whereas Wayne and Joe were ready to split up eighteen months earlier, now they looked forward to building up the band again. Zawinul expected all of the band members to soon relocate to Los Angeles, telling Leonard Feather, "Now you're going to hear a band, my friend! We can meet and rehearse two or three times a week—and I mean all the time, not just before we go on tour."[7] Joe called the current group "the best all-around band we have had. We can play anything and everything. Everybody is excited and everybody is trying to learn. Wayne is playing twice as good as he's ever played, and I'm doing my best to improve myself. It's an incredible little ensemble."[8]

Critical to the band's success was the musical rapport that Omar and Victor shared. "Omar and I had a special connection," Bailey affirmed. "In retrospect, my perception of why we played well together is how I like to describe each of us. We're jazz musicians, but not exactly jazz musicians. And we're funky, but not exactly funk musicians. I think we're both somewhere in the middle, so it's a natural fit. A lot of times, if I play with a pure, straight-ahead jazz drummer or a pure funk drummer, I feel like there's an element to what I do that doesn't fit with him. But with Omar, no matter what I play, what he plays will just fit, and vice versa."[9]

Victor was the perfect bass player for Weather Report at this stage, combining the funkiness of Alphonso Johnson with Jaco-like chops. More important, Victor gave the music space again. "As much as I loved Jaco, it was like lead bass," he said. "Everybody had to follow *his* energy. I never heard him sound like he was supporting everybody else. When I saw Weather Report, he was not listening to Wayne Shorter. It's not that I don't *think* he wasn't listening to Wayne; he *wasn't*. He was doing his own thing. That's not a criticism of him, because he was a very special presence, and a very powerful force that added a lot to our instrument. He added new colors to music that didn't exist before.

"But I felt like when I saw him, I didn't hear Wayne, and I was just as much a fan of Wayne's as I was of Jaco's. I wanted to hear Wayne, too. So I wanted to play more like Alphonso. And Alphonso was an influence on Jaco himself. A lot of what Jaco did, with the fretless, with effects, with chorus and delay and distortion, some of the phrasing, Alphonso was a direct predecessor to it, and it never gets mentioned. He was a *great* improviser. Even those long vamps, those long grooves that Joe would play, Alphonso kept it moving; it never got stagnant."[10]

"I think that's what made Victor in many ways a perfect candidate to play with Weather Report at that point," Hakim said. "To have the attention on the bass player kind of relax a little bit for Joe and Wayne, it was almost like they could think again. And Victor totally came to the table, because not only is he a great cat in terms of chops and facility, he's an *incredible* groove player. Very few bass players that I know swing harder than Victor Bailey, whether they're playing jazz or funk or rock, or even freakin' dance music with Madonna. Victor Bailey will fucking swing you into the ground with a groove. He is no joke.

"And at this point in the band, they deliberately got away from the concept of playing choruses over changes—the very traditional, jazzy thing. I remember Joe saying that the idea wasn't to create tunes that had a head and then three or four solos, but a head itself being a song. So in many ways, yes, there were tunes that were vamps, and primarily it was vamp-based solo sections. There were a few tunes that had harmonic movement, but it was definitely more open, conceptually, most of the time. Which, in an interesting way, made it sound more modern. So to have Victor Bailey there, who had the harmonic knowledge but the Philadelphia groove sense, it was this freakin' perfect combination."[11]

Omar carried himself with a maturity that belied his age. A steadfast vegetarian, he kept himself in good shape mentally and physically. "I remember Wayne and I were the two guys that would get up the earliest in the morning. I didn't drink or anything, so I'd basically head back to the hotel after the gig, listen to my music that I would carry with me, read, and then pass out. So I'd be up early and typically I would run into Wayne. Or sometimes I'd call him, or he'd call me, and we would hook up for breakfast and walk. And we had really cool, interesting talks. He would always want to talk about his family, his wife, his kids. Or we'd talk about movies. He loved movies. So we would talk about that kind of stuff. It was always fun and interesting to hang out with him. Conversations would be really weird. I wish I had a tape recorder for some of the stuff, because everybody who knows Wayne knows that he communicates in a unique way. But the feeling of hanging out with him was to hear him talk about the things that were important outside of music.

"And observing him playing every night, I realized that talking to Wayne and hearing him play were the same thing. It was an interesting realization for me—that I recognized his voice on the instrument from hanging out with him during the day. Exactly the way he communicated verbally, and expressed emotion verbally, would come through the horn in the same way. And then I thought, *that's it*: If you can connect your emotional state, your spiritual state, through your instrument in such a connected way, then that's everything. It's the stuff that you can't practice; you can only live it. And that's the thing that connects with people. There were times when he would play a solo and I counted four or five notes in the whole solo that he recombined in different shapes and different dynamics. I would even say that he brought us to tears on certain nights. So it was an intense experience to witness his genius every night."[12]

After a ten-day break, the band flew across the Atlantic, where they performed for several weeks, making their way to such far-flung locales as Yugoslavia and Israel. As an indication of what went into a Weather Report tour at this point, the production crew (not counting the musicians) consisted of eighteen members, including a manager, production manager, stage manager, and tour manager. The entire contingent navigated Europe in two buses, along with two trucks for the musical instruments, sound reinforcement, and stage lightening. Two caterers provided meals to order along the way.

As per custom, Weather Report wrapped up its European tour in England. *Crescendo International* sent a correspondent to the June 5 show in Manchester. "There are not enough superlatives to praise Weather Report's concert performance at the Palace Theatre, Manchester," he wrote. "With three new faces in the cast, the lineup produced such a refreshing, rhythmic sound that you would never think the band nearly split for good last year through internal argument."[13]

•

As he had done the previous year, Joe introduced a trio of new tunes to Weather Report's stage repertoire, and these formed the basis for the band's next album, *Domino Theory*. Building from their previous experience, the youngsters had little trouble absorbing the new music and putting their own stamp on it. "I think we had developed the 'OS' at that point," Hakim said. "It was easy to plug new music into that operating system. I had found my place in the band that I had fought for. Victor got more comfortable. And so as a result, I think Victor and I sound more comfortable. We sound like we had been on the road: tighter, grooving. Joe even told me this was the sound he was looking for from the rhythm section. He would say, 'Yeah, these tracks are smoking!'"[14]

In concert, the new material was played as a block after the set openers, "Procession" and "Fast City." As the audience caught its breath from that exhilarating start, Omar and José descended from behind their kits and sat down in front of the drum and percussion risers, donning a collection of hand instruments for the first of Joe's new tunes, which had the working title of "Singapore" (later changed to "The Peasant"). It is an evocative folk song built on a deceptively complex, serpentine melody that Joe and Wayne played in unison, their phrasing so clean that they melded into a single, unidentifiable timbre.

In addition to the melody, Joe worked out a percussion template for Omar Hakim and José Rossy on the Linn drum machine. "It was like a map of how this should be because it feels good to him," Rossy explained. "Once you start rehearsing, you're going to hear other things, and it becomes a different thing. But the feel of it would be the same because you captured the feel that he heard. The longer we worked together and the more we got to know what we were doing on stage, we just knew where things could go. So it was very helpful that he had those things in the drum machine as a guide to start from."[15]

The British television program, *The South Bank Show*, aired a documentary about Weather Report at about the time *Domino Theory* was released, and a good portion of it is devoted to the making of "The Peasant." Viewers see Joe at his Pasadena home, transcribing his original tape recording, and then the full band works out the instrumentation and feel during a rehearsal. In the voiceover, Joe gives one of his most expansive descriptions of his oft-stated credo of composition-by-improvisation:

> The way I compose is by improvising. I improvise, put it on tape, and then if I like it, I just take it and write it down for the band. Often I have long scores—seventeen, eighteen pages full of music.
>
> I want to avoid in my music to think so much about it, and I hardly ever do. But when it's there, you always hear it. You hear it when you do it. But if you think about it, it's gone. You cannot do that. You gotta be able to concentrate on what you are doing so strongly that you never will be interrupted by anything, and just go. And then there will be a whole composition, a whole song form, like a symphony. And that's possible with one thought, without never letting it go—just to work. But not *thinking*, just concentrating.
>
> After the improvisation, I usually put the tape away unless I immediately know that's a piece we are going to be using. And then just work

on it, write it down note for note. And the work will change to a point, but not very much.

Most of my pieces, I'm totally stubborn about it, because I don't want to change the inspiration because I believe it's given to you; you ought to respect it. What I try to do is to get as close to the original idea with the interpretation.[16]

Joe's original improvisation for "The Peasant" was about two-and-a-half minutes long, so he added a middle section on which he utilized a new addition to his keyboard rig to produce the sound of a pan flute. Just before the tour commenced, he acquired an E-mu Emulator, one of the first "affordable" digital samplers (original price tag: $10,000, about $25,000 in 2020). Unlike synthesizers, which create sound using oscillators and filters, the Emulator played digital recordings of other musical instruments or sound sources, not unlike a drum machine. More crucially, the Emulator allowed musicians to record their own samples, which were stored on five-inch floppy disks. For the pan flute, all Joe had to do was record one note of a given pitch into the Emulator and—voilà—he could play it up and down the keyboard. Not only that, the Emulator offered eight-voice polyphony, so Joe had an entire section of pan flutes at his command.

As soon as Joe got the Emulator, he tried out the samples that came with it, delighting in the realistic sounds. But he immediately wanted to make his own, so he summoned Jim Swanson to Pasadena. "We had a sample day at Joe's house," Swanson recalled. "We had the big kalimbas, some guitars he had. We were pulling stuff off the walls, all those ethnic percussion instruments. It was a sample safari, my friend. What really blew his mind was on one of the stock disks there was a keyboard split, so he was improvising into the sequencer with the Emulator, playing this piece, and I said, 'Now watch this, Joe,' and I threw in a drum-set disk. 'Wait a minute, this is a melody part played by drums? Whoa! I can do that?!' Every time we tried something new, he'd say, 'I can do that?'" They got twenty or thirty samples made, including the pan flute that Joe's father had given him.[17]

Incorporating the Emulator into live performance was tricky because only two samples could be loaded into the machine at a time, and they were split between the lower and upper ranges of the keyboard. Furthermore, the floppy disks also stored just two samples and it took several seconds to load them. "You have to pre-think your programs and put the disks in order," Joe said of the logistics. "Jim Swanson might run out on stage when the concentration is on the bass player and put a disk in. You can also load a couple of sounds, take the disk out, and put in the next disk. The first sounds remain in there as long as you don't hit the record button for the next sounds; one disk is ready to be loaded while the other is playing. That way I can keep ahead of it."[18]

In concert, "The Peasant" was followed by the second of Joe's new tunes, the irresistibly funky "D Flat Waltz." It is arguably the quintessential track of the Hakim-Bailey era. Victor called it "by far one of the best Joe Zawinul compositions ever," and his and Omar's playing "one of the best rhythm section performances ever."[19] At over eleven minutes in length, and with little harmonic movement, Bailey proved his mettle when it came to maintaining a groove while improvising along the way. "The key is to provide the bass function, but make it move; it's a feel thing," he later explained to Chris Jisi for *Bass Player* magazine. "Rhythmically, I make sure I'm always riding the drums—locking into a part of the kit or a pattern. Melodically, I keep my phrases and fills short, so the part remains in groove mode. And overall, I'm listening to the rest of the band for inspiration and material to react to."[20]

Omar found the tune similarly stimulating. "One of the things Joe liked is the funky waltz, and 'D Flat Waltz' is another chapter in the Zawinul funky waltz concept. It made sense to me. That rhythm was just something that I came up with, just feeling what he was doing. I always tell people Weather Report was one of the few gigs in my career that I've had to use everything that I knew about the instrument to make it happen. I had to play with the facility of a jazz musician, but with the power of a rock drummer, because Joe wanted to hear that impact, and he liked it. And so, as a result, I was trying to blend the funk and the bebop so to speak."[21]

Live, "D Flat Waltz" was also a feature for Wayne's tenor, and anyone who claimed that he wasn't playing much in those days just wasn't paying attention. Then there was the gamesmanship with the dynamics, where the band repeated the vamp several times, each more quietly than before, with the stage lights dimming right along with the sound. And just when the music was barely a whisper, it exploded for the climactic finale. "That whole thing of it getting softer and softer happened on a gig," Hakim explained. "Joe and I were making these faces, and sinking lower into the chairs. We were on stage laughing—cracking up—until it was real soft. One night, we did it about eight times and just kept getting softer. The humor of it was to come back full-out again, and to hear somebody scream in the audience."[22]

The third new tune they played was "Blue Sound–Note 3," a deliberately paced ballad in which Wayne spends the first minute demonstrating how to emote on the same two-note melody. (One writer observed that he'd pay the price of a ticket to hear Wayne play just *one*.) At the time, Joe liked to boast that with Wayne's sampled saxes in his Emulator, he could reproduce his partner's notes "more perfect than he can play it himself."[23] Perhaps Zawinul was overly enamored with his new toy, because one need only listen to Wayne's solo on "Blue Sound," with its honks and squeals and slurs—or any of Wayne's solos, for that matter—to realize that Wayne's expressive powers couldn't be captured in a single "perfect" sample, let alone one played from a keyboard.

That aside, Joe's solo is particularly unusual, with all manner of strange sounds emanating from his keyboards, like acoustic lightning bolts. He did this by setting up a bank of bizarre "out" (non-musical) patches on his Prophet-5; as he played the keyboard he would hit the eight program-select buttons, triggering abrupt timbre changes while holding down notes. In effect, he was playing the program buttons instead of the keys.[24]

•

Along with the Emulator, Joe added a Rhodes Chroma synthesizer to his rig. It was originally developed by ARP as its belated answer to the Prophet-5, but the synth maker filed bankruptcy before completing it and CBS bought the design and hired the engineering team for its Rhodes division. When the instrument came out in 1983, it quickly became a favorite of Zawinul's, owing to its rich polyphonic sound and a velocity-sensitive keyboard whose action was more akin to a piano than an organ. However, like a lot of instruments in those days, the Chroma suffered when subjected to the rigors of the road.[25]

So it was that Weather Report's 1983 tour of Japan is in part remembered for the Chroma self-destructing midway through the first concert. "The Chroma was notorious for a bad power supply and it literally went up in smoke," Jim Swanson recalled. "Smoke was coming out the back and Joe was waving at me and pointing. I said, 'Well, turn it off! Don't use that one!' So he had to shift everything and play all the Chroma parts on different keyboards. Afterwards, we quickly got ahold of CBS and said, 'Look, Joe's an endorser. You need to get us one of these things here *now*,' and they overnighted one from California. But when it showed up I realized, wait a minute, I don't have a backup for those patches. What a dummy. So I took the processor board out of the old one—it had a battery on it for the memory—and stuck it into the new Chroma, and sure enough, there were all the patches. The next day I bought a cassette data recorder and downloaded all of the Prophet and Chroma sounds so that I had a backup. This was the early eighties; that's the way it was done: cassette data dumps."[26]

When the band reached Osaka, Joe arranged to have a recording truck on hand. "There were some issues with getting into the studio in time to deliver the *Domino Theory* record to Columbia, and I remember there was a little bit of a panic," Omar Hakim recalls. "I remember the manager saying, 'You guys can't say that this is live, because we're not supposed to turn in a live album by the contract; we're supposed to turn in a studio album.' So there was a weird little issue there, but Joe and Wayne were like, 'We've got to get this done, so we're going to pull a truck up and we're just going to record this live,' because there was no other

Weather Report performing at the Live Under the Sky Jazz Festival in 1983. Photo: Shigeru Uchiyama / Whisper Not Photo Factory.

time and no other way to finish the tour, mix it, and turn it in on time as a studio recording."[27]

Three tracks from Osaka made it onto *Domino Theory*: "The Peasant," "D Flat Waltz," and "Blue Sound–Note 3." Of course, this wasn't enough for an LP, so once again Joe raided his oft-delayed solo album, including a tune he had kicking around for a few years. "Can It Be Done" is a sentimental ballad written by Willie Tee, Joe's old friend from New Orleans.[28] Sung by Carl Anderson, who was best known for his role as Judas in the rock opera *Jesus Christ Superstar*, the lyrics appealed to Joe's conviction that his own music and sound palette were unique. As *Domino Theory*'s album opener, it surely confounded Weather Report fans, but Joe had high hopes for it, telling *Billboard* that he felt it could be a number one pop song.[29] He permeated the track with unfamiliar synthesizer textures. If this was going to be a pop tune, it was going to be done Zawinul-style.

Another tune that was originally slated for Joe's solo album is the title track. It's basically Joe jamming against his outrageous (as Omar Hakim described them) programmed drum machine parts, which Hakim later augmented with overdubs. Wayne also brought in a couple of tunes. "Predator" is a medium-tempo feature for his tenor, augmented by Joe's synthesized countermelodies and a herky-jerky groove underneath. "Wayne hears those kinds of rhythms," Hakim said. "He handed me a little slip of paper one day and said, 'Check this out.' It had a different beat than [what was recorded] actually; I changed it up a little. Wayne will give you an outline and just say play what you hear. . . . So we were in the studio jamming and we struck up this groove."[30]

The introduction features some bass slapping by Victor—"the only tune in the history of Weather Report where the bass player plays with some slapping," he noted. "And that bass line was the bass line to one of my songs. After I played it, I tried to give it up, but Joe wanted to use it. I wanted to play something else, because I'm like, 'Well, now I can't use it in my song.'" Victor was also struck by Wayne's juxtaposition of harmony and melody in this tune. "The most incredible thing I can tell you about that song is when it gets to the melody, my bass line is in D flat, but the melody is in G. How Wayne did that, to this day I still don't know."[31]

Wayne's other tune is "Swamp Cabbage," with its signature "yoo-hoo" sound effect. "Those sounds were taken from a Fairlight," Jim Swanson said. (The Fairlight CMI was a forerunner to the Emulator and preceded it to market, but was considerably pricier and not suitable for the road.) "I was working at Fairlight and I took one up to Joe's house. We started running through all the sounds, and he said, 'I gotta get this.' So we rolled a 24-track tape, and we recorded sounds out of the Fairlight and dumped them back into the Emulator. So the 'yoo-hoos' and the helicopter coming out of the swamp at the end, that's where those came from."[32]

•

Like its predecessor, *Domino Theory* was greeted by mixed reviews, and given the held-over lineup, a sense of déjà vu. Leonard Feather described it as a "four-star effort—not the group's crowning achievement, but guaranteed to reveal new and intriguing aspects with every replaying."[33] Some critics, such as J. D. Considine, found much to admire in the album's attention to sonic detail and cohesive ensemble playing, while putting it in historical perspective. "Over the years, the band has appeared in various guises, ranging from headstrong avant-gardists to latent pop stars. Yet each successive musical identity seemed less a matter of evolution or growth than a sort of aesthetic restlessness. After fourteen years and a dozen albums, Weather Report still seems to be discovering itself anew."[34]

Although Wayne blew hard on tour and contributed two compositions to the album, he continued to be quizzed by journalists about his diminished role in the band. "I'm very involved with the life of the band," he protested in an interview with the *Milwaukee Sentinel.* "This means quite a few things apart from music, especially in the '80s—like business. You can't just take the afternoon off and do an album of your own. Joe and I will probably go out and do other things on our own. But whatever we do, Weather Report lays the groundwork and the foundation and the spirit for that."[35]

Wayne once again referred to his solo album, which he maintained was "a year or two away." He had also begun writing again, telling a reporter, "I've got a big, fat book of music that I've written, but it's not specifically Weather Report music. It could probably be orchestrated for some other element."[36] Joe had his mind elsewhere, too. "If you take your profession seriously, it takes so much to put in. To make one good record a year is a killer, and touring and being a family person and all, it takes something, you know. So, I have all this music already on tape. It's just for me to maybe get a year where I don't tour and where I don't necessarily have to come up with a Weather Report record or whatever. I will be able to do that. It will be no problem."[37]

If it sounded like they were getting the itch to do other things, it's because they were.

20 Sportin' Life

The last album you do for Columbia, really do something nice —
crazy but nice so you can go on and make your moves.

— Joe Ruffalo

FOR WEATHER REPORT, 1984 BEGAN MUCH AS 1983 DID, with a spring album release and a concurrent tour. The one difference was a change in personnel precipitated by José Rossy's departure. To fill his chair, Wayne initially brought in Frank Colón, a percussionist who grew up in Puerto Rico and had recorded with Milton Nascimento, among others. Colón rehearsed with the band for two weeks, but ultimately things didn't work out. As he later put it, "To this day, I'm still tight with Wayne, but they had two leaders. I didn't get along with one."[1]

With the U.S. tour about to commence (advanced advertising already included Colón's name), Joe and Wayne needed to act quickly. Omar Hakim and Victor Bailey were enthusiastic about another percussionist by the name of Mino Cinélu. At the time, Cinélu was best known for his work with Miles Davis, with whom he had toured since 1981. New York was Cinélu's home base and he frequently appeared in the clubs there. Omar and Victor heard him one night at Mikell's and were so taken by his playing that they called Joe from the club's payphone, holding out the receiver in the hopes that Zawinul would hear him, too. "You gotta hire this guy!" they raved.[2]

A self-taught musician, Cinélu was born and raised in the suburbs of Paris. His mother hailed from France, while his father was born in Martinique, a French island in the Caribbean. Music filled the two-room flat that Mino shared with his parents and older brothers, and he took up guitar at an early age. After leaving home just shy of his eighteenth birthday, Mino quickly became an in-demand session player, proficient on guitar, drums, and percussion. A year later he came to the United States for the first time, backing the Haitian singer, actress, and activist

Mino Cinélu at the 1984 Playboy Jazz Festival. Photo: © www.markbrady.com.

Toto Bissainthe at Carnegie Hall. While in town, he met Ron Carter, who in turn introduced him to a raft of other New York musicians. Cinélu left determined to come back, which he did in 1979. Two years later, Miles Davis tapped him for his comeback band.

Joe called Cinélu on the eve of Weather Report's tour. "I saw you at the Hollywood Bowl with Miles," he told him. "You were the only one playing!"[3] Fortunately, Miles was off the road at the time, so Mino was available. He arrived in L.A. just in time to participate in Weather Report's first music video, which featured an edited version of "Swamp Cabbage." It was an interesting choice, if for no other reason than that it wasn't one of Joe's compositions. But it's likely that the most important criterion was a tune that could fit within the three-and-a-half minute format that was typical of music videos at the time. So the band spent several hours in a fog-filled Hollywood soundstage, lip-syncing fourteen takes of the song. "I had to do a lot of remembering so I could look halfway like I did the record," Omar quipped.[4]

Four hours of tape and seventy-two camera shots were recorded before calling it a wrap so that Joe could leave in time to celebrate his wedding anniversary with Maxine later that evening.[5] The footage was combined with what were then considered innovative computer-generated effects, such as motion flare from Victor's bass strings, animated halos emanating from the musicians' heads and bodies, and compositing that makes them look like they are playing in a literal swamp. At one point, Wayne is even superimposed onto Omar's bass drum head. It all must have seemed cutting edge at the time, but it looks pretty hokey now.[6]

This wasn't the only video that Weather Report was a part of that year, although in the second case it was passive involvement. In the fall, Sony released a short film on VHS and Beta videocassettes titled *The Evolutionary Spiral*. It was an unusual and innovative piece for its time, wedding film footage and computer-generated animation around the theme of planetary evolution, with the first side of *Procession* serving as the soundtrack. While Sony touted it as the first of its kind for the home video market, it was originally made for a live event hosted by a northern European advertising agency.[7]

Meanwhile, with the "Swamp Cabbage" taping behind them, the band set off for what would be its final performances in the United States, following the well-trod path from California to the East Coast and back. "I joined the band with no rehearsals," Cinélu recalled. "We did the video for 'Swamp Cabbage' for the whole afternoon, so I knew that tune pretty well. And then on the tour bus Joe showed me the charts and Omar explained things to me, and it was just overwhelming. Joe's charts—we are talking about sixteen parts of percussion, it was not even a score. I don't even know what it was. So he said he would give me cues for this and that and whatever. I told Joe before the first gig, 'Listen, I'm going to mess up, but I'm not gonna be shy about it,' and he kind of liked that. So sometimes they stopped, and guess what? I was still playing—so another five seconds, eight seconds of solo. And I'm looking at Joe, and he couldn't help laughing. And so little by little we learned about each other. I had great affinity with Joe. We both came from Europe. We both had to fight our way through. We had to play. Nobody cut us slack, so we had that in common."[8]

Mino added just the right touches of color to what was already a full rhythmic palette. His contributions sound entirely organic, but were the result of a thoughtful process. "Omar was so incredible, I thought the band didn't even need a percussionist," Cinélu later said. "He's somebody who's got a vast and copious vocabulary, and so much energy. I didn't see how I could do anything with such a drummer, so I had to adapt. I started to learn his style because I'm a drummer as well. So I found my way around. I changed my style totally, which I like to do, actually. I try to adapt on each project."[9]

This went beyond the obvious of not stepping on each other's playing. Cinélu built a percussion kit whose sounds complemented Omar's in terms of frequency range and timbre. If Omar had a snare drum of a certain size, Mino picked one of a different size; the same for his cymbals. He incorporated ethnic instruments, such as the udu, an African pottery drum capable of producing a variety of sounds

Weather Report performs at the 1984 Playboy Jazz Festival. Photo: © www.markbrady.com.

and pitches, while also embracing the new electronic drums just hitting the market. It was a kit that seemed to grow daily. "The more the evolution of the music, the more I hear sounds," Mino said. "So I had total carte blanche with Miles, with Weather Report, and most bands. They know I'll come with ideas. I dwarfed Omar's drums with electronics, acoustics. I had hand drums. I had drums with sticks. I had kicks. I had bells on the foot. I was out of his range, complementing his range totally."[10]

In concert, the band kicked things off with "D Flat Waltz" and "Procession," after which "Swamp Cabbage" and "Two Lines" received lengthy workouts. The latter included an extended bass solo in which Victor copped a few tricks from Jaco's bag, such as accompanying himself using a digital delay unit. But Bailey definitely put his own stamp on it, interspersing harmony chords with nimble melodic lines, backed by Cinélu on percussion. Only the most zealous Pastorius fans would deny that these solos were virtuoso performances. After "Two Lines," things cooled off with "Blue Sound–Note 3," while "Predator" highlighted Cinélu's lightning-fast hands on congas, as well as his facility with the new Simmons electronic drums, all capped by a stunning triangle solo.

Some tunes on the set list were in their second or third year in the live book, so the band avoided boredom by switching up forms, relying on improvisational exploration. Carl Anderson joined them for many U.S. dates, coming on stage to sing "Can It Be Done," and then returning for the encore rendition of "Where the Moon Goes," which included an eerie-sounding vocoder band introduction.

After a return trip to the Playboy Jazz Festival in June, the band hit the European festival circuit. When they got back, the Summer Olympics was underway in Los Angeles, and Weather Report performed for the Olympic Village at UCLA. Joe had originally wanted to be part of the opening ceremony with Wayne, but he was excited to do this, reminding everybody, "We're at the Olympics, man!"[11] But few in the village took notice. "There might have been twenty-five people when we played," Victor recalled. "I think most of the athletes weren't really there to go and hear music. They were training, and there were not that many people, just sitting on the lawn in front of the stage. Which was not a problem. I'm honored to say that I was at the Olympics, you know."[12]

Several weeks later, Weather Report made its final tour of Japan. By this time, Joe and Wayne's duets were exquisite ten- to fifteen-minute affairs, semi-symphonic in scope, improvised but seemingly organized in movements, running the gamut from avant-garde abstraction to classical romanticism. With Joe's synthesizer arsenal more capable than ever, he could single-handedly emulate an entire orchestra, earthbound or otherwise, with long, bell-like tones that seemed to stretch while they rang, a string section here, brass there, then together, and even timpani pounding forth from his keyboards. For his part, Wayne relied on his singular, gorgeous tone on soprano to produce staccato bursts, flighty melodic leaps, and flutters that morphed into long, pensive lines.

Nearly all the duets of this era are lost to history, but one was preserved on the video release, *Japan Domino Theory: Weather Report Live in Tokyo*. It is an extraordinary performance, and when it concludes even Joe and Wayne appear taken aback by what transpired. Wayne cocks his head to the side, as if knowing that he had just taken part in something transcendent, but too shy to publicly acknowledge it. Glancing back at Joe with a grin that he is ultimately unable to contain, Wayne walks over to him, where they exchange words and a handshake. It was one of Weather Report's last performances, and judging by their body language, Joe and Wayne both seemed to know it.

•

Between tours, the band got in a few days of studio time for their next album, *Sportin' Life*. They cut two tracks on the first day: "Corner Pocket" and "Pearl on the Half-Shell." The former leads off the album and sets the tone for what is a funky, upbeat record. Certainly the rhythm section enjoyed this tune. "'Corner Pocket' was one that me and Omar really loved," Victor recalled. "It's just a groove—that funk and R&B part and putting down a groove like that. That was what Omar and I did. We loved that."[13]

On the record, "Corner Pocket" opens with an odd, spoken tongue-twister introduction, which Joe later added in an overdubbing session using a small chorus of singers. "I have no idea what that is, but I always loved that," Bailey remarked. "Maybe the singers were going through something and sped up? Whatever it is, it was amazing. I remember hearing that for the first time—that wasn't there when

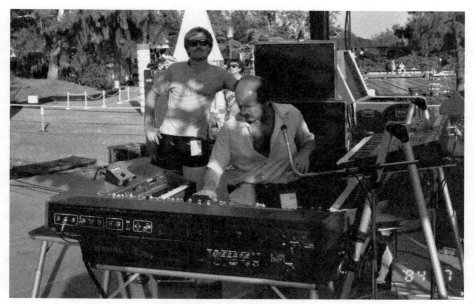

Jim Swanson wth Joe at sound check for the Olympic Village show in 1984. Photo: Jim Swanson—Zawinul's Keyboard Engineer.

we did our part."[14] To American ears, at least, it sounds liked gibberish—what Joe called vocal bebopping—but it was actually a word game he played as a child. The saying roughly translates to, "There's a fly sitting on the wall, and I have to catch this fly." This explains why there is a buzzing sound in the introduction, which is carried through to the rest of the tune. The humor—the game of it—is that when the phrase is repeated, all the vowels are replaced with another vowel.

Whatever it was, it was a challenge for the singers—both the introduction and the syncopated ensemble passages elsewhere in tune, which *were* vocal bebopping. Bobby McFerrin was among the foursome who sang it. At the time, he had just released his second album, *The Voice*, firmly establishing him as a singular artist with exceptional range and improvisational skills. Working with him intrigued Joe and vice versa.

"There were four singers who had never sung together before," McFerrin told Brian Glasser. "It was a real task, because of course we all approached it in a very different way and we were working on these incredible lyrics or sounds or language that had been written. I was a big fan of Weather Report, and one of the things I liked about Zawinul's writing was it had a very Third World feel, like in this song. He integrates those sounds and feelings into his music. So we worked steadily for hours. I remember that the four of us couldn't quite get it together, so he had me do it alone, and then I guess he had the others do it alone, too."[15]

The other tune recorded on the first day was Wayne's "Pearl on the Half-Shell," which leads off the flip side of the LP. By this time, Wayne had gotten a Yamaha portable keyboard, which he partially credited for reinvigorating his writing process. Not only did its sounds cause Wayne to think of ideas, it was small enough to take on the road, allowing him to compose on airplanes and in hotel rooms. As a result, the songs were "just pouring out of me," he said not long after *Sportin' Life* was released.[16] "Pearl on the Half-Shell" was one of the tunes Wayne wrote on the Yamaha, playing the melodies slowly to make up for his limited keyboard chops. In the studio, the band brought it up to tempo and Omar and Victor provided a funky bottom with "a little more groove," as Bailey put it.[17]

With those two tunes in the can, the band went out to dinner. When they returned to the studio later that evening, Victor picked up his bass and started fiddling around with Marvin Gaye's song "What's Going On." "That was on my original demo that I sent to Joe," he said. "I had a whole arrangement where I played the melody, and I did a scat solo with the fretless bass, which is one of the things Joe and Wayne were most impressed by on my demo. So I started playing that melody and Joe said, 'Let's do that.'"[18]

Gaye died while the band was on tour, so that might also have had something to do with it. "Joe loved Marvin Gaye," Omar said. "He really respected him. I remember bringing Marvin Gaye's new album, *Midnight Love*, on the tour bus. It was his last album. There was a ballad on that record that Joe liked, and he asked me to play it over and over again on the bus. I could see why he dug it, the way the harmony was moving in it. Joe dug that. But when you think about it, Joe dug R&B and he was a great writer of commercial music."[19]

Whatever the inspiration, it was an unusual choice for a Weather Report album. Only twice before had the band covered a tune from an outside composer, one of which was by the peerless Duke Ellington while the other had never been recorded before. But "What's Going On" was a multimillion-selling R&B song that virtually every Weather Report fan would have heard on the radio. Nevertheless, the band approached it in its own way, with a relaxed but funky feel while Joe played the melody using a timbre somewhat reminiscent of an accordion (as he often did). The results are entirely satisfying.

The rest of the tracks on *Sportin' Life* were made without the full band on hand. Mino Cinélu's tune "Confians" is an example, with Cinélu overdubbing parts on guitar, bass, and drums. "Joe asked me if I had any music, and I had a demo cassette of 'Confians,'" Mino recalled. Joe listened to it and told Mino that he wanted to record it, asking for a copy of the tape so he could transcribe the keyboard part. Mino wanted to play those parts himself, but Joe wouldn't have it. "Nobody plays keyboards but me in this group," he insisted.[20]

"So those flute things are my lines," Mino said. "Victor was not there when we started to work on it, so I grabbed his bass—it was an old Fender jazz bass, which at the time was not in great condition—and I just did a guide bass. The bass line

Joe's keyboard rig in 1984. At top: ARP Quadra, Prophet-5, the external keyboard for the Oberheim Eight Voice, and below that, Jim Swanson's Oberheim "OB-Brain Box," which contained the keyboard input panel and electronics, programmer, and two mini sequencers. The small box next to the Prophet 5 is an external modulation source for the Quadra. At right: Auxiliary keyboard for the Korg VC-10 Vocoder, Prophet T-8, and Rhodes Chroma. At bottom: the E-mu Emulator, underneath which is a cabinet containing the rest of the Oberheim Eight Voice. Hidden behind the stage monitor at left is the vocoder. Also note the array of foot pedals, which Joe used to control the volume of each keyboard. Photo: Jim Swanson—Zawinul's Keyboard Engineer.

was simple and I was fine with it, but I thought I could have done a better job with my own bass. But when I came back to do a better bass line, Joe said, 'I like it, leave it alone.' And Omar wasn't there, so I did the drums on the tune as well, and the guitar. Afterwards, when Omar and Victor came, they did the choir in the background."[21]

"Confians" is a deeply personal song to Mino, drawing from his childhood experience. By his own admission, he grew up under difficult circumstances and found refuge in music. "Without music I would not be here," he said. "Music was my everything—my confidant, my soul mate, my guide."[22] The lyrics "came in one night. They're written in Creole from Martinique, with a few expressions from Guadeloupe and a few words from Haiti. The lyrics are really about me following a dream. For so many years, I was crushed by my folks. I had to leave. I left home for Paris with my drums and my bongos and my guitar. I used to play in the streets. I used to steal food. I didn't always sleep on a bed. I expressed all of who I was through the music. Those lyrics talk about the struggle."[23]

"Face on the Barroom Floor" is a poignant duet written by Wayne in the

tradition of "Blackthorn Rose" and "Five Short Stories." It has one of those evocative titles that he often came up with. Some were from his fertile imagination,
while others, like *I Sing the Body Electric*, were co-opted from other works. That
seems to be the case here, as "The Face on the Barroom Floor" is the title of a late
nineteenth century poem written by Hugh Antoine d'Arcy. It tells the tale of a
painter who loses his lover to one of his portrait subjects—a story of sadness that
is rendered in Wayne's music. The poem subsequently inspired a country song; a
well-known painting in Central City, Colorado; and even a chamber opera.

As for the music, after Joe and Wayne recorded to a click track, Zawinul added the synthesizer accompaniment based on Wayne's manuscript. "He had the
song written out so neatly," Joe told Josef Woodard. "I took a piece of paper and
orchestrated it for me. I hadn't changed a single note of what he had written. I
looked at the way the melodies were running. He came back in about an hour,
and the piece was like you hear it on the record."[24]

The balance of the album was done at Joe's home studio, which benefited from
an upgrade in technology in the form of MIDI-equipped keyboards. MIDI (an
acronym for Musical Instrument Digital Interface) was introduced to the public
at the January 1983 NAMM show, the "golden spike moment" occurring when
keyboards from Roland and Sequential Circuits were connected via a cable and
played each other's sounds. Up to that point, the various synth makers each developed their own schemes for connecting their devices, but no standard existed for
general interoperability. Despite some grumbling from the various manufacturers
who were naturally invested in their own technologies, MIDI quickly established
itself, and virtually all keyboards released from 1983 on were MIDI-equipped.
Soon, personal computers also came with MIDI interfaces, leading to a wave of
new software and hardware products that changed the face of music production.

It took some time for Joe to acquire MIDI technology. In a lengthy interview
that appeared in the March 1984 issue of *Keyboard* magazine, Zawinul didn't
acknowledge MIDI at all, save for Jim Swanson mentioning the possibility that
Joe might get his two Prophet-5s retrofitted with MIDI so they could trigger each
other. But just months later, Joe's options had expanded considerably. Either he
had instruments that came with MIDI built-in, such as the new Prophet T8, or he
was able to get them talking to each other via upgrades or aftermarket adapters.
Compared to the way things had been before, it was almost like another world.
Zawinul likened MIDI to "the gunshot at the start of a 100-yard dash" in terms
of unleashing new creative options.[25] Swanson was a big help to Joe, building a
MIDI adapter for the Emulator and a custom switchbox that let Zawinul control
the connections between devices from a central point.

"Ice-Pick Willy," Hot Cargo," and "Indiscretions" were among the first batch
of tunes Joe played with his MIDI setup. Instead of overdubbing various parts

The timestamp on the photo indicates that Joe and Wayne are celebrating Zawinul's fifty-second birthday, somewhere in Europe. Photo: Jim Swanson—Zawinul's Keyboard Engineer.

on top of each other via multitracking, Joe would set up rhythms on his drum machines and jam along, playing everything live in one shot, layering the sounds of multiple synthesizers played from a single keyboard. Afterward, Wayne, Bobby McFerrin, and the other musicians overdubbed additional parts, but Joe didn't need to. Furthermore, by capturing his playing in a MIDI sequencer, Joe could then feed a MIDI track into an entirely different device from which it was played. For instance, on "Ice-Pick Willy" he played his MIDI-recorded melody into the Emulator, which was loaded with a drum set disk. The result was Joe's melody line rendered through orchestrated percussion.

It's clear that Joe was taking the composition-by-improvisation method further than ever. With MIDI and a multitude of drum machines, sequencers, and interconnected keyboards, he had largely become self-sufficient. The next question was, could he do it all in real time in front of an audience? It wouldn't be long before he would seek to find out.

•

Sportin' Life was dressed in a colorful art deco–style jacket depicting what appear to be chic globetrotting tourists. It conveyed a sense of exoticism, that this music has international appeal. Even though several tunes on *Sportin' Life* are largely of Joe's creation (as opposed to the full band), there is still a satisfying cohesiveness about the album. It was Joe's most successful blend to date of drum machines, sequencers, and live instruments. "It was a very, very organic album,"

Cinélu said. "A lot of things were played live, and then a lot of overdubs after that. I think it was sometimes an orgy of overdubs and machines, but at some point, mixed down, it's part of the sound, and it's an organic chaos, if you want."[26]

The reviews were strong, as well. *Down Beat* called it the band's finest effort of the post-Jaco era. Even those who dismissed *Procession* and *Domino Theory* found much to like. Given such a strong effort, *Sportin' Life* would have been a fitting way to conclude Weather Report, whose Columbia contract ended with this record. As Joe Ruffalo put it to Zawinul, "The last album you do for Columbia, really do something nice—crazy but nice so you can go on and make your moves."[27] Joe and Wayne must have felt like they had accomplished that. If only things were that simple.

21 This Is This

With or without Wayne, with or without Columbia, we're gonna keep going.

—Joe Zawinul

IN MARCH 1985, JOE AND WAYNE HOSTED THE PRESS for a round of interviews at the Columbia Records offices in the Century City district of Los Angeles. The purpose was to promote *Sportin' Life*, which was just reaching record stores. But the album's release was overshadowed by the news that Weather Report was on indefinite hiatus. "We're not going to tour with the band this year," Joe confirmed. "We're putting it on the back burner for a while."[1]

After years of talking about their desire to work on individual projects, Joe and Wayne planned to do just that. Of course, precipitating this decision was their expiring Columbia contract, which freed them from the annual grind that had defined their musical lives for the past fourteen years. Wayne was already in the studio making *Atlantis*, his first album since 1975's *Native Dancer*, and Joe was anxious to do likewise. In the meantime, Zawinul insisted that Weather Report would remain an ongoing entity. "The group will reorganize later, but it's important for the public to get a break from it for a while, and important for us to make our separate statements. Now is the time; if we don't do it now we may never do it!"[2]

After finishing *Atlantis*, Wayne spent several weeks in Paris filming *'Round Midnight*, a theatrical movie directed by Bertrand Tavernier. The plot revolves around a fictional American jazz musician played by Dexter Gordon, loosely based on Charlie Parker and Bud Powell. The centrality of jazz to the story demanded that Tavernier use real musicians instead of actors, which greatly enhances the authenticity of the film. Despite the endless waiting between takes, Wayne had a great time getting to know Gordon better and hanging out with old bandmates

Zawinul performing his one-man show at the Warfield Theatre in San Francisco, May 24, 1986. Photo: © www.markbrady.com.

Ron Carter, Herbie Hancock and Tony Williams.

Joe took his one-man act to Europe—"just me, my four synthesizers, four drum machines, and a bunch of foot pedals."[3] It was the biggest challenge—and greatest risk—of his career. But he felt that technology had reached the point where he could single-handedly fulfill all the roles his music demanded by triggering pre-programmed drum and sequenced patterns while playing the rest on his synthesizers. The difficulty of the task is illustrated in a video from 1985, in which Joe rehearses a solo version of "Corner Pocket" while struggling to trigger the drum machine program changes at the correct moment—a performance in itself—and mixing it all with his feet.[4] It required a lot of memorization and practice, not to mention an extraordinary balance of left- and right-brain thinking.

Joe's solo record, *Dialects*, released in 1986, still stands as a tour de force of electronic music—technically breathtaking and original. But when he took the music to the stage, he battled the public's perception of his performance. Audiences were naturally skeptical of the machines, apt to believe that Zawinul was merely cueing prerecorded music. He later said that audiences appreciated his efforts when they could see his hands, but were skeptical when they could not. "People simply didn't believe what I was doing," he recalled. "I was booed one time in Berlin. I mean, if I wasn't a strong person as I am, I would have just given up or left the bandstand."[5]

The reviews were not kind. One journalist called Joe's concert "the disappointment" of Debrecen Jazz Days, a festival in Hungary. "The master seemed somewhat lost in making the instruments work properly; often it took long minutes to find every tone, rhythmic pattern, and sound volume needed for an improvisation. After a while it became boring witnessing Zawinul's heroic but rarely successful effort at coordinating music and technology."[6] And this was a show in which everything worked. One concert never got off the ground because of equipment malfunctions, while another was abruptly canceled minutes after it began when a critical piece of gear broke down.

October brought the release of *Atlantis* and the first concerts of Wayne's newly formed quartet, which included Tom Canning on keyboards, Gary Willis on electric bass, and Tom Brechtlein on drums. Booked into small clubs and absent the touring trappings to which Weather Report was accustomed, these were nevertheless among the most anticipated jazz shows of the year. Remarkably, it was the first time in Wayne's career that he led a band of his own, and the news sent a buzz through the jazz world.

While the quartet offered plenty of space for Wayne to blow, the many critics and fans hoping to hear a resumption of Wayne's 1960s Blue Note sound were disappointed. *Atlantis* is carefully composed and orchestrated, with no room for improvisation, even from Wayne—a jazz version of chamber music. In concert, Wayne played the material with greater freedom than on record, but he largely ignored his older compositions. Furthermore, Wayne didn't shed himself of electronic instrumentation, nor did he play much tenor. One could almost hear the buzz fizzle into an exasperated sigh.

Instead, those same critics and fans found what they were looking for in trumpeter Wynton Marsalis. Since his Columbia debut in 1982, the charismatic twenty-four-year-old had become a star in both classical and jazz circles, thanks to his virtuosic technique and Columbia's marketing machine. His new offering, *Black Codes (From the Underground)*, was released at around the same time as *Atlantis* and won two Grammys to go along with the four Marsalis had previously received. (Two were for his classical performances, making him the first musician to win simultaneous jazz and classical Grammy Awards.) Marsalis was, and is, a vehement jazz traditionalist whose own band was strongly derivative of Miles Davis's second great quintet. The liner notes to *Black Codes* even cite Wayne as one of the composers upon which Marsalis hoped to pattern himself.

Given the debt to Wayne that Marsalis and his band expressed both verbally and musically, it was inevitable that *Black Codes* and *Atlantis* would be compared, sometimes in joint reviews. Wayne, having failed to live up to his own past in the eyes of his critics, found himself in the position of having Marsalis and the so-called Young Lions do it for him. As one writer put it, "It's ironic that while members of the Marsalis band acknowledge the immense influence of the 1960s-style Shorter on their music, Shorter himself seems to be spinning his wheels."[7] At the same time, the revived Blue Note label reissued some of Wayne's classic albums of the sixties, so he also wound up competing with himself.

Wayne took the criticism stoically and forged ahead with a series of concerts in Europe later that fall. He was in Poland when he received the devastating news that his daughter, Iska, suffered a grand mal seizure and died.[8] Wayne played as planned, drawing strength from the audience. "When I went on stage that night, it became a warm, fireside sort of thing," he said. "It was like [the crowd] was my family. I'll never forget that."[9] Wayne chose to finish the tour and didn't return to Los Angeles for the funeral, which took place a week later. Instead, Herbie Hancock stood in for him.

Struggling to find meaning in Iska's death, Wayne took solace in his practice of Buddhism, which holds that life does not begin at birth nor end at death. "In the last weeks before she died, she was laughing and saying something over and over," he said. "She was trying to say goodbye to us and she was happy about it. She knew that her mission was complete." Much as Iska's birth hastened Wayne's break from Miles, her death reinforced his plans to move forward without Weather Report. He said he would never forget that Iska taught him that it's "life first and music second," but now it was time to reestablish himself as a leading voice of jazz. "All those years when you wondered about Wayne Shorter not stepping out and laying back in the background? Well, I was tilling the soil."[10]

•

Whether or not Wayne and Joe had plans of ever regrouping again, their hand was forced by Columbia, which exercised its option for one more album. According to Joe, the label did so on the last possible day in which it was contractually entitled.[11] This was not welcome news for either man, as they were heavily involved in their own projects. Wayne was booked into December, so when Joe got back to Los Angeles after his fall trip to Europe, the task fell to him to get the record done. Weather Report hadn't existed for over a year, and Corvalan-Condliffe scrambled to assemble a band and studio schedule for the end-of-year holiday season. Victor Bailey and Mino Cinélu were available, but Omar Hakim was on tour with Sting. So Joe called on Peter Erskine, who welcomed the opportunity even as he wondered what happened with Omar.

After his four-year separation from Zawinul, Erskine found working with Joe to be "a much more pleasant task" than before.[12] Peter was still living in New York, so he flew out to L.A. a couple of times, staying at a short-term apartment complex not far from Sound Castle Studios, where the recording took place. As it developed, Erskine was instrumental enough in getting the album done that he was rewarded with a co-producer credit (though it didn't come with any financial remuneration). "Whatever ideas I had, I was trying to help Joe realize some of what he was doing," Erskine said, downplaying his role. "And I seem to recall I made some helpful suggestions, but I was just kind of there. But it was nice to get a co-producer credit. I thought that was kind of cool."[13]

Joe also knew that he needed a substitute for Wayne, who had no music to offer and, save for a single session, was uninvolved in the production. Zawinul had improvised a tune (later titled "Man with the Copper Fingers") that had a guitar-like quality to the melody, and it made him think of Carlos Santana. "This is a guy who can play a melody," Joe said. "The music always comes first and then the choice of who is going to play it. And he, I must admit, really surprised me to be a hell of a good musician, because I always thought he was not that trained of a musician, you know?"[14]

Santana also figures prominently on the title track, "This Is This," which leads off the record. It's basically a groove with an uncharacteristically strong backbeat that he improvises over. Despite the catchy synthesized horn riff, it isn't one of Joe's strongest works. Like "Man with the Copper Fingers," it slips perilously close to routine fusion fare—something Weather Report had consciously avoided to this point.

Elsewhere, Joe contributes an abbreviated tune called "Face the Fire," which is characterized by Erskine and Cinélu's funky beat and the wordless, quasi-tribal vocal chant performed by a quartet of singers. (According to Erskine, when Joe played a rough cut for Maxine, she commented, "When are you going to write a song that has real English lyrics?"[15]) Zawinul also composed a schmaltzy ballad, "I'll Never Forget You," in honor of his parents, but it suffers in comparison to similar pieces that he had already recorded with Weather Report.

The best of Zawinul's tunes were saved for the end of the record. "Update" is a blistering improvisation in which Joe just whales on synthesizers. Listening to it, one would never know that it was constructed with overdubs, but Joe had already recorded his parts when Erskine added his. "I just went in, he said go ahead, and I just played it. I kind of learned it by ear and gave it a shot. And I think that might have been just one take."[16] The walking bass line by Victor Bailey proved just how adept he had become at holding the groove on Joe's one-chord jams. As he later said, "You could give me a chord chart, or you could write out eighteen bars right now and put some chords in there, and I could stand here for the next seventy-two hours and play those and never repeat myself and have a fat groove every time around."[17]

This Is This closes with "China Blues," a sultry tune whose title was inspired by the Kathleen Turner character in the 1984 movie, *Crimes of Passion*—or perhaps more specifically, the movie poster, which Joe felt evoked a similar mood to his tune. "China Blues" includes many of Zawinul's signature compositional elements—the evenly accented bass drum on every beat and an improvised melody line that weaves its way through perpetual variations. It's also interesting that he chose to use electronic voices, probably from the Emulator, as opposed to human singers as on "Face the Fire," but it works to maintain the mysterious vibe.

In addition to Joe's pieces, Victor and Mino each got a tune on the record. For Victor, this had been a long time coming, as he'd been trying to get Joe and Wayne to record one of his compositions all along, to no avail. "I played them everything I had," Bailey said. "They just didn't respond to it. At the time, I thought they just weren't getting it."[18] One of his pieces was called "Consequently." "I used to play it at sound checks, and we used to fool around with it. Joe would play the chords, and I would improvise. I don't remember exactly how we came to do it on the record, but it's something we used to play around with."[19]

Given Victor and Omar Hakim's tight hookup, it's fitting that this is the only tune on *This Is This* on which Omar plays. And since it was Victor's tune, he was also allowed to mix it. "That's the only song in my entire history with the band that really sounds the way I sound," he said. "In the mix, the sound was never my sound, and the concept of the bass was never my concept. I'm talking about the tone of my bass, as well as the concept. When I played my bass solo, that's the way that I sound."[20]

Mino's tune is "Jungle Stuff, Part I." "I had a cassette on the tour bus and Joe said, 'Okay, let's do that.' And he wanted to use that cassette, actually, to play on top of it. I thought it would be more organic to do that, and then the tune came out and it's interesting."[21] "Jungle Stuff" is the only track on *This Is This* that truly features Wayne, who plays a beautiful soprano solo that elevates the tune substantially. Wayne appears in a couple of other pieces, but it's not until the end of the LP's first side that listeners hear from him. There was no hiding his absence from fans and critics.

Overall, the sessions were disjointed, with the musicians filtering in and out. "I wasn't even there when Wayne overdubbed," Erskine said. "I was out of town and came back and the sax parts were on."[22] "Jungle Stuff" was completed without Cinélu present; he and the band exchanged cross-country notes regarding the various mixes in progress. Omar Hakim has only vague memories of his participation. "By that time, I had moved on, and the session is a blur. I don't even remember it, honestly."[23]

When *This Is This* came out in June of 1986, it was pretty well slammed by the critics. Eric Snider in the *Tampa Bay Times* offered an accurate and succinct summary: "Given the choice of having one last Weather Report album or not having it, I'll take *This Is This*. I just wish it could have been better."[24] Disappointed fans wound up altering the record's title to *This Is Shit*. Reminded of this many years later, Zawinul had to concede the point. "Well, somehow it was a shit record. But still, if you listen to the music today, tremendously good things are on it."[25]

So in the end, it wasn't like the gang got back together for one last hurrah.

"All the arrangements were very difficult, the studio time ran away, and we noticed that everything was pieced together," Joe said. "We just were not a band anymore."[26]

•

Even before *This Is This* was finished, Joe's thoughts turned to taking a group out to support it. With a stateside tour of his solo act scheduled for the spring of 1986, he eyed a return to Europe in the summer, with the United States to follow. But if he was going to do so, it would be without Wayne. And it would be without the name Weather Report.

Joe's hopeful optimism aside, it's clear that Wayne had every intention of leaving Weather Report behind as soon as *Sportin' Life* was done. He said as much during interviews when he began touring with his own band. Asked in October 1985 about the possibility of Weather Report regrouping, he replied, "There would be no reason to get back together but to make new hits. The Beatles had more reason to get back together; a lot of groups have better reasons to get back together."[27] That didn't sound like someone looking forward to a reunion.

The moment of truth came early in 1986, when Wayne contested Joe's use of the Weather Report name and news of the split spilled into the press. "I didn't know until a couple of weeks ago that Wayne is booked so far ahead," Zawinul groused to Leonard Feather. "I can't wait another year for him to decide it's time for us to tour again. So we'll definitely go out—but there will be no saxophonist, because nobody can replace Wayne."

The article went on to say, "Having devoted fifteen years of his life to Weather Report, Zawinul says he has no intention of letting it fall apart." Nor was there any animosity between him and Shorter. "Wayne and I are friends," Joe said. "It's just that he's had a taste of being a leader on his own, and he wants to be out there doing his thing. That's fine; but with or without Wayne, with or without Columbia, we're gonna keep going."[28]

And so Joe did. He retained the same management (Wayne was now working with David Rubinson, Herbie Hancock's longtime manager), the same road crew, and the same touring conditions. Because of the name dispute, Joe had to come up with an alternative, and he didn't stray far from the original, choosing Weather Update. "The name, I believe, was Maxine's idea," Peter Erskine recalled. "When Joe announced it in the studio, we all thought, great, that's a clever name. It seemed funny. It had a little wink in it. But a lot of fans were not happy with the fact that 'Weather' appeared in the name at all."[29]

Of course, it was meant to mollify jittery concert promoters who feared that without Weather Report's name recognition, Joe's band would fail to attract the large audiences his fee demanded. "I would've preferred to keep the name Weather Report," Zawinul explained, "but the way we'll advertise our concerts people

Display ad for a Weather Update concert in St. Louis in 1986.

will know who we are."[30] As it developed, posters in Italy advertised "Weather Report" in a large font, with a very small "Update" tucked in between. Even several months later, when the band toured the United States, it was sometimes identified as "Weather Report/Update." (One newspaper advertisement had the "Report" in Weather Report crossed out and "Update'd" scrawled next to it.[31])

Peter Erskine, Victor Bailey and Bobby Thomas were all onboard for the upcoming tours, but the big question was how to replace Wayne. Carlos Santana's playing on *This Is This* suggested a guitarist who was a powerful soloist in his own right, but Zawinul had another concept in mind. "I wanted to have a guitar take over some of those rhythm lines I played with Weather Report," he said. "My left hand was always busy playing lines. And I was concentrating on most melodies I play by myself, so I don't have to play the same way. Wayne and I played excellent together, but when we played ensemble we phrased it together. When I played the melodies alone, I could change them. I could make the ensembles different every night. And that's what I really liked about that concept."[32] In effect, Joe wanted the harmonic and melodic freedom that he enjoyed when he improvised alone, with the rest of the band effectively taking over the role of his machines.

The first guitarist he sought was John Scofield, a well-regarded jazz musician with R&B and funk influences. By 1986, Scofield was an established bandleader with dozens of credits behind him, including several of his own albums, and had just come off a three-year stint with Miles Davis. Around the time that Joe revealed his plans for Weather Update to Leonard Feather, Scofield confirmed his participation in interviews.[33] But eventually negotiations broke down and Zawinul chose to end the relationship before they played a note.

Joe then turned to Steve Khan, a guitarist who came up in the New York fusion scene playing with the Brecker Brothers, Mike Mainieri, and David Sanborn, among others. After releasing three fine albums for Columbia, Khan took a stylistic turn in 1980 with *Evidence*, a solo album in which he layered electric and acoustic guitar parts on such classic tunes as Wayne's "Infant Eyes" and Joe's "In a Silent Way." Thereafter, he set aside his Telecaster for the pure tone of a Gibson ES-335 and established Eyewitness, an innovative band known for its chemistry, interplay, and grooves. Joe heard them in Japan during a Weather Report tour.

"We were playing at the Pit Inn [a well-known jazz club in Tokyo]," Khan recalled. "And I don't think I knew Joe was in the audience. I probably would have been scared to death knowing that he was there. But I guess we left a real, lasting impression on him, so when he called me about being in the band, I thought he wanted me to be some version of what he heard with that group. At the time, I was playing with a very clean guitar sound, very pared down, not a hint of fusion playing. And I was excited about it, because I loved Joe's writing and his music."[34]

Thus began a three-month odyssey that Khan later described as "one of the great musical and personal experiences of my life. But also, one of the great, great disappointments!"[35] It started with the run-up to the first concert, which Khan recounts here:

Joe didn't send me very much music, and I wasn't sure what was going to happen. So I started transcribing almost the history of Weather Report, writing out all the music, now with guitar parts—basically transcribing the tunes and what Wayne was playing, as best I could. I made a huge notebook and I kept asking Joe questions about things, but he didn't really answer anything. So we all flew to Vienna, where we had a week to rehearse. In the jazz-fusion business, this was an incredible luxury. Weather Report—now Weather Update—was a real organization, a huge machine, so it could afford to do something like that.

Joe had just released *Dialects*, so he wanted to play some music from that. And for the first three days, and maybe into the fourth day, I didn't play a note. All Joe did was rehearse all these sequenced drum machines with Peter, and a little bit of Victor and Bobby Thomas, trying to make it groove with these machines. He wanted to go from the way he had been creating music in his home, which was basically him playing alone. And there were things that were unbelievably complex. So we spent all this time and, honestly, I sat there doing nothing, waiting for him to say, "Okay, let's play something we know."

Now we're two days away from having to play in front of people, and we had no music. Peter and I were close friends by that time, and of course I was friendly with Victor—it was my first time working with Bobby—and we would sit at dinner together and I would say, "What the fuck is this? What are we doing?" I mean, I had never seen anything like this. Peter was getting pissed off, too. We all understood what it took to put together great music; it's not easy. And Peter had been a part of some of the greatest Weather Report ever. So it was getting to the point where it was scary—like, what's going to happen?

Finally Joe says, "Well, okay, let's start doing some stuff here," and he didn't really have any music in front of him. So I had my notebook and I started going through it, but he didn't want to play any of the old stuff. Everything in that book, he'd say, "No, we're not going to do that." "Well, what about 'Domino Theory'?" "No, we're not going to do that." "What about 'Black Market'?" "No, we're not going to do that." I almost went through the entire book and he just said no to everything.

So finally we put together a set of music and somehow—I don't know how we did it—we survived that first concert. We never did play things like "Birdland" or "Black Market" or any of the really famous tunes. The most famous thing we did was a medley of "Badia" and "Boogie Woogie Waltz."[36]

Not only did Khan find the band's choice of music lacking, he also struggled with his role in it. "I think Joe had a very primitive view of what the guitar is and what it can do. And I think in many ways, though he wasn't sure about it in Weather Update, he was really looking for someone who played a sort of disco kind of rhythm guitar—and I don't mean that in the most pejorative way—and someone who was more of a fusion-style guitarist. And when I entered the picture, the music was already loud with just Joe and Peter playing. So then you add bass, and there was no way a modern or contemporary-jazz-guitar sound was going to cut through this band. I thought I'd gotten rid of playing fusion-style guitar years ago, and now I was forced to dredge that up because it was the only way to cut through the band. So on the one hand I was fighting against what I didn't want to do as an individual artist, but then being forced into a position where I had to do what seemed right for the music."[37]

Meanwhile, Erskine had to deal with the machines. As Khan saw it, Erskine was handcuffed from the start. "If you look at it, before he ever played a note—and this was said at the rehearsals—every sixteenth note was covered," Khan said. "Multiple things were going *dig-a-dig-a-dig-a-dig-a*. So what are you supposed to do when *every* rhythmic subdivision is already being played by something, whether it's four tambourines or sixteen conga drums? Peter said, 'Can't we just play?' And Joe didn't want to do that. He thought this was going to be something new, to bring the way he played at home to the stage."[38]

Had this been 1978, Joe would have probably gotten into Erskine's head, but eight years on Peter was much more experienced and self-assured. "At this point in time, I was somewhat immune," he said. "I had gone back to working with Joe with eyes open, and I felt better equipped to work with him. I was a lot more confident than I'd been before. And you know, it was kind of fun, but because of the machines and everything, it was a little bit limiting. This was really where the one-chord Afro-beat vamp thing started kicking in more and more, and when he finally got the band with guys like Paco Séry, they were great. They made that stuff come alive. I know with me, after a while, I'd just kind of go, 'This is dumb. I can't keep doing this.'"[39]

Weather Update's debut took place in Joe's hometown of Vienna. Joe was rightly considered a star there, and this being the first concert without Wayne, interest was especially high, and the band held a press conference before the show. All five members were on the dais, but Joe did most of the talking. At one point, a journalist asked, "Mr. Zawinul, so what do you think about rock?"

"I don't think about it," Joe replied.

Attempting to elicit a more expansive response, the reporter tried again. "Well, but what do you listen to?"

"I listen to myself!"[40]

"When I heard that, I laughed," Khan remembered, "but inside I was saying to myself, 'Jesus Christ, what an arrogant son of a bitch.' One answer after another—it didn't matter what the question was—it all came off as this gruff guy. But that moment was really significant to me, because I started to realize that Joe's so great because he *doesn't* listen to anything else. All he hears is what's coming from himself, and that's why he was completely true to himself. Yes, it's great to have an open mind and listen to all the music that's out there, but in the final analysis, if you don't hear your own music—the music that exists inside of you—then you will never have a musical personality or style. And when you look at Joe's body of work, it is rich with personality and style."[41]

Most of Weather Update's tunes came from *This Is This* and *Dialects*. The former wasn't Zawinul's best material, while the latter wasn't meant for a live band. Erskine and Khan lobbied for some of Weather Report's classic tunes, to no avail. At one point on the tour bus, Peter brought some videotapes of Weather Report that his father had made, with sound provided by Brian Risner. As they all watched a concert from 1978, Joe turned to Peter and said softly, "You know what, man? We were playing better music back then."[42]

As the tour went on, Joe and Khan developed a duet version of "In a Silent Way." Joe loved what Khan had done with the tune on *Evidence*, and in concert they started with a free improvisation that ultimately led into the "Silent Way"

Zawinul reviews Steve Khan's book of Weather Report transcriptions during a game of gin rummy. Regarding the card games, Khan later said, "I kicked Joe's ass all over Europe, he wouldn't let me leave the table!" Photo: Peter Erskine.

melody. "When I joined the band," Khan said, "I didn't realize that Joe had perfect pitch, which is a great thing, because he had completely amazing ears and a really unique sense of harmony. I remember one night he said, 'Listen, Steve. You can play whatever you want in the front there. Play anything you like, anything you hear. It doesn't matter, because I have the greatest ears in the history of music—greater than Mozart.' This is exactly what he said to me. And of course, I was like, okay Joe, sure.

"But because he had perfect pitch, there was nothing I could play that he wouldn't hear. And so as that piece developed, I would just go out there and close my eyes and start to play. I didn't even look at him; I just played. And he would sit over there listening, and eventually I would start to hear the most beautiful orchestra come in behind me, and we could go all over the place before working our way into 'In a Silent Way.' It was a beautiful moment.

"We had an outdoor concert in Europe, and he came up to me afterwards and said, 'You know, Steve, I have to tell you, tonight was one of the greatest concerts in the history of Weather Report'—he used the name Weather Report—'because tonight we had the Shorter connection, you and me. It was there. I felt it. We had it.' And when he talked to you in that voice [a unique mixture of a black American jazz musician with a heavy Austrian accent], it was hard not to laugh sometimes. But there were moments like that where I was happy that he heard something that he liked. It always felt special to play that duet with him."[43]

Sadly, that special moment came to an abrupt end during the U.S. tour, thanks to the great Weather Update truck heist. "I don't know what happened, but I think a couple of the guys went to get the truck and pulled it up to a Holiday Inn," Khan recalled. "They ran upstairs to get their bags, and in the five or ten minutes they were gone, the truck got stolen. The next thing I know, we're being told that all of the equipment is gone and the concert for that night is canceled. So we sat in some shitty hotel lounge waiting to hear from the police, and we heard different things—you know, they spotted the truck on the freeway and so on. It was almost like losing your children. When they finally found the truck, some equipment was missing and I was pretty much the biggest loser. I lost two guitars, including the acoustic guitar that I used on those duets with Joe. Both of my amps were gone. I think Victor lost something, and I think Joe lost a briefcase that had a lot of samples in it. Lucky for me, I had my main guitar in the room, so I didn't lose that. But our duet with the acoustic guitar was gone."[44]

Overall, Weather Update is barely remembered today—a transitional band if ever there was one: not Weather Report, but not quite another thing, either. They toured with John McLaughlin's reincarnated Mahavishnu Orchestra, which then included Bill Evans, Jim Beard, Jonas Hellborg, and Danny Gottlieb. "John's band would open for us," Khan said, "and the truth is—and I'm not talking about the level of musicianship or anything like that—but in my opinion we got blown off the stage every night because their preparation was completely together in terms of having a book of music and pacing a set. And we didn't have that. If there was some vagary in our presentation, we weren't going to do well, and it made for some very long nights.

"In contrast to that, when things did go well, there were moments that were really wonderful, that in some ways I'll never forget. One of the best things was at sound checks, when it would just be Joe and Peter playing, very much like the piece 'Update' on *This Is This*. And it was just burning; it was killing. That was some of the best music I heard during those seven weeks, and it happened almost every day. The two of them would just start playing something—never anything really recognizable—and it was incredible. If the five of us played like that, it would have been great. But of course, Joe didn't want to do that except at sound check."[45]

At the end of the year, Erskine offered an optimistic view of the band's future to *Down Beat*: "This group has more going for it potentially than the last few editions of Weather Report, basically because we're all just a little older and wiser. Joe's going for something, and he's going for it with a determination I've never seen before." Erskine added that they hoped to do a new record in early 1987, but at some point Joe realized that he needed to make a clean break. Weather Update didn't get the response that he hoped for—attendance at the 5,870-seat Greek Theatre in Los Angeles was a dismal 1,600, for example[46]—and it's likely that once he examined the balance sheet, he realized that it couldn't continue.

And so Weather Update, like Weather Report itself, went out quietly, without fanfare—without really ending, for that matter. Peter Erskine relocated to Los Angeles under the assumption that he would be working with Zawinul well into the future. But as he settled into his new home, he read a *Down Beat* article in which Dennis Chambers mentioned that Joe had invited him to join his new band. This was news to Erskine, so he jotted off an angry note to Zawinul, who apologized while confirming that it was true (although nothing ever materialized with Chambers).

Likewise, Khan never got any official word regarding his status. "At the end of the tour, everything seemed to be headed toward recording and going out next year. But I think when Joe sat down to look at the ledger—the black ink and the red ink—he realized that he had to make some changes. I remember just sort of hearing, oh, Joe's got a new band, and that's what he did. Like Peter, I thought it would be long-term. I was working on all this equipment with Ralph Skelton, and I had this rack built because I felt like that was the direction the music was going, and I wanted to be prepared for it. So the next thing I know I had this big refrigerator-sized rack, and I never even got to play it with Weather Update. I went through this whole thing thinking I'm going to be in this band for five years, and then *kapoof*—it was gone."[47]

"It was a good band," Joe said. "A Weather Report without Wayne Shorter. . . . And that's it—after this tour, the Weather Report era was over."[48]

PART V

Epilogue

22 Transitions

The most important living composer in jazz.

—Ben Ratliff

ON APRIL 25, 1986, JOE BROUGHT HIS ONE-MAN SHOW to Carnegie Hall. During the sound check, he had a couple of friendly visitors: Jaco Pastorius and Manolo Badrena. With Jaco's need for Zawinul's approval undimmed, he bought a new suit for the occasion and was on his best behavior, helping Joe get his sound together before the concert that evening. Jaco looked good, Joe thought. But his outward appearance was deceiving. Since leaving Weather Report, Jaco's life had spiraled out of control in ways that no one could have predicted, much less imagined.

His post–Weather Report career began promisingly enough, as he led his Word of Mouth big band and smaller aggregations through the early months of 1982. But a major turning point in Jaco's personal life occurred when Ingrid gave birth to twin boys that June. What should have been a joyous event in the couple's lives turned divisive as Ingrid insisted that Jaco not be around the children when he was drinking, which by then was most of the time. It drove a wedge in their marriage that never healed and they eventually divorced. Still, the big band's appearance at Avery Fisher Hall on June 27, 1982, showed that Jaco remained at the top of his game. Accompanied by special guest Toots Thielemans, the band blazed through a two-hour set "that practically burst at the seams in rich, chunky horn-based climaxes augmented by the steel drum of Othello Molineaux," per the *New York Times*.[1]

When many of those same musicians accompanied Pastorius on a brief tour of Japan two months later, it was a different story. Peter Erskine had witnessed Jaco's erratic behavior with Weather Report, but even he was unprepared for the sight that greeted him at the airport for the flight across the Pacific. Pastorius had

Peter Erskine and Jaco Pastorius enjoying better times with Weather Report. Photo: Peter Erskine.

cut his trademark long hair in a jagged crew cut and stuck pieces of electrical tape to his cheeks—to "hold my face together," he explained. Taken aback, Erskine walked over to say hello. "Hiya, fatso," Pastorius replied, an edge of hostility in his voice.[2]

On the day of the first concert, Jaco disappeared. With just minutes to show time, nervous band members wondered if they should leave. Then at the last second, Jaco sauntered through the dressing room as if nothing was amiss and nonchalantly walked on stage. The rest of the band followed and after Jaco quickly tuned up, they hit. The concert was such a success that afterward Erskine hugged Pastorius with tears in his eyes. But more antics followed. Jaco left the stage in the middle of another performance, and he later made headlines throughout Japan after throwing his bass into Hiroshima Bay. At one point, he drove a motorcycle into a hotel lobby, fell off, and passed out. "It was pretty awful," Erskine remembered of the tour. "And it was scary. It was like a different person than the guy I met down in Miami that night with Maynard's band. The look in his eyes . . . everything just seemed wrong."[3]

Some speculated that his estrangement from Ingrid and the twins led to his acting out. Ingrid had been his constant companion on the road, but with two newborns, she refused to go on this trip. Erskine remembered that on the flight to Japan, Pastorius took a seat next to him, grabbed the sports section of the newspaper, and circled the word "Twins" in all of the references to the Minnesota Twins baseball team, as well as the word "base" in the baseball articles. Obviously, the situation with Ingrid and his children weighed on him. (Jaco named the double

LP produced from the tour *Twins I & II—Live in Japan 1982.*)

Jaco also felt the pressure of leading his own band—and a very large one, at that—in a land that adored him. Furthermore, he brought his daughter Mary on the trip. Perhaps it was all too much to handle, leading him to revert to his Jaco-the-prankster persona, in which everything was done to effect, with the ultimate goal being the "total wipe," a term that he and his teenage pals used to describe dangerous or outrageous stunts.

Whatever demons Jaco was battling, bizarre incidents piled up one atop another. Late in 1982 while on tour in Italy, Jaco was partying at a hotel when he decided to walk across a second floor balcony banister wearing nothing but a bath towel. Moments later, everyone heard a thud, then a groan. When they went to the balcony to see what happened, they saw Jaco lying on the ground, writhing in pain. He had broken his arm and cracked his pelvis in four places.

Jaco's appearance with the Word of Mouth Big Band at the 1984 Playboy Jazz Festival was disastrous. It was a highly anticipated set, with many of L.A.'s music-industry elite in attendance. By then, Pastorius had lost his Warner Bros. contract, so a good performance could demonstrate that he was worth the risk to another label. But Jaco arrived at the Hollywood Bowl obviously under the influence, and trashed the dressing room. Once on stage, he ignored the set list, knocked over equipment, and turned his amplifier to full blast before hurling his bass to the floor, producing a thunderous howl. The other musicians were so embarrassed, they left the stage one by one until Jaco was alone. Ten minutes into the set, the master of ceremonies, Bill Cosby, signaled for the crew to revolve the circular stage. It was the Hollywood Bowl equivalent of getting the hook. This being well before the Internet, those in attendance had little inkling of Jaco's mental state and found the whole spectacle bewildering. Many booed as he disappeared from view.

A few months later, Pastorius was the subject of a cover story for *Guitar Player* magazine. The author, Bill Milkowski, knew firsthand the true extent of Jaco's physical and mental decline, but kept it from readers. Like many of Jaco's peers and supporters, Milkowski was hopeful that the bassist would turn himself around, and even lent his support in getting Pastorius a new record deal, but Jaco sabotaged all such efforts.

By the time Joe saw him at Carnegie Hall, Pastorius was living on the streets—drunk, dirty, belligerent—a danger to himself and to others. When word of his condition got back to his brother Gregory, he came up from Florida to see for himself. Shortly thereafter, Gregory persuaded Jaco to check in to the psychiatric ward of Bellevue Hospital for evaluation. He was diagnosed with bipolar disorder, for which he used alcohol as a form of self-medication.

Jaco remained at Bellevue for eight weeks, after which he was released to the custody of Brian Melvin, a drummer who lived in the San Francisco Bay Area. Pastorius spent several weeks on the West Coast and for a time lived a healthy lifestyle. But when his girlfriend Teresa Nagell got pregnant and decided to have an abortion, Jaco began drinking again and the downward spiral resumed. In January 1987, he moved back to Florida, where he was declared legally indigent and wound up living in Fort Lauderdale's Holiday Park. He was arrested nine times in nine months, on charges ranging from vagrancy to driving a stolen car around the park's running track.

Some of Jaco's friends and family members tried to stage an intervention. At one point, Bob Bobbing drove him to a resort in the Florida Keys, thinking that a weekend away would do Pastorius some good. "We had a great time, swimming with the porpoises at Hawks Cay, and all the food was being delivered at the house," Bobbing said. "He was great. He even played in the lounge that night. Totally normal." But Jaco's well-being was illusory. "On the way back, he got depressed, thinking about reality and what he was coming back to. He didn't want to talk anymore, and he was holding his chin." At one point, they stopped for gas. "He went into the gas station and came out manic and swaying, and I thought, *What the fuck happened?* I went inside and there was a cap on the floor; the bottle was in the trash. Basically, two swallows and he was already in a manic state. I said, 'That's it, man!' I didn't understand it. I got pissed off and dropped him off at Holiday Park. It was the last time I ever saw him."[4]

One of Jaco's favorite ploys was to jump on stage uninvited during someone else's gig, demanding to sit in or otherwise disrupt the performance. The last time he did so was on the night of September 11, 1987, while Carlos Santana performed at the Sunrise Musical Theater in Fort Lauderdale. Jaco was quickly removed by security and escorted out to the street. Angry and humiliated, he eventually made his way to Wilton Manors just north of Fort Lauderdale, where he attempted to gain entry to the members-only Midnight Bottle Club. An altercation ensued and when the police arrived they found Jaco unconscious, lying face down on the sidewalk in a pool of blood. His skull was fractured, as were several facial bones. His right eye was dislodged from its socket, his left arm was badly injured, and there was significant internal bleeding.

The club's manager, a twenty-five-year-old martial artist named Luc Havan, insisted that Jaco sustained those injuries when he fell and hit his head, but the evidence showed that he had been badly beaten. After lying in coma for several days, Jaco died on September 21, 1987. He was thirty-five years old. Havan was charged with second degree murder, but subsequently pleaded guilty to the reduced charge of manslaughter and served four months in prison—"one month for each child he left fatherless," as Ingrid pointedly put it.[5]

Not long after Jaco's death, Joe reflected on his life in an interview with *Down*

Beat's Josef Woodard:

> I loved Jaco. Every time I think of him, I smile. He was one of the nicest
> people I've ever known, and he did things nobody ever did. When my
> parents had their golden wedding anniversary, in the tiny village where I
> come from, he and Ingrid sent the biggest flower arrangement you've ever
> seen. He bought me an accordion one birthday. He was a very thoughtful
> human being. He had a good soul and good character. . . . He was a total
> gentleman, and I thought he was going to get it together. I miss the guy.[6]

•

Before embarking on the next phase of his career, Zawinul took a detour when
he agreed to a series of duo piano concerts with Friedrich Gulda. They played a
repertoire of classical pieces, including Johannes Brahms's *Variations on a Theme
by Haydn*, as well as some of their own compositions. Zawinul admitted that his
motivation for doing so was in part "a financial thing," calling the money involved
"mind-boggling" compared to what he was used to making.[7]

The windfall from these concerts set the stage for the formation of Joe's new
band, the Zawinul Syndicate. After the Weather Update experience, Zawinul
wiped the slate clean, recruiting musicians who had no prior connection to
Weather Report. He also recorded his first post–Weather Report album for Columbia, *The Immigrants*. However, things got off to a rocky start when the record
was recalled due to licensing issues related to the tune "No Mercy for Me," which
was essentially "Mercy, Mercy, Mercy" with new lyrics.

The Immigrants also marked the recording debut of the Pepe, an instrument
that Zawinul conceived and which was brought to fruition by Korg. The Pepe was
wind-controlled, using the mouthpiece from a melodica and operated with a set
of accordion-like buttons along the side of its body. Joe played fairly convincing
horn solos on it, triggering samples of Wayne's soprano, for instance. On a technical level, Joe's "saxophone" solos played on the Pepe were an impressive feat, but
they paled compared to the real thing. Joe would have been better off utilizing
sounds that *evoked* acoustic instruments instead of emulating them. This became
more of an issue on the Syndicate's second album, *Black Water*, which includes a
Thelonious Monk medley. Unlike Weather Report's delightfully warped version
of "Rockin' in Rhythm," Joe's seemingly inerrant ear fails him here as his re-cre-
ation of acoustic horns comes off as mechanical and hokey.

The live edition of the Zawinul Syndicate got underway in June 1988. "Our
first concert was in New Jersey, and it was funny because the power was so weird
that the keyboards went up and down," Joe said. "It was the weirdest concert, in
one of those funny nightclubs, hardly any people there. I mean, it was tough in
the beginning. We had to start over, but it didn't take long. People liked the band

immediately. We didn't sell that many tickets, but the people who came to see us were knocked dead."[8]

With the release of the third Syndicate album, *Lost Tribes*, in 1992, Joe's Columbia contract was not renewed. Scott Henderson, Joe's guitarist in the early years of the band, observed that the Syndicate records "came at a time when Joe wasn't really being treated that well by CBS. I think Joe's glory days with the company were long gone. . . . I thought, *Here's Joe being treated like a jerk by his record company.*"[9] Whatever the case, Zawinul's albums failed to generate much excitement, and sales were lackluster. As one label executive remarked, Joe's records "presented a problem at retail," meaning they didn't fit into any marketable category.[10] *Lost Tribes* wasn't acoustic jazz, and it certainly wasn't smooth jazz. Once again, Zawinul faced a crossroads in his career.

Around this time, Joe was asked to produce a new album by the Malian singer Salif Keita. Although Keita had earned an international reputation with his 1987 release, *Soro*, which combines traditional West African music with Western funk and R&B influences, Zawinul didn't know who he was. "I never heard his name, so I said they should send me some material. And I listened to the cassette, and the first tune I didn't like at all. But when I had just finished with the first tune, my son Erich called me. He said, 'So Dad, what are you up to?' I said, 'Well, this African guy—they sent me this cassette of his. His name is Salif Keita, but I don't like that shit at all.' And Erich said, 'Dad, do me a great favor: Listen further, because this is the king of Africa. He is incredible.' And he was right. I listened to the next song ['Waraya'], and I was sold on that project."[11]

Their collaboration resulted in *Amen*, which became the best-selling world music album of 1991. To say that Joe was producer understates his contributions. He also arranged all the music and performed on the record. It was a significant event in Zawinul's musical journey. "I improvised the arrangements from the lead tracks that Salif sent, and then I went to Paris to rehearse it with the band. And when the musicians came to rehearsal, there was Paco Séry on drums, Étienne M'Bappé on bass, Kanté Manfila on guitar—all these great musicians. And they loved the music immediately. We had so much fun. That was for me the most personal and nicest experience of all the records I've made. They were the kindest, the most open people. And I was struck by how well they played the rhythms because I put my own things in there." That Zawinul would find an instant affinity with these musicians was not a coincidence, as he would come to learn. "'Black Market' was for twenty years the theme song of the Radio Dakar jazz hour," he said. "They grew up with 'Black Market,' 'Nubian Sundance' from *Mysterious Traveller*, all the Weather Report songs."[12] The records circulated among the musicians there via bootleg cassettes; they thought Zawinul was a Zulu name.

After *Amen*, Joe tapped the African musical talent based in Paris, leading to

The Zawinul Syndicate in 2006. Left to right: Joe Zawinul, Aziz Sahmaoui, Alegre Corrêa, Paco Séry, Sabine Kabongo, Linley Marthe, and Jorge Bezerra Jr. Photo: Curt Bianchi.

the mature stage of the Syndicate that prevailed to the end of his life. "When we would hit Paris, he would spend most of his time hanging out with the African musicians," recalled Bobby Thomas, who reunited with Joe in the Syndicate. "He *loved* African music and drumming."[13]

The first manifestation of this was Zawinul's 1996 album *My People*. Several years in the making, *My People* was Joe's most overt attempt to fuse his own musical sensibilities with those from other cultures. In addition to utilizing members of Keita's band—and Keita himself—Joe performs a duet with the Russian throat singer Bolot Bairyshev (the two-and-a-half-minute track is part of a mesmerizing live performance that went on for over twenty minutes). Another tune includes some of the hippest yodeling committed to disc with the Austrian folk group Broadlahn. *My People* is a high point in the Zawinul discography and marked Joe's embrace of a truly international cast of musicians.

Along the way, Joe indulged in substantial side projects. He composed a symphony, *Stories of the Danube*, which includes an orchestrated version of "Unknown Soldier," and he was commissioned to write and perform a concert-length piece memorializing the victims of Mauthausen, Austria's largest Nazi concentration camp. The latter was performed live at the camp on the fiftieth anniversary of its opening. The last album of new music that Joe made was *Faces & Places*, released in 2002. For Zawinul fans, it was a sumptuous feast. Like *My People* before it, Joe's inspiration was global. The compositions, he said, were "my impressions of the many peoples and places I have visited; their moods, songs, laughter, dances;

the sights and sounds of the daily lives I have glimpsed or imagined as I've toured around the world."[14] Utilizing the resources of digital multitracking, *Faces & Places* is thick in texture and color, crafted with Zawinul's typical attention to detail.

Nevertheless, Joe's music was best experienced live, and the last Syndicate line-up was the most potent of them all. Paco Séry—an extraordinary drummer from the Ivory Coast who seemed born to play Joe's music—and Linley Marthe formed one of the most exhilarating drum-and-bass tandems that Zawinul ever fielded. Joining them were vocalist Sabine Kabongo, Jorge Bezerra Jr. on percussion, Alegre Corrêa on guitar and vocals, and Aziz Sahmaoui on percussion and vocals. Together they took on Joe's hippest grooves at breakneck tempos, with dynamics that went from a whisper to a roar. The band is documented on the 2007 live set, *75*, recorded during Joe's last tour of Europe.

•

Meanwhile, Wayne's fears that his compositional well had dried up proved unfounded, and he released *Phantom Navigator* in 1987 and *Joy Ryder* a year later. The reviews were mixed, the reception tepid, and Columbia quietly dropped him from the label. (According to one article, the albums failed to sell more than 20,000 copies each.[15]) Wayne didn't make another record until 1995's *High Life*.

In the interim, Wayne found a lucrative gig of his own when he teamed up with Carlos Santana in the summer of 1988. It was an unorthodox pairing, but it worked, and Wayne made enough money from the tour that he could concentrate on writing music while limiting his public appearances. One such occasion was on July 10, 1991, when Miles Davis assembled seventeen current and former bandmates, including Joe and Wayne, for a rare career retrospective. Six weeks later, Miles gave his last concert at the Hollywood Bowl. It coincided with Wayne's fifty-eighth birthday, so he and Ana Maria attended the performance with some friends, including Joni Mitchell. Before the show, they visited with Miles in his dressing room. Perhaps sensing that his time was short, Miles spoke to Wayne with purpose. "You need to be exposed," he told Wayne, emphasizing that he was one of the last jazz giants, and he shouldn't let people undervalue him.[16] When Miles died the next month, his words took on added weight.

"I had a feeling that he was saying something for the last time, and he knew that I had a battle in front of me," Wayne told Michelle Mercer. "The battle was against the whole of the corporate world, and the marketing system, against the simple thing that's easy to market. He knew that I had to take it on myself to find a way to be exposed. And I had to do it legitimately, not using any controversy or skulduggery to get exposed. So after that conversation, I acted in that way."[17]

In the immediate years after Davis's death, Wayne continued to maintain a low profile. He did a tribute to Miles tour with Herbie Hancock, Ron Carter, and Tony Williams (with the young trumpeter Wallace Roney stepping in for

Davis), which reminded people of what they wanted to hear from Wayne, even if he wasn't the same player he was in the sixties. But aside from that, he took a break from performing, remaining at his home in the Hollywood Hills as if he were on a sabbatical. "We don't have patrons of the arts anymore, but I was going to make believe I had one for two years," he said. "I said I'm going to see what it feels like to stay home for two years and just think about anything that I want to think about, and then I'll do a record."[18]

In January 1994, Wayne was ready to begin work on *High Life*. He enlisted the aid of Rachel Z, a classically trained jazz pianist who was a member of Steps Ahead, to help flesh out the complex orchestration using MIDI-equipped computers and synthesizers. Wayne later employed thirty members of the Los Angeles Philharmonic for the recording and brought in Marcus Miller to produce the album. (Miller had by then produced three albums for Miles Davis.) It was the most ambitious project Wayne had undertaken. In the press materials that accompanied *High Life*, he bragged, "Every note on the album is written except for my solos. All the bass lines, the hand positions on the keyboards, all of it."

High Life received a Grammy Award for Best Contemporary Jazz Performance, but it also revived the controversy regarding Wayne's post–Miles Davis career. In short, it wasn't what the cognoscenti wanted and Wayne was savaged in a *New York Times* article written by Peter Watrous. Titled "A Jazz Generation and the Miles Davis Curse," with an illustration of Miles and Wayne splayed across the front page of the Sunday Arts & Leisure section, the article dismissed *High Life* as "an eager-to-please instrumental pop album," and "a pastel failure and a waste of [Wayne's] enormous talent; it is as if Picasso had given up painting to design greeting cards."[19]

While acknowledging that Wayne's "most durable influence" was compositional, including "a completely new harmonic vocabulary," Watrous ignored those aspects of *High Life*, unable to get past the backbeats and synthesizer gloss. It was an incredibly condescending indictment given the depth of Wayne's contributions to music. Watrous then pivoted to attack the entire fusion movement spawned by Miles Davis—the "curse" being that a generation of influential musicians had abandoned the jazz tradition and bore the responsibility for stifling its development for their successors.

With the weight of the *Times* behind him, Watrous was a powerful figure in jazz criticism. One A&R executive recalled that some labels would send him mixes of albums *before* they were finished in order to get his opinion of them. But in the aftermath of the *High Life* review, the jazz community rallied around Wayne. John Ephland, the managing editor of *Down Beat*, directly took on Watrous's "superficial analysis" in an editorial titled "One for Wayne."[20]

Nevertheless, the review stung, and it lingered in the form of other writers asking Wayne to respond to it. When a reporter from the *Los Angeles Times* called for an interview a week or so later, Wayne intentionally conflated the paper with its East Coast counterpart. "They're the same," Wayne bristled. "They're of the same kindred spirit. All media controls all art—throughout history." Having gotten that out of the way, Wayne insisted that Watrous's comments were "not worth speaking about. He hasn't lived the feeling, lived the life, lived in the neighborhood ghetto. He doesn't know the necessities that were needed to predicate the birth of modern jazz."[21] In another interview with the Associated Press six months later, Charles Gans noted that Wayne is "good-humored and amiable, but a harder edge creeps into his voice when confronted with such criticism. He deeply resents 'criticism by dictatorship'—an attempt to decree that what he should be doing is returning to playing mainstream acoustic jazz."[22]

Wayne took the music of *High Life* on the road, but his septet struggled to bring the arrangements to life. Keyboardist Adam Holzman called the charts "probably the most difficult and dense pile of music I've ever had to learn for a long tour."[23] Wayne eventually pared down to a quartet and took a much looser approach to the material while injecting a few old tunes into his sets, albeit in radically altered form. Nevertheless, the overarching theme of Wayne's post–Weather Report years was his quest for a band that could fulfill his musical vision. Ten years on, he still hadn't found it.

•

Rumors of a Weather Report reunion began almost as soon as the band ended. Especially in Europe, promoters tried to entice Joe and Wayne to reunite with offers of a big payday, none of which panned out. Then in 1990, the two played together for the first time since 1984 at a Jaco Pastorius tribute in Spain, prompting Joe to talk about "some sort of reunion." He suggested a billing of "Zawinul Syndicate featuring Wayne Shorter." Terms and setting were negotiated, but nothing came of it.[24]

The idea picked up steam in 1996. Joe had been without a record deal since the release of *Lost Tribes*, and he visited the offices of Verve Records, where Wayne had recently signed. Verve was interested in signing Joe, too, and proposed a piano trio recording of Duke Ellington tunes. A Syndicate release could come after that, and then a project with Wayne. Guy Eckstine, who headed Verve's A&R at the time, remembered that Joe "really, really loved" the idea of the Ellington project, but he insisted on releasing *My People* first, so discussions didn't go any further.[25] Of course, Joe remembered it differently, telling Anil Prasad, "They wanted me to sign up, but only to play acoustic piano on the first record and only Duke Ellington's music. I got up and left."[26] (*My People* was released on the independent German label ESC Records.)

Around that time, *Down Beat* published a full-page news item touting Weather Report's eminent reunion, quoting both Joe and Wayne. "We want to make a new record with new music," Zawinul said. "And on tour, we'll probably play the new music, as well as recalling some of the old tunes." Joe even went so far as to name Paco Séry and Alex Acuña as members of the new band. Wayne was more circumspect. "Yeah, Joe and I are on that path," he said. "But we're not going to just jump in, do something to get instant gratification, do something that's intended to last for just a couple of seconds."[27]

Given their long association with Columbia Records, which by this time was part of Sony Music Entertainment, it made the most sense to do a Weather Report reboot with that label. But an indication of Joe and Wayne's sincerity—or lack thereof—was their outlandish asking price: $1 million each.[28] Needless to say, negotiations went nowhere.

Any further talk of a reunion was quashed in mid-July when Wayne's wife, Ana Maria, was killed in the explosion of TWA Flight 800 off Long Island. Wayne was on tour in Europe at the time, but he returned home immediately, his life shaken to its core. Ana Maria was his staunchest advocate. She fell in love with Wayne's music before she fell in love with the man. After fulfilling a commitment to tour Japan, Wayne didn't resurface until months later when he and Herbie Hancock made the duet album *1+1*. Recorded in Hancock's living room, it was a cathartic experience. "Ana Maria is all over the record, from beginning to end," Hancock said. "And not just in Wayne's playing, but in my playing, in the sound of the whole thing. But not in any reference to the plane crash. It felt more like Ana Maria was on the record, inside both of us somehow. And, in that sense, it captured her spirit, or maybe not captured, but had her spirit as a part of the music."[29]

Wayne emerged from his period of mourning with a renewed sense of purpose. "When my wife passed away, I felt like I wasn't concerned with career and excellence and the star system and 'Are you doing something musically valid?'" he told Ben Ratliff of the *New York Times*. "All I want to do is listen to the conversation of life through what I'm doing with music, and the books I'm reading. Everything I'm touching, there's something my wife is telling me, and I gotta listen. She's saying that there's something more than money, real estate, the old shell game. I just want to have a comprehension of the essence of life, to have a cognizance."[30]

Wayne undertook an international tour with Hancock, but mostly concentrated on writing, including commissions for symphony and jazz quartet. When it came to performing these pieces live, he tried out a new group of musicians consisting of John Patitucci on bass, Brian Blade on drums, and Danilo Pérez on piano. Significantly, it was an all-acoustic group—the first that Wayne had ever led. Word of Wayne's new band preceded him to New York, where his June 2001 appearance at the JVC Jazz Festival was highly anticipated.

Patitucci, Blade, and Pérez are impressive players in their own rights. Collec-

Wayne performs with his quartet at the 2001 JVC Jazz Festival. Left to right: Danilo Pérez, Wayne Shorter, John Patitucci, and Brian Blade. Photo: © Hiroyuki Ito / Hulton Archive / Getty Images.

tively, they had the cachet of an all-star group, but their respect for Wayne caused them to set aside their egos. As Ratliff wrote, Wayne's sidemen "seemed scarily committed to the opportunity of making a perfect band for Mr. Shorter, almost ready to die for it." In reviewing the JVC show, Ratliff added that Wayne "was more engaged than he has seemed in at least the last five years."[31] In short, Wayne was having fun.

The next month, he took the group to Europe, where the band jelled into one of the best improvising units in jazz. Out of the tour came the album *Footprints Live!*, released in 2002. *Jazz Times* magazine called it "the new acoustic Shorter album that's been waiting to happen since 1967."[32] Two hallmarks of the quartet were the freedom Wayne gave to his musicians, and the band-driven spirit of collective improvisation, which he likened to his improvised duets with Zawinul, only with four people instead of two.[33] These were themes that Wayne had pursued throughout his career, going back to his days with Miles Davis, as well as the early incarnation of Weather Report. When Brian Blade told *Jazz Times* that it's "almost scary how much freedom we get," he echoed the words of the musicians who played on Wayne's Blue Note albums.

With the quartet serving as his base, Wayne's career experienced a renaissance. As early as 1998, writers began describing him as "the most important living composer in jazz."[34] Soon that designation was applied routinely, and Wayne has come to be regarded as arguably the preeminent jazz musician of the twenty-first century. Prestigious awards followed: A National Endowment for the Arts Jazz

Master Fellowship in 1998, a Lifetime Achievement Award from the Thelonious Monk Institute of Jazz in 2013, a Grammy Lifetime Achievement Award in 2014, a Guggenheim Fellowship in 2016, a Polar Music Prize in 2017, and Kennedy Center honors in 2018.

Joe didn't attain such lofty status. He remained uncompromising in pursuit of his musical vision, and unlike Wayne and many of their fusion era contemporaries, he never did a return-to-acoustics turn. That put him out of step with prevailing trends in the United States, where Joe's brand of music fell out of favor, stuck in the no-man's-land between smooth and traditional jazz. Consequently, his greatest recognition came from Europe, where attitudes toward jazz were more encompassing. He eventually transferred his business base to Vienna, even opening a club there in 2004.

In his native country, Zawinul was considered a national hero—the recipient of the 2000 Hans Koller Austrian State Prize, the Silver Medal for Meritorious Service to the Republic of Austria, and the 2002 Ring of Honor awarded by the City of Vienna. The Austrian postal service honored him with a special stamp in 2004, and he was the official Austrian goodwill ambassador to seventeen African nations. Nevertheless, Joe's U.S. booking agent remembered it being "a deep personal disappointment" to Zawinul that aside from a handful of jazz clubs mainly on the coasts, he had no place to perform in the country where he discovered himself as a jazz musician.[35]

23 Legacy

The word "jazz" to me means "creative music."

—Wayne Shorter

RIGHT AROUND THE TIME THAT WEATHER REPORT DISBANDED, Gary Giddins wrote about the "renaissance of jazz" that was then taking place. Jazz artists, especially young ones, were looking past the stylistic excesses of the '60s and '70s (the avant-garde, as well as fusion, though Giddins didn't mention the latter) and taking inspiration from the music's traditional repertoire. Jazz, he wrote, had "turned neoclassical. Musicians weaned on the free jazz of the '60s now sift '20s classicism, '30s swing, '40s bop, and '50s soul for repertoire and expressive wisdom. They are, in effect, going home again."[1]

Since then, the neoclassicists have dominated the jazz narrative and Wynton Marsalis quickly became their de facto spokesman, "anointed as the musical messenger who might well save jazz from extinction by resurrecting its endangered tradition of creative improvisation," according to a 1983 profile in *Ebony* magazine.[2] He is now the most recognizable jazz musician of his generation. In addition to being an articulate and tireless champion for "real jazz," Marsalis has used his influence and celebrity to attack those outside the mainstream, often in personal terms, denouncing the avant-gardists as "charlatans," while dismissing fusion as "a decline" motivated by financial gain.[3]

Unsurprisingly, neither Joe nor Wayne had much use for such pronouncements. Like Zawinul, one of Marsalis's musical heroes is Duke Ellington. The highest praise that Ellington bestowed on the musicians he most admired was "beyond category," a term that applied equally well to himself. Wayne often used similar terms when describing jazz. "The word 'jazz' to me means 'creative music,'" he said. And "the extended meaning means, really, 'no category.'"[4]

Joe and Wayne also took issue with the related repertory movement, personified by Jazz at Lincoln Center, where Marsalis has served as artistic director since 1987. While emulating performance patterns of the past preserves jazz in one sense, "it's not what I consider preserving the spirit of jazz," Wayne said. "For me, preserving the spirit of jazz means change. That's what jazz is—breakthrough. And for all those young people who want to play like something that was played before, to preserve it, I would say maybe it's better to preserve the process of discovery."[5]

Joe was more pointed. "The jazz which is being played by the Young Lions, who are not young any longer, is one of the most boring periods," he said in 2003. "They know how to play their instruments very, very well—perhaps better than most—but without any trace of personality. If you can't recognize a musician after four bars—who he is, by himself—then he ain't got it. That doesn't mean that he can't be a master musician and all that, but there is something above that."[6]

When the Ken Burns documentary *Jazz* aired on PBS in 2001, it gave the neo-classicists their imprimatur. Spread across ten episodes (nineteen hours in total), Louis Armstrong, Duke Ellington, and to a lesser degree the young Miles Davis are the central figures of the film. After covering Davis's 1959 recording *Kind of Blue*, Burns summarizes the remaining forty years of jazz (up to that point) in a single final episode. Jazz in the seventies is depicted as moribund, emphasized by the passing of Armstrong and Ellington early in the decade. In the words of Branford Marsalis, "jazz just went away for a while." Ultimately, the savior who resuscitates it in the final scenes is none other than Branford's brother, Wynton, who is one of the film's central storytellers. Fusion is given a scant five minutes of airtime, all centered on Miles Davis. Weather Report, the dominant force of its era, isn't mentioned at all (although "Birdland" is included in the companion five-CD box set).

In dismissing the fusion period, Burns hewed to a view shared by many historians who see fusion as an unfortunate product of its time—a wrong turn that ultimately arrived at a dead end. Martin Williams, a respected critic who did much to canonize jazz by curating *The Smithsonian Collection of Classic Jazz*, captured this sense in his 1989 book, *Jazz in Its Time*: "[Wynton Marsalis], and some others, seem to see the whole fusion thing as a kind of commercial opportunism and artistic blind alley, maybe even a betrayal of the music, on the part of everyone involved, on the part of record companies, record producers, and the artists themselves. . . . Although it may have produced some good music, the fusion effort seems to me largely over and was even something of a mistake."[7]

Despite the concerted efforts to delegitimize bands like Weather Report, Joe certainly saw Weather Report as well within the jazz continuum, even with all of its stylistic inputs. "I do feel that we're coming from jazz, that the music is inventive and very powerful rhythmically, which is what jazz is all about," he said

In 2007, the Percussive Arts Society hosted a panel session, dubbed The Drummers of Weather Report, at the Percussive Arts Society International Convention. The participants, left to right: Chester Thompson, Skip Hadden, Ndugu Chancler, Alex Acuña, Omar Hakim, and Peter Erskine. Photo: Percussive Arts Society.

in 1982. "The difference between what we do and what you might call straight-ahead jazz is, first, our rhythmic ideas are coming from everywhere, from all over the world; and second, that the energy of the rock age has affected us very positively."[8] Despite attempts to marginalize Weather Report, Joe called it the last serious movement in jazz—"The last one really where you can say, hey, this was something different and something which has lasting power and longevity."[9]

Weather Report's power and longevity have proven themselves in the decades since its demise. In lieu of a reunion, Joe promised that a box set of previously unreleased material would be forthcoming, at times claiming it would be a whopping eight CDs, including studio outtakes and live concert tracks.[10] But interminable delays made it seem like the Holy Grail to Weather Report fans, who ultimately had to content themselves with the two-disc *Live & Unreleased*, released in 2002. It includes material taken from five concerts spanning the years 1975 to 1983, plus alternate tracks from the *Night Passage* sessions at the Complex. As the first official Weather Report release since *This Is This*, it was a welcome addition to the band's discography, if not the blockbuster that Joe had optimistically predicted.

Four years later, Legacy Recordings put out the box set *Forecast: Tomorrow*—a three-CD compilation culled from the band's sixteen Columbia albums. Although it serves as a good overview of Weather Report's career arc, serious fans already had this music in their collections, save for a handful of tracks. Nevertheless, *Fore-*

cast: Tomorrow includes two gems: a one-hundred-page booklet with unpublished photographs and commentary, and a concert-length DVD of Weather Report's 1978 appearance in Offenbach, Germany. The footage had circulated among tape traders for years, but this was the first official video of any of the band's performances for the U.S. market. (A LaserDisc was released in Japan in 1984, covering a portion of a 1983 concert there.) These releases, as well as a round of remastered CDs and box sets of Weather Report's classic albums, were tangible acknowledgments of the group's relevance by Legacy Recordings, the division of Sony Music Entertainment that manages Columbia's back catalog.

With interest in Weather Report reinvigorated, Joe decided to do something he never did: look back. The inspiration came from the 2002 International Association of Jazz Educators Conference in Long Beach, California, where Zawinul received the first International Jazz Award from the European Jazz Festivals Organization. As part of the festivities, the WDR Big Band played a handful of Joe's tunes from Weather Report and beyond, arranged and conducted by Vince Mendoza. A follow-up concert, billed as "The Music of Weather Report," took place at the 2002 Leverkusener Jazztage.

Zawinul didn't perform with the big band at either of these events—Scott Kinsey handled the keyboard duties—but they planted the seeds for a collaboration that took place in 2005. Joe asked Mendoza to craft more arrangements so that he could put together a concert-length set. More crucially, concerned that the big band "might sound a little stiff," Joe insisted on leading it himself and brought in his own rhythm section consisting of Weather Report and Zawinul Syndicate alumni. Nor did he allow the band's horns to replace his keyboards. Instead, they coexisted side-by-side, with Joe controlling the ensemble like he did his own bands, using hand signals to cue ensemble passages and improvisational sections. The result was an unqualified success—a big band that grooved as only Zawinul could, roaring through Weather Report classics like "Black Market" and "Boogie Woogie Waltz." The first concerts, which took place at Joe's club in Vienna, were recorded and released in 2006 as the double-CD *Brown Street*.

Aside from those projects benefiting from Joe's direct involvement, it seemed for years as though no one else was willing or able to address Weather Report's music entirely on his or her own terms. As Scott Kinsey put it, "The definitive versions of those songs have already been done—the first time—so it's a little hard to reinterpret them."[11] Nevertheless, there have been some inspired reinventions, among the first being those of Dutch keyboardist and composer Michiel Borstlap, who reconfigured several Weather Report tunes in an acoustic context on the album *Body Acoustic*, released in 1999. He even got Joe's blessing. "I like it and I am pleased to hear young musicians trying different approaches," Zawinul wrote in the liner notes. "Weather Report music always had little hidden treasures and

Michiel as well as the other players seem to recognize these."[12]

A year later, keyboardist Jason Miles paid homage to the band with *Celebrating the Music of Weather Report*, a collection of eleven of the group's best-known pieces performed by a who's who of the fusion world. Miles put his own spin on the material, suffusing it with high production values and smoothing out the rough edges. "I felt that not only the music, but the recorded sound of the Weather Report albums was interesting for the '70s, but that if these compositions were to be successful today they had to be adapted—particularly the grooves—to fit current tastes," he explained at the time.[13] As a consequence, he engendered the ire of hardcore Weather Report fans who heard *Celebrating* as a pale imitation of the real thing.

Joe wasn't thrilled about it either, but then he found fault with most interpretations of his music, Borstlap being the rare exception. Peter Erskine tells a story of recording "Dream Clock" for his 1988 album *Motion Poet*. "I spent most of my budget on that tune because I had a sense of responsibility to honor Jaco; he had died not too many years before that. And also, it was the first time I recorded one of Joe's tunes. Vince Mendoza did an incredible arrangement, and I spent a lot of time on it. I flew out to California, partially because I wanted to play it for Joe. So I drove out to Pasadena and I played it for him. He listened, and when the song was done, all he said was, 'It's too slow. Come on, let's have a drink.'"[14]

Tribute projects continue to be released well into the twenty-first century. In 2008, the Metropole Orchestra, under the direction of Vince Mendoza, produced a concert program of Joe's compositions, mostly from the Weather Report era, portions of which were released on the 2010 album *Fast City*. It's hard to imagine any fan expecting to ever hear "Jungle Book" or "Nubian Sundance" rendered live by an orchestra, but the results are spectacularly satisfying. Another reinterpretation of Weather Report came at the hands of radio.string.quartet.vienna, whose live performances of Joe's pieces were captured on the 2013 album *Posting Joe—Celebrating Weather Report—live*. An extraordinarily resourceful group that wrings sound out of its instruments in every possible way, *Posting Joe* again demonstrates the richness of Weather Report's compositions and their ability to withstand even the most radical departure from the original recordings.

As the fiftieth anniversary of Weather Report's founding nears, interest remains strong. Its music is being played by new generations of musicians in bands sporting names like Sweetnighters, Plaza Real, and Mr. Gone. Tribute albums continue to be made, such as *Weather or Not* by Gerry Gibbs and Thrasher People, which spent three weeks atop the JazzWeek radio charts in 2017. Jason Miles has taken his *Celebrating the Music of Weather Report* concept to festival stages in the United States to rave reviews. Along with the former members of the Zawinul Legacy Band, which was organized by Joe's eldest son, Anthony, Scott Kinsey pays homage to the maestro on his 2019 album *We Speak Luniwaz*. Miroslav Vitous remains a staunch champion of the "we always solo and we never solo" ethos with his 2009 album *Remembering Weather Report* and its 2016 follow-up, *Music of Weather Report*.

There's no reason to think this trend won't continue. One of the delightful aspects of Weather Report's discography is that it offers multiple entry points to listeners. For some, the band's first two albums were groundbreaking approaches to group improvisation, but the subsequent turn to funk was a bridge too far. For others, it's the opposite. A large portion of fans tend to think the band started and ended with Jaco Pastorius, while a smaller contingent of devotees regard the Pastorius era as one of excess that didn't serve the music well. Yet others find all of the band's music indispensable.

Perhaps more significantly, musicians continue to take inspiration from Joe and Wayne's *approach* to music, which was free of artificial constraints imposed upon them by critical dogma. "Weather Report was a part of legitimizing that it's all music, regardless of the medium and the types of instruments you are using," said Nicholas Payton, whose deep and broad musical roots have led him to reject the term "jazz" to describe his own music, preferring instead "Black American Music."

"Whether or not we're plugged in, we're still creating art on a high level," Payton argues. "Joe Zawinul by this point has become one of the greatest proponents of using electronic keyboards for creating timbre. Who did more than him in that respect, even now, forty years later? Few have reached that apex of what could be done with keyboards texturally. It was like what Duke Ellington was doing, and Billy Strayhorn was doing—you could hear that that's where he was coming out of, especially when they did tunes like 'Birdland,' harkening back to this familiar, bygone era. They were able to bring that part of the music in because of their deep roots and deep connections to a Cannonball Adderley or a Miles Davis, which a lot of the other fusion bands perhaps didn't have. They were sort of like first generation rockers or experimenters. They had their feet firmly placed in the roots of straight-ahead, but were also young men of the time and had leanings towards more experimental things. It's very easy for people to try to delegitimize groups like Weather Report for using electronic music or for not swinging in a 4/4 sense, but to me, it's all music, and that's one of the important things that they did. They encompassed everything and shed light to the future."[15]

"Some of Weather Report's real influence is yet to be felt," Steve Khan says. "Over time, you'll see more guys do other stuff with it—someone like Scott Kinsey, who is brilliant all by himself, but completely understands Joe Zawinul in a way even I can't and carries it forward in his own way. Or someone like Scott Henderson, who has taken a lot of Joe's tunes—some really difficult ones—and translated them to a guitar trio setting, which is really tough to do. So it's like two different approaches to taking Joe's music to another place. I think people will still be questioning what Joe was doing for decades—and I'm talking about *very* musical people."[16]

"I think as time goes on, Weather Report's music will constantly be rediscovered by people, and it will offer potent things," Peter Erskine adds. "Not just for musical enjoyment, but in terms of how a group of musicians could get together and create new music. The legacy of the band runs very deep, even if the tide of neoclassicism in jazz washed away some of the imprints that Weather Report made in the general music consciousness. Whether we view it through the historical lens or not, it stands the test of time really well. Weather Report endures. I mean, with rare exception—there might be a couple of tunes here and there—you can try on just about any Weather Report track and you'll still look good in it. You try on a lot of other music from that period and it looks like you're wearing the silliest bell-bottoms and hairstyle you can imagine. And Joe and Wayne recognized that. They knew that."[17]

24 The Last Duet

You go safe, then, my dearest friend.

—Sabine Kabongo

"THIS MAY BE THE LAST TIME YOU GET TO PLAY WITH DAD."[1] Those words hung in the air as Wayne rode to the Veszprém Castle, a medieval complex located about an hour's drive from Budapest, Hungary. The date was August 1, 2007.[2] That evening, Joe was scheduled to perform what would be the penultimate concert of his life. Six weeks later, he would die from complications related to Merkel cell carcinoma, a rare form of skin cancer.

Joe had been dealing with the illness for several years, but only his family and closest confidants knew. Despite a friendship that went back almost fifty years, Wayne himself had only learned about it weeks earlier. "The only thing that he said to me was something really quick: 'I've got this cancer, man.' He just kind of tossed it off. Not that he was in denial. It was more like he was talking about a nuisance. That was Joe."[3]

With the Zawinul Syndicate, Joe had embarked on this, his last European tour, seven weeks earlier. As was typical of his summers, he hopped from festival to festival, performing twenty-five times in forty-two days. That might seem like a fairly grueling schedule for a seventy-five-year-old man, but it was a leisurely jaunt across the continent by Joe's standards. That spring, for instance, he played the same number of shows—mostly one-nighters in clubs—in just thirty-three days. And it had been that way for years.

To most observers, Joe seemed indestructible, a force of nature who would outlast us all. His work ethic was legendary, and though his lithe, athletic frame had thickened with age, he remained a vigorous man into his eighth decade. So when word of his deteriorating physical appearance made its way to the Internet, it was alarming. Marco Piretti, who had interviewed Zawinul face-to-face several times in the preceding years, saw the Syndicate in Italy and wrote to an email list that Joe had lost weight and was weak. Most concerning, he needed a wheelchair to reach the stage. The concert was great, but when Piretti saw Zawinul backstage after the show, he was exhausted. "It seems to be a very difficult moment in his life," Piretti wrote. "I think that all Zawinul supporters should be near to him, with their affection and their prayers."[4]

It *was* a difficult moment for him. His wife, Maxine, passed away on July 26, when the band was in Rome. The concert went on as scheduled, with a notable addition: Joe closed the show by performing "Hymn" from his *Mauthausen* album—a tribute to Maxine that he repeated for the remainder of the tour. That concert was the first of four in consecutive nights, each in a different Italian city. With setup, sound check, interviews, and the performance itself, Joe might spend eight hours or more at the venue. Along with traveling from city to city by bus, it was unquestionably taxing for someone undergoing cancer treatment.

Sabine Kabongo had been a member of Joe's band for five years and saw the toll it took up close. "The medication for cancer is really heavy," she said. "You have all of the secondary effects, so it was a little bit difficult for him, in the sense of—he could not eat properly. So he got weaker and weaker. In the meantime I thought, we have to stop the tour, so he can go to the hospital and get rechecked and everything. But we ended up the tour, because he wanted to end up that tour. You know, it's the old school."[5] So Joe and the band soldiered on. When they got to Veszprém, they noticed that Wayne was scheduled to perform there the next evening. An urgent call was placed to Wayne's management to see if he might arrive in time to see his musical partner of so many years one last time.

The Syndicate's performance took place in the castle's main square, with the baroque building of the Archbishop's Palace serving as the backdrop. "It was a big, big audience in the open air—a clear night," remembered Risa Zincke, Zawinul's longtime manager. "Everybody realized when Joe came on stage that he was very sick, but still, the music was fresh and full of power. I don't know how he made it. Then, after a break, Wayne came out to him."[6] As the audience and the other musicians reacted with cheers, Wayne walked over to Joe, who remained seated behind his bank of keyboards, wrapped in a coat despite the hot stage lights and the warmth of the summer evening. The two men shook hands and embraced. It was one of the few times they had shared a stage since the Weather Report days.

"Joe didn't know that we had arrived," Wayne said. "We came into the venue behind the bandstand. I was with the band that I have now [with Danilo Pérez, John Patitucci, and Brian Blade] plus the members of the Imani Winds. I went up on the stage without Joe seeing me and walked up behind him. He turned around from his keyboards and looked up and smiled. And then we went into the introduction of 'In a Silent Way.'"[7]

It was the part that Joe's wife liked, the part that Miles Davis liked. Wayne recalled Joe saying that it reminded him of his grandparents. "I said 'all grandparents,' all out there in the pastures or the woods—the Vienna woods or whatever country you live in—and your grandparents out there making a way for their grandchildren before they leave. That's what that's about, and we did it—we had our last conversation together right there."[8]

As they started to play, "the whole audience, a big place full of people, went silent," remembered Zincke. "Nobody was breathing, it was so quiet. And it was like they were talking together. They knew it was the last time, so it was really a heartbreaking moment. When they finished playing, there was nobody talking or even clapping. Nothing. It was magic. *Really magic*. I still could cry when I think about that."[9]

Some of the Syndicate musicians remained on stage to watch the two masters up close, but Sabine Kabongo preferred a more private vantage point. "Unlike some of my colleagues, I hesitated to sit close as I did not want to disturb their intimacy, so I found the right distance and the perfect lonely spot." Regardless of where they were, it was an electric moment for all of them. "Beyond the musical conversation they engaged in, I could hear each and every word," Kabongo remembered. "Beyond both their stance and body attitudes and expressions, I could feel the love and respect they had for each other. There was gravity, humor, memories, private jokes. Joe was clearly telling him, 'I'm fine, that's right, I'm leaving. I'm ready. I'm not afraid.' To which Wayne answered, 'All right then, if it is so, I'll let you go. You go safe, then, my dearest friend.'"[10]

They played for nearly thirteen minutes. "It was very concise and to the point," Wayne said. "Very eye-to-eye, that kind of thing."[11] When they had said everything they wanted to say to each other, they brought the music to a close as smoothly as if there was a score in front of them. Joe rose to his feet for the first time of the night, sharing a private moment with Wayne before taking a microphone and expressing his thanks for their years of friendship.

"To me, it wasn't a case of two jazz legends who made history meeting again," Kabongo said, "but more like two powerful souls doing what they loved to do together. Those two were connected on the highest level for sure, and not for one second did I feel the many years that had flowed down the river, previously to this magical and very emotional encounter. At the end of it, I stayed a little far from them. I really thought this should be intimate and private. I don't think they had more to talk about than what they did on stage. The obvious doesn't need words and is speechless; staring into each other's eyes is way more appropriate."[12]

"When Joe's band finished, they announced to the effect that this was one of his last performances," Wayne said. "I hadn't left the stage yet, and everybody in the band was crying. It was like a send-off. But Joe wanted it to be a party! I didn't know he was sitting in a wheelchair at the keyboard, but his son rolled him out, and then we followed. Backstage, after it was over, he had a blanket over him, and he met Danilo Pérez—Joe liked the way Danilo played—and the women from the Imani Winds. Beautiful women. Joe always told me that one reason why he came to the United States was that he wanted to meet somebody like Lena Horne, who he saw in the movies when he was a kid. So I said, 'Hey Joe, here's four Lena Hornes right here!' And he just cracked up. That was the last time we spoke."[13]

Two nights later, on Friday, August 3, Joe performed his last concert, in Güssing, Austria. On Sunday he was admitted to the Wilhelmina Clinic in Vienna, where he struggled to regain his strength.[14] At first his progress was hopeful. "He was believing and hoping that he would come back and have a couple of years to work on music," Zincke said. "This was his wish. He knew after Maxine died that nothing would be the same anymore. He didn't want to go back to the U.S. without her there. He knew his life had changed completely, but he wanted to stay to make music. He really was thinking that until only two weeks before he died."[15]

"I'm not afraid of death," Zawinul once said. "The reason could be that I grew up in an environment in which I was always exposed to death every day for years. Experiencing bomb attacks in the night and day and actual war in your country is very different than watching a war a thousand miles away from your home. We had the war right there in my house."[16]

Joe died in Vienna on September 11, 2007. Not long afterward, Wayne was asked if he'd like to hear a recording of their final performance. "I don't need to," he replied. "I remember every note."[17]

25 Reflections

Weather Reporters on Weather Report.

Alphonse Mouzon:

> We rehearsed so much that what we played was natural. It was sponta-
> neous, continuous improvisation, which is good because it was fresh.
> Themes and motifs were brought to the sessions and we expanded and
> improvised on them, and we'd play them and play them. We could sound
> the same but different each time. Joe would tell me what to play, but I
> listened and played my own way. I just made it different. That's why he
> loved me. When I left the band, they went through so many drummers
> because they couldn't deal with Joe telling them what to do. I just took it
> in stride and said, "Okay . . ."[1]
>
> *After leaving Weather Report, Alphonse Mouzon replaced Eric Gravatt in
> McCoy Tyner's band. Mouzon is perhaps best known for the fusion albums he
> made in the 1970s, not to mention his flamboyant attire. He also acted, with
> roles in the motion pictures* That Thing You Do! *and* The Dukes. *He died
> in 2016 from complications related to cancer.*

Barbara Burton:

> I enjoyed the experience. And when you know what you've done, there's a
> kind of peace that comes along with that. I really went out of my way to
> come up with some interesting stuff, like the bubble effects on "Morning
> Lake," and stuff like that. I just knew I had done a good job. I knew the
> music flowed, and I knew that it was class A work. I was happy that I
> had it because it was a chance to be creative, and I'm always looking for
> a chance to do something different and new. It was nice, it really was.[2]
>
> *Barbara Burton went on to play drums, vibes, and percussion with many*

name acts during her career, including Marvin Gaye, Roberta Flack, and the Temptations.

Airto:

Overdubbing is always more challenging than playing live. A lot of musicians don't think so. They think it is the opposite, but in reality, I think the overdub situations are more demanding. Say Picasso paints something beautiful, and it's already done, and then he says, "Now you do your part. Just paint whatever you think is lacking." It's the same thing. I always felt that it was harder because the energy is not there, the energy that exists when musicians play together. So it was kind of challenging.

I recorded for three days, and the music was good—very good. But it was kind of electronic, even though Miroslav was playing acoustic, and Wayne was acoustic, and Alphonse Mouzon was playing drums. Joe was doing a lot of electronic stuff, which to me was kind of alien because I was playing jazz and jamming and everything. That was really the first time that I had played with an electronic keyboard player. So anyway, I played for three days, and then Joe said that he wanted me to go on the road with them and play percussion.[3]

Airto has lent his talents to innumerable records, virtually defining the role of hand percussionist for future generations of musicians. He has also recorded under his own name and led his own bands, which often include his wife, vocalist Flora Purim.

Eric Gravatt:

It didn't really surprise me [that Joe and Wayne remained together for fifteen years]. Wayne is like water. Joe was the cup and Wayne was the water. And they had a nice working relationship like that. Wayne is so amenable to almost anything that happens, because he's so shy and well mannered, and so proficient. Art Blakey once said that everybody in his band has gone on to be a leader except the one man that was qualified to do that, and he played his dick off and he's got music hanging out his ass. And that's Wayne Shorter. [*laughs*][4]

Eric Gravatt retired from the State of Minnesota Department of Corrections in 2001. He reunited with McCoy Tyner and finally made an album under his own name, Fire on the Nile, *with guitarist Dean Magraw.*

Ralph Towner:

That was such a creative time in New York. All the musicians would go there to play with other good musicians, and you would find out how good you were pretty quickly by who you were playing with. It was just a collection of all kinds of people from all over—all the really great English musicians, Dave Holland, John McLaughlin . . . Indian percussionists, Brazilian percussionists. There were all these different kinds of music starting to be heard. It was really open. Most of those players had tremendous roots in jazz—Joe, especially, and Wayne with Miles—and that was all part of the mix. And like Miles and Joe and Wayne, the whole idea was extended; we weren't just doing the same standards and stuff. It was an extension of improvisation. People with really good ears can understand that what we were doing was an extension of the history. It was a great creative period.[5]

Ralph Towner is one of the most distinctive guitarists and composers in jazz history. He co-founded the group Oregon in 1971.

Brian Risner:

For as many synth players as there are now, Joe is the one guy that never sounded electronic. He approached making sounds in an orchestral sense. He let his ear drive him, and it would lead him to create the sound of an instrument that you could actually visualize, like a thirty-foot trombone. It was a synthesizer, and at times it could be electronic, but it always sounded acoustical. He put the air into the instrument. You can't think of him as a keyboard player. He was a *musician*. He could pick up anything and make it sing.[6]

After Weather Report, Brian Risner toured with Miles Davis, among others, before settling in Los Angeles, where he specializes in sound design and sound editing for television and movie studios.

Herschel Dwellingham:

One day [in 1973] my friend Richard Reid came to me and said, "I need to take you somewhere. Oh, man, you gotta come hear this." So he made me get in the car and go to downtown Boston. I went in the record store and people started screaming and clapping. I said, "What the hell is happening, Richard?" He said, "I want you to hear something." So they put *Sweetnighter* on, and then I remembered that I had played on it. I was playing on so many records and doing so many sessions that I didn't remember, you know? So I listened to it, and I said, "Wow. Damn. That's the album?" And overnight that album made me famous.[7]

After a thriving session career in New York, Herschel Dwellingham relocated to his hometown of Bogalusa, Louisiana, where he runs a music studio and production company. In 2019 he formed the Sweetnighters Band and released the album Soul Bass, *which features "Mercy, Mercy, Mercy," "Boogie Woogie Waltz," "Palladium," and a handful of Dwellingham originals.*

Andrew White:

> I was riding down the street in Las Vegas, riding in one of my luxury cars—my Las Vegas thing—and I got to the corner of Sahara and Las Vegas Boulevard and I heard this music coming out of a record store in a little mall on the corner. I heard the bass at the traffic light, and that's when I said, "Hey wait a minute, I got to go check this out." They were playing that thing *loud*, playing it on big speakers out in the parking lot. I said, "Shit, listen to that bass." I know my music, and I never heard this. I got out and went in there. I said, "Whatcha all playing?" And they called me by name. I ain't know none of them people. They said, "That's you!" And that's how I found out [*Sweetnighter*] was out.[8]
>
> *Andrew White operated Andrew's Music for nearly five decades until his death in November 2020.*

Steve "Muruga" Booker:

> I learned a lot from them. Joe would tell me, "I notice you're like the Indian guys; you know, if I'm going fast, you go fast like the tablas." But he said, "If I'm going fast, you go the complete opposite; then we'll give dimension to the music." Wayne would say, "Look at who you're playing to, and then bring the attention back to yourself. And then look at another part of the theater at somebody else, and bring the attention back to yourself. Do that to every spot in the theater: right, left, up, down, back, front. Then they'll all think that you're looking at them, and you're bringing their awareness back to you, to what you're doing."
>
> It was a very high experience. Everything was laid out, whatever the band needed was there; you didn't have to worry about anything. They treated us all on a very high level. I want you to know that. I want to give credit where credit is due.[9]
>
> *Steve "Muruga" Booker has performed in a number of contexts. In 1980, he met George Clinton, and subsequently participated in many Parliament-Funkadelic and P-Funk All-Stars recordings. Muruga eventually returned to Detroit, where he operates his own music studio.*

Greg Errico:

> I didn't know this at the time, but I found out from an interview Wayne did that he and Joe had been talking about wanting to give the band a younger presence and infuse some different elements of music, so I guess

I was the perfect guy for it. I know one thing: For me, it was just a wonderful experience because after Sly, I took a year off. I mean, I was kind of burned out. I probably turned down more stuff than I'd like to admit during that year. And when Weather Report came along, I didn't even realized how wonderful an opportunity it actually was until I got into it. I really enjoyed traveling the world with them. Whether it be the musical experience or the exposure to different audiences, it was a whole different vibe, a whole different paradigm. I really enjoyed it.[10]

Greg Errico has led or contributed to a variety of projects, ranging from big band jazz to Sly and the Family Stone tributes. He was inducted into the Rock and Roll Hall of Fame in 1993.

Ishmael Wilburn:

It was a crazy experience. I was not roadworthy. They had to teach me some things. It was a learning experience on the road, like jazz drummer 101. Joe and Wayne were like uncles to me. They taught me a lot. Wayne was really calm on stage. When he grabbed that horn and started soloing, it was like, *whew*. I remember lying down on the floor in Devonshire Sound when they recorded "Blackthorn Rose." It was one of the most beautiful things. Every time I think about that song and Wayne doing those solos, I think of birds fluttering in the spring air. I was lying on the floor in the back of the studio, just listening to them record that. What a moment.[11]

Ishmael Wilburn still lives in Philadelphia. After retiring from the corporate world, he does occasional gigs and enjoys his grandchildren.

Bradie Speller:

Joe was always searching, and that's the thing that I loved about the music. It was always fresh. Not one night was ever the same with those guys. I mean, sometimes I was wondering, *What the hell are we playing now?* Because it wasn't set. It was like, "Get out here and play some shit." That was Joe's mantra: "Play some shit."

Bradie Speller is a corporate executive in Atlanta, Georgia. He's still involved in music, fronting the band Bradie Speller and Climate Change.

Skip Hadden:

I was really pleased when *Mysterious Traveller* became the album of the year for *Down Beat* magazine. I was like, yeah, maybe nobody knows but me, but it was a validation. It is with great satisfaction that the tunes that I played on have been chosen repeatedly in the 'best of' Weather Report releases and fusion music mixes around the world. It is truly a joy to be included with such distinctive players. And when I came up here [to teach at Berklee] in '82, the reason was because that music was popular and they wanted someone who could do that. And I'm still there now, so it worked out good.[12]

Skip Hadden continued performing for several years before devoting himself to teaching. He has a master's degree in education and has been a faculty member at the Berklee College of Music since 1982.

Alphonso Johnson:

Joe Zawinul is probably one of the most unique human beings I've ever met. He was kind of like Jekyll and Hyde at the same time. He would always be the warmest person, and yet very single-minded about what he wanted and what he wanted to do. Just a very complete person and very unique.

Wayne is indescribable. I've never met anybody like him. He's kind of like from another planet, in a nice way. He's like Miles in a sense; he doesn't talk in direct terms. He talks in nuances and metaphors. *Constantly.*

Most of what we recorded, we wouldn't start at the beginning of what was on paper. Joe would start something or Wayne would start something, and they would start being playful, and I would jump in, and the drummer would finally jump in, and they would hit the record button. And then somebody would play a theme and then oh, we're at that part of the song. And then later they would edit it together.[13]

Alphonso Johnson went on to perform and tour with numerous high-profile jazz and rock bands during his career, including Santana and Phil Collins. After surviving a cancer scare in 2007, Alphonso went back to school and earned a degree in Music Education from California State University, Northridge. He now teaches at the University of Southern California.

Shawn Hart:

I met Joe and Wayne at Bob Devere's place on Long Island. And I honestly think I was hired for the road manager's gig because Joe wanted me to teach him how to shoot a jump shot. He was knocked out by the fact that I seemed to freeze in midair in Bob's backyard before launching the ball. And I just thought, yeah, great, I'll show you whatever I've got, Joe. But I really didn't know these guys, nor did I know the music, when I met them at the airport in Detroit to join the tour.

Dom Um Romão was a revelation to me. He came off the plane with all this gear, and this beautiful set of luggage made from wine-colored leather. And he had at least three pieces of it, like a wardrobe bag and two suitcases. I didn't know exactly how many folks we would have to transport, so I'd rented a Chrysler Town and Country station wagon, and I had everybody's luggage in the wagon except Dom Um's. There was so much luggage that I had to put his on the rack on top where I intended to tie it in.

Now, I had recently come from Central America, where I had been on a boat for sixteen months, and I knew how to tie things down. But Dom Um insisted that he was going to tie it down. Dom Um could be a little obstinate. He was amicable about the conversation, but he needed to do it his way, so he tied everything onto the top of the Chrysler. We start down the expressway towards town, and Dom Um's luggage slides off the rack and drops into at least two lanes of traffic. The cars behind are squealing their brakes trying to avoid running over this stuff, and I pull over to the side of the road. As soon as I stop on the shoulder, Dom Um bolts from the back seat and onto the highway to retrieve his bags. My first thought was, *This is not a good start to this tour. If I get this guy killed, it's not going to bode well for my future with the band.* So I rushed out to help him get his stuff off the road a little more quickly and get him back into the car.

That's where it began, and it was often like that; a traveling circus sort of affair, all of which I remember fondly, although often with amazement and amused resignation.

Shawn Hart went on to tour internationally with Grover Washington Jr., then migrated to the magazine publishing industry where he worked as a writer, editor, and production director. He is now retired and living in Philadelphia with his wife, Kari.

Darryl Brown:
Joe Zawinul was a very interesting guy—extremely talented. He was the conductor of the band, almost like an orchestral conductor. He was very specific with us—what a person should play, when he should play it, how he should play it. Joe was neat offstage as well. He was a great swimmer. When we were on the road, he was always in the pools at the hotels. I remember Joe took me to a Japanese restaurant and introduced me to chopsticks. I had never seen those. He showed me how to hold them and said, "As a drummer, you should have no problem with this." So I grabbed the chopsticks and said to myself, "Well, I guess I'm going to just get it right," doing that competition thing with Joe. I never thought

it would spread over to something like chopsticks.

We went to see the George Foreman–Muhammad Ali fight. Joe loved the fights, loved boxing. He loved the concept of champions. He would always tell us, "We are the baddest band on the planet. We are the champions, bar none." I don't know what Wayne thought when he was saying these things, but this was very motivating for me. He insisted we have a really strong presence on stage. He would say, "I want you guys to play to the back of the room. I want you to play for that little dude with the five dollar seat all the way in the back." And I think he was trying to say that when we played, it would be powerful and it would radiate through the entire room.[14]

After his stint with Weather Report, *Darryl Brown remained in the music business a few years longer, notably doing Stanley Clarke's* School Days *tour and recording on Clarke's album* I Wanna Play for You. *Brown eventually returned to college and earned his medical degree from Drexel University College of Medicine. He subsequently practiced medicine for many years in the Phoenix, Arizona area before passing away at the end of 2017. The mark he made on his community is evident in the many online messages that were posted in response to his obituary.*[15]

Chuck Bazemore:

Right before rehearsal we always sat down and talked around the table, had something to eat. That was great. This way you could feel one another and get the chemistry going. We studied our charts, studied the music, what we had to do. And they were trying to go into like a funk band. That's why they called me. In Philadelphia I was known for my foot because I had a unique style. They called me Heavy Sound Chuck Bazemore.[16]

Chuck Bazemore resides in "The City of Brotherly Love," where he is a successful businessman.

Leon "Ndugu" Chancler:

That whole period of how music was made is gone. That was one of the greater times in music because you had openness to all elements and genres of music, and could input them into any situation. And the beauty of that era was that freedom in the hands of guys that had that depth in those genres. They could take that music and make it anything, from avant-garde to funk to Latin to Brazilian to straight-ahead jazz to *anything*, right at the drop of a dime, because all of it was bred in their musical scope.[17]

Leon "Ndugu" Chancler became one of the most sought-after studio drummers in the world, recording with artists ranging from Michael Jackson to Frank Sinatra. He was also a champion of music education and taught at USC before his death from cancer in 2018.

Bruce Botnick:

Of course, Joe was *La Patrón* (the boss), but he was cool because he never, to my recollection, used the word *no* in a negative way. He seemed open to something good coming along. One thing I loved about Joe is that when he heard it, he knew. Joe always had that vision in his head, whether it was right for this album or for the next album—he always had that kernel. He and Wayne had gotten together and had arrangements in their minds, but they left it totally open to happenstance, to good things happening. Joe was the personification of, *Let's not kill it before it gets out of the cradle.* He would leave it open, and then he would know that if he went too far, he was able to pull back.[18]

Bruce Botnick is a legendary recording engineer and producer, best known for his work with the Doors, Buffalo Springfield, and the Beach Boys. He has also recorded and mixed the scores for over one hundred movie soundtracks.

Alyrio Lima:

There were times that Joe would start playing all alone, improvising in the best of the bests, and Wayne would blow with such a gentleness that made the same tune be totally fresh—new and unexpected. That was the trademark of that band—freedom to play the beauty of life. They had the courage to be new and were very successful in doing so. I love them and am grateful to their music artistry and their patience to us youngsters at the time, to play the beautiful notes, in front without rushing, pushing without forcing the beat ahead—alive and swinging like a motherfucker.[19]

Alyrio Lima continued touring and recording with name jazz musicians for the rest of the 1970s, after which he became a disciple of the Indian spiritualist Rajneesh, with whom Lima maintained a close relationship until the latter's death in 1990. Alyrio now lives in Brazil.

Chester Thompson:

There was a feel about the recordings. For one thing, it was the way you listened. I remember a distinct moment that affected everything I have done since. I think we were playing "Gibraltar" and I was just listening to Wayne. I'm playing with the headphones on, but mentally, it was like

I was in my living room listening to this amazing band. And then I had this thought. It was like, *You're not paying attention to what you're doing,* because I was grooving on what I was hearing. And it's so funny because the moment I had that thought, I heard the drummer start to go left. And all of sudden I realized, well, that's me, and I was able to not blow the take. I heard that first inkling of something, but caught it.

And I realized for the first time that that's the way to listen—to be so totally absorbed in the music that's going on, you've got to listen as though you're in the audience, not the one playing. And I think I did that okay on stage, but because I didn't grow up in the studios like some of the L.A. guys and people who grew up in the recording centers, it was a turning point for me. That's something I'll always be grateful for.[20]

After parting with Weather Report, Thompson joined the touring company of The Wiz. A year later, Phil Collins called, and Chester joined the band Genesis. In addition to numerous studio recordings, Thompson was for many years an adjunct professor at Belmont University in Nashville, Tennessee, before retiring in 2018.

Narada Michael Walden:

I can't judge anybody, but I can certainly tell you, as far as musicians walking on this earth, there are no higher than Joe Zawinul and Wayne Shorter. They come no more supremely tuned. They come no more supremely inspired. They come no more developed on their instruments. They can be free on their instruments and have complete command of the rainbow, command of the heaven, command of the hell, and can go back and forth at will. *At will.* And if you can't go with them, you ain't on the scene. And those who *are* on the scene, it's because they understand it. Joe and Wayne are the elite, the very top. They are the elite.[21]

Narada Michael Walden became a hugely successful record producer, working with a who's who of the music industry. He has been nominated for eight Grammy Awards, winning three, including Producer of the Year in 1987 for Whitney Houston's album Whitney.

Bob Cavallo:

I grew to love those guys, and I think they liked us. I just made sure they could pay their rent and operate and play. And we did pretty good for them; we did improve circumstances. I think they were making more money when we had them than at any other time. And if you listen to the album *Heavy Weather*, "Birdland" was the reason it got attention, but the record itself was the most accessible record I think they every made. I was so proud to be part of that.[22]

Along with his partners Joe Ruffalo and Steve Fargnoli, Bob Cavallo produced Prince's feature films, Purple Rain *and* Under the Cherry Moon. *Cavallo later became chairman of the Disney Music Group before retiring in 2012.*

Alex Acuña:

We had an incredible time on the road. A lot of laughs, a lot of fun, a lot of music, a lot of this and that, and all the things that the industry—the entertainment business—offers to all of the musicians. Especially in Europe, Weather Report was like the Beatles of jazz. Every time we played, it was like, Wow! Weather Report! Everybody was screaming, even with Chester and Alphonso. We played four or five nights in Paris, five thousand people every night, people outside waiting.

And Joe and Wayne—this is very important—remember that I came from Puerto Rico to Las Vegas to Los Angeles, and I'm playing with one of the heaviest bands in the whole world, Weather Report. And this is the only band that when you became a member of the band, you were a *member* of the band. You were not Joe and Wayne's drummer or percussionist. You were a Weather Report *member*.

I had a little problem after I left Weather Report. I don't want to mention the names, but some guitar players that had a little name hired me to play with them, and they go in first class, and I go in regular class in the back. And when they did the interviews, they just interviewed them. See, I was raised in a band with Weather Report that when Joe and Wayne were interviewed, they said you also have to interview Jaco. And you also have to interview Alex. And you also have to interview Manolo.

They were very generous with us, Joe and Wayne. Joe was the first person in my life that invited me to go first class in an airline. He said, "Alex, I want to take you to New York a couple of days before we play. We fly in first class." That was Joe.[23]

Alex Acuña settled in the Los Angeles area, where he has applied his talents to innumerable recordings, television shows, and motion pictures. He is the recipient of an emeritus Most Valuable Player award from the National Academy of Recording Arts and Sciences. But if you ask him, he will tell you that he is most proud of the five children that he raised with his wife, Diana.

Alan Howarth:

Having listened to the band improvise on those same tunes hundreds of times, there were moments that were literally music from the Gods, where I heard the best stuff *ever*. And it just came and went. If you weren't there, you missed it. And that I take into my own musical palette moving forward as a composer and a sound designer and all the film stuff that I do now. What I learned from them, you couldn't buy, and you can't put in a bottle. You had to be there as a witness and have it repeat over and over again, so you knew their patterns and how they did it. And that's in my head. When I go, it goes.[24]

Right after his stint with Weather Report, Alan Howarth parlayed his knowledge of synthesizers into a gig doing sound design for the Star Trek *theatrical films. Nowadays, Howarth is best known for his composing collaborations with film director John Carpenter.*

Peter Erskine:

When I joined the band, fitness was a big part of the whole macho thing. I mean, Joe was taking boxing lessons. He was in good shape—very good shape. And Jaco, of course, would compete any way he could when it came to physical prowess. They would always be bragging, trying to one-up each other. And Wayne had put on the middle age paunch already. His hair was graying, and Jaco would always make jokes. "Wayne, you painting the kids' bedroom ceiling again?" And then all of a sudden Wayne's hair would be all black again, and Jaco would say, "Wayne got himself some Grecian Formula last week" or something. So as much as I know they loved and revered Wayne and cherished him, he was sort of the odd guy out, just on that alone.

And yet, for all their obsession about fitness, Wayne outlasted everybody and proved to have a more enduring creative output. Wayne has now been a leader of a band that has lasted longer than Weather Report, which is a testament not only to the strength of his creativity, but to his innate personal strength and charisma as a bandleader. And he's incredibly modest. You know, the thought occurs to me that Joe and Jaco's interest in spirituality was, at best, kind of gimmicky. I mean, they dabbled at numerology, and they bragged that they had copies of *The Urantia Book*, and they liked quoting this and that. But Wayne was the only person who practiced any adherence or devotion to anything that represented something greater than himself. And if you look at Weather Report, it worked for him, and there might be a lesson in that.[25]

Peter Erskine is perhaps the most-recorded jazz drummer of his generation, appearing on over seven hundred albums and film scores. He and his wife Mutsy (whom he met during Weather Report's 1978 tour of Japan) operate Fuzzy Music, a sort of modern day equivalent of Andrew's Music. The

424 / ELEGANT PEOPLE

author of several books, Erskine is also Director of Drumset Studies at the Thornton School of Music, University of Southern California, where he was honored with the 2015 Associates Award for Artistic Expression, the highest honor the faculty bestows on its members for significant artistic impact.

Robert Thomas Jr.:

Now that Joe's gone, I realize what an incredible friend and mentor I had. These kinds of people are rare, especially with his style of writing music. I went to a great school with that man and I have a lot to show for it. When you look at the cast of musicians that have been in that band, it's the best of the best on the planet. What an honor for a bebop conga player to be in that category. So I'm just always very thankful. And I'll keep playing his music and paying my respects to one of the greatest artists that ever lived. And that comes from my heart—every single word. What a journey, man. And it's not over, because the world still loves his music. That's what keeps him alive.[26]

Robert Thomas Jr. still makes his home in South Florida, where he teaches and gigs. He remains the only bebop hand drummer in the world, still confounding the local congueros.

Omar Hakim:

Weather Report was a great experience. First of all, it was a freakin' dream come true. I graduated in 1977 from Music and Arts High School, and five years later I'm in Weather Report—five years after graduating high school. I was busy, doing a lot, but I didn't see that coming.

And you want to hear something really interesting? When I was on the road for the first tour with Joe, I got offered David Bowie's Serious Moonlight tour. Huge money. I had never seen that kind of money for playing drums. And I asked myself, "Well, who played drums with David Bowie?" And I couldn't think of anybody. Then I thought, okay, Dennis Davis. I knew Dennis Davis played on "Fame," but he was the only one that I could think of off the top of my head.

Then I said, "Well, I'm in this band, Weather Report. Who played drums in Weather Report?" And I could name a bunch of cats: Dom Um Romão, Manolo, Alex, Peter, Chester Thompson, Narada Michael Walden, Eric Gravatt—a long list of drummers. So I said, "This is where I need to be right now." That money would have come in handy at that moment, but for some reason I understood the value of being considered in that lineage of Weather Report drummers. I mean, it's a list of cats that I love, so to be a part of the list was just mind-blowing at that age.[27]

Omar Hakim has worked with the biggest names in virtually every genre of music, both in the recording studio and on stage. In addition to his performing and recording career, he chairs the Berklee percussion department.

Victor Bailey:

Weather Report opened doors. I remember at the time thinking that once you're in that group, you have a name for life—you have an instant name. Everybody all over the world knows who you are, and it will last forever. And it's proven to be true, no matter what else I do or have done. I'm a part of music history. I wish I could say I was Joe and Wayne, the guys who created it and who changed music, but I was a part of it, and that will never go away.[28]

Victor Bailey is the only musician to join Joe in Weather Report, Weather Update, the Zawinul Syndicate, and the WDR Big Band with Joe Zawinul. In his later years, Victor taught at his alma mater, the Berklee College of Music. He died in 2016 from complications related to Charcot-Marie-Tooth disease.

José Rossy:

Those guys worked together like one. Ideas came from Wayne, and Joe added his take to it, and with no effort it came out like a piece. Joe had unlimited creativity. That man would think it and play it. Every night there were different things happening without talking about it. It would just happen together. And Wayne—what a sweet human being; he was just the best, and his compositions were angelic.

And they were counting on us to just play. I mean, it was never like, this is what you have to do here—we were never told exactly what to play. We would just feel and hear what's going on, and create our own part, and they seemed to like it. There weren't any rules or anything. They had the format of the tunes and it sounded like it was totally orchestrated. But then somewhere around it we would create stuff to go with it, adding other pieces to it, and put it together to make it sound like Weather Report. And it was unbelievable, always.[29]

José Rossy lives in Texas about an hour north of Dallas where he runs his own music studio and does occasional gigs—"domesticated, but playing," he says.

Jim Swanson:

Doing the inverted keyboard and the cycling voices on the Oberheim and all that stuff, it was always about Joe doing mental athletics. He was a very athletic guy, and just to exercise his brain in that way was very challenging to him. It was really fun to work together with him like that. I could technically enable him to do what he artistically wanted to do. We worked together very well in that sense. And I think he respected me to the end of his life for that, because of all the gizmos that I came up with for him—the MIDI switchers and all the other stuff. He truly respected me for that.

And we were lifelong friends. It was a great privilege in my life to be a friend of Joe Zawinul's. One of the last things he ever told me when I went out to his house in Malibu was, "You know, Jim Swanson, I'm glad I know you." I'll take that to my heart. "I'm glad I know you, Jim Swanson." It was that kind of friendship. My kids grew up knowing him as Uncle Joe. We would go to New Year's Eve parties at his house and visit on the weekends. My son would play with his grandson, Simon. My wife was a good friend of Maxine's. They would sit in the family room and watch movies, and Joe and I would go out to the studio and do stuff. It was always a family mentality and environment with the band and crew. It was a great, great experience in my life, and I'll always remember it.[30]

Jim Swanson is an electrical engineer in Southern California. He has designed or contributed to many audio and musical devices during his career, including some one-of-a-kind items for Zawinul.

Mino Cinélu:

Those guys were such opposites—more opposite than yin and yang. And yet, what they did together was fabulous. You have one who could hear everything, and one who could find melodies on the spot on anything. That sounds like a good recipe if you just leave it at that. Then you've got the fact that they both played with Miles, so that's a good way to hear things. You had two geniuses together, but also, you had two kids. Those guys were two kids, except one was not acting like it in front of other people. But Joe was a kid; that's what's so wonderful. And Wayne, we all know. So two kids, with all due respect.

It's still something that years from now we will say, "Wow, I saw that; I heard that; I met them." And for some of us, "I played with them." I am part of this whole thing—Weather Report and Miles. I'm proud of this legacy. Not too shabby for a kid who left his home at seventeen years old with six dollars in his pocket and has been on his own since.[31]

Mino Cinélu has worked with countless artists in the pop, R&B and jazz genres, including Sting and Kate Bush. An endlessly creative musician, Mino continues to perform live and on record.

Steve Khan:

There was a stretch where a couple of gigs in Italy got canceled, which probably never would have happened to Weather Report, but it happened to Weather Update. So we were in this little town for a week called Civitanova Marche on the Adriatic Coast of Italy—literally a one-street town. It was a hundred degrees out and we were in a hotel that had no air conditioning. It was brutal. It was driving all of us completely fucking nuts. So the band got together—everybody but Joe—and we decided to pay the bus driver to take us to Florence to go to the da Vinci Museum. We just had to get out of there; we couldn't take it anymore.

We made our plans and the day came, and as we were all heading out to the bus, Joe walked into the hotel with his typical kind of Western gunslinger swagger. So Peter, with that beautiful innocence of his, said, "Hey Joe. We're taking the bus to Florence to the da Vinci Museum. You wanna soak up some culture with us?" And Joe looked at him and bellowed, "I don't need no fucking culture. I *am* culture!"

You could think about what he said for weeks. And when the whole relationship has come and gone, he *is* culture. We're sitting here thirty-two years later, and I remember it like it was yesterday. I'll never forget that.[32]

Steve Khan is considered one of the great jazz guitarists, having maintained a standard of excellence for over forty years. In addition to his own albums, he has also enjoyed a prolific career doing session work.

Miroslav Vitous:

I enjoyed all of the music we played until *Sweetnighter*, when we started with "Boogie Woogie Waltz" and all that stuff. It was not my cup of tea, let's face it. It really didn't ring with my musicality because I was asked to go back to jail, to a slave role, at that point. And I guess my natural feeling was, why should I go back to jail when we are playing some creative music? My soul didn't want to do that at all. That was so obvious.

I will tell you an interesting story. When God created jazz music, the bass player was the only person who could not play the instrument. The piano player could play like a maniac, the drummer was fantastic, the horn players were cooking on their instruments, but the bass player could hardly play. Most of them were actually trombone players who picked up the bass because there were no bass players. So the bass went *boom-boom-boom-boom* because that was all he could do.

So then imagine somebody who comes to this music who can really play the bass—*it's really a drag.* But an even more interesting thing: when you really start playing the bass, it completely changes the music. So in a way, I'm very lucky, because when I came and started playing the bass like I play the bass, I was the first one to do it, aside from Scott LaFaro and a few others before me. In that sense, it really came together in my time, so I was really lucky because I had a free territory. No one did anything like that before me, not really.[33]

In 1979, Miroslav Vitous began teaching at the New England Conservatory, and subsequently became chairman of the jazz department. In 1988, he relocated to Europe and developed the Miroslav Vitous Symphonic Orchestra Samples *CD-ROMs, one of the first and best sample libraries of its kind. Ultimately, Miroslav came full circle with 2003's* Universal Syncopations, *an album that many observers compared favorably to* Infinite Search. *He now resides in the country of his birth and is working on his own memoir.*

Wayne Shorter:

We were doing things that had nothing to do with a tune here, a tune there. One thing we didn't want to do was consciously repeat something; we wanted the variety of things to be presented on these albums. . . . What we did in general—with the music then and those albums—was just profound. We were taking a chance at that time without any support from Columbia Records really, knowing that it would take fifteen or twenty years to gather a wide audience.[34]

Joe Zawinul:

We were able, with that band, to get an incredible power and we turned on so many people through this music. It was unbelievable. And for that, I will always be happy.[35]

Acknowledgments

THIS BOOK IS THE CULMINATION of my lifelong passion for Weather Report and Joe Zawinul. It began in 1976, when I read a five-star review of *Black Market* in *Down Beat* magazine and purchased a copy of the LP at the local record store. At the time, I was in the thrall of Chick Corea's band, Return to Forever, but *Black Market* was a revelation. Thereafter, I bought each of Weather Report's albums as they were released and wound up purchasing their back catalog as well.

Living in Los Angeles, I had the privilege of attending many Weather Report concerts, including the Long Beach show that yielded most of the material for *8:30*. Seeing Jaco sliding around on the stage still brings a smile to my face. I also saw the Hakim-Bailey band three times, and that group took a second seat to no one.

In 1999, I founded the website Zawinul Online (www.zawinulonline.org), initially as a clearinghouse for online material about Joe, and later as a repository for news and my own articles. When I woke up on Tuesday, September 11, 2007, I learned from an email that Joe had died. On that day I created the Joe Zawinul Memorial Page as a place for fans to post their personal tributes. That page is still live and can be found at www.zawinulonline.org/memorial/.

In 2001, I established the website Weather Report: The Annotated Discography (www.weatherreportdiscography.org). As I describe in this book's introduction, these websites opened the door to my interviews with Joe, paving the way for all the others. These interviews took place over a span of many years, starting with my first session with Zawinul in 2003.

There are many people who helped me bring this book to fruition, but first I must sincerely thank everyone who agreed to be interviewed. One of the great joys of this project has been hearing their stories firsthand. I have become friends with some of them, while others died in the intervening years. I hope this book honors their stories. I am indebted to them.

I interviewed the following individuals: Alex Acuña, Arma Andon, Victor Bailey, Chuck Bazemore, Lou Beach, Gene Bertoncini, Bob Bobbing, Steve "Muruga" Booker, Bruce Botnick, Darryl Brown, Barbara Burton, Bob Cavallo, Ndugu Chancler, Mino Cinélu, Frank Cuomo, Herschel Dwellingham, Guy Eckstine, Wayne Edwards, Greg Errico, Peter Erskine, Ed Freeman, Bob Glassenberg, Gary Grainger, Eric Kamau Gravatt, Gerry Griffith, Skip Hadden, Omar Hakim, Billy Hart, Shawn Hart, Alan Howarth, Alphonso Johnson, Steve Khan, Scott Kinsey, Bill Laswell, David Less, Maria Booker Lucien, Roy McCurdy, Dave McMacken, Airto Moreira, Alphonse Mouzon, Alison Mills Newman, Nan O'Byrne, Nicholas Payton, Roger Powell, Brian Risner, José Rossy, Wayne Shorter, Janis Siegel, Bradie Speller, Jim Swanson, Robert Thomas Jr., Chester Thompson, Ralph Towner, Jerri Trandem, Jack Trompetter, Miroslav Vitous, Narada Michael Walden, Andrew White, Ishmael Wilburn, Joe Zawinul, and Risa Zincke.

Several others responded to my questions via email, sometimes at length. Those that I corresponded with are: Brad Blanchard, Bobby Colomby, Frank Colón, Johnny Conga, Heinz Czadek, Darius Fischer, Rob Freeman, David Friedman, Laurie Goldstein, Sonny Greenwich, Jamey Haddad, Kenny Klimak, Sabine Kabongo, Alyrio Lima, Mark Mawrence, Vince Mendoza, Mike Nock, Dan Phillips, Doug Ramsey, John Sanna, Tom Stroud, and Jim Wilke.

A few of my interview subjects went above and beyond. Brian Risner, the chief meteorologist, supported my efforts from the beginning and has become a friend. We've had more conversations about Weather Report than I can count. I hope I did right by the band, Brian. Alex Acuña, Alphonso Johnson, Wayne Shorter, Robert Thomas Jr., Miroslav Vitous, and Joe Zawinul were all kind enough to grant me multiple interviews. Peter Erskine indulged my questions three times in face-to-face settings while also responding to my many questions via email. Another friend is Jim Swanson, with whom I spent many afternoons talking Weather Report over beers and tacos. And then there's Herschel Dwellingham. I have yet to get to Bogalusa, but one of these days I will. Thanks, Herschel, for being Herschel.

I must thank Brian Digenti for arranging my first interview with Zawinul in 2003. If it wasn't for that, I don't know that I would have pursued this book at all. Brian, you got the ball rolling.

Many others supported my efforts over the years, and I am most grateful. One of those is Tom Wilmeth, author of the book, *Sound Bites: A Lifetime of Listening*. I cannot begin to tell you how generous Tom was with his time. I have never met him in person, but an email inquiry regarding a piece he had written about Jaco Pastorius led to him copy editing an early draft of my manuscript. He also provided me with a transcript of his 1980 interview with Eric Gravatt.

Yet another supporter of my work has been Anil Prasad, the founder of Innerviews (www.innerviews.org), the Internet's first and longest-running music magazine. Andy Forward was of great help in providing archival concert recordings. Holly Trechter, a dear friend and a former staffer at Stanford University, helped me procure periodical articles. Jim Dustin assisted with graphic design. Shawn Hart lent me his eye for detail. Gerhard Hauer helped with German-to-English translations. Koji Tanaka and Atsuko Yamura provided Japanese-to-English translations. Many years ago, Thomas Kober provided me with an English translation of a Zawinul documentary that aired on German television.

I am grateful to all of the photographers who contributed images for this book, starting with Shigeru Uchiyama, who opened his archive of Weather Report photographs to me. Likewise, Peter Erskine, Brian Risner, and Jim Swanson were generous in allowing me to choose photos from their collections. My additional thanks to Michael Wilderman, Lisa Tanner (on behalf of her father, Lee Tanner), and Mark Brady for the use of their photographs.

Readers of early manuscripts of this book include George Cole, Peter Erskine, Rick Mattingly, Anil Prasad, Shawn Hart, and Tom Wilmeth. I must acknowledge my copy editor, Matt DeMazza, who took to this project enthusiastically. When I brought the manuscript to him, he had never heard of Weather Report, but he checked them out on Spotify and became a fan. Any errors that crept into the manuscript as a result of my endless tinkering are my own. My thanks to John Cerullo at Rowman & Littlefield for championing this book, and to Barbara Claire and Carol Flannery for shepherding it through the publishing process.

In addition to the research tools found at institutions of higher learning, such as the Entertainment Industry Magazine Archive, the following websites were valuable in doing research: newspapers.com, newspaperarchive.com, awardsandshows.com, and David A. Gleason's amazing website, worldradiohistory.com. I would also like to acknowledge the many journalists who created a historic record of the band. Their work helped immeasurably in adding meat to the bones of this book. I am especially grateful for the kindness and generosity of Brian Glasser and Gunther Baumann.

Many afternoons were spent researching and writing at the Dr. Martin Luther King Jr. Library in San José, California. Additional research was conducted at Stanford University, the University of California at Los Angeles, and the Institute of Jazz Studies at Rutgers University. Other institutions that responded to my requests include Monmouth University, which houses the Bruce Springsteen Special Collection; the Special Collections Archive at the University of Idaho Library; and the Briscoe Center for American History at the University of Texas at Austin.

Assistance in arranging interviews or connecting me to interview subjects was provided by David Agnew; Judi Bohn; Diana Booker; Mike Charlasch; Alisse

Kingsley, Muse Media; Tom Korkidis, International Music World; Steve Netsky, Ed Keane Associates; Tina Pelikan, ECM; Anna M. Sala, AB Artists Management; and David Stanoch.

Others who provided assistance along the way: E. Taylor Atkins; Tony Bacon; John Bowen; Adam Budofsky, Editorial Director at *Modern Drummer*; Susan Burneson, Dolph Briscoe Center for American History at the University of Texas at Austin; Lukas Camenzind; Eileen Chapman, Associate Director of the Center for the Arts, Monmouth University; Robert Collins; Max Dax; Dan Del Fiorentino, the Music Historian for NAMM; Michael Fitzgerald; Mark Frandsen; Mark Gilbert, editor of *Jazz Journal*; Will Groves, editor in chief at Music Radar; Shawn Hart; Danny Kastner; Mark Kidel; Alex Livadas, Sony Music Entertainment; David Lusterman, String Letter Publishing; Rick Mattingly; Tony Palkovic; Ted Panken; Mark Parsons; Ingrid Pastorius; Dina Pearlman, Executive Director of the Alan R. Pearlman Foundation; Matt Peiken; Marco Piretti; Jeff Potter; Jeffrey Pepper Rodgers; Monk Rowe, Hamilton College Fillius Jazz Archive; David Schroeder, New York University; Elliot Sears; Steve Shepherd; Dore Stein; Erin Stoddart, Special Collections and Archives, University of Idaho Library; Thomas Tierney, Sony Music Archives Library; David Vandagriff; George Varga; Larry Wayte; Anthony Zawinul; and Ivan Zawinul.

I want to thank my wife, Sue, for her encouragement and support. Sue, you mean the world to me.

And finally, my apologies to my sister, Susan, for all the loud music.

Appendix A 1970 Timeline

Feb 6	Joe's last studio session with Miles Davis.
Mar 6–7	Wayne's last live performances with Miles Davis.
March	Miroslav records Larry Coryell's album *Spaces*. He meets engineer David Baker, with whom he works over the next several months to record the tracks that form the album *Purple*. Zawinul participates in some of these sessions.
Apr 3	Wayne records *Moto Grosso Feio*. Miroslav is on the session.
Aug 6, 10, 12	Joe records *Zawinul*. Miroslav is on the sessions.
Aug 26	Wayne records *Odyssey of Iska*. Alphonse Mouzon is on the session.
Late August	Miroslav leaves for Japan with Herbie Mann. While there, he sells the tracks that are later released as the album *Purple*, and gets an offer to join Miles Davis.
Sep 1–13	Cannonball Adderley residency at Shelly's Manne-Hole in Los Angeles. Joe gets an offer to join Miles Davis.
Sep 11	While in Japan, Miroslav records *Green Line* with his Herbie Mann bandmates.
Late September	After returning from Japan, Miroslav plays one gig with Miles Davis. Later, he calls Wayne, asking if he would be interested in forming a band.
Oct 3–4	Cannonball Adderley and Miles Davis perform on back-to-back nights at the Pacific Northwest Jazz Spectacular in Seattle. Miles asks Joe to play with him, but Zawinul declines because Miroslav is not there. Joe tells the promoter he is forming a band with Wayne Shorter.

Oct 5–6	Joe's last recording sessions with Cannonball for the album *The Price You Got to Pay to Be Free*.
Oct 6–8	Miroslav and Alphonse Mouzon record with Eugene McDaniels for the latter's album *Headless Heroes of the Apocalypse*.
Oct 13	Wayne's *Creation* session for Blue Note, with Miroslav, Mouzon, McCoy Tyner, and Barbara Burton.
Oct 24	*Melody Maker* announces that Joe is leaving Cannonball Adderley to form a band with Wayne, Miroslav, Mouzon, and Woody Shaw.
Oct 28	Overdubs for *Zawinul* with Wayne, Miroslav, Woody Shaw, and Hubert Laws.
November	Miroslav's last recording sessions with Herbie Mann, for the album *Memphis Two-Step*.
Dec 2–8	Joe's last performances with Cannonball Adderley at the Apollo Theater. Miroslav and Alphonse Mouzon are on the same bill, supporting Eugene McDaniels.
December	Joe, Miroslav and Mouzon record tracks for Tim Hardin's album *Bird on a Wire*. The producer is Ed Freeman, who photographed the covers for *Zawinul* and the first Weather Report album.
Dec 10	*Down Beat* reports that Joe is leaving Cannonball to form a band with Wayne, Miroslav, Mouzon, and "trumpeter David Lee."

Appendix B Live Band Personnel

This listing does not include musicians who sat in with the band for single performances.

Jun–Sep 1971
Joe Zawinul (keyboards), Wayne Shorter (saxophones), Miroslav Vitous (acoustic and electric bass), Alphonse Mouzon (drums), Dom Um Romão (percussion)

Oct 1971–Jun 1973
Zawinul, Shorter, Vitous, Eric Gravatt (drums), Romão

Jun–Nov 1973
Zawinul, Shorter, Vitous, Greg Errico (drums), Romão

Nov–Dec 1973
Zawinul, Shorter, Vitous, Ishmael Wilburn (drums), Romão
Bradie Speller (congas) joined the band for some performances.

Jan–May 1974
Zawinul, Shorter, Alphonso Johnson (electric bass), Wilburn, Romão

Jun–Nov 1974
Zawinul, Shorter, Johnson, Darryl Brown (drums), Romão
Romão left the band before the last performances of 1974. Other drummers joined Brown on the bandstand at various times.

Feb–Oct 1975
Zawinul, Shorter, Johnson, Chester Thompson (drums), Alyrio Lima (percussion)

Oct–Nov 1975
Zawinul, Shorter, Johnson, Thompson, Alex Acuña (percussion)
Acuña took over percussion at the start of the fall European tour.

Apr 1976–Nov 1977
Zawinul, Shorter, Jaco Pastorius (electric bass), Acuña (drums), Manolo Badrena (percussion)
Badrena departed before the last concerts of 1977, after which the band performed as a quartet.

Jun 1978–Jan 1980
Zawinul, Shorter, Pastorius, Peter Erskine (drums)

Jan 1980–Jul 1981
Zawinul, Shorter, Pastorius, Erskine, Robert Thomas Jr. (percussion)
Thomas joined the band on Jan. 24, about a week into the U.S. tour.

Jun 1982–Aug 1983
Zawinul, Shorter, Victor Bailey (electric bass), Omar Hakim (drums), José Rossy (percussion)

Mar–Oct 1984
Zawinul, Shorter, Bailey, Hakim, Mino Cinélu (percussion)
Carl Anderson (vocals) appeared with the band for some U.S. performances.

Bibliography

Books

Abernethy, David. *The Prophet from Silicon Valley: The Complete Story of Sequential Circuits*. Auckland, NZ: AM Publishing New Zealand, 2015.

Anderson, Iain. *This Is Our Music: Free Jazz, The Sixties, and American Culture*. Philadelphia: Univ. of Pennsylvania Press, 2007.

Atkins, E. Taylor. *Blue Nippon: Authenticating Jazz in Japan*. Durham, NC: Duke Univ. Press, 2001.

Bailey, Philip, with Keith Zimmerman and Kent Zimmerman. *Shining Star: Braving the Elements of Earth, Wind & Fire*. New York: Penguin, 2014.

Baker, David N., Lida M. Belt, and Herman C. Hudson. *The Black Composer Speaks*. Metuchen, NJ: The Scarecrow Press, 1978.

Balliett, Whitney. *Improvising: Sixteen Jazz Musicians and Their Art*. New York: Oxford Univ. Press, 1977.

Baumann, Gunther. *Zawinul: Ein Leben aus Jazz*. Salzburg; Frankfurt am Main; Wien: Residenz-Verl., 2002.

Carr, Ian. *Miles Davis: The Definitive Biography*. New York: Thunder's Mouth Press, 1998.

Cogan, Jim and William Clark. *Temples of Sound: Inside the Great Recording Studios*. San Francisco: Chronicle Books, 2003.

Cohodas, Nadine. *Queen: The Life and Music of Dinah Washington*. New York: Billboard Books, 2006.

Cole, Bill. *Miles Davis: A Musical Biography*. New York: William Morrow, 1974.

Coryell, Julie, and Laura Friedman. *Jazz-Rock Fusion: The People, The Music*. New York: Delacorte Press, 1978.

Cuscuna, Michael, and Michel Ruppli. *The Blue Note Label: A Discography, Revised and Expanded*. Westport, CT: Greenwood Press, 2001.

Davis, Clive, with Anthony DeCurtis. *The Soundtrack of My Life*. New York: Simon & Schuster, 2013.

Davis, Clive, with James Willwerth. *Clive: Inside the Record Business*. New York: William Morrow, 1975.

Davis, Miles, with Quincy Troupe. *Miles, the Autobiography*. New York: Simon & Schuster, 1989.

Edwards, Wayne. *Can't Touch This: Memoirs of a Disillusioned Music Executive*. Bloomington, IN: AuthorHouse, 2015, Kindle.

Erskine, Peter. *No Beethoven: An Autobiography & Chronicle of Weather Report*. FUZZ/E/BOOKS, 2013.

Fellezs, Kevin. *Birds of Fire: Jazz, Rock, Funk and the Creation of Fusion*. Durham, NC: Duke Univ. Press, 2011.

Giddins, Gary. *Rhythm-a-ning: Jazz Tradition and Innovation in the '80s*. New York: Oxford Univ. Press, 1985.

Giddins, Gary, and Scott DeVeaux. *Jazz*. New York: W. W. Norton, 2009.

Ginell, Cary. *Walk Tall: The Music & Life of Julian "Cannonball" Adderley*. Milwaukee: Hal Leonard Books, 2013.

Ginell, Cary. *The Evolution Of Mann: Herbie Mann and the Flute in Jazz*. Milwaukee: Hal Leonard Books, 2014.

Glasser, Brian. *In a Silent Way: A Portrait of Joe Zawinul*. London: Sanctuary Publishing, 2001.

Glasser, Brian. *In a Silent Way: A Portrait of Joe Zawinul*. 2nd ed. London: As Long As It's Hot, 2009.

Gluck, Bob. *The Miles Davis Lost Quintet and Other Revolutionary Ensembles*. Chicago: Univ. of Chicago Press, 2016.

Gluck, Bob. *You'll Know When You Get There: Herbie Hancock and the Mwandishi Band*. Chicago: Univ. of Chicago Press, 2012.

Goldberg, Joe. *Jazz Masters of the Fifties*. New York: Da Capo Press, 1980.

Goldsher, Alan. *Hard Bop Academy: The Sidemen of Art Blakey and the Jazz Messengers*. Milwaukee: Hal Leonard, 2002.

Harper, Colin. *Bathed In Lightning: John McLaughlin, the 60s and the Emerald Beyond*. London: Jawbone Press,

2014.

Hancock, Herbie, with Lisa Dickey. *Possibilities*. New York: Viking Penguin, 2014.

Harrison , Max, Eric Thacker, and Stuart Nicholson. *The Essential Jazz Records Volume 2: Modernism to Postmodernism*. London: Mansell Publishing, 2000.

Hentoff, Nat. *The Jazz Life*. Cambridge, MA: Da Capo Press, 1975.

Hobsbawm, Eric. *Uncommon People: Resistance, Rebellion and Jazz*. New York: The New Press, 1998.

Jisi, Chris, ed. *Bass Player Presents the Fretless Bass*. New York: Backbeat Books, 2008.

Jones, LeRoi (a.k.a. Amari Baraka). *Black Music*. New York: William Morrow, third printing, 1970.

Kahn, Ashley. *Kind Of Blue: The Making of a Miles Davis Masterpiece*. New York: Da Capo Press, 2000.

Kolosky, Walter. *Power, Passion and Beauty: The Story of the Legendary Mahavishnu Orchestra, the Greatest Band That Ever Was*. Cary, NC: Abstract Logix Books, 2006.

Kringel, Chris. *Fretless Bass*. Milwaukee: Hal Leonard, 2007.

Lees, Gene. *Cats of Any Color: Jazz, Black and White*. New York: Da Capo Press, 2001.

Litweiler, John. *The Freedom Principle: Jazz After 1958*. New York: W. Morrow, 1984.

Marmorstein, Gary. *The Label: The Story of Columbia Records*. New York: Thunder's Mountain Press, 2007.

Martin, Linda, and Kerry Segrave. *Anti-Rock: The Opposition to Rock 'n' Roll*. Hamden, CT: Archon Books, 1988.

Mathieson, Kenny. *Cookin': Hard Bop and Soul Jazz, 1954–65*. Edinburgh: Canongate Books, 2000.

Mercer, Michelle. *Footprints: The Life and Work of Wayne Shorter*. New York: J. P. Tarcher/Penguin, 2004.

Milkowski, Bill. *Jaco: The Extraordinary and Tragic Life of Jaco Pastorius*. Deluxe ed. San Francisco: Miller Freeman Books, 2005.

Neumüller, Robert. *Joe Zawinuls Erdzeit: Interviews für ein Portrait*. Weitra: Verl. Publ. PN°1, Bibliothek der Provinz, 2009.

Nicholson, Stuart. *Jazz-Rock: A History*. New York: Schirmer Books, 1998.

Nisenson, Eric. *Blue: The Murder of Jazz*. New York: Da Capo Press, 1997.

Patterson, James T. *Grand Expectations: The United States, 1945–1974*. New York: Oxford Univ. Press, 1996.

Pinch, Trevor, and Frank Trocco. *Analog Days: The Invention and Impact of the Moog Synthesizer*. Cambridge, MA: Harvard Univ. Press, 2002.

Porter, Lewis. *John Coltrane: His Life and Music*. Ann Arbor, MI: Univ. of Michigan Press, 1998.

Ratliff, Ben. *Coltrane: The Story of a Sound*. New York: Farrar, Straus and Giroux, 2007.

Rodgers, Jeffrey Pepper. *Rock Troubadours: Conversations on the Art and Craft of Songwriting*. San Anselmo, CA: String Letter Publishing, 2000.

Rosenthal, David H. *Hard Bop: Jazz and Black Music, 1955–1965*. New York: Oxford Univ. Press, 1992.

Ruppli, Michel. *Atlantic Records: A Discography, Volume 2*. Westport, CT: Greenwood Press, 1979.

Ruppli, Michel. *Atlantic Records: A Discography, Volume 3*. Westport, CT: Greenwood Press, 1979.

Salazar, Max. *Mambo Kingdom: Latin Jazz in New York*. New York: Schirmer Trade Books, 2002.

Sheridan, Chris. *Dis Here: A Bio-Discography of Julian "Cannonball" Adderley*. Westport, CT: Greenwood Press, 2000.

Small, Mark, and Andrew Taylor. *Masters of Music: Conversations with Berklee Greats*. Boston: Berklee Press, 1999.

Svorinich, Victor. *Listen to This: Miles Davis and Bitches Brew*. Jackson, MS: Univ. Press of Mississippi, 2015.

Szwed, John. *So What: The Life of Miles Davis*. New York: Simon & Schuster, 2002.

Terry, Clark, and Gwen Terry. *Clark: The Autobiography of Clark Terry*. Berkeley: Univ. of California Press, 2011.

Trethewey, Ken. *Weather Report: Electric Red*. Cornwall, UK: Jazz-Fusion Books, 2012.

Waters, Keith. *The Studio Recordings of the Miles Davis Quintet, 1965–68*. New York: Oxford Univ. Press, 2011.

Wein, George, with Nate Chinen. *Myself Among Others: A Life in Music*. Cambridge, MA: Da Capo Press, 2003.

White, Andrew. *Everybody Loves the Sugar—The Book*. Washington, DC: Andrew's Music, 2001.

Williams, Martin. *Jazz in its Time*. New York: Oxford Univ. Press, 1989.

Wilmeth, Tom. *Sound Bites: A Lifetime of Listening*. United States: MuleShoe Press, 2016.

Yamashita, Kunihiko. *Joe Zawinul: On the Creative Process*. Tokyo: Rittor Music, 2006.

Yudkin, Jeremy. *Miles Davis, Miles Smiles, and the Invention of Post Bop*. Bloomington, IN: Indiana Univ. Press, 2008.

Yoshio, Matsushita. *All About Weather Report*. Japan: Shinko Music Entertainment, 2014.

Liner Notes

Belden, Bob. Liner notes to *E.S.P.* Miles Davis. Columbia Legacy CK 65683, 1998, CD.

Belden, Bob. Liner notes to *Miles in the Sky*. Miles Davis. Columbia CK 65684, 1998, CD.

Belden, Bob. "Annotations." Liner notes to *Miles Davis Quintet 1965–1968*. Miles Davis. Sony Legacy/Columbia C6K 67398, 1998.

Belden, Bob. Liner notes to *The Complete In a Silent Way Sessions*. Miles Davis. Columbia C3K 65362, 2001.

Bobbing, Bob. Liner notes to *Portrait of Jaco: The Early Years, 1968–1978*. Jaco Pastorius. Holiday Park Records, 2002.

Coolman, Todd F. "The Quintet." Liner notes to *Miles Davis Quintet 1965–1968*. Miles Davis. Sony Legacy/ Columbia C6K 67398, 1998.

DeMichael, Don. Liner notes to *Weather Report*. Weather Report. Columbia PC 30661, 1971

Erskine, Peter. Liner notes to *The Legendary Live Tapes: 1978–1981*. Weather Report. Sony Legacy/Columbia 88875141272, 2015.

Feather, Leonard. Liner notes to *74 Miles Away*. Cannonball Adderley. Capitol ST 2822, 1967.

Feather, Leonard. Liner notes to *Odyssey of Iska*. Wayne Shorter. Blue Note, BST 84363, 1971.

Hentoff, Nat. Liner notes to *The Big Beat*. Art Blakey & the Jazz Messengers. Blue Note 4029, 1960.

Kopp, Bill. Liner notes to *The Price You Got to Pay to Be Free*. Real Gone Music RGM-0453, 2016.

Leeds, Alan. Liner notes to *Weather Report Live & Unreleased*. Columbia/Legacy C2K 65525, 2002.

Miller, Hal. "Weather Report." Liner notes to *Forecast: Tomorrow*. Weather Report. Columbia/Legacy 82876 85570 2, 2006.

Wong, Herb. Liner notes to *Super Nova*. Wayne Shorter. Blue Note BST 84332, 1969.

Zawinul, Joe. Liner notes to *Body Acoustic*. Michiel Borstlap. EmArcy 538 976-2, 1999.

Audio and Video

The Midnight Special, Season 5, episode 23. Aired Jun. 10, 1977, viewable at https://youtu.be/tQAW9fsauT8.

The South Bank Show. Season 7, Episode 11. Originally aired Mar. 11, 1984 on ITV.

Kidel, Mark, prod. *Joe Zawinul: A Musical Portrait*. Bristol, England: Calliope Media Ltd, 2005.

Shepherd, Steve, prod. *Punk Jazz: A Portrait of Jaco Pastorius*. BBC, originally aired over Radio 3, Nov. 1998.

Online Content

"Conversation with Peter Erskine." NYU Steinhardt Jazz Studies. Jan. 26, 2016. https://youtu.be/U-yvLOck-GC0.

"Pi Corp Interview with Guy Bickel." http://psychedelicbaby.blogspot.com/2013/02/pi-corp-interview-with-guy-bickel.html, Feb. 3, 2013.

"Residents, Patients Mourn Death of Longtime CG Doctor." *Casa Grande Dispatch*. https://www.pinalcentral. com/casa_grande_dispatch/area_news/residents-patients-mourn-death-of-longtime-cg-doctor/article_ bafb5a2b-6779-572d-809c-57381946b60a.html. Dec. 18, 2017.

Blumenthal, Bob. "In Conversation with Wayne Shorter." Jazz.com. Mar. 21, 2008. http://www.jazz.com/fea-tures-and-interviews/2008/3/21/in-conversation-with-wayne-shorter.

Brown, Dr. Anthony. McCoy Tyner Smithsonian Jazz Oral History Program NEA Jazz Master interview tran-script. Smithsonian National Museum of American History . Dec. 7–8, 2011. https://amhistory.si.edu/ jazz/Tyner-McCoy/Tyner_McCoy_Transcript.pdf.

Buzby, Pat. "Miroslav Vitous' Infinite Search for Universal Syncopations." jambands.com. http://www.jambands. com/features/2004/01/29/miroslav-vitous-infinite-search-for-universal-syncopations. Jan. 29, 2004.

Collins, Chris. "Joe Zawinul." International Association of Jazz Educators. May 2000. https://web.archive.org/ web/20070416154936/http://www.iaje.org/article.asp?ArticleID=84.

Cox, Tony. "The Journey of Jazz Great Joe Zawinul." NPR. http://www.npr.org/templates/story/story.php?sto-ryId=9495945. Apr. 10, 2007.

Dax, Max. "Joe Zawinul." Alert. http://www.waahr.de/texte/joe-zawinul. Originally published in *Alert*, No. 8, Oct. 2002, 88–96.

de Wilde, Laurent. "Joe Zawinul." http://www.laurentdewilde.com/article/joe-zawinul.html. Jan. 1, 2012.

Dread, Dennis. "Robots at the Factory: The Alan Howarth Interview (Part I)." http://dennisdread.blogspot. com/2014/09/robots-at-factory-alan-howarth.html.

Erlich, Reese. "Wayne Shorter: A Jazz Artist for All Time." Into the Music. http://www.abc.net.au/radionational/ programs/intothemusic/wayne-shorter-a-jazz-artist-for-all-time/3178038. Feb. 28, 2009.

Eskow , Gary. "Jason Miles Pays Tribute to Weather Report." *Mix*. https://www.mixonline.com/recording/jason-miles-pays-tribute-weather-report-373782. Jan. 1, 2000.

Floyd, John. "Soul Salvation." *Miami New Times*. Jan. 9, 1997. http://www.miaminewtimes.com/news/soul-sal-vation-6361042.

Giddins, Gary. Interview transcript for *Jazz: A Film By Ken Burns*. PBS. Apr. 9, 1996. http://www.pbs.org/jazz/ about/pdfs/Giddens.pdf.

Haga, Evan. "Bright Moments with John McLaughlin." *Jazz Times*. Aug. 22, 2016. https://jazztimes.com/fea-tures/bright-moments-with-john-mclaughlin/.

Heckman, Don. "The Making of Weather Report's *Heavy Weather*." Recording Academy Grammy Awards. Dec. 16, 2013. http://www.grammy.com/news/the-making-of-weather-reports-heavy-weather.

Held, Pablo. "Peter Erskine." Pablo Held Investigates. https://pabloheldinvestigates.com/peter-erskine/. Jan. 16, 2019.

Iverson, Ethan. "Interview with Wayne Shorter." Do the Math. Apr. 2015. https://ethaniverson.com/interview-with-wayne-shorter/.

Jackson, Joshua. "Wayne Shorter: The Newark Flash." WBGO. Feb. 8, 2011. http://www.wbgo.org/checkout-jazz/wayne-shorter-the-newark-flash.

Jenkins, Willard. "Paquito D'Rivera: NEA Jazz Master (2005)." Smithsonian Jazz Oral History Program NEA Jazz Master interview transcript. Smithsonian National Museum of American History. Jun. 11–12, 2010. http://amhistory.si.edu/jazz/Drivera-Paquito/D'Rivera_Paquito_%20Interview_Transcription.pdf.

Johnson, David. "The Great Columbia Jazz Purge: Coleman, Evans, Jarrett, and Mingus." Jun. 29, 2015. http://indianapublicmedia.org/nightlights/great-columbia-jazz-purge-coleman-evans-jarrett-mingus/.

Jung, Fred. "A Fireside Chat with Miroslav Vitous." All About Jazz. http://www.allaboutjazz.com/php/article.php?id=619&pg=1#.UN-7YbQqWbA. Oct. 10, 2003.

Jung, Fred. "A Fireside Chat with Wayne Shorter." JazzWeekly. https://web.archive.org/web/20030310023833/http://jazzweekly.com/interviews/wshorter.htm. 2003.

Khan, Steve. "Tributes." http://www.stevekhan.com/tributes.htm.

Korman, Nina. "In Good Hands." *Miami New Times*. Oct.15, 1998. https://www.miaminewtimes.com/music/in-good-hands-6387533.

Levitin, Daniel. "A Conversation with Joni Mitchell." https://jonimitchell.com/library/originals/jmOriginal_460.pdf.

Milkowski, Bill. *Faces & Places* release info. ESC Records. https://www.esc-records.de/public/artist/releaseset_en.php?subby=3&cd=25&artist=15, 2002.

Milkowski, Bill. "Joe Zawinul: Long-Distance Weather Report." *Jazz Times*. Jun. 2002. http://www.jazztimes.com/columns_and_features/web_exclusive/joe_zawinul_interview/index.cfm.

Milkowski, Bill. "Wayne Shorter Interview." Abstract Logix. Jun. 12, 2005. http://www.abstractlogix.com/interview_view.php?idno=75.

Musto, Russ. "Artist Profiles: Eric Kamau Grávátt." All About Jazz. http://www.allaboutjazz.com/php/article.php?id=22927#.UtTNQZGkkVs. Sep. 15, 2006.

Oberheim, Tom. Oral History Interview. National Association of Music Merchants. https://www.namm.org/library/oral-history/tom-oberheim. 2005.

Palkovic, Tony. "Joe Zawinul Interview, Part 2." http://www.tpradioshow.com/interviews.htm, Feb. 2003.

Panken, Ted. "Joe Zawinul's 79th Birthday Anniversary." July 7, 2011. https://tedpanken.wordpress.com/2011/07/07/joe-zawinuls-79th-birthday-anniversary/.

Prasad, Anil. "Joe Zawinul: Man Of The People." Innerviews. 1997. https://www.innerviews.org/inner/zawinul.html.

Prasad, Anil. "Miroslav Vitous: Freeing The Muse." Innverviews. 2004. http://innerviews.org/inner/vitous.html.

Prasad, Anil. "Adam Holzman: Optimistic Evocations." Innerviews. 2016. https://www.innerviews.org/inner/holzman.html.

Rekas, Stephen. "An Interview with Emmett Chapman, Inventor of the Chapman Stick." http://archive.guitar-sessions.com/dec05/luthier/luthier-dec05.pdf.

Rubin, Paul. "The Wizard of Austria." *Phoenix New Times*. https://www.phoenixnewtimes.com/music/the-wizard-of-austria-6421076. Mar. 25, 1999.

Schwartz, Steve, and Michael Fitzgerald. "Chronology of Art Blakey (and the Jazz Messengers)." May 1996–July 6, 2008. http://www.jazzdiscography.com/Artists/Blakey/chron.htm.

Schuller, Geri. "Joe Zawinul Interview." http://www.geraldschuller.com/datei/menu/discographie/discografie/2004/joezawinul.htm. 2004.

Soka Gakkai International-USA, https://www.sgi-usa.org.

Sturcken, Robert. "Allyn Robinson Discusses Jaco Pastorius with Robert Sturcken." Aug. 1, 2012. https://www.youtube.com/watch?v=fKH0EDCs2Ng.

Swenson, John. "Jazz Condition—UPI Arts & Entertainment." UPI. https://www.upi.com/Jazz-Condition-UPI-Arts-Entertainment/27491017876553/. Apr. 3, 2002.

Thompson, Scott H. "Fusion Revolutionary." *Playbill*. Oct. 20, 2006. http://www.playbillarts.com/features/article/5430.html.

Van Gelder, Rudy. NEA Jazz Master interview transcript. http://amhistory.si.edu/jazz/VanGelder-Rudy/Rudy_Van_Gelder_Interview_Transcription.pdf.

Walters, John L. "Joe Zawinul Profile." Unknown Public. http://www.unknownpublic.com/writing/zawinul2.html. 2002.

Walters, John L. "CD Review: *Weather Report—The Legendary Live Tapes 1978–1981*." London Jazz News. Apr. 11, 2016. http://www.londonjazznews.com/2016/04/cd-review-weather-report-legendary-live.html.

Weiner, Natalie. "Wayne Shorter on Miles Davis, Kanye West, & the Music of the Future." *Billboard*. http://www.billboard.com/articles/news/6568518/wayne-shorter-miles-davis-kanye-west-the-music-of-the-future, May 15, 2015.

Wikane, Christian John. "'Music Is More Than Just Notes': An Interview with Mino Cinélu." *Pop Matters*. https://www.popmatters.com/188598-we-want-mino-an-interview-with-mino-cinelu-2495581330.html. Feb. 17, 2015.

Williamson, Clive. "Interview with Clive Williamson BBC." 1978. http://jacopastorius.com/features/interviews/

interview-with-clive-williamson-bbc/.

Wise, Brian. "Wayne Shorter Speaks." Rhythms: Australia's Roots Music Monthly. Mar. 5, 2010. https://web.archive.org/web/20100408022623/http://www.rhythms.com.au/features/default,id,13972.aspx.

Zuckerman, Alicia. "When Metheny Met Jaco and the Old Miami Days." WORN, Feb. 6, 2014. http://www.wlrn.org/post/when-metheny-met-jaco-and-old-miami-days.

Zwerin, Mike. "Joe Zawinul: Austrian Funk and Weathered Funk." Culturekiosque. Jul. 9, 1998, http://www.culturekiosque.com/jazz/miles/rhemile15.htm.

Zwerin, Mike. "A Cocky, Eclectic Jazzman, Recalling Zawinul." Sep. 13, 2007. http://mikezwerin.com/html/notepad.php?pad=53.

Newspaper and Magazine Articles

"As Rock Stalls at Crossroads, Jazz Breaks Through All Across Board." *Variety.* Mar. 1, 1972, 1, 70.

"Big Col Promo Sets Sights on Weather Report." *Billboard.* Apr.24, 1971, 6.

"CBS Jazz Product Hits Youth Pay Dirt." *Billboard.* Mar. 18, 1972, 4.

"CBS Fails to Prevent Warners from Issuing Pastorius' Solo Album." *Variety.* May 6, 1981, 181, 185.

"Classic Tracks: 'Birdland' by Weather Report." *Mix.* Jun. 1995, 163, 173–75.

"Col Push on Jazz Catalog." *Billboard.* Oct. 28, 1972, 3.

"Devere to Col. A&R Staff." *Variety.* Apr. 24, 1968, 57.

"Grammy Time Is Gripe Time; See Brush of New Jazz Faces." *Variety.* Jan. 29, 1975, 59.

Iska Shorter Funeral Announcement. *Los Angeles Times.* Oct. 30, 1985.

"Joe Zawinul Hospitalized in Vienna." Associated Press. Aug. 7, 2007.

"Live Reviews." Review of Weather Report, Palace Theatre, Jun. 5, 1983. *Crescendo International.* Aug. 1983, 8.

"Teazers." *New Musical Express.* Apr. 5, 1975, 47.

"Teens Dig Jazz." *Down Beat.* Jan. 21, 1960, 13.

"Triad & Transition Talk with Weather Report." *Triad Radio Guide.* Chicago: Triad Prod., Aug. 1973, 15, 38–39, 50–51.

"Jazz at the 12th Gate." *Down Beat.* Oct. 25, 1973, 10.

"NARAS Rep Denies 'Safe' Picks in Grammy Jazz Nominations." *Variety.* Feb. 5, 1975, 77.

"Potpourri." *Down Beat.* Dec. 19, 1974, 11.

"Triad & Transition Talk with Weather Report." *Triad Radio Guide* (Chicago: Triad Prod). Aug. 1973, 39.

"Weather Report Marks 1st Year." *Billboard.* Mar. 4, 1972, 14.

"Who Brought the Funk?" Down Beat News. *Down Beat.* Sep. 13, 1973, 10.

"Zawinul Leaves." *Melody Maker.* Oct. 24, 1970, 3.

"Zawinul Quits Cannon to Co-Lead New Group." Down Beat News. *Down Beat.* Dec. 10, 1970, 11.

Aiken, Jim. Review of *Mr. Gone. Contemporary Keyboard.* Jan. 1979, 64.

Andrews, Colman. "Black Market, Wayne Shorter & Weather Report #6." *Phonograph Record Magazine.* Apr. 1976, 50–51.

Armbruster, Greg. "Zawinul: Continued Hot, Chance of Record Highs." *Keyboard.* Mar. 1984, 44–59.

Armbruster, Greg. "Jim Swanson, Zawinul's Keyboard Manager." *Keyboard.* Mar. 1984, 51.

Aronowitz, Al. "Weather Report: The First Real Supergroup?" *Melody Maker.* May 15, 1971, 35.

Baker, Michael. "Eric Kamau Gravatt: Interview with a Legend." *Modern Drummer.* Oct. 1996, 116–24.

Ball, Nancy. "Music in Mid-America." *Kansas City Star.* May 11, 1973.

Bangs, Lester. Review of *In a Silent Way.* Miles Davis. *Rolling Stone.* Nov. 15, 1969, 33.

Bangs, Lester. Review of *Odyssey of Iska. Rolling Stone.* Dec. 23, 1971, 68, 70.

Bangs, Lester. Reviews of *Zawinul* and *Weather Report. Rolling Stone.* Aug. 5, 1971.

Barber, Lynden. "Passage to Old Peaks." *Melody Maker.* Nov. 11, 1980, 18.

Bell, Max. Review of *Mr. Gone. New Musical Express.* Oct. 21, 1978, accessed from Rock's Back Pages, http://www.rocksbackpages.com/Library/Article/weather-report-imr-gonei.

Benarde, Scott. "Metheny: Commerciality Comes Without Compromise." *Ft. Lauderdale News.* Nov. 18, 1984.

Beuttler, Bill. "Peter Erskine: Steppin' Out." *Down Beat.* Dec. 1986, 16–18, 69.

Birnbaum, Larry. "Weather Report Answers Its Critics." *Down Beat.* Feb. 8, 1979, 14–16, 44–45.

Blumenfeld, Larry. "Editor's View: First Meetings and Points of Departure." *Jazziz,* 4.

Blumenthal, Bob. "Jaco Pastorius: Tempest In A Bass." *Rolling Stone,* May 5, 1977, 24, 26.

Blumenthal, Bob. "The 8 Year Weather Report." *Rolling Stone.* Dec. 28, 1978–Jan. 11, 1979, 60, 65–68.

Bohen, Jim. "Showtime." *Daily Record* (Morristown, NJ). Jan. 18, 1980.

Bouchard, Fred. "Miroslav Vitous: Both Sides of the Bass." *Down Beat.* Sep. 1984, 18–20, 63.

Bourke, Brian G. "A change in the Weather." *Syracuse Herald American.* Sep. 7, 1986.

Bourne, Mike, Gary Giddins, Peter Keepnews and Joe Klee. "Message from Newport/NYC." *Down Beat.* Sep. 13, 1973, 32–35.

Brabenec, Jerry. "Weather Report's High Tech Cosmopolitanism." *Ann Arbor Sun.* Mar. 30, 1983.

Breskin, David. "24 Shorter Solos." *Musician.* Jul. 1981, 54–62.

Broadhurst, Judith. "A Jazz Fest Is Born." *Santa Cruz Sentinel*. Jun. 16, 1989.
Brodacki, Krystian. "The Original Batman: Wayne Shorter Remembers Miles Davis." *Jazz Forum*. No. 132, 1992, 24–29.
Brodacki, Krystian. "Joe Zawinul: Jazz Is a Black Music." *Jazz Forum*, No. 134, 1992, 21–23.
Brodowski, Pawel. "Miroslav Vitous' Infinite Search. *Jazz Forum*. No. 80, 1983, 44–50.
Brodowski, Pawel. "Alphonse Mouzon: 'Music Is Also a Business.'" *Jazz Forum*. No. 81, 1983, 20–25.
Brodowski, Pawel. "I'll be back!!!' *Jazz Forum*. No. 98, 1986, 36–40.
Brodowski, Pawel. "Michael Brecker: A Spirit of Discovery." *Jazz Forum*. No. 115, 1988, 30–35.
Brodowski, Pawel. "Coolin' It with Wynton Marsalis." *Jazz Forum*. No. 121, 1989, 30–35, 57.
Brown, Mick. "Singing the Body Electric." *Sounds*. Aug. 7, 1976, 16–18.
Bruton, Hugo. "Weather Report: Hugo Bruton Forecasts Long Balmy Periods." *International Musician and Recording World*. Jan. 1981, 51–53.
Carlberg, Robert. "Joe Zawinul Interview." *Electronic Musician*. May 1986. 44, 46, 48, 69.
Campbell, Mary. "Joe Zawinul's Album First in 15 Years." Associated Press, *Baytown Sun*. May 26, 1986.
Case, Brian. "John McLaughlin: Phew!—This is a Jolly Interesting Article!" *New Musical Express*. Feb. 1, 1975.
Case, Brian. "This Man Is Watching Out for Custard Pies." *New Musical Express*. Aug. 7, 1976, 20–21.
Case, Brian. "The Face with the Bass." *New Musical Express*. Jun. 12, 1976, 22.
Chambers, Jack. Review of *I Sing the Body Electric*. *Coda*. No. 12, 1973, 27–28.
Clarke, Sebastian. "And Now... The Weather." *Black Echoes*. Aug. 14, 1976, 12–13.
CM. "Weather Report." *The Wire*. Spring 1983, 4.
Cobb, Nathan. "Weather Report: Jazz That Rocks." *Boston Globe*. Aug. 27, 1972.
Colón, Frank. "Dom Um Romão." *Modern Drummer*. Nov. 1990, 58–62, 119.
Conover, Willis. "Conover in Europe, Part I: Jazz Festival In Prague." *Down Beat*. Jan. 13, 1966, 15–17.
Conover, Willis. "Viennese Cookin.'" *Down Beat*. Aug. 11, 1966, 23–26.
Considine, J. D. "In 13th Album, Weather Report Remains as Unpredictable as Ever." *Baltimore Sun*. Mar. 4, 1984.
Cook, Richard. "High Wind in Birdland: Weather Report's Procession." *New Musical Express*. Mar. 19, 1983, accessed from Rock's Back Pages, https://www.rocksbackpages.com/Library/Article/high-wind-in-bird-land-weather-reports-iprocessioni.
Cosford, Bill. "Jazz Group Puts Sun in Your Life." *Miami Herald*. May 3, 1976.
Crouch, Stanley. "Play the Right Thing." *The New Republic*. Feb. 12, 1990, 30–37.
Crouse, Timothy. "600 Lames Wreck Newport Festival." *Rolling Stone*. Aug. 5, 1971, 10
Cuscuna, Michael. "Weather Report." *Jazz & Pop*. Jul. 1971, 12–15.
Czadek, Heinz. "Joe Zawinul." *Jazz Forum*. Aug. 1972, 46–47.
Dallas, Karl. "The Sunny Weatherman." *Melody Maker*. Dec. 6, 1975, 46.
Dallas, Karl. "Weather Report: Sunny." *Melody Maker*. Oct. 15, 1977, 9.
Dallas, Karl. Review of Weather Report at the Rainbow Theatre, London. *Melody Maker*. Oct. 15, 1977, 18.
Dallas, Karl. "Weather Report: MM Band Breakdown." *Melody Maker*. Oct. 29, 1977, 56–57.
Daly, Mike. "'We're the Kings,' He Says." *The Age* (Melbourne, Aus.). Jul. 15, 1978.
Davis, Barry. "Mr. World Music." *Jerusalem Post*. Jun. 21, 2001.
Davis, Clive. "Davis Receives Standing Ovation at Radio Forum with His Speech." *Billboard*. Aug. 24, 1974, 10.
Davis, Peter. "Weather Report: Fine and Warm." *Crescendo International*. Jun.–Jul. 1984, 12–13.
Denselow, Robin. "Weather Report." *The Guardian*. Jul. 29, 1976.
De Van, Fred. Review of *Tale Spinnin'*. *Audio*. Feb. 1976, 83–84.
DeVault, Russ. "Return of Wayne Shorter." *Atlanta Constitution*. Dec. 7, 1985.
DeVault, Russ. "John Scofield Brings Quartet to Town Tonight." *Atlanta Constitution*, Feb. 21, 1986.
Diliberto, John. Review of *Procession*. *Down Beat*. Jun. 1983, 32–33.
Diliberto, John. "Zawinul: The Siren Song of Synths." *Down Beat*. Aug. 1984, 16–19.
Doerschuk, Bob. "Miles Davis: The Picasso of Invisible Art." *Keyboard*. Oct. 1987, 67–77, 80–81.
Dorham, Kenny. Review of *E.S.P.* Miles Davis. *Down Beat*. Dec. 30, 1965, 34.
Dove, Ian. "Aborted Newport Jazz Hits Record Companies." *Billboard*. Jul. 17, 1971, 58.
Ephland, John. "On the Beat: One for Wayne." *Down Beat*. Nov. 1996, 6
Ephland, John. "Alex Acuña: Command in All Directions." *DRUM!* Jan. 2011, 55–59.
Erving, Spottswood. "Jaco Pastorius: The Eccentric from the Everglades." *Musician*, May 1983, 14, 17, 116.
Fadden, James. "A Jazz Video Report from Concept to Wrap." *Back Stage*, Sep. 28, 1984, 37B.
Feather, Leonard. "Viennese Scores in U.S. Jazz Group." *Los Angeles Times*. Mar. 21, 1967.
Feather, Leonard. "Cannonball Keeps the Jazz Spirit Afloat." *Los Angeles Times*. Aug. 13, 1967.
Feather, Leonard. "Mann Unit at Marty's on the Hill." *Los Angeles Times*. Dec. 8, 1967.
Feather, Leonard. "Blindfold Test: Herbie Hancock." *Down Beat*. Sep. 18, 1969, 28.
Feather, Leonard. "Miles Davis: Ahead or Rocking Back?" *Los Angeles Times*. May 17, 1970.
Feather, Leonard. "The Year of Jazz." *Melody Maker*. Dec. 30, 1972, 12–13.
Feather, Leonard. "A Sunny Weather Report." *Los Angeles Time.*, Sep. 28, 1973.
Feather, Leonard. "Crossover Albums." *Billboard*. Feb. 8, 1975, 25.

Feather, Leonard. "Weather Report Thundering." *Los Angeles Times*. May 7, 1975.

Feather, Leonard. "Weather Report: An Aural Rainbow." *Los Angeles Times*. Jun. 6, 1976.

Feather, Leonard. "Jazz, Si! Show Builds a Bridge to Cuba." *Los Angeles Times*. May 29, 1977.

Feather, Leonard. "In Search of a Definition for the 1970s." *Los Angeles Times*. Dec. 30, 1979.

Feather, Leonard. "Playboy Jazz—A Sag in the Swing." *Los Angeles Times*. Jun. 23, 1981.

Feather, Leonard. "Hurricane Joe Et Al. in San Diego." *Los Angeles Times*. Jun. 3, 1982.

Feather, Leonard. "Weather Report Tops Itself." *Los Angeles Times*. Jun. 21, 1982.

Feather, Leonard. "Weather Report Blows Up a Storm." *Los Angeles Times*. Apr. 18, 1983.

Feather, Leonard."Jazz Album Briefs." *Los Angeles Times*. Apr. 1, 1984.

Feather, Leonard. "A New Life, New Plans, New Values." *Los Angeles Times*. Oct. 14, 1984.

Feather, Leonard. "Forecasters Report No More Weather Till 1986." *Los Angeles Times*. May 5, 1985.

Feather, Leonard. "Prepare for a Change in the Weather Report." *Los Angeles Times*. Mar. 2, 1986.

Feather, Leonard. "Weather Report in New Guise." *Los Angeles Times*. Sep. 29, 1986.

Feather, Leonard. "Keyboardist Joe Zawinul: From Weather Report to Rap." *Los Angeles Times*. Feb. 18, 1990.

Feather, Leonard, and Jeff Atterton. "Jazz." *Melody Maker*. Mar. 6, 1971, 6.

Feuer, Ron. "Jazz Beat." *Billboard*. Sep. 13, 1975, 33.

Flans, Robyn. "Alex Acuña." *Modern Drummer*. Oct. 1990, 18–23, 80, 82, 84, 86, 88, 90.

Flippo, Chet. "Rocking Havana." *Rolling Stone*. May 3, 1979, 62–64.

Freedland, Nat. "Cross over the Bridge from Jazz to Pop—That's the Happy Object." *Billboard*. Jun. 23, 1973, 54.

Freedland, Nat."Herbie Hancock; A Crossover Artist Who Feels None the Worse for the Trip." *Billboard*. Jun. 29, 1974, 40.

Gans, Charles J. "Jazz Master Wayne Shorter Won't Be Bound by Tradition." *Daily Oklahoman*, May 17, 1996.

Garland, Phyl. "Musical Genius Reaches Top at 21." *Ebony*. Mar. 1983, 29–30, 32, 34.

Gilbert, Mark. "Wayne Shorter." *Jazz Journal International*. Apr. 1986, 8–9.

Gilbert, Mark. "Wayne Shorter." *Jazz Journal International*. Mar. 1996, 6–7.

Gilbert, Mark. "Joe Zawinul." *Jazz Journal International*. May 1998, 12–13.

Gill, Andy. "Weather Report; Hammersmith Odeon." *New Musical Express*. Nov. 29, 1980, 52–53.

Gill, John. "The Genius of Gray Haired Men." *Sounds*. Nov. 29, 1980 (from clipping in the collection of the Institute of Jazz Studies at Rutgers Univ.).

Gitler, Ira. "The Family of Mann: Herbie Mann Talks with Ira Gitler." *Down Beat*. Nov. 28, 1968, 15–17.

Glassenberg, Bob. "Studio Track." *Billboard*. Aug. 21, 1971, 4.

Glassenberg, Bob. "Weather Report: Breezy." *Billboard*. Jun. 5, 1971, 18.

Gonzalez, Fernando. "An All-Star Big Band in Coastal Collusion." *Boston Globe*. Aug. 24, 1990.

Graham, Samuel. "Backbeat: The New Jaco." *High Fidelity*. Mar. 1984, 76–77, 85.

Graham, Samuel, and Sam Sutherland. "The Coast." *Record World*. Sep. 30, 1978, 35.

Green, Susan. "Weather Report." *Burlington Free Press*. Nov. 2, 1978.

Griffith, Mark. "Eric Kamau Gravatt: Tracking Down and Learning from a Legend." *Percussive Notes*. Dec. 2006, 18–19, 21.

Hadekel, Peter. "Marsalis Shifts Gears with Brash, Bold LP." *Montreal Gazette*. Oct. 24, 1985.

Hale, James. "Night Passage, Joe Zawinul's Friends, Colleagues Pay Tribute to the Late Keyboard Giant." *Down Beat*. Dec. 2007, 13–14.

Hall, Stanley. "Chester Thompson: Up For The Challenge." *Modern Drummer*. Jan. 1983, 14–17, 64–67.

Hardman, Dale. "Miroslav Vitous: The 'Report' Is Good!." *Down Beat*. Feb. 14, 1974, 16, 38.

Heckman, Don. "Jazz-Rock Is Played by Weather Report." *New York Times*. Apr. 23, 1972.

Heckman, Don. Review of *8:30*. *High Fidelity*. Nov. 1979, 150.

Heckman, Don. Review of *Night Passage*. *High Fidelity*. Feb. 1981, 102.

Heckman, Don. "Duet for One." *Los Angeles Times*. Jun. 29, 1997.

Heckman, Don. "Joe Zawinul, 75: Influential Jazz Keyboardist Led Weather Report." *Los Angeles Times*. Sep. 12, 2007.

Heldenfels, R. D. "Weather Report a Band for All Seasons." *Daily Press* (Newport News, VA). Nov. 11, 1977.

Henderson, Bill. "Weather Report: Singing in the Rain." *Black Music & Jazz Review*. Jun. 1978, 10–13.

Henderson, Bill. "Meteorology and Me: The Joe Zawinul Interview." *Black Music & Jazz Review*. Dec. 1978, 8–9.

Hendricks, Jon."Weather Report: Doin' Fine." *San Francisco Chronicle*. Feb. 17, 1973.

Higgins, Jim."Wayne Shorter, Uncloistered." *Milwaukee Sentinel*. Apr. 1, 1983.

Heron, W. Kim. "Band Basks in 13 Years of Fair Weather for Fusion." *Detroit Free Press*. Mar. 30, 1983.

Hohman, Marv. Review of *Moto Grosso Feio* and *Mysterious Traveller*. *Down Beat*, Nov. 7, 1974.

Hohman, Marv. "Do the Funky Renaissance with Alphonse Mouzon." *Down Beat*. Dec. 4, 1975, 15–16, 42.

Holden, Stephen. "Word of Mouth Sound: Richly Pan-American." *New York Times*. Jun. 29, 1982.

Hunt, Dennis. "Weather Report into Sounds of Hard Rock." *Los Angeles Times*. Feb. 23, 1973.

Hunt, Dennis. "Weather Report's Cloudy Image." *Los Angeles Times*. Nov. 19, 1978.

Jackson, Blair. "Fusion Giants Weather Report." *BAM*. Jun. 3, 1983, 42–43.

Jerome, Jim. "Havana Jam '79." *People Weekly*. Mar. 19, 1979, 34–37.

Jisi, Chris. "Alphonso Johnson, Fusion Revolutionary." *Bass Player*. Apr. 1992, 23–29.

Jisi, Chris. "Three Views of a Secret: The Reissues of 'Jaco Pastorius' & What You Won't Hear." *Bass Player*. Nov. 2000, 66, 68, 70.

Jisi, Chris. "Jaco's Finest Hour." *Bass Player*. Sep. 2007, 32–33, 39–40, 94–95.

Jisi, Chris. "A Remark They Made: The Bass World Remembers Joe Zawinul." *Bass Player*. Jan. 2008, 42–48.

Johnson, Sy. "Interview: Joe Zawinul." *Changes in the Arts*. Mar. 1973, 22.

Johnson, Sy. "Zawinul from Birdland to 'Birdland.'" *Jazz*. Vol. 2, No. 1, Fall 1977, 46–51.

Jordan, Pat. "Who Killed Jaco Pastorius?" *GQ*. Apr. 1988, 268–73, 309–12.

Kahn, Ashley. "Wayne Shorter: Face of the Deep." *Jazz Times*. Jun. 2002, 44–49, 51–52, 120–21.

Kahn, Ashley. "Updated Weather Report." *Jazz Times*. Jun. 2002, 50.

Kart, Larry. Review of *In a Silent Way*. Miles Davis. *Down Beat*. Oct. 30, 1969, 20–21.

Kart, Larry. Review of *Odyssey of Iska*. Wayne Shorter. *Down Beat*. Nov. 25, 1971, 22–23.

Kelleher, Ed. Review of Weather Report and Al Di Meola, Beacon Theatre, New York. Talent in Action. *Billboard*. May 28, 1977, 49.

Keller, Larry. "Killer of Pastorius Free after Four Months." *Ft. Lauderdale Sun-Sentinel*, Jul. 4, 1989.

Kevorkian, Kyle. "Chasing the Jazz Train: When Does a Trend become a Trap?" *Keyboard*. Feb. 1990, 71–76.

Kirb. Review of Dr. John and Weather Report, Beacon Theatre. "Concert Reviews." *Variety*. Nov. 3, 1971, 43.

Kirb. Review of Ike & Tina Turner Revue, Weather Report, Quinames Band, and Banchee. "Concert Reviews." *Variety*. Dec. 1, 1971, 46.

Klee, Joe H., and Will Smith, Review of *Sweetnighter*, Down Beat. Jul. 19, 1973, 20.

Kohlhaase, Bill. "When Shorter Dissects His Jazz, He Breaks It Down to Its Essence." *Los Angeles Times*. Oct. 26, 1995.

Lake, Steve. "Weather Report: Outlook Sunny." *Melody Maker*. Jul. 20, 1974, 51.

Lake, Steve. Review of Weather Report at the New Victoria Theatre. "Caught in the Act." *Melody Maker*. Dec. 6, 1975, 28.

Lake, Steve. "Jazzscene: Our Music… It's So Simple!" *Melody Maker*. Dec. 20, 1975, 33.

Laurence, Paul. "Recording the Electric Bass." *Recording Engineer/Producer*. Jun. 1977, 60, 62, 64, 66, 68, 70, 72–75,

Leer, King. "Weather Report." *Changes*. Aug. 15, 1971, 24.

Le Gendre, Kevin. "The Alchemist." *Jazzwise*. Jun. 2002, 22–27.

Less, David. Review of *Mr. Gone*. Down Beat. Jan. 11, 1979, 22.

Liska, A. James. "Wayne Shorter: Coming Home." *Down Beat*. Jul. 1982, 21–23, 66.

Liska, A. James. "On the Road with Weather Report." *Down Beat*. Oct. 1982, 21–23, 66.

Litweiler, John. Review of *Super Nova*. Down Beat. Aug. 20, 1970, 26–27.

Logan, Tim. "Wayne Shorter, Double Take." *Down Beat*. Jun. 20, 1974, 16–17, 38.

Lubin, Tom. "Profile: Producer Ron Malo." *Modern Recording & Music*. Sep. 1981, 52–59.

Lowe, Allen. "Profiles: Some People Behind the Music: Barry Harris." *Down Beat*. Jul. 14, 1977, 19.

Lyons, Len. "Weather Report: Mysteries of the Organism." *Musician Player & Listener*. Feb. 15–Mar. 31, 1977, 22–25.

Lyons, Len. "Josef Zawinul Keyboard Magician." *Keyboard*. Sep. 1977, 26–28, 38, 40.

Lyons, Len. "Brian Risner: Zawinul's Equipment Expert." *Keyboard*. Sep. 1977, 28.

Lyons, Len. "This Year's Weather Report." *High Fidelity*. Sep. 1978, 115–18.

Macintosh, Adrian. "Wayne Shorter: Putting It in the Weather Report Rack." *Jazz Forum*. Apr. 1976, 44–45.

MacKinnon, Angus. "Joseph Zawinul, Future Primitive." *New Musical Express*. Nov. 15, 1980, 23–24.

MacKinnon, Angus. "The Body Electric Gets Rewired." *New Musical Express*. Nov. 22, 1980, 43.

Mandel, Howard. "Joe Zawinul: 'My Prime Is Coming!'" *Down Beat*. Jan. 1999, 30–32.

Mandel, Howard. "Now Voyager." *The Wire*. Jul. 1996, 21–24.

Marlowe, Jon. "Jaco Pastorius' Sound Goes National." *Miami News*. May 7, 1976.

Mattingly, Rick. "Peter Erskine." *Modern Drummer*. Jan. 1983, 8–13, 43–54.

Mattingly, Rick. "PASIC 2007 Panel: The Drummers of Weather Report." *Percussive Notes*. Dec. 2007, 8–15.

McDonald, Ian. "Hot News on Weather Report." New Musical Express. Jun. 23, 1973, 44.

Meyer, Frank. "Rhythm, Blues of Cuba Under Fidel's Baton." *Variety*. Mar. 7, 1979, 1, 178.

Micallef, Ken. "Wayne Shorter: Speak No Evil—About Drummers." *Modern Drummer*. Sep. 2003, 106–10.

Milano, Dominic. "Tom Oberheim, Designer of Synthesizers." *Contemporary Keyboard*. May 1977, 20–21, 32, 34.

Milkowski, Bill. "Larry Coryell: Back to the Roots." *Down Beat*. May 1984, 16–18, 68.

Milkowski, Bill. "Jaco Pastorius, Bass Revolutionary." *Guitar Player*. Aug. 1984, 58–68.

Milkowski, Bill. "Requiem for Jaco." *Musician*. Dec, 1987, 86–90, 92–102.

Mitchell, Charles. "'Bim, bang, boing, slam, pop, z-i-i-ing!': The Anatomical Signatures of Airto." *Down Beat*. Nov. 8, 1974, 18–19, 44.

Mitchell, Joni. "Jaco by Joni." *Musician*. Dec. 1987. 91, 100, 122.

Moon, Tom. "Saxophonist Wayne Shorter Takes Cautious Steps Back into Spotlight." *Arizona Daily Star*. Nov.

13, 1985.

Moore, Carman. "The New Thing Meets Rock." *New York Times*. Aug. 9, 1970.

Morgan, A. J. "Weather Report: Increasingly Warm & Sunny." *Crawdaddy*. Oct. 1975, 30–31.

Morgenstern, Dan. "Herbie's Mann-Made World." *Down Beat*. Dec. 10, 1970, 14–15, 42.

Morgenstern, Dan. "Weather Report: Outlook Bright and Sunny." *Down Beat*. May 27, 1971, 14–15, 42.

Morgenstern, Dan. "No Jive from Clive." Afterthoughts. *Down Beat*. Sep. 16, 1971, 18, 46.

Morgenstern, Dan. "'Different Strokes,' Music Is a Beautiful Game." *Down Beat*. Mar. 15, 1973, 18.

Murphy, Ray. "Weather Report with the Hot Numbers." *Boston Globe*. Jul. 15, 1981.

Murtha, Tom. "Weather Report Quintet Raises New Hope on Jazz Barometer." *Minneapolis Star*. Feb. 13, 1973.

Nash, Margo. "Coming Home." Jersey Footlights. *New York Times*. Feb. 24, 2002.

Nicholson, Stuart. "Joe's Public." *Jazzwise*. Sep. 2002, 22–27.

Nooger, Dan."Ain't Blue No More." Riffs. *Village Voice*. Dec. 28, 1972, 36.

Nusser, Richard. "Magic Music." Riffs. *Village Voice*. Oct. 28, 1971, 52.

Oliver, Kitty. "Show Business Marriages: Living, Loving in Limelight." *Miami Herald*. May 15, 1977.

Ouellette, Dan. "Bitches Brew, Miles Davis' Bitches Brew: Reissue and Box Set of the Year." *Down Beat*. Dec. 1999, 32–37.

Palmer, Bob. Review of *I Sing the Body Electric*. *Rolling Stone*. Jul. 6, 1972, 55.

Palmer, Bob. Review of *Mysterious Traveller*. *Rolling Stone*. Aug. 1, 1974, 50.

Palmer, Robert. "Big Apple Grapevine: Weather Report." *Real Paper*. Sep. 30, 1978.

Palmer, Robert. "Survivors in Jazz-Rock Disclaim It." *New York Times*. Jun. 11, 1982.

Panken, Ted. "Unfinished Business." *Jazziz*. September 2003, 34–39.

Pareles, Jon. "Weather Report." *Musician Player & Listener*. Apr.–May 1980, 18–19.

Pareles, Jon. "Rock: Weather Report Sings." *New York Times*. Mar. 21, 1983.

Pareles, Jon. "Jazz Swings Back to Tradition." *New York Times*. Jun. 17, 1984.

Pareles, Jon. "Pop/Jazz." *New York Times*. Apr. 25, 1986.

Pekar, Harvey. Review of *Infinite Search*. *Down Beat*. Jun. 25, 1970, 23–24.

Peters, Sam. "Jazz Records." *The Guardian*. Aug. 16, 1972.

Podolinsky, Gil. "Weather Report: An Interview with Joe Zawinul and Engineer Brian Risner." *Modern Recording*. Nov. 1977, 32–37.

Potter, Jeff. "Manolo Badrena." *Modern Percussionist*. Sep.–Nov. 1986, 8–13, 34–35, 37.

Protzman, Bob. Review of Weather Report at the Guthrie Theater, Minneapolis. Caught in the Act. *Down Beat*. May 24, 1973, 29.

Protzman, Bob. "Profile: Eric Gravatt." *Down Beat*. Jul. 17, 1975, 32.

Radel, Cliff. "Legends Keep Jazz Alive." *Cincinnati Enquirer*. Jul. 11, 1982.

Rambali, Paul. Review of Weather Report at the Rainbow Theatre, London. On the Town. *New Musical Express*. Oct. 15, 1977, 51.

Rambali, Paul. "Boing." *New Musical Express*. Nov. 19, 1977, accessed from Rock's Back Pages, http://www.rocksbackpages.com/Library/Article/boing.

Ramsey, Doug. Review of *Zawinul*. Joe Zawinul. *Down Beat*. Sep. 16, 1971, 33–34.

Ratliff, Ben. "With This Composer, The Work Is Never Done." *New York Times*. Apr. 22, 1998.

Ratliff, Ben. "JVC Jazz Festival Review; At 67, Inspiring a Quest for Perfection." *New York Times*. Jun. 30, 2001.

Rensin, David. "Weather Report: Fair Weather Jazz Fans Leave Them Alone." *Rolling Stone*. Sep. 27, 1973, 24.

Rhodes, Larry. "Audience Didn't Need Theatrics at Weather Report's Norfolk Show." *Daily Press* (Norfolk, VA). Mar. 18, 1983.

Robinson, Leroy. "Blue Note's Butler Adds New Image." *Billboard*. Jul. 13, 1974, 28, 36.

Rockwell, John. "A Strong New Front Lends Bright Touch to Weather Report." *New York Times*. Jul. 9, 1974.

Rodgers, Jeffrey Pepper. "My Secret Place: The Guitar Odyssey of Joni Mitchell." *Acoustic Guitar*. Aug. 1996, 40–43, 48–55.

Roerich, Damon. "Jaco Pastorius, The Bassist Interviewed." *Musician Player & Listener*. Aug. 1980, 38–42.

Rohter, Larry. "Weather Report: Amplified Jazz." *Washington Post*. Jul. 15, 1974.

Rozek, Michael. "Alex Acuña: Transcending All Influences." *Modern Drummer*. May 1982, 12–15, 61–62, 64.

Santosuosso, Ernie. "Weather Report's Three-Tiered Sound." *Boston Globe*. Jul. 24, 1971.

Seligman, Adam Ward. "A Different View: Joe Zawinul." *Modern Drummer*. Apr. 1997, 110–12.

Russell Shaw. Review of *Magical Shepherd*. *Down Beat*. Jul. 15, 1976, 32.

Shore, Michael. "Omar Hakim." *Musician*. Mar. 1986, 60–66, 85.

Shorter, Wayne. "Creativity and Change." *Down Beat*. Dec. 12, 1968, 20–22.

Shuster, Fred. "Groove Gangster: Joe Zawinul." *Down Beat*. Jun. 1992, 21–23.

Silvert, Conrad. "Weather Report Heads Down Thunder Road." *Rolling Stone*. May 5, 1977, 24.

Silvert, Conrad. "Wayne Shorter: Unlimited Imagination." *Down Beat*. Jul. 14, 1977, 15–16, 58–59.

Silvert, Conrad. "Joe Zawinul: Wayfaring Genius." *Down Beat*. Jun. 1, 1978, 13–15.

Silvert, Conrad. "Joe Zawinul: Wayfaring Genius—Part II." *Down Beat*. Jun. 15, 1978, 20–22, 52–53, 56, 58.

Sinker, Mark. "Manhattan Transfer: Clean-Cut Agony." *The Wire*. Jun. 1988, 26.

Smith, Arnold Jay. "Bass Lines: Crystal Gazing with a Bonanza Of Experts." *Down Beat*. Jan. 27, 1977, 14–16,

42–43.

Snider, Eric. "Weather Report's Wayne Shorter Interviewed." *Music*. Mar. 3, 1983, 12–14.

Snider, Eric. Review of *This Is This*. *Tampa Bay Times*. Jul. 27, 1986.

Snider, Martin. "Weather Report: Favorable." Club Review. *Record World*. May 13, 1972, 27.

Sohmer, Jack. "Two Forays into Jazz-Rock: Weather Report is Fine." *Miami Herald*. May 7, 1977.

Solothurnmann, Jurg. "Joseph Zawinul: A Space Musician." *Jazz Forum*. Apr. 1976, 40–43, 46.

Stein, Bradford J. "Joe Zawinul: Part 1 of a Two Part Interview." *California Jazz Now*. Jun. 1993, 9–10, 26.

Stein, Bradford J. "Joe Zawinul: Part 2 of a Two Part Interview." *California Jazz Now*. Jul. 1993, 14–16, 31.

Stephens, Greg. "Weather Report Takes on New Talent." *Austin American-Statesman*. Mar. 4, 1983.

Stern, Chip. "And Now for This Year's Weather Report." *Musician Player & Listener*. Feb. 1979, 22–24, 64.

Stern, Chip. Review of *Procession*. *Musician*. May 1983, 88.

Stewart, Zan. "Weather Report to Re-Form." Riffs. *Down Beat*. Apr. 1996, 14.

Stewart, Zan. "Heaven's Door." *Down Beat*. May 2002, 20–25.

Stook, John. Review of *Weather Report* (1982). *Musician*. Jun. 1982, 80, 82.

Suber, Charles. "The First Chorus." *Down Beat*. Nov. 8, 1973, 6.

Sumrall, Harry. "Jazz-Rock 'Fusion Music' Comes of Age." *Washington Post*. Nov. 8, 1978.

Sutherland, Sam. "Fusion Controversy Boring to Zawinul." *Billboard*. Apr. 11, 1981, 32, 42.

Sutherland, Sam. "Weather Report: No Tour This Year." *Billboard*. Apr. 6, 1985, 42.

Sutherland, Sam. "Zawinul Weathers Changes." *Billboard*. May 10, 1986, 22–23.

Sweeting, Adam. "Order from Liberty." *Melody Maker*. Nov. 29, 1980, 12.

Szantor, Jim. Review of *Bitches Brew*. Miles Davis. *Down Beat*. Jun. 11, 1970, 20–21.

Szantor, Jim. Review of Weather Report at the Brown Shoe (Chicago). *Down Beat*. Oct. 26, 1972, 31.

"Teens Dig Jazz." Music News. *Down Beat*. Jan. 21, 1960, 13–14.

Tesser, Neil. Review of *Heavy Weather*. *Down Beat*. May 19, 1977, 23.

Tesser, Neil. "Jaco Pastorius, The Florida Flash." *Down Beat*. Jan. 27, 1977, 12–13, 44.

Thiers, Walter. "The Scene Livens Up." Swinging News/Argentina. *Jazz Forum*. No. 24, 1973, 14.

Tiegel, Eliot. "Who Will Own the Soul 70's?" *Billboard*. Aug. 22, 1970, 24, 26.

Tiegel, Eliot. "'Extended Energy' Jazz Energizes New Wave of Enthusiasm." *Billboard*. Apr. 29, 1972, 13–14, 20.

Tiegel, Eliot. "Repackages Pack Their Own Sales Wallop as U.S. Labels Broaden Their Jazz Coverage." *Billboard*. Jun. 23, 1973, 48, 50, 52, 56.

Tiegel, Eliot. "Jazzmen Fusing Rock into Music for Wider Appeal." *Billboard*. Jun. 1, 1974, 1, 10.

Tiegel, Eliot. "Does it Sell? That's the Criterion for Jazz Issues." *Billboard*. Jan. 6, 1979, 10, 75.

Tingen, Paul. "From a Whisper to a Scream." *Mojo*. Sep. 2001, 44–52.

Tolleson, Robin. "Omar Hakim: Going for the Feeling." *Modern Drummer*. Dec. 1984, 14–17, 80–90.

Townley, Ray. "The Mysterious Travellings of an Austrian Mogul." *Down Beat*. Jan. 30, 1975, 15–17, 37.

Townley, Ray. Review of *Black Market*. *Down Beat*. Jul. 15, 1976, 26.

Trask, Simon. "Hey Joe!" *Music Technology*. Jan. 1992, 36–43.

Turi, Gabor. "Debrecen Jazz Days." *Jazz Forum*. No. 97, 1985, 23.

Underwood, Lee. "Airto and His Incredible Gong Show." *Down Beat*. Apr. 20, 1978, 15–16, 41.

Underwood, Lee. Review of Weather Report at the Civic, Santa Monica, California. Caught! *Down Beat*. Feb. 22, 1979, 40–41.

Underwood, Lee. "Tony Williams: Aspiring to a Lifetime of Leadership." *Down Beat*. Jun. 21, 1979, 20–21, 54, 60.

Varga, George. "Weather Report Has Clear Sailing." *San Diego Union*. Apr. 14, 1985.

Varga, George. "Wayne Shorter's Quiet Time Engenders Long-Awaited Album." *San Diego Union*. Oct. 6, 1985.

Varga, George. "Zawinul Weathers It Very Well: LP May Make Things Happen for Jazzman." *San Diego Union*. Mar. 9, 1986.

Varga, George. "Sportin' Life." *Jazz Times*. Apr. 2007, 52–57.

Wanamaker, George. "Weather Report Spins Tales." *Los Angeles Free Press*. Jul. 4–10, 1975.

Watrous, Peter. "Jazz View; A Jazz Generation and the Miles Davis Curse." *New York Times*. Oct. 15, 1995.

Watts, Michael. "Hot Weather Report." Caught In The Act. *Melody Maker*. Jul. 14, 1973, 48.

Waz, Joe. "Pat Metheny: The Incredible String Man," *Jazz Forum*, No. 54, 1978, 38–42.

Waz, Joe. Review of *Mr. Gone*. *Jazz Forum*. No. 59, 1979, 48.

Weisel, Joe. "Weather Report Overblown." *Stars and Stripes*. Oct. 1, 1977, 19.

Weiskind, Ron. "Weather Report: Clear Rhythms, Hot Solos." *Pittsburgh Post-Gazette*. Jun. 17, 1982.

Weiss, David. "New Sounds & Traditions from New York's Hot Percussionist, Frank Colón." DRUM! Aug.–Sep. 1997, 72–78.

Welch, Chris. "Weather Report: Myth & Magic." *Melody Maker*. Oct. 14, 1978, 50, 61.

Welding, Pete. "From Vienna with Love, Joe Zawinul." *Down Beat*. Nov. 17, 1966, 23–25.

Wessel, Harry. "Great Southern Audience in Tune with Weather Report's Sound." *Orlando Sentinel Star*. May 7, 1977.

West, Hollie I. "McCoy Tyner Quartet." *Washington Post*. May 13, 1971.

West, Hollie I "Andrew White . . . Musician." *Washington Post*. Jun. 11, 1971.

West, Hollie I. "Weather Report." *Washington Post*. Nov. 4, 1971.
West, Hollie I. "Eric Gravatt: Drumming Up Some New Ground Rules for Jazz." *Washington Post*. Nov. 5, 1972.
Whyte, Bert. Review of *Tale Spinnin'*. Tape & Turntable. *Audio*. Feb. 1976, 106.
Williams, Martin. "Jazz: Some Old Favorites Are Back." *New York Times*. Jan. 18, 1970.
Williams, Richard. "Wayne Waxes Strong." *Melody Maker*. May 23, 1970, 20.
Williams, Richard. "Weather Report: A Bleak Outlook." *Melody Maker*. Oct. 23, 1971, 40.
Williams, Richard. "Weather Man: Joe Zawinul Talks to Richard Williams." *Melody Maker*. Jul. 29, 1972, 12.
Williams, Richard. "Shorter Story." *Melody Maker*. Aug. 5, 1972, 22.
Wong, Jo-Ann. "Weather Report Plays Up a Storm." *Deseret News*. Apr. 12, 1983.
Woodard, Josef. "Josef Zawinul: Doing Something about the Weather." *Mix*. Jul. 1983, 89–92, 99.
Woodard, Josef. "Joe Zawinul Spars with the Muse." *Musician*. Jun. 1985, 48–52, 56, 58, 97.
Woodard, Josef. "Joe Zawinul: The Dialects of Jazz." *Down* Beat. Apr. 1988, 16–19.
Woodard, Josef. "Weather Report: Storm Surge." *Down Beat*. Jan. 2001, 22–29.
Woodard, Josef. "Shifting Winds." *Down Beat*. Jan. 2001, 26.
Woodard, Josef. "Boogie Woogie Big Time." *Down Beat*. May 2007, 28–30, 32–33.
Yanow, Scott. "The Wayne Shorter Interview." *Down Beat*. Apr. 1986, 17–18, 56–57.
Zabor, Rafi. Review of *Mr. Gone. Musician*. Dec. 1978, 38.
Zawinul, Josef, as told to Greg Armbruster. "The Evolution of Weather Report." *Keyboard*. Mar. 1984, 49–51.
Zink, Jack. "A Three-Block Trip from Rags to Riches." *Ft. Lauderdale News and Sun-Sentinel*. May 16, 1976.
Zink, Jack. "'Vultures' Keep Jaco Busy." *Ft. Lauderdale News*. Jul. 1, 1977.
Zipkin, Michael. "Weather Report's Dance of the Elements." *BAM*. Oct. 29, 1978, 24–27.
Zulaica, Don. "The Drummers of Weather Report." *DRUM!* Oct. 2006, 70–72, 74–79.
Zwerin, Mike. "Disaster Area." State of Mind. *Down Beat*. Jul. 27, 1967, 13.

Academic Theses and Dissertations

Cooper, Alan. "Making the Weather in Contemporary Jazz: An Appreciation of the Musical Art of Josef Zawinul." Ph.D. thesis, Univ. of Southampton, 2012.
Frandsen, Mark Steven. "Forecasting Fusion at Low Frequencies: The Bass Players of Weather Report." Ph.D. diss., Texas Tech Univ., 2010.
Wayte, Lawrence A. "Bitches Brood: The Progeny of Miles Davis's 'Bitches Brew' and the Sound of Jazz-Rock." Ph.D. diss., University of California, Los Angeles, 2007.

Other Documents

Wilmeth, Tom. Eric Gravatt unpublished interview transcript. May 8, 1980.

Discography

A list of recordings mentioned in this book. Dates are those of the albums' first release. For tracks, personnel listings, and recording data for the sixteen Weather Report albums produced from 1971 to 1986, see this book's companion website, www.weatherreportdiscography.org.

The Cannonball Adderley Quintet Featuring Nat Adderley. *The Cannonball Adderley Quintet in San Francisco* (Riverside RLP 12-311), 1960.
The Cannonball Adderley Quintet Featuring Nat Adderley. *Them Dirty Blues* (Riverside RLP 12-322), 1960.
The Cannonball Adderley Quintet. *Mercy, Mercy, Mercy! Live at "The Club"* (Capitol ST 2663), 1967.
The Cannonball Adderley Quintet. *74 Miles Away / Walk Tall* (Capitol ST 2822), 1967.
The Cannonball Adderley Quintet. *The Price You Got to Pay to Be Free* (Capitol SWBB-636), 1970.
The Cannonball Adderley Quintet. *Cannonball in Japan* (Capitol Jazz CDP 7 93560 2), 1990.
Count Basie and His Orchestra. *Basie's Beatle Bag* (Verve V-8659), 1966.
The Beatles. *Magical Mystery Tour* (Capitol SMAL-2835), 1967.
The Beatles. *Sgt, Pepper's Lonely Hearts Club Band* (Capitol 4CL-2653), 1967.
The Beatles. *Abbey Road* (Apple PCS 7088), 1969.
Art Blakey Quintet. *A Night at Birdland, Vol. 3* (Blue Note BLP 5039), 1954.
Art Blakey & the Jazz Messengers. *Art Blakey and the Jazz Messengers* (Blue Note BLP 4003), 1959.
Art Blakey & the Jazz Messengers. *The Big Beat* (Blue Note BLP 4029), 1960.
Art Blakey & the Jazz Messengers. *Free for All* (Blue Note BLP 4170), 1965.
Art Blakey & the Jazz Messengers. *Africaine* (Blue Note LT-1088), 1981 (recorded in 1959).
Art Blakey's Jazz Messengers. *Live in Leverkusen—The Art of Jazz* (In+Out, IOR 77028-2), 1995.
Borstlap, Michiel. *Body Acoustic* (EmArcy 538 976-2), 1999.
James Brown and the Famous Flames. "Papa's Got a Brand New Bag" (King 45-5999), 1965.
James Brown and the Famous Flames. "I Got You (I Feel Good)" (King 45-6015), 1965.
Byrd, Donald. *Black Byrd* (Blue Note BN-LA047-F), 1973.
Carlos, Wendy. *Switched-On Bach* (Columbia Masterworks MS 7194), 1968.
Clarke, Stanley. *School Days* (Nemporer NE 439), 1976.
Clarke, Stanley. *I Wanna Play for You* (Nemperor KZ2 35680), 1979.
The Billy Cobham / George Duke Band. *"Live" on Tour in Europe* (Atlantic SD 18194), 1976.
Coltrane, John. *My Favorite Things* (Atlantic 1361), 1961.
Corea, Chick. *Now He Sings, Now He Sobs* (Solid State SS 18039), 1968.
Coryell, Larry. *Spaces* (Vangard Apostolic VSD-6558), 1970.
Davis, Miles. *Porgy and Bess* (Columbia CS 8085), 1959.
Davis, Miles. *Kind of Blue* (Columbia CL 1355), 1959.
Davis, Miles. *Sketches of Spain* (Columbia CL 1480), 1960.
Davis. Miles. *E.S.P.* (Columbia CS 9150), 1965.
Davis. Miles. *Miles Smiles* (Columbia CL 2601), 1967.
Davis. Miles. *Nefertiti* (Columbia CS 9594), 1968.
Davis, Miles. *Miles in the Sky* (Columbia CS 9628), 1968.
Davis, Miles. *Filles de Kilimanjaro* (Columbia CS 9750), 1969.
Davis, Miles. *In a Silent Way* (Columbia CS 9875), 1969.
Davis, Miles. *Bitches Brew* (Columbia GP 26), 1970.
Davis. Miles. *The Complete In a Silent Way Sessions* (Columbia Legacy C3K 65362), 1991.

Davis, Miles. *The Complete Live at the Plugged Nickel 1965* (Columbia Legacy CXK 66955), 1995.
Davis, Miles. *The Studio Recordings of Miles Davis 1965–'68* (Columbia Legacy C6K 67398), 1998.
Miles Davis All Stars. *Walkin'* (Prestige PRLP 7076), 1957.
Miles Davis + 19. *Miles Ahead* (Columbia CL 1041), 1957.
Di Meola, Al. *Land of the Midnight Sun* (Columbia PC 34074), 1976.
Duke, George. *The Aura Will Prevail* (Pausa PR 7042), 1975.
Earth, Wind & Fire. *That's the Way of the World* (Columbia), 1975.
Erskine, Peter. *Motion Poet* (Denon CY-72582), 1988.
Ferguson, Maynard *Conquistador* (Columbia PC 34457), 1977.
Gaye, Marvin. *What's Going On* (Tamla TS-310), 1971.
Gaye, Marvin. *Midnight Love* (CBS 85977), 1982.
Gerry Gibbs and Thrasher People. *Weather or Not* (Whaling City Sound WCS 091), 2017.
Gulda, Friedrich, and Joe Zawinul. *Music for Two Pianos* (Capriccio 67 175), 1988.
Hancock, Herbie. *Head Hunters* (Columbia KC 32731), 1973.
Hancock, Herbie. *Speak Like a Child* (Blue Note BST 84279), 1968.
Hancock, Herbie, and Wayne Shorter. *1+1* (Verve 314 537 564-2), 1997.
Hardin, Tim. *Bird on a Wire* (Columbia C 30551), 1971.
Harrison, George. *Electronic Sound* (Zapple 02), 1969.
Henderson, Eddie. *Inside Out* (Capricorn CP 0122), 1974.
Henderson, Joe. *Canyon Lady* (Milestone M-9057), 1975.
Hunter, Ian. *All American Alien Boy* (Columbia PC 34142), 1976.
James, Bob. *Two* (CTI CTI 6057 S1), 1975.
Jarre, Jean-Michel. *Oxygène* (Polydor PD-1-6112), 1976.
Joel, Billy. *Piano Man* (Columbia KC 32544), 1973.
Johnson, Alphonso. *Moonshadows* (Epic PE 34118), 1976.
Keita, Salif. *Soro* (Mango CCD 9808), 1987.
Keita, Salif. *Amen* (Mango 162 539 910-2), 1991.
Khan, Steve. *Evidence* (Arista Novus AN 3023), 1980.
Kinsey, Scott. *We Speak Luniwaz* (Whirlwind WR4743), 2019.
Lewis, Ramsey. *The In Crowd* (Argo LP-757), 1965.
The Lovin' Spoonful. *Do You Believe in Magic* (Kama Sutra KLP 8050), 1965.
Magraw, Dean, and Eric Kamau Gravatt. *Fire on the Nile* (Red House RHR CD 273), 2014.
The Mahavishnu Orchestra. *The Inner Mounting Flame* (Columbia KC 31067), 1971.
The Mahavishnu Orchestra. *Birds of Fire* (Columbia KC 31996), 1973.
Mangione, Chuck. *Land of Make Believe* (Mercury SRM-1-684), 1973.
The Manhattan Transfer. *Extensions* (Atlantic SD 19258), 1979.
Mann, Herbie. *Memphis Underground* (Atlantic SD 1522), 1969.
Mann, Herbie. *Muscle Shoals Nitty Gritty* (Embryo SD 526), 1970.
Mann, Herbie. *The Wailing Dervishes* (Atlantic SD 1497), 1967.
Mann, Herbie, and Tamiko Jones. *A Mann & A Woman* (Atlantic SD 8141), 1967.
Marsalis, Wynton. *Black Codes (From the Underground)* (Columbia CK 40009), 1985.
Marcus, Steve, and Miroslav Vitous, Sonny Sharrock, and Daniel Humair. *Green Line* (Nivico SMJX 10109), 1971.
McDaniels, Eugene. *Headless Heroes of the Apocalypse* (Atlantic SD 8281), 1971.
McFerrin, Bobby. *The Voice* (Elektra Musician 9 60366-1-E,), 1984.
McLean, Don. *American Pie* (United Artists UAS-5535), 1971.
Metheny, Pat. *Bright Size Life* (ECM MSE 1073), 1976.
Metropole Orkest / Vince Mendoza. *Fast City—A Tribute to Joe Zawinul* (BHM 1050-2), 2010.
Miles, Jason. *Celebrating the Music of Weather Report* (Telarc CD-83473), 2000.
Mitchell, Joni. *Court and Spark* (Asylum 7E-1001), 1974.
Mitchell, Joni. *Hejira* (Asylum 7E-1087), 1976.
Mitchell, Joni. *Don Juan's Reckless Daughter* (Asylum BB-701), 1977.
Mitchell, Joni. *Mingus* (Asylum 5E-505), 1979.
Mitchell, Joni. *Shadows and Light* (Asylum BB-704), 1980.
Monteux, Pierre, conductor. *The Rite of Spring* (RCA Victor Red Seal LM-1149), 1951.
Montgomery, Wes. *Goin' Out of My Head* (Verve V6-8642), 1966.
Moreira, Airto. *Seeds on the Ground—The Natural Sounds of Airto* (Buddah BDS 5085), 1971.
Mouzon, Alphonse. *Mind Transplant* (Blue Note BN-LA398-G), 1975.
Pastorius, Jaco. *Jaco Pastorius* (Epic PE 33949), 1976.
Pastorius, Jaco. *Word of Mouth* (Warner Bros. BSK 3535), 1981.
Pastorius, Jaco. *The Birthday Concert* (Warner Bros. 9 45290-2), 1995.
Pastorius, Jaco. *Portrait of Jaco—The Early Years, 1968–1978* (Holiday Park Records), 2002.
Pastorius, Jaco. *Modern American Music…Period! The Criteria Sessions* (Omnivore OVLP-84/6651016075),

2014.
Jaco Pastorius Big Band. *Twins I and II—Live in Japan 1982* (Warner Bros. WPCR-10609-10), 1999.
Ponty, Jean-Luc. *Upon the Wings of Music* (Atlantic SD 18138), 1975.
Presley, Elvis. "Heartbreak Hotel" (RCA Victor EPA-821), 1956.
radio.string.quartet.vienna. *Posting Joe—Celebrating Weather Report—live* (ACT 9553-2), 2013.
Rypdal, Terje, Miroslav Vitous, and Jack DeJohnette. *Terje Rypdal / Miroslav Vitous / Jack DeJohnette* (ECM 1125), 1979.
Sanborn, David. *As We Speak* (Warner Bros. 9 23650-1), 1982.
Mongo Santamaría. *Mongo at Montreux* (Atlantic SD 1593), 1971.
Mongo Santamaría. *Up from the Roots* (Atlantic SD 1621), 1972.
Santana, Carlos, and John McLaughlin. *Love, Devotion and Surrender* (Columbia KC 32034), 1973.
The Seventh Century. *The Seventh Century* (Al Segno AS 3733), 1971.
Shank, Bud, and Bob Cooper. *European Tour '57* (Lone Hill Jazz LHJ10246), 2006.
Shorter, Wayne. *Introducing Wayne Shorter* (Vee Jay VJLP 3006), 1959.
Shorter, Wayne. *Night Dreamer* (Blue Note BLP 4173), 1964.
Shorter, Wayne. *Juju* (Blue Note BST 84182), 1964.
Shorter, Wayne. *The All Seeing Eye.* (Blue Note BST 84219), 1966.
Shorter, Wayne. *Speak No Evil* (Blue Note BST 84194), 1966.
Shorter, Wayne. *Adam's Apple* (Blue Note BST 84232), 1966.
Shorter, Wayne. *Schizophrenia* (Blue Note BST 84297), 1969.
Shorter, Wayne. *Super Nova* (Blue Note BST 84332), 1969.
Shorter, Wayne. *Odyssey of Iska* (Blue Note BST 84363), 1971.
Shorter, Wayne. *Moto Grosso Feio* (Blue Note BN-LA014-G), 1974.
Shorter, Wayne. *The Soothsayer* (Blue Note LT-988), 1979 (recorded 1965).
Shorter, Wayne. *Etcetera* (Blue Note LT-1056), 1979 (recorded 1965).
Shorter, Wayne. *Atlantis* (Columbia CK 40055), 1985.
Shorter, Wayne. *Phantom Navigator* (Columbia CK 40373), 1987.
Shorter, Wayne. *Joy Ryder* (Columbia CK 44110), 1988.
Shorter, Wayne. *High Life* (Verve P2-29224), 1995.
Shorter, Wayne. *Footprints Live!* (Verve 589 679-2), 2001.
Shorter, Wayne, Featuring Milton Nascimento. *Native Dancer* (Columbia PC 33418), 1975.
Sinatra, Francis Albert, and Antonio Carlos Jobim. *Francis Albert Sinatra & Antônio Carlos Jobim* (Reprise 1021), 1967.
Tonto's Expanding Head Band. *Zero Time* (Embryo SD 732), 1971.
Tyner, McCoy. *Focal Point* (Milestone M-9072), 1976.
Tyner, McCoy *Inner Voices* (Milestone M-9079), 1977.
Various artists. *Havana Jam* (Columbia PC2 36053), 1979.
Various artists. *The Smithsonian Collection of Classic Jazz* (Smithsonian Collection P6 11891), 1973.
Various artists. *Keys to the Crescent City* (Rounder CD 2087), 1991.
Vitous, Miroslav. *Infinite Search* (Embryo SD 524), 1970.
Vitous, Miroslav. *Purple* (CBS / Sony SOPC 57101-J), 1970.
Vitous, Miroslav. *Mountain in the Clouds* (Atlantic SD 1622), 1972.
Vitous, Miroslav. *Magical Shepherd* (Warner Bros. BS 2925), 1976.
Vitous, Miroslav. *Miroslav* (Arista AF 1040), 1977.
Vitous, Miroslav. *Universal Syncopations* (ECM 1863), 2003.
Vitous, Miroslav. *Music of Weather Report* (ECM 2364), 2016.
Miroslav Vitous Group w/ Michel Portal. *Remembering Weather Report* (ECM 2073), 2009.
Washington, Dinah *What a Diff'rence a Day Makes!* (Mercury SR-60158), 1959.
Washington, Grover, Jr. *Mister Magic* (Kudu KU 20), 1975.
Weather Report. *Weather Report* (Columbia C 30661), 1971.
Weather Report. *I Sing the Body Electric* (Columbia KC 31352), 1972.
Weather Report. *Sweetnighter* (Columbia KC 32210), 1973.
Weather Report. *Mysterious Traveller* (Columbia KC 32494), 1974.
Weather Report. *Tale Spinnin'* (Columbia PC 33417), 1975.
Weather Report. *Black Market* (Columbia PC 34099), 1976.
Weather Report. *Heavy Weather* (Columbia PC 34418), 1977.
Weather Report. *Mr. Gone* (ARC JC 35358), 1978.
Weather Report. *8:30* (ARC PC2 36030), 1979.
Weather Report. *Night Passage* (ARC JC 36793), 1980.
Weather Report. *Weather Report* (ARC FC 37616), 1982.
Weather Report. *Procession* (Columbia FC 38427), 1983.
Weather Report. *Domino Theory* (Columbia FC 39147), 1984.
Weather Report. *Japan Domino Theory—Weather Report Live in Tokyo* (CBS/Sony 78LM 30), 1984.

Weather Report. *Sportin' Life* (Columbia FC 39908), 1985.
Weather Report. *This Is This* (Columbia FC 40280), 1986.
Weather Report. *Live & Unreleased* (Columbia, Legacy C2K 65526), 2002.
Weather Report. *Forecast: Tomorrow* (Legacy, Columbia 82876 85570 2), 2006.
Weather Report. *Live at Montreux 1976* (Eagle Eye Media EREDV629), 2007.
Weather Report. *Live in Berlin 1975* (Art of the Groove MIG 80020), 2011.
Weather Report. *The Columbia Albums 1971–1975* (Legacy, Columbia 88691993422), 2012.
Weather Report. *The Columbia Albums 1976-1982* (Legacy, Columbia 88697 93940 2), 2014.
Weather Report. *The Legendary Live Tapes: 1978–1981* (Legacy, Columbia 88875141272), 2015.
White, Andrew. *Who Got de Funk?* (Andrew's Music AM-4), 1973.
Wilson, Nancy, and the Cannonball Adderley Quintet. *Nancy Wilson / Cannonball Adderley* (Capitol T 1657), 1961.
Wonder, Stevie. *Music of My Mind* (Tamla T 314L), 1972.
Wonder, Stevie. *Talking Book* (Tamla 319L), 1972.
Wonder, Stevie. *Innervisions* (Tamla T 326L), 1973.
Wonder, Stevie. *Fulfillingness' First Finale* (Tamla T6-332S1), 1974.
Zawinul, Joe. *The Rise & Fall of the Third Stream* (Vortex 2002), 1968.
Zawinul, Joe. *Zawinul* (Atlantic SD 1579), 1971.
Zawinul, Joe. *Dialects* (Columbia FC 40081), 1986.
Zawinul, Joe. *My People* (Escapade Music ESC 03651-2), 1996.
Zawinul, Joe. *Stories of the Danube* (Philips 454 143-2), 1996.
Zawinul, Joe. *Mauthausen* (ESC EFA 03666-2), 2000.
Zawinul, Joe. *Faces & Places* (ESC EFA 03679-2), 2002.
Zawinul, Joe. *Brown Street* (Heads Up International HUCD 3121), 2007.
Zawinul, Joe. *75* (Heads Up International HUCD 3162), 2009.
Zawinul, Joe, and the Austrian All Stars. *His Majesty Swinging Nephews 1954–1957* (RST RST-91549-2), 1992.
Joe Zawinul Trio. *To You With Love* (Strand SL 1007), 1961.
The Zawinul Syndicate. *The Immigrants* (Columbia CK 40969), 1988.
The Zawinul Syndicate. *Black Water* (Columbia CK 44316), 1989.
The Zawinul Syndicate. *Lost Tribes* (Columbia CK 46057), 1992.

Notes

Sources are cited in full the first time they are referenced in each chapter. Subsequent citations in the same chapter are shortened.

Introduction

1 Joe Zawinul personal interview, Sep. 15, 2003.
2 Zawinul interview, 2003.
3 Zawinul interview, 2003.
4 Zawinul interview, 2003.
5 Wayne Edwards, *Can't Touch This: Memoirs of a Disillusioned Music Executive* (Bloomington, IN: AuthorHouse, 2015), Kindle, loc. 1941–48.
6 Bob Blumenthal, "The 8 Year Weather Report." *Rolling Stone*, Dec. 28, 1978–Jan. 11, 1979, 65.
7 Josef Woodard, "Weather Report: Storm Surge," *Down Beat*, Jan. 2001, 22.
8 Gary Giddins interview, Apr. 9, 1996 (accessed Apr. 24, 2013), http://www.pbs.org/jazz/about/pdfs/Giddens.pdf, 19–20.
9 Stuart Nicholson, *Jazz-Rock: A History* (New York: Schirmer Books, 1998), 181.
10 Victor Bailey telephone interview, Feb. 18, 2014.
11 Chester Thompson telephone interview, Dec. 22, 2014.
12 Judith Broadhurst, "A Jazz Fest Is Born," *Santa Cruz Sentinel*, Jun. 16, 1989.
13 Barry Davis, "Mr. World Music," *Jerusalem Post*, Jun. 21, 2001.
14 Wayne Shorter telephone interview, Dec. 23, 2008.
15 Omar Hakim telephone interview, Feb. 25, 2014.

1   Joe

1 Bradford J. Stein, "Joe Zawinul: Part 1 of a Two Part Interview," *California Jazz Now*, Jun. 1993, 9.
2 Stein, "Joe Zawinul: Part 1," 9.
3 Jon Pareles, "Pop/Jazz," *New York Times*, Apr. 25, 1986.
4 Joe Zawinul personal interview, Sep. 15, 2003.

5 Paul Rubin, "The Wizard of Austria," *Phoenix New Times*, Mar. 25, 1999 (accessed Jan. 15, 2020), https://www.phoenixnewtimes.com/music/the-wizard-of-austria-6421076.
6 Mike Zwerin, "Joe Zawinul: Austrian Funk and Weathered Funk," Culturekiosque, Jul. 9, 1998 (accessed May 18, 2015), http://www.culturekiosque.com/jazz/miles/rhemile15.htm.
7 Zwerin, "Joe Zawinul."
8 Brian Glasser, *In a Silent Way: A Portrait of Joe Zawinul* (London: Sanctuary Publishing, 2001), 19.
9 Krystian Brodacki, "Joe Zawinul: Jazz Is a Black Music," *Jazz Forum*, No. 134, 1992, 22.
10 Richard Williams, "Weather Man: Joe Zawinul Talks to Richard Williams," *Melody Maker*, Jul. 29, 1972, 12.
11 Zawinul interview, 2003.
12 Zawinul interview, 2003.
13 Mike Zwerin, "A Cocky, Eclectic Jazzman, Recalling Zawinul," Sep. 13, 2007 (accessed Feb. 15, 2019), http://mikezwerin.com/html/notepad.php?pad=53.
14 Stein, "Joe Zawinul: Part 1," 9.
15 Zawinul interview, 2003.
16 Zawinul interview, 2003.
17 Barry Davis, "Mr. World Music," *Jerusalem Post*, Jun. 21, 2001.
18 Zawinul interview, 2003.
19 Stein, "Joe Zawinul: Part 1," 10.
20 Zawinul interview, 2003.
21 Zawinul interview, 2003.
22 Zawinul interview, 2003.
23 Len Lyons, "Josef Zawinul, Keyboard Magician," *Keyboard*, Sep. 1977, 28.
24 Zwerin, "A Cocky, Eclectic Jazzman."
25 Mark Small and Andrew Taylor, *Masters of Music: Conversations with Berklee Greats* (Boston: Berklee Press, 1999), 92–93.
26 Conrad Silvert, "Joe Zawinul: Wayfaring Genius," *Down Beat*, Jun. 1, 1978, 15.
27 Silvert, "Wayfaring Genius," 15.
28 Davis, "Mr. World Music." A recording was made from this tour, *European Tour '57*, Lone Hill Jazz (LHJ10246), 2006.
29 "The First *Down Beat* Hall of Fame Scholarship," *Down Beat*, Jan. 9, 1958, 47.
30 Silvert, "Wayfaring Genius," 15.
31 Willis Conover, "Viennese Cookin'," *Down Beat*, Aug. 11, 1966, 23.
32 Silvert. "Wayfaring Genius," 15.
33 Pete Welding, "From Vienna with Love, Joe Zawinul," *Down Beat*, Nov. 17, 1966, 24.
34 "Hall of Fame Awards," Music News, *Down Beat*, May 15, 1958, 9.
35 Silvert, "Wayfaring Genius," 15.
36 Zawinul interview, 2003.
37 In George Wein's autobiography, he describes how Zawinul almost came to the United States in 1958 as part of the International Youth Band, which Wein organized with Marshall Brown for a performance at the Newport Jazz Festival. Wein and Brown were intent on including musicians from across Europe, but finding one from Swit-

zerland proved difficult. "We could find no suitable musicians in Switzerland, one of our target countries. Fortunately, we did find a good Swiss pianist by the name of George Gruntz—in Milan. Our problem seemed to have been solved, but another arose when we discovered a more desirable pianist in Austria, a young man by the name of Josef Zawinul. What could we do? There were a number of good musicians in Austria, but only one capable player from Switzerland. And so it was that we chose George Gruntz over Joey Zawinul for the International Youth Band." George Wein and Nate Chinen, *Myself Among Others* (Cambridge, MA: Da Capo Press, 2003), 184.

38 Tony Cox, "The Journey of Jazz Great Joe Zawinul," NPR, Apr. 10, 2007 (accessed Jan. 25, 2016), http://www.npr.org/templates/story/story.php?storyId=9495945.
39 Stein, "Joe Zawinul: Part 1," 10.
40 Zan Stewart, "Heaven's Door," *Down Beat*, May 2002, 23.
41 Welding, "From Vienna," 24.

2 Wayne

1 Mark Gilbert, "Wayne Shorter," *Jazz Journal International*, Apr. 1986, 8.
2 Kevin Le Gendre, "The Alchemist," *Jazzwise*, Jun. 2002, 25.
3 Scott Yanow, "The Wayne Shorter Interview," *Down Beat*, Apr. 1986, 18.
4 Le Gendre, "Alchemist," 25.
5 Gilbert, "Wayne Shorter," 1986, 9.
6 Margo Nash, "Coming Home," Jersey Footlights, *New York Times*, Feb. 24, 2002.
7 Dialogue drawn from Bob Blumenthal, "In Conversation with Wayne Shorter," Jazz.com, Mar. 21, 2008 (accessed Jan. 8, 2015), http://www.jazz.com/features-and-interviews/2008/3/21/in-conversation-with-wayne-shorter.
8 Tim Logan, "Wayne Shorter, Double Take," *Down Beat*, Jun. 20, 1974, 16.
9 Conrad Silvert, "Wayne Shorter: Unlimited Imagination," *Down Beat*, Jul. 14, 1977, 58.
10 Blumenthal, "Conversation with Wayne Shorter."
11 Blumenthal, "Conversation with Wayne Shorter."
12 Le Gendre, "Alchemist," 25.
13 Leroi Jones (a.k.a. Amiri Baraka), *Black Music* (New York: William Morrow, third printing, 1970), 81.
14 Silvert, "Unlimited Imagination," 16.
15 Mark Gilbert, "Wayne Shorter," *Jazz Journal International*, Mar. 1996, 6.
16 Silvert, "Unlimited Imagination," 16.
17 Fred Jung, "A Fireside Chat with Wayne Shorter," JazzWeekly, 2003 (accessed Jan. 3, 2015), https://web.archive.org/web/20030310023833/http://jazzweekly.com/interviews/wshorter.htm.
18 Bill Milkowski, "Wayne Shorter Interview," Abstract Logix, Jun. 12, 2005 (accessed Jul. 5, 2014), http://www.abstractlogix.com/interview_view.php?idno=75.

19 Yanow, "Wayne Shorter Interview," 56.
20 A. James Liska, "Wayne Shorter: Coming Home," *Down Beat*, Jul. 1982, 18–19.
21 Yanow, "Wayne Shorter Interview," 56–57.
22 Gilbert, "Wayne Shorter," 1986, 9.
23 Lewis Porter, *John Coltrane: His Life and Music* (Ann Arbor, MI: Univ. of Michigan Press, 1998), 138.
24 Ben Ratliff, *Coltrane: The Story of a Sound* (Farrar, Straus and Giroux, 2007), 128.
25 Porter, *John Coltrane*, 138.
26 Alan Goldsher, *Hard Bop Academy: The Sidemen of Art Blakey and the Jazz Messengers* (Milwaukee: Hal Leonard, 2002), 59.
27 Michelle Mercer, *Footprints: The Life and Work of Wayne Shorter* (New York: J. P. Tarcher/Penguin, 2004), 71.
28 Jones, *Black Music*, 83.
29 Brian Glasser, *In a Silent Way: A Portrait of Joe Zawinul* (London: Sanctuary Publishing, 2001), 252.
30 Heinz Czadek, "Joe Zawinul," *Jazz Forum*, Aug. 1972, 46.
31 Glasser, *In a Silent Way*, 252–53.
32 Jones, *Black Music*, 85.
33 Silvert, "Unlimited Imagination," 16.
34 Joshua Jackson, "Wayne Shorter: The Newark Flash," WBGO, Feb. 8, 2011 (accessed Nov. 13, 2014), http://www.wbgo.org/checkoutjazz/wayne-shorter-the-newark-flash.
35 Chris Collins, "Joe Zawinul," International Association of Jazz Educators, May 2000 (accessed Jan. 1, 2015), https://web.archive.org/web/20070416154936/http://www.iaje.org/article.asp?ArticleID=84.

3 Apprenticeship

1 Leonard Feather, "A New Life, New Plans, New Values," *Los Angeles Times*, Oct. 14, 1984.
2 Details can be found at http://www.laurentdewilde.com/article/joe-zawinul.html. The album is *To You with Love* by the Joe Zawinul Trio (Strand SL 1007), recorded Sep. 1959.
3 Nadine Cohodas, *Queen: The Life and Music of Dinah Washington* (New York: Billboard Books, 2006), 325.
4 Mary Campbell, Associated Press, "Joe Zawinul's Album First in 15 Years," *Baytown Sun*, May 26, 1986.
5 Brian Glasser, *In a Silent Way: A Portrait of Joe Zawinul* (London: Sanctuary Publishing, 2001), 66.
6 Cohodas, *Queen*, 326.
7 In some interviews, Joe has said that right after he started with Washington they went into the studio to record her hit tune, "What a Diff'rence a Day Makes." Actually, she recorded it in Feb. 1959 and the single had already risen to the top of the charts by the time Joe joined her. However, shortly after Joe was hired, he participated in the recording of Washington's follow-up LP, also titled *What a Diff'rence a Day Makes!* Cohodas,

Queen, 305–7, 328.

8 Cohodas, *Queen*, 353–54.

9 Cohodas, *Queen*, 211.

10 Cohodas, *Queen*, 365.

11 Gunther Baumann, *Zawinul: Ein Leben aus Jazz* (Salzburg: Residenz-Verlag, 2002), 62.

12 Baumann, *Zawinul*, 62.

13 Glasser, *In a Silent Way*, 70.

14 Campbell, "Joe Zawinul's Album."

15 Steve Schwartz and Michael Fitzgerald, accessed Jan. 13, 2020, "Art Blakey Chronology (and the Jazz Messengers)," https://jazzmf.com/art-blakey-chronology-and-the-jazz-messengers/.

16 Lee Underwood, "Tony Williams: Aspiring to a Lifetime of Leadership," *Down Beat*, Jun. 21, 1979, 54.

17 Michelle Mercer, *Footprints: The Life and Work of Wayne Shorter* (New York: J. P. Tarcher/Penguin, 2004), 73.

18 Mark Gilbert, "Wayne Shorter," *Jazz Journal International*, Apr. 1986, 9.

19 Nat Hentoff, liner notes to *The Big Beat*, Art Blakey & the Jazz Messengers, Blue Note 4029, 1960.

20 Gene Lees, *Cats of Any Color: Jazz, Black and White* (New York: Da Capo Press, 2001), 170.

21 Alan Goldsher, *Hard Bop Academy: The Sidemen of Art Blakey and the Jazz Messengers* (Milwaukee: Hal Leonard, 2002), 63.

22 Kenny Mathieson, *Cookin': Hard Bop and Soul Jazz, 1954–65* (Edinburgh: Canongate Books, 2000), 29.

23 Sy Johnson, "Zawinul from Birdland to 'Birdland,'" *Jazz*, Fall 1977, 49.

24 Ted Panken, "Joe Zawinul's 79th Birthday Anniversary," Jul. 7, 2011 (accessed Jan. 4, 2015), https://tedpanken.wordpress.com/2011/07/07/joe-zawinuls-79th-birthday-anniversary/.

25 Howard Mandel, "Joe Zawinul: 'My Prime Is Coming!'" *Down Beat*, Jan. 1999, 32.

26 Pete Welding, "From Vienna with Love, Joe Zawinul," *Down Beat*, Nov. 17, 1966, 23.

27 Panken, "Joe Zawinul's 79th."

28 Welding, "From Vienna," 25.

29 Joe Zawinul personal interview, Sep. 15, 2003.

30 Zawinul interview, 2003.

31 Pawel Brodowski, "I'll be back!!!" *Jazz Forum*, No. 98, 1986, 37.

32 From an interview for *Joe Zawinul: A Musical Portrait*, Mark Kidel, prod., Calliope Media/BBC, www.calliopemedia.co.uk/.

33 Welding, "From Vienna," 25.

34 Greg Armbruster, "Zawinul: Continued Hot, Chance of Record Highs," *Keyboard*, Mar. 1984, 45.

35 Joe Zawinul telephone interview, Jan. 1, 2004.

36 Zawinul interview, 2004.

37 Leonard Feather, "Viennese Scores in U.S. Jazz Group," *Los Angeles Times*, Mar. 21, 1967. Additional background from Leonard Feather, "Cannonball Keeps the Jazz Spirit Afloat," *Los Angeles Times*, Aug. 13, 1967.

38 Zawinul interview, 2004.

39 Cary Ginell, *Walk Tall: The Music & Life of Julian "Cannonball" Adderley* (Milwaukee: Hal Leonard, 2013), 120.

40 Joe can be heard playing "Mercy, Mercy, Mercy" on acoustic piano on *Cannonball in Japan* (reissued on CD in 1990), recorded live in Tokyo on August 26, 1966.

41 Zawinul interview, 2003.

42 Zawinul interview, 2003.

43 Zawinul interview, 2003.

44 Ginell, *Walk Tall*, 123–24; *Billboard*, Mar. 4, 1967, 24.

45 Feather, "Cannonball Keeps."

46 *Billboard*, Aug. 19, 1967.

47 Zawinul interview, 2003.

48 John L. Walters, "Joe Zawinul Profile," Unknown Public, 2002 (accessed Mar. 18, 2007), http://www.unknownpublic.com/writing/zawinul2.html.

49 Baumann, *Zawinul*, 73.

50 Leonard Feather, "Blindfold Test: Herbie Hancock," *Down Beat*, Sep. 18, 1969, 28.

51 Ashley Kahn, *Kind of Blue: The Making of a Miles Davis Masterpiece* (New York: Da Capo Press, 2000), 71.

52 Kahn, *Kind of Blue*, 181.

53 Leonard Feather, liner notes to *74 Miles Away*, Cannonball Adderley, Capitol ST 2822, 1967.

54 Zawinul interview, 2003.

55 Ginell, *Walk Tall*, 122.

56 Cited in Iain Anderson, *This Is Our Music: Free Jazz, the Sixties, and American Culture* (Philadelphia: Univ. of Pennsylvania Press, 2007), 28.

57 For a detailed analysis of "The Soul of a Village," see Alan Cooper, "Making the Weather in Contemporary Jazz: An Appreciation of the Musical Art of Josef Zawinul," PhD thesis, University of Southampton, 2012.

58 Sy Johnson, "Zawinul from Birdland to 'Birdland,'" *Jazz*, Fall 1977, 49.

4 Miles

1 A. James Liska, "Wayne Shorter: Coming Home," *Down Beat*, Jul. 1982, 20.

2 Natalie Weiner, "Wayne Shorter on Miles Davis, Kanye West, & the Music of the Future," *Billboard*, May 15, 2015 (accessed May 30, 2015), http://www.billboard.com/articles/news/6568518/wayne-shorter-miles-davis-kanye-west-the-music-of-the-future.

3 Reese Erlich, "Wayne Shorter: A Jazz Artist for All Time," *Into the Music*, Feb. 28, 2009 (accessed Jul. 5, 2014), http://www.abc.net.au/radionational/programs/intothemusic/wayne-shorter-a-jazz-artist-for-all-time/3178038.

4 Weiner, "Wayne Shorter on Miles Davis."

5 Miles Davis with Quincy Troupe, *Miles, the Autobiography* (New York: Simon & Schuster, 1989), 263.

6 Gary Giddins and Scott DeVeaux, *Jazz* (New York: W. W. Norton, 2009,) 411–12.

7 Davis, *Autobiography*, 270.

8 The show took place on Sep. 4, 1964. According to advertisements that appeared in the *Los Angeles Times*, as well as the *Times's* review of the show (published on Sep. 6, 1964), the billing included the Miles Davis Quintet, the Gerry Mulligan Quartet, the João Gilberto quartet, and Nina Simone.

9 Weiner, "Wayne Shorter on Miles Davis."

10 Herbie Hancock with Lisa Dickey, *Possibilities* (New York: Viking Penguin, 2014), 78.

11 Weiner, "Wayne Shorter on Miles Davis."

12 Davis, *Autobiography*, 276.

13 John Szwed, *So What: The Life of Miles Davis* (New York: Simon & Schuster, 2002), 241.

14 Hancock, *Possibilities*, 60.

15 *Time*, Jun. 27, 1960.

16 Joe Goldberg, *Jazz Masters of the Fifties* (New York: Da Capo Press, 1980), 231. Davis was especially withering in his comments about Eric Dolphy and Cecil Taylor in a *Down Beat* blindfold test that year. (The blindfold test is a long-running column in which participants are asked to comment on musical selections without being told who is playing them.) Recognizing a Dolphy cut, Miles hissed, "nobody else could sound that bad!" And of Taylor, he exclaimed, "Take it off! That's some sad _____, man." *Down Beat*, Jun. 18, 1964, 31.

17 Szwed, *So What*, 255.

18 Weiner, "Wayne Shorter on Miles Davis."

19 Kenny Dorham, review of *E.S.P.*, *Down Beat*, Dec. 30, 1965, 34.

20 Bob Belden, liner notes to *E.S.P.*, Columbia Legacy CK 65683, CD, 1998, 13.

21 Eric Snider, "Weather Report's Wayne Shorter Interviewed," *Music*, Mar. 3, 1983, 14.

22 Rudy Van Gelder, NEA Jazz Master interview transcript, Nov. 5, 2011, http://amhistory.si.edu/jazz/VanGelder-Rudy/Rudy_Van_Gelder_Interview_Transcription.pdf, 20.

23 Michelle Mercer, *Footprints: The Life and Work of Wayne Shorter* (New York: J. P. Tarcher/Penguin, 2004), 104.

24 Ted Panken, "Unfinished Business," *Jazziz*, Sep. 2003, 36–37.

25 Nat Hentoff, liner notes to *The Big Beat*, Art Blakey & the Jazz Messengers, Blue Note 4029, 1960.

26 Victor Bailey telephone interview, Feb. 18, 2014.

27 Mark Gilbert, "Wayne Shorter," *Jazz Journal International*, Apr. 1986, 9.

28 Hancock, *Possibilities*, 92.

29 Hancock, *Possibilities*, 92.

30 Ian Carr, *Miles Davis: The Definitive Biography* (New York: Thunder's Mouth Press, 1998), 204.

31 Todd F. Coolman, "The Quintet," liner notes to *Miles Davis Quintet 1965–1968*, Sony Legacy/Columbia C6K 67398, CD, 1998, 40.

32 Davis, *Autobiography*, 275–76.

33 Jeremy Yudkin, *Miles Davis, Miles Smiles, and the Invention of Post Bop* (Bloomington, IN: Indiana Univ. Press, 2008), 63.

34 Davis, *Autobiography*, 273.

35 Zan Stewart, "Heaven's Door," *Down Beat*, May 2002, 24.

36 Bob Blumenthal, "The 8 Year Weather Report." *Rolling Stone*, Dec. 28, 1978–Jan. 11, 1979," 65.

37 Ray Townley, "The Mysterious Travellings of an Austrian Mogul," *Down Beat*, Jan. 30, 1975, 17.

38 Eric Nisenson, *Blue: The Murder of Jazz* (New York: Da Capo Press, 1997), 196.

39 Mark Gilbert, "Wayne Shorter," *Jazz Journal International*, Mar. 1996, 7.

40 James T. Patterson, *Grand Expectations: The United States, 1945–1974* (New York: Oxford Univ. Press, 1996), 372.

41 For examples of the response to rock 'n' roll in the pages of *Down Beat*, see Leonard Feather, May 4, 1955, 6; Nat Hentoff, May 30, 1956, 12; Ralph Gleason, July 11, 1956, 34; Barry Ulanov, January 23, 1957, 40. For a broader overview of the negative reaction to rock 'n' roll by jazz and established popular artists, as well as industry executives, see Linda Martin and Kerry Segrave, *Anti-Rock: The Opposition to Rock 'n' Roll* (Hamden, CT: Archon Books, 1988).

42 "Teens Dig Jazz," *Down Beat*, Jan. 21, 1960, 13.

43 Eric Hobsbawm, *Uncommon People: Resistance, Rebellion and Jazz* (New York: The New Press, 1998), 282, 284. At the same time, rock/pop accounted for about 75 percent of sales, according to the 1972 *Billboard International Music Industry Directory*.

44 David H. Rosenthal, *Hard Bop: Jazz and Black Music, 1955–1965* (New York: Oxford Univ. Press, 1992), 169.

45 Nat Hentoff, *The Jazz Life* (Cambridge, MA: Da Capo Press, 1975), vii. An additional hit was the premature death of John Coltrane in July 1967 at the age of 42. By then Coltrane had become the most important jazzman of the sixties, providing leadership for modern jazz and especially the avant-garde.

46 Per Martin and Segrave, "One of the most virulently anti-rock people was Mitch Miller, the chief producer, or artist and repertoire man, at Columbia Records. For him rock music was the 'glorification of monotony' and with its 'illiterate' lyrics was aimed at the twelve- to fifteen-year-olds. Miller boasted proudly that none of Columbia's hits were rockers and he accepted losing the twelve- to fifteen-year-olds but was ready to welcome them back to Columbia's fold later, when they had developed 'taste.'" Martin and Segrave, *Anti-Rock*, 46.

47 Between 1958 and 1961, for example, Mitch Miller released eleven albums in his *Sing Along* series, with total sales of over 4.5 million units. Gary Marmorstein, *The Label: The Story of Columbia Records* (New York: Thunder's Mountain Press, 2007), 252.

48 Clive Davis with James Willwerth, *Clive: Inside the Record Business* (New York: William Morrow, 1975), 75.

49 Kevin Fellezs, *Birds of Fire: Jazz, Rock, Funk and*

the *Creation of Fusion* (Durham, NC: Duke Univ. Press, 2011), 65.

50 Fellezs, *Birds of Fire*, 66.

51 Carr, *Miles Davis*, 222.

52 The earliest uses of the hyphenated phrase "jazz-rock" that I have found appear in the pages of *Variety*. See Army Archerd, "Just for Variety," *Variety*, Sep. 7, 1965, 2; and "R&R Evolution: Jazz-Rock and Even Show-Rock," *Variety*, Dec. 22, 1965, 49. For a thorough history of jazz-rock, see Stuart Nicholson, *Jazz-Rock: A History* (New York: Schirmer Books, 1998).

53 Scott Yanow, review of *Goin' Out of My Head*, Wes Montgomery, AllMusic, accessed Jun. 6, 2016, https://www.allmusic.com/album/goin-out-of-my-head-mw0000192283.

54 Davis, *Autobiography*, 298.

55 Bob Belden, "Annotations," liner notes to *Miles Davis Quintet 1965–1968*, Miles Davis, Columbia C6K 67398, 1998, 88–89.

56 Bob Doerschuk, "Miles Davis: The Picasso of Invisible Art," *Keyboard*, Oct. 1987, 69.

57 Bob Belden, liner notes to *The Complete In a Silent Way Sessions*, Miles Davis, Columbia C3K 65362, 2001, 48.

58 Davis, *Autobiography*, 289.

59 Bob Belden, liner notes to *Miles in the Sky*, Miles Davis, Columbia CK 65684, 1998.

60 Keith Waters, *The Studio Recordings of the Miles Davis Quintet, 1965–68* (New York: Oxford Univ. Press, 2011), 243.

61 In one interview, Joe said it was the day after he returned to New York. Max Dax, "Joe Zawinul," *Alert*, No. 8, Oct. 2002 (accessed Jun. 20, 2019), http://www.waahr.de/texte/joe-zawinul.

62 Dax, "Joe Zawinul."

63 Dax, "Joe Zawinul."

64 Dax, "Joe Zawinul."

65 Anecdote related by Zawinul in a German television documentary.

66 Paul Tingen, "From a Whisper to a Scream," *Mojo*, Sep. 2001, 47.

67 Angus MacKinnon, "Joseph Zawinul, Future Primitive," *New Musical Express*, Nov. 15, 1980, 23.

68 Conrad Silvert, "Wayne Shorter: Unlimited Imagination," *Down Beat*, Jul. 14, 1977, 59.

69 Bob Belden, *The Complete In a Silent Way Sessions*, 64.

70 Tingen, "Whisper to a Scream," 48.

71 Bob Belden, *The Complete In a Silent Way Sessions*, 77.

72 The rehearsal take can be heard on *The Complete In a Silent Way Sessions*. Joe's score is reproduced in Kunihiko Yamashita, *Joe Zawinul: On the Creative Process* (Tokyo: Rittor Music, 2006), 188–89. It includes the note "slow bossa nova."

73 Brian Case, "John McLaughlin: Phew!—This Is a Jolly Interesting Article!" *New Musical Express*, Feb. 1, 1975 (accessed from Rock's Back Pages, http://www.rocksbackpages.com/Library/Article/john-mclaughlin-phew--this-is-a-jolly-interesting-article).

74 Davis, *Autobiography*, 296–97.

75 Tingen, "Whisper to a Scream," 48.

76 Lester Bangs, review of *In a Silent Way*, Miles Davis, *Rolling Stone*, Nov. 15, 1969, 33.

77 Jim Szantor, review of *Bitches Brew*, Miles Davis, *Down Beat*, Jun. 11, 1970, 20–21.

78 An example of such a letter is reproduced in Victor Svorinich, *Listen to This: Miles Davis and Bitches Brew* (Jackson, MS: Univ. Press of Mississippi, 2015), 130.

79 Svorinich, *Listen to This*, 113.

80 Joe's score is reproduced in Yamashita, *Joe Zawinul: On the Creative Process*, 214–16, and Svorinich, *Listen to This*, 88–90.

81 Bob Belden, "Session-By-Session Analysis," liner notes to *The Complete Bitches Brew Sessions*, Miles Davis, Sony Music Entertainment, 1998, 129.

82 Erlich, "Jazz Artist for All Time."

83 Tingen, "Whisper to a Scream," 46.

84 Dan Ouellette, "*Bitches Brew*: The Making of the Most Revolutionary Jazz Album in History," *Down Beat*, Dec. 1999, 37.

85 Carman Moore, "The New Thing Meets Rock," *New York Times*, Aug. 9, 1970.

86 Bill Cole, *Miles Davis: A Musical Biography* (New York: William Morrow, 1974), 103–6.

87 Dan Morgenstern, "No Jive from Clive," Afterthoughts, *Down Beat*. Sep. 16, 1971, 18.

88 Clive Davis with Anthony DeCurtis, *The Soundtrack of My Life* (New York: Simon & Schuster, 2013), 86.

89 Davis, *Soundtrack of My Life*, 87.

90 For example, the heading of the Columbia ad for *Filles de Kilimanjaro* in the May 31, 1969, issue of *Rolling Stone* read, "You May Like Jazz, but Not Even Know It."

91 Svorinich, *Listen to This*, 116–18.

92 Davis, *Autobiography*, 298.

93 John Litweiler, *The Freedom Principle: Jazz after 1958* (New York: W. Morrow, 1984), 223. The common perception that Miles turned commercial at the request of Columbia was established by the mid-1970s. For example, in early 1975, Leonard Feather wrote, "Miles Davis was advised in the late 1960s that he would have to come up with something more commercial if he wanted to sell records; accordingly, he abandoned his subtle jazz experimentations in favor of a series of LPs to which rock fans, young blacks and the new jazz-rock audience in general were able to relate." *Billboard*, Feb. 8, 1975, 25.

94 Stanley Crouch, "Play the Right Thing," *The New Republic*, Feb. 12, 1990, 30.

95 David Rensin, "Weather Report: Fair Weather Jazz Fans Leave Them Alone," *Rolling Stone*, Sep. 27, 1973, 24.

96 Chris Welch, "Weather Report: Myth & Magic," *Melody Maker*, Oct. 14, 1978, 61.

97 Simon Trask, "Hey Joe!" *Music Technology*, Jan. 1992, 43.

5 Miroslav

1 Willis Conover, "Conover in Europe, Part I: Jazz Festival in Prague," *Down Beat*, Jan. 13, 1966, 15.
2 Conover, "Jazz Festival in Prague," 16.
3 Miroslav Vitous telephone interview, Feb. 21, 2015.
4 Many biographies of Vitous identify Jelinek as Jírí Jerinek.
5 Iain Anderson, *This Is Our Music: Free Jazz, the Sixties, and American Culture* (Philadelphia: Univ. of Pennsylvania Press, 2007), 24.
6 Vitous interview, 2015.
7 Conover, "Viennese Cookin'," 26.
8 Vitous interview, 2015.
9 Vitous interview, 2015.
10 Vitous interview, 2015.
11 Vitous interview, 2015.
12 Vitous interview, 2015.
13 Fred Bouchard, "Miroslav Vitous: Both Sides of the Bass," *Down Beat*, Sep. 1984, 63.
14 Vitous interview, 2015.
15 Maria Lucien telephone interview, Mar. 22, 2017.
16 The date of the performance was Aug. 11, 1967.
17 Clark Terry and Gwen Terry, *Clark: The Autobiography of Clark Terry* (Berkeley: Univ. of California Press, 2011), 204.
18 Miroslav Vitous telephone interview, Apr. 26, 2007.
19 Anil Prasad, "Miroslav Vitous: Freeing the Muse," Innerviews, 2004 (accessed Jul. 19, 2014), http://innerviews.org/inner/vitous.html.
20 Cary Ginell, *The Evolution of Mann: Herbie Mann and the Flute in Jazz* (Milwaukee: Hal Leonard Books, 2014), 103.
21 Ginell, *The Evolution of Mann*, 103.
22 Dan Morgenstern, "Herbie's Mann-Made World," *Down Beat*, Dec. 10, 1970, 14.
23 Ginell, *The Evolution of Mann*, 108.
24 Leonard Feather, "Mann Unit at Marty's on the Hill," *Los Angeles Times*, Dec. 8, 1967.
25 Fred Jung, "A Fireside Chat with Miroslav Vitous," All About Jazz, Oct. 10, 2003 (accessed Dec. 29, 2012), http://www.allaboutjazz.com/php/article.php?id=619&pg=1#.UN-7YbQqW-bA.
26 Wayne Shorter, "Creativity and Change," *Down Beat*, Dec. 12, 1968, 21.
27 Herb Wong, liner notes to *Super Nova*, Blue Note BST 84332, 1969.
28 Richard Williams, "Wayne Waxes Strong," *Melody Maker*, May 23, 1970, 20.
29 Quoted in Colin Harper, *Bathed in Lightning: John McLaughlin, the 60s and the Emerald Beyond* (London: Jawbone Press, 2014), 348.
30 For example, in May 1970, Leonard Feather wrote of Miles: "As can be deduced from his current album [*Bitches Brew*], he is creating a new and more complex form, drawing from the avant-garde, atonalism, modality, rock, jazz and the universe. It has no name, but some listeners have called it 'space music.'" Leonard Feather, "Miles Davis: Ahead or Rocking Back?", *Los Angeles Times*, May

17, 1970. Other uses of the term—describing Grateful Dead to Pink Floyd, and later, Herbie Hancock and Weather Report—can be found in trade papers such as *Billboard* in the early 1970s (see *Billboard*, Apr. 29, 1972; May 13, 1972; Jun. 1, 1974).
31 John Litweiler, review of *Super Nova*, *Down Beat*, Aug. 20, 1970, 26–27.
32 Harvey Pekar, review of *Infinite Search*, *Down Beat*, Jun. 25, 1970, 23–24.
33 Pat Buzby, "Miroslav Vitous' Infinite Search for Universal Syncopations," jambands.com, Jan. 29, 2004 (accessed Dec. 28, 2012), http://www.jambands.com/features/2004/01/29/miroslav-vitous-infinite-search-for-universal-syncopations.
34 Vitous interview, 2007.
35 Buzby, "Miroslav Vitous' Infinite Search."
36 Morgenstern, "Herbie's Mann-Made World," 14.
37 "Album Reviews," *Billboard*, Aug. 8, 1970, 20.
38 Morgenstern, "Herbie's Mann-Made World," 14; Vitous correspondence, Aug. 2016.
39 Miroslav says that Mann's account in *Down Beat* is not accurate. When he and Sharrock informed Mann that they had accepted their offers from Miles, Mann "was so hurt that he changed this fact [claiming to fire Vitous] in his preference. He also wrote in the long interview [in *Down Beat*] that I was taking over his band so he had to fire me. He was devastated by all this." Vitous correspondence, Aug. 2016.
40 Vitous interview, 2007.

6 Shoviza

1 Richard Williams, "Shorter Story," *Melody Maker*, Aug. 5, 1972, 22.
2 "Trigger man" from Michelle Mercer, *Footprints: The Life and Work of Wayne Shorter* (New York: J. P. Tarcher/Penguin, 2004), 141.
3 Krystian Brodacki, "The Original Batman: Wayne Shorter Remembers Miles Davis," *Jazz Forum*, No. 132, 1992, 25.
4 Williams, "Shorter Story," 22.
5 Although the album's liner notes state the recording date as Aug. 26, 1970—which is the same day that Wayne recorded his next Blue Note album, *Odyssey of Iska*, but with completely different personnel—*The Blue Note Label: A Discography* lists the recording date as Apr. 3, 1970, which is accepted as correct. Michael Cuscuna and Michel Ruppli, *The Blue Note Label: A Discography, Revised and Expanded* (Westport, CT: Greenwood Press, 2001) Miroslav Vitous is mentioned in the liner notes, but not on the album jacket's personnel listing. Micheline Pelzer is misidentified as Michelin Prell.
6 Michael Cuscuna, "Weather Report," *Jazz & Pop*, Jul. 1971, 14; Williams, "Shorter Story," 22.
7 Tim Logan, "Wayne Shorter, Double Take," *Down Beat*, Jun. 20, 1974, 17.
8 Ralph Towner telephone interview, May 13, 2014.

9 Gene Bertoncini telephone interview, Sep. 26, 2016.

10 *Promises, Promises* opened on Broadway on Dec. 1, 1968. The pit band featured a number of jazz musicians, including Friedman, trumpeters Al Porcino and Joe Newman, and Chuck Israels on bass. Harold Wheeler conducted. Bobby Thomas originally held the drum chair, but was later replaced by Billy Cobham and Alphonse Mouzon. When Mouzon joined the company at age nineteen, he was the youngest musician on Broadway.

11 Alphonse Mouzon email correspondence, Sep. 2016.

12 Bertoncini interview, 2017.

13 Bertoncini interview, 2017.

14 David Friedman email correspondence, Sep. 2016.

15 Leonard Feather, liner notes to *Odyssey of Iska*, Wayne Shorter, Blue Note, BST 84363.

16 Lester Bangs, review of *Odyssey of Iska, Rolling Stone*, Dec. 23, 1971, 68, 70.

17 Larry Kart, review of *Odyssey of Iska, Down Beat*, Nov. 25, 1971, 22–23.

18 Gil Podolinsky, "Weather Report: An Interview with Joe Zawinul and Engineer Brian Risner," *Modern Recording*, Nov. 1977, 33.

19 Ted Panken, "Joe Zawinul's 79th Birthday Anniversary," Jul. 7, 2011 (accessed Jan. 4, 2015), https://tedpanken.wordpress.com/2011/07/07/joe-zawinuls-79th-birthday-anniversary/.

20 Roy McCurdy telephone interview, May 22, 2016.

21 Bob Glassenberg, "Studio Track," *Billboard*, Aug. 21, 1971, 4.

22 It is said that the sounds on "Arrival in New York" are from Joe's tune "Country Preacher," recorded by Cannonball Adderley, but slowed down.

23 Brian Glasser, *In a Silent Way: A Portrait of Joe Zawinul* (London: Sanctuary Publishing, 2001), 126.

24 The near nineteen-minute version of "Recollections" was recorded on February 6. It appears on the Davis album *Big Fun*, released in 1974, a compilation of music that Miles recorded between 1969 and 1972. Joe's handwritten score for "Recollections" is reproduced in Kunihiko Yamashita, *Joe Zawinul: On the Creative Process* (Tokyo: Rittor Music, 2006), 296.

25 "Zawinul Quits Cannon to Co-Lead New Group," *Down Beat*, Dec. 10, 1970, 11.

26 Session data in *Atlantic Records: A Discography, Volume 2* indicates that on Aug. 6, 1970, "In a Silent Way" and "Doctor Honoris Causa" were recorded with the following personnel: Woody Shaw (trumpet), George Davis (flute), Earl Turbinton (soprano sax), Joe Zawinul and Herbie Hancock (electric piano), Miroslav Vitous and Walter Booker (bass), Billy Hart and David Lee (percussion). On Aug. 10, the same group, minus Davis, Turbinton and Vitous, plus Joe Chambers and Jack DeJohnette (percussion) recorded "Arrival in New York" and "Directions" (the latter was not released). On Aug. 12, the original group,

plus Chambers (percussion) and DeJohnette (melodica) recorded "His Last Journey" and "Double Image." On Oct. 28, overdubs on "Arrival" were recorded using Hubert Laws (flute), Woody Shaw, Wayne, and Miroslav. By then, Joe, Wayne, and Miroslav had agreed to form their as-yet unnamed band. Michel Ruppli, *Atlantic Records: A Discography, Volume 2* (Westport, CT: Greenwood Press, 1979), 376, 377.

27 The two albums were released within weeks of each other. *Billboard* included *Zawinul* in its review of new albums on May 15, 1971, and *Weather Report* on June 5, 1971.

28 Lester Bangs, reviews of *Zawinul* and *Weather Report*, *Rolling Stone*, Aug. 5, 1971.

29 Doug Ramsey, review of *Zawinul*, *Down Beat*, Sep. 16, 1971, 34.

30 The *Purple* album jacket says that the music was recorded at Apostolic Studios on August 25, 1970, but per correspondence with Miroslav, it was done over multiple sessions rather than a single day. In an interview with Anil Prasad, Miroslav said the tracks were done over a period of six months. Plus, that date is suspect because it was around the time that Miroslav departed for Japan with Herbie Mann. Anil Prasad, "Miroslav Vitous: Freeing the Muse," Innerviews, 2004 (accessed Jul. 19, 2014), http://innerviews.org/inner/vitous.html; Vitous correspondence, Aug. 2016.

31 Miroslav Vitous telephone interview, Apr. 26, 2007.

32 "New Records in the World," *Jazz Forum*, No. 20, Dec. 1972, 106.

33 Brodacki, "The Original Batman," 25–26.

34 See Iain Anderson, *This is Our Music: Free Jazz, the Sixties, and American Culture* (Philadelphia: Univ. of Pennsylvania Press, 2007), Chapter 4, "The Musicians and Their Audience."

35 Stuart Nicholson, *Jazz-Rock: A History* (New York: Schirmer Books, 1998), 58.

36 Mike Zwerin, "Disaster Area," State of Mind, *Down Beat*, Jul. 27, 1967, 13.

37 Bob Gluck, *You'll Know When You Get There: Herbie Hancock and the Mwandishi Band* (Chicago: Univ. of Chicago Press, 2012), 80.

38 Williams, "Shorter Story," 22.

39 Richard Williams, "Weather Man: Joe Zawinul Talks to Richard Williams," *Melody Maker*, Jul. 29, 1972, 12.

40 The Adderley band played two weeks at Shelly's Manne-Hole, Sep. 1–13, 1970. A week later they played the Monterey Jazz Festival; parts of their performance are included in Clint Eastwood's movie, *Play Misty for Me*. On Saturday, Oct. 3, Cannonball performed at the Pacific Northwest Jazz Spectacular in Seattle. Miles played there the next evening. Joe also did a Sunday afternoon jazz piano workshop with Herbie Hancock, Keith Jarrett, and Bill Evans. Chris Sheridan, *Dis Here: A Bio-Discography of Julian "Cannonball" Adderley* (Westport, CT: Greenwood Press, 2000), 434–35; Steven F. Brown, "Caught in the Act," *Down*

Beat, Jan. 7, 1971, 31–32.

41 Jim Wilke correspondence, Jan. 2017.

42 Dan Morgenstern, "Weather Report: Outlook Bright and Sunny," *Down Beat*, May 27, 1971, 14.

43 Vitous interview, 2007.

44 Williams, "Shorter Story," 22. Joe and Wayne have given conflicting accounts of how their dialogue unfolded. This is Wayne's recollection from a 1972 interview, not long after the events occurred.

45 Len Lyons, "This Year's Weather Report," *High Fidelity*, Sep. 1978, 116.

46 Vitous interview, 2007.

47 Barry Altschul described the operation of the band as "collective everything. Everyone had a job to do in the band: librarian, business . . . we were also kind of a commune. We were on the road together with our families—those who had families—and we cooked, we had little cookers with us, bought fresh vegetables and brown rice and shit. And anyone who wanted to eat meat, that's what they did, but still, we were all like a family. So, we were very tight." Bob Gluck, *The Miles Davis Lost Quintet and Other Revolutionary Ensembles* (Chicago: Univ. of Chicago Press, 2016), 121.

48 Whitney Balliett, *Improvising: Sixteen Jazz Musicians and Their Art* (New York: Oxford University Press, 1977), 194.

49 Ray Townley, "The Mysterious Travellings of an Austrian Mogul," *Down Beat*, Jan. 30, 1975, 17.

50 Wayne Shorter telephone interview, Mar. 27, 2015.

51 A. J. Morgan, "Weather Report: Increasingly Warm & Sunny," *Crawdaddy*, Oct. 1975, 31.

52 Vitous interview, 2007.

53 Bertoncini interview, 2017.

54 "Zawinul Leaves," *Melody Maker*, Oct. 24, 1970, 3.

55 "Zawinul Quits Cannon," 11. This mistake was repeated in *Melody Maker*, Mar. 6, 1971, 6.

56 John Swenson, "Jazz Condition—UPI Arts & Entertainment," UPI, Apr. 3, 2002 (accessed Jun. 20, 2019), https://www.upi.com/Jazz-Condition-UPI-Arts-Entertainment/27491017876553/. Turbinton can be heard on B. B. King's album *Live in Japan*, recorded in Mar. 1971, and the studio albums *Guess Who* and *L.A. Midnight*, both released in 1972.

57 The session took place on October 13, 1970. A *Down Beat* blurb at the end of 1974 noted the unreleased album's existence. "Potpourri," *Down Beat*, Dec. 19, 1974, 11.

58 Max Dax, "Joe Zawinul," http://www.waahr.de/texte/joe-zawinul. Originally published in *Alert*, No. 8, Oct. 2002, 88–96. Translated from German by Curt Bianchi.

59 In an interview years later, Nat Adderley complained about the manner in which Joe left the band: "The only departure that left a bad taste was Joe Zawinul's because it seemed to have been plotted in an underhand manner." Chris Sheridan, *Dis Here: A Bio-Discography of Julian "Can-*

nonball" Adderley (Westport, CT: Greenwood Press, 2000), 199. David Axelrod was offended, too. "Joe didn't give Cannon any notice. I liked Joe a lot, but that was really wrong. He had been planning on leaving for some time with Wayne Shorter and Miroslav Vitous." Cary Ginell, *Walk Tall: The Music & Life of Julian "Cannonball" Adderley* (Milwaukee: Hal Leonard Books, 2013), 141. Ginell writes that Zawinul's departure "had been imminent for some time," calling it a "calculated escape." Ginell, *Walk Tall*, 140.

However, Joe committed to Wayne and Miroslav in early October and his plans were publicly reported before the month was out. Joe continued to perform with Adderley into December, so it seems Joe gave Cannonball plenty of notice, especially considering that the quintet was off for five weeks following Joe's final dates with them.

Roy McCurdy offers his own take on the matter. "No, [Joe] didn't leave in an underhanded way. We knew he was going to leave. We knew what his plans were. There were no hard feelings that I remember. Cannon and Joe were very close. Joe and Nat weren't as close as Cannon and Joe were, but everybody in the band was close. It was like a family. It was fine. We knew he was going to leave and Cannon had to have time because he was preparing to have somebody else come into the band at that time." McCurdy interview, 2016.

60 The bill for the Apollo shows, from Dec. 2 to Dec. 8, consisted of Roberta Flack, Cannonball Adderley, Les McCann, Joe Williams, Letta Mbulu, and Gene McDaniels. (Ed Ochs, "Soul Sauce," *Billboard*, Dec. 12, 1970, 42.) The tracks for *Headless Heroes of the Apocalypse* were recorded at Regent Sound Studios, Oct. 6–8, 1970. Michel Ruppli, *Atlantic Records: A Discography, Volume 3* (Westport, CT: Greenwood Press, 1979), 13.

61 Joe Zawinul personal interview, Sep. 15, 2003.

7 Weather Report (1971)

1 Dan Morgenstern, "No Jive from Clive," *Afterthoughts, Down Beat*, Sep. 16, 1971, 18.

2 Clive Davis, "Davis Receives Standing Ovation at Radio Forum with His Speech," *Billboard*, Aug. 24, 1974, 10.

3 Clive Davis with James Willwerth, *Clive: Inside the Record Business* (New York: William Morrow, 1975), 143.

4 The $90,000 figure comes from an interview Joe gave to Geri Schuller. http://www.geraldschuller.com/datei/menu/discographie/discografie/2004/joezawinul.htm, accessed Aug. 13, 2016.

5 Gunther Baumann, *Zawinul: Ein Leben aus Jazz* (Salzburg: Residenz-Verlag, 2002), 107. Translated from German by Curt Bianchi.

6 Adrian Macintosh, "Wayne Shorter: Putting It in the Weather Report Rack," *Jazz Forum*, Apr. 1976, 45.

7 Wayne Shorter telephone interview, Dec. 23, 2008.

8 Leonard Feather and Jeff Atterton, "Jazz," *Melody Maker*, Mar. 6, 1971, 6.

9 Shorter interview, 2008.

10 Dan Morgenstern, "Weather Report: Outlook Bright and Sunny," *Down Beat*, May 27, 1971 14.

11 Miroslav Vitous telephone interview, Apr. 26, 2007.

12 Wayne Shorter telephone interview, Mar. 27, 2015.

13 Brian Glasser, *In a Silent Way: A Portrait of Joe Zawinul* (London: Sanctuary Publishing, 2001), 132.

14 Don DeMichael, liner notes to *Weather Report*, Columbia PC 30661, 1971.

15 Alphonse Mouzon correspondence, Jan.–Feb. 2014.

16 Vitous interview, 2007.

17 The Seventh Century met weekly in the basement of the Village Gate. In 1971, they produced a self-titled album, although Burton didn't perform on it (Al Segno Records AS 3733).

18 Barbara Burton telephone interview, Nov. 12, 2014.

19 Burton interview, 2014.

20 Burton interview, 2014.

21 DeMichael, *Weather Report* liner notes.

22 Len Lyons, "Josef Zawinul Keyboard Magician," *Keyboard*, Sep. 1977, 28.

23 Greg Armbruster, "Zawinul: Continued Hot, Chance of Record Highs," *Keyboard*, Mar. 1984, 49.

24 Shorter interview, 2015.

25 Freeman got to know Joe through *American Pie*. "Nat Adderley had a rehearsal studio and I rented it out for a couple of things, just on an hourly basis," Freeman recalled. "One of the things I rented it for was to rehearse *American Pie*, and somewhere in the course of that I met Joe. I remember having a conversation with him about *Sgt. Pepper's* at the time. He had apparently not paid much attention to pop music and I remember having this sort of stirring conversation with him about how pop music was really getting creative and inventive, and he should pay attention to it. It was a conversation about integrating jazz and pop music, which is exactly what happened."

Freeman later asked Joe to do a session for Tim Hardin's album *Bird on a Wire*, and Joe brought along Miroslav and Alphonse Mouzon. "We had hung out and we were casually, socially connected, and I asked him to play on the album," Freeman said. "At the time he was certainly amenable to doing sessions for double scale and I paid him an arranging fee, too. Tim was not on these sessions. I wouldn't trust Tim Hardin anywhere near a live band. [*laughs*] Tim Hardin was drop dead brilliant; he was just impossible to work with, that's all. So there was very little direction for Joe. I remember Joe sort of being disgusted because I didn't have a written arrangement for it. He did a head arrangement for the introduction and pretty much arranged the whole thing on the spot. He was an enormously talented guy." Ed Freeman

telephone interview, Jul. 25, 2016.

26 Freeman interview, 2016.

27 Vitous interview, 2007.

28 Mouzon correspondence, 2014.

29 Alphonse Mouzon telephone interview, Apr. 27, 2015.

30 Dr. Anthony Brown, McCoy Tyner Smithsonian Jazz Oral History Program NEA Jazz Master interview transcript, Smithsonian National Museum of American History, Dec. 7–8, 2011 (accessed Apr. 27, 2019), https://amhistory.si.edu/jazz/Tyner-McCoy/Tyner_McCoy_Transcript.pdf.

31 Mouzon interview, 2015.

32 According to Brian Risner, the reason the cover of the Rhodes was removed in these early videos was to create a stable base for the ring modulator (the top of the Rhodes case was arched) and to provide Joe with access to the tines, which he would physically manipulate.

33 Brian G. Bourke, "A change in the Weather," *Syracuse Herald American*, Sep. 7, 1986. The ring modulator can be heard on "Devastatement" and "Alto Sex" on Adderley's album *The Price You Got to Pay to Be Free* (Capitol Records SWBB-636).

34 Vitous interview, 2007.

35 Morgenstern, "Outlook Bright and Sunny," 14–15.

36 Morgenstern, "Outlook Bright and Sunny," 15.

37 Morgenstern, "Outlook Bright and Sunny," 42.

38 Anil Prasad, "Miroslav Vitous: Freeing the Muse," Innerviews, 2004 (accessed Jul. 19, 2014), http://innerviews.org/inner/vitous.html.

39 Morgenstern, "Outlook Bright and Sunny," 15.

40 Mouzon interview, 2015.

41 Morgenstern, "Outlook Bright and Sunny," 15.

42 Airto Moreira telephone interview, Aug. 20, 2016.

43 Mouzon interview, 2015; email correspondence, May 2015.

44 Mouzon interview, 2015.

45 Dan Morgenstern, "'Different Strokes,' Music Is a Beautiful Game," *Down Beat*, Mar. 15, 1973, 18.

46 Frank Cuomo telephone interview, Nov. 11, 2016.

47 Mouzon interview, 2015.

48 Mouzon interview, 2015.

49 Darryl Brown telephone interview, Feb. 15, 2014.

50 Chris Collins, "Joe Zawinul," International Association of Jazz Educators, May 2000 (accessed Jan. 1, 2015), https://web.archive.org/web/20070416154936/http://www.iaje.org/article.asp?ArticleID=84.

51 Monk Rowe, Don Alias interview for the Fillius Jazz Archive at Hamilton College, New York, NY, January 6, 2002.

52 Rowe, Don Alias interview.

53 Charles Mitchell, "'Bim, bang, boing, slam, pop, z-i-i-ing!': The Anatomical Signatures of Airto," *Down Beat*, Nov. 8, 1974, 19.

54 "Big Col Promo Sets Sights on Weather Report," *Billboard*, Apr. 24, 1971, 6.

55 King Leer, "Weather Report," *Changes*, Aug. 15, 1971, 24.

56 Leer, "Weather Report," 24.
57 Al Aronowitz, "Weather Report: The First REAL Supergroup?" *Melody Maker*, May 15, 1971, 35.
58 According to *Billboard*, one of the performances took place on May 25. The said it included Dom Um Romão, but Airto confirmed in an interview that he performed at this event. Bob Glassenberg, "Weather Report: Breezy," *Billboard*, Jun. 5, 1971, 18; Moreira interview, 2016.)
59 Leer, "Weather Report," 24.
60 Hollie I. West, "Weather Report," *Washington Post*, Nov. 4, 1971.
61 Glassenberg, "Weather Report: Breezy"; Bob Glassenberg telephone interview, May 28, 2015.
62 Reese Erlich, "Wayne Shorter: A Jazz Artist for All Time," *Into the Music*, Australian Broadcasting Corp., Feb. 28, 2009 (accessed Jul. 5, 2014), http://www.abc.net.au/radionational/programs/intothemusic/wayne-shorter-a-jazz-artist-for-all-time/3178038">www.abc.net.au/radionational.
63 Morgenstern, "Outlook Bright and Sunny," 42.
64 Michael Cuscuna, "Weather Report," *Jazz & Pop*, Jul. 1971, 14.
65 Display ad for *Weather Report*, *Down Beat*, Jul. 22, 1971, 10.
66 Display ad for *Weather Report*, *Rolling Stone*, Jun. 24, 1971.
67 Display ad for *Weather Report*, *Record World*, Jun. 12, 1971, 9.
68 Don Zulaica, "The Drummers of Weather Report." String Letter Publishing, *DRUM!*, Oct. 2006, 72.
69 Richard Williams, "Weather Report: A Bleak Outlook," *Melody Maker*, Oct. 23, 1971, 40.
70 Cuscuna, "Weather Report," 13.
71 Dialogue drawn from an interview Airto gave to Terry Bozzio. "The Art of Drumming with Airto Moreira," video interview, Drum Channel, accessed Oct. 6, 2018, https://drumchannel.com/show/the-art-of-drumming-with-airto-moreira/.
72 Moreira interview, 2016.
73 Frank Colón, "Dom Um Romão," *Modern Drummer*, Nov. 1990, 62.
74 The date of the Penn State performance was Jun. 9. Display ad, *Daily Collegian*, Jun. 2, 1971.
75 Conrad Silvert, "Joe Zawinul: Wayfaring Genius—Part II," *Down Beat*, Jun. 15, 1978, 22.

8 I Sing the Body Electric

1 Most bootleg recordings of Weather Report's appearance at Ossiach date it to July 27, 1971. However, the Third International Music Forum took place from June 25 to July 5.
2 See "Rock Too Much for Newport," *Rolling Stone*, Aug. 9, 1969, 10; "Rock at Newport: Big Crowds, Bad Vibes," *Down Beat*, Aug. 21, 1969, 40; and "Rock, Jazz and Newport: An Exchange," *Down Beat*, Dec. 25, 1969, 22.
3 Timothy Crouse, "600 Lames Wreck Newport Festival," *Rolling Stone*, Aug. 5, 1971, 10.
4 Crouse, "600 Lames," 10.
5 Ian Dove, "Aborted Newport Jazz Hits Record Companies," *Billboard*, Jul. 17, 1971, 58.
6 Heinz Czadek, "Joe Zawinul," *Jazz Forum*, Aug. 1972, 47.
7 Ernie Santosuosso, "Weather Report's Three-Tiered Sound," *Boston Globe*, Jul. 24, 1971.
8 Bob Glassenberg, "Studio Track," *Billboard*, Aug. 21, 1971, 4.
9 Miroslav Vitous telephone interview, Apr. 26, 2007.
10 Barbara Burton telephone interview, Nov. 12, 2014.
11 Alphonse Mouzon telephone interview, Apr. 27, 2015.
12 Pawel Brodowski, "Alphonse Mouzon: 'Music Is Also a Business,'" *Jazz Forum*, No. 81, 1983, 21–22.
13 Mouzon interview, 2015. Among the earliest of Mouzon's recorded compositions were "Climax" on Mongo Santamaría's 1971 album *Mongo at Montreux*, and "Virtue" on Santamaría's *Up from the Roots* LP, released the next year.
14 Mouzon interview, 2015.
15 Brian Glasser, *In a Silent Way: A Portrait of Joe Zawinul* (London: Sanctuary Publishing, 2001), 140.
16 Eric Gravatt telephone interview, Mar. 13, 2020.
17 Gravatt interview, 2020.
18 Pawel Brodowski, "Michael Brecker: A Spirit of Discovery," *Jazz Forum*, No. 115, 1988, 34.
19 The first mention I found of Gravatt's name in print was in the May 9, 1968, edition of the *Philadelphia Inquirer*, which identified him as the central figure in the Howard University student-made film-within-a-film "Color Us Black," which aired on the public television program *NET Journal*.
20 Bob Protzman, "Profile: Eric Gravatt," *Down Beat*, Jul. 17, 1975, 32.
21 Michael Baker, "Eric Kamau Gravatt: Interview with a Legend," *Modern Drummer*, Oct. 1996, 117–18.
22 Mark Griffith, "Eric Kamau Gravatt: Tracking Down and Learning from a Legend," *Percussive Notes*, Dec. 2006, 20–21.
23 Griffith, "Eric Kamau Gravatt," 21.
24 Griffith, "Eric Kamau Gravatt," 18.
25 Gravatt interview, 2020.
26 Gravatt interview, 2020.
27 Maria Booker Lucien telephone interview, Mar. 22, 2017.
28 As an upstart promoter (perhaps compounded by the fact that it was run by women), Bow Wow faced some headwinds. Talent agencies didn't want to work with them, so they went directly to the artists, which further alienated the agencies. At the time, the Beacon wasn't the premier concert venue it would later become, so in order to distinguish themselves in a crowded field, Bow Wow strove to give their productions cachet. On the sidewalk, below the marquee, a band and dancers regaled concertgoers who were greeted inside by "foxy looking usherettes," as the *Village*

Voice described them. It was all an effort to "boost the neighborhood's karma a few notches," which was showing the effects of urban blight. Richard Nusser, "Magic Music," Riffs, *Village Voice*, Oct. 28, 1971, 52.

29 Gunther Baumann, *Zawinul: Ein Leben aus Jazz* (Salzburg: Residenz-Verlag, 2002), 108.

30 Mouzon interview, 2015.

31 Richard Williams, "Weather Man: Joe Zawinul Talks to Richard Williams," *Melody Maker*, Jul. 29, 1972, 12.

32 Ken Micallef, "Wayne Shorter: Speak No Evil—About Drummers," *Modern Drummer*, Sep. 2003, 110.

33 Roy McCurdy telephone interview, May 22, 2016.

34 Kirb., review of Dr. John and Weather Report, Beacon Theatre, "Concert Reviews," *Variety*, Nov. 3, 1971, 43.

35 Richard Nusser, "Magic Music," Riffs, *Village Voice*, Oct. 28, 1971, 52.

36 Kenny Klimak email correspondence, Jan. 2017.

37 Kirb., review of Ike & Tina Turner Revue, Weather Report, Quinames Band, and Banchee, "Concert Reviews," *Variety*, Dec. 1, 1971, 46.

38 Booker Lucien interview, 2017.

39 Gravatt interview, 2020.

40 Joe actually had incidental experience with an electronic music synthesizer before the ARP 2600. He and a fellow musician who lived in his building, violinist and composer Arnold Black, bought an EMS VCS 3 Putney. It was a small device without a keyboard, and used a pin-and-matrix interface in order to configure it. Joe didn't get far with it, saying it "took a day to get even one sound" and it "created little radio-type sounds." (Mary Campbell, Associated Press, "Joe Zawinul's Album First in 15 Years," *Baytown Sun*, May 26, 1986.)

    Despite Joe's comments, one should not assume the Putney was a toy. For example, it was use extensively by Jean-Michel Jarre on his most famous work, *Oxygène*, released in 1976. Jarre briefly demonstrates the Putney in this YouTube video: https://youtu.be/ctOhwRGdVvo.

41 Joe Zawinul personal interview, Sep. 15, 2003.

42 Zawinul interview, 2003.

43 *Switched-On Bach* was released under Carlos's given name, Walter. The album won Grammys in 1970 in the categories Album of the Year—Classical, Best Classical Performance—Instrumental Soloist(s) with or without Orchestra, and Best Engineered Recording—Classical.

44 Pre-dating *Abbey Road* was Harrison's avant-garde LP, *Electronic Sound*, which consists of two long tracks produced with a Moog synthesizer.

45 Trevor Pinch and Frank Trocco, *Analog Days: The Invention and Impact of the Moog Synthesizer* (Cambridge, MA: Harvard Univ. Press, 2002), 232.

46 Other notable early users of the ARP 2600 included Stevie Wonder, Pete Townshend, Herbie Hancock, and Edgar Winter, who featured it on his hit, "Frankenstein." Wonder had his control panel labeled in braille, although Tom Oberheim remembers hearing that Wonder could feel the silkscreened, painted lettering on the standard 2600 control panel in order to identify the various sliders.

47 Roger Powell personal interview, Jan. 28, 2004.

48 Powell interview, 2004.

49 Jack Trompetter telephone interview, Feb. 1, 2017.

50 Baumann, *Zawinul*, 110.

51 From an interview for *Joe Zawinul: A Musical Portrait*, Mark Kidel, prod., Calliope Media/BBC, www.calliopemedia.co.uk/.

52 Zawinul interview, 2003.

53 Powell interview, 2004.

54 Ralph Towner telephone interview, May 13, 2014.

55 Max Harrison, Eric Thacker, and Stuart Nicholson, *The Essential Jazz Records Volume 2: Modernism to Postmodernism* (London: Mansell Publishing, 2000), 605.

56 Towner interview, 2014.

57 "Weather Report Marks 1st Year," *Billboard*, Mar. 4, 1972, 14.

58 E. Taylor Atkins, *Blue Nippon: Authenticating Jazz in Japan* (Durham, NC: Duke University Press: 2001), 209.

59 Hollie I. West, "Eric Gravatt: Drumming Up Some New Ground Rules for Jazz," *Washington Post*, Nov. 5, 1972.

60 Glasser, *In a Silent Way*, 144.

61 *Billboard* indicated that *Live in Tokyo* was scheduled for Japanese release by CBS/Sony on April 21, 1972. *Billboard*, Apr. 1, 1972, 44.

62 For instance, when Richard Williams reviewed Weather Report at Ronnie Scott's in London, he wrote that Romão's "traditional melody on the berimbau, incorporating a little dance, was one of the highlights." Richard Williams, "Cool Weather," *Melody Maker*, Jul. 22, 1972, 42. When the *Village Voice*'s Dan Nooger reviewed a Weather Report performance near the end of 1972, he noted that the group's "only concession to theatricality (or perhaps simply our presence)" was when Romão danced down the center aisle while playing "a metal-strung bow with an exotic gourd rattle," referring to the berimbau. Dan Nooger, "Ain't Blue No More," Riffs, *Village Voice*, Dec. 28, 1972, 36.

63 Hal Miller, "Weather Report," liner notes to *Forecast: Tomorrow*, Columbia/Legacy (82876 85570 2), 2006, 46.

64 Gravatt interview, 2020.

65 Hollie I. West, "McCoy Tyner Quartet," *Washington Post*, May 13, 1971.

66 Gravatt interview, 2020.

67 Gravatt interview, 2020.

68 Hollie I. West, "Eric Gravatt: Drumming Up Some New Ground Rules for Jazz," *Washington Post*, Nov. 5, 1972.

69 Tom Wilmeth, Eric Gravatt unpublished interview transcript, May 8, 1980.

70 Glassenberg, "Studio Track," 4.
71 Vitous interview, 2007.
72 The studio take was released in 2006 as part of the box set *Forecast: Tomorrow*. It is also included as a bonus track on the version of *I Sing the Body Electric* in the box set *The Columbia Albums 1971–1975*, released in 2012.
73 "Devere to Col. A&R Staff," *Variety*, Apr. 24, 1968, 57.
74 Michael Cuscuna, "Weather Report," *Jazz & Pop*, Jul. 1971, 14.
75 Apparently none of the established New York City jazz clubs—the Village Vanguard being the most prominent—booked Weather Report. Perhaps they objected to amplified jazz (although the Vanguard did book Herbie Hancock in those days). Or maybe Joe and Wayne didn't want to play at venues associated with the jazz establishment, hoping to attract a different audience.
   At about the same time Weather Report inked its deal with Columbia Records, John McLaughlin also signed with the label. His experience with Clive Davis was similar to Weather Report's. "Clive said, 'I know Miles likes you. He's got you on his recordings.' And then he asked, 'What are you going to do?' I said, 'This band is going to be killer. Whether you sign me or not, somebody's going to sign me, and we're going to make some great music,' He said, 'John, I love the way you talk. Let's sign.'" Walter Kolosky, *Power, Passion and Beauty: The Story of the Legendary Mahavishnu Orchestra, the Greatest Band That Ever Was* (Cary, NC: Abstract Logix Books, 2006), 60.
76 *Village Voice*, Mar. 30, 1972, 53.
77 Martin Snider, "Weather Report: Favorable," Club Review, *Record World*, May 13, 1972, 27.
78 Baumann, *Zawinul*, 109.
79 Walter Thiers, "The Scene Livens Up," Swinging News/Argentina, *Jazz Forum*, No. 24, 1973, 14.
80 Richard Williams, "Shorter Story," *Melody Maker*, Aug. 5, 1972, 22.
81 Display ad, *Village Voice*, Dec. 21, 1972, 58.
82 Bob Palmer, review of *I Sing the Body Electric*, *Rolling Stone*, Jul. 6, 1972, 55.
83 Jack Chambers, review of *I Sing the Body Electric*, *Coda*, No. 12, 1973, 27–28.
84 "Pi Corp Interview with Guy Bickel," Feb. 3, 2013 (accessed Jul. 5, 2014), http://psychedelic-baby.blogspot.com/2013/02/pi-corp-interview-with-guy-bickel.html.
85 Dennis Dread, "Robots at the Factory: The Alan Howarth Interview (Part I)," accessed Feb. 15, 2017, http://dennisdread.blogspot.com/2014/09/robots-at-factory-alan-howarth.html.
86 Brian Risner personal interview, Jul. 5, 2007.
87 Risner interview, 2007.
88 Risner interview, 2007.
89 Brian Risner telephone interview, Jan. 14, 2004.
90 Dan Nooger, "Ain't Blue No More," 36.
91 Powell interview, 2004.
92 Joe Zawinul telephone interview, Jan. 1, 2004.
93 Risner interview, 2004.

9   Sweetnighter

1 Michelle Mercer, *Footprints: The Life and Work of Wayne Shorter* (New York: J. P. Tarcher/Penguin, 2004), 148.
2 *Down Beat*'s categories changed over the years. From 1972 to 1975, Weather Report won the Jazz Combo category. Starting in 1976, the category was changed to Acoustic Jazz Group, and Weather Report won that every year through 1982. In 1983, *Down Beat* introduced the Electric Jazz Group category, which Weather Report won that year and the next. *I Sing the Body Electric* placed fourth for best album, well behind the Mahavishnu Orchestra's *The Inner Mounting Flame*, which *Down Beat* readers voted their favorite jazz *and* pop album.
3 Don Heckman, "Jazz-Rock Is Played by Weather Report," *New York Times*, Apr. 23, 1972.
4 Bill Henderson, "Weather Report: Singing in the Rain," *Black Music & Jazz Review*, Jun. 1978, 11.
5 Bob Protzman, review of Weather Report at the Guthrie Theater, Minneapolis, "Caught in the Act," *Down Beat*, May 24, 1973, 29.
6 Jim Szantor, review of Weather Report performance at the Brown Shoe (Chicago), Caught in the Act, *Down Beat*, Oct. 26, 1972, 31.
7 Sy Johnson, "Interview: Joe Zawinul," *Changes in the Arts*, Mar. 1973, 22.
8 "CBS Jazz Product Hits Youth Pay Dirt," *Billboard*, Mar. 18, 1972, 4.
9 Eliot Tiegel, "Jazzmen Fusing Rock into Music for Wider Appeal," *Billboard*, Jun. 1, 1974, 10.
10 Eliot Tiegel, "'Extended Energy' Jazz Energizes New Wave of Enthusiasm," *Billboard*, Apr. 29, 1972, 14. In 1974, Bruce Lundvall, then Columbia's marketing vice president, said that the "straight ahead blowing kind of record by an established artist has a limited sales potential from 10,000 to 20,000." Eliot Tiegel, "Repackages Pack Their Own Sales Wallop as U.S. Labels Broaden Their Jazz Coverage," *Billboard*, Jun. 23, 1973, 48).
11 Eliot Tiegel, "Who Will Own the Soul '70s?" *Billboard*, Aug. 22, 1970, 26. The article states that Cannonball Adderley's album *Country Preacher* sold 127,000 copies, reaping $90,000 in sales.
12 Dan Morgenstern, "No Jive from Clive," Afterthoughts, *Down Beat*, Sep. 16, 1971, 46.
13 See http://indianapublicmedia.org/nightlights/great-columbia-jazz-purge-coleman-evans-jarrett-mingus/, accessed Mar. 2, 2017.
14 Josef Zawinul as told to Greg Armbruster, "The Evolution of Weather Report," *Keyboard*, Mar. 1984, 49. As far as Wayne being on the same wavelength as Joe, one reporter observed that while Zawinul "does most of the talking" in describing the necessity of these changes, Wayne, "obviously a little more reserved by nature, backs up all of Joe's points." Steve Lake, "Weather Report: Outlook Sunny," *Melody Maker*, Jul. 20, 1974, 51.
15 Tom Wilmeth, Eric Gravatt unpublished inter-

view transcript, May 8, 1980.

16 Zawinul, "Evolution of Weather Report," 49.

17 Josef Woodard, "Shifting Winds," *Down Beat*, Jan. 2001, 26.

18 Eric Gravatt telephone interview, Mar. 13, 2020.

19 Zawinul, "Evolution of Weather Report," 49.

20 See http://www.eldredgeatl.com/2016/07/23/dancing-on-the-tables-a-celebration-of-the-athens-atlanta-music-scene-starring-the-b-52s-the-fans-the-brains-glenn-phillips-and-some-act-named-r-e-m/, accessed Mar. 1, 2017; and "Jazz at the 12th Gate," *Down Beat*, Oct. 25, 1973, 10.

21 Brian Case, "This Man Is Watching Out for Custard Pies," *New Musical Express*, Aug. 7, 1976, 21.

22 Herschel Dwellingham telephone interview, Mar. 13, 2017.

23 Dwellingham telephone interviews, Dec. 3, 2013; Mar. 13, 2017.

24 Dwellingham interview, 2013.

25 Dwellingham interview, 2013.

26 Dwellingham interview, 2013.

27 Hollie I. West, "Andrew White . . . Musician," *Washington Post*, Jun. 11, 1971.

28 Andrew White telephone interview, Jul. 14, 2017.

29 White interview, 2017.

30 Muruga Booker telephone interview, Dec. 23, 2013.

31 Booker interview, 2013.

32 Booker interview, 2013.

33 Gravatt interview, 2020.

34 Gravatt interview, 2020.

35 Gravatt interview, 2020.

36 Miroslav Vitous telephone interview, Feb. 21, 2015.

37 Maria Lucien believes that the title was an homage to Joe's good friend (and Maria's ex-husband) Walter Booker, who called his home studio Boogie Woogie Studio. Maria Booker Lucien interview, Mar. 22, 2017.

38 You might think this was thanks to his jazz background, but White says no, playing funk was completely separate from playing jazz. Nevertheless, he clearly exhibits a lot of creativity in his bass playing, which made him an excellent fit for what Weather Report was trying to do.

39 Dwellingham interview, 2013.

40 Booker interview, 2013.

41 Andrew White, *Everybody Loves the Sugar—The Book* (Washington, DC: Andrew's Music, 2001), 386.

42 Joe Zawinul telephone interview, Jan. 1, 2004.

43 Len Lyons, "Brian Risner: Zawinul's Equipment Expert," *Keyboard*, Sep. 1977, 28.

44 Brian Risner personal interview, Jun. 1, 2014.

45 Ray Townley, "The Mysterious Travellings of an Austrian Mogul," *Down Beat*, Jan. 30, 1975, 17.

46 A low-frequency oscillator is one tuned to a low frequency, usually sub-audible, in order to produce a repeating pulse or sweep that could affect other parts of the synthesizer to produce vibratos, tremolos, or rhythmic timbral changes.

47 Risner interview, 2014.

48 Booker interview, 2013.

49 Stuart Nicholson, *Jazz-Rock: A History* (New York: Schirmer Books, 1998), 170.

50 Brian Glasser, *In a Silent Way: A Portrait of Joe Zawinul* (London: Sanctuary Publishing, 2001), 151.

51 Zawinul interview, 2004.

52 Rick Mattingly, "PASIC 2007 Panel: The Drummers of Weather Report," *Percussive Notes*, Dec. 2007, 10.

53 Gunther Baumann, *Zawinul: Ein Leben aus Jazz* (Salzburg: Residenz-Verlag, 2002), 114.

54 Booker interview, 2013.

55 White interview, 2017.

56 Zawinul interview, 2004.

57 Vitous telephone interview, Apr. 26, 2007.

58 Booker interview, 2013. The album credits on *Sweetnighter* go into detail for each song, but there are some omissions. For instance, Dom Um Romão isn't credited as playing on "Adios," even though he clearly does.

59 Sebastian Clarke, "And Now... The Weather," *Black Echoes*, Aug. 14, 1976, 13.

60 Risner interview, 2014.

61 Dwellingham interview, 2017.

62 Brian Risner telephone interview, Jan. 14, 2004.

63 White interview, 2017.

64 Gravatt interview, 2020.

65 Dwellingham interview, 2013.

66 White interview, 2017.

67 This mistake was made in most of the reviews of *Sweetnighter*. For example, in *New Musical Express*, Ian MacDonald wrote that Miroslav was "forced to play out of position as a funky linkman between the front line and the defending percussionists." Ian McDonald, "Hot News on Weather Report," *New Musical Express*, Jun. 23, 1973, 44.

68 "Who Brought the Funk?" *Down Beat* News, *Down Beat*, Sep. 13, 1973, 10. Actually, Miroslav did play acoustic bass on "125th Street Congress"—you can clearly hear him get down on arco at the 8:34 mark, for example—but White's point stands.

69 White interview, 2017.

70 Dwellingham interview, 2013.

71 Jon Hendricks, "Weather Report: Doin' Fine," *San Francisco Chronicle*, Feb. 17, 1973.

72 Dennis Hunt, "Weather Report into Sounds of Hard Rock," *Los Angeles Times*, Feb. 23, 1973.

73 Tom Murtha, "Weather Report Quintet Raises New Hope on Jazz Barometer," *Minneapolis Star*, Feb. 13, 1973.

74 Risner interview, 2004.

75 Risner interview, 2004.

76 Risner interview, 2014.

77 Risner interview, 2004.

78 Risner interview, 2014.

79 Risner interview, 2004.

80 Brian Risner personal interview, Jul. 5, 2007.

81 Eliot Tiegel, "Jazzmen Fusing Rock into Music for Wider Appeal," *Billboard*, Jun. 1, 1974, 10.

82 Leonard Feather, "The Year of Jazz," *Melody Maker*, Dec. 30, 1972, 12–13.

83 *Variety*, Mar. 1, 1972, 1.
84 Eliot Tiegel, "'Extended Energy' Jazz Energizes New Wave of Enthusiasm," *Billboard*, Apr. 29, 1972, 14.
85 "Best selling" from Nat Freedland, "Cross over the Bridge from Jazz to Pop—That's the Happy Object," *Billboard*, Jun. 23, 1973, 54. 300,000 from Leroy Robinson, "Blue Note's Butler Adds New Image," *Billboard*, Jul. 13, 1974, 28.
86 Leonard Feather, "Crossover Albums," *Billboard*, Feb. 8, 1975, 25.
87 *Birds of Fire* was nominated for a 1974 Grammy in the category Best Pop Instrumental Performance. It lost to Eumir Deodato's *Also Sprach Zarathustra (2001)*. The same year, *Black Byrd* was nominated in the category Best Rhythm & Blues Instrumental Performance, the winner being Ramsey Lewis's *Hang On Sloopy*. *Head Hunters* was nominated in 1975 for Best Pop Instrumental Performance, losing to Marvin Hamlisch's *The Entertainer*.
88 "Grammy Time Is Gripe Time; See Brush of New Jazz Faces," *Variety*, Jan. 29, 1975, 59.
89 "NARAS Rep Denies 'Safe' Picks in Grammy Jazz Nominations," *Variety*, Feb. 5, 1975, 77.
90 Sam Peters, "Jazz Records," *The Guardian*, Aug. 16, 1972.
91 Nathan Cobb, "Weather Report: Jazz That Rocks," *Boston Globe*, Aug. 27, 1972.
92 The *Down Beat* jazz-rock issue dates were Nov. 9, 1972; Nov. 8, 1973; and Nov. 7, 1974.
93 Charles Suber, "The First Chorus," *Down Beat*, Nov. 8, 1973, 6.
94 Eliot Tiegel, "Repackages Pack Their Own Sales Wallop as U.S. Labels Broaden Their Jazz Coverage," *Billboard*, Jun. 23, 1973, 48.
95 "Col Push on Jazz Catalog," *Billboard*, Oct. 28, 1972, 3.
96 *Billboard*, Jun. 23, 1973, 45.
97 Tiegel, "'Extended Energy' Jazz," 14.
98 Joe H. Klee and Will Smith, reviews of *Sweetnighter*, Record Reviews, *Down Beat*, Jul. 19, 1973, 20.
99 Nancy Ball, "Music in Mid-America," *Kansas City Star*, May 11, 1973.
100 Zawinul, "Evolution of Weather Report," 49.
101 Gravatt interview, 2020.
102 Vitous interview, 2007.
103 Greg Errico telephone interview, Mar. 10, 2014.
104 "Triad & Transition Talk with Weather Report," *Triad Radio Guide* (Chicago: Triad Prod.), Aug. 1973, 39.
105 Errico interview, 2014.
106 Gravatt interview, 2020.
107 Michael Baker, "Eric Kamau Gravatt: Interview with a Legend," *Modern Drummer*, Oct. 1996 124.
108 Russ Musto, "Artist Profiles: Eric Kamau Gravatt," All About Jazz, Sep. 15, 2006 (accessed Dec. 28, 2013), http://www.allaboutjazz.com/php/article.php?id=22927.
109 Bob Protzman, "Profile: Eric Gravatt," *Down Beat*, Jul. 17, 1975, 32.
110 Gravatt interview, 2020.
111 Baker, "Eric Kamau Gravatt," 124.
112 Adam Ward Seligman, "A Different View: Joe Zawinul," *Modern Drummer*, Apr. 1997, 112.

10 Mysterious Traveller

1 Mike Bourne, Gary Giddins, Peter Keepnews and Joe Klee, "Message from Newport/NYC," *Down Beat*, Sep. 13, 1973, 34.
2 Michael Watts, "Hot Weather Report," Caught in the Act, *Melody Maker*, Jul. 14, 1973, 48.
3 Greg Errico telephone interview, Mar. 10, 2014.
4 Errico interview, 2014.
5 Errico interview, 2014.
6 From the Soka Gakkai International description of its practice of Nichiren Buddhism at http://www.sgi-usa.org/basics-of-buddhism/, accessed Mar. 25, 2020.
7 Nat Freedland, "Herbie Hancock; A Crossover Artist Who Feels None the Worse for the Trip," *Billboard*, Jun. 29, 1974, 40.
8 David N. Baker, Lida M. Belt, and Herman C. Hudson, *The Black Composer Speaks* (Metuchen, NJ, 1978), 120.
9 Michelle Mercer describes in detail Wayne's acceptance of Buddhism. Michelle Mercer, *Footprints: The Life and Work of Wayne Shorter* (New York: J. P. Tarcher/Penguin, 2004), 150–57.
10 Karl Dallas, "The Sunny Weatherman," *Melody Maker*, Dec. 6, 1975, 46.
11 Errico interview, 2014.
12 Dallas, "Sunny Weatherman," 46.
13 Dallas, "Sunny Weatherman," 46.
14 Conrad Silvert, "Weather Report Heads Down Thunder Road," *Rolling Stone*, May 5, 1977, 24.
15 Adam Ward Seligman, "A Different View: Joe Zawinul," *Modern Drummer*, Apr. 1997, 111.
16 Errico interview, 2014.
17 Errico interview, 2014.
18 Leonard Feather, "A Sunny Weather Report," *Los Angeles Times*, Sep. 28, 1973.
19 Brian Risner telephone interview, Jan. 14, 2004.
20 Progressive jazz bands were a common item on the college circuit, whose FM radio stations were receptive to playing their music. But a more practical reason was cited by *Variety*: "One important factor is that the prices for jazz are generally lower than for a hit pop combo." "As Rock Stalls at Crossroads, Jazz Breaks Through All across Board," *Variety*, Mar. 1, 1972, 70.
21 Errico interview, 2014.
22 Ishmael Wilburn telephone interview, Mar. 9, 2014.
23 Wilburn interview, 2014.
24 Wilburn interview, 2014.
25 Wilburn interview, 2014.
26 Wilburn interview, 2014.
27 Wilburn interview, 2014.
28 Bradie Speller telephone interview, Apr. 17, 2017.
29 Speller interview, 2017.
30 Speller interview, 2017.
31 Speller interview, 2017.

32 Silvert, "Weather Report Heads Down," 24.

33 Josef Zawinul as told to Greg Armbruster, "The Evolution of Weather Report," *Keyboard*, Mar. 1984, 49.

34 Skip Hadden Skype interview, Apr. 17, 2017.

35 Conrad Silvert, "Joe Zawinul: Wayfaring Genius—Part II," *Down Beat*, Jun. 15, 1978, 52.

36 Scott Kinsey personal interview, Jul. 6, 2007.

37 Wilburn interview, 2014.

38 Skip Hadden email correspondence, Nov. 2013; interview, 2017.

39 Hadden correspondence, 2013.

40 Hadden interview, 2017.

41 Funkadelic and Graham Central Station performed at the Whisky a Go Go December 12–16, 1973. "Today's Calendar," *Los Angeles Times*, Dec. 12, 1973.

42 Hadden correspondence, 2013.

43 Brian Risner personal interview, Jun. 1, 2014.

44 Risner interview, 2014.

45 Some listeners and musicians have suggested that the crowd noises came from the Rose Bowl just below Joe's house. Others thought that it came from a bullfight. Brian Risner believes Joe merely used a sound effects stock library.

46 Silvert, "Wayfaring Genius—Part II," 53.

47 Wilburn interview, 2014.

48 Hadden interview, 2017.

49 Hadden interview, 2017.

50 Risner interview, 2014.

51 Wilburn interview, 2014.

52 Miroslav Vitous email correspondence, May 2017.

53 Hadden interview, 2017.

54 Hadden interview, 2017.

55 The personnel listing on the back cover matches the musician portraits, so it doesn't include Hadden. However, Hadden is credited on the LP's inner sleeve for "Nubian Sundance" and "Mysterious Traveller."

56 Hadden interview, 2017.

57 Hadden interview, 2017.

58 Hadden correspondence, 2013; interview, 2017.

59 Hadden interview, 2017.

60 Miroslav Vitous telephone interview, Feb. 21, 2015. The suddenness of the move was inadvertently brought to light by *Down Beat* magazine. In an interview in the February 14, 1974, issue (on newsstands around the middle of January), Miroslav was asked what kind of future he saw for himself in Weather Report. He replied, "A great future! We're going to be playing together for quite a while unless something completely unexpected happens." At the end of the article was a postscript: "In the time since this interview, the completely unexpected did indeed happen. At press time, we received word that Miroslav Vitous had left Weather Report, and that he would be replaced by Al Johnson, formerly bassist with the Chuck Mangione Quartet." Dale Hardman, "Miroslav Vitous: The 'Report' Is Good!" *Down Beat*, Feb. 14, 1974, 38.

It was considered such big news that *Down Beat* ran a couple of follow-up news items in the ensuing months. "Revised Forecast—Miroslav Leaves Weather Report," *Down Beat* News, *Down Beat*, Feb. 28, 1974, 8; "Vitous Plans Band for '75," *Down Beat* News, *Down Beat*, Jun. 20, 1974, 10.

61 Miroslav Vitous telephone interview, Apr. 26, 2007.

62 George Varga, "Sportin' Life," *Jazz Times*, Apr. 2007, 56.

63 Vitous interview, 2007.

64 Stuart Nicholson, *Jazz-Rock: A History* (New York: Schirmer Books, 1998), 171.

65 Vitous interview, 2007.

66 Vitous interview, 2007.

67 Pawel Brodowski, "Miroslav Vitous' Infinite Search," *Jazz Forum*, No. 80, 1983, 47. In Zawinul's account in *Ein Leben aus Jazz*, Miroslav got together with Bob Devere and together they sued Joe and Wayne for $100,000, settling for a sum of $50,000 or $60,000. Gunther Baumann, *Zawinul: Ein Leben aus Jazz* (Salzburg: Residenz-Verlag, 2002), 115.

68 According to *Billboard*, Vitous formed a band in 1975 with Grainger, Alex Acuña, and keyboardist Ron Feuer. "Jazz Beat," *Billboard*, Sep. 13, 1975, 33.

69 Russell Shaw, review of *Magical Shepherd*, *Down Beat*, Jul. 15, 1976, 32.

70 Arnold Jay Smith, "Bass Lines: Crystal Gazing with a Bonanza of Experts," *Down Beat*, Jan. 27, 1977, 43.

In what was described as his first appearance since Weather Report, Miroslav performed with a second bassist "to fill in during his frequent lead playing." Phil DiMauro, "California Soul Invades New York Successfully," *Cash Box*, Mar. 13, 1976, 33.

71 Brodowski, "Miroslav Vitous," 48.

72 Alphonso Johnson personal interview, Jul, 25, 2008.

73 Alphonso Johnson telephone interview, Jan. 26, 2015.

74 Johnson interview, 2015.

75 Johnson interview, 2008.

76 Nicholson, *Jazz-Rock*, 171–72.

77 Joe Zawinul personal interview, Sep. 15, 2003.

78 Wayne Shorter telephone interview, Dec. 23, 2008.

79 Johnson interview, 2015.

80 Sebastian Clarke, "And Now... The Weather," *Black Echoes*, Aug. 14, 1976, 12.

81 Brian Glasser, *In a Silent Way: A Portrait of Joe Zawinul* (London: Sanctuary Publishing, 2001), 257.

82 Johnson interview, 2008.

83 Dan Morgenstern, "Weather Report: Outlook Bright and Sunny," *Down Beat*, May 27, 1971, 14.

84 Steve Lake, "Weather Report: Outlook Sunny," *Melody Maker*, Jul. 20, 1974, 51.

85 Marv Hohman, review of *Moto Grosso Feio* and *Mysterious Traveller*, *Down Beat*, Nov. 7, 1974,

86 Bruce Botnick telephone interview, Jul. 27, 2017.
87 You can spot the Minimoog in the video *Live in Berlin 1975*. Joe never touches it.
88 Joe Zawinul telephone interview, Apr. 1, 2004.
89 Brian Risner personal interview, Jul. 15, 2017.
90 Bill Milkowski, "Joe Zawinul: Long-Distance Weather Report," *Jazz Times*, Jun. 2002 (accessed Nov. 21, 2006), http://www.jazztimes.com/columns_and_features/web_exclusive/joe_zawinul_interview/index.cfm.
91 Josef Woodard, "Josef Zawinul: Doing Something about the Weather," *Mix*, Jul. 1983, 91.
92 Risner interview, 2004.
93 Johnson interview, 2015.
94 Johnson interview, 2008.
95 Johnson interview, 2015.
96 Johnson interview, 2008.
97 Silvert, "Weather Report Heads Down," 24.
98 Bob Palmer, review of *Mysterious Traveller*, *Rolling Stone*, Aug. 1, 1974, 50.
99 Shawn Hart telephone interview, Aug. 26, 2020.
100 Hart interview, 2020.
101 Hart interview, 2020.
102 Wilburn interview, 2014.
103 Wilburn interview, 2014.
104 Johnson interview, 2008.
105 Johnson interview, 2008.

11 Tale Spinnin'

1 Ted Panken, "Joe Zawinul's 79th Birthday Anniversary," Jul. 7, 2011 (accessed Jan. 4, 2015), https://tedpanken.wordpress.com/2011/07/07/joe-zawinuls-79th-birthday-anniversary/.
2 Rick Mattingly, "Peter Erskine," *Modern Drummer*, Jan. 1983, 49.
3 Darryl Brown telephone interview, Feb. 15, 2014.
4 Brown interview, 2014.
5 John Rockwell, "A Strong New Front Lends Bright Touch to Weather Report," *New York Times*, Jul. 9, 1974.
6 Larry Rohter, "Weather Report: Amplified Jazz," *Washington Post*, Jul. 15, 1974.
7 Nancy Ball, "Music in Mid-America," *Kansas City Star*, May 11, 1973.
8 Brown interview, 2014.
9 Alphonso Johnson personal interview, Jul. 25, 2008.
10 Brown interview, 2014.
11 Brown interview, 2014.
12 Brown interview, 2014.
13 Brown interview, 2014.
14 Brian Risner email correspondence, Jun. 2017.
15 Brown interview, 2014.
16 Alphonso Johnson telephone interview, Jan. 26, 2015.
17 Brown interview, 2014.
18 Brown interview, 2014.
19 Alyrio Lima email correspondence, Jul. 2017.
20 Chuck Bazemore telephone interview, Jun. 27, 2017.
21 Bruce Botnick telephone interview, Jul. 27, 2017.
22 George Duke's *The Aura Will Prevail* was recorded at Paramount Recording Studio in January 1975, around the same time that Weather Report recorded *Tale Spinnin'*. According to Chester Thompson, Duke found out about Alphonso through him. "I loved *Mysterious Traveller*; I used to play it all the time. And somehow George Duke hadn't heard *Mysterious Traveller*, so when he heard 'Cucumber Slumber' he said, 'Man, who is that bass player? You got his number?' George immediately called him because he was getting ready to go into the studio and wanted Alphonso on it." Chester Thompson telephone interview, Dec. 22, 2014.
23 Rick Mattingly, "PASIC 2007 Panel: The Drummers of Weather Report," *Percussive Notes*, Dec. 2007, 9.
24 Leon "Ndugu" Chancler telephone interview, Dec. 22, 2008.
25 Johnson interview, 2008.
26 Botnick interview, 2017.
27 Mattingly, "Drummers of Weather Report," 13.
28 Mattingly, "Drummers of Weather Report," 10–11, 13.
29 Botnick interview, 2017.
30 Chancler interview, Dec. 22, 2008.
31 Chris Kringel, *Fretless Bass* (Milwaukee: Hal Leonard, 2007), 4.
32 Mark Steven Frandsen, "Forecasting Fusion at Low Frequencies: The Bass Players of Weather Report." PhD diss., Texas Tech University, 2010, 152.
33 Chris Jisi, ed. *Bass Player Presents the Fretless Bass* (New York: Backbeat Books, 2008), 34.
34 Chris Jisi, "Alphonso Johnson, Fusion Revolutionary," *Bass Player*, Apr. 1992, 27.
35 Jisi, "Alphonso Johnson," 27.
36 Johnson interview, 2015.
37 Johnson interview, 2015.
38 Johnson interview, 2015.
39 Johnson interview, 2008.
40 Wayne Shorter telephone interview, Dec. 23, 2008.
41 Shorter interview, 2008. Wayne remembered Joe bringing up the Krampus character from European folklore, and the band actually recorded a tune of Joe's titled "Krampus." It was originally intended for *Tale Spinnin'*, with spoken words by Wayne and Joe. We know this because the inner sleeve on early pressings had a track listing that included this tune, as well as a different sequence of tracks from the LP itself. (A sticker covered the incorrectly printed track list on the album jacket.) The sequence printed on the inner sleeve was, Side A: "Freezing Fire," "Badia," "Krampus," and "Lusitanos." Side B: "Between the Thighs," "Five Short Stories," and "Man in the Green Shirt."
42 Shorter interview, 2008.
43 Shorter interview, 2008.
44 Shorter interview, 2008.
45 Jurg Solothurnmann, "Joseph Zawinul: A Space Musician," *Jazz Forum*, Apr. 1976, 43.
46 Johnson interviews, 2008, 2015.

47 Trevor Pinch and Frank Trocco, *Analog Days: The Invention and Impact of the Moog Synthesizer* (Cambridge, MA: Harvard Univ. Press, 2002), 184.

48 Brian Risner personal interview, Dec. 28, 2008.

49 Chancler interview, Dec. 22, 2008.

50 Shorter interview, 2008.

51 Gunther Baumann, *Zawinul: Ein Leben aus Jazz* (Salzburg: Residenz-Verlag, 2002), 57.

52 Leon "Ndugu" Chancler telephone interview, Dec. 30, 2008.

53 Bradley Dupont Blanchard email correspondence, Jul. 2017.

54 Blanchard correspondence, 2017.

55 Blanchard correspondence, 2017. As an indication of Joe's prowess and love of unusual instruments, the same year he acquired his Mzuthra, Zawinul happened to hear the innovative guitarist Emmett Chapman playing his own invention, the Chapman Stick, at the Five Spot in Manhattan. Zawinul had to try it for himself. "He picked up my instrument after the show, stood up on a table and played some impressive rhythms," Chapman later recalled. It is said that Zawinul purchased one of the first examples from the first production run of six Sticks in 1974, though he never played it on record or live. Stephen Rekas, "An Interview with Emmett Chapman, Inventor of the Chapman Stick," accessed Jul. 23, 2017, http://archive.guitarsessions.com/dec05/luthier/luthier-dec05.pdf.

56 Shorter interview, 2008.

57 Shorter interview, 2008.

58 Bill Milkowski, "Joe Zawinul: Long-Distance Weather Report," *Jazz Times*, Jun. 2002 (accessed Nov. 21, 2006), http://www.jazztimes.com/columns_and_features/web_exclusive/joe_zawinul_interview/index.cfm.

59 Chancler interview, Dec. 22, 2008.

60 It is interesting to contemplate what the album would have sounded like with Chuck Bazemore. In that regard, Alyrio Lima offers his perspective: "The difference was that Ndugu played in front and Chuck was a funk drummer used to playing behind the beat," Lima explained. "You see, the main difference between Weather Report and the other bands was the way of playing the beat. You hit the note on top of the beat and not on the downbeat. It is very subtle but it makes a huge difference in the way that the phrase or the rhythm is played. It was new, fresh, and unheard of except for Miles's bands after his outstanding quintet with Tony, Ron, Wayne and Herbie." Lima correspondence, 2017.

61 A. J. Morgan, "Weather Report: Increasingly Warm & Sunny," *Crawdaddy*, Oct. 1975, 31.

62 Fred De Van, *Tale Spinnin'* review, *Audio*, Feb. 1976, 83.

63 De Van, *Tale Spinnin'* review, 84.

64 Bert Whyte, *Tale Spinnin'* review, Tape & Turntable, *Audio*, Feb. 1976, 106.

65 Botnick interview, 2017.

66 Botnick interview, 2017.

67 Chancler interview, Dec. 30, 2008.

68 Stanley Hall, "Chester Thompson: Up for the Challenge," *Modern Drummer*, Jan. 1983, 15.

69 Thompson interview, 2014.

70 Thompson interview, 2014. Percussionist Jamey Haddad was also present and recalls that the other drummer was Woody "Sonship" Theus. Theus, who died in 2011, was known as a relentlessly energetic drummer, so Thompson's comment that the other drummer didn't do as well on the ballad reinforces Haddad's recollection. Jamey Haddad email correspondence, Jul. 2018.

71 Johnson interview, 2015.

72 "Teazers," *New Musical Express*, Apr. 5, 1975, 47.

73 Thompson interview, 2014.

74 Hall, "Chester Thompson," 16.

75 Thompson interview, 2014.

76 Risner personal interview, Jul. 15, 2017.

77 Lima correspondence, 2017.

78 Lima correspondence, 2017.

79 Thompson interview, 2014.

80 Leonard Feather, "Weather Report Thundering," *Los Angeles Times*, May 7, 1975.

81 Michael Zipkin, "Weather Report's Dance of the Elements," *BAM*, Oct. 29, 1978, 26.

82 Josef Woodard, "Shifting Winds," *Down Beat*, Jan. 2001, 26.

83 Thompson interview, 2014.

84 Thompson interview, 2014.

85 Dialogue drawn from Mattingly, "Drummers of Weather Report," 9; Alex Acuña telephone interview, Oct. 5, 2017; John Ephland, "Alex Acuña: Command in All Directions," *DRUM!*, Jan. 2011, 57.

86 Alex Acuña telephone interview, Feb. 21, 2014.

87 Ephland, "Alex Acuña," 56.

88 Acuña interview, 2017.

89 Acuña interviews, 2014 and 2017.

90 Thompson interview, 2014.

91 Ulish Carter, "Jazz Concert Too Long and Boring to Be Good," *Pittsburgh Courier*, Nov. 1, 1975.

92 Johnson interview, 2008.

93 Steve Lake, review of Weather Report at the New Victoria Theatre, "Caught in the Act," *Melody Maker*, Dec. 6, 1975, 28.

94 Johnson interviews, 2008 and 2015.

12 Black Market

1 Bob Cavallo telephone interview, Jan. 11, 2017.

2 Brian Glasser, *In a Silent Way: A Portrait of Joe Zawinul* (London: Sanctuary Publishing, 2001), 199.

3 Cavallo interview, 2017.

4 Alan Leeds, liner notes to *Weather Report Live & Unreleased*, Columbia/Legacy C2K 65525, Jun. 2002.

5 Cavallo interview, 2017.

6 Chester Thompson telephone interview, Dec. 22, 2014.

7 Dave McMacken telephone interview, Aug. 28,

2017.

8 Don Heckman, "The Making of Weather Report's *Heavy Weather*," Recording Academy Grammy Awards, Dec. 16, 2013 (accessed Mar. 27, 2015), http://www.grammy.com/news/the-making-of-weather-reports-heavy-weather.

9 Colman Andrews, "Black Market, Wayne Shorter & Weather Report #6," *Phonograph Record Magazine*, Apr. 1976, 50.

10 In this context, the term polyphonic synthesizer generally refers to a true, general-purpose synthesizer with the classic oscillator-filter-amplifier-envelope architecture. There were other polyphonic keyboards, including the Hammond organ and various instruments marketed as "string synthesizers", but they were based on different technology that limited their capabilities. As such, they aren't considered true polyphonic synthesizers.

11 Brian Risner personal interview, Jun. 1, 2014.

12 Leonard Feather, "Weather Report: An Aural Rainbow," *Los Angeles Times*, Jun. 6, 1976.

13 Brian Risner personal interview, Sep. 4, 2017.

14 Andrews, "Black Market," 51.

15 James Hale, "Night Passage: Joe Zawinul's Friends, Colleagues Pay Tribute to the Late Keyboard Giant," *Down Beat*, Dec. 2007, 13.

16 Leeds, *Weather Report Live & Unreleased*.

17 Michael Zipkin, "Weather Report's Dance of the Elements," *BAM*, Oct. 29, 1978, 26.

18 Len Lyons, "Josef Zawinul Keyboard Magician," *Keyboard*, Sep. 1977, 38.

19 Lyons, "Keyboard Magician," 26.

20 Details of Adderley's death can be found in Cary Ginell, *Walk Tall: The Music & Life of Julian "Cannonball" Adderley* (Milwaukee: Hal Leonard Books, 2013), 155–59.

21 Brian Risner personal interview, Jul. 5, 2007.

22 Thompson interview, 2014.

23 Bill Milkowski, "Joe Zawinul: Long-Distance Weather Report," *Jazz Times*, Jun. 2002 (accessed Nov. 21, 2006), http://www.jazztimes.com/columns_and_features/web_exclusive/joe_zawinul_interview/index.cfm.

24 Leeds, *Weather Report Live & Unreleased*.

25 Alex Acuña telephone interview, Feb. 21, 2014.

26 Johnson's first album was titled *Moonshadows*. Its inner sleeve indicates that it was recorded in January and February 1976 at the Sound Labs and Wally Heider's Studio.

27 Milkowski, "Long-Distance Weather Report."

28 Alphonso Johnson telephone interview, Jan. 26, 2015.

29 Thompson interview, 2014.

30 Philip Bailey with Keith Zimmerman and Kent Zimmerman, *Shining Star: Braving the Elements of Earth, Wind & Fire* (New York: Penguin, 2014), 105.

31 Narada Michael Walden telephone interview, Apr. 1, 2015.

32 Walden interview, 2015.

33 Walden interview, 2015.

34 Walden interview, 2015.

35 Pat Jordan, "Who Killed Jaco Pastorius?" *GQ*, Apr. 1988, 271.

36 Bill Milkowski, *Jaco: The Extraordinary and Tragic Life of Jaco Pastorius*, deluxe ed. (San Francisco: Miller Freeman Books), 2005, 11.

37 Karl Dallas, "Weather Report: Sunny," *Melody Maker*, Oct. 15, 1977, 9.

38 Samuel Graham, "Backbeat: The New Jaco," *High Fidelity*, Mar. 1984, 77.

39 Neil Tesser, "Jaco Pastorius, the Florida Flash," *Down Beat*, Jan. 27, 1977, 13.

40 Some of Jaco's Cochran bandmates remember him being in the band for a period of nine or ten months, but Bill Milkowski documents the duration at twenty weeks, starting in July 1972 and ending with Jaco's last gig on December 2. Milkowski, *Jaco*, 46.

41 John Floyd, "Soul Salvation," *Miami New Times*, Jan. 9, 1997 (accessed Oct. 6, 2018), http://www.miaminewtimes.com/news/soul-salvation-6361042.

42 Milkowski, *Jaco*, 41.

43 Milkowski, *Jaco*, 44.

44 Chris Jisi, ed., *Bass Player Presents the Fretless Bass* (New York: Backbeat Books, 2008), 47–48.

45 For examples of Jaco performing with Graves during his Weather Report years, see the *Ft. Lauderdale News*: Aug. 9, 1976; Aug. 27, 1976; Jan. 20, 1977; Jan. 22, 1977. *Miami Herald*: Jun. 15, 1977; Jun. 26, 1977; Jul. 23 1978. *Miami News*, Jun. 24, 1977.

46 From an interview conducted by Steve Shepherd for his BBC radio series "Punk Jazz—A Portrait of Jaco Pastorius."

47 Bill Milkowski, "Requiem for Jaco," *Musician*, Dec, 1987, 90.

48 Shepherd, "Punk Jazz."

49 Chris Jisi, "Three Views of a Secret: The Reissues of 'Jaco Pastorius' & What You Won't Hear," *Bass Player*, Nov. 2000, 70.

50 Alicia Zuckerman, "When Metheny Met Jaco and the Old Miami Days," WORN, Feb. 6, 2014 (accessed Oct. 6, 2018), http://www.wlrn.org/post/when-metheny-met-jaco-and-old-miami-days. Metheny also recalled that his first gig in Fort Lauderdale was at Bachelors III with Jaco and drummer Danny Gottlieb backing singer Lorna Luft. "During every break we would go into a back room and play old Coltrane tunes. The room was right next to her dressing room. She hated it. We almost got fired." Scott Benarde, "Metheny: Commerciality Comes Without Compromise," *Ft. Lauderdale News*, Nov. 18, 1984.

51 Risner interview, 2007.

52 Milkowski, *Jaco*, 85.

53 Risner interview, 2007.

54 Risner interview, 2007.

55 Jaco later explained that he had gone back to the Gusman to pick up gear that he had left behind from his earlier performance. Dallas, "Weather Report: Sunny," 9.

56 Tony Palkovic, "Joe Zawinul Interview, Part 2," Feb. 2003 (accessed Apr. 10, 2015), http://www.tpradioshow.com/interviews.htm.

57 Dallas, "Weather Report: Sunny," 9.

58 Joe Waz, "Pat Metheny: The Incredible String Man," *Jazz Forum*, No. 54, 1978, 41.

59 Chris Welch, "Weather Report: Myth & Magic," *Melody Maker*, Oct. 14, 1978, 61.

60 Tony Palkovic, "Zawinul Interview, Part 2."

61 Josef Zawinul as told to Greg Armbruster, "The Evolution of Weather Report," *Keyboard*, Mar. 1984, 50.

62 Palkovic, "Joe Zawinul Interview, Part 2."

63 "Shepherd, "Punk Jazz."

64 In Joe's version of the story, the phone message got morphed into a telegram, but Thompson confirms that it was a telephone message.

65 Thompson interview, 2014.

66 Thompson interview, 2014.

67 Acuña interview, 2014.

68 A limiter prevents a signal from going over a certain threshold, effectively keeping the signal from getting too loud. In the days discussed here, it was an analog circuit, but nowadays it is typically a digital effect.

69 Chris Jisi, "Jaco's Finest Hour," *Bass Player*, Sep. 2007, 33.

70 Walden interview, 2015.

71 Palkovic, "Zawinul Interview, Part 2."

72 Julie Coryell and Laura Friedman, *Jazz-Rock Fusion: The People, The Music* (New York: Delacorte Press,) 1978, 27–28.

73 Tesser, "The Florida Flash," 13.

74 Thompson interview, 2014.

75 Brian Risner telephone interview, 2017.

76 Shepherd, "Punk Jazz."

77 Risner interviews, 2007, 2014.

78 Acuña interview, 2014.

79 Bob Bobbing telephone interview, Mar. 4, 2018.

80 Milkowski, *Jaco*, 88.

81 Risner interview, 2017.

82 Ray Townley, review of *Black Market*, *Down Beat*, Jul. 15, 1976, 26.

13 Heavy Weather

1 Chester Thompson telephone interview, Dec. 22, 2014.

2 Alex Acuña telephone interview, Feb. 21, 2014.

3 Acuña interview, 2014.

4 Acuña interview, 2014.

5 Thompson interview, 2014.

6 Thompson interview, 2014.

7 Monk Rowe, Don Alias Interview for the Fillius Jazz Archive at Hamilton College, New York, NY, January 6, 2002.

8 Jeff Potter, "Manolo Badrena," *Modern Percussionist*, Sep.–Nov. 1986, 13.

9 John Sanna email correspondence, Jun. 2017.

10 Tom Wilmeth, *Sound Bites: A Lifetime of Listening* (United States: MuleShoe Press, 2016), 288.

11 Damon Roerich, "Jaco Pastorius, the Bassist Interviewed," *Musician Player & Listener*, Aug. 1980, 42.

12 From an interview conducted by Steve Shepherd for his BBC radio series "Punk Jazz—A Portrait of Jaco Pastorius."

13 Bill Cosford, "Jazz Group Puts Sun in Your Life," *Miami Herald*, May 3, 1976.

14 Bob Bobbing telephone interview, Mar. 4, 2018.

15 Jack Zink, "A Three-Block Trip from Rags to Riches," *Ft. Lauderdale News and Sun-Sentinel*, May 16, 1976.

16 Jon Marlowe, "Jaco Pastorius' Sound Goes National," *Miami News*, May 7, 1976.

17 Leonard Feather, "Weather Report: An Aural Rainbow," *Los Angeles Times*, Jun. 6, 1976.

18 "Paris," *Variety*, Jul. 28, 1976, 69.

19 George Duke Online, http://www.georgeduke.com/1970s.html, accessed Jun. 21, 2017.

20 Mick Brown, "Singing the Body Electric," *Sounds*, Aug. 7, 1976, 18.

21 Robin Denselow, "Weather Report," *The Guardian*, Jul. 29, 1976.

22 Brown, "Singing the Body Electric," 16.

23 Denselow, "Weather Report."

24 Jurg Solothurnmann, "Joseph Zawinul: A Space Musician," *Jazz Forum*, Apr. 1976, 46.

25 Bob Blumenthal, "Jaco Pastorius: Tempest in a Bass," *Rolling Stone*, May 5, 1977, 24.

26 Jeffrey Pepper Rodgers, *Rock Troubadours: Conversations on the Art and Craft of Songwriting* (San Anselmo, CA: String Letter Publishing), 2000, 48.

27 Rodgers, *Rock Troubadours*, 38.

28 Rodgers, *Rock Troubadours*, 50. Jaco once described his contribution to *Hejira* in much simpler terms: "It was a gig. I bailed her out of a lot of trouble." Simon Balderstone, "Outlook Sunny for this Stormy Ensemble," *The Age*, Jul. 8, 1978.

29 Joni Mitchell, "Jaco by Joni," *Musician*, Dec. 1987, 91.

30 Mitchell, "Jaco by Joni," 100.

31 Tom Oberheim, oral history interview, National Association of Music Merchants, 2005 (accessed Nov. 25, 2017), https://www.namm.org/library/oral-history/tom-oberheim.

32 Bob Cavallo telephone interview, Jan. 11, 2017.

33 Sy Johnson, "Zawinul from Birdland to 'Birdland,'" *Jazz*, Fall 1977, 49.

34 Johnson, "Zawinul from Birdland to 'Birdland,'" 49.

35 Oberheim, NAMM oral history.

36 Tom Lubin, "Profile: Producer Ron Malo," *Modern Recording & Music*, Sep. 1981, 56.

37 Paul Laurence, "Recording the Electric Bass," *Recording Engineer/Producer*, Apr. 1977, 75.

38 Brian Risner personal interview, Jul. 15, 2017.

39 Bill Milkowski, *Jaco: The Extraordinary and Tragic Life of Jaco Pastorius*, deluxe ed. (San Francisco: Miller Freeman Books), 2005, 96.

40 "Classic Tracks: 'Birdland' by Weather Report," *Mix*, Jun. 1995, 173, 174.

41 Blair Jackson, "Fusion Giants Weather Report," *BAM*, Jun. 3, 1983, 43.

42 Gil Podolinsky, "Weather Report: An Interview with Joe Zawinul and Engineer Brian Risner," *Modern Recording*, Nov. 1977, 36.

43 Acuña Interview, 2014.
44 Acuña Interview, 2014.
45 Acuña Interview, 2014.
46 Acuña Interview, 2014.
47 Max Salazar, *Mambo Kingdom: Latin Jazz in New York* (New York: Schirmer Trade Books, 2002), 92.
48 Michelle Mercer, *Footprints: The Life and Work of Wayne Shorter* (New York: J. P. Tarcher/Penguin, 2004), 49.
49 Acuña Interview, 2014.
50 Alex Acuña telephone interview, Oct. 7, 2020.
51 Chris Jisi, "Jaco's Finest Hour," *Bass Player*, Sep. 2007, 33.
52 Acuña interview, 2014.
53 Jisi, Chris. "Jaco's Finest Hour," 33.
54 Jisi, Chris. "Jaco's Finest Hour," 33, 35.
55 Leonard Feather, "Keyboardist Joe Zawinul: From Weather Report to Rap," *Los Angeles Times*, Feb. 18, 1990.
56 Johnson, "Zawinul from Birdland to 'Birdland,'" 47, 49.
57 See *Snoopy's Jazz Classiks on Toys, Gurkha Parade* by the Band of the Brigade of Gurkhas, and *Talking Hands* (1997) by Acoustic Mania (Antonio Forcione and Neil Stacey)
58 Lou Beach telephone interview, Nov. 2, 2017.
59 Other successes from this campaign included Return to Forever's *Musicmagic*, which hit number 35 on *Billboard*'s top LP chart, Jeff Beck's *Jeff Beck with the Jan Hammer Group Live*, which peaked at 23, and Maynard Ferguson's *Conquistador*, which topped out at 22.
60 There's a photograph of Wayne and Joe receiving their gold record plaques at a Columbia Records convention on page 58 of the Aug. 19, 1978, issue of *Record World* magazine. It's also interesting to note that *Billboard* considered *Heavy Weather* to be the fifth best selling jazz album of 1977. The top four were *In Fight* by George Benson; *Free as the Wind* by the Crusaders, *Breezin'*, also by Benson; and Jean-Luc Ponty's *Imaginary Voyage*. The gold record plaque anecdote comes from Ingrid Pastorius's former website, Ingrid's Unofficial Jaco Pastorius Cyber Nest, accessed Jul. 10, 2014, http://www.jacop.net:80/goldrecord.html.
61 Neil Tesser, review of *Heavy Weather*, *Down Beat*, May 19, 1977, 23.

14   Mr. Gone

1 Greg Armbruster, "Zawinul: Continued Hot, Chance of Record Highs," *Keyboard*, Mar. 1984, 56.
2 The entire program can be seen on YouTube at https://youtu.be/tQAW9fsauT8. Weather Report also played "Teen Town" for the show.
3 Howarth's instructor was Phil Dodds, who ran the service department at ARP. In that role, Dodds was on the set of the 1977 motion picture *Close Encounters of the Third Kind*, managing the ARP 2500 that was used in the film. The director,

Steven Spielberg, cast him on the spot as the audio engineer who plays the five-note melody of alien tones.
4 Alan Howarth telephone interview, Jun. 1, 2016.
5 "Near Concorde proportions": Ed Kelleher, review of Weather Report and Al Di Meola, Beacon Theatre, New York, Talent in Action, *Billboard*, May 28, 1977, 49. (The Concorde was a supersonic jetliner that began flying in 1976. It was initially banned from some airports because it was so loud during takeoff.) "Mind-bending volume": Joe Weisel, "Weather Report Overblown," *Stars and Stripes*, Oct. 1, 1977, 19.
6 Robyn Flans, "Alex Acuña," *Modern Drummer*, Oct. 1990, 86.
7 "Long-haired rockers" and "aging jazz aficionados" from R. D. Heldenfels, "Weather Report a Band for All Seasons," *Daily Press* (Newport News, VA), Nov. 11, 1977.
8 Performances of "Sophisticated Lady" and "Loch Lomond" noted in Jack Sohmer, "Two Forays into Jazz-Rock: Weather Report is Fine," *Miami Herald*, May 7, 1977.
9 Jack Zink, "'Vultures' Keep Jaco Busy," *Ft. Lauderdale News*, Jul. 1, 1977.
10 Bill Milkowski, *Jaco: The Extraordinary and Tragic Life of Jaco Pastorius*, deluxe ed. (San Francisco: Miller Freeman Books), 2005, 60.
11 Alex Acuña telephone interview, Feb. 21, 2014.
12 Anil Prasad, "Joe Zawinul: Man of the People," *Innerviews*, 1997 (accessed Sep. 12, 2003), https://www.innerviews.org/inner/zawinul.html.
13 Maria Booker Lucien telephone interview, Mar. 22, 2017.
14 Brian Glasser, *In a Silent Way: A Portrait of Joe Zawinul* (London: Sanctuary Publishing, 2001), 256.
15 Herbie Hancock with Lisa Dickey, *Possibilities* (New York: Viking Penguin, 2014), 84.
16 Howarth interview, 2016.
17 Bob Bobbing telephone interview, Mar. 4, 2018.
18 Pat Jordan, "Who Killed Jaco Pastorius?" *GQ*, Apr. 1988, 273.
19 Gerry Griffith telephone interview, Sep. 24, 2015.
20 Howarth interview, 2016.
21 Detail about the age at which manic-depression surfaces comes from Jordan, "Who Killed Jaco Pastorius," 309–10.
22 Jordan, "Who Killed Jaco Pastorius," 309.
23 From an interview conducted by Steve Shepherd for his BBC radio series "Punk Jazz—A Portrait of Jaco Pastorius".
24 Statistics are from Foundations Recovery Network, an organization for treating people with a dual diagnosis of substance addition and mental health disorders. See http://www.dualdiagnosis.org/bipolar-disorder-and-addiction/.
25 Karl Dallas, review of Weather Report at the Rainbow Theatre, London, Caught in the Act, *Melody Maker*, Oct. 15, 1977, 18.
26 Paul Rambali, review of Weather Report at the Rainbow Theatre, London, On the Town, *New*

Musical Express, Oct. 15, 1977, 51.

27 Paul Rambali, "Boing," *New Musical Express*, Nov. 19, 1977 (accessed from Rock's Back Pages, http://www.rocksbackpages.com/Library/Article/ boing).

28 Howarth interview, 2016.

29 Howarth interview, 2016.

30 Bob Blumenthal, "The 8 Year Weather Report," *Rolling Stone*, Dec. 28, 1978–Jan. 11, 1979," 68.

31 Colman Andrews, "Black Market, Wayne Shorter & Weather Report #6," *Phonograph Record Magazine*, Apr. 1976, 50.

32 Brian Case, "This Man Is Watching Out for Custard Pies," *New Musical Express*, Aug. 7, 1976, 21.

33 Howarth interview, 2016.

34 Samuel Graham and Sam Sutherland, "The Coast," *Record World*, Sep. 30, 1978, 35.

35 Conrad Silvert, "Joe Zawinul: Wayfaring Genius—Part II," *Down Beat*, Jun. 15, 1978, 58.

36 Jeff Potter, "Manolo Badrena," *Modern Percussionist*, Sep.–Nov. 1986, 13.

37 Alex Acuña telephone interview, Oct. 7, 2020.

38 George Wanamaker, "Weather Report Spins Tales," *Los Angeles Free Press*, Jul. 4–10, 1975.

39 Karl Dallas, "Weather Report: MM Band Breakdown," *Melody Maker*, Oct. 29, 1977, 57.

40 Michelle Mercer, *Footprints: The Life and Work of Wayne Shorter* (New York: J. P. Tarcher/Penguin, 2004), 181.

41 George Varga, "Wayne Shorter's Quiet Time Engenders Long-Awaited Album," *San Diego Union*, Oct. 6, 1985.

42 David Breskin, "24 Shorter Solos," *Musician*, Jul. 1981, 58.

43 Spottswood Erving, "Jaco Pastorius: The Eccentric from the Everglades," *Musician*, May 1983, 14, 16. Another explanation for the *Mr. Gone* title comes from Wayne: "We were in the studio and I was playing a part on my saxophone and Jaco said, 'Man, that's just like—Mr. Gone.'" Elena Jarvis, "Weather Report 'Gone' to Jazz Heaven," *Colorado Springs Gazette Telegraph*, Dec. 8, 1978.

44 There's a YouTube clip of Erskine performing "Gonna Fly Now" live with Ferguson on the Mike Douglas television show at https://youtu. be/zHd3vzyM1fw.

45 "Conversation with Peter Erskine," NYU Steinhardt Jazz Studies, Jan. 26, 2016 (accessed Jun. 23, 2019), https://youtu.be/U-yvLOckGC0.

46 Peter Erskine personal interview, Nov. 4, 2006.

47 Erskine interview, 2006.

48 Peter Erskine, *No Beethoven: An Autobiography & Chronicle of Weather Report* (FUZZ/E/BOOKS, 2013), 13.

49 Erskine interview, 2006.

50 Angus MacKinnon, "Joseph Zawinul, Future Primitive," *New Musical Express*, Nov. 15, 1980, 24.

51 Len Lyons, "This Year's Weather Report," *High Fidelity*, Sep. 1978, 117.

52 See Clive Williamson, "Interview with Clive Williamson BBC," 1978, http://jacopastorius.com/ features/interviews/interview-with-clive-william-

son-bbc/, accessed Jan. 3, 2015.

53 Lyons, "This Year's Weather Report," 117.

54 See Herbie Hancock with Lisa Dickey, *Possibilities* (New York: Viking Penguin, 2014), 103.

55 Bill Milkowski, "Jaco Pastorius, Bass Revolutionary," *Guitar Player*, Aug. 1984, 65.

56 Williamson, Pastorius interview.

57 Damon Roerich, "Jaco Pastorius, the Bassist Interviewed," *Musician Player & Listener*, Aug. 1980, 40.

58 Ken Trethewey, *Weather Report: Electric Red* (Cornwall, UK: Jazz-Fusion Books, 2012), 99.

59 Sharon Todd, "One Little Song Adds Up to a Lot for Clemson Musician," *Greenville News and Piedmont*, Mar. 18, 1979.

60 Erskine interview, 2006.

61 Erskine interview, 2006.

62 Erskine interview, 2006.

63 Erskine interview, 2006.

64 Erskine interviews, 2006 and Feb. 24, 2018.

65 Erskine interview, 2018.

66 Erskine interviews, 2006 and 2018.

67 Rick Mattingly, "Peter Erskine," *Modern Drummer*, Jan. 1983, 8–9.

68 Mattingly, "Peter Erskine," 9.

69 "Conversation with Peter Erskine," NYU Steinhardt Jazz Studies.

70 Erskine interview, 2006.

71 "Conversation with Peter Erskine," NYU Steinhardt Jazz Studies.

72 Erskine interview, 2006.

73 Erskine interview, 2006.

74 Alias's name was actually printed "Don Arias," but it's clear they meant Don Alias. *Japan Times*, May 26, 1978, 8.

75 Dennis Hunt, "Weather Report's Cloudy Image," *Los Angeles Times*, Nov. 19, 1978.

76 Bill Henderson, "Meteorology and Me: The Joe Zawinul Interview," *Black Music & Jazz Review*, Dec. 1978, 8.

77 Howarth interview, 2016.

78 Howarth interview, 2016.

79 Susan Green, "Weather Report," *Burlington Free Press*, Nov. 2, 1978.

80 Hunt, "Weather Report's Cloudy Image."

81 Harry Sumrall, "Jazz-Rock 'Fusion Music' Comes of Age," *Washington Post*, Nov. 8, 1978; Max Bell, review of *Mr. Gone*, *New Musical Express*, Oct. 21, 1978, accessed from Rock's Back Pages, http:// www.rocksbackpages.com/Library/Article/weather-report-imr-gonei.

Among the negative reviews was Joe Waz's in *Jazz Forum*, in which he referred to the album as "a most interesting failure." (Joe Waz, *Jazz Forum*, No. 59, 1979, 48.) In *Musician*, Rafi Zabor described the album as "remarkably empty, easily the band's least interesting effort." (Rafi Zabor, *Musician*, Dec. 1978, 38.)

Positive reviews came from Jim Aikin in *Keyboard* magazine: "*Mr. Gone* possesses, in equal parts, accessible, hummable tunes, sophisticated jazz progressions and phrasings, a thick, gritty electronic sound, and a direct, almost primitive rhythmic drive." (Jim Aiken, review of *Mr. Gone*, *Contemporary Keyboard*, Jan. 1979, 64.) Robert Palmer, writing in the *Real Paper*, described *Mr. Gone* as "more nourishing" than *Heavy Weather*. (Robert Palmer, "Big Apple Grapevine: Weather Report," *Real Paper*, Sep. 30, 1978.)

82 Jim Cogan and William Clark, *Temples of Sound: Inside the Great Recording Studios* (San Francisco: Chronicle Books, 2003), 121.

83 Erskine interview, 2006.

84 Brian Risner telephone interview, Dec. 23, 2017.

85 Michael Zipkin, "Weather Report's Dance of the Elements," *BAM*, Oct. 29, 1978, 27.

15   8:30

1 Bob Bobbing telephone interview, Mar. 4, 2018.

2 Kitty Oliver, "Show Business Marriages: Living, Loving in Limelight," *Miami Herald*, May 15, 1977.

3 "Conversation with Peter Erskine," NYU Steinhardt Jazz Studies, Jan. 26, 2016 (accessed Jun. 23, 2019), https://youtu.be/U-yvLOckGC0.

4 Peter Erskine personal interview, Jan. 26, 2014.

5 Peter Erskine personal interview, Nov. 4, 2006.

6 Don Zulaica, "The Drummers of Weather Report," String Letter Publishing, *DRUM!*, Oct. 2006, 77.

7 Erskine interview, 2006.

8 Erskine interview, 2006.

9 Alan Howarth telephone interview, Jun. 1, 2016.

10 Peter Erskine personal interview, Feb. 24, 2018.

11 Chip Stern, "And Now for This Year's Weather Report," *Musician Player & Listener*, Feb. 1979, 23.

12 Erskine interview, 2006.

13 David Less, review of *Mr. Gone*, *Down Beat*, Jan. 11, 1979, 22.

14 Larry Birnbaum, "Weather Report Answers Its Critics," *Down Beat*, Feb. 8, 1979, 14.

15 Josef Woodard, "Weather Report: Storm Surge," *Down Beat*, Jan. 2001," 26.

16 David Less telephone interview, Apr. 24, 2018.

17 Bill Henderson, "Meteorology and Me: The Joe Zawinul Interview," *Black Music & Jazz Review*, Dec. 1978, 8.

18 Lee Underwood, review of Weather Report at the Civic, Santa Monica, California, Caught! *Down Beat*, Feb. 22, 1979, 40.

19 Peter Erskine, *No Beethoven: An Autobiography & Chronicle of Weather Report* (FUZZ/E/BOOKS, 2013), 103.

20 Erskine interview, 2018.

21 Conrad Silvert, "Weather Report Heads Down Thunder Road," *Rolling Stone*, May 5, 1977, 24.

22 Mike Daly, "'We're the Kings,' He Says," *The Age* (Melbourne, Aus.), Jul. 15, 1978.

23 Brian Case, "The Face with the Bass," *New Musical Express*, Jun. 12, 1976, 22.

24 Kyle Kevorkian, "Chasing the Jazz Train: When Does a Trend become a Trap?" *Keyboard*, Feb. 1990, 73–74.

25 Conrad Silvert, "Joe Zawinul: Wayfaring Genius—Part II," *Down Beat*, Jun. 15, 1978, 56, 58.

26 Allen Lowe, "Profiles: Some People Behind the Music: Barry Harris," *Down Beat*, Jul. 14, 1977, 19.

27 Erskine interview, 2006.

28 Peter Erskine recounts this story at length in his book, *No Beethoven*, 105–7.

29 Dennis Hunt, "Weather Report's Cloudy Image," *Los Angeles Times*, Nov. 19, 1978.

30 Hugo Bruton, "Weather Report: Hugo Bruton Forecasts Long Balmy Periods," *International Musician and Recording World*, Jan. 1981, 53.

31 Erskine interview, 2018.

32 From an interview conducted by Steve Shepherd for his BBC radio series "Punk Jazz—A Portrait of Jaco Pastorius."

33 Bobbing interview, 2018.

34 Leonard Feather, "Jazz, Si! Show Builds a Bridge to Cuba," *Los Angeles Times*, May 29, 1977.

35 Feather, "Jazz, Si!."

36 Chet Flippo, "Rocking Havana," *Rolling Stone*, May 3, 1979, 62.

37 Jim Jerome, "Havana Jam '79," *People Weekly*, Mar. 19, 1979, 34.

38 Jerome, "Havana Jam," 35, 37.

39 Erskine interview, 2006.

40 Erskine interview, 2018.

41 Frank Meyer, "Rhythm, Blues of Cuba under Fidel's Baton," *Variety*, Mar. 7, 1979, 178.

42 Willard Jenkins, "Paquito D'Rivera: NEA Jazz Master (2005)," Smithsonian Jazz Oral History Program NEA Jazz Master interview transcript, Smithsonian National Museum of American History, Jun. 11–12, 2010 (accessed Feb. 5, 2018), http://amhistory.si.edu/jazz/Drivera-Paquito/D'Rivera_Paquito_%20Interview_Transcription.pdf.

43 Flippo, "Rocking Havana," 64.

44 Evan Haga, "Bright Moments with John McLaughlin," *Jazz Times*, Aug. 22, 2016 (accessed Feb. 5, 2018), https://jazztimes.com/features/bright-moments-with-john-mclaughlin/.

45 Erskine interviews, 2006 and 2018.

46 Erskine interview, 2006.

47 Meyer, "Cuba under Fidel's Baton," 178.

48 Jerome, "Havana Jam," 37.

49 Meyer, "Cuba under Fidel's Baton," 178.

50 Flippo, "Rocking Havana," 64.

51 Jerome, "Havana Jam," 37.

52 Jerome, "Havana Jam," 34.

53 Erskine interview, 2006.

54 Erskine interview, 2018.

55 Joe Zawinul personal interview, Sep. 15, 2003.

56 Erskine interview, 2018.

57 Josef Woodard, "Boogie Woogie Big Time," *Down Beat*, May 2007, 33.

58 Erskine interview, 2018.

59 Erskine interview, 2018.

60 Zawinul interview, 2003.

61 Erskine interviews, 2006 and 2018.

62 Erskine, *No Beethoven*, 117.

16 Night Passage

1 Jim Bohen, "Showtime," *Daily Record* (Morristown, NJ), Jan. 18, 1980.
2 Eliot Tiegel, "Does It Sell? That's the Criterion for Jazz Issues," *Billboard*, Jan. 6, 1979, 10.
3 Leonard Feather, "In Search of a Definition for the 1970s," *Los Angeles Times*, Dec. 30, 1979.
4 Josef Zawinul as told to Greg Armbruster, "The Evolution of Weather Report," *Keyboard*, Mar. 1984, 50.
5 Peter Erskine personal interview, Feb. 24, 2018.
6 Peter Erskine personal interviews, Nov. 4, 2006; Jan. 26, 2014.
7 Peter Erskine, liner notes to *The Legendary Live Tapes: 1978–1981*, Sony Legacy/Columbia 88875141272, 2015, CD.
8 Jon Pareles, "Weather Report," *Musician Player & Listener*, Apr.–May 1980, 18–19.
9 Angus MacKinnon, "The Body Electric Gets Rewired," *New Musical Express*, Nov. 22, 1980, 43.
10 Erskine interview, 2014.
11 Erskine interview, 2014.
12 Pareles, "Weather Report," 19.
13 Peter Erskine, *No Beethoven: An Autobiography & Chronicle of Weather Report* (FUZZ/E/BOOKS, 2013), 217–18.
14 Erskine interviews, 2006 and 2018.
15 "Conversation with Peter Erskine," NYU Steinhardt Jazz Studies, Jan. 26, 2016 (accessed Jun. 23, 2019), https://youtu.be/U-yvLOckGC0.
16 Erskine interview, 2006.
17 The benefit took place in Miami on Sunday, Sep. 23, 1979. (*Miami News*, Sep. 21, 1979.) Salas can be heard on the Pastorius CD, *The Birthday Concert*.
18 Robert Thomas Jr., telephone interview, Jan. 21, 2014.
19 Thomas interview, 2014.
20 Thomas interview, 2014.
21 Thomas interview, 2014.
22 Erskine interview, 2014.
23 Thomas interview, 2014.
24 Thomas interview, 2018.
25 Thomas interview, 2014.
26 Nina Korman, "In Good Hands," *Miami New Times*, Oct. 15, 1998 (accessed Feb. 7, 2014), https://www.miaminewtimes.com/music/in-good-hands-6387533.
27 Jordan, "Who Killed Jaco Pastorius," 309.
28 Joe Zawinul personal interview, 2003.
29 Erskine interview, 2014.
30 Hugo Bruton, "Weather Report: Hugo Bruton Forecasts Long Balmy Periods," *International Musician and Recording World*, Jan. 1981, 53.
31 Erskine interview, 2014.
32 Adam Sweeting, "Order from Liberty," *Melody Maker*, Nov. 29, 1980, 12.
33 Scott Kinsey personal interview, Jul. 6, 2007.
34 Erskine interview, 2014.
35 Erskine interview, 2014.
36 Ingrid Pastorius, quoted at https://www.weatherreportdiscography.org/night-passage/, accessed

Jun. 3, 2019.
37 Erskine interview, 2014.
38 Erskine interview, 2014.
39 Erskine, *No Beethoven*, 223.
40 John L. Walters, "CD Review: Weather Report—The Legendary Live Tapes 1978–1981," *London Jazz News*, Apr. 11, 2016 (accessed Mar. 18, 2018), http://www.londonjazznews.com/2016/04/cd-review-weather-report-legendary-live.html.
41 Brian Risner correspondence, Nov. 2020.
42 John Gill, "The Genius of Gray Haired Men," *Sounds*, Nov. 29, 1980 (from a clipping in the collection of the Institute of Jazz Studies at Rutgers University).
43 Andy Gill, "Weather Report; Hammersmith Odeon." *New Musical Express*. Nov. 29, 1980, 52.
44 Lynden Barber, "Passage to Old Peaks," *Melody Maker*, Nov. 11, 1980, 18.
45 Don Heckman, review of *Night Passage*, *High Fidelity*, Feb. 1981, 102.
46 Bruton, "Long Balmy Periods," 53.

17 Weather Report (1982)

1 Brian Risner interview, Dec. 23, 2017.
2 The $200,000 figure comes from "CBS Fails to Prevent Warners from Issuing Pastorius' Solo Album," *Variety*, May 6, 1981, 185.
3 Bill Milkowski, *Jaco: The Extraordinary and Tragic Life of Jaco Pastorius*, deluxe ed. (San Francisco: Miller Freeman Books), 2005, 128–29.
4 Peter Erskine personal interview, Jan. 26, 2014.
5 Sam Sutherland, "Fusion Controversy Boring to Zawinul," *Billboard*, Apr. 11, 1981, 32, 42.
6 Sutherland, "Fusion Controversy Boring," 42.
7 Peter Erskine personal interview, Feb. 24, 2018.
8 Erskine interview, 2014 and 2018.
9 Erskine interviews, Nov. 4, 2006, and 2018.
10 From an interview conducted by Steve Shepherd for his BBC radio series "Punk Jazz—A Portrait of Jaco Pastorius."
11 Erskine interview, 2018.
12 Erskine interview, 2018.
13 Erskine interview, 2018.
14 Erskine interview, 2018.
15 Gunther Baumann, *Zawinul: Ein Leben aus Jazz* (Salzburg: Residenz-Verlag, 2002), 131.
16 Erskine interview, 2018.
17 Milkowski, *Jaco*, 134.
18 Leonard Feather, "Playboy Jazz—A Sag in the Swing," *Los Angeles Times*, Jun. 23, 1981.
19 Erskine interview, 2014.
20 Erskine interview, 2014, 2018.
21 Ray Murphy, "Weather Report with the Hot Numbers," *Boston Globe*, Jul. 15, 1981.
22 Erskine interview, 2014.
23 Erskine interview, 2014.
24 Brian Risner personal interviews, Sep. 4, 2017; Apr. 5, 2018.
25 Risner interview, 2018.
26 Robert Thomas Jr., telephone interview, Jan. 21,

2014.

27 Erskine interview, 2014.

28 To put the Linn's price in perspective, a Toyota Corolla could be had for less than $4,000 in 1980.

29 Rick Mattingly, "Peter Erskine," *Modern Drummer*, Jan. 1983, 12, 43. Erskine was so intrigued by the Linn that he lent his efforts to Tom Oberheim, whose DMX drum machine hit the market soon after the LM-1. "I met Tom Oberheim at some gigs and I recorded one of my drum sets in a small jingle studio on Highland in Hollywood on a quarter-inch Technics tape machine. I think they kept the bass drum that they had done at Oberheim, but the snare, tom, cymbals, tambourine, and hi-hat were mine. That was used on a lot of hit records. And I was paid a DMX; I got one. I kind of got ripped off on that. [*laughs*]" (Erskine interview, 2014.)

30 Angus MacKinnon, "Joseph Zawinul, Future Primitive," *New Musical Express*, Nov. 15, 1980.

31 Jim Swanson personal interview, Jan. 27, 2014.

32 Baumann, *Zawinul*, 144.

33 One such ad appeared in the *Orlando Sentinel* on Sep. 25, promoting a concert on Oct. 25. The *Sentinel* issued a cancellation notice on Oct. 16. The Oct. 2 issue of the *Cleveland Plain Dealer* reported that tickets for Weather Report's Nov. 3 appearance in Cleveland would go on sale the following Monday. The very next day the *Plain Dealer* noted that the concert had been canceled.

34 Josef Zawinul as told to Greg Armbruster, "The Evolution of Weather Report," *Keyboard*, Mar. 1984, 50.

35 John Stook, review of *Night Passage*, *Musician*, Jun. 1982, 80, 82.

36 Samuel Graham, "Backbeat: The New Jaco," *High Fidelity*, Mar. 1984, 77.

37 Blair Jackson, "Fusion Giants Weather Report," *BAM*, Jun. 3, 1983, 43.

18 Procession

1 CM, "Weather Report," *The Wire*, Spring 1983, 4.

2 Gunther Baumann, *Zawinul: Ein Leben aus Jazz* (Salzburg: Residenz-Verlag, 2002), 144.

3 Peter Erskine personal interview, Jan. 26, 2014.

4 Rick Mattingly, "Peter Erskine," *Modern Drummer*, Jan. 1983, 49.

5 Brian Glasser, *In a Silent Way: A Portrait of Joe Zawinul* (London: Sanctuary Publishing, 2001), 227.

6 A. James Liska, "On the Road with Weather Report," *Down Beat*, Oct. 1982, 22.

7 Michael Shore, "Omar Hakim," *Musician*, Mar. 1986, 62.

8 Omar Hakim telephone interview, Feb. 25, 2014.

9 Robin Tolleson, "Omar Hakim: Going for the Feeling," *Modern Drummer*, Dec. 1984, 80.

10 Hakim interview, 2014.

11 Hakim interview, 2014.

12 Hakim interview, 2014.

13 Hakim interview, 2014.

14 Victor Bailey telephone interview, Feb. 18, 2014. According to the biography on Victor's former website, the demo tape included "a version of Marvin Gaye's 'What's Going On,' with bass melody and scat bass solo, a multitracked version of the Beatles' 'She's Leaving Home,' a funk/thumb groove tune that I had written, and a burning live solo on 'Giant Steps.'"

15 José Rossy telephone interview, Feb. 1, 2014.

16 Josef Zawinul as told to Greg Armbruster, "The Evolution of Weather Report," *Keyboard*, Mar. 1984, 51.

17 Hakim interview, 2014.

18 Bailey interview, 2014.

19 Rossy interview, 2014.

20 Jim Swanson telephone interview, Apr. 23, 2018.

21 Swanson interview, 2018.

22 Hakim interview, 2014.

23 Cliff Radel, "Legends Keep Jazz Alive," *Cincinnati Enquirer*, Jul. 11, 1982.

24 Tolleson, "Omar Hakim," 87.

25 Hakim interview, 2014.

26 Liska, "On the Road," 21.

27 Swanson interview, 2018.

28 Leonard Feather, "Hurricane Joe Et Al. in San Diego," *Los Angeles Times*, Jun. 3, 1982.

29 Bailey interview, 2014.

30 Bailey interview, 2014.

31 Hakim interview, 2014.

32 Ron Weiskind, "Weather Report: Clear Rhythms, Hot Solos," *Pittsburgh Post-Gazette*, Jun. 17, 1982.

33 Mark Sinker, "Manhattan Transfer: Clean-Cut Agony," *The Wire*, Jun. 1988, 26.

34 Janis Siegel telephone interview, Jul. 18, 2016.

35 Leonard Feather, "Weather Report Tops Itself," *Los Angeles Times*, Jun. 21, 1982.

36 Glasser, *In a Silent Way*, 232.

37 Hakim interview, 2014.

38 Tom Moon, "Saxophonist Wayne Shorter Takes Cautious Steps Back into Spotlight," *Arizona Daily Star*, Nov. 13, 1985.

39 Josef Woodard, "Josef Zawinul: Doing Something about the Weather," *Mix*, Jul. 1983, 92.

40 Greg Armbruster, "Zawinul: Continued Hot, Chance of Record Highs," *Keyboard*, Mar. 1984, 58.

41 Rossy interview, 2014.

42 Bailey interview, 2014.

43 Bailey interview, 2014.

44 "Rhythm changes" refers to a 32-bar chord progression derived from George Gershwin's "I Got Rhythm." Many subsequent jazz tunes were based on this progression and it is one of the standard forms that jazz musicians are expected to know.

45 Bailey interview, 2014.

46 Hakim interview, 2014.

47 Siegel interview, 2016.

48 Blair Jackson, "Fusion Giants Weather Report," *BAM*, Jun. 3, 1983, 42.

49 Brian Risner personal interviews, Jun. 1, 2014; Sep. 4, 2017.

50 Hal Miller, "Weather Report," liner notes to *Forecast: Tomorrow*, Columbia/Legacy (82876 85570 2), 2006, 78.
51 Hakim interview, 2014.
52 Jim Swanson personal interviews, Jan. 31, 2004; Jan. 27, 2014.
53 Joe attributed the poor sales of *Weather Report* to the fact that the band didn't tour in support of it, and "it came out at a funny time, so it didn't materialize." Woodard, "Doing Something," 90.
54 W. Kim Heron, "Band Basks in 13 Years of Fair Weather for Fusion," *Detroit Free Press*, Mar. 30, 1983.
55 Richard Cook, "High Wind in Birdland: Weather Report's *Procession*," *New Musical Express*, Mar. 19, 1983 (accessed from Rock's Back Pages, https://www.rocksbackpages.com/Library/Article/high-wind-in-birdland-weather-reports-iprocessioni).
56 John Diliberto, review of *Procession*, *Down Beat*, Jun. 1983, 32–33.
57 Chip Stern, review of *Procession*, *Musician*, May 1983, 88.

19 Domino Theory

1 Larry Rhodes, "Audience Didn't Need Theatrics at Weather Report's Norfolk Show," *Daily Press* (Norfolk, VA), Mar. 18, 1983.
2 Jon Pareles, "Rock: Weather Report Sings," *New York Times*, Mar. 21, 1983.
3 Jerry Brabenec, "Weather Report's High Tech Cosmopolitanism," *Ann Arbor Sun*, Mar. 30, 1983.
4 Jo-Ann Wong, "Weather Report Plays Up a Storm," *Deseret News*, Apr. 12, 1983.
5 Blair Jackson, "Fusion Giants Weather Report," *BAM*, Jun. 3, 1983, 42.
6 Leonard Feather, "Weather Report Blows Up a Storm," *Los Angeles Times*, Apr. 18, 1983.
7 Leonard Feather, "Zawinul, Shorter Sound the Future," *Los Angeles Times*, May 1, 1983.
8 Josef Zawinul as told to Greg Armbruster, "The Evolution of Weather Report," *Keyboard*, Mar. 1984, 51.
9 Victor Bailey telephone interview, Feb. 18, 2014.
10 Bailey interview, 2014.
11 Omar Hakim telephone interview, Feb. 25, 2014.
12 Hakim interview, 2014.
13 "Live Reviews," review of Weather Report, Palace Theatre, Jun. 5, 1983, *Crescendo International*, Aug. 1983, 8.
14 Hakim interview, 2014.
15 José Rossy telephone interview, Feb. 1, 2014.
16 "Weather Report," *The South Bank Show*, season 7, episode 11, originally aired Mar. 11, 1984, ITV Archive.
17 Jim Swanson personal interview, Jan. 27, 2014.
18 Greg Armbruster, "Zawinul: Continued Hot, Chance of Record Highs," *Keyboard*, Mar. 1984, 56.
19 Mark Steven Frandsen, "Forecasting Fusion at

20 Chris Jisi, "A Remark They Made: The Bass World Remembers Joe Zawinul," *Bass Player*, Jan. 2008, 48.
21 Hakim interview, 2014.
22 Robin Tolleson, "Omar Hakim: Going for the Feeling," *Modern Drummer*, Dec. 1984, 90.
23 Jackson, "Fusion Giants," 42.
24 Swanson interview, 2014.
25 None of the early synthesizer manufacturers that Joe relied on during his Weather Report years survived the 1980s. Oberheim went into bankruptcy in 1985, while Sequential Circuits failed in 1988. Coupled with Moog Music's bankruptcy in 1987, it was the end of the classic analog synthesizer industry in the United States. Nowadays the instruments manufactured by these companies are highly coveted by collectors and musicians.
26 Jim Swanson telephone interview, Apr. 23, 2018.
27 Hakim interview, 2014.
28 Willie Tee later recorded his own unaccompanied version of "Can It Be Done," which appears on the compilation album *Keys to the Crescent City*, issued by Rounder in 1991.
29 Sam Sutherland, "Fusion Controversy Boring to Zawinul," *Billboard*, Apr. 11, 1981, 42.
30 Tolleson, "Omar Hakim," 85.
31 Bailey interview, 2014.
32 Swanson interview, 2014.
33 Leonard Feather, "Jazz Album Briefs," *Los Angeles Times*, Apr. 1, 1984.
34 J. D. Considine, "In 13th Album, Weather Report Remains as Unpredictable as Ever," *Baltimore Sun*, Mar. 4, 1984.
35 Jim Higgins, "Wayne Shorter, Uncloistered," *Milwaukee Sentinel*, Apr. 1, 1983.
36 Jackson, "Fusion Giants," 42.
37 Josef Woodard, "Josef Zawinul: Doing Something about the Weather," *Mix*, Jul. 1983, 99.

20 Sportin' Life

1 David Weiss, "New Sounds & Traditions from New York's Hot Percussionist, Frank Colón," *DRUM!*, Aug.–Sep. 1997, 77.
2 Mino Cinélu Skype interview, Jun. 25, 2018.
3 Cinélu interview, 2018.
4 Robin Tolleson, "Omar Hakim: Going for the Feeling," *Modern Drummer*, Dec. 1984, 88.
5 James Fadden, "A Jazz Video Report from Concept to Wrap," *Back Stage*, Sep. 28, 1984, 37B.
6 The video can be seen on YouTube at https://youtu.be/MF7_h-AhS1U, accessed Jun. 27, 2018.
7 Mark Mawrence email correspondence, Jul. 29, 2015.
8 Cinélu interview, 2018.
9 Cinélu interview, 2018.
10 Cinélu interview, 2018.
11 Opening ceremony anecdote from Leonard Feather, "Zawinul, Shorter Sound the Future," *Los Angeles Times*, May 1, 1983.

Low Frequencies: The Bass Players of Weather Report." PhD diss., Texas Tech Univ., 2010, 163.

12 Victor Bailey telephone interview, Feb. 18, 2014.
13 Bailey interview, 2014.
14 Bailey interview, 2014.
15 Brian Glasser, *In a Silent Way: A Portrait of Joe Zawinul* (London: Sanctuary Publishing, 2001), 246.
16 Lloyd Sachs, "Shorter to Pour Out Renewed Spirit Here," *Chicago Sun-Times*, Nov. 19, 1985.
17 Bailey interview, 2014.
18 Bailey interview, 2014.
19 Omar Hakim telephone interview, Feb. 25, 2014.
20 Cinélu interview, 2018.
21 Cinélu interview, 2018.
22 Cinélu interview, 2018.
23 Christian John Wikane, "'Music Is More than Just Notes': An Interview with Mino Cinélu," *Pop Matters*, Feb. 17, 2015 (accessed Jul. 1, 2018), https://www.popmatters.com/188598-we-want-mino-an-interview-with-mino-cinelu-2495581330.html.
24 Josef Woodard, "Joe Zawinul Spars with the Muse," *Musician*. Jun. 1985, 56.
25 Sam Sutherland, "Zawinul Weathers Changes," *Billboard*, May 10, 1986, 23.
26 Cinélu interview, 2018.
27 Woodard, "Joe Zawinul Spars," 52.

21   This Is This

1 Sam Sutherland, "Weather Report: No Tour This Year," *Billboard*, Apr. 6, 1985, 42.
2 Leonard Feather, "Forecasters Report No More Weather Till 1986," *Los Angeles Times*, May 5, 1985.
3 Mary Campbell, Associated Press, "Joe Zawinul's Album First in 15 Years," *Baytown Sun*, May 26, 1986.
4 The video can be found at https://youtu.be/xc-qQ1pYWtlM, accessed Jul. 25, 2018.
5 Joe Zawinul personal interview, Sep. 15, 2003.
6 Gabor Turi, "Debrecen Jazz Days," *Jazz Forum*, No. 97, 1985, 23.
7 Peter Hadekel, "Marsalis Shifts Gears with Brash, Bold LP," *Montreal Gazette*, Oct. 24, 1985.
8 Michelle Mercer places the date of Iska's death as October 25, 1983. *Footprints: The Life and Work of Wayne Shorter* (New York: J. P. Tarcher/Penguin, 2004), 206. However, the correct year of 1985 is corroborated by a funeral announcement that appeared in the *Los Angeles Times* on Oct. 30, 1985, and in an interview with Wayne in the Dec. 7, 1985, issue of the *Atlanta Constitution*.
9 Russ DeVault, "Return of Wayne Shorter," *Atlanta Constitution*, Dec. 7, 1985.
10 Russ DeVault, "Return of Wayne Shorter."
11 Gunther Baumann, *Zawinul: Ein Leben aus Jazz* (Salzburg: Residenz-Verlag, 2002), 149–50.
12 Peter Erskine, *No Beethoven: An Autobiography & Chronicle of Weather Report* (FUZZ/E/BOOKS, 2013), 151.
13 Peter Erskine personal interview, Jan. 26, 2014.
14 Robert Carlberg, "Joe Zawinul Interview," *Electronic Musician*, May 1986, 46, 48.
15 Erskine interview, 2014.
16 Erskine interview, 2014.
17 Mark Steven Frandsen, "Forecasting Fusion at Low Frequencies: The Bass Players of Weather Report." PhD diss., Texas Tech University, 2010, 157.
18 Frandsen, "Forecasting Fusion," 154.
19 Victor Bailey telephone interview, Feb. 18, 2014.
20 Bailey interview, 2014.
21 Mino Cinélu Skype interview, Jun. 25, 2018.
22 Erskine interview, 2014.
23 Omar Hakim telephone interview, Feb. 25, 2014.
24 Eric Snider, review of *This Is This*, *Tampa Bay Times*, Jul. 27, 1986.
25 Baumann, *Zawinul*, 151.
26 Baumann, *Zawinul*, 151.
27 George Varga, "Wayne Shorter's Quiet Time Engenders Long-Awaited Album," *San Diego Union*, Oct. 6, 1985.
28 Leonard Feather, "Prepare for a Change in the Weather Report," *Los Angeles Times*, Mar. 2, 1986.
29 Peter Erskine personal interview, Feb. 24, 2018.
30 George Varga, "Zawinul Weathers It Very Well: LP May Make Things Happen for Jazzman," *San Diego Union*, Mar. 9, 1986.
31 Display ad, *St. Louis Post Dispatch*, Aug. 24, 1986.
32 Joe Zawinul personal interview, Feb. 16, 2007.
33 Russ DeVault, "John Scofield Brings Quartet to Town Tonight," *Atlanta Constitution*, Feb. 21, 1986.
34 Steve Khan telephone interview, Jul, 15, 2018.
35 Steve Khan, "Tributes," accessed Jan. 13, 2020, http://www.stevekhan.com/tributes.htm.
36 Khan interview, 2018.
37 Khan interview, 2018.
38 Khan interview, 2018.
39 Erskine interviews, 2014 and 2018.
40 Khan interview, 2018.
41 Khan interview, 2018.
42 Erskine interview, 2014.
43 Khan interview, 2018.
44 Khan interview, 2018.
45 Khan interview, 2018.
46 Leonard Feather, "Weather Report in New Guise," *Los Angeles Times*, Sep. 29, 1986.
47 Khan interview, 2018.
48 Baumann, *Zawinul*, 151.

22   Transitions

1 Stephen Holden, "Word of Mouth Sound: Richly Pan-American," *New York Times*, Jun. 29, 1982. The concert has been preserved on the album *Truth, Liberty & Soul—Live in NYC: The Complete 1982 NPR Jazz Alive! Recording*, released by Resonance Records in 2017.
2 Peter Erskine, *No Beethoven: An Autobiography & Chronicle of Weather Report* (FUZZ/E/BOOKS, 2013), 220.
3 Bill Milkowski, "Requiem for Jaco," *Musician*,

Dec, 1987, 97.

4 Bob Bobbing telephone interview, Mar. 4, 2018.

5 Larry Keller, "Killer of Pastorius Free after Four Months," *Ft. Lauderdale Sun-Sentinel*, Jul. 4, 1989.

6 Josef Woodard, "Joe Zawinul: The Dialects of Jazz," *Down Beat*, Apr. 1988, 17.

7 Zawinul audio recording, provenance unknown.

8 Joe Zawinul personal interview, Feb. 16, 2007.

9 Stuart Nicholson, "Joe's Public," *Jazzwise*, Sep. 2002, 25.

10 Larry Blumenfeld, "Editor's View: First Meetings and Points of Departure," *Jazziz*, 4.

11 Zawinul interview, 2007.

12 Zawinul interview, 2007.

13 Robert Thomas Jr., telephone interview, Aug. 1, 2018.

14 Bill Milkowski, *Faces & Places* release info, ESC Records, 2002 (accessed Sep. 16, 2018), https://www.esc-records.de/public/artist/releaseset_en.php?subby=3&cd=25&artist=15.

15 Peter Watrous, "Jazz View; A Jazz Generation and the Miles Davis Curse," *New York Times*, Oct. 15, 1995.

16 Daniel Levitin, "A Conversation with Joni Mitchell," accessed Jun. 28, 2019, https://jonimitchell.com/library/originals/jmOriginal_460.pdf.

17 Michelle Mercer, *Footprints: The Life and Work of Wayne Shorter* (New York: J. P. Tarcher/Penguin, 2004), 233.

18 Charles J. Gans, Associated Press, "Jazz Master Wayne Shorter Won't Be Bound by Tradition," *Daily Oklahoman*, May 17, 1996.

19 Watrous, "The Miles Davis Curse."

20 John Ephland, "On the Beat: One for Wayne," *Down Beat*, Nov. 1996, 6.

21 Bill Kohlhaase, "When Shorter Dissects His Jazz, He Breaks It Down to Its Essence," *Los Angeles Times*, Oct. 26, 1995.

22 Gans, "Jazz Master Wayne Shorter."

23 Anil Prasad, "Adam Holzman: Optimistic Evocations," Innerviews, 2016 (accessed Oct. 5, 2018), https://www.innerviews.org/inner/holzman.html.

24 Fernando Gonzalez, "An All-Star Big Band in Coastal Collusion," *Boston Globe*, Aug. 24, 1990.

25 Guy Eckstine telephone interview, Aug. 2, 2018.

26 Anil Prasad, "Joe Zawinul: Man of the People," Innerviews, 1997 (accessed Sep. 12, 2003), https://www.innerviews.org/inner/zawinul.html.

27 Zan Stewart, "Weather Report to Re-Form," Riffs, *Down Beat*, Apr. 1996, 14.

28 Gunther Baumann, *Zawinul: Ein Leben aus Jazz* (Salzburg: Residenz-Verlag, 2002), 155.

29 Don Heckman, "Duet for One," *Los Angeles Times*, Jun. 29, 1997.

30 Ben Ratliff, "With This Composer, the Work Is Never Done," *New York Times*, Apr. 22, 1998.

31 Ben Ratliff, "JVC Jazz Festival Review; At 67, Inspiring a Quest for Perfection," *New York Times*, Jun. 30, 2001.

32 Ashley Kahn, "Wayne Shorter: Face of the Deep," *Jazz Times*, Jun. 2002, 46.

33 Wayne Shorter telephone interview, Dec. 23, 2008.

34 Ratliff, "With This Composer."

35 Brian Glasser, *In a Silent Way*, 2nd ed. (London: As Long as It's Hot), 297.

23 Legacy

1 Gary Giddins, *Rhythm-a-ning: Jazz Tradition and Innovation in the '80s* (New York: Oxford University Press, 1985), xi–xii.

2 Phyl Garland, "Musical Genius Reaches Top at 21," *Ebony*, Mar. 1983, 29.

3 "Charlatans" from Jon Pareles, "Jazz Swings Back to Tradition," *New York Times*, Jun. 17, 1984. "A decline" from Pawel Brodowski, "Coolin' It with Wynton Marsalis," *Jazz Forum*, No. 121, 1989, 34.

4 Krystian Brodacki, "The Original Batman: Wayne Shorter Remembers Miles Davis," *Jazz Forum*, No. 132, 1992, 26.

5 Mark Gilbert, "Wayne Shorter," *Jazz Journal International*, Mar. 1996, 7.

6 Joe Zawinul personal interview, Sep. 15, 2003.

7 Martin Williams, *Jazz in Its Time* (New York: Oxford Univ. Press, 1989), 46–47, 56.

8 Robert Palmer, "Survivors in Jazz-Rock Disclaim It," *New York Times*, Jun. 11, 1982.

9 Ted Panken, "Joe Zawinul's 79th Birthday Anniversary," Jul. 7, 2011 (accessed Jan. 4, 2015), https://tedpanken.wordpress.com/2011/07/07/joe-zawinuls-79th-birthday-anniversary/.

10 Very few unreleased studio tracks have been released over the years. According to Peter Erskine, the band had a practice of erasing the tapes of unused material. See Pablo Held, "Peter Erskine," Pablo Held Investigates, Jan. 16, 2019 (accessed Jan. 14, 2020), https://pabloheldinvestigates.com/peter-erskine/.

11 Scott Kinsey personal interview, Jul. 6, 2007.

12 Joe Zawinul, liner notes to *Body Acoustic*, Michiel Borstlap, EmArcy, 538 976-2, 1999, CD.

13 Gary Eskow, "Jason Miles Pays Tribute to Weather Report," *Mix*, Jan. 1, 2000 (accessed Sep. 30, 2018), https://www.mixonline.com/recording/jason-miles-pays-tribute-weather-report-373782.

14 Peter Erskine personal interview, Jan. 26, 2014.

15 Nicholas Payton telephone interview, Nov. 16, 2016.

16 Steve Khan telephone interview, Jul, 15, 2018.

17 Peter Erskine personal interview, Feb. 24, 2018.

24 The Last Duet

1 Don Heckman, "Joe Zawinul, 75: Influential Jazz Keyboardist Led Weather Report," *Los Angeles Times*, Sep. 12, 2007.

2 Although the CD/DVD *75th* lists the date of Wayne and Joe's performance in Veszprém as August 2, 2007, the actual date was August 1. Confirmation can be found at the Veszprém Festival website's 2007 program, which can be

viewed online at https://veszpremfest.hu/en/photos/4-2007, accessed August 4, 2018.

3 Heckman, "Joe Zawinul, 75."

4 Marco Piretti, Aug. 1, 2007, https://groups.yahoo.com/neo/groups/zawinulfans/conversations/messages/1394.

5 Robert Neumüller, *Joe Zawinuls Erdzeit: Interviews für ein Portrait* (Weitra: Verl. Publ. PN°1, Bibliothek der Provinz, 2009), 126.

6 Risa Zincke telephone interview, Jun. 13, 2014.

7 Wayne Shorter telephone interview, Mar. 27, 2015.

8 Brian Wise, "Wayne Shorter Speaks," *Rhythms: Australia's Roots Music Monthly*, Mar. 5, 2010 (accessed Dec. 16, 2014), https://web.archive.org/web/20100408022623/http://www.rhythms.com.au/features/default,id,13972.aspx.

9 Zincke interview, 2014.

10 Sabine Kabongo correspondence, Jun. 2014.

11 Heckman, "Joe Zawinul, 75."

12 Kabongo correspondence, 2014.

13 Shorter interview, 2015.

14 Associated Press, "Joe Zawinul Hospitalized in Vienna," Aug. 7, 2007.

15 Zincke interview, 2014.

16 Anil Prasad, "Joe Zawinul: Man of the People," Innerviews, 1997 (accessed Sep. 12, 2003), https://www.innerviews.org/inner/zawinul.html.

17 Brian Glasser, *In a Silent Way*, 2nd ed. (London: As Long as It's Hot), 324.

25 Reflections

1 Alphonse Mouzon telephone interview, Apr. 25, 2015; email correspondence, Feb. 2014.

2 Barbara Burton telephone interview, Nov. 12, 2014.

3 Airto Moreira telephone interview, Aug. 20, 2016.

4 Eric Gravatt telephone interview, Mar. 13, 2020.

5 Ralph Towner telephone interview, May 13, 2014.

6 Brian Risner telephone interview, Jan. 14, 2004.

7 Herschel Dwellingham telephone interview, Dec. 3, 2013.

8 Andrew White telephone interview, Jul. 14, 2017.

9 Muruga Booker telephone interview, Dec. 23, 2013.

10 Greg Errico telephone interview, Mar. 10, 2014.

11 Ishmael Wilburn telephone interview, Mar. 9, 2014.

12 Skip Hadden Skype interview, Apr. 17, 2017; email correspondence, Nov. 2013.

13 Alphonso Johnson personal interview, Jul, 25, 2008.

14 Darryl Brown telephone interview, Feb. 15, 2014.

15 "Residents, Patients Mourn Death of Longtime CG Doctor," *Casa Grande Dispatch*, Dec. 18, 2017 (accessed Mar. 22, 2020), https://www.pinalcentral.com/casa_grande_dispatch/area_news/residents-patients-mourn-death-of-longtime-cg-doctor/article_bafb5a2b-6779-572d-809c-57381946b60a.html. Brown's online obituary can be found at https://www.dignitymemorial.com/obituaries/chandler-az/darryl-brown-7653063.

16 Chuck Bazemore telephone interview, Jun. 27, 2017.

17 Ndugu Chancler telephone interview, Dec. 30, 2008.

18 Bruce Botnick telephone interview, Jul. 27, 2017.

19 Alyrio Lima correspondence, Jul. 2017.

20 Chester Thompson telephone interview, Dec. 22, 2014.

21 Narada Michael Walden telephone interview, Apr. 1, 2015.

22 Bob Cavallo telephone interview, Jan. 11, 2017.

23 Alex Acuña telephone interview, Feb. 21, 2014.

24 Alan Howarth telephone interview, Jun. 1, 2016.

25 Peter Erskine personal interview, Feb. 24, 2018.

26 Robert Thomas Jr., telephone interview, Aug. 1, 2018.

27 Omar Hakim telephone interview, Feb. 25, 2014.

28 Victor Bailey telephone interview, Feb. 18, 2014.

29 José Rossy telephone interview, Feb. 1, 2014.

30 Jim Swanson telephone interview, Apr. 23, 2018.

31 Mino Cinélu Skype interview, Jun. 25, 2018.

32 Steve Khan telephone interview, Jul. 15, 2018.

33 Miroslav Vitous telephone interview, Apr. 26, 2007.

34 Ashley Kahn, "Updated Weather Report," *Jazz Times*, Jun. 2002, 50.

35 Scott H. Thompson, "Fusion Revolutionary," *Playbill*, Oct. 20, 2006, http://www.playbillarts.com/features/article/5430.html.

Index